THE
BBC

A CENTURY
ON AIR

David Hendy is a writer, broadcaster and Emeritus Professor of Media and Cultural History at the University of Sussex, England. His book *Life on Air: A History of Radio Four* won the Longman–History Today Book of the Year Award and was nominated for the Orwell Prize.

ALSO BY DAVID HENDY

Radio in the Global Age

Life on Air: A History of Radio Four

Public Service Broadcasting

Noise: A Human History of Sound and Listening

THE BBC

A CENTURY ON AIR

DAVID HENDY

PUBLICAFFAIRS

New York

PublicAffairs
Hachette Book Group
1290 Avenue of the Americas, New York, NY 10104
www.publicaffairsbooks.com
@Public_Affairs

Printed in the United States of America
Originally published in hardcover in Great Britain in 2022 by Profile Books Ltd
First US Edition: March 2022

Published by PublicAffairs, an imprint of Perseus Books, LLC, a subsidiary of
Hachette Book Group, Inc. The PublicAffairs name and logo is a trademark of
the Hachette Book Group.

The Hachette Speakers Bureau provides a wide range of authors for speaking
events. To find out more, go to www.hachettespeakersbureau.com or
call (866) 376-6591.

The publisher is not responsible for websites (or their content) that are not owned
by the publisher.

Library of Congress Control Number: 2021948773

ISBNs: 9781610397049 (hardcover), 9781610397056 (e-book)

LSC-C

Printing 1, 2022

For Henrietta

Contents

LIST OF ILLUSTRATIONS

We would like to extend our thanks and gratitude to all the copyrightholders for allowing us to include the images in this book, and in particular to the BBC Photo Library for their assistance in sourcing, re-scanning and digitally re-mastering many of the pictures within.

Alamy: p. 111 Loudspeaker in General Strike © PA Images/Alamy; V is for Victory © Sueddeutsche Zeitung Photo/Alamy; p. 389. Anthony Eden © PA Images/Alamy; p. 456. Margaret Thatcher © PA Images/Alamy; p. 528. Greg Dyke © PA Images/Alamy

BBC: pp. 12, 21, 36, 55, 64, 67, 81, 88, 94, 101, 102, 130, 133, 150, 153, 160, 167, 171, 172, 181, 191, 199, 202, 206, 211, 215, 227, 231, 237, 269, 275, 281, 284, 299, 300, 302, 306, 318, 339, 348, 358, 375, 383, 402, 411, 427, 439, 441, 443, 453, 466, 489, 500, 514, 517, 559 © BBC

C. A Lewis *Broadcasting from Within* (1923) frontispiece, p. 7

Getty Images: p. 261. Frank Gillard recording © Photo by Leonard McCombe/Picture Post/Hulton Archive/Getty Images; p. 336. Scene from Dick Barton © Keystone/Getty Images; p. 403. Langston Hughes © Photo by Jan Persoon/Getty Images; p. 475. John Birt. Photo by John Minihan/*Evening Standard*/Getty Images; p. 539. Dame Janet Smith © Photo by Adrian Dennis – WPA Pool/Getty Images

National Portrait Gallery: p. 50. Hilda Matheson, photograph by Howard Coster © National Portrait Gallery

While every effort has been made to contact copyright-holders of illustrations, the author and publishers would be grateful for information about any illustrations where they have been unable to trace them, and would be glad to make amendments in further editions.

PREFACE

Is a history of the BBC even possible?

At a hundred years old, the British Broadcasting Corporation has already transmitted somewhere between ten and twenty *million* programmes. The precise total is unknown simply because any attempt at an accurate count would be too vast and complex a task for anyone to undertake. Back in 1957, Asa Briggs started to write an 'official' history of the Corporation. He took thirty-five years, five volumes, and nearly 4,000 pages to complete his mission. Even this Herculean effort, he said, offered '*a* history and not *the* history'.[1] In the years since the last volume of his magisterial study was published, broadcasting has become a round-the-clock, multi-channel phenomenon. The most dedicated listener or viewer in the world would stand no chance of catching more than a tiny slice of the BBC's daily output. What hope for the historian wanting to make sense of a century's worth of activity? The problem of selection is almost unbearable. Merely listing its programmes would occupy a shelf, doing justice to the story of their creation a whole library.

Still, the BBC demands our attention. We can't hope to understand modern Britain – its politics, its culture, its sense of itself – without understanding the role of the BBC in the life of the nation. In large parts of the world, public service broadcasters survive in the margins of national life, while state-run or commercial companies dominate the scene. Yet here is an institution that almost every Briton uses in one way or another; the tiny minority who don't will know about it – have views about it. Around the globe, it's long been seen as *the* embodiment of public service broadcasting, a template to emulate. To use the advertisers' favoured language, it is a powerful 'brand', conveying something about quality, reliability, accuracy. For listeners and viewers at home, the BBC is not just one broadcaster among many: it is *the* national broadcaster, possessing a quasi-mystical place in the national psyche. Public devotion can sometimes reach unnerving levels of intensity. The novelist Sebastian Faulks said of Radio 4 that its 'humane upper-middle-brow seriousness has done more both to define British society and to hold it together than any political or artistic movement of the last 100 years'. Another writer suggested that it is the BBC's historic position at the heart of our media ecology that has given Britain 'possibly the greatest single system of diverse, quality communication the world has ever seen'. A poll of men and women listed in *Who's Who* once found that the Corporation was regarded as more influential than Parliament or the Church of England. Although not actually a government-run broadcaster, it is a body so clearly aligned with the 'Nation' that it often *feels* to us like an organ of state, as if it were a creative arm of the civil service. It exists by Royal Charter, and the licence fee that funds it is set by ministers in Parliament. If nuclear war begins, the last voice of authority we will hear before Armageddon arrives is a Radio 4 announcer.[2]

All of which makes the BBC part of what we have come to call 'the establishment'. But in all sorts of meaningful ways it also belongs to *us*. This is not just about 'owning' the BBC because we pay for it directly through the licence fee. Public service broadcasting is always, in the most fundamental way, *for* us: its output has no value unless it's heard or seen, and broadcasters always have some kind of listener or viewer in mind as they go about their work. Broadcasters and their audience, it has been said, are like twin stars: they revolve around and substantially determine each other. For decades, our domestic routines – getting up, preparing meals, sitting together as a family, going to bed – have been marked and measured by the passage of our favourite radio and television programmes. The television playwright Dennis Potter recalled the BBC of his childhood days as 'paternalistic and often stuffily pompous', presenting itself in an almost priestly role. Yet at a crucial moment in his life it also 'threw open the "magical casement" on great sources of mindscape at a time when books were hard to come by, and when I had never stepped into a theatre or even a concert hall'. The images and sounds the BBC has brought into our homes have been the portal to other worlds, other ideas, other times, 'the tissue of our dreams, the warp and weft of our memories, the staging posts of our lives'.[3] Its status as a lofty national body in close embrace with the world of high politics has always co-existed with a cradle-to-grave role in our own domestic lives and emotional landscapes.

This dual identity is why the Corporation's former Director-General, Tony Hall, claimed that 'all the eddies and currents that make up Britain flow right through the BBC', and why Asa Briggs said that 'To write the history of broadcasting in the 20th century is in a sense to write the history of everything else'. It is also why the BBC has aroused not just intense devotion but fierce criticism. We expect so much of it that it always disappoints. The Corporation acts as a lightning rod, a place where some of our most fundamental anxieties about politics or taste or morality are displayed and fought over. Sebastian Faulks might revere Radio 4, but others have accused it of being no more than a mouthpiece for the middle-aged and the middle class, for 'Middle England' and everything that goes with such rhetorical terrain. Complaints over a particular programme or a particular channel are rarely parochial affairs. With a national press ever-ready to amplify the mildest of grumbles, they easily spin out of control. As the *Guardian* writer Charlotte Higgins puts it, 'The BBC is a battlefield that can be grim and dark and strewn with human wreckage. It is where the British gather to fight their most vicious culture wars.' The Corporation, she suggests, has always ricocheted from trouble to trouble – 'it has crisis in its bones'.[4]

These headline-grabbing flare-ups are an inevitable feature of the pages that follow. But one reason why this is a 'people's history' is that it attempts to trace the wider story of the BBC's tangled relationship with the public. The Corporation has always had to be utterly alive to the feelings of its audience as well as to the prevailing political climate. Its programme makers see their job as measuring the mood of the times, restlessly turning over social issues, spotting trends, nurturing new talent. The television and radio that emerges from this labour tells us what these programme makers thought about their viewers and listeners – that is, what they thought about *us*.

This is also a 'people's history' because it aims to bring into focus the men and woman who made the BBC what it is. It's too easy to dismiss all modern media as formulaic and machine-tooled. Some of it certainly is. But for the past hundred years, most programmes have been handcrafted – made by thinking, feeling, and often fallible human beings. Behind every programme lies a world of thought and debate. Only by reaching deep inside the BBC, and by trying to discover the backgrounds, the tastes, the prejudices, the ideals of those who have worked there over the decades, can we understand why the radio we listen to and the television we watch has become what it is today.

Seeing the broadcasters of the past as flesh and blood rather than as faceless functionaries, we can begin to see the BBC as one of the most extraordinary creative communities of the past century. David Attenborough remembers his induction as a young producer in the 1950s, and a colleague showing him a diagram of the Corporation's structure. 'It came as no surprise to me later to discover that he was also the author of an authoritative book on witchcraft in medieval England.' It's been said that one needs to understand medieval power politics to appreciate the Byzantine structure of the BBC and its proud tradition of territorial disputes. Over the years, the Corporation has attracted the attention of generations of sociologists, political scientists, anthropologists, historians and journalists. Few have been brave enough to summarise the BBC in a short sentence. After immersing herself in its life for many months, Charlotte Higgins decided that it was 'ungraspable in its entirety: it was like a city whose streets I had only partially explored, a place whose streetscape was so circuitous and complex that a lifetime would be too short to map it'. Asa Briggs, who really *did* spend a large part of his lifetime trying to map the Corporation, certainly possessed an encyclopaedic knowledge of its inner workings by the time he retired. But according to his fellow historian, Raphael Samuel, policy-making, rather than broadcasting, was the true subject of his work: his five-volume history, Samuel suggested, was perhaps too 'top-down' to do justice to 'radio's penny-a-liners, the freelance playwrights and scriptwriters, scraping a living in the republic of letters, the foreign correspondents, the old soaks at Bush House, gathered from the four corners of the world, doing their all-night stints, and comforting themselves with the bottle'. These men and women are part of the BBC's story as much as the high politics of government interference, official enquiries, administrative reorganisations, or the Olympian pronouncements of Governors and Director-Generals. This 'people's history' is a belated attempt to give them their due.[5]

Fortunately, the testimonies of those who 'made' the BBC reach down to us from the past. As an organisation obsessed with monitoring its own performance, the Corporation minuted almost every stage in its decision-making processes. Its written archives therefore contain hundreds of thousands of documents in which the thinking of staff has been captured in print at a level of detail the most punctilious civil servant would celebrate. But there's another, equally valuable resource – one of the Corporation's most underused treasures: the collection of several hundred oral history interviews with former staff that it has been quietly accumulating over the past half-century. These feature people – Directors-General, yes, but also editors, producers, presenters, engineers, secretaries, even telephonists and lift attendants – who were asked to talk candidly about their life and times. Their accounts don't just blow the dust off the written archives and bring them to life; they offer first-hand accounts that sometimes transform our understanding of key episodes in the BBC's past. Even if dates or names or the precise sequence of events are occasionally misremembered, almost every testimony provides priceless evidence of what it *felt* like to be in the BBC at a given moment of time: the look and smell and sound of a place, the small but telling details of working life, the atmosphere in the studio, the arguments that got in the way of normal business, the friendships and alliances that made good things happen, how grand policy was *really* interpreted on the factory floor. As a 'people's history', this book puts these accounts centre stage.

Everyone who has ever worked for the BBC will have a strong view as to its 'true' history. But what they thought of the BBC will have depended not only on their character, experience or outlook, as well as the precise date on which they entered the Corporation, but on the place that they occupied within the system. Their perspective would perhaps have changed as they moved upwards, across, or occasionally downwards. Which is why historians try to look at the scene from more than one angle. Getting to grips with 'the BBC' is like piecing together a vast jigsaw puzzle, and even then the final picture defies easy description. The distinguished critic Clive James once said that British television was 'too various to be fully absorbed by one mind ... The more you watched, the less likely you were to make wide-ranging statements'. Broadcasting, he suggested, could 'be reduced to a socio-political formula only at the price of distortion'.⁶

Even so, some things *can* be said with reasonable certainty. The media historian Jean Seaton has suggested that the BBC's story is one of men and women 'trying to make programmes that people like and that also – not in a preachy way (well only occasionally in a preachy way) – do them good'.⁷ This deceptively simple description provides one helpful starting point for the tale that unfolds over the following pages. A history of broadcasting is always partly about that long and continuing effort behind the scenes to discover formats and styles that somehow 'work' for the vast and unseen audience. But in the case of the BBC, it has always been much more than a matter of delivering programmes to people's homes as if they were electricity or gas or water: it has been about culture, morality, values, politics. Behind the Corporation's famous mission statement to 'inform, educate and entertain' lies a complex tangle of ideas, though one united around a vision of humanity's potential to change. That vision has been ferociously debated and continuously adapted. The struggle to hold on to some kind of guiding ethos while constantly bending under the strain of wider social forces lies at the heart of the BBC's story. The struggle matters because it's not just about the nature of the BBC itself; the Corporation's fate can be seen as emblematic of the kind of society we wish to preserve or create.

That's why it's no coincidence the story of the BBC begins in the early 1920s – many years after wireless had been discovered but in the lingering aftermath of a traumatic world war. And it's why, before we even begin to talk about the very first programmes that were broadcast, it's good to stand for a little while alongside those who had fought in the conflict and who were looking to build from the rubble a new and better world for the generations to come. It is through trying to understand their fears, their hopes, their passions and their values that we might just get a clearer picture, not just of *how* the BBC emerged in 1922 but *why*.

I

CRUCIBLE

1

MAKING A NEW WORLD

Soon we began to explore the possibilities of peace.
Where should we go? What should we do?

Cecil Lewis, pilot

London, early evening, Tuesday 19 December 1922.

The year is almost at an end, the working day nearly done, the light fading. The weather has been unseasonably kind recently, though it is getting colder and wetter just in time for Christmas. The windows of the big West End department stores – Selfridges, Whiteleys, Gamages, Swan and Edgar – are glowing invitingly, and a steady flow of customers wander inside. Those weary of shopping are searching for the comfort and warmth of the nearest Lyons Corner House – one of the city's 'palaces of pastry', promising decently priced food and a touch of opulence. Later, they might go to the theatre, to see one of the multitude of musical comedies and Christmas shows on offer: *Alice in Wonderland* at the Court Theatre, *The Lady of the Rose* at Daly's, 'comedy duets' from Muriel George and Ernest Butcher at the Coliseum. Those wanting to make a night of it might try to catch the *Midnight Follies* in a slightly risqué revue at the Hotel Metropole, or go dining and dancing into the small hours at the Hotel Cecil.

Yet, not everyone is embracing the pursuit of pleasure. Heads turned down, coats buttoned up, millions of Londoners are scurrying home for the night, whisked to the capital's ever-expanding suburbs by motorised buses and the Underground.

Through the windows there is just darkness – a chance, at least, to glance at the papers and catch up with the day's events. A grenade dating from 1914 has been found in a dustcart at Buckingham Palace. The new Italian prime minister, Mussolini, has announced the creation of a fascist militia. Lord Balfour is due to give a lecture on the possibility of telepathic communication. Unemployment is still rising.[1]

Not everyone is planning an evening of entertainment or leaving for home. Just a short walk from the Aldwych, squatting between the imperial grandeur of the recently widened Strand and the river Thames, is the Savoy precinct – a slightly seedy rectangle of narrow, sloping streets where a series of undistinguished offices are clustered. Here, three men stand huddled together, deep in thought.

They linger for a moment on the steps of the Institution of Electrical Engineers. Upstairs is a suite of eight unused rooms. They might be exactly what they are looking for: offices for what they call 'our enterprise'. They push through the heavy door and make their way up to the second and third floors. All three men are feeling distinctly jaded. They have spent the day scuttling around London visiting location after location, and this is their last hope. Now they are inside, it seems, alas, the worst of the lot: 'a depressing place' recently used for some mysterious medical activity. But they have to settle upon something, and have no option other than to take it. After all, time is of the essence. This new 'enterprise' is only a few weeks' old and already turning out to be even bigger, even more demanding than they had ever imagined. It urgently needs a new home.[2]

The address is No. 2 Savoy Hill. In three months' time they will have moved in and brought the building back to life. In a few years, they will have made it among the best-known addresses in Britain. For now, though, renting an office is just one of myriad concerns. They are feeling their way: setting out on 'uncharted seas'; trying, in fact, to work out what this new enterprise of theirs actually *is* – and what, with good fortune and effort, it might one day become.[3] For now, nothing is certain. Their work is startlingly novel, barely understood, precariously funded, and conducted with few people even knowing of its existence. Between them, the three men make up three-quarters of their company's employees. Yet they barely know each other. Two have only just begun sharing a makeshift office nearby; the third is meeting them for the very first time today; none knows whether they will get along, let alone succeed.

Their names are Cecil Lewis, John Reith and Arthur Burrows. Three men so different in appearance and temperament it would be hard to imagine. But something has brought each of them to Savoy Hill this December evening. What, exactly? An impulse among individuals still youthful enough to make something of themselves, to experience the thrill of risking their livelihoods in an unknown venture? A more noble desire, perhaps, to make good a world that seems to them – as it seems to many others in 1922 – to be in crisis?

All three have experienced the Great War at first hand. It is now four years since the cataclysm ended, but it continues to cast a long shadow, its effects unfurling slowly, unpredictably. Thousands of those who fought, unable to put into words what they went through, are declared still 'broken'. Thousands more still struggle to find a firm footing in adult life. And there is contagious talk of society sliding into barbarism, civilisation on the brink of collapse. Writers and thinkers, conjuring an idealised image of a rosy belle époque before the war, conclude sorrowfully that humanity's relentless progress has been shattered once and for all.[4]

Not everyone feels the same sense of despair. In the bookshops this season, a new collection of poems, *The Cud*, expresses a striking ambivalence towards the war's significance. 'War is abominable', says one of its verses. 'But it is also Tremendous! Prodigious! Exciting!'[5] For some, the war's aftermath has become not a cause for despondency but a spur to action. There is a fragile peace to uphold, mutual understanding to be nurtured, a new world to be built from the ashes of the old. The modern age might be disturbing. But it is also brilliantly inventive – alive with new technology, new marvels. And the three men now standing in Savoy Hill are starting to believe that *they*, at least, are lucky enough to possess the very means with which to make a profound difference to human affairs.

It will be a small operation at first, this new 'enterprise'. Before larger forces take over, Cecil Lewis, John Reith and Arthur Burrows will have a chance to mould it – and they will do so in their own image. They will define its essential purpose, set the direction of travel. It might be, as Lewis himself later claims, that none of them can yet 'grasp' *what* exactly they are doing. But they all know *why* they are doing it. Each had arrived at Savoy Hill that evening with a heavy baggage of tastes, beliefs, prejudices, hopes and experiences. 'We are all from birth ... the slaves of influence', Lewis thinks. 'Youth is the crucial time, for, once the mould has set, it is next to impossible to change it.'[6]

Which is why he now glances over his own shoulder with an eye to the not-too-distant past.

Cecil Lewis: the search for a 'greater guiding principle'

Cecil Lewis was the youngest of the three, just twenty-four, and, as one of his colleagues put it, 'an extremely good-looking young man, rather like Rupert Brooke'. Well over six feet tall, exuberant and quick-witted, married to the glamorous young daughter of an exiled White Russian general: in every way, he embodied what he in fact was – a flying ace of the Great War. Yet not all was what it seemed. His dashing looks and style, he later admits, had 'conspired to make the façade a good deal better than it really was'. Behind the 'high spirits and vitality' was a young man burdened by hidden trauma and a desire to do more in life than enjoy the 'vagabond and dilettante' existence that he knew could so easily ensnare him.[7]

When war had erupted, Lewis was a schoolboy of sixteen in Northamptonshire. He felt little patriotic fervour, but he did have a burning desire to fly. He devoured magazines such as *Flight* and *The Aero*, each issue filled with stirring accounts of

Cecil Lewis was still in his early twenties when he joined the BBC. He'd only recently turned seventeen when he became a pilot for the Royal Flying Corps back in 1915.

planes looping the loop at air displays, and of the brave, death-defying people who flew them. 'Pilots! There was magic in the very word!'[8]

By April 1916 – with only twenty hours of actual flight experience, and barely eighteen years old – he was in France flying reconnaissance patrols for the Royal Flying Corps. Over the next two and a half years, Lewis fought in the war's newest, strangest, most untested arena, the air. During the Somme offensive, he flew across the lines at a recklessly low altitude to gather information about troop movements. He hurled himself into frenzied dogfights with Baron von Richthofen's squadron of Red Albatrosses. And when London came under attack from German Gotha bombers, he launched his plane into the terrifying darkness of the night sky, equipped with nothing in the way of lights but his own torch.

Towards the end of 1917, he was on a dawn patrol: the worst time to head towards enemy lines, since it meant flying into the rising sun. As he grappled one-handed with a jammed gun, a German plane appeared from nowhere and opened fire. A 'white-hot rod was flicked along the round of my back', he recalled. It 'burned terribly'. A few minutes later he was back on the ground, being treated: 'A six-inch graze. No more.' He had been immensely lucky, and knew it, for the brutal reality was hard to ignore: for pilots like him, life expectancy was horribly short.[9]

Despite this, Lewis found it hard not to be seduced by the gut-wrenching thrill of it all. For a start, there was the startling novelty of viewing the world from 10,000 feet. The countryside stretched to the four horizons, dazzling in its 'wealth of soft colour, of light and shade', and the opposing lines far below almost touching each other, 'like two pieces of lace put together'. There was also the tactile thrill of the plane itself. Lewis would rhapsodise over the 'nice arrangement of instruments in the cockpit ... the handiness of the controls'. It was, he said, always 'grand to fly a well-thought-out machine'. Handling it brought a feeling of 'mastery over mechanism' – and through this, a sense also of 'mastery over space, time, and life itself'. It was as though man and machine became one, each enhancing the other. Lewis would feel 'keyed up to superhuman tension': 'in a state of awareness, of tremendous alertness, ready to act instantaneously should the need arise.'[10]

None of this could erase other feelings gnawing away, slowly sowing the seeds of doubt. By 1918 Lewis felt he had been living for years in 'the stretch or the sag of the nerves'. In the longer run, he admitted, many pilots had been reduced to 'a dithering state, near to imbecility'. The real cracks only started to show – and Lewis only realised how 'shaky and good-for-nothing' he was himself – when sent home to rest. What he experienced in those brief moments of domestic respite was 'not like a bodily fatigue from which you could completely recover, it was a sort of damage to the essential tissue of your being'.[11]

As the war progressed, Lewis also became increasingly uneasy about what he witnessed from his cockpit: not just sunlit vistas but a darker, more troubling landscape. Soaring over the Somme, he spied below the roiling mass of fighting men ranged against each other. 'There isn't much picturesque or visibly heroic to be seen in this war when you're in the air', he decided. Indeed, what was so shocking was the 'horrible futility': so many lives being lost to stake what was now visibly just 'a mile or two of earth'. 'Viewed with detachment', he concluded, the war 'had all the elements of grotesque comedy – a prodigious and complex effort, cunningly contrived, and carried out with deadly seriousness, in order to achieve just nothing at all.'[12]

When the Armistice came in November 1918, it was greeted back in Britain with a mix of joy and weary relief. As news reached Manchester, the streets surrounding Albert Square thickened with cheering factory workers. In Sunderland there were impromptu fancy-dress parties, and in the South Wales Valleys 'practically every house exhibited a flag'. For the millions of men still slowly making their way home from the scattered theatres of battle, peacetime prompted more complex emotions. Lewis confessed to a feeling of anti-climax, even 'to a momentary sense of regret'. He was not yet twenty-one. He had entered adulthood as a pilot. Disillusioned or not, it was hard to envisage any other livelihood. 'When you have been living a certain kind of life for four years, living as part of a single-minded and united effort, its sudden cessation leaves your roots in the air, baffled and, for the moment, disgruntled.' 'Where should we go? What should we do?' There was no past career to which he could return. 'There before me, like a clean sheet of paper, lay my life.'[13]

His first response was simply to embrace the joy of being alive and to make 1919 a year like no other, filling it with endless house parties, each one sparkling with youthfulness and glamour. 'We laughed, we danced, we lazed, we loved … headlong, feckless, wrapped in the golden moment like a bee in amber.' His next response was to flee. Before the year was out he had set off for Peking, where his job would be to train pilots for the engineering company Metropolitan-Vickers. He had never been to the Far East before, and the sights and smells and sounds of the city were instantly beguiling. He decorated his house in Chinese style and embraced the pace and patina of local life – relishing the hours he might spend listening attentively to a pet thrush singing under the willows or watching the artistry of a winter solstice firework display. But it was also unsettling. The 'wonder' of it all underlined just how 'flat, stale, unprofitable' western civilisation now appeared. And mixing with the city's small community of British immigrants, as his job demanded, only made matters worse. It was all bridge and tennis and polo and 'petty protocol'. In 1922, bored by their 'narrow outlook' and 'ill-informed superiority', he boarded a tramp steamer for home. His stay had been a revelation. It made him realise that life was too short to be 'wasted on fools who had no appetite for it'. He now wanted only one thing: 'to add my iota to the wisdom and beauty of the world'. And it was in Britain – 'back in the centre of things' – that he decided 'a wider sweep' awaited him, if only he knew where it could be found.[14]

But what might 'it' be, exactly? None of his musings quite cohered into a firm philosophy or belief. If one thing shaped his attitude to life more than anything else, it was the Western Front. And what he had learned from his 'self-taught degree' at 10,000 feet was this: the need for humanity to find some transcendent sense of purpose, some 'greater guiding principle', if it was to avoid 'floundering deeper and deeper into chaos'. Economies and trade and communications made the world utterly interdependent – or soon would do – and only some sort of profoundly internationalist outlook would succeed in 'co-ordinating and controlling the life of the planet'. Little of this was original. But in the immediate aftermath of the war, such ideas were being ventilated with a greater awareness of the need to find something, *anything*, that might challenge isolationism and protect the 'civic virtues' of peace and security. Post-war Britain echoed to the noise of doom-mongers trading powerful metaphors of decline, both spiritual and physical. Historians and social commentators pointed to a profound fracture with Victorian notions of continual progress, while scientists spoke of entropy, and eugenicists preached about the genetic 'degeneration' of the imperial race. Might the story of decay be a story that applied to *all* civilisations, even to that of present-day Europe? Was 'civilisation' itself now revealed to be only skin-deep? Lewis was unwilling to be defeated by such pessimism. It had been music and art and poetry that had first set him 'vibrating' as a schoolboy, and the same feeling had now returned. In a world shadowed by death, Lewis decided, it was the enduring power of *culture* that offered the only hope of immortality, simply because its 'vast credits' of wisdom and art would not be dead 'till the last man had forgotten them'.[15]

The tricky question remained of how to put such a grand manifesto into effect. What, he asked himself, could *he* – someone with no profession, no job, no training in anything other than flying, but also someone who was youthful, energetic, and in possession of 'a certain unfocused, undirected ability' – give 'in return for all this?'[16]

When the answer came, it was something of a surprise. Lewis had been back from China only a few weeks when the telephone rang. Through the crackle and hiss an old friend from his time with Metropolitan-Vickers relayed an intriguing tale. He had flown back from China via the United States, where he had witnessed something new and extraordinary – an exciting business opportunity, which, were it to take off in Britain, would require the involvement of someone 'artistic'. 'You know, Lewis,' he said, 'I think broadcasting's the thing for you.' 'Broadcasting,' Lewis replied. 'What on earth's that?'[17]

John Reith: a calling from God

When they met for the first time that day on the steps of 2 Savoy Hill, John Reith had even less idea about what 'broadcasting' was. In almost every other respect, however, he struck Lewis as possessing a frightening abundance of certainty and self-belief. 'He was in every sense a big man', Lewis remembered of his first encounter with Reith. 'I stood 6 ft. 4 in., Reith was even taller. A sort of lofty detachment surrounded him … He had a pronounced Scottish accent, a neatly rolled umbrella and very fine hands.' Lewis could also not help but notice a searing gash running all the way down the left side of his face. Combined with

John Reith, photographed in 1926, more than a decade after he had been shot in the face. In this image, the deep, three-inch scar is concealed by shadows. But Reith's wartime injury would cause him considerable pain and anxiety for many years.

his deep-set eyes and bushy brows, it gave an already sombre countenance the permanent hint of severity. But this forbidding appearance masked what one of his biographers called the 'vulnerable, uneasy, tangled core of the man within'. John Reith was brooding, pompous, arrogant, uncompromising and humourless. He was also capable of great kindness and loyalty. Above all, he was wracked with 'a progressive and almost pathological despair'.[18] He was as unlike Lewis as it was possible to be in his deep suspicion of art and culture. But he was just as restless, and at the still youthful age of thirty-three, equally determined to make up for years of lost time. Of the three men, he had the greatest sense of an extraordinary – and perhaps God-given – destiny to fulfil.

According to his daughter, Reith's childhood was always 'very present to him'. He had grown up in Glasgow in a deeply Christian household. His mother, Adah Mary, had been brought up in a Church of England tradition, and expressed her faith through constant good works: teaching factory girls to sew, organising concerts and lectures in Glasgow's poorer districts, visiting hospitals. His father, George, was the local minister of the Free Church of Scotland – though a Presbyterian who happened to hang on his study wall a picture not of John Knox but of the great High Anglican-turned-Catholic theologian, John Henry Newman. His reputation in the area was as a theological liberal, a great preacher, and, like his wife, a tireless promoter of good causes.[19]

Both of Reith's parents embodied that famous spirit of Christian charity and reforming zeal that characterised so much of late Victorian Britain. It was a time when ideas of 'rational recreation' were widespread, with charitably-minded individuals and civic leaders seeking to replace rough plebeian culture, such as drinking and gambling, with all sorts of 'improving' activities. Matthew Arnold had articulated this reforming spirit in his 1869 bestseller, *Culture and Anarchy*. The book had diagnosed a broken Britain in which the 'raw and half-developed' toiling masses were only ever a hair's breadth away from open revolt, while the middle classes were behaving like self-satisfied 'Philistines', and the aristocrats were too busy indulging their own pleasures. For Arnold, the country's only hope of salvation was culture, which entailed cultivating 'all sides of our humanity' through the pursuit of wisdom and beauty – or, as he put it, 'sweetness and light'. It was also about making sweetness and light *prevail* – making 'the best that has been thought and known in the world current everywhere'. It was no good just cultivating one's own tastes: if the world was to be left 'better and happier than we found it', a person had to 'carry others along' in the march towards perfection, 'continually doing all he can to enlarge and increase the volume of the human stream sweeping thitherward'.[20]

It was such High Victorian paternalism that saw new libraries and galleries and parks and education institutes springing up across Britain in the closing years of the nineteenth century. High Victorian paternalism and a muscular Christianity did not, however, make the big grey manse in which John Reith spent his childhood an especially happy place. Inside, there was strict adherence to the Sabbath. Psalms and prayers were said every morning and evening. His six siblings, much older than he was, shut themselves in their own rooms. It meant a great deal of loneliness, and a growing awkwardness in mixing with others. The teachers at his boarding school in Norfolk thought him surly; his own diagnosis was that he was simply 'longing for a real friend'. He dreamed of studying classics or philosophy or literature – 'almost anything that was an intellectual rather than a manual pursuit' – but his father arranged instead for him to be trained as a mechanical engineer and apprenticed to the big locomotive works in Glasgow's north-eastern suburbs.[21]

Reith was desolate. Yet there was consolation to be had in the spiritual realm. On long, solitary walks in the Cairngorms, he would imagine that he was hearing divine messages carried towards him on the wind – messages that might give some hint of his own destiny in life. His father's greatness, he felt sure, lay in his sheer goodness and integrity of purpose. Where on earth would his own greatness lie? All he knew was that he was 'to do something considerable' in the world. He also reflected on his father's warning: 'You will never be or do anything useful until you start thinking how you can serve others and learning to work with a will.'[22]

By the time war broke out, Reith, then twenty-five, was convinced that his own destiny was to lead men. He had, he later confessed, 'been looking forward to war, and for years'. Alas, the opportunity to test himself in the heat of battle turned out to be frustratingly short-lived. In the autumn of 1915, he was in the village of Cuinchy on the Western Front serving with the Royal Engineers when he was shot by an enemy sniper. The wound was bad enough to get him evacuated to London: a 'Blighty wound' that ended his war for good. 'I am more disgusted than I can say', he wrote to his mother from hospital. 'I was getting on so well and enjoying the work.'[23]

These words contained a perverse truthfulness. Before his spell with the Royal Engineers, Reith had been a transport officer organising supplies and the movement of men. He had been 'a somebody; an object of mystification, envy and respect … a power in the land'. At the Front, his commanding officers struggled to keep him in line. In his own mind, he knew that in exercising 'supreme responsibility for men' he could do better than anyone else. The slaughter of the Great War was as much a case study in mismanagement as it was a tragedy. His hero was one of the great strongmen of history: 'I wish there were an Oliver Cromwell in England now', he confided in his diary.[24]

But Reith's Blighty wound did at least allow him to demonstrate other extraordinary abilities. In January 1916 an old engineering contact got him a job in the United States, helping to run a Remington gun factory in Philadelphia that supplied the British Army. His mission over the following eighteen months was to speed up production without any reduction in quality. Within a matter of weeks, he was summarily sacking employees who agitated for better conditions or asked for a pay rise – and admitting that he 'enjoyed doing it'. As a battle-scarred war veteran, he was an object of great curiosity throughout the city, feted by financiers and industrialists and flattered into giving speeches at prominent social gatherings about the need in civic life for men of good character. Reith returned to Britain in April 1917 'full of self-confidence'. His factory experience had taught him how to 'force the pace', as he put it, while his speech-making and socialising had reawakened an interest in politics. He was now 'inordinately ambitious' to be of 'tremendous service' back home.[25]

As Cecil Lewis had discovered, however, the arrival of peace did little to clarify what precise form such service might take. Reith eventually accepted the job of general manager at Beardmore, a large engineering firm in Coatbridge just outside Glasgow. He would later claim that it was this experience that helped him 'get to know the conditions under which a very large part of the population worked'. Yet he swiftly put into practice the ruthless management style he had picked up in the United States. Shop stewards were closely monitored, and employees who failed to clock-in were dismissed. Such high-handed behaviour was not unusual at the time. Since the Russian Revolution of 1917, factory owners had been fretting constantly about the insurrectionary potential of organised labour. In their worst moments, they feared that thousands of men, not just brutalised by conflict but angered by the absence of that 'land fit for heroes' that Lloyd George's government had promised, might go on the rampage. In one sense, everyone was now under suspicion. The 1918 Representation of the People Act had expanded the electorate from just under eight million to over twenty-one million in one fell swoop: where, the middle classes wondered, were the guarantees that all these newly enfranchised men and women would think calmly and clearly now that they had joined the political realm? In any case, the atmosphere of distrust had become so bad at Reith's own firm that it had been flagged by the Ministry of Labour as a potential flashpoint. In January 1919, thousands of workers across 'Red Clydeside' went on strike to demand a shorter working week, better conditions and more jobs. There were fears that Glasgow might become 'Britain's Petrograd'.[26] At Beardmore, Reith rooted out what he called 'disruptive communistic activity' with a brutal efficiency that alarmed even his superiors. At the same time, he arranged lectures, canteen concerts and football matches for the staff. He even struck a deal with the local council to supply shop-floor employees with twenty new tied houses. Reith was deeply suspicious of organised labour. Yet he was also discovering first-hand how the carefully calibrated disbursement of the good things in life, something that Matthew Arnold had once advocated and his own parents practised, could stop class anger from boiling over.

There were other worries for Reith to navigate, less easy to fix and more nebulous in character. In 1922, he had sought weekly treatment at a psychological clinic at Glasgow's Western Infirmary, admitting that he felt as though he were now 'living in great anxiousness', haunted by 'demons of doubt, depression and even despair'. There was no single cause for this loss of mental equilibrium, nor could it easily be cured. Reith always maintained publicly that, while he was 'intensely sorry that friend after friend' had been lost, the war had had little lasting impact on him personally. Yet he was now among the 58,000 or so ex-service personnel receiving a ministry pension for neurasthenia.[27]

It was no coincidence that the signature trauma of the Great War itself was 'shell shock'. In the first months of the conflict, the sudden amnesia and extreme muscle tremors exhibited by many thousands of frontline soldiers had been understood merely as symptoms of physical damage to the brain caused by proximity to a shattering blast. Psychiatrists working in field hospitals had quickly established a more likely explanation: the prolonged emotional impact of trench warfare, with its constant noise and sleeplessness, the endless fear of death, the sheer bloody horror and grind.[28] Shell shock, in other words, looked like the most extreme manifestation of a wider problem: stress. Many ex-servicemen displayed a nervous strain – characterised by, say, anxiety, headaches, insomnia, restlessness, exhaustion, irritability – which was diagnosed as 'neurasthenia'. This was not solely a neurosis of war: it had first been diagnosed in the nineteenth century, and popularised by a New York physician, George Beard, and the leading psychologist, William James. Both men had warned that human nerves were being worn to shreds by modern life in general. The noise and dazzle and frenetic pace of the city, the speeding trains, the startling new rhythms and images of the electrical age: they were all creating a kind of shock to the system. The shock of war, with its unleashed brutalities, was merely the final straw.

Reith's medical reports show that in January 1920, he had started to become fearful of crowds and enclosed spaces. By September the following year, he was apparently exhibiting 'giddiness and sleeplessness and general depression of spirits'. His doctor also noted that he had 'marked general tremors to hands, eyelids and tongue' and easily became 'anxious and irritable'. By the end of 1922 he was described bluntly as 'mentally nervous and on edge'. It had all started with 'noises' in the ear as a direct result of that gunshot wound to the face, but as Reith himself explained, the trouble was 'not one which can be detected physically'. At this moment in his life, he was certainly also distressed at the recent death of his father and one of his sisters. He was anxious about his mother's health. As always, he was troubled by his own spiritual inadequacies. Above all, he was more distressed than ever that he had yet to find a job that lived up to the extraordinary potential he had seen in himself. Adjustment to a humdrum civilian life was clearly a source of strain for thousands of ex-servicemen. For someone such as Reith, a man over-brimming with self-belief, the feeling must have been particularly acute. Certainly, he now felt that working at the engineering plant was a 'horrid prostitution' of his unique talents. By the spring of 1922, the feeling had become so intolerable that he handed in his notice and abandoned Coatbridge for London. 'I am now conscious of abilities which almost overwhelm me', he complained, 'and yet nothing to do.'[29]

There was something he *wanted* to do: enter politics. As far back as 1914, Reith had decided that if there were things to do in the world, 'the greatest amount of influence' belonged to a government minister. From that point on he was, as he told his father, 'awfully keen to go into Parliament'. The only unresolved question was which party he should represent. At first, Reith had dallied with the Liberals. More recently, he had announced in a letter to a Labour MP that he might best serve his country by going into politics as a socialist. It was, however, a Conservative MP close to Lloyd George's fracturing coalition government, William Bull, who came forward first, offering Reith the role of political secretary. Reith signed up to fight what he called 'the Labour menace' in the forthcoming general election, though he confided in his diary that he remained, in essence, a Liberal. The profound differences between each party were apparently of less importance to him than whether any of them offered 'an unqualified, deliberate, manly and aggressive adoption of the principles expounded by Christ', and, in particular whether they advocated 'righteousness in every department of human activity'. Just as importantly, he was 'always susceptible to oratory'.[30] As with everything else, Reith's own political beliefs were complex and contradictory. The only certainty was that he always wanted to have an *effect*.

It was a striking piece of oratory that now offered Reith a way forward. One Sunday in October 1922, he went as usual to the evening service at the Presbyterian church in London's Regent Square. The minister held him spellbound with a sermon based on Ezekiel, all about God seeking a man to act as an outstanding example to others. 'I still believe', wrote Reith in his diary that night, 'that there is some great work for me to do in the world'. A week later, a small advert in the *Morning Post* caught his eye. A general manager was required, 'only applicants having first class qualifications' need apply. It was for an outfit he had never heard of: the 'British Broadcasting Company (in formation)'. Two months and one short interview later the job was his. After a brief return home to Glasgow, he was back in London and ready to begin what he now called his 'great work'.[31]

Arthur Burrows: the wonder of wireless

On that December evening at Savoy Hill, after the trio had finished looking around the building, Reith left Cecil Lewis to his own devices. It was Arthur Burrows whom he whisked off to his club for a drink, 'with intent to discover, without disclosing my ignorance, what I had become general manager of'.[32]

At first Reith had been rather 'mystified' by the man. At the age of forty, Burrows was very much the oldest of the group. He was also the most unassuming. Lewis found him soft, genial, very friendly, with a mellifluous voice – a 'sweet chap', but someone with little obvious presence or character or vision.[33] This was a wild underestimation of the man, for here was someone whose wartime career had given him the perfect combination of skills to transform this new joint venture from a mere technology into something with a powerful cultural or moral purpose. He brought to the group a cautious but egalitarian spirit. He was a little stolid, perhaps even timid; yet he was fair-minded, grounded, practical. And, in his own quiet way, driven by a passionate idealism.

Arthur Burrows had grown up in Oxford, where his father was a college porter, his mother a part-time teacher. Throughout his childhood, he had been surrounded by academics and always regarded the city's university with reverence. The undergraduates, however – especially the 'wealthy, arrogant and boorish' among them – would frequently treat his father offhandedly, and when it came to relations between Town and Gown, Burrows would always be firmly on the side of Town. He believed profoundly in education, but of the kind which usually took place outside a formal setting. When he left school at seventeen, his first job was teaching science at adult evening classes run by the local technical school; in his spare time he taught himself photography. After a year or two, he joined the local newspaper, the *Oxford Times*, where he did a little of everything: type-setting, maintaining the machinery, cycling around the city in hot pursuit of stories. In 1911 he moved on to the London paper, *The Standard*. And it was here that he discovered the rather arcane, somewhat mystical world of wireless.[34]

The technology had been around for decades. Its roots lay in the dots and dashes of Morse code that had pulsed back and forth along telegraph cables snaking across whole continents and ocean floors throughout the Victorian era: a fully fledged system of instant communication that had encircled the globe. It was after the German physicist Heinrich Hertz proved the existence of electromagnetic waves in the late 1880s that another technological leap forward seemed possible. A crucial breakthrough had been made in a lecture theatre in Arthur Burrows' home city of Oxford. There, in 1894, the British physicist Oliver Lodge sent the three short pulses of a single letter 'S' from one room to the next without any wires, thereby demonstrating to an excited public audience an important principle: that electrical signals could not just escape the confines of the telegraph cable and carry with them a flow of words radiating inaudibly through the open air; they could also be captured again by

Arthur Burrows, pictured in 1931. Cecil Lewis described him as a 'sort of plum pudding'. His genial demeanour made it easy to overlook the strength of his moral vision when it came to championing wireless as a technology to be used for the public good.

anyone with the right sort of receiving equipment.[35] It then fell to Guglielmo Marconi – a young Italian with little knowledge of physics but a limitless gift for self-promotion, as well as a family wealthy enough to bankroll him – to exploit this scientific knowledge commercially.

Barely out of his teens, Marconi had been eagerly reading up on the experiments of electrical pioneers around the world. By the autumn of 1895 – just a year after Lodge's demonstration in Oxford – he had assembled enough equipment to send signals wirelessly across the sprawling grounds of his family estate on the outskirts of Bologna. Early the following year, still only twenty-one years old, he left Italy for Britain, which, as the centre of a global empire and the world's leading naval power, seemed to present greater opportunities for attracting investment. Sending signals wirelessly at ever greater distances, he demonstrated that he had not just an intriguing scientific device but a practical *system* for international communication.

Marconi referred constantly to 'my invention', and within half a decade he had ensured that his name was virtually syn-onymous with wireless. In reality, he had a highly limited aesthetic vision of its future. In a speech to the Royal Institution in London in 1902, he announced blandly that wireless was 'certainly no more wonderful than the transmission of telegrams along an ordinary wire'.[36] His interest was with achieving 'point-to-point' communication between a single sender and a single receiver: wireless was merely another kind of private subscription service in which both sender and receiver could be charged for their transaction.

He was, however, relentless in pursuing the opportunities this presented for building a lucrative business, modifying the work of others, buying out their patents, or, if any rival systems emerged, trying to suppress or discredit them. By 1900, having secured the support of the General Post Office, which was in charge of all telegraphy within Britain, and under the ever-watchful eyes of Admiralty officials, he had succeeded in sending signals across Salisbury Plain, then the Bristol Channel, then the English Channel. Finally, towards the end of 1901, he managed to get a faint signal across the 3,000 miles of the Atlantic Ocean, a feat which suggested that by bouncing off the ionosphere wireless signals could travel right over the horizon. When news reached Britain a few days later – ironically, by telegram along the old submarine cable route – there was a ripple of astonishment. It was as though the whole world suddenly lay at the mercy of this new technology.

There was soon an eager pool of customers for Marconi's kit. Ever since the Titanic had sunk in April 1912, the Marconi Company had seen fit to fill the pages of one of its own publications, *Wireless World*, with ghoulish tales of terror at sea. Stories about stricken ships were reminders, as the magazine put it bluntly, 'of our dependence upon wireless telegraphy for the safe navigation of the ocean'.[37] As the prospect of war loomed, *Wireless World* had shifted emphasis, offering dire warnings about enemy powers gaining a cunning strategic advantage through newly constructed communication networks of their own.

When hostilities finally erupted in August 1914, the focus on wireless's strategic role quickly shifted from communication to propaganda. Germany deployed powerful transmitters on its own territory to broadcast a news service throughout the world several times a day. Stations in New York and New Jersey would pick this up and pass it on by telegraph to various domestic news agencies across America. The German version of events would then appear in hundreds of newspapers. All this was being closely monitored in London, where there were feverish articles about the 'mischievous' uses to which the technology was being put, about 'vast floods' of false reports being treated as fact by credulous newspapers, about lies spreading like 'poison gas'. In response, a so-called 'Neutral Press Committee' was established to co-ordinate the transmission of friendly news to overseas wireless stations and agencies. At Poldhu on the Cornish coast, a station issued a nightly bulletin to allied naval and merchant ships scattered throughout the oceans of the Northern Hemisphere.[38]

More discreetly, at the Marconi Company's Chelmsford works, a new Wireless Press Service also began to eavesdrop on behalf of the government. Its team of Morse code operators worked day and night to intercept and summarise the stream of messages radiating from Germany, which were then distributed across Whitehall. The man who ran this secret listening service was Arthur Burrows. It was here at Chelmsford that Burrows grew to appreciate the extraordinary potency of wireless as a means of spreading information – and, so it seemed, *dis*information.[39]

Marconi himself remained obsessed with wireless as a means of sending messages privately between a single transmitter and a single receiver, his mind stubbornly fixed on a Victorian notion of point-to-point telegraphy. That anyone with the right equipment might tune in and overhear messages intended for others was, as he put it, a 'critical flaw'.[40] The military authorities, too, only ever thought of wireless as another device for delivering confidential information speedily from one field of operation to another. Burrows, however, had noticed a different kind of wireless being forged in the heat of conflict. The demands of propaganda required that the millions of dots and dashes hurled into the ether by all sides, far from being kept private, needed to be scattered as widely as possible, reaching not an individual but a multitude. This was wireless as *broadcasting* – wireless where the leaky, uncontrolled, intrinsically public nature of the electromagnetic signal was no longer a defect but a strength.

Implicit, too, in this new concept of broadcasting was the intriguing notion that it had the power to change listeners' minds – and possibly lots of them at once. *Wireless World* had warned its readers that German messages did not have to be true in order to 'convince' people of their truthfulness. And their impact could be immeasurable on those who were especially 'curious' or 'disaffected'. The implications were unsettling. Yet also thrilling. For if wireless really was being used to radiate such disruptive messages to the widest imaginable audience, might it not also be used to reach equal numbers of people with messages of enlightenment and peace? Burrows certainly thought so. Wartime duties, he later recalled, 'confirmed in my opinion that in wireless there exists a factor, which, when more fully developed materially will alter for the better the social life of the people and international relations'.[41]

A suggestion from *Wireless World* in April 1917 that harmful propaganda should be countered by 'saturating the ether with truth ions' spoke to a broader sense of technological idealism taking root in the immediate aftermath of war. In Soviet Russia the visionary writer and former Red Army member, Velimir Khlebnikov, was preaching of wireless as a potential 'tree' of consciousness that would 'unite all mankind'. He imagined a central station from which 'The crests of waves in the sea of human knowledge' would roll outwards: news and lectures and information unleashed 'like the flight of birds in springtime', 'saturating' the countryside all around 'with a flood of scientific and artistic news' so that millions might experience 'the snowy heights of the human spirit'. Wireless, he concluded, would 'forge continuous links in the universal soul and mold mankind into a single entity'. Back in Britain, Arthur Burrows offered a more prosaic vision. He had emerged from the war as a life-long pacifist, and had only stayed at the Marconi Company to sell the idea of wireless as a civilian rather than a military technology. When the League of Nations held its first General Assembly in Geneva in November 1920 in an attempt to secure permanent international peace, it was Burrows who rushed to the Swiss city to set up and run an ad hoc wireless station so that newspaper journalists covering the event could send home their daily despatches. In the aftermath, he saw how wireless might become a 'platform' for 'the social life of the people'.[42]

In making this leap from private tool to public medium, wireless needed to undergo one further – and hugely important – transformation: it would only be truly accessible to large numbers of people if it could move beyond a language of dots and dashes and carry instead the actual sound of the human voice. Before the war, there had been only sporadic successes on this front. In America, an engineer called Reginald Fessenden had managed to transmit a few songs as early as Christmas 1906. In 1912, Burrows himself had written a story in the London *Standard* about 'hundreds' of amateur wireless operators across southern England who, expecting to eavesdrop on a stream of Morse code, had heard instead 'wafted scraps of melody and tantalising fragments of conversation' – evidence, he hinted, of hush-hush experiments in Slough and Crystal Palace.[43]

Such public experiments as there were had come to a halt at the outbreak of war, when the military took control of all wireless activity. But from his vantage point at the Wireless Press Service, listening in to all the electronic messages flying around the globe, Burrows occasionally caught the intriguing sound of human voices emanating from Berlin, and in 1915 a speech sent from Arlington in the United States to the Eiffel Tower in Paris, some 3,800 miles away. By the time peace had returned three years later, he felt confident enough to outline an astonishing – though now achievable – vision. 'Before we are many years older', he predicted, people would be listening in their own homes to 'concerts or the important recitals' from venues such as London's Albert Hall, and newspaper offices across the country would be hearing their local MPs speaking live in Parliament.[44]

Whether there was any real public demand for such fantastical things was another matter. The medium still belonged to the hobbyists – men and boys mostly, who, even before the war, had been assembling in their sheds or attics or spare rooms various cables, wires, switches and valves, so that they could privately eavesdrop on the thousands of messages already flying through the air. They were called 'listeners-in', because, strictly speaking, little of what they heard was intended for them in the first place. Some of these messages were official; others radiated out from training schools being set up by the Marconi Company to supply ships with their wireless operators. In time, yet more came from other hobbyists who had the equipment – and the necessary Post Office licence – to transmit as well as receive. It all had a very distinctive appeal. Just as Cecil Lewis had been mesmerised by the machinery of the planes he flew during the war, there was a real thrill in handling the arcane hardware of wireless. Clubs were formed throughout the country, membership usually open only to 'bona fide experimenters'. They were a cultish tribe who would have regarded Burrows' notion of concerts from the Albert Hall with bemusement, since, like Guglielmo Marconi himself, they showed little immediate awareness of the creative potential of the technology in their hands.[45] Nevertheless, there were by now enough listeners-in around to provide a useful testing ground for those, like Burrows, who wanted to take wireless in a new direction – enough, perhaps, to one day provide a ready pool of customers for whom companies like Marconi's might make available domestic wireless receivers. There was as yet no clear 'market' for the kind of thing Burrows had imagined. But it was possible one might be tickled into existence, especially if listeners-in knew that there was something more interesting than call signs or time signals wafting about – something, in fact, specifically intended *for* them, rather than something they simply happened to overhear.

Finding a practical means of achieving this marked a critical moment in the history of broadcasting in Britain. Towards the end of 1919, the Marconi Company's 'Publicity and Demonstration Department', which Burrows led, opened a new transmitter at its main works in Chelmsford, and over the course of ten days the following spring it 'radiated' two daily half-hour programmes, including what Burrows described as 'news and vocal and instrumental selections'. Reports soon came flooding back. The broadcasts had been heard clearly on ships a thousand miles or so away as well as by around four hundred 'experimenters' across Britain. Three months later, the celebrated singer Nellie Melba stood before the microphone at Chelmsford to recite three short pieces, preceded by what Burrows recalled as 'a prolonged trill' – the first of a series of demonstration concerts that continued throughout the rest of 1920. There was, as yet, nothing in the way of a regular service: the Post Office, still worrying about anything 'wasteful and frivolous' interfering with military signals, granted only a series of very temporary licences to transmit, and at year's end Chelmsford was asked to cease transmitting. Even so, its 'stunts', as Burrows called them, achieved a great deal more than simply providing Marconi engineers with feedback on the strengths and weaknesses of their technology. They had caught the attention of the press. They had even changed the mood among amateur listeners. In December 1921, sixty-three different wireless clubs petitioned the Post Office for a new service of 'speech and even music'.[46]

Officially, the Marconi Company's main business remained the sale of wireless telegraphy equipment to the newspaper industry and the government. It still regarded the brief snatches of news and music that had been sent out from Chelmsford as no more than a means of refining the technology of private communication. But within Marconi, Burrows now argued for a wholly new concept of wireless, writing in a confidential memo that it was precisely the 'radiation' of news and entertainment to a large but dispersed civilian audience, and the opportunity perhaps to levy some sort of hiring charge on all these listeners, which now presented the better business opportunity. Might it not use the 'substantial industrial base' it had created for peaceful purposes?[47]

In February 1922, cajoled by Burrows and buoyed by the combined enthusiasm of the wireless amateurs, the Marconi Company secured permission from the Post Office to open another new station, at Writtle, just a few miles from Chelmsford. In a small hut, a handful of engineers would spend the days tinkering with equipment and their evenings performing for anyone who cared to tune in. Their ringleader was Peter Eckersley, who had spent the war as a wireless operator in the Royal Flying Corps. Now, at precisely eight o'clock each evening the engineers would begin their transmissions by announcing the station call sign, 2MT: 'Hullo, CQ. Hullo, CQ. This is two emma tock, Writtle Calling'. Some gramophone records followed, each briefly introduced. As the weeks passed, more spontaneity and gaiety crept in: sing-songs and nursery rhymes, a dramatised scene from *Cyrano de Bergerac*, even a night of grand opera in which Eckersley himself sang all the arias.

From his London base in Marconi House, Burrows kept an attentive ear on proceedings. Some of the Writtle staff, he feared, were getting a little carried away with their 'spirit of farce and foolishness'. He wanted schedules of evening concerts to be advertised in advance and tighter arrangements to be put in place with record companies. In short, he was looking for something a bit more respectable – something that would more easily garner the support of the Post Office and its political masters. So his department arranged for a second transmitter to start broadcasting, this time from the top floor of Marconi

House itself. The new London station featured less music, more scripted talks, and lots of worthy items designed to impress 'distinguished visitors'. It was called 2LO – a name that would soon become iconic.[48]

By the middle of 1922 events had started to take on a momentum of their own. What had begun as a series of transmissions ostensibly designed to test and improve the technical capacities of wireless telegraphy was evolving into a form of wireless 'radiating' entertainment for its own sake. Regular programmes of music and talk were being hurled into the sky for anyone within a hundred miles or more to hear. Every now and then, something entirely new would be attempted – commentary on a boxing match, say, or a bedtime story. Tens of thousands of people around the country were tuning in every week to catch these transmissions. More and more businesses, too, were wanting to get in on the act: a plethora of firms selling domestic receivers, ranging from the basic to the luxurious; and, alongside Marconi, two other companies – Metropolitan-Vickers and Western Electric – prepared to launch their own stations in Manchester and London.

Little of this was happening as a direct result of 'consumer' pressure, let alone a grassroots movement: if anything, supply was creating demand, not the other way around. Yet the immense possibilities of wireless as a public medium were clearer by the month. This was the very moment that Cecil Lewis, just back from China, had learned from his friend that something extraordinary was taking shape in America. Burrows himself was in the habit of scanning American magazines and would already have known what Lewis was only just discovering: that on the other side of the Atlantic, newspapers and companies such as General Electric and Westinghouse were installing 'radiophone stations' in every city and arranging daily programmes of 'gramophone concerts', operas, even church sermons. An obvious commercial opportunity had been spotted: not just the chance to manufacture or sell receivers, but the chance to sell whole slices of airtime for advertising goods of every kind. American operators were also alive at this point to the grander cultural opportunities. As a senior manager at Westinghouse put it, radio was 'the only means of instantaneous collective communication ever devised': it was, he said, poised to 'bring happiness' into every human life.[49]

Etherites

In a Britain recovering from a long, devastating war, anything that promised collective happiness had a powerful utopian appeal. On the eve of the war, *Wireless World* had been full of blood-curdling talk of powerful transmitters seizing 'dominion in the ether'. By the summer of 1922, a new magazine, *The Broadcaster*, spoke with a more optimistic and inclusive voice. Its very first front cover featured a simple domestic scene: a family – well-dressed, smiling – listening to the wireless at home. Pictures inside showed a courting couple listening to a receiver while floating dreamily on a boat, people dancing to music on a passenger plane, and miniature radio sets worn as wristwatches. Articles talked breathlessly of radio introducing 'a humanizing note when scattered peoples are brought into closer contact' or providing a 'panacea' for all who were ill or lonely. In this new, exciting world, they suggested, terms such as 'wireless amateur' were inadequate. The new phrase could perhaps be 'Etherites': a label that might easily be applied to all – rich and poor, young and old, male or female, casual or committed – who made use of that 'same invisible wonder', the ether.[50]

By forging this link between wireless and the ether, *The Broadcaster* was breathing new life into the Victorian concept of an all-pervasive, invisible medium. Oliver Lodge himself had believed passionately that some vast intangible entity had to exist in order to explain how energy moved through the universe. Einstein's theories of relativity had since dispensed with the need for such thinking. Yet the ether, and with it the idea of a universal connective medium, was simply too useful a concept to disappear entirely. It provided not just a neat shorthand for the electromagnetic spectrum, but something that helped people think of the world as 'a coherent whole, instead of a chaotic collection of independent isolated fragments'. The ether was a space without hierarchy, without centre or boundary – a *public* space, which not only joined together separate realms of being but separate realms of thought. In the years after the war, Lodge had come to believe that wireless might facilitate 'international conversation and co-operation' precisely because it embodied the ether's ability to break through the barriers that had so recently 'retarded mutual understanding' to such devastating effect.[51]

Indeed, it was as Etherites that Cecil Lewis, John Reith and Arthur Burrows had come together for the first time at No. 2 Savoy Hill – even if they would not have described themselves in this way.

Cecil Lewis had taken to the air to see the world anew and had discovered that what he really wanted was the 'vast credits' of wisdom and art produced by humankind to be of service in helping civilisation endure. John Reith, too, had been grasping for some means of holding the looming chaos at bay by spreading the 'sweetness and light' so beloved of Matthew Arnold. Neither man knew quite how their ambitions might be fulfilled. But here, in Arthur Burrows' hands, was a piece of technology that might provide the answer – something that could reach into every corner of the land, indifferent to status and ability, capable of delivering enlightenment to all. Burrows spoke of wireless as a force for 'disarmament', as something that would 'assist the progress of civilization'. Newspapers, he pointed out, were highly partisan and failed utterly 'to circulate in the homes of all classes of Society and people of all tastes and temperaments'. Wireless, by way of contrast, might soon be received 'in any house or institution'; it embraced a potpourri of voices and opinions. In 'radiating amusement and instruction' it would help 'in spreading throughout the world a doctrine of common sense'. Thanks to wireless, the ether would soon be like a vast ocean filled with all manner of sounds and spirits, thoughts and messages. It would be a sea of possibility – synthesising ideas, advancing human understanding, building peace between peoples and nations. To men and women still unfamiliar with the science, it all spoke of something mysterious, magical, *exciting*. It was, an avid reader told *The Broadcaster*, something that filled one 'with wonder and awe'. 'You've started the fever in the brain', another wrote. 'It will prove catching. It will grow to an epidemic.'[52]

*

It must have been immensely satisfying for Arthur Burrows to know that after all his strenuous efforts everyone was now so excited by radio. But for a cautious man like him an epidemic would be the worst of all outcomes.

What was happening in the United States suggested the need for care. At the beginning of May 1922, the country had 219 registered radio stations. Only a month later the number was 318. By summer's end, there was talk of a 'jumble of signals', the 'blasting and blanketing of rival programmes', 'chaos of the ether'. The 'American experience', Burrows argued, showed what 'might result in a densely-populated country of small area like our own, if the go-as-you-please methods of the United States were copied'. He now persuaded his managing director, Godfrey Isaacs, that in Britain some sort of national 'public service' arrangement would be needed in which the various radio companies, including his own, worked 'under a measure of Government direction'. The General Post Office was reaching much the same conclusion. Four years of war had demonstrated the effectiveness of centralised administrative control of utilities such as health, coal and food, in harnessing national resources.[53] When it came to broadcasting, the precise form of oversight was less clear – save for the GPO's firmly expressed wish *not* to take direct responsibility for itself.

The issue was thrashed out in a series of meetings across the summer, between the GPO, the Imperial Communications

Committee, which represented the armed services and key government ministries, and the ever-expanding number of radio companies wanting to exploit the growing market for receivers. It was eventually agreed that some sort of organised service of music and educational talks was desirable, that advertising should be prohibited, and that 'clashing' over wavelengths needed to be avoided. There could be several radio stations positioned around the country. But since all broadcasting would be confined to a particular band of wavelengths and to certain times of day, there would need to be a single agency to ensure that the various stations did not interfere with each other. Co-operation between the radio companies would also prevent a commercial monopoly emerging – with the GPO's favoured solution being 'to make all the firms get together to form one Company for the purpose of doing the broadcasting'. These, then, were the practical considerations. But cultural ones were also discussed. For, as a senior GPO official later explained, it was agreed that 'If the ether was to be occupied, we hoped that it would be worthily occupied'.[54]

By summer's end agreement was reached. On Wednesday 18 October 1922, a consortium was formed, to be licensed by the GPO and open not just to the six largest firms who provided the initial capital of £100,000 but to each and every bona fide radio manufacturer in the country willing to pay £1 for an 'Ordinary Share'. Operational costs would be met from half of the 10-shilling licence fee that the GPO levied on all owners of domestic receivers, plus – to begin with – a modest royalty on the sale of sets. As the Postmaster-General explained, this new entity would 'have no business to secure': 'it will simply have to provide broadcasting programmes'.[55] The most straightforward aspect of all was its name. It was to be called the 'British Broadcasting Company' – or, for short, the BBC.

On the Friday before the BBC was formally born, a newspaper advertised the first few vacancies for senior roles at the new company. Arthur Burrows, who by now almost certainly knew more than anyone else in the land about the practicalities of broadcasting, secured the post of Director of Programmes. His deputy would be Cecil Lewis; his General Manager, and the man in overall charge, John Reith. Together, the three men constituted the original creative nucleus of British public service broadcasting. And No. 2 Savoy Hill would be where they would build their empire.

'Finally, a man comes home'

For Reith, the most profound revelation of all when he began his new job at the British Broadcasting Company was the complete lack of direction from above. 'There were', he explained, 'no sealed orders to open.' This simple fact had one profound and immediate consequence, as far as he was concerned. 'Almost everything depended upon the personality of those to whom, almost by chance, this service had been committed.'[56] Their beliefs, their prejudices, their fears, their hopes – the whole crooked timber of their humanity: twisted together, this made up the DNA of the BBC. It was to be an organisation bearing the traces of thinking, feeling, complicated individuals – an organisation shaped in *their* image.

But Cecil Lewis, John Reith and Arthur Burrows were not alone for long. They would soon be joined by dozens, then hundreds, of others – and the BBC would be shaped in the image of these men and women, too.

The Great War had touched an entire generation – though not always in predictable ways. It is why historians have written of 'one war, multiple memories'. They point out the 'morbid' atmosphere seeping through Britain – or, at least, its intellectual circles – in the aftermath of a terrifyingly brutal conflict. Yet they also describe a country that was far from being 'frozen in perpetual mourning'. For all those who despaired at the state of civilisation in the 1920s, there were many others determined to recast the world they had inherited, who refused to give in without a struggle and to accept that humanity was beyond redemption. It was to this latter group that Lewis,

Reith and Burrows – and many of those who now joined them – all emphatically belonged. Many still bore the obvious signs of battle. Reith himself had a face sufficiently scarred that he looked like 'a villain in a melodrama'. Lewis carried a six-inch gash on his shoulder. Among the other early BBC recruits were a remarkable number of ex-pilots. They included Lance Sieveking, who, after spending time in a German prisoner-of-war camp, still suffered from multiple ailments, including a weakened liver and stomach. Among those who had fought in the trenches, there was Derek McCulloch, who arrived at Savoy Hill blind in one eye and suffering severe pain in his limbs: he had been so badly injured in the war that when a German stretcher party found him lying in No Man's Land, they had shot him in the head to put him out of his misery.[57] Over the coming years there would be countless others walking the BBC's corridors with a pronounced limp or bearing some other injury inflicted during service at the Front.

It was, though, the invisible damage lurking beneath these physical wounds that mattered more in the longer run. The kaleidoscope of experiences accumulated through the four-year conflict lingered 'just below the surface' of many fighting men's consciousness, ready to emerge later in all sorts of behaviours and attitudes. An astute observer of those who would soon join the infant BBC was struck by the 'high proportion of young people … mainly men who had served in the war, and who – because of some awkward versatility or some form of fastidiousness, idealism, or general restlessness … never settled down to any humdrum profession'.[58] Sieveking for instance, like Reith, had been diagnosed with neurasthenia; every now and then, he would have suicidal thoughts and minor nervous breakdowns. Working alongside him was Lionel Fielden, who had fought at Gallipoli. It was there that Fielden had experienced what he called an 'elastic stretching of the nerves'. After peace was declared, he had worked for the League of Nations in Geneva, gone to art school, run a poultry farm, worked at the Treasury, and led a somewhat raffish life on the French Riviera – all while being

Savoy Hill at night in 1927. For the BBC's pioneering staff, many
of whom still carried the psychological baggage of wartime, the
building became what Lionel Fielden called 'a port in a storm'. His
colleague Lance Sieveking described it as 'a very jolly bedlam'.

'dogged by a recurrence of Gallipoli dysentery'. It was during
this extended period of 'wandering' that he first nurtured, as he
put it, 'some vague idea that I might blow out my brains in the
Casino'. 'I saw too many possible roads', Fielden thought, yet
was 'trained for nothing'. No wonder Maurice Gorham, who
joined the BBC in 1926, found that those around him needed
careful handling. 'Quite a lot of them suffered shell-shock ...

you never quite knew how they would react. And quite a lot of them drank . . . there were always some of my colleagues with whom it was never safe to do any business after lunch.'[59] The generation who founded the BBC were by no means wrecks. But their energy was of an unpredictable kind.

Many of these ex-servicemen showed a deep attachment to male companionship in the aftermath of the war. Some even betrayed a nostalgia for military life. Given the difficulties that adjusting to home life sometimes presented, it was often the workplace that offered most comfort. Sieveking was acutely aware on his arrival at the BBC that No. 2 Savoy Hill had been the very same building in which he had been demobbed from the Royal Air Force several years before. 'In it again,' he wrote, 'mobilised into another "Air Force".' When Fielden moved into the same building a little later, he, too, felt as if he had found somewhere familiar, a 'port in a storm'.[60] At the BBC, military titles would abound – and be used when people addressed each other formally. There was 'Captain Sieveking', 'Captain Lewis', 'Captain Eckersley'; there would soon be a 'Commander Goldsmith' and an 'Admiral Carpendale' and a 'Major Atkinson'; Reith would flit between 'Captain' and 'Major' – he was in dispute with the War Office on the matter of which of the two titles was correct. The collective memory of recent war service was going to be palpably present at Savoy Hill. And it mattered.

Yet if the generation that joined the BBC in the 1920s had learned anything from the war it was that it had had enough of taking orders. The military titles used at Savoy Hill spoke to a kind of *moral* authority that attached to those who had served. And there was also something more organic – and more *comradely* – at play: a recognition of shared experience and mutual understanding, which, if anything, cut across formal chains of command. At the very least, it created an atmosphere that helped those inside feel they were part of a community.

★

In what has been labelled an 'Age of Stress', it was unsurprising that many people responded to the perceived threat of instability by searching for ways of achieving the opposite. In culture, politics, psychology, even biology, there was much talk of equilibrium and of balance. It represented not a reactionary wish to halt progress, let alone to return to the old order, but rather a desire to find a way in which humanity as a whole might successfully navigate a changing world. For the founding generation who moved into No. 2 Savoy Hill, this meant that radio itself would be conceived as something requiring a delicate balancing act. Home and hearth – and, in particular, the comforts of the cosy fireside – would have an iconic place in the imagery of the BBC's first decade. Indeed, Reith said very explicitly that one of the prime goals in broadcasting would be to enable people to 'enjoy an evening at home'. The desire for life to be a bit more peaceable was widely felt, and it seemed reasonable to think that home was precisely where a process of *re*-civilising might begin. At the same time, there would be an impulse, more social-democratic than conservative in spirit, to bring to the British people through radio things that were new and perhaps a little bit unsettling, in the belief that this would also slowly but surely improve their lives. Having started his career knowing next to nothing about broadcasting, it would not be long before Cecil Lewis was rhapsodising about its huge, transformative potential. Before broadcasting, he asked, 'who went to concerts, who went to the opera? Only the people who could afford it'. 'The poor, the ordinary people in the street never heard an opera in their lives, never heard a symphony concert ... And then suddenly there it was, in their ears ... everybody's excitement and interest in life was lifted: they hadn't known; now they began to know.'[61]

It was a distinctly mixed bunch who were charged with creating this grand, emancipatory project. Very few were passionate, let alone knowledgeable, about wireless itself. For the waifs and strays, the damaged souls, the oddballs, idealists, pragmatists, moralists, military types, dilettantes, actors, journalists and pacifists who would shortly fill up the BBC, the technology of radio was beside the point. It was a means to an end. Fielden would describe the atmosphere of Savoy Hill as 'one-third boarding school, one-third Chelsea party, one-third crusade'. He would add that perhaps the element of crusade 'bulked a little larger', for there was 'the same feeling of dedication and hope which had characterised the League of Nations in its earliest days'. 'We may have been silly', he would say, 'but we were never complacent. And God save us, we really believed that broadcasting could revolutionize human opinion.'[62]

On that cold, dark evening of Tuesday 19 December 1922, as Cecil Lewis, John Reith and Arthur Burrows stood on the steps of No. 2 Savoy Hill, all this excitement still lay in the future. But what a future it promised to be! For many of those who were about to go through the building's portals, the war had been the most momentous event in their lives. For some it had been thrilling – a once in a lifetime experience. But now there was the possibility of a *twice* in a lifetime experience: the opportunity to be in on something else utterly new and untried. Suddenly, all those lost years of 'vague and stupid' youth turned out to be exactly suited to the task ahead. 'My experience', Lionel Fielden explained, 'disorderly and aimless as it might have seemed, fitted the BBC, as it then was, perfectly.' For its 'chief and greatest attraction' was that 'the shape of things to come was still fluid'. It was a place where mistakes would be constantly made and where every day would be an experiment. Lance Sieveking explained that he loved beginnings more than anything else. Like Cecil Lewis, he had been there for the beginning of flying; now – alongside Lewis and Reith and Burrows and Fielden and all the others – he would be there at the beginning of broadcasting. It was a new industry, a new institution, a new way of life, a new art form, even. It was in the crucible, 'blazing, volatile, as yet innocent of the mould.'[63]

2

RIDING THE TIGER

In the heart of London, civilised and organised to
death, there was a sudden flash – a gesture – made by a
handful of silly young men who had, with the aid of a
microphone, the ear of the world. And the irony of the
situation is that the world hardly realised what they were
up to!

                                        Cecil Lewis, broadcaster

The British Broadcasting Company took to the airwaves for
the very first time at six o'clock in the evening on Tuesday 14
November 1922.

Through the crackle of the ether, several thousand listeners
to Marconi's London station suddenly heard Arthur Burrows
enunciating what would soon become a familiar, even famous
refrain. 'Hullo, hullo, 2LO calling. 2LO calling. This is the British
Broadcasting Company. 2LO. Stand by for one minute please!'
After a brief pause, Burrows read a short news bulletin and
weather forecast. In fact, he read it twice – first at normal speed
then more slowly so that listeners at home could take notes.[1]

The launch date had been chosen carefully. The next day was
a general election and Burrows had hoped that the Company
would be up and running in time to transmit the results. As the
country went to the polling stations on the Wednesday, 2LO's
listeners were joined by several thousand more tuned in to
Western Electric's 5IT in Birmingham and Metropolitan-Vickers' 2ZY just outside Manchester. Like 2LO, these stations, along

with well over a thousand commercial wireless manufacturers, were now operating under the new and unfamiliar banner of the BBC.

The practicalities of getting to this point had been tortuous. In the days leading up to the launch, Birmingham had been enveloped in a fog so dense that engineers at 5IT had nearly fallen off the roof as they struggled to erect their transmitter. In London, Burrows' inaugural broadcast had been cobbled together on a shoestring. Since there were no journalists at 2LO, his script was simply copy from news agency wires. There was hardly anyone else around, aside from a handful of enthusiastic survivors from the old Marconi days. Cecil Lewis was about to turn up from Metropolitan-Vickers to provide a bit of badly needed artistic input. But John Reith would not be appointed as General Manager for another month. Burrows, in other words, was largely working alone. And neither the bulletin he read out that first night, nor the election coverage over the days that followed could accurately be described as anything like a national broadcasting service. Indeed, the whole event passed entirely unnoticed by huge swathes of the British public. The total number of listeners was measured in tens of thousands rather than millions. And there was next to no coverage of the launch in the press. Only the *Times* had bothered alerting its readers to the momentous events of the day. 'Preliminary "broadcasting" will be authorized from Marconi House this evening', it had announced plainly on an inside page of the Tuesday edition. The fact that the word 'broadcasting' had to be placed delicately in inverted commas demonstrated just how exotic the paper still judged the term to be.[2]

This was indeed a new and uncharted activity, where the boundaries of what was creatively possible were going to have to be discovered day by day. 'The beginning of everything', Cecil Lewis recalled, 'a thrilling and exciting time'. Having been given a tool of potentially immense power – something that needed careful handling if it was to do more good than harm – it was also, he hastened to add, a *terrifying* time. It felt like 'somebody had given us a tiger and we were obliged to ride this tiger down Piccadilly ... we didn't know where the hell it was going and what damage the tiger might do!'[3]

The search for respectability

It wasn't until the following spring that the Company would actually be moving into its new premises at No. 2 Savoy Hill. Through the winter months, the fledgling Company had therefore been squatting uncomfortably in the second floor of Magnet House, the General Electric Company's headquarters just off London's Kingsway. A dozen or so people were squeezed into a single room around three long tables pulled together. At one end was a tiny 'cubby hole', just large enough for another small table and equipped with its own telephone. This, Reith had taken for himself. There was no studio in the building: each evening, when broadcasting began, Arthur Burrows or Cecil Lewis or one of their new colleagues would have to rush downstairs, scurry to the corner of Aldwych and the Strand, and then head to the top floor of Marconi House, where the Company had been loaned the use of a box room just big enough for six people, kitted out with an upright piano and microphone. It was here that the 2LO transmitter, piercing the roof above, had been broadcasting a 'London' programme during the summer and autumn of 1922, and where another half-dozen staff now toiled in conditions no less cramped and dingy than back at Magnet House. 'Pandemonium reigned!', Lewis recalled, acknowledging happily the palpable sense of adventure to be found in such chaos.[4] But for a new company wanting to make an impression, it was all rather undignified. And for a company with the ambition to grow, it could not last. It was this that had prompted Lewis and Burrows to join Reith in a London-wide search for new premises.

The move to Savoy Hill in 1923 brought the BBC's fledgling staff a reassuring sense of permanence. The gardens of the Savoy Chapel were close by, offering the tantalising glimpse of a leafy oasis. But the discomforts were manifest. Being stuck in what was irreverently termed the 'backside' of the Institution of Electrical Engineers' headquarters caused their ears to throb 'with the twittering of countless starlings roosting' and their nostrils to twitch at the noxious scent of the river Thames drifting in through the windows. Young men and women had to patrol the corridors, discharging a fine mist of vapour to drive away the 'mosquitos', while rodents would scurry along the wainscoting. Even so, the building's slightly seedy location and lack of pretension had a strange charm. The ageing lift creaked and the stone staircase was narrow, but new linoleum flooring had been laid down in the second-floor offices, old stoves re-enamelled, and fashionable opal bowl lamps added. Fireplaces in the corner of each room offered a modicum of comforting warmth. There was a generously sized General Office for clerks and typists, a Board Room, two lavatories, even a cupboard equipped with a kettle for making cups of tea. Separate rooms were available for, among others, a Company Secretary, Company Accountant, Company Registrar, and a Publicity Manager. Peter Eckersley, the technical wizard behind many of the experimental broadcasts from Writtle in 1922, was now the BBC's Chief Engineer and accordingly entitled to a room of his own on the North Wing. Two doors along, the Company's most senior programme makers, Burrows and Lewis, were, for the moment, required to share. Reith himself was ensconced in a plush management corridor on the West Wing, his thickly carpeted room separated from the surrounding hubbub by a heavy glazed swing door. Here, he had a dedicated telephone switchboard operator and his own private waitress, who looked after him 'in a most maternal way'.[5] His personal secretary, Isabel Shields, freshly recruited from Cambridge University, had her own rather more modest annexe next door, while a room at the far end of the North Wing corridor was the domain of Olive May, who ran the telephone exchange.

It was more than adequate for a company with thirty or so employees, less so for a company that by the end of 1924 had more than four hundred. Within two years of moving in, the Company had spread upwards into the third floor, then downwards into the first, and finally sideways into a separate block next door, No. 4 Savoy Hill. This created badly needed space for a panoply of new arrivals and specialist departments, responsible for, among other things, Talks, Women's programmes, *Children's Hour*, 'Special Features' and Music, as well as a new listings magazine launched in 1923 called the *Radio Times*. It was not long before getting from one part of the building to the next meant navigating an intimidatingly complex series of staircases and corridors. Bustling and crowded, it was a place small enough for everyone to know everyone else. 'You were always running across artists and speakers and bandsmen and passing doors with red lights betokening ON THE AIR.'[6] 'Studio No. 3', for instance, was on the third floor, near to the Music department's office. 'Studio No. 1' was on the first floor, right next to a room for band musicians and only a few steps away from the engineers' area. Even if you were one of Savoy Hill's 'backroom' staff, you could never be far away from the actual business of broadcasting.

As for the precise nature of this 'business', finding raw material to fill the hours of transmission was at the heart of it all: a lot easier said than done. The first issue of the *Radio Times* promised listeners that London alone would broadcast every weekday from 11.30 a.m. till 12.30, then from 5 p.m. till 6.25 p.m., and finally from 7 p.m. till the 10.30 p.m. 'close down' – a total of six hours a day, week after week.[7] And the permitted hours of transmission would only expand from this point onwards. It all represented an awful lot of programmes needing to be made from scratch.

Staring at the blank spaces on a vast schedule 'grid' pinned to the wall of his office, Cecil Lewis immediately realised that he and his colleagues had just been appointed 'guardians and attendants of the most voracious creature ever created – the microphone'. Henceforth, the overriding fact of their professional existence was that this 'terrible and insatiable' monster

– the tiger, as Lewis called it – 'clamoured daily to be fed!' But the constant question was what exactly to feed it *with*. When the BBC was launched, Reith had said that 'The commission was of the scantiest nature ... A broadcasting service was expected, and had to be initiated and developed. We had to do it.' Board members who had appointed Reith had simply told him 'we're leaving it all to you.'[8] As General Manager, Reith would set the general course of direction; it was for others to turn his lofty ideals into reality. This meant that the task of building programmes now fell to Arthur Burrows, his deputy Cecil Lewis, and those gathered around them.

★

To begin with, there was no 'policy' to guide them because, as Lewis pointed out, 'We didn't know what we were doing, we were simply finding something which could be broadcast ... it was a sort of free for all in which everybody was free to come up with any idea that seemed likely to be any use.'[9]

Despite the BBC's first official transmission being a bulletin, the one thing Lewis firmly believed was that news and current affairs should play only a small part in the overall output. 'I wasn't wild about what was happening in the world ... I didn't really care what was happening in Abyssinia', he explained. 'What *I* was up to, *that* was interesting, and that meant drama ... a new artist or a big show or a big concert.' He spoke for many inside Savoy Hill when he said that 'we were hooked on the idea of entertainment ... we were an *entertainment* medium'.[10]

Over the next few months, output closely echoed what had been produced in an ad hoc way at Writtle or 2LO during the old Marconi Company days: sketches and skits from variety shows, book readings and scenes from stage plays, short musical recitals, the occasional talk or lecture. From the very start, children were generously supplied with stories and miniature dramas of their own in a daily *Children's Hour*, Burrows regularly playing the role of 'Uncle Arthur', Lewis the role of 'Uncle Caractacus'.

And there was a strong taste for 'stunts' – special outside broadcasts from glamorous or unusual locations, including the first-ever 'relay' of an opera from Covent Garden: Mozart's *The Magic Flute*.

Savoy Hill did not have a monopoly in the supply of such cheerful eclecticism. At 2ZY near Manchester, the first broadcasts under the aegis of the BBC consisted of a brief news bulletin followed by a reading of Oscar Wilde's *The Happy Prince*, some light music, and finally, the first results of the election. The Oscar Wilde story was read by 'the Lady of the Magic Carpet' – in reality, a local English teacher, 'Miss Bennie' – as part of a new series broadcast three or four times a week called *Kiddie's Corner*. One of 2ZY's biggest early hits was a regular satirical commentary on the day's events called *Algy's Priceless Piffle*, presented by the monocle-wearing local actor-impresario Victor Smythe, who also busied himself writing scripts, directing plays, reading the news, creating sound effects, and organising a stream of outside broadcasts from sporting events or local variety theatres. On occasions, a small house orchestra little bigger than a quartet would be squeezed into the station's studio, complete with its conductor, Dan Godfrey Junior, who would stand on a small rostrum, dressed in an old football jersey and plus fours 'sweating gigantically'.[11]

There was a similar frenzy of improvisation at 5IT in Birmingham, where staff had quickly thrown together a schedule of live music in which all sorts came before the microphone entirely unrehearsed. The station's resident engineer, Maurice Deloraine, recalled how little thought was given to the finished product. 'They just said "I'm going to play on the piano" or "I'm going to sing this particular song"; sometimes it was not very successful, but we didn't worry.' Within a few months, 5IT's menu had settled into a comfortable routine, with well-organised relays of live orchestra concerts or 'rhythmic dance bands', as well as a *Ladies' Corner* and a regular *Kiddie's Corner* of its own.[12]

Between November 1922 and October 1923, more BBC

stations were opened in Newcastle, Cardiff, Glasgow, Aberdeen and Bournemouth. Belfast followed a year later. None of them thought of themselves as mere 'outposts' of London. Indeed, they were determined to showcase the variety and strength of local talent. At 5SC in Glasgow, for instance, a staff of five provided adaptations of classics such as Walter Scott's *Rob Roy* alongside fixed slots for their four-strong house orchestra. In Cardiff, 5WA offered recitals, short plays, and uplifting literary nights, though most of the evening schedule was devoted to children's programmes and music, including male voice choirs, 'light airs, folk songs and arias from popular operas'. While the range of material was genuinely broad, the city's Lord Mayor noticeably chose to heap praise on the station's ability above all else to provide 'the poorest of the land' with 'the highest form of culture'. [13]

With little or no central direction, the men and women of these 'provincial' stations had not just crafted a workable schedule of radio programmes for their listeners; they were helping the BBC to become a prominent feature of local culture and politics, on its way to being as important to civic identity as, say, the *Manchester Guardian*, the Bournemouth Municipal Orchestra or the Birmingham Rep.

The Company could therefore look back on its first months of operation with immense satisfaction. Across the country, ad hoc arrangements were already mutating into something more ordered and respectable. In the eight stations that the Company controlled, people who had never previously met, who had no precedent to work upon and the most threadbare of budgets to work with, had shown what Arthur Burrows described as 'the extraordinary, but in the majority of instances unsuspected, possibilities of broadcasting'. [14]

But the challenge facing all production staff remained essentially the same: how to *keep* putting out programmes, week in, week out, month after month, and, just as importantly, to do so with a professionalism that would reflect well on the fledgling BBC. John Reith was already starting to formulate an overarching principle – one that clearly embedded in the

Company's mission the spirit of Matthew Arnold. The airwaves, he announced, should feature 'everything that is best in every department of human knowledge, endeavour and achievement'. But, even leaving aside the thorny issue of what exactly counted as 'the best', this was easier said than done. The resources to hand were meagre: licence fee income was extremely modest, especially with the Post Office taking a hefty slice. And neither broadcasting in general nor the BBC in particular had yet established a reputation that raised it above the more commercialised pleasures of cinema or music hall or popular journalism. As one magazine reminded its readers, it might well be that 'in the very near future whoever controls the wireless of the world will also control the world', but for now it remained the case that 'everyone seems to take Radio merely as another form of light entertainment'. The leading writers, artists and politicians of the day were not yet knocking on the door of No. 2 Savoy Hill to offer their services:[15]

Until they did, an anxious search for fresh material and affordable talent hung over everything. Indeed, it was this relentless search that would define more than anything else the skills required of a producer such as Lionel Fielden:

> To gather enough people – always new and more people – for the microphone meant a constant alertness: the reading (or at least skimming) of every new book, the seeing of every new play and film, the attendance at every party to which one was asked, the journeys around England, to points where one thing or another created interest – slums, unemployment, pageants, new factories, a murder trial, a scandal, anything and everything: but above all an ear constantly cocked, at parties, in buses or tubes, at exhibitions, in shops, in the street and on the farm, for the Promising Voice … Many people would think that our 'work' was not work at all, but a constant round of pleasure. But we could never forget it; every moment of experience could be grist to the microphone.[16]

It helped to have the 'right' kind of social connections, of course. It was precisely because Fielden had, as he frankly admitted, 'made the acquaintance of a great many distinguished people in various walks of life' that he was hired as a producer in the Talks department, bringing to Savoy Hill what was described as his 'Etonian-cum-Regency elegance'. The man who now shared his office, Lance Sieveking, brought a similarly dazzling array of contacts picked up during his war service and subsequent artistic dabblings: G. K. Chesterton, Paul Nash, Wyndham Lewis, Eddie Marsh, Geoffrey Fry, John Maynard Keynes, H. G. Wells, A. P. Herbert, Esmond Harmsworth. Acquaintances like these provided an entrée into the worlds, not just of art and literature, but of Whitehall, the universities, Bloomsbury, Fleet Street. Indeed, the BBC's Director of Publicity, Gladstone Murray, admitted that it was less Sieveking's ideas and more his 'stand in with the Harmsworths' that was of primary benefit to the BBC: it helped in any dealings with the perennially hostile *Daily Mail*.[17] Right from the start, *who* you knew mattered a great deal at the BBC: it helped keep the schedule ticking over.

Throughout the 1920s and 1930s, the programmes that depended most on close contact with the Great and Good were those produced by the BBC's small but growing 'Talks' department. Both Lionel Fielden and Lance Sieveking were prominent members. But their immediate boss, the Director of Talks, was Hilda Matheson – someone with impressive connections of her own when she arrived at Savoy Hill in 1926, and who would turn out to be a major figure in the Company's attempts to make programmes that were both topical and influential. Matheson had spent part of her childhood on the Continent, so she spoke fluent Italian and pretty good French and German – language skills that quickly proved immensely useful. During the war, she had been recruited to the newly established MI5, and later transferred to Rome, where she helped set up a British counter-espionage unit. The discretion and acute political sensitivity involved in such work paid dividends. In 1919, when Nancy Astor became the first woman to take her seat as an MP in the House

Hilda Matheson, the BBC's Director of Talks, sitting with her dog Torquhil. When not asleep in Matheson's office Torquhil was usually to be found in the rabbit warren of corridors, being taken for a walk by one of Savoy Hill's 'office boys'.

of Commons, Matheson was hired as her political secretary. 'We worked as one', Astor later explained. 'I might describe it as my zeal and her brain.' Matheson spent the next six years helping Astor with speeches and correspondence, and keeping her company in social gatherings at Clivedon or St James's Square. One of Matheson's own initiatives was organising regular 'at homes' where MPs of all parties and other leading figures could meet women and learn more about what they wanted from Parliament now many of them had the vote. It was at one such event that Reith first met Matheson. He was impressed by her sharp intelligence and her influential social networks, and decided almost immediately to recruit her. She brought to the Talks department a blend of brisk efficiency and common-room intimacy. Colleagues would describe how she would hurry along the corridors of Savoy Hill 'at a half run', then sit on the floor of her room with her dog Torquhil at her feet and gather her team around the gas fire. Fielden remembered Matheson as someone who 'never lectured, never laid down the law: she ran her department on a loose rein, encouraging, helping, sympathising, and yet keeping herself firmly in the saddle.' She set rigorous standards, while fostering a spirit of collegial informality.[18]

Under Matheson's influence, 'Talks' rapidly became the most exciting part of the BBC in which to work. Its efforts to get leading figures before the microphone involved 'constant alertness' and hyperactive social mixing. Sieveking's diary for 1926, for instance, reveals a heavy schedule of lunch dates – Eddie Marsh at Romano's one day, Osbert Sitwell at the Savoy Grill the next – and an even larger number of voice tests for potential contributors: Fred Astaire (who Sieveking notes as sounding 'no good'); Cecil Beaton ('very languid'); and Rhoda Power ('excellent'). Matheson, meanwhile, was busily booking appearances from MPs and government ministers. But it was her ability to draw members of the Bloomsbury circle into regular broadcasting that proved to be her greatest personal contribution. Both E. M. Forster and Desmond MacCarthy offered a flow of literary reviews, showing a willingness to discuss anything from railway bridges to Beau Brummel. Virginia Woolf consented to perform at the microphone on three occasions, once with her husband Leonard to discuss whether too many books were being written and published. Woolf's sometime lover, Vita Sackville-West, with whom Matheson also happened to be having an affair at the time, became one of Savoy Hill's most prolific contributors. Her talks ranged across travel, poetry and gardening. In June 1927, she even appeared on air with her husband Harold Nicolson to debate the meaning of marriage. 'The car of love' runs on pneumatic tyres, Nicolson told his listeners: there would be 'punctures' along the way. Then again, he added, marriage is perhaps better thought of as like a plant: 'It grows; it changes; it develops'. 'What I object to', Sackville-West riposted splendidly, 'is the tendency in men to regard *themselves* as the plant and the women as the soil.' Few talks were quite so rich in metaphor or subtext. Most days, listeners were more likely to come across 'Mrs Cawson, a mother of four', describing her landing at Dover after swimming the Channel, or 'A. J. Alan', offering delicately crafted tales such as 'My Adventure in Jermyn Street' or 'A Foggy Evening'.[19]

The general flavour of talks was light and ephemeral. This

did not stop it also being distinctly 'improving' at times. Some programmes aspired to be both at once, marking out a potentially fertile 'middlebrow' style. One outstanding example of this was *Music and the Ordinary Listener*, a long-running series launched in January 1926 in which Walford Davies introduced highlights from the classical canon. Persuading rather than lecturing, sharing secrets rather than handing down information, he was a master of the easy-going, informal manner. One of the BBC's announcers, Stuart Hibberd, would watch Davies out of the corner of his eye, moving effortlessly between playing the piano and speaking into the microphone. His notes appeared to be meticulously prepared and rehearsed, yet he somehow retained a sense of intimacy with all those tuning in at home, as if he were having a chat with an individual listener or family. 'Shut your eyes', wrote one reviewer, 'and Sir Walford might well be in the same room with you.'[20]

Davies's secret, Lionel Fielden reckoned, was simply that he was always 'his natural self'. If so, this was a rare achievement. Being 'natural' in the far from natural environment of a Savoy Hill studio was something that had to be worked at. For a long while, the rather tortuous means by which talks were produced led to a distinctly *un*natural style emanating from the nation's wireless sets. The problem was that technical limitations conspired with the BBC's sense of propriety. The ability to record and edit speech had still to be perfected, so all radio performances had to be live. Yet simply ad-libbing seemed just too risky. So every word of every programme was laboriously scripted. A straight monologue delivered by the most distinguished of writers could be entrusted largely to the author and would need only gentle tweaking by Matheson or Sieveking or Fielden. For most other speakers, a façade of spontaneity was achieved only by the most contrived methods. They were invited ahead of the broadcast to discuss the topic while a stenographer took notes. These would then be typed up so that the producer could smooth out and embellish what had been said. During the actual broadcast, the speaker would then have to follow this revised script, having been rehearsed thoroughly beforehand. Spontaneity became an awkward, stagey simulacrum of the real thing.[21] The producer's craft lay in minimising the inevitable gap between reality and artifice by ensuring that each script was well larded with dramatic pauses, jovial asides and chatty colloquialisms.

For Hilda Matheson, this remoulding of words was more than a technical necessity. It played a vital role in the developing art of broadcasting. Most studio guests were complete novices when it came to radio. They were used to writing for the page, not the ear. They were used to declaiming in theatres or lecture halls rather than talking intimately into a microphone. And they were discombobulated by the precision of the broadcasting schedule, which demanded a good sense of exactly how many words they had the time to utter. The producer's job, as Matheson saw it, was to make a good writer into a good talker – and turn a good talker into an even better one. A natural speaking style could not be left to chance: it needed to be created through skilfully crafting a script stripped of any declamatory tendency or verbosity, full of warmth and personality, and expressed in the most concise way possible. For her, no subject was out of bounds, but getting it across involved the trickiest of balancing acts. Reith had wanted 'the best' of everything to reach as many homes as possible. A talk that was too abstruse would merely preach to a minority of the already converted; a talk that lacked ambition would hardly represent 'the best' to begin with. Lionel Fielden described the task as one of constantly steering 'a course between vulgarity and obscurantism, pulling the one up and the other down, until a lucid and agreeable programme is obtained'.[22]

Not everyone made the grade. Lloyd George was a great public orator but lost all confidence in the studio without an audience in front of him, while Lytton Strachey's one disastrous audition at Savoy Hill revealed a crackling falsetto voice that sounded terrible at the microphone.[23] Then there were those who spoke well but were a nightmare to produce. Among the worst offenders on this score was the playwright George Bernard Shaw.

A stream of solicitous letters from a star-struck Cecil Lewis had prompted the playwright to visit for the first time in October 1924. Within a few weeks, Shaw was reading his own play, *O'Flaherty, VC*, live on-air, doing all the voices and even singing 'Tipperary'. It was, Lewis told him, 'the best thing that has ever been broadcast'. Over the following months and years, he was offered an unprecedented array of inducements to return to the microphone, but he repeatedly objected that, alas, he would not be able to speak freely on the BBC. The basis for this claim was that various official agreements under which the Company operated had implicitly banned it from discussing matters of controversy on air – in large part to placate the powerful newspaper lobby. This act of censorship was emphatically not of the BBC's own choosing, but the simple fact that the Postmaster-General could refuse to renew its licence if it transgressed, left the BBC with little option but to acquiesce with a horribly vague restriction that Shaw would never agree to observe.[24]

Relations reached their lowest ebb in October 1929, when the playwright kicked up an enormous fuss over a two-hour, full-cast production of *Captain Brassbound's Conversion*. A few days after the broadcast, and with generally favourable reviews being posted, Hilda Matheson had gently enquired whether he had tuned in. Alas, he had. 'Its infamy', Shaw thundered, 'was such that I hereby solemnly renounce, curse, and excommunicate everybody who had a hand in it.' His grumbles were manifold. Transmission had started at 9.35 p.m., which was far too late. The man playing Brassbound sounded like a woman. The woman playing Lady Cicely sounded like a man. 'If the producer has not already been shot', he declared, 'I will pay for the cartridges.' Lance Sieveking was among those who thought that in the end Shaw was just more trouble than he was worth. 'He seemed to think mere rudeness clever.' The producer of *Captain Brassbound*, Howard Rose, was less prepared to give up, and issued a detailed riposte. He was adamant that 'every line

George Bernard Shaw at the microphone in 1931. Producers were
eager to get the playwright on air, but Shaw had a tetchy relationship
with the BBC, complaining of censorship, demanding high fees, even
objecting to any restrictions on the length of time he had to speak.

of dialogue was clearly understood by everyone concerned',
and the two leads – Baliol Holloway and Gertrude Kingston –
had been approved by no less a figure than Shaw himself. It was
just 'a pity', he said pointedly, that 'Mr Shaw will not allow us
to cut'. 'I am on the classic list, like The Messiah or the Ninth
Symphony', the playwright had insisted pompously, 'and must
be made room for or done without.'[25]

The single most articulate critic of the BBC's mission to
make culture accessible to the 'ordinary' listener was Virginia
Woolf. The novelist was defiantly proud to be called a 'highbrow', a person of 'thoroughbred intelligence', as she put it,
'who rides his mind at a gallop across country in pursuit of an
idea'. She admired equally the 'lowbrow', someone of 'thoroughbred vitality who rides his body in pursuit of living at a

gallop across life'. What she could not abide was the merely 'middlebrow', embodied in the kind of person who lived not in Bloomsbury as she did but in, say, respectably dull South Kensington – a busybody who would create work neither well-written nor badly written, neither proper nor improper, but always somehow obscuring great art rather than shining a light on it. This disdain for the very process of mediation that was at the heart of broadcasting set Woolf squarely at odds with the whole Reithian project and its faith in people's ability to change – a belief that, with a little help and guidance, the British people might achieve 'a general intelligence and a higher culture'. This, she believed, was wasted effort, for art needed to be quarantined from the vulgarities of common taste. She called the BBC the 'Betwixt and Between Company' and dismissed Hilda Matheson as 'earnest ... drab ... dreary'. Her 'wooden-face', Woolf wrote, 'affects me as a strong purge, as a hair shirt, as a foggy day, as a cold in the head'.[26]

Matheson, who of course lived in South Kensington, knew full well what Woolf thought of her, and was tormented by the growing belief in her own mind that she really was 'a social failure, a blot'.[27] But she also knew how important it was that she and her staff kept courting famous writers and thinkers no matter how tricky they were to handle. The involvement of such eminent figures as Woolf or Shaw raised the intellectual standard of individual programmes. It also helped confer legitimacy on broadcasting among both establishment and progressive circles, enabling the Company to distinguish itself from the world of commercial mass entertainment, or, at the very least, get noticed.

By 1928, Lytton Strachey was reporting that every time he went to Cambridge the dinner table conversation seemed to revolve around God, Bernard Shaw, and the wireless. But there was a limit to what could be achieved, for the BBC could not afford to become the exclusive playground of the highbrows. As a letter writer to the *Radio Times* pointed out in May 1930, the schedule was still stuffed full with talks on 'how bats sleep, where

papier mâché comes from, common faults in humming, secrets
of sardine tinning, the evolution of braces' – programmes that
were all very diverting, and even no doubt occasionally fascinat-
ing, but not exactly representative of Reith's longed-for 'higher
culture'. Then again, they did not need to be. Reith himself had
said very clearly that no one was expected to listen to every
broadcast, and indeed that it was 'most important that light and
"entertaining" items' were always available to allow for some
'pleasing relaxation after a day's work'.[28]

Despite the BBC's search for respectability, it could have no
broader cultural impact unless it was also popular. Broadcasting
by its nature – and the BBC, by its own philosophy – set out to
reach, as Arthur Burrows put it, 'a million homes, ranging from
the palace to the humblest cottage'. This was not just about differences of class, but about differences in education, opinion,
age, mood, attention. Making programmes for this vast and
disparate audience was never, in Burrows' understated words,
a 'simple matter'. But nor, perhaps, was it altogether a futile
mission. Eight months earlier, in October 1929, *The Listener*
magazine had confidently announced in its editorial that the
intellectual's 'cautious and conservative' attitude to radio was at
last changing. The reason the *Listener* gave was an intriguing one:
that it was precisely through the mixing together in one place
of high-, low- and middlebrow fare that great ideas and great
art would reach a new audience while remaining unsullied. It
was 'the common man' who had 'popularised broadcasting and
thereby surrounded it with an atmosphere of genial anticipation
and pleasure'; the intellectual was now free 'to come along and
take his share of the good thing, and to transform it into a better
thing by claiming a place for "the things of the mind"'.[29] It was
an idealistic claim, and no doubt naïve. But it spoke loudly of the
BBC's lingering hopes: that a life of pleasure and a life of virtue
need not be opposed, that culture was not a static thing, that
supply could shape demand, and that through radio a 'common
culture' might one day be forged.

Entertaining the nation

Talks were not the only programmes taking time to find the right tone. Music was the mainstay of almost every station's schedule. But right from the start, Arthur Burrows had identified two not easily reconciled ambitions for the Company that echoed the dilemmas facing Matheson and her team. He calculated that among the 'vast audience' now available to radio, very few would have attended any 'high-class musical entertainment'. If wireless sets were to be sold in bulk and listeners' loyalty secured, most music on the airwaves needed to be 'of a really popular character'. At the same time, he saw a unique opportunity to 'lift' what he called the 'present standard of musical appreciation', by placing before these same listeners at least some work with which they were unfamiliar.[30]

The earliest schedules show this delicate balancing act at work. In the first week of October 1923, for example, London broadcast songs from a West End show, dance music from the ballroom of the Savoy Hotel, and a night of popular ballads from the Cavendish Singers. It also broadcast modern French chamber music and orchestral concerts featuring Massenet, Elgar, Dvořák and Strauss. Several programmes occupied something of a middle ground – the musical equivalent of Woolf's 'Betwixt and Between'. The 2LO Dance Band, for instance, entertained listeners on Saturday night with a busy concert of foxtrots, songs such as 'Down Vauxhall Way', and catchy moments from Puccini's *La Bohème*. This middle ground – 'good music of the popular variety' – was regarded as one way of squaring the circle between high- and lowbrow tastes, although Cecil Lewis was among those who believed that the emphasis should be tilted slowly but surely towards music of lasting value – music, as he put it, that 'gains fresh beauties at every hearing'. In the meantime, it was no good simply broadcasting the classics and hoping for the best. When the BBC had broadcast *The Magic Flute* in its opening weeks, Lewis offered listeners what he called 'some interpolation from the prompter's box at the side of the stage during the actual performance'. This novel procedure of offering the occasional résumé was justified, he suggested, because 'the vast majority of our listeners had never listened to opera before, and would have the greatest difficulty in following the plot'. A letter subsequently arrived at Savoy Hill threatening to shoot someone if the same interruptions were made during Wagner, but Lewis thought that a helping hand of the kind he had attempted would pay dividends in the longer term. 'I prophesy', he wrote in 1924, 'that ere many years have passed a Beethoven symphony or a piano concerto will be every bit as popular an item in our programmes as half-an-hour's dance music.'[31]

Getting the right balance of enjoyment and 'lift' in the schedules was one challenge; the organisational difficulty of getting such programmes on air in the first place was another. Savoy Hill, like the BBC's main regional stations, had its own small orchestra. Its musicians could just about squeeze into one of the studios to perform in a variety of guises: the 2LO Wireless Orchestra, the 2LO Dance Band, the BBC Military Band, the London Wireless Trio, and so on. This ensured a regular supply of music of a decent enough quality in reasonably controlled conditions. But transmissions from live stage shows, which had an extra cachet, were altogether more challenging. For *The Magic Flute*, the BBC had relied on just one microphone and a hastily installed phone line running from Covent Garden to the transmitter at Marconi House. By the time of the broadcasts from the Savoy Hotel a few months later, a whole network of dedicated lines had been installed beneath the pavements of the capital. Unfortunately, the efforts of the Company's engineers were sabotaged by waiters who tried to remove the equipment that had been placed discreetly on tables or under floral displays.[32]

Concert organisers remained deeply suspicious of broadcasting. The managing director of the Queen's Hall, William Boosey, feared that people would never pay to attend if they could listen in the comfort of their homes. Only after 1927 did he allow artists under his control to perform on the airwaves.

The British National Opera Company, which had organised the Covent Garden concert, was unusual in being supportive from the start. The fact that it sold more seats than usual that season confirmed the BBC's own claim that broadcasting represented a colossal amount of free publicity and created 'the desire to hear and see a performance, where before such desire never even existed'.[33] By the end of the 1920s, relations between the national broadcaster and the music industry had become much more harmonious, each side acknowledging the virtues of co-operation. And with the BBC's appointment of its own full-time music adviser and full-time conductor, as well as longer contracts and more rehearsal time for its own musicians, the range and quality of programmes on air had improved hugely.

In drama, as with music, the BBC's engineers had been eager from the start to link up with professional performances from London's West End. In 1923, they managed to prop a microphone up on the stage of the Hippodrome to broadcast excerpts from a production of *Cinderella* – the first of a number of such relays. Once again, the BBC's efforts were swiftly blocked by vested interests, when the country's biggest theatre managers decided to cease co-operation. Left fending for themselves, producers immediately opted to bring the cast for a production of *Twelfth Night* into Savoy Hill's own studios. It was, however, with the broadcast of *A Comedy of Danger*, eight months later in January 1924, that the notion of drama which was merely *on* the radio was replaced for the first time with drama that was genuinely *of* the radio. Specially written by the up-and-coming playwright Richard Hughes, it was set in the darkness of a coal mine after an accident – a dramatic conceit in which, for listeners at home as well as for the characters in the play, everything was revealed through sound alone.[34]

Soon after the *Danger* broadcast, 'R. E.' Jeffrey, who had made his name inside the BBC for having staged *Rob Roy* at the Glasgow studio, was appointed the Company's overall Director of Drama. His first act upon arriving in London was to fire a shotgun into the well of the main staircase at Savoy Hill to test whether it would sound authentic on-air. His discovery that it sounded more like the feeble popping of a champagne cork led to the appointment of the BBC's first specialist studio 'effects' operator, who manipulated a motley collection of mundane objects – potatoes in metal drums, tin baths, roller skates, matchboxes – to create a variety of sounds from creaking doors to cascading avalanches. At the same time, Jeffrey established the London Radio Repertory Players as a readily available pool of acting talent. He also compiled notes on 'Playwriting for Wireless Broadcast', which gave guidance to authors on how to help listeners build a 'mental picture' of the main characters and events. He suggested, for example, that when casting a play, use should be made of the widest range of voice styles, so that each character sounded distinctive at the microphone. Scripts, he added, should make frequent mention of each character by name and hint frequently about locations or people's appearances in the dialogue. If all this sounded a bit prescriptive, there was the promise that wherever language was used with subtlety radio drama would conjure in the listener's mind a sweeping imaginary canvas that no conventional theatre could hope to realise: 'it is possible', Jeffrey explained, 'to commence play action in, say, a room at a hotel, continuing with the same character ... down the stairs, in a taxi to wharf-side, across the gangway to a cutter, out to a liner, and conclude with possibly a wreck at sea.' Since 'each listener creates his own conception of such scenes', he added, these scenes would also assume for every single listener 'a reality which can be far greater than any effect provided on an ordinary stage'.[35]

Within two years of moving into Savoy Hill, the BBC was broadcasting two or three plays a week. About one in ten was categorised as 'classical or high-class', with Shakespeare providing the indispensable ballast. The rest were mostly routine comedies and lightweight dramas. On the evening of Monday 8 September 1924, for example, listeners were offered three short plays with musical interludes: *The Boatswain's Mate*, set in a bar; *A Minuet*, described as a 'Little Play in Verse'; and *The Philosopher of Butterbiggins*, about which the *Radio Times* reveals only that it was set in a 'Tenement' and that Jeffrey himself played the lead role as well as being the producer. They were all jolly enough and no doubt competently done. But it was only a matter of time before the BBC was lambasted by the critics for leaning too heavily on 'uninspired machine-made stories'. This was hardly surprising, given the Company's desperate need to fill airtime cheaply, the initial lack of engagement from a theatrical profession that still reckoned there was nothing in broadcasting but 'script reading and the equivalent of cigarette-money', and, above all, the lack of production experience inside Savoy Hill. Yet Jeffrey himself was partly responsible for this state of affairs. Despite all his efforts, he remained very much a man 'of the theatre'. It was only in 1929, when he was succeeded by Val Gielgud, that the creative boundaries were pushed more decisively. Gielgud brought to the task his very own sense of drama. He had marked the end of his studies at Oxford by eloping with the daughter of a Russian countess, and ever since had insisted on going around town sporting a scarlet-lined cloak and sword-stick. He was hardly a revolutionary figure, but he did at least cut a dash. And although he came from a family of actors, he had never spent enough time in the theatre to pick up its habits. Indeed, he felt unburdened by any tradition, and if anything inspired him it was what he called the 'pleasant happy-go-lucky amateurishness' of Savoy Hill itself. Gielgud's self-confidence, and his attachment to broadcasting as a creative enterprise, would prove decisive, both in ensuring his own long service at the BBC and in helping drama to become a solid fixture of the radio schedules for years to come.[36]

Savoy Hill: a village life

Drama programmes – like *Children's Hour*, like the musical concerts, like all the 'Talks' – did not, of course, just magically come together in the hands of one omnipotent individual. Once written, scripts needed to be copied, actors paid, studios booked.

Savoy Hill hummed with the hidden labour of an ever-expanding number of secretaries, typists, clerks, caterers, technicians,
office boys and commissionaires, all busily duplicating, opening
letters, writing contracts, serving refreshments, ushering people
along the winding corridors from lobby to office to studio and
back again. They, too, helped create the atmosphere of a pioneering community engaged collectively in an exciting and
important new venture.

They also happened to make the place less exclusively middle
class and masculine. In large parts of the building a predictable
division of labour held sway, accentuated by the presence of so
many ex-servicemen. Engineers – and the studio 'control rooms'
they inhabited – were exclusively male; secretaries, clerks or
typists – many of them gathered together in the General Office –
were predominantly female, while the dispensation of plentiful
tea was managed by a phalanx of charwomen treading the corridors from dawn to dusk. A small number of women managed to
secure positions of genuine authority. Alongside Hilda Matheson at Talks, there was Mary Somerville – another formidably
intelligent woman, barely out of Oxford – who ran the Schools
programmes. Women also occupied posts as drama producers or *Children's Hour* organisers. They oversaw the Reference
Library, the Registry, the Duplicating Section, the telephone
exchange. Indeed, during this period, women accounted for
roughly a third of the BBC's staff. Although women occupied
a disproportionate number of the lower-ranked posts, men and
women on the same grade usually received the same wage.[37]

At the very end of the North Wing on the second floor, the
telephone room was presided over by Olive May. She had joined
in March 1923, having been interviewed for the job by Reith. The
role of switchboard operator, he told her, was vitally important.
'You'll be rung by people from all parts of the world, from all
walks of life and often be the only contact between the BBC
and them ... they must be dealt with efficiently, quickly and
courteously.' The hours were long, since as well as the two-way
flow of business calls throughout the daytime, she had to deal

Staff sorting the post at Savoy Hill in 1930. 'Office boys' would open
and sort the first deliveries of the day but would be joined later
by women working in the General Office. By this stage, the BBC
employed about 200 waged female secretarial and clerical staff.

with listeners' calls long into the evening. At these moments,
Reith himself would occasionally drop by to drink some cocoa
or share some chocolates, while lonely engineers at one of the
BBC's regional stations would ring for a chat, hoping to relieve
the boredom of a quiet nightshift.[38]

In April 1924, growing pressure on office space meant that
May's telephone switchboard had to be moved to a new and
improved General Office in the South Wing of the second floor.
This large, airy room, with tall windows overlooking the Thames,
was the buzzing administrative nerve centre of the whole operation. One part – with the most daylight – was reserved for at least
eleven typists. Other sections, screened from the 'roar of the
typewriters', were used for general filing by Miss Banks, by the
cashier Miss Mallinson, and by the accountant Mr Harley. It was
here that the first work of the day was always done. Office 'boys'

would arrive at 8.30 a.m., an hour before everyone else, to open and sort the first postal delivery. Throughout the rest of the day, they would be rushing in and out, sorting fresh postbags, scurrying through the labyrinth of corridors and staircases to deliver hundreds of letters – incoming, outgoing and internal – to the growing number of staff offices. Some of these were occupied by administrators or engineers, others by programme makers. In all cases, the most senior ranked had their own secretaries. Hilda Matheson, for example, had Sheila Wynn-Williams; Peter Eckersley had a Miss Fortune, and the team putting together the *Radio Times* had a Miss Bryant. One of the editors of the *Radio Times*, Maurice Gorham, worked out that if he ever urgently needed any details of forthcoming programmes, it was best to ask one of the other secretaries, since she would usually know more than the producers themselves. They were all 'very clever', he realised, and 'did the work of two men'. He also thought that they brought a definite touch of glamour. For men, dark suits were the rule, along with pin-striped trousers, spats and bowler hats – except for Saturday mornings, when plus fours might be worn. The BBC secretaries were, as Gorham put it, altogether more 'decorative': 'high-heeled, sheer-stockinged, beautifully made-up'. They might not earn much, but he suspected they were being wined and dined and taken dancing 'every night'. He would watch entranced at the end of each day, as they took the lift down with the commissionaire Joe, a burly seventeen-stone ex-policeman, and said their goodnights to the receptionist, Bill, still busy turning away a stream of unsolicited callers in the entrance hall. Gorham would later follow in their footsteps, returning perhaps to one of his lunchtime haunts, Mooney's in the Strand, where he enjoyed 'the best bread and cheese in London, as well as Irish whiskey and the famous Dublin stout'. Others would retire to the Coal Hole next door for a few drinks, or head to a nearby picture house, before making their way home.[39]

As evening fell, and the building was emptied of its managers and office staff, the main hours of broadcasting began. Nearby, the machinery of the 2LO transmitter hummed with electricity, its valves giving off a dim, eerie glow. Inside Savoy Hill itself, the programme makers made final preparations and their performers started to arrive. In the 'drawing room' Colonel Brand, a red-faced, tennis-playing socialite, acted as host, dispensing gin and whisky from his 'entertainment cupboard' to any distinguished visitors as well as a fair few members of BBC staff.[40] It was, though, the studios on the first and third floors that were now at the sharp end of the whole operation, for it was here that the announcers and musicians and actors at last gathered before the microphone to put on the BBC's advertised schedule of programmes – live and sometimes entirely unrehearsed. These studios embodied more vividly than anywhere else Savoy Hill's ethos of improvisation and experiment – the business of working out through trial and error what exactly broadcasting was and how it might be achieved day in, day out.

Studio No. 3, which occupied a suite of interconnected spaces on the north side of the top floor, had been completed first. At the far end was a small 'Listening Room', where an engineer lurked. Next door was an assembly area for musicians to get ready to perform, then an artistes' waiting room tastefully furnished with settees, mahogany chairs, a writing table, and a small sign politely asking guests not to 'talk loudly'. A small anteroom absorbed any overflow. The main studio was a capacious 37 feet long and 18 feet wide. Its ceiling and walls were tricked out in seven layers of canvas – each separated by an air space of about one inch – and finished with ruched saffron-coloured netting. Thick blue pilasters were placed at regular intervals around the perimeter and featured clocks and atmospheric wall lighting. Circular tables, blue-and-gold-coloured settees and armchairs stood in semi-formal fashion on a thick fitted carpet, the odd pot plant or vase of flowers adding a homely touch. The room's real function was revealed by the grand piano in the corner, the small conductor's platform and the array of red warning lights. Standing right in the middle – impossible to miss – was an enormous microphone.[41]

An audition in Studio No. 3 in 1927. A producer can just be
seen in the small 'Listening Room' at the back of the studio.
The main studio was large, but its heavy curtains meant the
acoustics were as 'dead as mutton', and its airless atmosphere
made performing there a draining experience for everyone.

Although it looked impressive, as a working environment
Studio No. 3 stretched the patience of staff and performers to
breaking point. The heavy curtains on the walls – all four tons
of them – were designed to eliminate echoes, which they did
so effectively that guest speakers often struggled to hear their
own voices, and, disorientated, ended up losing all confidence
in their delivery. The room was also incredibly dusty. Fans had
been fitted to provide ventilation, but hummed so noisily that
the engineer in the Listening Room would have to switch them
off whenever a live transmission began. If a choir and orchestra
were in the studio for hours at a stretch, the atmosphere and the
heat would soon be 'appalling'.[42]

Microphones were still new and unfamiliar bits of technology. The earliest models, used in the old top-floor studio at Marconi House, had really been no more than telephone receivers slung from ceiling hooks or propped up on simple stands. It was their complete inability to cope with reverberation that had led the engineers to soundproof Studio No. 3 so ferociously. By the time the studio was pressed into service, a more advanced device had already been unveiled: the Magnetophone or, as Cecil Lewis called it affectionately, the 'jam jar'. It consisted of a heavy, round magnet in a thick rubber sling suspended within a box to protect it from undue electromagnetic interference. The box, or 'Faraday Cage', sat on a wooden stand fitted with casters so it could be wheeled around the studio floor at will. To give the contraption a more domestic feel, the whole thing was usually covered with a blue silk sheet. It allowed performers to move around freely and still be heard, but nothing could disguise its bizarre appearance, which resembled that of an old-fashioned meat safe. In its forbidding presence, even seasoned performers were often mortified. A young Vernon Bartlett, later one of the BBC's most assured journalists, was reportedly 'paralysed' at first. The Hollywood star Tallulah Bankhead apparently 'slid under the table in faints'.[43]

Dead acoustics, unbearable heat, bizarre-looking equipment. Such challenges called for unending improvisation. When Cecil Lewis was working with the theatre impresario Nigel Playfair on the first-ever series of full-length Shakespeare plays, they quickly decided to relocate: 'we played the entire *Hamlet* and the entire *As You Like It* in the corridor outside the studio, wheeling out the microphones … into the better acoustic of the plastered walls and open windows.' Adjustments also had to be made for performers trained to project their voices in a theatre or concert hall. Among the worst offenders was the Shakespearean actor Henry Ainley. On his first visit to Savoy Hill, he told Val Gielgud that since some two million people might be listening, he would really let himself rip. 'And he did', Gielgud recalled: 'I had to have two effects boys holding the sleeves to pull him away from

the microphone to prevent him blasting the whole place.' Lance
Sieveking tried to forestall future disasters by having a framed
notice placed beside the microphone warning guest speakers
that, 'If you *sneeze* or *rustle papers* you will DEAFEN THOU-
SANDS!!!!' But it was removed by Lionel Fielden when it turned
out to be even more intimidating than the microphone itself.[44]
The underlying message was clear: there was an art to using a
microphone that both producers and performers would have to
master if they were to succeed in this radio business.

When almost everything was being done for the first time,
slip-ups of all kinds were frequent. Microphones would often
break down, especially when temperatures inside the studio rose
dramatically. If the programme ground to an undignified stop,
'dead air' would prevail until a replacement microphone was
installed. In the interval an announcer would frantically attempt
to coax the studio pianola into life, although, as the announcer
John Snagge remembered, this brought its own problems. 'You'd
get the wrong roll onto the wrong machine. There was an
upright and a grand and if you put an upright onto the grand it
didn't play at all – and it used to go *boom boom boom* and *flip flip flip*
backwards.' The BBC quickly realised the advantages of having
an actual pianist on standby. The first was Cecil Dixon, who had
been trained at the Royal College of Music and was a noted
recitalist in her own right. For more than two decades after her
appointment in 1923, she was famous inside Savoy Hill for thousands of face-saving impromptu performances, as well as for
playing the role of 'Aunt Sophie' on *Children's Hour*. Such was the
BBC's insatiable demand for standby accompanists that at least
ten others were employed in London alone, and countless more
in its various regional stations. Among these later recruits were
some of the future stars of broadcasting, frequently profiled in
popular magazines: Jean Melville, for example, who would later
appear regularly on *Workers' Playtime*; and Doris Arnold, who,
having been plucked from her role as a typist in Savoy Hill's
Stores department, would later become the producer and presenter of *The Melody is There* and *These You Have Loved*.[45]

Not every break in transmission was unplanned. Once broadcasting had begun for the evening, the handful of studios were
in constant demand. At the end of each programme there was
a period of organised chaos, as one set of musicians and actors,
hurriedly rearranging furniture and microphones, made way for
a new set of performers. The BBC's engineers left a silent gap
on air lasting a quarter or even half an hour to accommodate
the changeover.[46] The ability to record and edit programmes
in advance would have been the ideal solution, but the existing
technology of recording on to wax and acetate gramophone
discs or steel wire was still too cumbersome and slow to keep
up with the hectic turnover of broadcasting. So all programmes
were still having to be performed live, warts and all, with no
possibility of 're-takes'.

Yet as Savoy Hill expanded, and staff became steadily more
confident in their craft, the teething troubles were gradually
overcome. Across the BBC's chain of stations, engineers stripped
back studio walls to add a little more 'brightness' to the acoustics. At Savoy Hill, the opening of 'Studio No. 1' on the first floor
offered a much more welcoming performance space. The 'meat
safe' eventually made way for the more reliable 'Reiss' carbon
microphones. And the changeover time between programmes
was steadily reduced to a well-rehearsed three minutes flat.
Above all, as more facilities came into service, transmissions
could more easily be switched from studio to studio as the evening's schedule unfolded.

Taking off

By the late 1920s, Savoy Hill was bubbling with confidence. A
small cadre of adventurous producers now decided that rather
than complain about the challenge of live broadcasting, they
would embrace its ephemerality. Rather than recycling the
works of the theatre or the concert hall, they would turn radio
into a bold new art of its own. They would forge a medium that
was complex, spectacular, attention-grabbing.

The leader of these young experimentalists was Lance Sieveking. Although he was technically a member of Hilda Matheson's Talks department, his irrepressible enthusiasm was beyond easy containment. At six foot six, the ex-pilot was the tallest man in the BBC aside from Reith himself. Always 'gesticulating wildly with huge hands that knocked over everything within reach', he carried a physical presence that announced him to his colleagues as someone 'talented and imaginative beyond the ordinary'. He loved new technology; he devoured the novels of Virginia Woolf, the surrealist photography of Francis Bruguière, and the Vorticist paintings of Wyndham Lewis; he was an avid viewer of the films of the German Expressionists and the Soviet pioneers of montage. Like all these artists, he wanted 'to mould the Future'.[47] Might the new medium of radio allow him, he wondered, to create in *sound* the kind of multilayered, fractured perspectives and complex narratives that were such a feature of the modernist works he so admired?

It would require deploying *several* studios at once, something now possible thanks to the arrival of Savoy Hill's first 'Dramatic Control Panel'. This elaborate mixing desk allowed a producer to sit alone and select the output of one or more studios scattered around the building with the simple flick of a switch. In February 1927, Cecil Lewis had used it for a two-hour adaptation of Conrad's *Lord Jim*, which the *Radio Times* described as 'a series of progressive mind-pictures' rather 'like an aural film'. Sieveking wanted to push this technology even further. Throughout 1927 and 1928, he had been grappling with a way to 'paint' in sound the inner mental turmoil of a character, dramatising the fragmented nature of consciousness. At 9.50 p.m. on the evening of Tuesday 4 September 1928, these experiments culminated in *Kaleidoscope*, a seventy-minute 'fantasy' that drew on episodes from his own life. Using all seven of Savoy Hill's studios, he created what the *Radio Times* called 'A Rhythm representing the Life of a Man from Cradle to Grave'.[48] It represented the high-water mark of radio experimentalism in the BBC's first decade.

The transmission began with an on-air announcement

warning listeners of the 'alarming' and 'tumultuous noise' to follow. The nameless protagonist was then pitched into a whirling montage of scenes that captured the struggle between 'Good' and 'Bad': idyllic seaside holidays in France, student days at Cambridge, courtship, laughter, dancing in cafes were cross-cut with echoes of war, financial crises, domestic betrayals. Vignette followed vignette – fragments of dialogue and poetry interspersed with the sounds of the city, countryside or battlefield. Clapping melted into the sounds of the sea, the passionate avowals of a lover became the sweet singing of a choir, dance tunes yielded to the symphonic grandeur of Beethoven. Behind the scenes, Savoy Hill hummed with a cast of more than a hundred spread out between studios on every floor and wing, including an orchestra, a quintet, a dance band, singers, sound-effects technicians, and even a young John Gielgud who had been drafted in as a last-minute replacement. At the centre of all this activity was Sieveking himself, hunched over the Dramatic Control Panel, his fingers dancing across the console, flicking knobs, turning on the red lights in each studio to 'cue in' every performer, fading the layers of sound up and down at breakneck speed. 'It was play, play, *play* the instrument if ever you did anything in your life.' Sitting in semi-darkness turning the dials and flicking the switches of the cockpit-like box of brown wood before him, he felt the same thrill of speed and accuracy and daring – the same emotional fever that came from the anticipation of high-wire combat – that he had experienced when taking an aeroplane into the sky during the war. 'The world was listening. No turning back now! We were off … Back with the joystick and up we go!'[49]

By eleven o'clock, the final notes of *Kaleidoscope* had faded into silence. Even a performance as spectacular as this could not escape what Sieveking called the 'ghastly impermanence' of a medium that 'melted as you looked and listened'. Yet he could see that *Kaleidoscope*'s ephemerality was also what made it special – indeed what made *all* radio special. For here was something that had been heard by listeners at the very moment it had come into existence, something that had forged a momentary but powerful 'mental contact' between artist and audience, a thrilling once-only experience that not even cinema could match.[50]

Something even more momentous had occurred, too. For as one of his Savoy Hill colleagues put it, this was *the* moment when radio, 'hitherto earthbound', had finally found its 'wings'. As for the future, Val Gielgud, who had acted as Sieveking's studio manager on the night, was now bursting with optimism. 'If the wings could only be grown', he said, there would surely be nothing to prevent this extraordinary new medium from 'soaring'.[51]

3

PROFESSIONALS

Whatever is done shall be well done.

John Reith, 1924

The creative innovation of *Kaleidoscope* was only possible, Lance Sieveking thought, because he had been working 'like an artist or a craftsman in the Middle Ages, employed by some large body like the Church, and set free to carve gargoyles ... to his heart's content'. As one of his admirers put it, he enjoyed the status of 'the irresistible amateur working in a field where there were as yet no experts'. Broadcasting was one of the most exhilaratingly unpredictable jobs on the market. It might involve capturing the sound of passing trains in the London Underground one moment, and having 'to act with your head in a kettle drum, upside down' the next.[1]

For the first five years of the BBC's existence, Sieveking's freedom to experiment was recognisably part of a wider ethos, where even bread-and-butter programme-making was infused with a willingness – born of necessity – to improvise. Cecil Lewis said that what he enjoyed most about the early days of the BBC was his immersion in 'unorganised methods ... handled by intelligent people'.

The microphone that is tied up with bits of string, the switches that are falling to pieces, and the gadgets that won't work unless they are coaxed by someone who knows how ... When something goes wrong and one has to step into the breach and talk nonsense for half an hour ... And best of all, when everything goes with a swing, because everyone pulls together and will put out their last ounce to achieve success.

Savoy Hill was, he suggested, a 'democracy of young pioneers' where it 'didn't matter who handled anything, as long as it was handled and handled well'.[2]

In *Vox*, a lively new magazine of radio criticism launched in 1929, the writer Compton MacKenzie described the BBC as 'the greatest amateur organisation this country has known since the General Staff at the beginning of the Great War'. Unlike the 'cynical professionalism' of Fleet Street or Hollywood, Savoy Hill was 'immune from commercial influence, superior to artistic coteries, and innocent of political prejudice' – a place where, despite all the modern technological wizardry, there clung the 'fragrant air of a bygone civilization', a place where something might still be created for the sheer love of it. Val Gielgud put it even more succinctly. Savoy Hill was 'casual, amateurish, uncertain of its status'. But, he added, it 'was alive'. 'Machine had not yet mastered man.'[3]

By 1929, though, the BBC had a payroll of more than 1,100.[4] It was also growing steadily in reputation. So the obvious question arose: when *would* machine begin to master man?

The 'Napoleon of Savoy Hill'

To many contemporaries there would be a simple explanation for any growing rigidity: the character of the man at the top – a man who, in the eyes of many observers, *was* the BBC. The newspapers had dubbed John Reith 'the Napoleon of Savoy Hill'. 'Before him all men tremble', one columnist wrote, describing a workforce that toiled 'under a system of military discipline'. 'No nonsense, no shirking, not the smallest degree of inefficiency is tolerated by the managing director.'[5]

Many of Reith's staff readily acknowledged a grain of truth

in the description, even if his great stature was distinctly *un*-Napoleonic. 'Reith not only towered, but intended to tower', one of them observed. They would watch in awe as Reith suddenly materialised in a doorway, his head scraping the lintel as he drew himself up to his considerable full height, beetled his brows, and turned his dour, scarred face towards them. He used his physical presence to intimidate people, to give tangible form to the role of 'being the great man'. It worked even at a distance. Three short rings always meant that it was Reith on the office telephone, which, as one member of staff recalled, one then picked up 'with a shaky hand'. A job interview was an opportunity to submit an applicant to a ritualised grilling. As the candidate entered his Savoy Hill office, Reith would sit behind a vast desk with his back to the light, or, more dramatically, stand in front of the open fire, brandishing a poker. He would then stride around the room 'like a giant bird, moving restlessly and jerkily', and, after fixing the poor interviewee with his 'staring, penetrating eyes', engage in a typically baffling line of questioning: 'Do you accept the fundamental teachings of Jesus Christ?' 'Have you any personal disability of character, any weakness, that you know of?' The intimidating manner had the effect of sifting out anyone who was either rebellious or faint-hearted.[6]

Successful candidates quickly became familiar with his aura of leadership. Reith appreciated the creativity that came with the exuberance of his young team, but he was determined to iron out the unevenness of their programmes. In July 1923, Reith brought in a retired rear admiral, Charles Carpendale, to be his deputy. With his brusque, quarterdeck manner, addressing junior staff as if they were delinquent ratings, 'Carps' quickly became the Company's enforcer. 'He would look through you with the coldest and most distant of stares, like a dowager duchess meeting a chimney-sweep in her boudoir.' A year later, Reith established a Control Board to formulate general company policy, and a Programme Board, which met weekly to review programme plans. Although Reith sat on neither of these committees, his influence was palpable. 'You could not be long in the BBC before you began to feel the force, the certainty, the vigour of Reith', one of Savoy Hill's announcers recalled. 'You found things being referred to him, you found judgements being made with reference to Reith's views, or with reference to the policy laid down by Reith ... that what should be done is what was jolly well *going* to be done.' Programmes tended to fall in line with Reith's personal predilections. His very first pronouncement on his appointment was that the BBC would 'observe Sundays', which meant an austere schedule of hymns, sermons and prayers that drove listeners to switch off in their hundreds of thousands.[7] Reith's aversion to modern art and drama, to dropped aitches and jazz, was equally evident. Staff awareness of these prejudices – re-enforced by Carpendale's own – guaranteed for the BBC a notably conservative manner and output from which whole areas of contemporary culture remained absent.

Yet there was a less well known Reith, given to great loyalty and kindness and unusually tolerant of anyone he thought talented. When he discovered that one employee was owed several weeks pay, he chased it up personally. When he learned that another had a dangerously ill child, he wrote a friendly note of sympathy. He may have been intimidating in job interviews, but he allowed himself to be overruled by those whose advice he respected. During his interview for an announcer's post, Harman Grisewood rubbed Reith up the wrong way by pronouncing the word 'gold' in what Reith judged to be some kind of 'Cockney'. 'I see you are just as bad as your cousin Freddie who also speaks with a southern accent', Reith complained, before adding, 'but *they* want you, they want you, they want you, and so I suppose they must have you.' Grisewood was completely taken aback. 'It was not exactly the picture of a formidable tyrant who gave his ruling and everybody quaked and obeyed.' Perhaps the most accurate assessment belonged to an assistant editor at the *Radio Times*, who described Reith as just 'intensely human'.[8]

Whatever people made of Reith, one overriding factor placed a practical limit on his power of intervention: there was very soon too much for one man – or even a small team of lieutenants – to watch over. 'You can have all the authorities and restrictions and committees and regulations' in the world, Lionel Fielden explained, 'but they are all defeated by the rapidity of successive programmes'. Reith's attention was also increasingly consumed by daily battles with politicians, the Post Office or the press over crises of funding or the right to broadcast on controversial topics. The bread-and-butter business of running programmes *had* to be delegated to others, and, in the last resort, this meant the actual producers in the studio. As Cecil Lewis put it, 'We had the whole thing left to ourselves'. 'One made the most appalling mistakes', a young producer admitted, but 'one was very rarely rapped over the knuckles'. As for Reith, he was 'never given credit for the amount of *liberty* he unleashed'.[9]

Many inside Savoy Hill tolerated Reith's crusading zeal because they were fellow crusaders themselves. They were not merely following orders, but bound to him by a loyalty born of shared conviction. Fielden recognised in Reith's BBC 'the same feeling of dedication and hope' that he had experienced working at the League of Nations. Richard Lambert, the socialist-minded pacifist who joined the education department at Savoy Hill in 1927, saw in the BBC a means of radically democratising British education. Charles Siepmann declared himself 'fanatically devoted' to a BBC that was ushering in a 'New Age of Cultural Communism', in which, 'for the first time in human history', everything ever written, every piece of music composed would be freely available to all. Even Lance Sieveking, who had drifted on to the payroll with little sense of purpose other than indulging his own aesthetic fancies, was swept along. 'To me the Things you stand for are Real Things,' he wrote to Reith in a private letter, 'and to serve under you an honour for any man.' Reith set the pace and direction, but there were plenty of staff who were only too willing to go along for the ride. 'We *all* had an active mission', was how Cecil Lewis put it. 'There was no question of it being just a job, it was *the* job.'[10]

'You'd better not put a foot wrong'

But what exactly *was* the job of the broadcaster now? The days of trial and error were largely over. Gut instinct about how to do things 'properly' was already cohering into well-practised routines, a shared set of assumptions – a shared institutional culture, even.

The BBC was now an established and respected institution. By the end of 1926, there were two million licence-holders and many more active listeners. Alongside the requirement for creative energy, there were all sorts of other demands of the job: understanding the limits of what the medium of sound could achieve; sensing the appropriate relationship between producer and contributor; and weighing-up the needs of the audience. Little was yet codified, but unspoken assumptions about what was acceptable inevitably set boundaries to artistic freedom. And for a few, especially those who had been among the pioneers, working life at the BBC would soon feel worryingly remote from the open, creative spirit of 1922.

Some of this pressure was there from the start. An immense feeling of responsibility came with the BBC's allotted role as guardian of radio technology. Arthur Burrows talked of the 'awful' thought of broadcasting to several million people simultaneously – 'awful', Cecil Lewis explained, simply because 'We didn't quite know what we'd got hold of'.[11] Broadcasting had so many 'permutations ... so many possibilities', he added, that it was natural to feel not just excited but also 'frightened' of what it might do. It was this feeling of unknown danger, Lewis suggested, that underpinned the BBC's conservative instincts during its first decade. 'We were a bit scared of it ... Reith was a bit scared of it, because it was quite clear that if you got some madman in front of the microphone he could do a hell of a lot of damage in two or three minutes, and there had to be some safeguard.' 'There was a great feeling of you'd better not put a foot wrong', but 'it wasn't Reith, it wasn't that anybody was wagging this big stick at us: it was just a general feeling'. One way not to put a foot wrong, Lewis thought, was to focus on music rather than news or current affairs, on the basis that 'music was totally uncontroversial, it could do no harm to anybody, it could only do them good'. The same compulsion to protect listeners explained the BBC's insistence on scripting talks programmes. The result, despite Herculean efforts to help speakers create on the printed page something finely tuned for the ear, was, Lewis conceded, 'very stuffy': no free-flowing conversation, no authentically earthy speech, no regional dialects or idiosyncrasies, no real spontaneity at all. But since *'everyone* was terrified' of the alternative, the lack of any serious challenge meant that it quickly became the norm.[12]

In his 1929 article Compton MacKenzie observed that a 'departmental' mindset was taking hold. Experiment, he said, had been displaced by routine; soon, routine would harden into a set of immutable rules in which the producer 'imagines he is no longer an amateur but a professional'. There was some truth in this claim – though insiders at Savoy Hill would have seen this development in a much more positive light. Over the years, new roles unique to broadcasting had emerged: managing studios, organising outside broadcasts, maintaining transmitters, typing up scripts and running orders for live programmes, creating sound effects. Producers had also steadily gained in confidence, as they realised that theirs really was a highly skilled – if sometimes under-appreciated – craft. Nominally, they were employed simply to play the role of midwives, bringing to the nation's airwaves with the minimum of fuss the work of others, whether famous writers, politicians or performers. Yet these same producers also happened to have strong tastes and passionately held views of their own. Their job was to be well-read, well-connected, alive to the currents of thought and creativity in literature, in the arts, in entertainment, in politics, and in society more broadly – and then somehow to introduce all this to the widest possible public. As radio worked best when it avoided drawing attention to itself, being a producer for the BBC usually involved a conscious act of self-effacement. This was why, despite making such a big splash at the time, Sieveking's 1928

A family listening to the wireless in their farm kitchen, 1936.
By now, 98 per cent of the population of the United Kingdom
could listen to the BBC on a fairly cheap set, and broadcasters
were increasingly interested in measuring the reactions of
the so-called 'ordinary listener' to their programmes.

epic, *Kaleidoscope*, turned out to be the exception rather than
the rule. Val Gielgud judged it a mistake to have 'tried out' on
the British public such a showy programme in which 'a few odd
young men were having a good deal of private fun' with their
knobs and switches, when, as the *Saturday Review* remarked, the
end result was simply 'too bothersome for the ordinary listener'.
What counted in the long run, Gielgud decided, was the work
of someone such as Howard Rose, a man 'quietly building, by
steady, unostentatious and perhaps prosaic methods, the regular
audience of the middle-class fireside'.[13]

This, perhaps, was *the* key element of the BBC's emerging
ethos: an acceptance that, by its very nature, broadcasting had
to work for listeners at home. The whole Reithian project – that
mission to 'carry into the greatest number of homes' everything

that was best – would come to nothing if millions of radio sets were not actually being switched on in the first place. The BBC had no choice but to be tuned in to its audience – what the so-called 'ordinary listener' liked and did not like, and how he or she listened.

Vital information on what Cecil Lewis called 'the home atmosphere' was in plentiful supply. Once a programme had been transmitted, 'shoals of letters' would arrive at Savoy Hill – by the end of the first year of operation some 2,000 a day. Meanwhile, the BBC's main switchboard handled some 20,000 incoming calls; its seven lines were so frequently overloaded that when it moved offices in 1924 three new lines had to be installed. In the same year a new 'Programme Correspondence' department began to summarise the letters and calls for a weekly report that was circulated throughout the building.[14]

Most of the listeners' concerns, especially in the early days, were about the often appalling quality of reception. Many thousands tuned in on small, fairly cheap crystal radio sets. As headphones were required, only one person could listen at a time, and catching a signal required not only setting up an elaborate aerial but constant fiddling with the fine metal wire, or 'cat's whisker', which connected with the crystal detector. On a good day, and with a fair amount of dexterity, the receiver might pick up programmes nicely from twenty miles away; beyond that, the hiss and crackle of so-called 'atmospherics' took its toll. Other listeners – and by the next decade, the vast majority of them – invested in more sophisticated 'valve' sets. The quality and reach of their reception improved with each extra valve. As, of course, did the price. The fancier sets, with two valves or more, could cost upwards of £18. But even a standard valve set was the equivalent of several weeks' average wages. Another alternative, especially popular among council-owned flats and housing blocks, was to subscribe to a relay exchange, in which each home had a loudspeaker connected to a central receiver: by the early 1930s, more than 130,000 Britons relied on this arrangement. Whatever the equipment, every listener suffered the curse of 'oscillation' – an irritating hum or whistle that erupted from every set across some thirty square miles whenever just one home-made wireless set was incorrectly tuned. At such moments, as many members of the public made clear in their letters and phone calls, 'the wailing and the grunting, the shrieking and the crying, made listening a torture'. The lesson for the programme makers was that fancy acoustic effects would invariably be lost in the ether, heard only as an indistinguishable 'mush' by the time they reached the listener at the fireside. The safest way to ensure that a performance cut through was a simple, uncluttered production technique and a bold, crisp delivery.[15]

In the longer run, solving the reception problem required building more transmitters. Having decided from the start that 'everyone should be able to hear one programme clearly on a cheap set', the BBC's Chief Engineer, Peter Eckersley, swiftly embarked on a wholesale upgrade of facilities. His first step was to boost transmitters at regional stations from a puny 1.5 kilowatts to a much more serviceable 10 kilowatts – in line with 2LO in London. 5WA in Cardiff was among the earliest to benefit. It meant that listeners in the industrial valleys of Monmouthshire and East Glamorgan could hear programmes from the Welsh capital for the first time – much to Reith's personal satisfaction: broadcasts to the coalfields, he hoped, would 'do much to combat the doctrines of Communism and Bolshevism so sedulously preached there'. Eleven new 'relay' stations were also established, which would further extend the BBC's reach by rebroadcasting material from the bigger stations: the idea was that Swansea would carry programmes from Cardiff, Sheffield would do the same for Manchester, and so on. The combination of relay stations, increasingly powerful transmitters, and more affordable, better-tuned and easier-to-operate valve sets meant that, by the 1930s, the BBC's listeners were less inclined to grumble about reception; their focus shifted to the content of the programmes themselves – feedback that helped producers to plan ahead. As one of them put it, 'Anything you read …

anything you heard, people's views, people's habits, when they listened, when they didn't listen. You began to assemble a great deal of information on which ... you based your judgements.'[16]

Yet listening to the audience was one thing, giving it exactly what it asked for quite another. Comments from the public were horribly contradictory, especially as the size and social range of the radio audience grew. In the very first edition of the *Radio Times*, a listener from Stockton-on-Tees thanked the BBC effusively for its 'most interesting talks' on subjects such as 'the Trojan Horse, the Plague of London, the Big Wind, etc'. Another, from Birmingham, asked whether the BBC thought 'ordinary people' were interested in 'lectures such as The Decrease of Malaria in Great Britain; How to Become a Veterinary Surgeon; The New Rent Act'. What about afternoon concerts or more request shows instead? 'Frankly,' he observed, 'the BBC are mainly catering for "listeners" who own expensive sets and pretend to appreciate and understand only highbrow music and educational "sob stuff".' The editor of the *Radio Times* replied as diplomatically as possible: 'In catering for all tastes serious subjects must be dealt with as well as the lighter side of life', but the BBC would nevertheless be 'untiring in its efforts to judge the requirements of the majority'. Reith set out the underpinning philosophy. Broadcasting should appeal 'to every kind of home' in the land, he said, but no one would be expected to listen to every single programme. The BBC's aim should be to satisfy 'the greatest number', but 'individual peculiarities' needed to be catered for occasionally, too. Indeed, he suggested, it might be good to be exposed to the tastes and ideas of others: 'We often dislike things intensely, or rather persuade ourselves we do, when we have actually never been brought into contact with them On the first occasion when, perforce, we are brought up against them, we are quite sure that our antipathy was justified, but next time perhaps they do not seem so bad, and gradually we may even come to appreciate them.'[17]

It was more than simply a question of 'balancing' the radio schedule, for the BBC regarded its relationship with the audience as in a constant state of *tension* – and purposefully so. Cecil Lewis believed that 'the public criticism to which it is constantly subjected' acted as a form of competition on the basis that 'there is always in a sense a rivalry between what the BBC has given, and what the man in the street wants'. This notion of 'rivalry' shaped his own day-to-day strategy for making programmes, since there was an underlying belief that the BBC served listeners best by giving them not what they wanted but what they *needed*. Channelling the spirit of Matthew Arnold, Reith argued that taste was a dynamic thing. 'The more one gets, the more one wants', was how he put it. The BBC's role was therefore to 'set the pace ... in advance of suggestions from without'. This desire to lead rather than simply follow was not just a fundamental principle for Reith. It was one that his most senior lieutenants also embraced as both desirable and practical. If there were '15 sorts of people in the office with 15 sorts of taste', Lewis reasoned, and those fifteen people were also kept 'constantly in touch with fresh and outside points of view', then a rough-and-ready policy was to hand: as long as 'you keep on the upper side of all those tastes you won't do so badly'.[18]

The unresolved question was exactly how *far* on the 'upper side' of public taste should the BBC's programmes be? For now, there was a consensus that, while the BBC could not afford to distance itself too much from public taste lest it lose its audience entirely, the great British public had to put its share of the work in too. When, for example, the BBC put on radio plays, listeners needed, in Val Gielgud's words, to 'take the trouble to concentrate'. Indeed, the BBC was quite explicit in its guidance to the home listener: to keep your mind from wandering, you might wish to turn the lights out, or settle into your favourite armchair five minutes before the programme starts; above all, you should remember that 'If you only listen with half an ear, you haven't a quarter of a right to criticize'. It was advice that represented a triumph of hope over reality. As radio became more and more a part of the furniture of British homes, listening to it steadily lost any sense of occasion: lovingly crafted programmes, which had to compete for attention with the hurly-burly of family life, were heard only haphazardly in the background. But it spoke eloquently, too, of the BBC's faith in the power of broadcasting to spread that elusive Arnoldian dream of sweetness and light.[19]

Harmony and discord

While the BBC's Chief Engineer, Peter Eckersley, busied himself building transmitters and opening relay stations, a simple but bold idea began to form in his mind. He realised that if all these transmitters and stations could be connected, then the BBC could share the same schedule across what would, in effect, be a single network. 'By using the trunk telephone wires,' Eckersley explained, 'a programme can be picked up anywhere and sent to some or all stations, there to be broadcast to the listeners nearby.' Such a system, he added hopefully, 'permits any number of permutations and combinations'. The scheme had begun within a few months of Eckersley's arrival at Savoy Hill. Regional link-ups were one early promise: it was Eckersley's cables that allowed the satellite station in Swansea to relay programmes from Cardiff, and its counterpart in Sheffield to rebroadcast programmes from Manchester. But more ambitious collaborations were also created. When news reached London in August 1923 of R. E. Jeffrey's exuberant production of *Rob Roy* in the 5SC studios at Glasgow, a repeat performance was requested, this time as a so-called 'simultaneous broadcast' or 'S.B': the cast duly reassembled on Saturday 6 October, and their efforts were heard that night on almost every station throughout Britain.[20]

The BBC's presence as a national broadcaster was enhanced further by the opening in July 1925 of a long-wave transmitter on a hill overlooking the Midlands town of Daventry. 5XX was the most powerful transmitter in the world. Its signal radiated for hundreds of miles in every direction, reaching some 85 per cent of the British population. The switching on of this transmitter with its own wavelength, so soon after the completion of a network of smaller, interconnected stations using different wavelengths, made it possible, with a little bit of coordination, to offer the British public a choice of *two* different radio services at the same time. Eckersley had the germ of the idea as early as 1924, but it did not reach fruition until the end of the decade, when a new generation of more powerful medium-wave transmitters had been erected. Listeners with good valve sets had been able for some time to listen to both their local station *and* London, either by tuning in to 2LO directly or to 5XX. But from March 1930, thanks to Eckersley's efforts, audiences could enjoy the 'National Programme' and its counterpart the 'Regional Programme'. It meant that after 6.40 p.m. on Monday 10 March, for instance, a listener in Birmingham could choose between a discussion of Schumann's piano music followed by a literature talk by Desmond MacCarthy on the National Programme or, as an alternative, some catchy Gilbert and Sullivan songs and other light classical tunes on the 'Midland Regional Programme'. A listener in London had the same choice, since 'London Regional' also transmitted the Gilbert and Sullivan programme as an 'S.B.' The BBC stressed that this new approach was intended not to divide the audience into different social classes or age ranges, but rather to accommodate the changing moods and appetites that any one listener might experience over the course of a day. The ultimate aim was to continue jumbling up the familiar and the new, providing for everyone a 'balanced' diet across the week.[21]

As yet, neither the National nor the Regional Programme was truly a universal service, since local variations persisted. Manchester, for example, might still opt to treat its own audience to something like *Northern Notions*, a medley of jolly music and verse featuring the Northern Wireless Orchestra, while Cardiff might offer its audience an hour or so of musical comedy from the National Light Orchestra of Wales. This was the moment, however, when that very first generation of city stations that had emerged in 1922 – 2LO, 2ZY, 5IT, 5SC and the rest – withered away as self-consciously separate entities, to be subsumed in the broader sweep of the Regional Programme. The *Radio Times* gamely assured readers that the new service

The 'simultaneous broadcast board' at Savoy Hill in 1926. Here,
every day, the complex, hour-by-hour and day-by-day scheduling
of output across the different local stations – and later, the
National and Regional Programmes – would be set out.

would be 'reserved for locally-inspired programmes'. Eckersley,
too, wanted its schedule to be 'typical of the taste and culture of
the Region it served'. But the main effect of the change was to
concentrate influence – administratively and culturally – in the
capital. The infrastructure of transmitters and telephone lines,
which had begun in 1923 with simultaneous broadcasting and
ended in 1930 with the Regional Programme, soon became a
tool for distributing London's output – and London's instructions – to the rest of Britain. Right from the start, local stations
had been required to broadcast nightly news bulletins supplied
along telephone lines from London; later, it was decided that
two complete evenings a week should be added, supplemented
by occasional 'London Special Nights'. With the introduction

of a fully fledged Regional arrangement, programmes started to be given a formal rating through the so-called 'phi-system'. Advance schedules from head office would allocate one star for those National Programme productions that should be considered for inclusion in the local Regional Programme; two stars for those that were strongly recommended; and three for those that were deemed compulsory on the basis of their outstanding significance. A process of 'diagonalisation' ensured that many other National Programme items were automatically given a repeat a few days later in the Regional schedule. In the meantime, Savoy Hill's departmental heads – including Charles Siepmann at Talks and Val Gielgud at Drama – insisted on their right to oversee all activity in their particular areas of programme-making, wherever in the country it was taking place.[22]

This assumption that London represented 'the best' was widely held, especially in Savoy Hill itself. Arthur Burrows decided that 'saturation point' had been reached in the use of local talent at what he called the 'provincial stations.' 'The whole entertainment industry is centred in London', he added: 'this fact has to be recognized.' Reith, too, complained to his station directors that he often saw people scheduled to appear in programmes 'whose status, either professionally or socially, and whose qualifications to speak, seem doubtful. It should be an honour in every sense of the word for a man to speak from any broadcasting station, and only those who have a claim to be heard above their fellows on any particular subject in the locality, should be put on the programme.'[23]

There was no explicit mention of London here: Reith was merely articulating a desire to improve the calibre of speakers in each location. But it carried the implicit message that even if London did not always *have* the best, it certainly *knew* best. Indeed, the creation of a centralised Programme Board in 1924 expressed the Managing Director's desire to supervise local stations more closely: all their programme plans now had to be submitted to the Board four weeks ahead of transmission. Meanwhile the aptly named Control Board, which included Reith's most senior lieutenants – Carpendale, Burrows and Eckersley included – became another instrument of central command. Soon memos were streaming out from head office with such words as 'sanction', 'authority', 'permission'. Driving this tangible tightening-up was Reith's conviction that as the BBC expanded its activities only what he called 'unified control' – and would later refer to as 'the brute force of monopoly' – could guarantee the maintenance of high standards. In his Manichean view of the world, the obvious response to the forces he saw ranged against him – populism, commercialism, political meddling – was to insist that any countervailing forces be made equally strong.[24]

One example of how this urge to control had an impact on the listener was the question of what sort of language should be used on-air. Reith had his own ideas, of course. But he could see the danger in relying exclusively on his own tastes. Since 1923, he had been setting up local and national advisory committees on religion, education, music, opera, women's programmes, and *Children's Hour*. They included distinguished experts in the relevant field – archbishops, university dons, the principals of leading music colleges, and the like. It was through a group such as this that Reith hoped both to tap opinion and mobilise support when it came to standards of speech. He took pride in the fact that the BBC had always 'made a special effort' to use announcers who could be 'relied upon to employ the correct pronunciation of the English tongue'. From 1926, however, their behaviour was to be heavily proscribed by a new Advisory Committee on Spoken English, which met thrice yearly to discuss 'debatable' words. Its membership included two founding members of the Society for Pure English. Its secretary was the phonetician Arthur Lloyd James, a man who prefaced one of his books with a telling quotation from Ben Jonson: 'Speech is the only benefit man hath to express his excellency of mind above other creatures. It is the Instrument of Society.' Lloyd James loved to use the metaphor of clothing when discussing the socially acceptable form of speech. 'The kilt', he once wrote, 'is as conspicuous in Piccadilly as the silk hat upon the moors; there are, however, occasions when a black tie is considered suitable by all classes.' Given this kind of thinking, his recommendations to the BBC were unsurprising. There are, he announced, varieties of pronunciation 'that are acceptable throughout the country, and others that are not'. What was deemed least 'distasteful' to most members of the public, was, he concluded, 'the current usage of educated speakers'. Reith's own formula was much the same: that BBC staff should generally speak with a 'southern' educated accent. This amounted to a barely modified form of Received Pronunciation, in which the hee-haw tones of 'BBC English' became only a touch more egalitarian-sounding than the King's English itself.[25] The senior ranks of the BBC had always been dominated by middle-class, public-school and Oxbridge types. Now it sounded like it, too.

Savoy Hill had already introduced other requirements: first, that its announcers, whose identities had hitherto been well known to the public, should remain anonymous; and second, that, in London at least, they should wear a dinner jacket while on duty as a courtesy to the live performers with whom they would be consorting. Anonymity, the dress code and correct pronunciation were all of a piece in creating a sense of propriety and projecting the image of the BBC's announcers as 'men of culture, experience and knowledge'. But the overall message was catnip to any newspaper columnist or cartoonist wanting to lampoon the BBC for its pomposity. The *Daily Mail's* radio critic declared that the increasingly bland presentational style had the 'bored, listless manner of a dying duck'. Compton MacKenzie's cutting accusation that the airwaves too often exuded a 'finicking, suburban, plus-fours gentility' was uncomfortably close to the truth.[26]

Ironically, when it came to spoken English, the BBC approach was largely in keeping with contemporary attitudes. In 1921, a national report into English teaching in schools had called for the inculcation of a standard 'free from provincialisms and vulgarisms'. In 1934, the grammarian Henry Wyld wrote of the 'superiority of Received Standard English'. Spurred on by self-help books that advocated 'a type of speech fitting for any occasion' as one of the best ways to get a job, many working-class Britons were encouraged to think of the BBC as setting the standard for how they should speak and behave. Indeed, Reith's own motivations also had a moral dimension. He reasoned that broadcasting could be of 'immense assistance' in ensuring that no one would have to 'go through life handicapped by the mistakes or carelessness of his own mispronunciation'.[27] It could help bring millions of Britons, hitherto marginalised and vulnerable, into the public realm of work, culture, ideas and debate. In his view, standardised pronunciation was an equalising force – a shining example of an undemocratic means to a democratic end.

Whatever the precise rationale, by the beginning of the 1930s the wider effects of centralisation and standardisation were starting to be felt. By broadcasting the same programmes at the same time to an audience drawn from every class, radio was helping to create a shared public life. The events in which millions of people participated now felt as though they were part of a 'national culture'. The BBC's schedules were routinely punctuated by live outside broadcasts that served to assert the identity of that culture: Trooping the Colour; the Lord Mayor's Banquet in London; the Shakespeare memorial celebrations at Stratford; the feast days of Britain's various patron saints; bank holidays, and so on. Once agreement had been reached with the newspaper owners in 1927, the BBC was also allowed to provide live coverage of the great set-piece events in the sporting calendar – Derby Day, Royal Ascot, Wimbledon, the Cup Final, the Grand National, the Boat Race. It was all very low-key and improvised to begin with. Lance Sieveking, who helped organise the very first live commentary – of an England–Wales rugby international at Twickenham in January 1927 – recalled a three-man team operating out of a small hut. But by the time of the coronation of King George VI at Westminster Abbey ten years later, the BBC's outside broadcast effort involved sixty engineers, fifty-eight microphones, 472 miles of cabling, and twelve tons of equipment. The aim by then was to ensure that the radio audience could eavesdrop on the event from as many different vantage points as possible: the listener at home was promised an experience which would surpass that of the crowd physically present on London's streets.[28]

Even between such landmark occasions, there were plenty of opportunities for people in the privacy of their own living rooms to imagine themselves part of a far larger community – to know that they were among countless others all hearing exactly the same thing at exactly the same time. One nightly ritual for millions was to catch the chimes of Big Ben at the beginning of the main evening news. Another, more intermittent, ritual began in May 1924, when the BBC first broadcast the song of a nightingale performing a 'duet' with the cellist Beatrice Harrison in her Surrey garden. Some 50,000 listeners wrote in to express their appreciation. Reith was thrilled that the nightingale had been heard 'all over the country, on highland moors and in the tenements of the great towns', unleashing 'a wave of something akin to emotionalism'. For him, this sublime sound of nature was a rare, noble, transcendent thing – a connection to the spiritual that anyone, no matter how poor or unlettered or housebound, could appreciate: it represented 'the best' just as much as did Shakespeare or a fine speech. And the British public seemed to agree. By popular demand, the song of the nightingale was heard on the BBC every springtime for nearly two decades.[29]

Since it was actually in the cold, dark winter months that listening – and buying new sets – peaked, the radio manufacturer's annual autumn trade exhibition, Radiolympia, marked the start of a 'wireless season' deliberately packed with Savoy Hill's choicest selection of plays, concerts and variety programmes. The culmination of these fireside months was Christmas, when the BBC provided listeners with a lavish celebration of 'home, hearth and happiness': church services, pantomimes, fancy productions of light opera, the very best dance bands, and live

Richard and Anne Renshaw send a Christmas Day message to their grandfather in New Zealand. Christmas Day was the culmination of the 'wireless season' and always featured live link-ups with absent friends in lighthouses, down coal-mines, or at parties being held across the Empire.

link-ups with 'absent friends' from far-flung places. On Christmas Day 1932, after years of trying, Reith persuaded a reluctant King George V to give the first in what would become an annual royal address: a special message to the peoples of Britain and the Empire. Speaking from Sandringham as nominal head of his own family, the King addressed himself to millions of other families listening in their own, rather more humble homes. It was almost as if in that single instant broadcasting symbolically bound together as one 'the family audience, the royal family, the nation as family'.[30]

These big occasions found a large, generally appreciative audience. But it was the BBC's sports coverage that appeared to have the biggest impact in working-class households. In January

1928 a 'clerk in a provincial city' shared with the *Radio Times* the details of his unspectacular life, in which he had far too little money to spend on entertainment.

> I'm only writing to say how much wireless means to me and thousands of the same sort. It is a real magic carpet. Before it was a fortnight at Rhyl, and that was all the travelling I did that wasn't on a tram. Now I hear the Boat Race and the Derby ... There are football matches some Saturdays, and talks by famous men and women who have travelled and can tell us about places ... But I do like best the running commentaries. You can just *see* the crowds.[31]

His enjoyment was vicarious, yet utterly real.

The BBC's impressive reach did not please everyone, not least because in its push for conformity it too often assumed a common national life that did not fully exist. Letters in the Northern Ireland papers, for instance, complained that there was always 'too much of the Irish pipe, the Irish jig, and the Irish atmosphere' in the BBC's broadcasts from Belfast – perhaps, it was hinted, because most of the staff working there hailed from England or Scotland. This was misleading. In reality, for most of the 1930s the BBC's Belfast base had, if anything, a distinctively unionist and Protestant outlook, which left many in the local nationalist and Catholic community feeling profoundly excluded. Its Regional Director, George Marshall, personified the difficulty. In 1936, he vigorously rejected London's suggestion of a regular and friendly exchange of programme material with Dublin. In the following year, he complained about a programme offered to Belfast by North Region called *The Irish* on the grounds that 'Irishmen as such ceased to exist after the partition'. As one local nationalist paper pointed out, it would not be long before 'anyone tuning into Belfast might take it for just another English station'.[32]

Elsewhere, the cheap-and-cheerful local items, quizzes and audience participation programmes of the pioneering days were long gone. Studio orchestras in Manchester, Birmingham, Glasgow and Cardiff, were scaled back or abolished entirely to make way for a new BBC Symphony Orchestra. Once again, plenty of voices spoke out against this kind of interference. On behalf of the National Federation of Music Societies, Thomas Beecham argued that the North was actually the most musical part of the whole country, and its listeners were therefore entitled to hear more – not less – from the Hallé, the Liverpool Philharmonic, or any of the countless choral societies then thriving in the region. But Savoy Hill remained resolute. Adrian Boult, the BBC's chief conductor and Director of Music, replied baldly that without central control there would be 'chaos'. Reith was slightly more emollient. He suggested that any local cultural loss would surely be offset by the gain in quality that came with extra programmes from London. The response revealed Reith's tin ear when it came to the nuances of culture, but it was at least consistent with his philosophy as to the BBC's purpose. The nation's airwaves must be used to bring 'the maximum benefit to the maximum number', he had always said. To which he could add, with growing confidence in the BBC's ability to deliver on another of its early promises: that 'whatever is done shall be well done'.[33]

The last days of Savoy Hill

The regions had every cause to grumble. But even in London, not all was sweetness and light.

On Saturday 9 June 1928, Lionel Fielden was in his office at Savoy Hill, scribbling a note to his friend and colleague Lance Sieveking. 'I am rapidly falling into dull and dismal bureaucratic ways', he confided. 'An atmosphere of heavy public service clings about the primrose, or sulphur walls ... this section is daily more conscientious and dreary.' Sieveking himself was in the south of France recovering from a nervous collapse. Two years later, Fielden suffered a 'shattering' breakdown of his own after three years of continuous overwork. Cecil Lewis, always restless, had already departed to pursue a life of writing and flying. When he began at the BBC in 1922, 'like all beginnings, it was a thrilling and exciting time', but he had been spending less and less time making programmes and more and more time sitting in committees. Arthur Burrows, too, had gone – back to Geneva to run the International Broadcasting Union and pursue his long-standing dream of using radio to foster global co-operation. As Director of Programmes he had faced a growing mountain of work that had begun to 'overwhelm' him. In 1929, it was Peter Eckersley's turn to leave, and, two years later, the head of Talks, Hilda Matheson.[34]

The constant striving for perfection was bound to undermine Savoy Hill's 'happy-go-lucky' working culture. Many, like Sieveking, stuck it for years, and thrived, even. But by the decade's end, the pioneers – the 'waifs and strays', the 'mixed flock of bohemians', the 'geniuses' and the 'misfits' – were starting to feel like a besieged minority. The 'stuffed shirts', it seemed, had taken charge. Peter Eckersley's younger brother, Roger, was settling in as the new Director of Programmes – a man regarded as kind but without imagination. His Assistant Director of Programmes, Cecil Graves, was a 'very uptight' ex-Guards Officer type, who was utterly loyal to Reith and impeccably orthodox in his taste. Joining them was Basil Nicolls, a dome-headed man who lurked in his office playing with magnets on his desk, who had become Director of Internal Administration – a post that, in its very title, betrayed the BBC's growing bureaucratic flavour. Everyone called him Benjie, which sounded affectionate, but his reputation was forbidding. Possessing a First in Classics from Christ Church, Oxford, he considered his education to be complete, and, according to Charles Siepmann, turned down 'anything imaginative' as automatically of no interest. Another colleague called him 'a most dangerous enemy ... a man of strong opinions who would hunt down somebody who he thought was an opponent'.[35] Above the triumvirate of Eckersley, Graves and Nicolls, of course, there remained Reith and his ultra-cautious deputy, Carpendale, both still firmly steering the ship.

This collective leadership induced a claustrophobic frustration among the BBC's more adventurous staff. From his eyrie in the *Radio Times* office, Maurice Gorham noticed the slow, steady spread of 'caste distinctions': subtle differences in decor – carpets 'blue for seniors, with mahogany furniture: the rest had grey hairline and oak' – or in the way the charladies served the tea – 'juniors a cup and saucer, seniors a pot on a tray'. Clerical and house staff were still permitted to use the same entrances and eat in the same canteen, but producers and managers, whom Nicholls called the 'officer' class, now enjoyed their own toilet facilities, access to first-class rail travel, an expense account and even an extra week's annual leave.[36]

What most stood out at the end of the decade was a new concern, perhaps even an obsession, with decorum. The BBC's status had changed in profound ways. It was bigger. It was doing more. The number of listeners was growing exponentially. The opening of extra transmitters and the regular coverage of big events was turning broadcasting into a nationwide phenomenon. Little more than a scientific curiosity when the BBC began, radio was now an all-pervasive feature of domestic life. A small but significant name change marked the BBC's more august status: on 1 January 1927, it switched from being a 'Company' to being a 'Corporation'.

This change in title represented much more than an administrative tidying up. The umbilical link with the radio set manufacturers that had been so important in 1922 had long since started to chafe. The vision, which Reith and his senior staff shared, of a 'public service operating upon a democratic policy', and of developing radio as a serious, professional craft, felt increasingly incompatible with the manufacturers' original, rather narrow goal of selling sets. The fact that the Post Office kept a sizeable proportion of the licence fees it collected was another constraint on the organisation's freedom of operation. A practical difficulty of this muddled status was that the newspaper owners resisted the BBC's efforts to increase its news coverage on the grounds that it was, after all, an 'ordinary business enterprise'. Reith disputed this. But the alternative of becoming a department of state held little appeal, and in any case neither the Post Office itself nor MPs of any party at Westminster were interested in taking on the responsibility. Reith's ambition instead was to make formal what the BBC was already effectively becoming under his stewardship: a public and independent body free wherever possible from interference by either business or government. There was widespread support for it to continue its monopoly over radio, given that the alternative was still reckoned to be chaos. The only proviso was that it should be accountable to the public *and* remain in what the *Times* called 'generous and humane hands'. It was a stipulation that Reith could reasonably claim to have met, and no one was surprised when in 1926 the government-appointed Crawford Committee recommended that the BBC be awarded public corporation status backed by a licence and Royal Charter. Once the recommendation had come into effect, a Board of Governors was appointed and Reith's title changed from Managing Director to Director-General. Although the emphasis was on continuity, the change of status was of immense significance. The Charter, which ran for a period of ten years, required the BBC to develop broadcasting 'to the best advantage and in the national interest', as if it were, in effect, part of the British constitution.[37]

As it developed a grander sense of its own character, it was perhaps only natural that its managers should feel there was a reputation that needed constantly to be defended. Peter Eckersley observed a 'corporate self-consciousness' that he thought would overwhelm the BBC in the end. Like a regiment, it had already become 'blind in its loyalty to itself and giving absolute obedience to a colonel'. Many who worked at the BBC admitted that it was impossible not to feel in awe of their employer. They would talk of the 'terrific prestige' that seemed to attach to the place, the feeling when one entered Savoy Hill of being 'in the presence of the great', the palpable sense there of a 'single-minded pursuit of excellence'. But in the same breath, they would speak of a 'current of self-satisfaction flowing around', an 'arrogance' that made the place impatient of criticism.[38]

The mixture of pride and prejudice, of pomposity and barely contained mischief that seemed so often to characterise the BBC was fully on show on the evening of Thursday 16 December 1926, when an enormous dinner dance was held to mark its coming rebirth as a Corporation. A hundred or so London staff, regional station directors, outgoing Company directors, incoming Governors, the Postmaster-General, Guglielmo Marconi, even the prime minister, Stanley Baldwin, all gathered at the glitzy Hotel Metropole, where the Charleston dance had made its British debut just a year before. Reith told the gathering that, against all the evidence, it was a family party. The prime minister then reminded everyone that despite the presence of so many famous guests, those who deserved the most recognition were the 'far more distinguished, silent, anonymous, obscure people' who had created broadcasting: the programme makers themselves. Even more welcome was the announcement that the hotel bar was free: most staff had expected the evening to be entirely dry. Soon after, Maurice Gorham recalled, the spirits were 'flowing like water'. By the end of the night, neither he nor any of his colleagues could remember much about the occasion. At work the next day, 'hardly a living being was to be seen'. 'The British Broadcasting Company may have come in like a lamb but it went out with a bang.'[39]

*

The days of Savoy Hill were now numbered. The building was full of character but bursting at the seams. Just as importantly, bigger and grander premises were needed to reflect the BBC's new status.

The search focused initially on a hotel in Trafalgar Square, then several locations along Park Lane. Finally, a site for a new building was chosen in Portland Place, just a few hundred yards north of Oxford Circus. It was flanked by All Souls Church to one

The reception in Broadcasting House, London, which was opened in 1932. The semi-circular space, lined with stone and marble and featuring plenty of Art Deco flourishes, was designed by Val Myer to create the impression of a calm, orderly and dignified institution.

side, Scott's Hotel on another, and a terrace of private houses on a third. It was narrow and awkwardly shaped, but with ingenuity, the BBC was assured, a building could be squeezed in which would prove itself 'worthy of housing a national institution'. An architect was chosen who promised a modern though 'dignified' design, and by the end of 1929 builders had set about digging deep into the ground. Three basement floors were created, descending forty feet below street level: 43,000 tons of sticky London clay was excavated and the water level artificially lowered. Above rose eight floors and a clock tower, topped by a vast turtle-back roof. The edifice presented the gently curved shape of an ocean liner, with a shimmering white façade and imposing bronze doors at its main entrance. Inside was a state-of-the-art 'sound factory' that included a large basement concert hall, a control room, a telephone exchange and twenty-two studios, each individually decorated with Art Deco flourishes to match their purpose – one,

A control cubicle on the sixth floor of Broadcasting House,
where programmes going out from both Studio 6B and
Studio 6C were monitored. Although spaces near the top
of Broadcasting House were often small, the stripped-down
modern interiors set new standards in British design.

for book talks, kitted out like a library; another, for religious programmes, designed as a chapel, and so on. All these studios were
located in a central tower, insulated from outside noise by a four-
feet-thick wall and row upon row of offices wrapped around the
building's outer edges. The *Daily Express* called it the 'brain centre
of modern civilization', the *Architectural Review*, the 'new Tower
of London'. The BBC called it simply 'Broadcasting House'. Its
staff took up residence in stages from September 1931. Finally, in
April 1932, the last 160 vans, loaded with 300 tons of equipment
and paperwork, turned up from Savoy Hill just as the artist Eric
Gill, dressed in beret, smock and hob-nailed boots, was putting
the finishing touches to his statue of 'The Sower' in the marbled
lobby. Reith knew it was a momentous occasion. He arranged to
be photographed at the old headquarters as he locked the doors
for the very last time.[40]

In paying tribute to its old home, the BBC described Savoy Hill as the place where it had 'spent its childhood and grew up to man's estate'. Adulthood was bound to be different. There would be excitement, but also a feeling of trepidation. For one thing, the Corporation was now expanding so rapidly that even Broadcasting House quickly proved to be too small. More ominously, the building had an aura of forbidding, stately authority. One of the BBC's young night pages, whose job it was to take visiting artistes to studios or run errands for producers, remembers racing along its endless curving corridors. 'Every door handle, tap, washbasin or anything else that could be polished was shining bright.' He would watch the commissionaires in the marble-clad lobby 'as smart and upright as guardsmen', standing to attention when Reith or Carpendale arrived each morning. A newly commissioned BBC coat of arms occupied prominent positions around the building, while a specially designed flag flew from the rooftop.[41]

Meanwhile, the weight of management felt just that fraction heavier. Reith's decision the following year to set up an entire administrative 'division' did not help. There was a whole new cadre of planners and accountants who, in their dealings with programme makers, 'had every incentive to say No and none to say Yes'. These administrators even had their own lifts; artistes or production staff wanting to go to studios had to go through an extra set of swing doors in the Broadcasting House reception to reach theirs. The feeling of division was pervasive. An engineer remembered his sorrow at finding himself suddenly 'more remote' from programme-making colleagues with whom he had previously been merrily cheek by jowl. Broadcasting House was modern and marvellous in its facilities and location, but the place was, Maurice Gorham thought, simply too 'stuck-up'. Worst of all, the 'old caste feeling' he had worried about during the dying days of Savoy Hill was 'stronger than ever'.[42]

Even so, the BBC could never be quite the vast, monolithic, authoritarian institution that people feared. It remained too complex, too busy, too sprawling, and, perhaps most importantly, too heavily populated by individualists for Reith's 'unity of control' to mutate into something truly totalitarian. The rules were multiplying, but insiders claimed that they were still 'not always adhered to'. Working life was more professional, but programmes were still made by thinking, feeling human beings. Whether they worked at Savoy Hill, Broadcasting House, or one of the regional stations, the BBC's staff were part of the turbulent stream of public life, required by the very nature of their job to try to understand the currents of thought and opinion swirling around them. Indeed, a spirit of mutual enterprise between broadcasters and the listeners was still palpable. There was no talk of the 'masses' inside Broadcasting House. Reith studiously avoided the term, as did most of his senior staff. The preferred descriptions of 'the ordinary listener' or 'the man in the street' spoke of a hard-wired determination to reach out to as many people as possible. As Lionel Fielden saw it, the goal of programme-making remained both simple and profound: to 'continually enlarge the listener's horizon'.[43] If there was mention of a collective 'general public', it was regarded not as inert but as a living community. Its sharply differing tastes, its foibles, its passions, its weaknesses: these had to be recognised, and, even if not fully accommodated, acted upon, *negotiated* with.

Meanwhile, in millions of homes around the country, radio had become a normal, taken-for-granted feature of daily life. For many Britons, the voice coming out of the loudspeaker in their living room was not that of a distant stranger but someone who might almost be regarded as part of the family. Reith took great satisfaction from the thought that the BBC still presented a friendly face. It was, he believed, a vital basis for its influence in the world.

Influence, like the relationship with listeners, was fragile, however. As an institution, the BBC now had a degree of permanence. Having started life as a company created by an act of the state, it had carved out an existence in that narrow but fertile space somewhere between 'Nation' and 'People'. But the changes that had culminated in its new existence as a Corporation were unlikely to be cost-free. By pulling away from some of its grassroots and drawing closer to the centres of power, the BBC risked opening up a divide with its audience. If the balance tipped too far away from the informality and friendliness upon which radio depended for its popularity, the BBC's mission to shape society for the better would surely falter.

What mattered most were the programmes it made. They were the real measure of the broadcaster's grasp of life beyond the studio wall, as it was lived by 'the ordinary listener'. When it came, in particular, to the charged world of politics, the test the BBC faced was to show that it could report the news accurately, debate controversy where it arose, and uncover injustice wherever it was found – all without incurring the wrath of those who had the power to damage it. When the country was divided as starkly as it was between the wars – by arguments over unemployment and the economy, and about democracy and its failings – the BBC was going to have to steer an especially difficult path: between government and people, between conservatives and progressives, between capitalists and workers. It would be impossible to satisfy everyone, but on several occasions the BBC would stumble badly. And at times, it would seem as if everything that had been achieved since 1922 might be undone in an instant.

4

US AND THEM

Everyone had something to tell his fellow-men, and a
point of view that deserved a hearing.

BBC producer Geoffrey Bridson, 1939

On Friday 18 April 1930, Wagner's opera, *Parsifal*, was being
broadcast live on the National Programme, the centrepiece
of the evening's wireless entertainment. At 8.45 p.m. a fifteen-
minute interlude had been scheduled for the evening news. But
when the time came, the announcer simply said 'There is no
news'. There was, it seemed, literally nothing worth reporting.
And little to be done other than fill the allotted slot with some
lovely piano music before returning listeners to the delights of
Parsifal.

In some respects, it *was* a quiet news day. After all, it was
Good Friday. The printing presses of the main national newspapers were idle, and the news agencies that supplied the BBC's
newsroom were offering only a skeleton service. Yet the world
had not really ceased to turn. In Glasgow, there were two terrible fires: one in a tenement that had left many families homeless;
another at a factory that had injured eight firemen. In Bradford,
6,000 textile workers were on strike, and in South Wales, several
thousand miners had just been given redundancy notices. Hundreds of men who had already lost their jobs were on a 'hunger
march' from Yorkshire to London. Meanwhile in Karachi, police
had opened fire on demonstrators against British rule. There
was also ominous news coming from Thuringia in Germany: a

recently elected local government minister from the party of a certain 'Herr Adolf Hitler' was calling for all 'alien influences' to be removed from public life and for severe penalties to be introduced for anyone 'interbreeding' with Jews.[1]

How had such stories failed to register?

One answer was that the BBC was still playing catch-up after years of being blocked from covering news properly. Back in 1922, Britain's anti-competitive newspaper proprietors had extracted from the fledgling Company a promise not to broadcast any news before 7 p.m. With no working journalists of its own, the BBC was limited to reading out a bulletin supplied each evening by Reuters. Since Reith believed profoundly in broadcasting's power to bring every single citizen 'first-hand knowledge of the events which make history', he regarded this restriction as intolerable. The most persistent stumbling block he faced in trying to overturn it concerned the treatment of politically sensitive subject matter. The BBC's very first licence from the Postmaster-General required it to broadcast programmes to his 'reasonable satisfaction'. The phrase was vague, but the Postmaster-General had offered some elaboration in 1923, when he told Parliament that it was undesirable for broadcasting to allow 'speculation' on controversial matters: if the BBC ignored this rule of thumb, then its licence was unlikely to be renewed. Even after the BBC's transformation into a Corporation in 1927, it was required to abstain from 'topics of political, religious or industrial controversy'. Having explained that opposing views would always be 'stated with equal emphasis and lucidity', Reith argued that the continued absence of controversy from the airwaves was a 'devitalising influence' and that the BBC had already demonstrated that it could handle such matters responsibly. The Post Office finally relented. On Monday 5 March 1928, it lifted the 'ban on controversy', recognising the 'loyal and punctilious manner' in which the BBC had met its obligations.[2]

For most of the BBC's history, changes in both programmes and policy were a result of evolution rather than revolution. But its emergence as a 'loyal' purveyor of news had been transformed dramatically and decisively by a single event back in May 1926: the General Strike, when millions of workers had attempted to bring the country to a standstill in support of Britain's miners, and the government had responded with a concerted effort to orchestrate public opinion against the action. The sudden and widespread hunger for up-to-date information had thrust the medium of radio into the national consciousness as never before and had allowed the BBC to force its entry into the world of daily journalism. Yet it was in the course of those nine eventful days in May that the BBC's ambition to broadcast opposing views 'with equal emphasis and lucidity' had also been found wanting. It was a failure which would cast a long shadow over its reporting of social affairs for years to come.

The General Strike

The grievances that led to the General Strike had been festering for years. Ever since 1919, Britain's coal miners had faced successive attempts by the colliery owners to cut jobs and wages. Their struggle had become more than a matter of protecting income: it was a battle for 'the acknowledgement that those who laboured were contributing to the country's wealth and thus deserved to share in it'. The immediate cause of the dispute was the owners' threat in 1925 to impose drastic wage reductions. Stanley Baldwin's Conservative government offered a subsidy to prevent an immediate strike, but then withdrew it nine months later. While the colliery owners used the interval to build up their stockpiles of coal, the hawks in the cabinet, led by Winston Churchill, saw an opportunity to 'smash the unions'. On Saturday 1 May, with no sign of the owners backing down, and fearing the damage to the wider labour movement if the miners were forced to capitulate, the Trades Union Congress reluctantly called a general strike in their support. It had no interest in 'holding the country to ransom', as Britain's newspapers suggested. It even wrote to the cabinet on the Sunday offering to co-operate in the distribution of essential foods. But the mood quickly polarised. That night, the *Daily Mail* prepared an editorial headlined 'For King and Country'. In inflammatory language, it accused the TUC of transforming an industrial dispute into revolutionary action aimed at 'subverting the rights and liberties of the people' – action that needed to be met with 'the utmost firmness'.[3]

Reith had seen the as yet unpublished editorial. He called 10 Downing Street, only to be told that the government had withdrawn from its negotiations with the unions. Just after 1 a.m., he used a phone line in his flat near the Houses of Parliament to broadcast to the country that the strike was on and that a state of emergency would be announced after daybreak. Savoy Hill now had less than twenty-four hours to prepare. Since transport workers were to be called out, the BBC's non-essential staff were given a week's wages and sent home, while others were encouraged to stay in central London with friends. Two 'saloon charabancs' were hired to ferry female staff and members of the orchestra around town. Inside Savoy Hill itself, canteen hours were extended to ensure that hot meals were available for anyone staying in the building overnight. Rotas were rearranged, contact details collected, and spare candles made ready for power cuts.[4]

On Monday, with the strike poised to start, the Controller, Admiral Carpendale, telephoned regional station directors, telling them that the BBC was now considered an essential service. Henceforth no member of staff could volunteer for any other duty. During the main news bulletin, Stuart Hibberd read out a statement by the strike's organisers that if the government was willing to resume negotiations a settlement could still be reached. He went on to describe an 'atmosphere of intense excitement' in the House of Commons earlier that day, when the prime minister accused the TUC of 'going nearer to proclaiming civil war than we have been for centuries past'.

The first full day of the strike actually began not with violent insurrection but an eerie silence. Railway stations were empty, the London Underground at a standstill, bus services abandoned. Upwards of 1.75 million workers in transport, printing, iron and steel, power stations and chemical factories had come out in support of a million miners. Thousands of textile workers across Lancashire had also downed tools. The country, the BBC told its listeners, was in 'almost complete industrial paralysis', but, it added, the government's effort to orchestrate tens of thousands of strike-breakers meant that milk and food were being distributed successfully by car or lorry, and some train services were still running with the help of volunteer drivers.

The BBC's schedule maintained a reassuring familiarity for the rest of the day: the usual lunchtime music, programmes for schools in the afternoon, *Children's Hour*, then, after dinner, plenty of dance tunes. But there were now five news bulletins instead of the usual two: at 10 a.m., 1 p.m. and 4 p.m., as well as at 7 p.m. and 9.30 p.m. Since the press had been mostly shut down, the Post Office had waived its restrictions on the BBC's news output for the duration of the strike. The vast public appetite for up-to-date information on a rapidly changing crisis had suddenly given the BBC a completely new role.

A team of five men and five women was hastily assembled to work in shifts around the clock, gathering, rewriting, compiling and typing up news items. Stories were garnered from the countless telegrams that now streamed in from local strike organisers, regional government officers, newspapers and listeners. The BBC relied on the main news agencies for most of its information, but a direct line was established to the Admiralty Office, where the Deputy Chief Civil Commissioner, John Davidson, was in charge of government news. Three BBC staff were also based at the Admiralty, including the Company's Director of Publicity, Gladstone Murray. The whole frenetic operation was co-ordinated at Savoy Hill, where Reith was often present, casting a beady eye over scripts. The sheer volume of news meant that bulletins were soon lasting an unprecedented three-quarters of an hour. Many who had previously resisted the lure of radio now hurriedly bought their own sets or clustered around receivers installed in high-street shops. 'The sensation of a general strike', Beatrice Webb wrote in her diary, 'centres around the headphones of the wireless set.'

Strike-breakers at a government centre in London 'for
the maintenance of essential services' listening to a radio
broadcast, May 1926. With most newspapers temporarily shut
down, millions of Britons – whether supporting the General
Strike or not – relied on the BBC for basic information.

Staff at Savoy Hill could not help but feel they were engaged
in work of the utmost national importance. Though Stuart
Hibberd read many of the bulletins, even the BBC's most senior
figures – Reith himself, Carpendale, Peter Eckersley – took turns
before the microphone. The building itself was under round-
the-clock guard, the place thick with special constables. The
press had mentioned the dangers of the BBC being taken over
by subversives. Yet under the terms of the licence it was the
government that ultimately had the power to commandeer the
Company outright or require it to broadcast certain messages.
Neither Baldwin, nor Ramsay MacDonald in his time, had shown
any desire to exercise this right, but there were now others in

the cabinet with more dangerous instincts – the Chancellor of the Exchequer, Winston Churchill, chief among them. He had just launched the *British Gazette*, a crudely partisan newspaper full of hysterical reports about misbehaving strikers. Why, he wondered, should the BBC not be turned into a radio version?

On the evening of Wednesday 5 May, the Home Secretary, William Joynson-Hicks, had turned up at Savoy Hill to broadcast an appeal for more volunteer special constables. 'Jix', as he was commonly called, used the opportunity to tell Reith that Churchill was on the warpath. Immediately after breakfast the next day, Reith went with John Davidson to see the prime minister in the Cabinet Room at 10 Downing Street. 'Baldwin was on the other side of the table from us, walking up and down smoking a pipe, and I was making a passionate appeal the Government should leave the BBC alone and trust to me.' Baldwin offered to put the issue to his ministers later that day in a special committee, which he allowed Reith to attend. When Reith arrived he was pleased to hear the Home Secretary read a statement of support from Baldwin. But then Churchill 'burst out, fulminating against the BBC's continuing independence – "absolutely wrong!"' After further heated debate in which Churchill showed no sign of giving ground, the Home Secretary was forced to report back to cabinet that no agreement had been reached. Reith left the room 'immensely disappointed', knowing the threat of takeover still hung over the BBC. A few hours later, he sent Davidson a short note making one last-ditch appeal. The BBC, he wrote, had spent more than three years earning 'the goodwill and affection of the people'. To commandeer it now, or even hamper its work, would be counter-productive, even calamitous. He then offered an assurance. 'Assuming the BBC is for the people, and that the Government is for the people, it follows that the BBC must be for the Government in this crisis too.' On this basis, Reith wrote, the BBC should be trusted to help in sustaining essential services and counteracting any 'spirit of violence and hostility', while also being allowed to run a news service with a reputation for 'sincerity and impartiality'. In response to the note there was only official silence. 'For several days, we just didn't know where we were ... there was no decision one way or another.'

Reith calculated that the BBC now needed to tread very carefully. The timing could hardly have been worse since the government-appointed Crawford Committee, which had been investigating the BBC's constitutional status for the past year, had only recently decided to recommend that it become a Corporation and be granted more financial independence: these recommendations still awaited government approval.

When Churchill phoned Savoy Hill to demand that the BBC broadcast the sound of the *British Gazette* rolling off the printing presses, Reith refused. Thereafter, the government largely got its way. The only speakers allowed on air were those making announcements of an anti-strike nature. On the evening of Saturday 8 May, the prime minister himself spoke to the nation – not from the Savoy Hill studios, but from Reith's own home. Earlier that day, the government had secured a dramatic victory when a fleet of armoured cars and troops broke through picket lines at the London docks to deliver food supplies to a distribution centre in Hyde Park. Confident he had the upper hand, Baldwin now drove home his advantage. He told listeners that the General Strike was an attack by the TUC on the national 'community', an attempt to 'starve us into submission'. It needed to be called off 'absolutely and without reserve'. If it continued there could be no settlement of the mining dispute. 'I am a man of peace', he concluded. 'But I will not surrender the safety and the security of the British constitution.' Reith was standing behind the prime minister throughout this short broadcast. Indeed, he had helped him finalise his script: 'I am a man of peace' were words that came from Reith, not Baldwin. And Reith believed it was this broadcast, more than anything else, that 'broke' the strike.

The Labour leader, Ramsay MacDonald, was livid. On the Monday, he phoned Reith asking to be allowed on-air. He wanted to tell the British public that the Labour movement had 'striven with might and main' to avert a dispute, that it was a strike 'conducted by men and women of goodwill', and that it would be called off if the government undertook to prevent the mining industry from further lowering the living standards of its employees and their families. MacDonald declared himself willing to change 'any word or form of expression' in this message, but Reith submitted it to Davidson as it was, with a strong recommendation that the Labour leader be allowed to speak. Davidson's reply was that Downing Street was 'quite against' MacDonald being given a slot, although the final decision was, of course, Reith's. It was now Reith's turn to be angry. 'They will not say we are to a considerable extent controlled', he wrote in his diary that night, 'and they make me take the onus of turning people down ... it puts me in a very awkward and unfair position.'

It wasn't the first use of the government's unspoken veto. On Friday 7 May, the Archbishop of Canterbury had asked to broadcast a statement on behalf of 'official Church opinion in this country'. It called for a 'spirit of fellowship' and a mutual agreement to suspend hostilities 'simultaneously and concurrently'. Although this contradicted the official government position, which was that the strike needed to be called off *before* any negotiations began, Reith regarded it as an 'unexceptional' appeal for the government to be 'generous and large-minded'. Yet when it was shown to Baldwin, he passed a message back to Reith that 'the Prime Minister would rather you didn't'. Reith knew that he had no real choice but to comply with the government's wishes. 'I told the Archbishop I was sorry, I wouldn't agree to his broadcasting ... I hated it.' As for the Archbishop, he made crystal clear 'how serious a matter' the rejection was. Reith knew that it was 'the PM's difficulties with the Winston lot' that had forced him to compromise the BBC's position. 'There was I, in the invidious position of having to arbitrate between the Prime Minister of the country and the Archbishop of Canterbury because I was so frightened of what Churchill would make of it.' 'If I had allowed the Archbishop to make that statement against the wishes of the Prime Minister', Churchill 'would have succeeded in swinging the Cabinet over to taking possession of the BBC ... That's why I did what I didn't approve of myself doing.'

Reith's only consolation was that the BBC did at least retain some control over its news bulletins. In their running orders, a distinction was drawn between announcements that the BBC was obliged to make on behalf of the government and regular items staff deemed to be free of partisanship. The former would be introduced on air with words such as 'We are *instructed* by the Deputy Chief Commissioner to make the following announcement ...', with the rest left to project a more even-handed tone. This meant that over the nine days of the strike, the BBC did manage to report several statements by union leaders as well as those by the government; it even quoted the TUC complaining about the non-appearance of the Archbishop of Canterbury. Yet the nuanced distinction Savoy Hill sought to make between propagandist announcements from the government and information written in-house would have been lost on many listeners. Lengthy official statements urging 'loyal citizens' to 'assist the government' or calling for additional volunteers to guard food convoys were being read out by the BBC's announcers. To all intents and purposes it would have sounded as if it was *always* the BBC speaking.

As the strike dragged on, the degree of self-censorship forced upon the BBC intensified. On Thursday 6 May, the day Churchill had spoken out against the broadcaster's independence, an internal directive told staff that the BBC was 'in a state of suspense, with a certain natural bias towards the Government side'. Twenty-four hours later, a further chilling effect had taken hold. 'The position is still one of suspense', staff were now told, but 'with a move towards the right': censorship of the TUC 'should be more rigid than formerly', with any quotations 'confined to the advocacy of restraint and the avoidance of disorder'.

The BBC tried valiantly to persuade listeners of its reliability. An 'editorial interlude' broadcast on Wednesday 5 May urged the public to stop spreading rumours based on what they had read in the papers. How, the announcer asked, would anyone ever know if something were true? The answer, he suggested, was blindingly obvious: 'Ladies and Gentlemen, if you hear it on the wireless, it is so!' But it clearly wasn't, and many listeners knew it wasn't. Flora Hutchings wrote in from Birmingham to say she had listened to Baldwin's Saturday night broadcast and wanted to know 'if it is not possible for one of the TUC representatives to give us the other side of the argument'. A Mr Lees in Bury, warned that as far as the working men of his town were concerned, it would 'take a long time of care for you to remove the bad impression and feeling of contempt that these people are left with'. One of the most excoriating letters of complaint, from the Labour MP Ellen Wilkinson, was later published in the *Radio Times*. Having travelled all over the country and addressed innumerable public meetings, she said, she could only report that 'Everywhere the complaints were bitter that a national service subscribed to by every class should have given only one side.' 'Personally,' she went on, 'I feel like asking the Postmaster General for my licence fee back.'

Only a swift end to the General Strike could prevent a further erosion of trust. Fortunately for the BBC, the second week saw both sides edging uneasily towards a deal. Sunday's and Monday's bulletins brought news of railwaymen and printers in several parts of the country returning to work. On Tuesday, the latest in a series of enormous convoys broke through the picket lines to deliver several hundred tons of meat to London's Smithfield Market. The following day, the BBC broadcast a vivid eyewitness account, describing how the lorries – some 125 in total – had been driven by strike-breakers under armed escort. As they rumbled through Silvertown, Canning Town and Poplar, listeners were told, 'Mounted and foot police were in considerable force … there were also little batches of military, all wearing steel helmets and armed.' Accounts such as these made uncomfortable news for the strike's supporters, and the TUC's national leadership was increasingly despondent about its chances of winning. By early afternoon that same day its General Council had capitulated: the General Strike over.

Reith himself was in Savoy Hill reading the lunchtime news on air when the agency report came through. Stuart Hibberd, who had been in the makeshift newsroom upstairs, rushed to the studio and placed it in front of his Managing Director. 'He paused, read it through, and reflected, then signed to me for a pencil and wrote on the back of the paper: "Get this confirmed by 10 Downing Street".' After ten minutes, Reith was able to return to the microphone and let the country know that the strike was indeed at an end. Three hours later, a much fuller account of the day's dramatic events could be provided. Reith read out statements from the TUC and Downing Street and reminded listeners that the miners themselves were still out on strike. After reading messages from the King and the prime minister, he gave a brief address of his own. 'Our first feelings on hearing the termination of the General Strike must be of profound thankfulness to Almighty God', he began. He spoke of the nation's 'happy escape' being due in large part to a 'personal trust in the Prime Minister'. 'As for the BBC,' he added, 'we hope your confidence in, and goodwill to us have not suffered. We have laboured under certain difficulties, the full story of which may be told someday.' He went on to conjure up the spirit of William Blake. With a small orchestra playing in the studio, he recited four verses, closing with the famous lines:

> *I will not cease from mental flight;*
>   *Nor shall my sword sleep in my hand*
> *Till we have built Jerusalem*
>   *In England's green and pleasant land.*

The bulletin ended with the usual weather forecast. A 'complex depression' was moving across the country, Reith warned. 'Further outlook: unsettled.'

★

Reith admitted many years later that during the nine turbulent days of the General Strike he had been 'most happy throughout'. 'I do not say that I welcome crises,' he added, 'but I do welcome the opportunities they bring.'

At a critical moment in the country's political life the BBC had shown the ability of broadcasting to provide a vital national service. Though the Post Office's ban on reporting matters of 'controversy' was swiftly reimposed and the number of news bulletins scaled back, the machinery for a BBC news-gathering department had been established. Reith had also seen off the very real threat of a government takeover. His personal calculation had been that almost any price was worth paying to prevent this calamity. The accommodations with officialdom had been 'embarrassing', but they had kept Churchill at bay and allowed the BBC to provide a news service that, though incomplete, had been factually accurate as far as it went. As one confidential BBC memo put it, 'our news was "doped" only by suppressions, not by fabrications'. In this way, Reith believed the BBC had been able to dispel misinformation, avoid panic, and contribute 'perhaps decisively' to what he called 'the attitude of understanding without which goodwill could not be restored'. Clearly, not every listener felt the same. The systematic absence of certain speakers had been widely noticed. And the goodwill of the Labour Party and the trades unions now appeared thoroughly spent. But for hundreds of thousands of Britons, tuning in to the BBC had suddenly become part of what it was to be an informed citizen.

The other vitally important result of the strike for the BBC was that its 'good conduct' had avoided jeopardising final approval of the Crawford Report. In July, the government accepted the report's recommendation that the BBC should become a Corporation: Reith's long-held desire to transform the BBC from a private business into a public body could go ahead.

Yet it was obvious that the BBC had paid a heavy price for retaining its formal independence. In a detailed communiqué to senior staff on 15 May, just three days after the dispute's collapse, Reith admitted that the constraints forced on the broadcaster had made it 'impossible' to provide the kind of service the BBC had originally envisaged: 'non-political' public messages every night and speeches not just from the prime minister but from 'Labour leaders ... and so on'. Later, Reith conceded that although the BBC had not been 'definitely commandeered' during the crisis, it had certainly been 'interfered with'. It was a tacit acknowledgement that the government's right to seize control of the BBC in an emergency represented an ongoing challenge to the BBC's independence. For, as Reith's behaviour during the strike had demonstrated, the mere threat of takeover had been 'a powerful inducement for compliance'. By deferring any final decision over the BBC's status until after the dispute, the government had been free to deploy what John Davidson called 'unofficial control': the BBC could keep operational autonomy on the tacit understanding that it would continue broadly serving the government's purposes. This set a precedent for future crises. Moreover, since politicians had been given a powerful lesson on radio's remarkable ability to provide direct access to a large slice of the electorate, it was now that they started taking a closer interest in broadcasting as a tool for managing public opinion. In the second half of the 1920s contact between central government and broadcasters became routine, with ministries creating publicity departments, setting up briefings, and arranging the circulation of official reports in advance of publication to selected journalists. Whitehall preached the doctrine that such work, being in the national interest, was 'politically and ideologically neutral'. For their part, the broadcasters thought of themselves as partners in what was a joint enterprise: educating the listening public to participate in the democratic process.

The nine days of close coordination between the BBC newsroom and the Admiralty Office, where Davidson had worked with the BBC's Director of Publicity Gladstone Murray, drafting announcements, vetting agency copy, drafting bulletins,

was supposed to have been a temporary arrangement. But soon
after the strike, Murray wrote a letter to Davidson in which he
recalled their time together as 'a privilege and a pleasure'. 'It
will not be for want of trying on my part if the pleasant associa-
tions thus established are not perpetuated', he added. 'I feel very
strongly that in the national interest it is more than desirable
that your contact with our service both official and unofficial
should become permanent.' This was an extraordinary act of
submission. And, to give him his due, Reith quickly decided that
Murray was being 'unduly influenced' by Davidson and could
no longer be fully trusted. In Reith's mind the BBC existed in
a realm floating above party politics, offering a model of good
governance from which the creaking machinery of the state
might have something to learn. At the same time, he desperately wanted respectability and status for broadcasting, which
meant that no matter how much he claimed to distrust power,
authority and wealth, he always, as he put it, 'had to be in association with them … in order to accomplish what I wanted to
accomplish for the BBC'.

Temperament, social connection and personal standing
oiled the machinery of these relationships. In May 1926, Reith
had been living in Barton Street, a few minutes' walk from Parliament and Lambeth Palace. Davidson just happened to live
three doors down on the same street. 'I knew him pretty well',
Reith admitted. Reith's remarkable inside knowledge of government tactics during the strike was partly a result of having
met the prime minister socially on several occasions. There was
mutual respect: Reith appreciated Baldwin's commitment to
broadcasting; Baldwin saw Reith as a natural ally in his campaign to improve the moral climate of Britain. A similar sense
of 'fellow feeling' could be detected in Reith's relationship with
the Leader of the Opposition, Ramsay MacDonald.

Such personal affinities reinforced Reith's determination that
the BBC, as a national broadcaster, should behave in the 'national
interest'. This was not quite the same as supporting politicians
unconditionally. In the case of the strike, Reith believed that the

government had been 'acting for the people' and upholding law and order, which was why he thought the BBC had to be 'for the government' too. But he hinted that there might, theoretically, be instances when the government was judged to be *not* acting in the national interest and the BBC would then be required to act differently. It was, though, hard to imagine this happening easily. Savoy Hill was riddled with middle-class attitudes and, worse, largely ignorant of the realities of working-class life. Someone such as Lance Sieveking could boast of being brilliantly attuned to all the fashionable artistic trends of the era but happily confess that the 'rights and wrongs' of industrial disputes remained to him 'a mystery'. Throughout the strike the BBC had aligned itself with the government as much out of social instinct as contractual obligation.

A few days after it ended, the prime minister wrote to Reith to offer 'a special word of thanks for the great help and service which the BBC rendered to the Government during the emergency'. Credit, he explained, was due not just to Reith himself but to 'all who helped' in discharging what he called this 'heavy responsibility'. On this occasion, at least, Baldwin proved as good as his word. As Reith set off for a well-deserved holiday in France, a pile of engraved cigarette cases turned up at Savoy Hill. They had been given, so one insider later revealed, 'by grateful government departments to loyal BBC staff'.

Radio on the dole

By the end of 1926, Britain's miners were either back at work, facing even harsher conditions than before, or finding that they had been made redundant in their absence. By the time a wider economic depression took hold at the end of the decade, throwing people out of work in the factories and mills that made up the country's industrial heartlands, the prospect of finding alternative employment had become grimly remote for many millions of ordinary Britons.

The experience of John Evans was sadly all too typical

of the 1930s. A middle-aged miner made redundant from the Gilfach colliery in South Wales, he would tramp the countryside in search of work, keeping his wife and four children fed and clothed with credit from the local Co-op and unemployment benefit from the Labour Exchange – until, that is, his benefit was cut, and then taken away altogether thanks to a new government Means Test that started to take into account the earnings of his two young sons. To heat his home, Evans would walk to isolated outcrops of coal, stretch out on the ground and scratch together a few lumps to carry home. Lying in pools of water to reach the seams, he would get soaked from head to foot, and start to suffer severe chest problems. Worst of all, there seemed little prospect of change. Politicians, John Evans decided, 'do not care a brass farthing for the bottom dog'.[5]

It was wireless that now gave Evans and people like him the opportunity to tell their stories. In 1934, their accounts were captured for broadcast and then reprinted in the pages of the Corporation's upmarket weekly journal, the *Listener*. The magazine's editor, Richard Lambert, had, before joining the BBC in 1927, spent several years with the Workers' Educational Association teaching Yorkshire steelworkers and railwaymen. 'I used to stay in the homes of my students', he explained, and 'gradually imbibed from the atmosphere in which I worked a sympathy with their point of view'. Lambert was part of a progressive, reforming British middle class that made its presence felt during the interwar years – on radio, as well as in print. At about the same time as Lambert's 'memoirs of the unemployed' appeared in *The Listener*, the essayist J. B. Priestley wrote *English Journey*, his celebrated account of travelling through the country's shires, towns and cities. Priestley described the 'silent rusting shipyards' of Tyneside and suggested that 'If T. S. Eliot ever wants to write a poem about a real wasteland instead of a metaphysical one', it was to this corner of the country that he should go. He reported how Jarrow was thick with 'enforced idleness, poverty and misery', its menfolk hanging about on the streets in their 'hundreds and thousands'. Wherever Priestley went, he detected a profound change in attitudes and behaviours: juveniles driven by boredom to petty theft, an older generation abandoning hope and embracing fatalism, young men seduced by Oswald Mosley's thuggish Black Shirt fascists, or, like 'Bob' in Newcastle, drawn to communism. 'There are a good many Bobs about', Priestley noted, 'especially in the north'. Before long 'there will probably be a great many more'. At the BBC, Lambert, too, worried that people who had been treated as disposable were withdrawing from the shared values of an enlightened democracy. He fretted at 'the recrudescence of violence, the revival of long-sleeping prejudices, the upset of values in our civilization'. 'If hunger does not make rebels,' he warned, 'it makes what is worse – criminals or listless unbelievers in the validity of our civilization. These unemployed men and women are decent people. We are losing their help in building up our common life.'[6]

Talk of a 'common life' spoke directly to Reith's credo, that broadcasting should spread 'enjoyment on the one hand ... assimilation on the other'. It also echoed the Director-General's interest in using the public airwaves to improve the quality of national debate. If 'the industries of the country suffer from the ignorance which prevails concerning them', he had pointed out, then 'there are the means at hand whereby the ignorance may be dispelled'. The General Strike had revealed all too starkly that few of Lambert's BBC colleagues truly understood working-class life from the inside. But in the aftermath of the 1929 crash, and, equally importantly, after the introduction of the intrusive Means Test, it was increasingly plain to anyone with a social conscience that grinding poverty was the experience of a growing number of Britons, and, just as importantly, that its cause lay with government policy rather than personal fecklessness. It was equally clear that unless the country's politicians recognised this fact, and unless the human toll of unemployment was better understood by the British public at large, any hope of a 'common life' was but a pipe dream. Lambert recognised this. So too did others at the BBC who lived and breathed

'the great liberal tradition': staff who felt that their own education 'made it an obligation upon them to enlighten other people
less enlightened in the ways that they should go'.[7] Collectively,
they ensured that an influential strand of deeply conscientious
broadcasting – progressive, sometimes even radical, in outlook –
was able to thrive. Indeed, thanks to these producers it was often
the BBC that was in the vanguard of raising social awareness,
providing a lead that writers, film-makers and social campaigners would later follow.

In London, it was usually the Talks department that was
busiest on this front. After Hilda Matheson left in 1931, frustrated
by Reith's conservatism, her replacement, Charles Siepmann,
continued the socially engaged tradition she had fostered. After
graduating from Oxford, Siepmann had gone into the prison
service with the hope of improving the education of boys locked
up in borstals. Visiting their homes had given him his first experience of slum life. 'It made an appalling impression on me', he
later explained. He had joined the BBC in 1927, he said, precisely
'to do something': he talked of radio as having 'revolutionary
powers'. 'I was concerned that broadcasting should become the
medium by which people became aware of the world they were
living in … that the BBC, being a new institution and a new
means of education should be on the cutting edge of contemporary problems and contemporary life.'[8]

Siepmann first worked in the Adult Education department,
as Richard Lambert's deputy. There, under Matheson's guidance, the two men set up hundreds of local 'wireless discussion
groups', in which listeners would meet in church halls, libraries
and working-men's clubs to talk about the programmes they had
just heard. The aim was to create an informal and friendly environment in which the 'plain man' might follow up the advice of
experts and 'decide and debate … all matters of policy'. Within
three years, an elaborate network of regional organisers had
been formed and some 70,000 pamphlets were being printed for
each of the discussion groups' three annual 'terms' of study.[9]

By the time Lambert had moved on to the *Listener* and

Siepmann had taken over from Matheson, the BBC could boast an impressive stream of programmes for the discussion groups to chew over. The hottest topic by far was unemployment, which had risen to alarming levels. In 1931, nearly a quarter of British adult male workers and a fifth of adult women were recorded as being out of work. In January that year the National Programme broadcast a series of high-profile talks on the 'problem of unemployment'. Guest speakers included John Maynard Keynes, Seebohm Rowntree, and Stanley Baldwin, now Leader of the Opposition. Two months later, the director of the London School of Economics, William Beveridge, presented a six-part evening lecture series on the 'disease' of unemployment. There was another talk on the subject the following year from the philosopher Sandie Lindsay, then the Master of Balliol in Oxford, which coincided with the latest and biggest wave of Hunger Marchers treading their weary way to London from all corners of the country in protest at yet another round of benefit cuts. Beveridge used the series very effectively to appeal to the nation's conscience by challenging the myth, doggedly propagated by many politicians and newspapers, that the poor caused their own poverty through bad judgement or idleness. But the challenge facing Talks was to find a less academic, more inclusive approach to the problem. For his 1934 series on *Industrial Britain*, the professor of industrial relations at Cambridge, John Hilton, was asked by producers to undertake a preparatory tour of roughly one hundred factories, mills and mines to get a feel for the views of people on the shop floor. In Lincoln, Sheffield, Derby, Nottingham, Leeds, Newcastle, Glasgow, Dagenham and Oxford, he talked with workers about their jobs, their methods, their troubles, their plans, their hopes.[10] Another series the same year, the twelve-part *Time to Spare*, went further still. Its first episode opened with a quotation from Priestley's recently published *English Journey* and advised listeners on how they might offer friendship and help to the unemployed. Subsequent weeks put the testimonies of the unemployed themselves centre stage. Their words were carefully transcribed and polished by BBC staff, but the very act of giving the microphone to working-class people so that they could give their own account of their experience was a significant innovation.

The sense of steady progress was halted in its tracks in 1935, after a major reshuffle at Broadcasting House in which Siepmann was replaced as head of Talks by the much more conservative figure of Richard Maconachie, a man who had just completed six years as British Minister in Kabul, where he had been responsible for a series of 'Kiplingesque' deeds on the Indian frontier. Under Maconachie, the department's collective will to deal with contentious issues rapidly withered and died. When a programme on the Means Test was planned in 1936, Maconachie not only referred the idea to Reith and the Governors, but allowed the Ministry of Labour to see the script and point out any observations it might care to make before the final version was broadcast. Another proposal, for an ambitious 'social survey' of Britain, was scotched completely after its producer was warned that the department did not 'want to get into the difficulties such as a couple of years ago when we were doing a series dealing with the actual conditions of the unemployed'.[11]

By now, it was all too easy for voices on the left to describe the BBC as a place remote from reality, 'knowing nothing of the masses, and caring less'. Yet the boundary-pushing series of the previous few years had shown that there were at least some programme makers who cared a great deal. As one historian has pointed out, Whitehall itself had 'made no serious attempt to investigate the social consequences of unemployment'. It was left to a variety of voluntary groups and enterprising organisations – from Penguin Books and the Left Book Club through to *Picture Post* and Mass Observation – to report on the social crises of the age and probe the failings of national policy. The BBC's Talks department had been an unofficial part of this movement, too. Yet, as its output became steadily more anaemic in character from the mid-1930s onwards, the charges of remoteness and ignorance of working-class life were progressively harder to deny. Charles Siepmann had begun his career at the BBC believing that broadcasting would be *the* means by which people were 'exposed to the realities' of the world in which they lived – that it would be 'the great medium of social consciousness'. By 1935 he looked around Broadcasting House and concluded that throughout the whole domain of talks, news, and education programmes, it was the forces of reaction that were now firmly in the ascendant.[12]

Seed time in the North

Fortunately, the BBC was an organisation with tentacles that stretched well beyond its London headquarters. And it was possible, despite Reith's policy of unified control or the enervating influence of figures such as Maconachie, for small, tightly knit groups of programme makers in places such as Edinburgh, Cardiff, Birmingham and Bristol, to strike a different tone. This independent spirit was at its fiercest, however, in the North Region based at Manchester. It was here during the 1930s that a vision of broadcasting's possibilities, even more radical than Matheson's or Siepmann's or Lambert's, took root and flourished. While London retreated, Manchester produced some of the most inventive and exciting radio the BBC had ever made.

The catalyst for this success was Archie Harding, a talented feature producer who was appointed North Region's Director of Programmes in 1933. Harding had been working contentedly in London, steadily building a reputation, until his production of *New Year Over Europe*, broadcast on the last day of 1932, attracted unwelcome controversy. The programme had offered a spectacular sound panorama of a dozen capital cities, but in a mood at odds with the festive occasion it had also hinted darkly at a continent sliding towards war. After complaints from the Polish ambassador about the programme's depiction of Warsaw, Reith had summoned Harding to his office. 'You're a very dangerous man, Harding', he announced. 'I think you'd be better up in the North, where you can't do so much damage.' It was said that on his arrival in Manchester, Harding – large, jaunty, with a penchant for well-tailored clothes – was 'so distinctively Oxford, that he had only to open his mouth and Deansgate turned round in astonishment'. Yet this middle-class 'champion of the proletariat' quickly found himself utterly at home.[13]

Manchester, Harding decided, was Britain's Leningrad. The city and its people were everything that his reading of Friedrich Engels had led him to expect. Like many of the 'Cotton Towns' that encircled it, here was a place with large pockets of industrial poverty, languishing in the backwash of the Depression as though it were 'the waning capital of a grimly autonomous Northern republic'. Yet it had a mercantile class with money to spend and a vigorous culture that included the Palace theatre, Hallé concerts at the Free Trade Hall, Thomas Beecham's Operatic Society and its own national newspaper in the form of the *Manchester Guardian*. As the centre of the BBC's North Region, Manchester was in a league of its own. Its headquarters in Piccadilly served two million licence-fee payers – an audience twice that of the BBC's Midland Region, and four times greater than Scotland's. Administratively, its domain stretched from the Scottish borders in the north to the Potteries and Lincolnshire in the south, encompassing a remarkable range of local cultures, dialects and habits. The fifteen or so programme makers who worked there had ready access to high-class repertory drama in Manchester and Yorkshire, countless colliery brass bands, variety stars from the seaside resorts of Blackpool and Scarborough, lecturers working at modern universities in Sheffield, Liverpool and Leeds; and they had, for inspiration and subject matter, the Lakes, the Yorkshire Dales and the Peak District, alongside some of the largest factories and mines in the country. There was little real unity to any of this, but the one characteristic in common, according to the local broadcasters, was that the typical northerner was virile, blunt, outspoken and kindhearted.[14] For a political radical such as Archie Harding it all added up to the perfect location for testing his most profound belief: that if it could somehow be made available to *everyone* the microphone would be an invention no less revolutionary than the printing press.

His first priority was to gather up a few kindred spirits. Among his first recruits was Geoffrey Bridson, a twenty-three-year-old writer who was, as Ezra Pound inimitably put it, busy 'raging in the back-streets' of Manchester. Bridson was deeply suspicious at first. 'I mentally bracketed the BBC with Parliament, the Monarchy, the Church and the Holy Ghost', he confessed. The BBC was no less suspicious of Bridson. Word came back from London that there was some administrative reluctance to employ him because he was thought to be 'rather politically-minded'. But finally it was agreed that Bridson's 'extreme value' as a feature writer outweighed what London officials referred to as the 'subsidiary' question of his politics. In June 1935, he became a Feature Programme Assistant. 'I had joined the Club', he announced: 'the BBC now had its Bolshevik.' 'It seemed to me', Bridson explained, 'that since its inception, broadcasting by the BBC had been the exclusive concern of "us", and listening the lucky privilege of "them".'[15] Over the following four years he would work with Harding's unbending support, to try to change this state of affairs by bringing to the airwaves vivid and sympathetic slices of northern life in an extraordinary series of features and documentaries.

Among the most celebrated was Bridson's quartet of features on the major industries of the North, *Steel*, *Cotton People*, *Wool* and *Coal*, which spliced together music, verse, and location recording to create epic evocations of working life. Their style evolved in subtle but important ways. *Steel* had conjured very poetically the heroic quality of mass production, but somehow neglected to give the actual labourers a voice. In contrast, *Coal* would be advertised as the 'story of a way of life' in which 'the men and women of a Durham mining town will speak for their work and themselves'. Bridson spent a month down the mines and staying in miners' homes, collecting recordings to provide background atmosphere. The young actor and theatre activist, Joan Littlewood – another of Archie

Geoffrey Bridson and Joan Littlewood joining workers and pit
ponies down a Durham mine as research for their epic 1938
feature, *Coal*. Littlewood, proud of her working-class origins,
mocked the BBC for its pomposities but proved to be a frequent
and supportive collaborator with its North Region producers.

Harding's inspired recruits to North Region – would accompany him. Her role was to chat to the miners and their families while Bridson made detailed notes of their conversations. But rather than convert these notes into fully fledged scripts, the usual BBC practice, he and Littlewood would simply rehearse the miners and their families in their own homes, getting them used to the presence of the microphone, and then invite them to speak spontaneously during the live transmission itself. At 7.30 p.m. on Thursday 17 November 1938, the miners and their wives were duly assembled in the BBC's Newcastle studio to play their parts, with Joan Littlewood acting as presenter and interviewer, and a colliery band playing occasional music in the background. For a full hour, the studio was linked to London, allowing *Coal* to be broadcast to several million listeners on the National Programme.[16]

This was a daring break from the BBC tradition of stilted reading aloud from the page, yet it carried obvious risks. When Bridson asked the miners to 'talk freely' about their work and life, they talked so freely that a colleague had to dash into the studio with a cardboard sign scrawled with the words, 'Do not say "Bloody" or "Bugger".' When the conversation then juddered to a halt, the cardboard sign was hastily removed and the miners told to carry on as before. Down in London, Broadcasting House expressed such displeasure at the breach of decorum that Bridson briefly feared for his job, but the programme provoked an immediate and sympathetic response from listeners. Money came pouring into the Newcastle office from around the country, and Bridson arranged for it to be distributed among the Durham miners without it coming to the attention of the Means Test inspectors. Bridson's star at the BBC was now rising fast. His 1938 annual staff appraisal noted the 'unique combination of imagination and earthy under-standing' he brought to his job. The following year it called him 'the most important feature writer in the Corporation'. Programmes such as *Coal*, Bridson wrote, 'gave millions of listeners a new realisation of the true dignity and importance of men and women like themselves'. Above all, he said, they 'proved that everyone had something to tell his fellow-men ... a point of view that deserved a hearing'.[17]

With Harding's encouragement, others at North Region were pushing hard in the same direction. There was also, for instance, Ewan MacColl, the son of an unemployed Glasgow steelworker who had travelled south in search of work and been spotted by a BBC producer as he busked outside a Manchester theatre. After being invited in for an audition, he had been given the role of 'Voice of the People' in Bridson's very first produc-tion back in 1934, a poetic celebration of the May Day tradition of social protest. Bridson loved how MacColl had 'snarled out in seething anger' the words of his script with a 'vigorously proletarian voice'.[18] Like Littlewood, he would become a regular contributor to the Region's programmes.

As would Olive Shapley. At the beginning of the 1930s, she was a 'blood-and-thunder' socialist finishing her undergraduate studies in Oxford. In between lectures and tutorials, she had found time to set up the October Club – effectively a front for the Communist Party. After graduating she trained to be a nursery teacher in the slum areas of Deptford. It was there, she said, that she 'learned the smell of dirt and old clothes and hard poverty'. While she was looking for a permanent teaching job, her mother spotted an advert for the post of *Children's Hour* organiser at the BBC in Manchester. 'But mother,' she blurted out in horror, 'I hate the wireless.' Shapley nevertheless applied and got the job.[19]

Harding greeted her upon her arrival at the Piccadilly studios in December 1934. He 'put out his hand', she recalled, and simply said, "Welcome, comrade".' It was a typically mischievous way of acknowledging the status the small group of producers and contributors he had gathered around him now collectively enjoyed: rebellious outliers within an organisation invariably identified with the status quo. This was certainly no communist cell in the literal sense. With Harding, Bridson reckoned, 'radio came first; politics were a slightly cynical runner-up'. What Shapley was after was authenticity. Every night, when she returned to her digs, her landlady would chat to her endlessly with a lively northern wit. 'I became almost obsessed with the idea of getting people like her on the air. Her jokes seemed to me so much better, so much funnier, than the jokes the scriptwriters wrote, and her point of view on almost anything was worth having.' In *Coal*, Bridson had pioneered the unscripted conversation, but the final result, Shapley thought, was still a contrived studio-bound version of 'reality'. She now hit on the idea of deploying a striking but underutilised bit of BBC kit: the 'Mobile Recording Unit'. An enormous seven-ton van, it contained inside two turntables, each with three discs. A four-minute-long recording could be cut into a single disc.

Olive Shapley talking to Mrs Emerson in the colliery village
of Craghead, County Durham, 1939. The producer lived with
the Emerson family for a week before travelling with her to
a mining village in France. 'I was fascinated by the nuts and
bolts of other people's jobs and lives', Shapley explained.

As one disc finished on the first turntable, recording could continue with another disc on the second. In this way, the van could
capture up to twenty-four minutes of sound in one trip. During
the making of Steel, Bridson had used it to record background
noise. Now, Shapley wanted to use it to record people speaking
in their own homes and workplaces or outside in the streets.[20]
In April 1938 she took the BBC van to a Yorkshire market town,
and, trailing a lengthy microphone cable, recorded her entirely
impromptu encounters with the shoppers and shopkeepers
she met. The finished programme, £.s.d. – A Study in Shopping,
was introduced on-air by a native Yorkshireman who worked at
North Region as an announcer and actor: Wilfred Pickles. The
introduction Shapley wrote for him set the informal, friendly,

unpretentious tone for which Pickles would soon become famous:

> Good evening everybody. Before we get going in this shop-
> ping programme there are one or two things I want to tell
> you about it. Now it's what I'd call a 'Homely' programme.
> No flourish of trumpets about it, you know, but the sort
> of programme you'll recognise yourself in maybe. The
> records you're going to hear were made at a little town
> called Sowerby Bridge. Sowerby Brigg I call it, coming
> from that part of the country myself.[21]

Over the next year Shapley worked with Pickles, Littlewood and MacColl to produce a remarkable series of documentaries – on homeless people, long-distance lorry drivers, canal workers, miners' wives. They offered listeners a kaleidoscope of voices and opinions and stories that joyfully cast aside the distinction between 'us' and 'them'. Producers, presenters, listeners, inter-viewees were treated not as mutually exclusive social groups, but as one and the same. When Pickles used the word 'we' it really did sound as if he meant it.

In July 1939, Shapley's work culminated in a feature that was more explicit than any of her previous work in its advocacy for the downtrodden. *The Classic Soil* borrowed its title from Frie-drich Engels, who had described Manchester as the classic soil in which capitalism flourished. Working with Littlewood, Shapley wanted 'to show that the lives of people had not changed' in any real way since Engels wrote *The Condition of the Working Class in England*. Their hour-long programme interspersed readings from Engels' book describing the dreadful living conditions of the nineteenth-century proletariat with recordings of working-class people sharing desperate accounts of getting by in 1930s Manchester and Salford. 'Nobody could stay politically neutral' after seeing the things she had seen, Shapley explained. Worried about the overall tone of the finished programme, she took the precaution of inviting the head of Features in London, Laurence

Gilliam, to hear it before transmission. He rang her up to denounce what he called 'a disgraceful programme'. Then after a brief pause, he added, 'but I like it – and I'm putting it out.'[22]

'Our battle for the radio feature had been won', Shapley said. She had never thought of her programmes as political in the strictest sense. They were much more 'about people and conditions – and they were honest'.[23] In a conservative decade, being honest about the conditions in which a great many British people lived turned out to be controversial. Yet to the BBC's credit, Shapley and North Region's other radical programme makers were offered institutional support – sometimes rather reluctantly in London, but always enthusiastically in Manchester. The remarkable series of social documentaries they made, under the beneficent guidance of Archie Harding, were a reminder that not every part of the BBC machine reflected establishment values. There was space for troublemakers behind the scenes, and for grittiness, even a little subversion, on air.

Rightward turn

Manchester's achievements could not hide how fearfully hard it was to nurture radical ideas at the BBC as the 1930s progressed. Since the election of a Conservative-dominated National Government in October 1931, the mood of a country in the grip of depression and mass unemployment had become increasingly sullen and reactionary. The governing class feared the danger of political extremism infecting British public opinion, and, despite the more obvious threat from Fascism, devoted most of its energy to tracking down alleged subversives on the left. Politicians were also emboldened in their belief that the BBC's business was now their business too. 'The conservative forces began to operate very early on', Charles Siepmann claimed – 'forces that I think were far more sinister in their effects on the BBC than anybody has ever realised.'[24]

Siepmann himself certainly felt scrutinised. Reith's attitude towards him had always been one of grudging acceptance.

'I don't trust you, and I don't *distrust* you', he had told Siepmann on his appointment as Director of Talks. Yet Reith was
now answerable to a Board of Governors, members of which
were all too familiar with rumours that the Conservative
Party viewed Siepmann as a Communist. Siepmann's confidential staff files correctly noted that there was 'no reason to
think that his political outlook inclined towards Communism'.
He regarded his own value to the BBC as being a necessary if
rather isolated 'counterweight' to its overwhelmingly conservative tendencies. But that did not prevent him from falling out
with the BBC's Director of Publicity, Gladstone Murray, who,
having maintained the intimate relationship he had built up
with Conservative politicians and newspaper barons during the
General Strike, lost no opportunity to mutter his dark suspicions about Siepmann over drinks at the Carlton Club. Neither
the Governors nor Reith wanted these doubts about the BBC's
neutrality to get out of hand. In 1934, Siepmann suddenly found
himself sidelined when John Coatman, a former police official
on India's North West Frontier – someone with a reputation as
a 'sound Conservative' but no experience of journalism – was
put in charge of 'News and Topicality'. This department was
officially part of Siepmann's Talks empire, but Coatman treated
it as his own domain. Disturbed by his new colleague's 'surly
… resentful … and insubordinate' behaviour, Siepmann took
the exceptional step of complaining directly to the Governors.
But the response that Gladstone Murray engineered behind the
scenes was to give News full independence under Coatman and
to move Siepmann to an invented job as Director of Regional
Programmes. He later left the Corporation for America.[25]

Another bizarre appointment was that of the mysterious
ex-army officer and friend of the royal family, Captain Alan
Dawnay, who in 1933 was parachuted in to take up the influential post of Controller of Programmes. This 'sweet … simple
soldier', Siepmann recalled, was 'utterly at sea' in Broadcasting
House. But there was more to Dawnay than met the eye. Half
his salary was paid for by the War Office and he met regularly

with senior officials at the security service MI5. The Control-ler's true role, it appeared, was to conduct detailed vetting of 'every officer in the BBC', with a particular focus on detecting any communist infiltration. Dawnay soon retired from the BBC on grounds of poor health, but his brief sojourn was yet one more example of how the centre of political gravity in the Cor-poration's upper echelons had shifted firmly to the right. As one of Siepmann's old producers, John Green, put it, by the end of the 1930s, 'Kipling's empire was fully in charge'.[26]

Direct political interference in the BBC's programmes was rare, though not entirely unknown. In 1932, the Talks department was preparing a series featuring people who had played signifi-cant if relatively obscure roles in the Great War. Among those they had tracked down was Captain Ernst Hashagen, a German submarine commander responsible for sinking a British ship and taking its captain prisoner. The plan was to bring Hashagen to the studio to meet his former captive so that the two men could 'talk about the old days' together. Word reached the cabinet. Within hours the Postmaster-General was on to Broadcasting House insisting the BBC should not go ahead because it would offend public opinion. The Governors were sufficiently intim-idated to insist that the talk be stopped – even though Reith himself had already approved the programme. It was precisely this subtle form of informal pressure – and the Governors' instinctive tendency to side with the politicians – that could be so intangible yet so pervasive in its effect on programme makers. Reith himself always maintained that although there were 'quite a number of disagreements' with the government at this time, 'practically all of them were settled amicably'. If so, the role as the BBC's Chairman of the Governors played by the emollient figure of John Whitley, the former Speaker of the House of Commons, proved crucial. Although it was in breach of the principle that Governors should remain at arm's-length from day-to-day decisions, Reith invited Whitley to meetings of the Control Board. He calculated, correctly, that this would educate the Chairman – and through him the other Governors

– about the complexities of the BBC's work. Reith referred to it as providing 'good cover'.[27] The arrangement was not quite watertight. It was, after all, Whitley who had yielded to political pressure over the German submarine commander's appearance. But over time the existence of a Board of Governors in tune with a Director-General promised to be a useful shock-absorber between Corporation and government whenever flashpoints arose.

*

In any case, these high-level political manoeuvrings over topical programmes were often something of a local problem in broadcasting terms. There was lots of other stuff on the wireless: dance music, classical music and opera, children's programmes; schools' programmes; adult education programmes; comedy, variety and music hall; religion; sport; and outside broadcasts. The BBC ran magazines such as the *Radio Times* – the biggest-selling weekly in Britain – and the *Listener*. It was starting to broadcast programmes around the world. Soon, it would even be dipping its toes in the new medium of television. Each of these areas raised thorny editorial issues of selection and balance and taste, but it was only really news and topical affairs that attracted the constant scrutiny of politicians. Day-to-day, broadcasting was something that routinely required decisions to be taken on the spur of the moment without referring them upwards through the editorial chain. The gut instinct behind these decisions naturally relied on some internalised notion of what was right for the BBC, but it was never quite uniform. News looked to official sources for its sense of what mattered; Schools broadcasting took their guidance from professional educationalists; religious broadcasting relied on the churches; and the drama and music producers moved in the world of commercial entertainment. A diversity of programming remained a key tenet of Reithianism: broadcasting offered a *mixed* diet so that 'the plain man' might become the rounded, balanced citizen that modern democracy required. That stated mission to 'educate, inform, and entertain' was not just an idle expression.

A striking feature of the BBC in the 1930s was that while many of its programmes offered a somewhat stiff and conservative view of the world, others had a far more intimate, friendly relationship with listeners. The North Region had repaired some of the damage done to the BBC's reputation during the General Strike by making a concerted effort to get the 'ordinary' listener on air. But when it came to securing not just the trust but the *devotion* of a national audience there was a limit to what could be achieved by news or talks or documentaries alone, no matter how progressive their style. Entertainment was even more crucial to the BBC's success. By 1939, there were some nine million licence-holders, representing nearly three-quarters of all households in Britain – almost thirty-four million people. As the BBC's audience had grown, so too had the proportion of listeners who were working class. Many producers recognised that programming had to reflect this change. The BBC could no longer preach *at* its working-class listeners; it needed to embrace and enjoy working-class life in all its variety – and on its own terms. In popular entertainment, of course, the BBC faced an even greater challenge than in news: everyone had to feel not just 'represented' but distracted, amused, *moved*. When pleasure was such an individual matter, and tastes in music and humour so fickle, achieving *that* was going to stretch the BBC's resourcefulness to the limits.

5

STARDUST

We want entertainment, not instruction. Cannot a
meeting of protest be called? I am afraid it would require
a very large space.
Letter from 'A Sufferer', London *Evening Standard*, 1928

'Too much education, too many lectures ... too many uninteresting items, such as Elizabethan music, new-fangled songs,
weird quartettes and quintettes, groaning Chamber Music quite
unappreciated by the public, readings from unknown poets ...
talks on subjects which are of no interest ...' So went the bru-
tally dismissive assessment of one of the BBC's own directors,
Witt Burnham, in 1925. Nine years later, the same charge was
being levelled by the Cambridge professor of political science,
Ernest Barker. The BBC, he complained, was broadcasting too
much 'modern music' and too many '*avant-garde* philosophies'.
'Programmes entertain us too loftily.'[1]

In the decade between these two damning indictments, the
letters pages of Britain's newspapers and magazines were regularly filled with similar gripes. One request overwhelmed all
the others: please could there just be more dance music, more
laughter, more glamour, more *fun*?

Yet the BBC's own figures showed that in 1925, 'groaning'
chamber music actually made up less than 1 per cent of its
output, while 'popular' or 'dance' music accounted for as much
as a third. Over the next decade the proportion of light entertainment crept steadily upwards.[2]

How, then, to explain the glaring gap between perception and reality? One explanation was that people were responding to a stubborn caricature sustained by the press of an institution deliberately dismissive of popular taste. The reputation was not entirely undeserved. A deeply held principle of the BBC, one which had been imbibed so deeply that it had been absorbed into the woodwork, had been set out by Reith back in 1924: that to exploit broadcasting 'for the purpose and pursuit of "entertainment" alone' 'would have been a prostitution of its powers and an insult to the character and intelligence of the people'. Unlike the commercial world of entertainment, the BBC could never be just a factory of dreams.[3] The problem was that while it constantly strove for some balance between edification and pleasure, most listeners wanted radio that supplied nothing *but* entertainment.

These were the decades in which Britons increasingly thought of work as the means to a life of leisure and enjoyment, not an end in itself. Going to see a film was hugely popular. In the 1930s, a town the size of Bolton could sustain fourteen cinemas, each offering customers a few hours' entertainment for as little as tuppence a seat. Dancing was the other great national passion, and, like cinema-going, crossed the social spectrum. It was the era of the nightclub and of the dance craze – the jogtrot, the shimmy, the Black Bottom, the Charleston. 'Going to the Palais' meant a touch of affordable glamour, a chance to mingle across the sexes, and a whole evening of non-stop live music. By the end of the 1930s nearly seven out of every ten adults in Britain were regularly heading off to dances; some teenagers would go three or four times a week. As one young man explained, 'To escape from the murky darkness of the streets into the lighted dance halls was the highlight of my week.' 'When you leave school,' it was said, 'you learn to work, to smoke, to bet and to dance.'[4]

Faced with a public appetite like this, it was far from easy to choose the right *kind* of entertainment to broadcast. Taste was not just tricky to pin down, it was so terribly divisive: 'one man's meat is another's poison', as Reith himself acknowledged. Unable to offer a multitude of specialised channels, the BBC still conceived of listeners as members of a single community – the so-called 'great audience'. The Director-General's approach was to suggest that most of the BBC's programmes should seek to satisfy 'the greatest number' of listeners, while a minority of programmes catered for what he called 'individual peculiarities'. And he hoped that broadcasting might one day break down these 'water-tight compartments' of culture so that initial antipathy gave way to appreciation. If the listeners' liking for, say, melodious orchestral music were to be nudged towards something a little more sophisticated, then perhaps one day they might seek out the classical repertoire. It was a delicate process. 'The BBC must lead, not follow, its listeners,' Reith explained, 'but it must not lead at so great a distance as to shake off pursuit.'[5]

'We can't let you broadcast that!'

Even if the BBC was to meet the burgeoning public demand for entertainment at some mystical halfway point, there were practical obstacles to overcome. The biggest thorn in the BBC's side was Britain's commercial entertainment industry. Just as the press magnates had feared the potential of broadcasting to cause a loss of newspaper sales, so West End impresarios worried about a collapse in box office receipts if their most profitable shows were freely available to listeners in the comfort of their own homes. There had been a series of acrimonious disputes from the start. Theatre managers often banned BBC microphones from their stages or inserted gagging clauses into artists' contracts prohibiting them from performing on radio. In 1928, the BBC reached agreements with George Black of the General Theatre Corporation and Oswald Stoll of the Moss Empires chain, which made possible a series of live relays from hit shows. But Black, in particular, remained suspicious, and was prone to imposing intermittent and arbitrary bans.[6]

Performers, too, felt ambivalent about broadcasting.

Comedians, especially, found the experience of telling jokes in a noiseless, windowless studio without an audience horribly disorientating. They also fretted about a single nationwide broadcast using up material that could otherwise be recycled over many months on tour.

From the BBC's perspective, a major issue was creating something that worked *as* radio. Popular stage entertainment was not just visual; it was frequently ribald. Roger Eckersley, one of the BBC's most senior controllers, explained the dilemma: 'a jest in doubtful taste heard in the parlour, within the bosom of the family, has a different effect from the same joke heard by a lot of happy people in the atmosphere of the Music Hall.' The BBC was also aware that it served an extremely varied national audience. Producers, Hilda Matheson explained, needed to 'take into account grandmothers and schoolboys, navvies and invalid ladies, town and country, north and south, rich and poor, sophisticated and unsophisticated'. Since the BBC was never going to please *everyone*, it often tried instead not to offend *anyone*. Artists were warned against using phrases like 'Damn' or 'My God', and told not to make jokes about 'Scotsmen, Welshmen, clergymen, drink or medical matters'. The BBC's exaggerated sense of propriety was wittily captured in a 1932 song by Norman Long, 'We Can't Let You Broadcast That'. With little sense of irony, the BBC immediately banned it.[7]

All could have been well, perhaps, if the BBC had been left to feel its way forward in private. But aside from the steady flow of letters from listeners, the BBC also had to face the often acerbic judgements of the professional radio critics. Jonah Barrington at the *Daily Express*, Sydney Moseley at the *Daily Herald*, and Collie Knox at the *Daily Mail* were three of the most influential. As Fleet Street was opposed to the expansion of broadcasting, it was no coincidence that these critics tended to berate the BBC at the slightest opportunity. Complaints intensified with the launch in January 1934 of a glossy new magazine called *Radio Pictorial*. Threaded through the photo spreads, tittle-tattle, celebrity profiles and lifestyle features about radio personalities were attacks

on the Corporation for its commitment to 'uplift' and its failure
to give listeners exactly what they wanted. 'Is the BBC Wasting
Your Money?', one headline asked in an article revealing supposedly shocking details of the earnings of actors and dance bands.
'Is Britain's Radio Talent Being Wasted?' asked another.[8]

From August that year *Radio Pictorial* provided its readers
with a brand-new feature: the programme schedules of some
of the biggest European commercial radio stations. For years,
listeners across southern England had been able to eavesdrop on
any number of private operators based in places like Hilversum,
Paris, Toulouse, Lyons or Athlone. Now, two of the biggest
were ramping up their efforts: Radio Normandie, which had
been broadcasting from the small French town of Fécamp since
the mid-1920s, and Radio Luxembourg, which had launched a
regular English-language service towards the end of 1933. Both
had recently attracted the financial backing of Leonard Plugge,
a businessman and future Conservative MP who had created
the 'International Broadcasting Company' to buy airtime and,
he hoped, undermine the BBC's monopoly. Increasingly, these
commercial stations also received support from *Radio Pictorial*
itself. 'One Sunday afternoon when both the National and the
Regional were very boring,' a typical piece began, 'I accidentally
turned the set knob to the long-wave position':

> Idly, I turned the tuning knob and heard a friendly voice
> speaking in English and announcing a popular light music
> programme. By the tone of the transmissions, I could tell
> that it was not any BBC station to which I had previously
> listened. But the music was good, so I did listen. It turned
> out to be an advertiser's sponsored programme from
> Luxembourg.[9]

The article would have struck a nerve with vast swathes of
the British public, who had long regarded the BBC's Sunday
schedule as dreary beyond measure. Reith believed that Sundays
needed to be marked as different from the rest of the week in

order for them to be restorative – 'quiet islands on the tossing sea of life', as he put it. For years, nothing was broadcast at all on Sunday mornings, save for a brief time signal and weather forecast or the occasional live relay from a church service. Even when programmes got going in the afternoon it was all a bit heavy. On Sunday 19 January 1930, for instance, the BBC's 2LO and 5XX transmitters offered their listeners a live relay of Bach's Church Cantata No. 13 from the Guildhall School of Music in London, a Bible reading, a dramatisation of Laurence Housman's 'The Temptation of Juniper', a military band concert featuring music from Strauss, Gluck, Beethoven and Liszt, a religious service in Welsh from a Swansea tabernacle, another service from Westminster Congregational Church, an appeal for *The Week's Good Cause*, the news, and – as the centrepiece of the evening schedule – a Light Symphony Concert of music from Mozart and Dvořák. The evening closed with an *Epilogue*, which on this occasion posed the question, 'Lord, what is Man?'[10]

Sundays on Radio Normandie and Radio Luxembourg could not have been more different. With generous sponsorship from companies like Ponds beauty products or Colgate toothpaste, they were able to broadcast dance music, popular songs and variety non-stop from breakfast to midnight. Regular series included a 'Dr Fu Manchu' radio drama, all-star variety in the *Rinso Music Hall* programme, George Formby in a show presented by the makers of FEEN-A-MINT, and the hit tunes of *The Kraft Show* with Billy Cotton. As the *Advertiser's Weekly* boasted, with only slight exaggeration, 'A Sunday's sponsored broadcasting from Luxembourg, Normandie and Lyons often contains more stars than the BBC broadcast in a whole week'.[11]

The impact on the Corporation's ratings was as dramatic as it was inevitable. On weekdays, most of the audience stayed loyal. But every Sunday two-thirds switched to the commercial stations; by mid-afternoon, Radio Luxembourg alone had some four million Britons tuning in, many of them young, female and working-class. It was clear that some kind of decisive response was in order.

The birth of Variety

The Corporation's approach to popular entertainment had already been evolving, albeit at a glacially slow pace. Since 1929, the 'Productions Department', responsible for light entertainment, had been led by Val Gielgud. Though his passion was drama, Gielgud at least recognised that music hall and variety, with their mix of comedy, music and speciality acts, had a huge appeal. In 1930, he created separate 'Revue' and 'Vaudeville' sections, which went on to make two of the BBC's most popular series of the decade: *Music Hall* – described in the *Radio Times* as 'a Vaudeville programme of the more robust type' – and *Kentucky Minstrels*, a 'Real Old Time' blackface revue.[12] The most significant change, however, came in 1933 with the creation of a single Variety department quite separate from Drama. This became the responsibility of Eric Maschwitz, a breezy thirty-three-year-old who had all the qualities necessary to energise the BBC's popular entertainment output for the rest of the decade.

Maschwitz had joined the BBC in 1926, working on outside broadcasts and then as editor of the *Radio Times*, but his first love had always been show business. After Cambridge and the Footlights, he had worked as a stage manager, spending his spare time watching the likes of 'Les Camellia Girls', a 'cockney "sister act"' at the Olympia music hall. He also wrote original musical plays of his own. His first production, a 'Romantic Operetta' called *Good Night Vienna*, was broadcast by the BBC in January 1932. It contained 'every sugary cliché imaginable', Maschwitz admitted, but the film rights were snapped up the very next day.[13] In 1936, he would go on to enjoy his biggest hit with *These Foolish Things*, which included the song 'A Nightingale Sang in Berkeley Square'.

His first act at Variety was to move a large slice of the department out of Broadcasting House completely. He persuaded the BBC to let him have St George's Hall, a large theatre just around the corner that had been the home since the 1860s of numerous vaudeville acts. It provided the perfect location for staging big live audience shows, but also 'a pleasant sense of escape from the growing formality' of headquarters. Once a week, he would have to scurry back to Broadcasting House for a meeting of the almighty Programme Board. The atmosphere, he recalled, was much like 'the hushed solemnity of a Cabinet conference'. He would then return to St George's Hall for a meeting with his own staff, where he would gather up 'the most assorted and co-operative collection of characters ever assembled' and face a stream of 'questions, answers, criticisms, suggestions, complaints'. Informality was the order of the day. 'I encouraged my band of incorrigible bohemians to call me by my first name and to break into my office at any hour of the day or night ... I also drank with them ... We were friends.'[14]

The energy released by Maschwitz – and the extra money thrown his way – helped the BBC turn a corner. Soon, his staff were delivering 'sixteen hours a week chock full of vitality'. In January 1933 there had been only twenty-eight variety programmes a month on air. By January 1935, that number had more than doubled to sixty-one. A year later, it was eighty-seven. Maschwitz's producers worked sixteen-hour days, which often took them to the verge of breakdown. One member of staff, who supplied entertainment shows from Manchester, talked of being 'so worn out' after a day's work that the only way to keep going was by regularly taking Benzedrine.[15]

Maschwitz had to tread carefully around certain BBC sensibilities. Radical change to the Sunday policy, for instance, continued to be blocked not just by Reith himself but by the Religious Broadcasting department and the influential Central Religious Advisory Committee. Despite some relaxation from 1930, the overall flavour remained 'as dankly entertaining as a damp Sabbath in a Lowland village'. The best Maschwitz could do was to tinker around the edges. In March 1934, he got permission to include extracts from musical comedies and light operas, and, from October 1936, music from the BBC Theatre Organ in St George's Hall. But only in 1938, when Maschwitz had already left and Reith himself was about to leave, did the BBC finally extend Sunday's broadcasting hours to the mid-morning. [16]

Variety's efforts to lighten the rest of the week's schedule were more successful, thanks largely to a noticeable thaw in the theatre industry's traditionally frosty attitude. Maschwitz's strategy 'was to gather theatre and music-hall people into the broadcasting fold'. His own successes on the stage demonstrated very publicly that 'not all broadcasters lived in a private world of their own'. His producers were encouraged to spend more time out and about, to offer better fees, to dangle the promise of big spreads in the *Radio Times*. Variety could also point out, of course, that radio appearances amounted to free publicity on a massive scale. In 1938, George Black offered his reasons for finally granting access to his considerable theatre empire. 'Formerly we had to deal at Broadcasting House with what I might term the cuff and collar brigade', he explained. 'Now there is a set of very nice fellows there, who do understand something of the business.' Henceforth, from Monday through to Saturday, the BBC's schedules were sprinkled with the likes of Eddie Cantor at St George's Hall, and French and Russian singers at the Ritz. Listeners could enjoy George Burns, Gracie Allen or The Boswell Sisters, even a live relay from the London Palladium or the Victoria Palace Theatre. In Manchester, North Region launched a Monday-night cabaret show, *After Dinner*, which the *Radio Times* described as an 'entertainment to accompany the nuts and wine, good-night coffee, or during the last laze with a cigarette in the hour before turning-in'.[17]

By this stage, the BBC was doing more to nurture artists of its own, in the hope of creating entertainment that might also prove more 'radiogenic'. The establishment of a Radio Repertory Company back in 1923 had been one means of avoiding an overreliance on the commercial sector. But a wider stable of performers was also emerging: individuals who had cut their teeth on the wireless and whose acts were now firmly associated in the public mind with the BBC. Elsie and Doris Waters, who had first taken to the airwaves in March 1927, and whose most famous creation was the double act 'Gert and Daisy', were in this category. So too was Mabel Constanduros, a remarkably adaptable writer and performer who the critics declared a 'born broadcaster'. As a member of the Rep, Constanduros had discovered that 'Behind the blessed shelter of the microphone you can be whatever character you choose ... anything from a child of six to an old woman of eighty'. Disappointed by the poor quality of many of the scripts on offer, she began to write and perform her own comic monologues. She then invented a whole cockney family: *The Buggins*. There was Mrs Buggins – a 'good-natured, much tried housewife'; Gran'ma Buggins – 'an old tartar if ever there was one'; and the two Buggins children. But the cast of characters grew: neighbours occasionally appeared, as would an Aunt Maria who 'came from the North'.[18] Not only did this fantasy family allow Constanduros to act as many as seven parts at one go; it also allowed her to start writing whole sketches rather than just short monologues. *The Buggins* were a comic creation that made her one of the first national celebrities of radio. But, more significantly, in showing how a variety of scenarios could be created while providing a reassuring continuity in character and setting, they offered a pioneering example of what would later be called 'situation comedy'.

Maschwitz now made an equally imaginative intervention of his own. Searching for a new hit series to fill the most high-profile slot of the whole week – Saturday evening – he created a one-stop 'shop window', which brought to the microphone a medley of people, famous or unknown, who either lived in London or were passing through, and packaged them up in something lively, inclusive and glamorous. The result was *In Town Tonight*, first broadcast at 7.30 p.m. on Saturday 18 November 1933. The *Radio Times* marked its debut with a sumptuous illustration showing the West End skyline dotted with twinkling stars and warm pools of street lighting, the programme's title arching cheerily across the dark horizon in large, glowing letters. The programme itself worked hard to exude 'an air of informality and friendliness'. Listeners were met with a brisk opening montage of sound: the music of Eric Coates's *Knightsbridge March*; the roar of London's traffic; a flower-girl murmuring

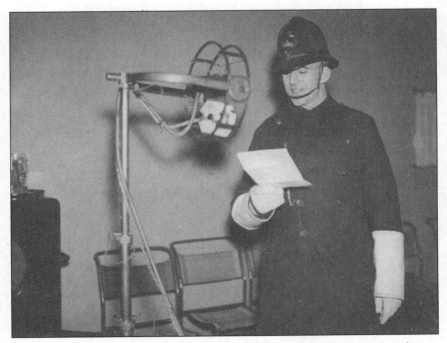

A policeman does a turn before the microphone for *In Town Tonight*,
1934. Like most guests, he would be met afterwards by dozens of
autograph-hunters gathered outside Broadcasting House in the hope
of catching a famous actor or musician as they left the show.

'sweet violets'; and the announcer Freddie Grisewood uttering
a 'stentorian shout' of 'stop!' After several more editions, one
of the BBC's young night pages, John Daligan, was brought in
to add a fresh layer of drama to this already distinctive signature tune by playing the role of a newspaper seller. The list of
guests who appeared in the first series was revealingly eclectic.
It included: the Hollywood star, Cary Grant; Mrs Nelson, the
chimney sweep; Charles Harrison, the 'Human Ostrich' who
ate anything from lit cigarettes to broken glass; the dance-band
leader, Cab Calloway; Betty Baxter, who ran a late-night coffee-
stall on the Thames Embankment; an American tenor famous
for singing in the bath (performing live in one of Broadcasting
House's own bathrooms); a rat-catcher from Madame Tussauds;

and five visiting yodellers from Austria. There were also outside broadcasts from, among other places, the lion house at London Zoo and the West India Docks.[19]

As one of its early producers explained, the watchword for *In Town Tonight* was: 'Not too many film stars, nor too many strange occupations, but contrast!' Each guest would have about fifteen minutes of rehearsal time before they appeared on air, during which time they would practise delivering a script based on earlier conversations. The BBC still hesitated to allow complete spontaneity before the microphone. But for most guests the script was merely a prop to prevent them 'drying up'. Producers wanted a 'natural' performance – though ideally one that conformed to stereotype. When the producer Jack Cannell was looking for a late-night coffee-seller, he wanted someone whose voice was 'sufficiently Cockney'. For an 'old-time barmaid', he spent nine weeks slogging around London's pubs until he found a woman who was 'buxom and buoyant'.[20]

Contrived or not, the formula proved so successful that by the end of the decade, a staggering twenty million people were tuning in. *In Town Tonight* was slick, topical, chatty, genial, *talked about*. Its linking together of lots of short, disparate items made it the harbinger of a new and highly adaptable radio format: the so-called 'magazine' show. Such was its appeal that variations of it could soon be found across the schedule. In Manchester there was *Owt abaht Owt*, which first appeared on the Regional Programme in May 1934, and was described as a 'Broadcast Magazine, for the North, by the North, and about the North'. Three years later, National Programme listeners were introduced to *At the Black Dog*, a chat show that used the conceit of being set in a 'West End pub'. Its use of sound effects to conjure up the right setting owed much to both *In Town Tonight* and the pioneering work of Mabel Constanduros many years before. But it also pointed the way forward to a series that would become one of the creative pinnacles of radio entertainment. Launched in January 1938, *Band Waggon* flaunted an increasingly bizarre range of acoustic devices to weave a surrealist fantasy of two 'resident' comedians, played by Arthur Askey and Richard Murdoch, living in a chaotic flat at the top of Broadcasting House. It relied heavily on running aural gags, including the hilariously misplaced use of sound effects for thunderclaps, pigeon coos, and doors slamming. The *Listener*'s radio critic, Grace Wyndham Goldie, reckoned that *Band Waggon* – which she described perceptively as a portrait of 'living in a lunatic asylum of a very logical kind' – was 'the most imaginative' of any series put out by the BBC. After hearing it, she rang up Askey to tell him how the programme allowed listeners sitting by their fireside to 'participate in unreality'. 'But, of course', he replied. 'Radio's a magical medium … I can make millions of listeners think that I'm up among the stars sitting on a circular saw.'[21] The public themselves took a while to warm to *Band Waggon*. But the fact that its pleasures were cumulative rather than instantaneous was probably why it ended up being a popular as well as a critical success. What allowed listeners to be 'in' on all the jokes was the steadily deepening understanding of character and setting that they would gain from being loyal fans.

Band Waggon, even more than *In Town Tonight*, was just the kind of show the BBC had been waiting for in order to face down all the intense commercial competition from Luxembourg. With its skilfully woven blend of the new and the predictable, and its ability to appeal across classes, its greatest value was that it made a lot of people laugh time and time again. It also demonstrated how far BBC light entertainment had come since its early and somewhat second-hand relationship with the stage. Allowed the freedom, by and large, to run Variety in their own way, Eric Maschwitz and his band of producers had sprinkled on to the radio schedules some welcome stardust. The fact that the BBC was now at the very heart of the British entertainment industry was revealed in dramatic fashion at the beginning of 1938. At the Victoria Theatre in London, a show called *Me and My Girl* had been doing so badly that it was on the verge of closing. When the BBC relayed a

The Hollywood film star Cary Grant in 1938, making a guest
appearance in the BBC's hit series, *Band Waggon*, alongside its two
regular performers, Richard Murdoch (left) and Arthur Askey (right).

live broadcast of an excerpt, the theatre's box office was suddenly overwhelmed by demand for tickets. *Me and My Girl* ended up running for over 1,600 performances. Its hit song, 'The Lambeth Walk', was soon being requested in every dance hall up and down the country.[22]

Dancing the night away

The BBC had never really neglected popular music. In fact, for years, it had invested enormous resources and allocated a great deal of airtime to it. When the 2LO Dance Band was formed in March 1923, it was only the first in a long line of similar outfits block-booked to fill large stretches of the afternoon and evening schedules: listeners would be able to tune in most days and hear live concerts from the likes of the Savoy Orpheans and the Savoy Havana Band, or the BBC Dance Orchestra led by Jack Payne or

Henry Hall – musicians of decent quality, perfectly capable of
playing the public's latest favourite tunes.

Yet the BBC had always been keen to demonstrate that its
bands were a cut above the rest, even when playing the popular
stuff. As for the music itself, 'dance', though an ill-defined category, was regarded as essentially American, and this clearly
discomfited many at the Corporation who worried constantly
about 'hot' styles, including 'swing' and jazz, sneaking their
way across the Atlantic and on to the nation's airwaves. They
also fretted about American styles of presenting. A 1932 relay
from New York of a show called *Famous Stars of American Radio*
prompted the *Radio Times* to raise its editorial eyebrows at the
programme's air of 'confidential familiarity ... the almost undi-
luted sentimentality ... We ourselves felt slightly faint before
the hour was over'. Jazz itself was never 'banned' outright. It
was recognised that there was a small but devoted audience for
it, and Reith had said, had he not, that even 'individual peculiarities' had to be catered for. But few at the BBC, or indeed the
country at large, knew much about it. It was American in origin,
which by extension made it vulgar. And behind certain assumptions about its moral dangers lurked a barely disguised racial
prejudice. Official BBC policy deemed 'blackface' performances
of the *Kentucky Minstrels* perfectly acceptable, as were 'Negro
spirituals', but the 'tone and rhythm' of jazz was capable of
being dismissed as a 'step back to ... the jungle'. The BBC's strategy was to eliminate the music's most undesirable features by
creating a pared-down version, shorn of suggestibility or indeed
any individuality. As the band leader Jack Hylton explained to
Radio Times readers, without a hint of embarrassment, before
ever allowing his band to play them on-air he would 'orchestrate'
jazz tunes 'in a manner altogether different from the ordinary
commercial arrangement'. Jazz was also sanitised by treating it,
somewhat warily, as a connoisseur genre. The London editor of
Gramophone magazine, Christopher Stone, was commissioned
to devote the occasional programme to what was called 'hot
American dance music', though he confessed to being unable to

play it without a 'faint scoff' in his voice. There was a bit more enthusiasm on show from Charles Chilton, a young assistant in the Gramophone department, who, from 1937, was allowed to present a late-night series, *Swing Time*. There was support, too, for bands that could be presented as home-grown practitioners, such as 'Ken "Snake-Hips" Johnson and His West Indian Dance Orchestra', described by the *Radio Times* as an 'all-British combination consisting of West Indian Negroes'. The BBC even promoted Continental European dance music as an alternative to what the *Radio Times* called 'the jazz bacillus' from America. 'The Orchestra of the Café Collete', which began in July 1933, allowed listeners to enjoy some '*unjazzlike rhythms*' in the atmosphere of a Parisian cabaret, complete with background chatter in French, the popping of champagne corks, and the sound of a waiter calling supper orders down a lift shaft to the kitchen – an entirely imaginary soundscape conjured up by technicians and actors in a basement studio of Broadcasting House. The most popular programmes with the audience, though, tended to be those which were relayed directly from the United States and featured the top performers of the time – among them Count Basie, Gena Krupa, Benny Goodman, and Joe Marsala, and their respective bands.[23]

If there was one thing more farcical than the BBC's curmudgeonly relationship with jazz, it was its contorted response to 'crooning', the new singing style that favoured an intimate, almost whispered delivery and which was rapidly gaining popularity among male performers such as Rudy Vallee and Bing Crosby. It was damned twice over: for its American origins and its alleged effeminacy. The case for the prosecution had been laid out in a biting article published in the *Radio Times* in February 1933. The singer of today, it thundered, 'knows neither restraint nor reticence ... Once we are rid of the crooner ... popular songs will be vital and robust again ... only then will we have songs fit for men'. From his lofty position as the BBC's Controller of Programmes, Cecil Graves pronounced crooning to be a 'particularly odious form of singing' – and suggested that it should be obliterated from the radio schedule entirely. Fortunately, the difficulty of agreeing a watertight definition of the style, and the impossibility of monitoring every performance, meant that such edicts were largely unenforceable. Crooning, like jazz, continued to be broadcast successfully *in spite of* disapproval from the top – proof that, even in Reith's day, rigid statements of policy rarely represented the last word. Managers were sometimes willing to turn a deaf ear, while lower down the hierarchy producers who showed sufficient enthusiasm and tenacity could find a way round the system.[24]

The BBC's most influential musical intervention was to push for a general 'lightening' and 'sweetening' of dance music across the board, so that by the end of the decade musical comedy, operetta, ballads, film scores, organ recitals, solos, palm-court trios, 'seaside' music, military bands, brass bands, and small orchestras playing classical highlights had all been homogenised into a capacious category of 'light' music that became the centre of gravity in the BBC's output. Fred Hartley, the leader of one of the most popular light orchestral quintets of the era, articulated the overall philosophy: 'neither highbrow, nor lowbrow but broadbrow, as one must be in catering for the great wireless audience'. And it was Henry Hall's BBC Dance Orchestra that carried the flag for this broadbrow art on to the nation's airwaves. Between March 1932, when Hall took over from Jack Hylton, and the end of 1939, the Dance Orchestra appeared over 400 times on the National Programme and at least 300 times on the Regional Programme. Hall's efficient and inoffensive orchestrations appalled the musical aficionados of the *Melody Maker* who complained they 'had no personality'. Yet many listeners welcomed music of a consistent tempo and quality which they could dance to. And in halls across the country, what young dancing couples now requested the house bands to play more than anything else was the music they had heard on the wireless.[25]

The BBC was not just the nation's biggest supplier of light entertainment; it was starting to be thought of by the public as an entertainer, first and foremost. The Variety department deserved huge credit for this. It had distinguished itself by being that rare thing in the BBC of the 1930s: a collection of enthusiasts who took popular culture and working-class tastes seriously. There was still plenty of harrumphing from above whenever something displeasing came up. But in the end, programmes usually went ahead with only minor changes. As Eric Maschwitz acknowledged, there were, in reality, few hard and fast rules 'to tell us what might or might not be permitted'.[26]

As for Reith's ideal listener – the man or woman lapping up everything on the wireless from Bing Crosby to Bach – this, alas, turned out to be largely a figment of the BBC mind. But the underpinning notion of a 'common culture' lived on in the Variety department's determination to broadcast shows that appealed across age, sex and class. *In Town Tonight* and *Band Waggon* had been outstanding examples. But for Eric Maschwitz it had been music, above all else, that had reached the widest range of listeners; he believed it was therefore music, above all else, that should always be the 'mainstay' of the BBC's output. 'Popular music cannot be lightly dismissed', he explained. 'To the rhythm of it people work and march and fall in love.'[27]

Magic rays of light

For much of the 1930s, millions of listeners continued to regard radio as the most convenient – and the most *modern* – means of keeping informed or being entertained. No one doubted that broadcasting meant radio – or that radio had a long and glorious future. Yet since the mid-1920s a growing number of experimenters and entrepreneurs had been taking the first faltering steps towards making 'television' a workable technology. And despite an initial reluctance to get involved, it was the BBC's patronage of this new medium which ensured that it developed into a full-blown service of public entertainment in less than a decade.

The underlying concept of transmitting moving images through the air had been explored by innumerable scientists around the world since the late nineteenth century. But it was in April 1924, in a tiny attic workshop in the seaside town of Hastings, that the first real breakthrough was achieved. Using an old tea chest, an empty biscuit box, several hatboxes, countless darning needles, and a pile of scrap timber – all lashed together with sealing wax and string, and smothered in a dense tangle of wires – a young Scottish engineer, John Logie Baird, had managed to shine a beam of light through a rapidly spinning disc punched with holes, and thereby display the faint, wobbly silhouette of a Maltese Cross on a screen just a few feet away.[28]

Over the next few years, with the financial backing of investors who sensed an opportunity to make money, Baird embarked on a series of experiments in his new London workshops, each slowly improving both picture quality and the distances over which his images might travel. In August 1926, the first domestic 'Televisor' set went on sale – at the hefty price of 30 guineas. And, although there were still no actual programmes to watch, it seemed as if a whole new consumer market was about to open up.[29]

The BBC was keeping a watchful but highly dubious eye on these proceedings. Reith acknowledged that television was 'bound to come' and he was under a lot of pressure from the GPO to show support for Baird's enterprise; the issue was about timing and resources. One of Reith's senior engineers, Harold Bishop, had seen Baird's experiments. He decided that the young Scotsman was getting 'interesting results' but, alas, 'not very much of real value'. By which Bishop meant 'value as a *service* to the British public'. Like many others at the BBC, he worried that Baird's technology was still too primitive to win public acceptance. The precipitous launch of a system that fell short of expectations risked killing off the new technology at birth. In July 1928, the BBC put out a public statement, explaining that only when television technology had reached the stage 'where some form of service which will benefit listeners may be guaranteed' would it be 'prepared, subject to the co-operation of the Postmaster-General, to co-operate'.[30]

Despite this, the BBC offered Baird the occasional use of its transmitter on the roof of Selfridges department store in Oxford Street for some experimental broadcasts. The first of these took place on the morning of 30 September 1929, before 2LO had really got going for the day. In Baird's small Long Acre 'studio', three performers sat down on a typist's chair, one after the other, each looking at a hole in the wall opposite to meet the gaze of the 'spotlight' scanning beam as it rushed across their face, left to right, top to bottom, twelve and a half times a second. The resulting images of their head and shoulders then hurtled along telephone wires to Savoy Hill, before being re-routed to the Selfridges transmitter, and from there broadcast wirelessly across a mile or so of London sky back to Long Acre, where a gaggle of invited guests huddled around a screen roughly one-and-a-half-inches tall and one inch wide. Because only one wavelength was available – the medium-wave slot used for the BBC's radio programmes – pictures could not yet be synchronised with sound: each performer was seen first and only heard later.[31]

It was a shaky start. From March 1930 additional transmitters were made available, which allowed the BBC to synchronise sound and image. Serious thought was also given to making the broadcasts more interesting. The Baird company hired Harold Bradley, who probably deserves the title of the world's first television 'director', to stage puppet shows, piano recitals, and even cartoons being drawn live.[32] But it was one of the BBC's own producers, Lance Sieveking – who had done so much to test the creative limits of radio – who now stepped forward with the most ambitious idea so far for demonstrating television's artistic potential. Prompted by his boss, Val Gielgud, he unveiled a plan to stage the world's first television play.

Sieveking had been fantasising about an opportunity like this for years. Back in 1913, when he was seventeen, he had visited the Scala cinema in London to witness the 'Kinoplastikon', a novelty act creating 'singing, talking, moving picture figures in solid stereoscopic relief' – an adaptation, in fact, of the

Rehearsals in Baird's studio for what is claimed to be the first television
play in the world: Lance Sieveking's 1930 production of *The Man
with the Flower in His Mouth*. Sieveking (standing, back left) described
the broadcast as plunging 'lightheartedly into unknown waters'.

Victorian 'Pepper's Ghost Trick', which used smoke and mirrors
to project images into the air. Having experienced 'the terrific
thrill of being present when a miracle is performed', Sieveking
had wanted ever since 'to play' with a 'huge mad toy' like the
Kinoplastikon. Baird's extraordinary new device seemed to fit
the bill. And so, in the summer of 1930, Sieveking did what he
had always done: 'I seized this new opportunity with both hands
– and with both feet.'[33]

His play was broadcast at 3.30 p.m. on Monday 14 July. Luigi
Pirandello's bleak avant-garde drama about cancer, *The Man
with the Flower in His Mouth*, was hardly a crowd-pleasing choice,
but it had the advantage of needing only one setting – a late-
night café somewhere in Italy – two speaking parts, some music
and a voice-over. Even so, Sieveking had to work out some of
the basic 'grammar' of television. He discovered that images

generated by Baird's equipment would blink and stutter if an actor moved too quickly in front of the camera. So he devised a way of making a 'cut' or 'fade' between scenes by placing a large chequered board in front of the camera at the appropriate moment. To make the actors' faces stand out clearly, he discovered that thick yellow greasepaint, with strokes of dark blue or green around the eyes, nose and lips, worked best. The hardest challenge was squeezing two actors into the same tightly framed shot. His solution was to position them face to face so closely that their noses almost touched. For scenery, he got his friend, the painter Richard Nevinson, to do some black-and-white line drawings on cardboard.[34]

On the actual day of the broadcast, a marquee was erected on the roof of Baird's Long Acre headquarters. Inside this makeshift auditorium some forty or so invited guests watched the performance taking place four floors below on a giant screen made out of two thousand tiny electric bulbs. The broadcast lasted twenty-seven minutes. As Sieveking himself popped up in the closing scene, the screen, which had become red-hot, began to melt. The next day the reporter from the *Times* described an experience that sounded more like a Victorian magic lantern display than the birth of a modern new medium. Staring at the ghostly, juddering image, he said he had felt as though he were 'prying through a keyhole at some swaying, dazzling exhibition of the first film ever made'. The reporter from the *Observer* was a little more prescient. 'Like the squeakings of the first phonograph and the flickerings of the first moving-pictures,' he wrote, 'the beginnings of Television must not be judged by actual performance; they must rather be regarded as signs and portents of marvels yet to come.' The only truly damning response to the broadcast came in a letter to Sieveking from his old wartime friend, Hugh Kingsmill Lunn. 'How sinister it all looks', Lunn told him. 'Don't let the science go too far, I beg you ... People will soon be carrying some bloody little gadget which will enable them to pick out any absent friend and see exactly what he or she is doing. Stop it, while there's yet time, *please*.'[35]

*

Television was not yet an unstoppable force, but it was certainly gathering momentum. In the two years following Sieveking's extravaganza, the BBC started to take a more decisive lead in shaping its future. It arranged for Baird Television to broadcast live pictures from its studios near Waterloo Bridge and to carry footage of radio programmes featuring Jack Payne's band. It also transmitted outside broadcasts from the Epsom Derby for two years running, despite viewers having complained that the horses and riders looked 'like out-of-focus camels'. Then, only months after moving into Broadcasting House, the Corporation set aside a basement studio, 'Studio BB', which had been lavishly designed for dance music performances. Here, from Monday 22 August 1932, it began to transmit hour-long television broadcasts up to four times a week.[36]

A small in-house team was gathered together: the BBC's first-ever dedicated television engineer, Douglas Birkinshaw; two engineers who had joined from Baird's London laboratory, Tony Bridgewater and Desmond Campbell; a former member of the Gramophone department, Eustace Robb, in the role of producer; and George Grossmith, who acted as creative adviser. Together they set out to make broadcasts that would test the technology *and* entertain viewers. A steady procession of actors and performers already made famous by radio were game enough to venture down from the upper floors of Broadcasting House to the dark and untidy basement studio, put on the strangest of make-up, and perform before the blinding gaze of the camera's beam. Josephine Baker was among the first to appear. Others in her wake included ballet dancers, high-kicking chorus lines, and Sally the Seal, who blew a saxophone and wiggled her flippers for the cameras. There were plenty of breakdowns and mishaps, but it was through this sustained period of trial and error that the craft of television slowly and surely took hold: week by week, camera movements were improved, the principles of floor management were developed, and techniques of lighting and make-up professionalised.[37]

The BBC team had soon accumulated more television pro-gramme-making experience than anyone else in the world. So it was a shock when, in March 1934, their work was brought to an abrupt halt. To outsiders it looked like an unprovoked, destruc-tive act, which betrayed the BBC's ultimate lack of commitment. In reality, the decision reflected the deep anxiety of senior staff about the long-term effectiveness of Baird's technology.

Despite several years of vigorous salesmanship, television was still no nearer to becoming truly popular. When the BBC had begun its experimental broadcasts in September 1929, the audience had consisted of thirty or so well-heeled viewers living in London or the Home Counties. Several thousand viewers had tuned into the first transmissions from Broadcasting House in 1932. But this was still paltry stuff compared to a national radio audience of five and a half *million* licence-fee holders. Only the BBC could afford to keep doggedly making programmes for the few in the hope of one day creating demand from the many. But the expert assessment of its own engineers was that Baird's mechanical scanning system was already reaching the limits of its potential. With a screen no bigger than a postcard and with images that still made people look as if they were 'in a heavy and persistent shower of rain', it was just too primitive to provide the basis for a mass product. Baird's cameras generated pictures of a mere thirty lines, which were not nearly enough to create satisfying visual detail. His system was also designed for use on medium wave, the same wavelength the BBC already used for its radio broadcasts. If even half-good pictures were to be pro-vided, the television signal would leave no room in the ether for anything else. The obvious solution, if the right system could be developed, was to use the ultra-short-wave range. But Baird's backers had been in a rush: it was medium wave that had pro-vided the short-term fix, so their business remained wedded to it. This meant that even if cameras could be improved at the studio end, there was still a strict upper limit to the picture quality at the receiver end, and it was, as Eckersley put it, 'an insult to the public' to pretend otherwise. It seemed only logical to conclude that since the images were never going to improve, it was no longer worth transmitting them at all. In the last analysis, the Baird system threatened what the BBC saw as the 'democratic foundation of British broadcasting', the basic tenet of which was 'the greatest good for the greatest number'.[38]

What finally killed off the BBC's commitment to Baird was the discovery of a much more promising alternative. Scientists working for EMI in America and Marconi in Britain had been secretly developing the cathode ray tube, an electronic rather than mechanical device that generated 'high definition' images with 405 lines and used higher frequency wavelengths. Once BBC engineers became aware of this new system, it quickly became obvious to them that a superior technology had arrived. Suspending the Baird transmissions in March 1934 provided the opportunity they needed to take stock – and, most likely, change direction.

Unfortunately, the great leap forward that the cathode ray tube represented was rather less obvious to Post Office officials and government ministers. They, too, were ruminating on television's future. And, unlike the BBC, they were keen to keep supporting Baird on the basis that his was a wholly British-owned enterprise. Baird had also helped his own cause by hurriedly coming up with a new 240-line standard, a last-ditch attempt to compete with Marconi and EMI. The result of these machinations was the Selsdon Inquiry, set up by the government to advise on how to proceed. The formal recommendation it came up with in January 1935 was an awkward, and ultimately unworkable, compromise: the Corporation itself should run a regular and permanent television service for the nation using *both* the new electronic system *and* Baird's modestly improved mechanical system.[39]

Alexandra Palace on the slopes of north London's Muswell Hill was the home chosen for this new operation. The former 'People's Palace' had been a place of lavish entertainment throughout the 1880s and 1890s, but its glory days were long gone. When the BBC engineer Desmond Campbell arrived to assess the building in the summer of 1935, he found it to be in 'the most dreadful mess'. Thousands of rats scurried through cavernous halls filled only with dilapidated slot machines, flea-bitten stuffed animals, peeling posters advertising tea dances, and the scattered debris of its time as a prisoner-of-war camp. Its location, on the other hand, was ideal. Ultra-high frequencies demanded clear sight lines to the horizon. And here was a building already a good 306 feet above sea level, which meant that once the BBC's vast latticed-steel transmitter mast was in place, the whole edifice soared over 600 feet into the sky – some 200 feet higher even than St Paul's Cathedral. This pretty well guaranteed that viewers across the capital and many miles beyond would receive its signal. The BBC leased a corner of the building and filled it with control rooms, scenery docks, carpenters' workshops, dressing rooms, offices and a canteen. The most important new facilities installed were two large studios on the first floor: Studio A, with Marconi-EMI equipment, and Studio B with Baird's.[40]

The basement studio crew from Broadcasting House formed the core of the new technical team at Alexandra Palace. Gerald Cock, who had proved a spirited and inventive head of the BBC's outside broadcasts since the Savoy Hill days, was appointed the first 'Director of Television', while the day-to-day running of programmes fell to Cecil Madden, a young producer of radio variety shows who had also organised live stunts for *In Town Tonight*.

It was Cock and Madden who set out a practical vision for the new television service. They faced a difficult balancing act. Formally, they had little autonomy: television was just one small part of the BBC's larger Programme Division and was therefore directly answerable to the Controller of Programmes, Cecil Graves, whose office was six miles away in Broadcasting House. Although Cock and Madden were radio men who brought with them all sorts of ideas and practices imbided from years of working in the older medium, they desperately wanted to put the stamp of difference on their new venture, creating as much distance as they could between the tightly knit group at 'Ally Pally' and the cautious regime of Graves at Broadcasting House.

Both men believed that a priority for a visual medium such as theirs was to find announcers with a 'pleasant personality' – by which they meant announcers with the right *appearance*. After an advert was placed in the *Daily Telegraph*, well over a thousand applicants were whittled down to a trio of successful candidates: Leslie Mitchell, a debonair *Movietone News* commentator and former actor, whom the *Daily Mail* described as a 'Television Adonis'; Elizabeth Cowell, who had modelled for the fashion designer Norman Hartnell; and Jasmine Bligh, who came from a vaguely aristocratic family with royal connections and had four years' theatre experience. Cock told the newspapers proudly that the two women – the one 'dark, Latin', the other 'blond, Nordic' – had been 'selected for their looks above everything else': both, he added, were 'easy to photograph'.[41]

When Gerald Cock summoned his team to the Council Chamber of Broadcasting House one morning in August 1936, he reassured them that although there was still lots to do, they had plenty of time to prepare: they would not be going on air until November. By the time they had reassembled in Alexandra Palace later that same afternoon, this comforting timetable had already been shredded. No sooner had Madden sat down in his office than he received a call from Gerald Cock with some alarming news. The Radiolympia show at Earls Court had television sets on sale for the first time, but without any programmes to watch it seemed that no one was in the mood to splash out. 'They want us to rescue them', Cock told Madden: 'You open in nine days.' The leisurely launch he was expecting had just been snatched away, though Madden regarded the turn of events as providential. 'It gave us no time to think and become self-conscious.'[42]

So it was in a devil-may-care spirit that Alexandra Palace first took to the air at 11.45 a.m. on Wednesday 26 August 1936 with Helen McKay singing a specially written theme song. A series

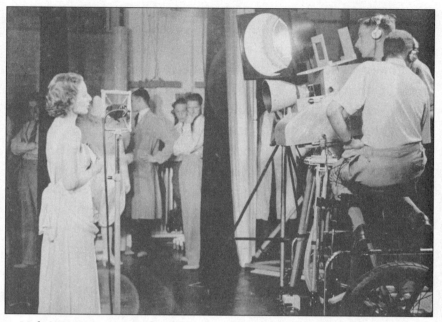

Helen McKay singing for the camera on *Here's Looking at You*, the first
television programme broadcast from Alexandra Palace in August
1936. Visitors to the annual Radiolympia exhibition in Earls Court
could watch the show by entering seat-less, darkened viewing boxes.

of breakdowns meant it wasn't until the following day that the
full variety show that had originally been planned, called *Here's
Looking at You*, was broadcast. After a brief burst of Duke Elling-
ton's 'Solitude', Leslie Mitchell stepped before the camera to
introduce Helen McKay once more. She was followed in quick
succession by the Three Admirals, a tuxedo-clad male trio from
the Cole Porter show *Anything Goes!*, a pair of Chilean dancers,
and Pogo the pantomime horse. Hyam Greenbaum's Television Orchestra provided the backing music. Over the next eight
days, a similar package of vaudeville, newsreels and extracts
from current British and American films was transmitted for
one hour twice a day every day.[43]

'It improved daily and by the end was reasonable', Madden
recorded modestly. The papers were rather more carried
away. The *Times* praised the programmes for their 'perfect

synchronization of sound and vision'. 'The miniature variety show', the *Observer* reported, 'was a gem'.[44] The most prescient eyewitness account came from the *Listener*'s radio critic, Grace Wyndham Goldie. She asked her editor, Rex Lambert, if she could go to Alexandra Palace to watch a broadcast taking place. 'Look,' he had told her, 'television is going to be of no importance in your lifetime or mine, and I don't want you going up there wasting your time on it.' She went nevertheless. Sitting quietly in a corner, looking at a monitor with one eye and at what was happening on the studio floor with the other, she decided that the production was terrible, the reception awful. But she was convinced that 'this was going to be one of the most important influences that had ever been created':

> So, I got out of the studio and I took the bus down to Wood Green tube station and got into a public telephone box and rang up Rex Lambert and I said, 'This is absolutely terrific, I must, must, must write about it, please let me. So, he said, 'Oh, all right!'[45]

At Radiolympia itself, television sets were placed in the foyer for customers to watch as they perched on tiered seats. Visitors could also queue for a minute's viewing in specially darkened booths reminiscent of a Victorian peep show. Fewer watched at home for the simple reason that all the Televisors that had been sold over the past decade were designed for Baird's now redundant thirty-line system. Anyone who wanted to see the Radiolympia broadcasts needed to invest in brand-new models such as the 'Marconiphone 701'. This consisted of a large mahogany cabinet containing a cathode ray tube so long it could only be installed vertically, its wide end facing the ceiling. There was a safety element to this strange arrangement, since if a tube were to explode – an event considered quite likely – any shattered glass would fly upwards rather than shooting across the room. It also meant that a tilted mirror had to be mounted on the lid of the set so that the images coming out of the tube were visible.

The most crucial element of the whole design, however, was a small switch that allowed users to flick between 405-line and 240-line transmissions. This was needed because, to meet the Post Office requirement that it use both the Marconi-EMI and Baird systems, the BBC opted to alternate its broadcasts between the two in a fixed pattern: on certain days, programmes would be made on 405 lines in the Marconi-EMI-equipped Studio A; on others, on 240 lines in the Baird-equipped Studio B.[46]

The arrangement was mildly inconvenient for 'lookers-in'. For those working at Alexandra Palace it was utterly insane. Staff knew from experience that with the Marconi-EMI system the 'Emitron' electronic cameras were better and more reliable, the lighting was decent, even everyday make-up could be used. The Baird process produced lower-quality results and was clunkier to operate. Announcers would have to sit in darkness to face the unremitting beam of a spotlight, and there was no escape from the grotesque make-up. Most bizarrely, an 'intermediate film' process was needed, which involved capturing each scene first on a roll of celluloid, and then developing and printing it, before anything could even be transmitted. The whole process took no more than ninety seconds, but it was hard to think that this was 'live' television. The only people who welcomed it were the actors and singers themselves. If they were quick enough, they could run backstage to watch their own performance.[47]

The tortuous obligation to alternate studios was still in place when, two months later, the world's first regular 'high-definition' television service officially began. At 3.30 p.m. on Monday 2 November, the BBC Television Orchestra began playing, and the musical comedy star Adele Dixon took to the studio floor to sing 'Magic Rays of Light'. She was followed by the African American duo, Buck and Bubbles, and six Chinese jugglers, the Lai Founs, before the service shut down for five hours at 4 p.m.

Dixon's song was not, in fact, the very first item to be broadcast that day. Half an hour before Dixon took to the studio floor, Madden had been required to produce a 'pretty dull' programme of short speeches from the BBC Chairman, the

Postmaster-General, Lord Selsdon, and the respective chairmen of Baird's and EMI. The aim was to honour briefly some of those who had helped guide television to this important stage in its development. John Logie Baird was in the building somewhere, too, but by some oversight had not been invited to join them in the studio, and was left wandering the corridors. Four weeks later he was to suffer a further indignity. Crystal Palace, which contained all his laboratory equipment, caught fire. The inferno was so large that it could be seen from the other side of London. At Alexandra Palace, BBC staff and visiting artists rushed outside on to the terrace to watch in horrified silence. A vital part of their own history was disappearing before their eyes.

*

Television's experimental phase was coming to an end. Alexandra Palace now fell into a routine; the weekly schedule printed in the *Radio Times* soon became as reassuringly familiar to the public as that of the BBC's National or Regional Programmes. Television took to the air twice daily, from 3 to 4 p.m., and then again from 9 till 10 p.m. Gerald Cock had ruled that there should be breaks between individual programmes in order to 'avoid eye strain' for those watching at home, and the extended early-evening break was designed to avoid interfering with viewers' domestic life, including mealtimes and children's bedtimes. The schedule included health tips, recipe suggestions, fashion parades, and talks on such subjects as home improvements, animal care, art exhibitions or books, as well as ten-minute editions of *British Movietone News*: the BBC did not yet have its own television news department. It was a diet dominated by straightforward variety and popular entertainment, much of it of a surprisingly high quality. Although Cecil Madden's budget when the service began was only £100 a week, he had wanted television's first full week to be 'as big and as fast and as good' as possible, and had managed to put on air Marie Rambert's ballet

A 1939 performance at Alexandra Palace of *The Sleeping Princess*
by the Vic-Wells Ballet company and starring Margot Fonteyn.
Cecil Madden thought ballet was perfect for television. 'The
close-up', he claimed, 'could humanise the whole conception'.

company, scenes from the West End play, *Marigold*, and a full-
scale cabaret. It sent a useful message to Broadcasting House
about the scale of his ambition.[48]

According to one estimate, a total of 386 plays were broadcast over the next three years. Among the critical highpoints
were scenes from T. S. Eliot's *Murder in the Cathedral*, a full-cast
production of *Cyrano de Bergerac*, and a live relay from the West
End production of J. B. Priestley's *When We Are Married*. The
start of Sunday programming in 1938 proved a big help, since
it was the one day of the week when stage actors were generally free. The Sunday play therefore became a weekly artistic
highlight – a chance, as Madden put it, to do a 'proper, three-act
play' that everybody might watch and talk about. On several
occasions members of the Birmingham Rep would travel by bus
to Alexandra Palace to recreate their stage performances before
the BBC cameras. Most other productions featured the cast of
West End shows. It was a time when London was overflowing

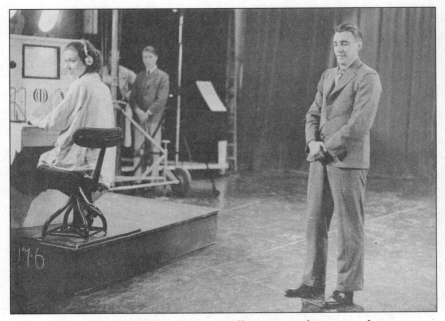

The 'Switchboard Girl', Joan Miller gets ready to introduce
the well-known aircraft designer Frederick Crocombe as a
guest on *Picture Page*. The series was described in the *Listener*
as offering viewers 'something of everything and nothing for
long. It is, in fact, a kind of high-speed television circus.'

with American talent, which meant that Madden could entice
to the studio an impressive range of leading artistes to appear
in variety series such as *Starlight* and *West End Cabaret*. On Saturday 25 February 1939, the first edition of a new series, *Harlem
in Mayfair*, was broadcast live from the popular West End night-
spot, the Florida Club. It featured, among others, Adelaide
Hall performing with the distinguished Nigerian musician
Fela Sowande in what the *Radio Times* described as 'a coloured
cabaret'. Others who appeared later in the series included Paul
Robeson, Elisabeth Welch and Fats Waller.[49]

The most popular and critically lauded programme of all
was the magazine show *Picture Page*, which ran twice a week for
a grand total of 262 editions. The very first *Picture Page* had actually been transmitted, somewhat surreptitiously, on Thursday 8

October 1936, nearly a month before the BBC's television service was formally launched. Cecil Madden had conceived the series along the lines of *Gossip Hour*, a bright and breezy show he had produced for radio. The format represented a mix of the traditional variety show and appearances from an eclectic array of topical guests who would be interviewed by the announcer Leslie Mitchell. The first edition included a busker, a model, the racing tipster 'Prince Monolulu', a suffragette, the holder of the world's altitude record, and 'Prestwick Pertana' the Siamese cat. To link each item smoothly Madden and his team got the Canadian actor Joan Miller to sit at a mocked-up 'telephone exchange'. 'You're through!' she would announce cheerily as she 'switched' the viewer to each celebrity. To cue Miller in, it later emerged, the studio director would give her a mild shock through wires attached to her ankles. The effect on viewers was equally electric. The *Daily Telegraph*'s critic declared *Picture Page* 'a brilliant success'. Writing in the *Listener*, Grace Wyndham Goldie called it 'one long triumph'. 'There is something of everything and nothing for long ... It is, in fact, a kind of high-speed television circus.' By 1939, according to Madden, 'all over London people used to poke each other and say "You're through, this is Picture Page"'. Given the minuscule number of television sets in circulation, this was obviously a wild exaggeration. But when BBC researchers conducted an audience survey in January 1937, *Picture Page* stood out for the favourable comments it received. According to one respondent, it was what made Thursdays 'stay at home night'. The only topic that stirred people up more was interference caused by passing motor cars.[50]

On Wednesday 12 May 1937, barely six months after its inauguration, the television service offered a glimpse of the nation at its most grand and formal when it joined radio in covering the coronation of King George VI. The Archbishop of Canterbury had banned cameras from Westminster Abbey itself, so the BBC's only television outside broadcast unit took up position at Hyde Park Corner, from where it was able to show the royal procession passing Marble Arch before continuing down

Constitution Hill. Baird's old engineer, Tony Bridgewater, who was in charge, described how 'everything was devised as we went along'. Perhaps as a result of the steady downpour, Bridgewater's equipment failed just moments before the King's carriage came into view. What brought it back to life, he later explained, was the simple expedient of hitting it as hard as possible. As a result, the broadcast stayed on the air and an estimated 10,000 viewers caught sight of a half-hearted smile from the King as he passed by.[51]

*

The Coronation was the kind of complex, makeshift exercise that helped the BBC discover the precise mix of technology and skills that would be required for the large-scale outside broadcasts of the future. But as Joan Miller, from *Picture Page*, pointed out, at Alexandra Palace, '*every* programme was a way of finding out how to do the thing'. Life inside the ramshackle home of television had eased, anyway, since February 1937, when the Post Office finally let the BBC wriggle out of its painful commitment to using the old Baird system every other week. There was still a multitude of other technical issues to solve. Cameras, for instance, showed images upside down in their viewfinders: operators had to develop an instinct for wheeling to the right whenever they wanted to follow an actor who appeared to be going to the left, and for pointing the camera 'upwards' to catch something happening near the floor. Nor was it possible yet to 'cut' from one camera to another: live shows had to be elaborately choreographed in advance to allow for fades that lasted for several agonising seconds. But Ally Pally was no longer an inconveniently located satellite of Broadcasting House. It was a creative centre of its own, a 'hive of enormous enthusiasm' where staff thought of themselves, like the pioneers of Savoy Hill, as buccaneers heralding a new era. Programme makers wholeheartedly embraced popular culture and the world of commercial entertainment, yet remained true to a Reithian

philosophy of surprising audiences and widening their horizons.[52] Ballet shared the screen with boxing, Rebecca West
starred alongside fire-eaters, an interview with John Piper might
be followed by a man ripping telephone directories in half. It
was an enthusiastic blending of high-, low- and middlebrow
that drew its inspiration from the BBC's radio traditions. Under
figures such as Eric Maschwitz, the older medium had already
made great strides in trying to reflect the kaleidoscope of public
tastes. The influence on television of shows like *Music Hall* and
In Town Tonight was obvious. And it was years of hard-won experience in the studios of Savoy Hill, Broadcasting House and St
George's Hall that lay behind the sheer confidence with which
the BBC's small but growing television team were now throwing themselves at their craft.

By 1939 it would have seemed to everyone at Alexandra
Palace as if television could only go from strength to strength.
Programmes were more polished by the week, the schedule
more varied than ever, public interest growing steadily. The
number of people owning sets had also grown to nearly 20,000.
It was even predicted that by Christmas that year as many as
100,000 sets might be sold.

It was not to be. On 30 September 1938, the BBC's television cameras had been at Heston airfield to capture the moment
when the prime minister Neville Chamberlain returned from
Munich bearing a piece of paper that promised 'peace for our
time'. Eleven months later, Douglas Birkinshaw was the engineer in charge at Alexandra Palace when at ten in the morning
he received a message from Broadcasting House: all transmissions should cease at the end of the morning schedule. As a
Mickey Mouse cartoon finished, Birkinshaw walked into the
control room and flicked some switches. Shortly after midday
the BBC's service came to a grinding halt.[53] With little ceremony,
television had closed down completely and would not reopen
again for nearly seven years. It was Friday 1 September 1939, and
Britain was on the verge of war.

II

WAR

6

UNDER SIEGE

The War came and of course everything really went into the melting pot.

Mary Lewis, duplicating clerk, BBC

At lunchtime on Thursday 24 August 1939, the editor of the *Radio Times*, Maurice Gorham, was in the back garden of his house overlooking the harbour in Dublin. As he painted a kitchen table with creosote, watching it soak in under the scorching sun, the telephone rang with a message from the BBC's Controller of Public Affairs, Stephen Tallents. He was to come back to Broadcasting House immediately. The Soviet Union had signed a non-aggression pact with Hitler's Germany, conflict in Europe was imminent, and the BBC was putting itself on a war footing.

Gorham caught the evening ferry. 'When I got to the office the next morning there was a high state of tension.' As he arrived in Portland Place, dozens of BBC staff were being squeezed into cars and buses: Variety, *Children's Hour*, and Religion were heading to Bristol; others, including Drama, Music, and Features, were going to Wood Norton Hall, a country house that stood in leafy grounds outside the Worcestershire town of Evesham. There was a whiff of subterfuge in the air. No one outside the BBC was supposed to know of this exodus, and especially not about Wood Norton. If anyone mentioned the BBC's country retreat they would refer gnomically to the mythical 'Hogsnorton'.[1]

The people of Evesham had only just been warned that they

would have a host of strangers billeted on them. Rumours had been circulating locally that Wood Norton was to be a home for the Duke and Duchess of Windsor or the Emperor of Abyssinia. In fact, Corporation staff had been quietly sequestered inside the building since Easter. The place had once belonged to the Duke of Orleans, and within its wood-panelled rooms, richly decorated with fleurs-de-lis, engineers had spent the summer laying down cables and lashing up makeshift studios and offices. In the grounds they had assembled several wooden huts, each one festooned with aerials. By the time staff from Broadcasting House began arriving at the end of August, there were already six fully functioning studios and a control room. Other facilities would follow. Soon, more than a quarter of the BBC's workforce were stationed here, turning out well over a thousand programme items a week.[2] Listeners would never know, but for the next few years, whenever they tuned in to their favourite programme and heard the words 'This is London', they were often listening not to Broadcasting House but a stately manor deep in the English countryside.

'This country is at war'

The BBC had been preparing for war for more than half a decade. As early as September 1933, Reith was told by the Cabinet Secretary, Maurice Hankey, that something needed to be done to 'prepare the country for what they would have to do in the event of air-raids'. The following year the Director-General appointed a committee to prepare the BBC for bombing and civil disturbance. By the end of 1936, security fencing and steel shutters started appearing at several BBC premises; after the Munich Crisis of 1938, staff were despatched to scour the country for buildings in which facilities and staff could be relocated away from London. Employees were now divided into three categories: 'A', those whose work for the BBC would be vital if war was declared; 'B', those who were to go home and await a summons; and 'C', those whose services would no longer be required and

A man stands guard in a Broadcasting House reception heavily barricaded
by bricked-up windows and sandbags. With the threat of bombing
raids and a widespread fear of Fifth Column infiltrators, the protection
of key BBC buildings was a constant worry throughout the war.

who would be encouraged to join the armed forces or a civilian
defence organisation. Some staff were already being redeployed:
a group of television engineers had been despatched to the RAF
base at Bawdsey in Suffolk to help speed up the development of
Britain's early-warning radar system.[3]

All this planning was supposed to be discreet. But by the
summer of 1939, no one at Broadcasting House could avoid the

sense of imminent crisis. Mary Lewis, who helped run the BBC's busy Duplicating Section, remembers 'seeing all the secret stuff as to what the BBC was going to do': 'one realised the situation was so bad that one couldn't really plan ahead.' John Daligan, who worked as a lift attendant, knew matters were coming to a head when new anti-gas and blast-proof doors were installed to protect the building's entrance and lorries suddenly arrived with a call-out for volunteers to fill hundreds of sandbags. Dutifully turning up with shovel in hand, Daligan found himself paired with Adrian Boult, the BBC's distinguished Director of Music. 'He was as friendly and pleasant as he'd always been', he remembered. 'We both enjoyed our unusual task.' As a category 'C' employee, Daligan would be enlisted with the Royal Artillery in a matter of days. As for Boult, he was packed off to Bristol along with the BBC Symphony Orchestra.[4]

The BBC's extraordinary effort to remove its staff to provincial outposts reflected two long-held assumptions about the coming war: first, that any aerial attack would be aimed at major population centres; and second, that it would be swift and annihilating. Though the most lurid scenarios, involving the complete destruction of entire cities, were highly fanciful, the notion had stuck that London was particularly vulnerable to a 'knockout blow'. Internal BBC documents warned staff that Germany was unlikely to give Britain the luxury of an actual declaration of war: 'an air attack literally out of the blue is very possible.' 'How many of the attacking aircraft get through', it added, 'must remain a matter of conjecture, but at best life in London would be extremely unpleasant.'[5] The decision to disperse its technical and human infrastructure was designed to ensure that no matter how bad things got in the capital the shutdown of Britain's entire broadcasting operation would be avoided.

There were, however, a few wrinkles in the plan. The sudden arrival of so many BBC staff put an immediate strain on relations with the people of Evesham. Billeting – of military personnel, factory workers, civil servants – was a widespread feature of the war, and almost always a source of contention, since hosts frequently grumbled about the extra mouths to feed while lodgers often felt that they were being offered second-rate rations and sub-standard rooms with little privacy. There were sharp clashes of lifestyle to contend with, too. Mary Lewis was among the first to arrive from London and experience the sheer randomness of local arrangements. 'I was met by a harassed Billeting Officer who said, "oh yes, now let me think, yes, you'll be in High Street, a double-bed, but the girl you're sharing with is on nights and you're on days, so it will be perfectly all right".' Val Gielgud grumbled about being allocated a 'vile' billet, where the landlady seemed to regard him as 'a medieval *condottiere* likely to steal the silver and ravish the daughter'.[6]

Wood Norton itself had some of the pioneering spirit of Savoy Hill. A highly disparate group of people – drama producers, musicians, actors, engineers – had been thrown together in the grounds of an isolated house with little to do but make the most of it. When the day's work was done, they could stroll across magnificent manicured lawns or talk long into the night with new-found friends. As one of the BBC's announcers, Bruce Belfrage, explained, 'Sharing the common view that we would all most probably be blotted out by the Luftwaffe during the first few weeks of war, we decided to adopt the principle of "Eat, drink and be merry".'[7]

Back in London, the Luftwaffe had also been playing on the minds of the BBC's most senior engineers. They had long worried that the very same transmitters used to broadcast programmes might also guide enemy planes to their targets. The Air Ministry had actually deemed the risk so severe that it wanted broadcasting shut down completely during hostilities. Since 1936 the BBC had been working on a simple but effective solution. The various medium-wave transmitters scattered around the British countryside were clustered into two 'synchronised' groups – Northern and Southern – and within each group every transmitter would broadcast on exactly the same wavelength. This meant that an enemy bomber would be unable to get a reliable 'fix' on any one location until it was within twenty-five miles of a particular transmitter. Only then would RAF Fighter Command alert the BBC to close down the transmitter concerned, denying the Luftwaffe vital information while still allowing listeners to receive a weaker but still serviceable signal from more distant transmitters in the same synchronised group. The BBC's high-power long-wave facility at Droitwich had to cease completely because there were no other transmitters working on the same wavelength to act as spoilers. The same was true of Alexandra Palace.[8]

The silencing of Droitwich and the synchronisation of the remaining transmitters had a profound impact on the public. It meant that the BBC could no longer offer listeners *both* the National Programme *and* the Regional Programme in all its various local identities: there would have to be a new unitary service for everyone. Given that the switchover to this new system would only come in response to an anticipated air attack, it also meant that whatever the British people heard on the wireless would henceforth offer the clearest indication that war really was about to begin.

By the end of August 1939, the BBC's meticulously worked-out plans were in place. Sealed instructions had been circulated to key staff. Around the country, millions of listeners now kept their radios switched on, waiting for news. In order to 'relieve the tension', a retired nurse in Sussex, Muriel Greenway, avoided the wireless altogether, spending the day in Brighton. 'I know I can do nothing, and feel I must guard my own nerves and health', she wrote in her diary. 'What is to come, will come.' But the very next morning, the last day of August, she was back home in Steyning listening to the first announcements that schoolchildren would be evacuated from major cities. 'Am rather sorry I listened,' she wrote, 'as it may mean a sleepless night.'[9] On Friday 1 September, listeners heard that German forces had invaded Poland and a full blackout would be implemented nationwide that night. It felt like a tipping point. In Romford, Essex, a seventeen-year-old girl who was helping out at the

local school watched as a wireless set was hurriedly installed
in the staffroom: 'Our headmistress decreed that someone was
to be in the room all the time, in readiness for any special radio
message.' At 11 a.m., she went in herself:

> There were three others there and together we listened
> to the announcement that 'serious developments in the
> international situation' had occurred. As the details of the
> Poland air raids were unfolded, one of the staff, an intend-
> ing missionary, kept muttering to herself and clicking her
> tongue ... All four of us knew it was virtually war. At break
> everyone was asking everyone else. 'Have you heard the
> news?' or 'Has there been any more news?'

Later, after supper, the girl's mother stopped her going
outside. 'If we die, we all die together.' With nothing better to
do, she went to bed early, leaving her father downstairs glued to
the wireless.[10]

It was on Friday 1 September, too, that the BBC switched to
a full-scale war footing. Listeners learned for the first time of the
wavelength changes that would be introduced imminently as a
result of what were called 'purely technical considerations'. By
7 p.m., key staff at every transmitter station and studio, including the senior control room engineer in Broadcasting House,
had been instructed to switch over to the new synchronised
system. The National and Regional Programmes were replaced
by a new unified 'Home Service'. Meanwhile, select members
of 'Category A' staff received telephone calls telling them to
open their sealed envelopes with more detailed instructions.
Godfrey Talbot, a young reporter then stationed in Birmingham, was told to head to Broadcasting House and join the news
team there. 'I was the only idiot going into London ... the road
coming up north was nose-to-tail solid with refugees: people
with their cars loaded to the gunwales and with beds and prams
on the roof ... I've never been so frightened in my life.' Olive
Shapley went down to London with her husband, John Salt,

who had been summoned to work on broadcasts to Europe. On the train they met another North Region colleague, Donald Boyd. Shapley remembers him white-faced with fear. His family, he explained, had headed off into the country leaving their pet rabbits behind. Before packing his bags, he had had to strangle them all.[11]

Most of those already in London were preparing to get out. On his last day in Broadcasting House before joining his fellow reservists, John Daligan sensed the change of mood. 'It was as if a weight of doubt and uncertainty had been lifted from every-one's shoulders ... people were saying with a sense of relief to each other that at least we knew where we stood now.'

> For the rest of the afternoon there was a great coming and going about the offices as people moved around to say their farewells to each other, and grade and class barriers broke down. Kisses and handshakes abounded and it was all very wonderful ... most of us decided to have one last fling in town that night and report in the morning. As soon as the pubs opened at 5.30pm, we went along to the Cock Tavern and were joined to our surprise by many of the people who had been bidding us farewell in the afternoon and who probably were not in the habit of calling in pubs. It was a hot September evening and because there were so many of us the landlord opened a bar upstairs for us. It was a memorable occasion, with more kisses and hugs and tears that grew more earnest as night went on. Few of us could remember very clearly how we got home and what made it more difficult was that it was the first night of the blackout, which even sober men found difficulty navigating in.[12]

After all this, Sunday's formal announcement that Britain really was at war seemed like a foregone conclusion. The BBC nevertheless handled it with appropriate solemnity. Wood Norton was on standby, but Broadcasting House remained in charge. The control room, from which all incoming and outgoing lines were co-ordinated, had been moved from its exposed position under the mansard roof of the eighth floor into a new and much safer location in the basement. In the Cabinet Room of 10 Downing Street, microphones had been set up since first thing. At a quarter past eleven, the control room faded out the sound of Bow Bells and switched on the live feed from Downing Street. The BBC's announcer read out two short sentences on the piece of paper in front of him: 'This is London. You will now hear a statement by the Prime Minister.' And then Neville Chamberlain began speaking in a sombre, weary voice. Germany, he explained, had failed to respond to Britain's deadline to withdraw from Poland, and consequently Britain was at war with Germany. He warned of the days of 'stress and strain' to come before finishing with a peroration on the righteousness of the battle ahead: 'It is evil things that we shall be fighting against: brute force, bad faith, injustice, oppression, and persecution. And against them, I am certain that the right will prevail.' After his statement, a series of government announcements was read out. People were to keep off the streets as much as possible and carry their gas masks. Large sporting events would cease immediately. Places of entertainment would close until further notice. Details were given of how air-raid or poison-gas warnings would be made and how the public should respond. The special broadcast ended just before 11.30 a.m. with the national anthem.[13]

In Broadcasting House, staff had assembled in the concert hall to listen, 'men and women all huddled together'. Godfrey Talbot remembers an 'awful feeling' in his stomach. 'We all thought London was going to be bombed to hell straight away.' Across the south-east air-raid sirens sounded in false alarm, sending thousands scurrying to find shelter. In a surreal twist, the warning signal that went off at Wood Norton consisted of 'The Teddy Bear's Picnic' blasted through loudspeakers. As soon as it was heard, all the producers, actors, administrators, secretaries and engineers promptly did as they were told and ran into the nearby woods to lie down in pairs. The day ended with a special message from a German radio station. 'Hello, the BBC at Evesham', it announced cheerily. 'Are you settling in comfortably?'[14]

The 'Bore' war

The apocalypse that everyone feared – and which the BBC had meticulously planned for – did not materialise. Poland was overrun, but French and British forces on the Western Front remained on the defensive, waiting for the Germans to make the first move. With cinemas and theatres shut, sporting fixtures cancelled, the blackout, and all the disruptions to ordinary life ordered by officialdom, the British people now relied more than ever on the wireless to keep them amused as well as informed. Alas, what they heard was largely anodyne and dull.

The wartime aims of the BBC were to maintain public morale and be 'the vehicle for official announcements and the radiation of reliable news'. Everyone had expected the second role to dominate in the first few days, but for now there turned out to be so little real news to report that the public had to endure repetitive bulletins interspersed with seemingly endless hours of organ music from Sandy MacPherson. As for maintaining public morale with 'good entertainment', that had been severely compromised by the loss of hundreds of staff to the services and by the distinctly primitive facilities at its two main retreats, Wood Norton and Bristol. Outside broadcasts were impossible because the telephone cables they relied on had been reserved for urgent government communications. Full-cast dramas, complicated live shows, elegant features: all these carefully crafted productions had to make way for a schedule of 'simple programmes'. To cap it all, of course, there was now just one radio service for the whole country.[15]

The public reaction was one of bitter disappointment. In Sussex, Muriel Greenway wrote in her diary for Thursday 14 September 1939 that she had turned off her radio 'in despair'. 'They say they have ten thousand records, and as far as I can see,

nine thousand nine hundred are high-toned music or the slop-
piest jazz.' Her frustration – and it was almost certainly widely
shared – was that while she loathed almost everything she heard
she could not really cope *without* the radio, either. Her diary
entry for 24 November recorded that she had been 'lost' after
her set was broken for three weeks. 'I feel as though a friend
has gone from the house, and I can hardly bear the silence or
the knowledge that I can't get any news no matter what is happening.' She would, she wrote, 'never grumble' again about the
BBC, though within days her diary resumed its usual litany of
complaints about inane entertainment and the lack of well-done
drama. In the *Daily Mail*, Collie Knox attacked the Home Service's 'paucity of ideas', and even the BBC's own *Radio Times*
joined the fray, publishing several sharp letters from otherwise
loyal listeners. 'I cannot believe that the miserable skeleton
paraded before us as the "BBC Home Service" represents the
best effort of which the Corporation is capable', raged one. 'We
should like to know if you keep Sandy MacPherson chained up
in the dungeons'.[16]

Unsurprisingly, thousands started tuning in nightly to
German radio just to 'relieve the boredom and dullness'. The
Nazis broadcast English-language programmes nine times a
day from Hamburg, Bremen and Zeesen. And it was one of
Hamburg's presenters, the former Conservative Party activist
and Mosley supporter William Joyce, speaking in a voice memorably described as 'Cholmondeley-Plantagenet out of Christ
Church', who quickly became the star attraction. Night after
night, 'Lord Haw-Haw' enlivened the blackout with his opening
lines, 'Germany calling, Germany calling, Germany calling',
before launching into a rambling attack on Chamberlain's government or expressing phoney concern for British workers. His
broadcasts were compelling for the way they jumbled together
hilariously unbelievable rumours with snippets of tittle-tattle
that were all too convincing. An internal BBC report acknowledged that there were unfortunately 'some elements of truth'
in Joyce's talks. 'There *is* a social problem in Great Britain, there

are economic difficulties.' It was because of this, the report concluded, that 'the fiction becomes less apparent'. By February
1940, Joyce's novelty was starting to wear off, and from May,
when Germany invaded the Low Countries, his attraction
waned dramatically. Yet throughout that first winter of the war,
somewhere between a quarter and a third of the British population listened regularly. Even British troops seemed to prefer him
to the BBC. At one anti-aircraft battery, a general who had been
watching the men and women under his command, described
how they were always 'pretty bored' in the evenings until it was
time for Lord Haw-Haw. 'The whole room gets up and gathers
round the wireless. After it is over, they go back to their games.'[17]

*

Most people thought the BBC guilty of misjudging the national
mood. The reality was more complicated. Quite apart from the
hidden difficulties over resources, the Corporation was having
to deal with a government constraining its freedom of action
behind the scenes.

In 1935, Whitehall's Committee of Imperial Defence had
stated that in the event of war, the government would assume
'effective control of broadcasting and the BBC' via a new Ministry of Information. The Corporation readily accepted its
responsibility to strengthen, as it put it, 'the moral and material
resources of the British public to bear the strain of war and to
carry it through to a successful end'. Yet it believed, too, that
to become a government mouthpiece putting out unmitigated
propaganda would be counter-productive. The 'only way to
strengthen the morale of the people whose morale is worth
strengthening', the BBC's senior news editor, R. T. Clark pronounced, 'is to tell them the truth and nothing but the truth,
even if the truth is horrible'.[18]

In the end it was agreed that the Ministry of Information
would officially 'guide' the BBC but delegate day-to-day censorship to senior staff at the Corporation. The degree of oversight

The BBC newsroom in 1941. A year earlier it had been moved from the second floor of Broadcasting House to the building's basement, creating an atmosphere of permanent night-time. R. T. Clark is standing at the back near a bunk bed where staff might get some sleep during long shifts.

varied according to programme genre. To avoid the release of information which might unwittingly aid the enemy, news output came under direct ministry control, although the BBC's 'Home News Editor' assumed responsibility for approving each individual bulletin. Most other material – talks, plays, features, variety shows, and so on – was required to stick faithfully to previously agreed scripts. Since most programmes were live, a 'switch-censor' system was introduced: each studio control room had a copy of the script with orders to switch off the microphone 'instantaneously' if any deviation occurred. To reduce misunderstanding, several BBC staff were seconded to the Ministry of Information, while others headed in the opposite direction. Hence Pat Ryan was 'Home Adviser' to the BBC on behalf of the Ministry, yet also worked for the Corporation: he actually became its 'Controller (Home)' from May 1940 and was described by a senior Corporation figure as '50 per cent our man'. R. T. Clark, meanwhile, talked of the newsroom as 'virtually' a 'section of the Ministry', but also claimed that no 'formal' censorship was in place 'other than that applied to newspapers'. The boundaries were blurred, the rules opaque. But this did at least allow room for interpretation.[19]

The necessity of censorship on security grounds was widely accepted. It 'often seemed unreasonable and irritating', Maurice Gorham conceded, but 'I had a horror of breaking it; you felt you might be the means of men losing their lives'.[20] Alec Sutherland, who worked in the BBC's Recorded Programmes department, remembered the three 'very simple' rules that broadcasters followed:

> No correspondent could use numbers: he couldn't say 'I took a 173 bus' because that might be a clue of some kind. He couldn't say anything about the weather. He couldn't say anything about where a bomb had landed: he couldn't say 'I'm standing at the corner of such and such a place' where there'd just been an incident.[21]

As for the 'switch-censors', Gorham thought the mere fact of their presence 'made people more careful'. Trust between broadcaster and government was clearly a vital ingredient in this arrangement, and it was not always present. Although the BBC's first wartime Director-General, Frederick Ogilvie, acknowledged that everything his staff did was now subservient to the war effort, the government was often reluctant to acknowledge the BBC's expertise in translating raw information into compelling programmes. Winston Churchill continued to nurse his grudges and make 'very offensive' remarks about the Corporation in private. On one occasion the senior controller on night duty at Broadcasting House heard the red emergency phone in front of him bursting unexpectedly into life, and when he picked it up found himself speaking to the prime minister himself. 'And what the Prime Minister said was, "I take strong exception to an item which I have just heard in the Nine o'clock News".' The Controller politely pointed out that this was impossible since it was still only 8.50 p.m. For once, Churchill was rendered speechless. Yet it was clear that even when he had his facts wrong or was temporarily 'indisposed' he was keen to interfere. Fortunately for the BBC it was the Minister of Information, not Churchill, who was responsible for day-to-day guidance. And with Brendan Bracken in the post from the middle of 1941, the Corporation found itself working with someone who usually trusted the broadcaster's own discretion in interpreting censorship policy.[22]

In 1939 and 1940, this smoothly functioning relationship still lay in the future. During the first months of the war, the government gave every impression of wanting to make the BBC's already difficult job even harder. The Ministry of Information kept delaying news releases. It also insisted on seeing in advance the names of all contributors to forthcoming programmes, even musicians, which meant long delays in getting clearance. The inevitable result was that producers opted for the same pre-approved artistes again and again. The repertory companies sequestered at Wood Norton and Bristol proved invaluable reservoirs of talent – so much so, in fact, that each member was soon appearing about ten times a week. Barely two months into the war, the actor Maurice Denham had clocked up a staggering total of 225 appearances on his own. Worst of all, the government required the BBC to broadcast a long list of appeals and exhortations from Whitehall, encouraging the British people, among other things, to make do and mend, put their savings into war bonds, stop sneezing, cut down on food waste, conserve fuel in the home, or grow their own vegetables by digging for victory. If the various ministries had their way, the entire day's radio schedule would have been filled with endless dreary pep talks or fake 'news flashes' delivered by officials. When it came to food rationing, the Corporation was keen to draw the line: it had far too much experience of its own in creating programmes with popular appeal to let Whitehall take over completely. The government's 'Food Economy' campaign, launched in the spring of 1940, was aimed at what officials called the 'feckless fringe' of housewives, those who were 'careless, extravagant, lazy, and completely uninterested in the whole business of keeping house or looking after their families' health'. The BBC transformed this hectoring approach into *Feed the Brute*, an upbeat series of five-minute sketch shows starring 'Gert and Daisy', the comic creations of Elsie and Doris Waters. Each episode saw the pair dispensing advice on using leftovers in favourite recipes or on nourishing alternatives to meat. The BBC's resident gardening presenter, 'C. H.' Middleton, would also pop up, talking enthusiastically about potatoes and onions as 'munitions'. As the war intensified and food supplies tightened further in June 1940, the BBC launched *The Kitchen Front* as a daily advice programme. The Ministry established general policy and content, the BBC chose contributors and shaped the overall presentational style. Its producer, Janet Quigley, emphasised the need for entertainment and variety. 'All our efforts would be defeated', she argued, 'were housewives to feel that the morning cookery talks were "official".' There would be plenty of solid advice: making cheese from sour milk, recipes that worked with dried eggs, how to cook radish tops and bracken fronds. But it was appearances by Gert and Daisy, 'Mrs Buggins' – the comedy working-class housewife played by Mabel Constanduros – and breezy health talks from Charles Hill, the 'Radio Doctor', which leavened the mix. Hill reckoned that it was being allowed a personality and style of his own that made the difference. His scripts were dictated rather than written, and delivered with the minimum of revision or rehearsal, even if that meant that grammatical errors or indelicacies were left in. 'There was always, I think, an expectation that one would use a naughty word', he recalled. 'One gardener was heard to remark to a friend of mine, "I always listen to that there Radio Doctor. He be going to say 'shit' one Friday".'[23]

Up to seven million tuned in to Hill's talks, a good five million to *The Kitchen Front*. Together these programmes helped countless households to eke out the weekly ration – and in doing so made the rationing system itself a more palatable wartime measure. The *Daily Express* raged about 'government control gone mad'. But series like *The Kitchen Front* gave credit to working-class families for the sacrifices they were making and valued 'making do' as a shared experience. At the start of the war, Tom Harrisson, who, as founder of Mass Observation, was far better placed than most Whitehall ministries to assess the national mood, described official rhetoric as being full of an 'ingrained contempt for the civilian masses'. The BBC, at least, was presenting the 'civilian masses' as the backbone of a nation on whose efforts victory depended. If anything, it was middle-class snobberies that were now being chastised on air. 'Don't come over all superior at the mention of fish-and-chips', the Radio Doctor told listeners. 'It's not only very tasty and very sweet – it's first-class grub'.[24]

*

The BBC was discovering more and more whose voices breathed empathy, which tones and accents delighted or offended. Getting this right mattered. Enlisting public support was the BBC's primary role, and the ease with which it could be gained – or lost – was revealed starkly in June 1940 by the contrasting reactions to two well-known radio performers: Churchill, in his new role as prime minister, and the writer J. B. Priestley. Both men were responding to the evacuation of the British Expeditionary Force from Dunkirk and the collapse of France, though in very different ways.

On Tuesday 4 June, Churchill gave a stirring speech to the Commons. Despite a 'colossal military disaster', he told MPs, Britain would go on whatever the cost. 'We shall fight on the beaches, we shall fight on the landing grounds, we shall fight in the fields and in the streets, we shall fight in the hills; we shall never surrender ...' Some in the Chamber thought the fine oratory an 'elaborate cover-up' for failure. As Parliament did not permit the live broadcasting of its proceedings, the rest of the country could pass judgement only from second-hand accounts in BBC news bulletins. The reaction was muted. People thought it a good speech; it just failed to cheer them up. Nella Last, a housewife from Barrow-in-Furness, confessed in her diary to having 'felt rather grave and rather sad about things unsaid rather than said'. As for the soldiers landing bedraggled and disorientated on the south coast, they were already 'seething ... dismayed ... savagely wounded in their pride ... seeking relief in bitter criticism of those set over them'. When France fell two weeks later, Churchill was pressured by his Minister of Information to speak on the radio, even though he 'didn't seem to see the point'. He repeated the speech he had given in Parliament that day, asking the nation to brace itself for the coming struggle, 'and so bear ourselves that if the British Commonwealth and Empire lasts for a thousand years men will still say, "This was their finest hour".' Alas, it was not Churchill's finest hour. He had resented being pressured to go before the microphone, and it showed. He 'just sulked', the junior minister Harold Nicolson noted in his diary. 'As delivered in the House of Commons, that speech was magnificent ... But it sounded ghastly on the wireless. All the great vigour he put into it seemed to evaporate.' Churchill really could do better than this. And it was noticeable that when he next spoke on the radio he was, for once, able to provoke near-unanimous public approval. It was no coincidence that on this occasion he downplayed his obsession with Empire and the British 'race', and talked more inclusively of 'a war of peoples and causes', of ordinary soldiers and civilians.[25]

This was the kind of language that listeners had already heard – and liked – in radio talks by Priestley. His reflections on Dunkirk were broadcast in a special Wednesday edition of *Postscript*, a series offering short personal commentaries immediately after the nine o'clock news. Originally conceived as a rival attraction to Lord Haw-Haw, *Postscript* offered a lesson in the power of downplayed propaganda. BBC producers had wanted something that would 'give our side of the picture' without resorting to 'exaggerated' rhetoric. Their first pick as presenter, the barrister Maurice Healy, had been a disaster: viciously anti-German, patrician, tactless. To illustrate the wartime sacrifice of working people, he talked about a barrister friend whose income had dropped by £1,000. Desperate for 'a contrast in voice, upbringing and outlook', the BBC drafted in Priestley. With his mellow Yorkshire accent and down-to-earth manner, he offered a wry optimism that turned his appearance before the microphone on 5 June into a popular sensation. He framed Dunkirk as a 'miserable blunder' that had ended as an 'epic of gallantry' and contrasted the soulless efficiency of the German war machine with the plucky British, who had improvised their way to safety with hundreds of small boats sailing into 'the inferno, to defy bombs, shells, magnetic mines, torpedoes, machine-gun fire'. 'And our great-grandchildren,' he concluded, 'when they learn how we began this War by snatching glory out of defeat, and then swept on to victory, may also learn how the little holiday steamers made an excursion to hell and came back glorious.' Churchill's response to Dunkirk had been to ask the nation to carry on and make ever greater effort. Priestley's broadcast recognised the sacrifices already made; it saw reasons for hope, even celebration, describing things not only as they were but as they might be. Above all, it forged allegory from the everyday. That flotilla of little ships symbolised the coming together of ordinary British citizens. It pushed what Priestley called 'the official and important personages' into the background and put 'the people' – their 'spirit ... sense, courage and endurance' – centre stage.[26]

The twenty editions of *Postscript* that Priestley went on to present were soaked in talk of Britain's – or, more often, England's – friendliness and tolerance, its fair-mindedness and humour, its patience and calm, its timeless landscape and its deep tradition of peace and freedom. There were large dollops of folksy myth-making in all this. But it was undeniably effective: it was what people certainly wanted – and perhaps needed – to hear. A Staffordshire miner told the BBC that Priestley's 'voice and manner appeal to the working man', while a railway clerk in

Swindon praised him for being 'easy to understand, sincere and honest'. In a clear dig at the country's political elite, Graham Greene, in the *Spectator*, suggested that Priestley 'gave us what the other leaders have failed to give us – an ideology'. For senior Conservative politicians, this was precisely the problem. They caught a whiff of socialism in Priestley's broadcasts, and were particularly discomfited by his talk of a brighter, fairer future. If no burden is too great for the people, Priestley had told listeners, then 'there can't be too rich and too great a reward' for them when all this was over. When Priestley returned for a second series of *Postscript* in 1941 with a promise that his programmes would be 'aggressively democratic', the Conservatives' backbench 1922 Committee protested. The Corporation's subsequent decision not to renew Priestley's contract was explained away in blandly reassuring terms: he was being 'rested' not sacked. But his removal from *Postscript* was nevertheless a victory, both for Churchill, who disliked Priestley's articulation of ultimate war aims, and reactionary figures in the BBC's own hierarchy, such as Richard Maconachie, who had always worried over the 'definite social and political views' the writer had been able to disseminate so successfully.[27]

Victory through harmony

In their brief existence, Priestley's contributions to *Postscript* had symbolised the BBC's shifting position between government and 'the People'. The simple need to keep listeners tuned in trumped every other concern. And it was clear that the British people wanted a BBC that not only sounded a bit more like them but also *understood* them, perhaps even *sympathised* with them. When it came, the BBC's embrace of popular – even explicitly working-class – culture, was not always motivated by purely instrumental concerns: there were many on the payroll who had long believed that the national broadcaster had a duty to reflect the country in all its social diversity. Geoffrey Bridson, who had produced those celebrated portraits of industrial life in the

Workers' Playtime, broadcast in May 1942 to Home and Forces listeners from an unidentified aircraft factory somewhere in Britain. Government ministries wanted the series to include lots of pep talks, but the BBC's Variety department insisted on offering entertainment without strings.

1930s, was *primus inter pares* in this category, and responsible for launching one of the Home Service's biggest wartime hits, *Billy Welcome*. The series featured Wilfred Pickles in the role of genial host travelling the length and breadth of the land to encounter 'ordinary' country folk and tap into their stoic humour through a bit of quick and cheery cross-talk. The basic idea, Bridson explained, was to celebrate the continuity of country life and how it offered something pleasant 'when life in the towns gets drab or difficult or just plain boring'.[28]

The BBC's raft of so-called 'factory' programmes were

also designed to do far more than deliver endless exhortations to increase output. *Workers' Playtime* brought an 'all-star cast of radio and music hall artists' to a different factory canteen several times a week for a live lunchtime broadcast. Within two years of its launch, 257 factories had been visited and 270,000 workers entertained face to face. *Works Wonders*, a series devised in Manchester by Victor Smythe, not only featured munition workers performing their own songs and comedy routines, it even invited workers to produce the show for themselves. The BBC acknowledged that the standards of such amateur performers would 'inevitably be fairly low': what counted was that 'the public takes them to their heart'. The factory series that made the biggest impact of all was *Music While You Work*, first broadcast on Sunday 23 June 1940. For half an hour, twice daily, everyone toiling away on Britain's production lines was promised 'no interruptions by announcements' and nothing but unobtrusive 'rhythmical music'. It was hoped that the new series would not just 'emphasis the drive towards production' but also 'relieve the tedium of work'. Providing this apparently monotonous diet was a challenge for a Variety department that had been drilled to believe that radio demanded bundles of personality and constant changes of tempo and mood. If production lines were to keep moving efficiently any thought of 'subtlety' or 'artistic value' had to be abandoned. 'From the point of view of the general listener we are asking for a *bad* piece of programme building', producers were told. Once it had been refined, the formula proved hugely successful. By the end of the war, some 9,000 large factories and nearly 40,000 smaller factories and workshops were tuning in regularly. Productivity was often up a little. More importantly, munitions workers said that *Music While You Work* helped 'brighten things up'. Millions more listened at home as they did their household chores.[29]

The significance of these factory programmes for public morale was obvious. Introducing *Workers' Playtime* in 1941, the Minister of Labour, Ernest Bevin, told listeners that it was the kind of show that 'makes us *all* feel that we are working

together in the common cause to win this war'. But the programmes marked yet another cultural shift inside the BBC: a
greater willingness to abandon deeply held artistic instincts
about propagating 'the best' and to accept that, for now at least,
what people wanted mattered more. The enthusiasm with
which audiences embraced *Music While You Work* underscored
how radio needed, in the words of John Snagge, to 'take people
away from thinking about the war'.[30]

Music was one means of escape. Comedy was another. The
extraordinary popularity of the wartime series *It's That Man
Again* – *ITMA* – was yet more proof that after an uneven start
the BBC's programme makers were increasingly agile about
tapping into the popular mood. The series had been launched
in the summer of 1939 to such a tepid reaction that it was very
nearly cancelled. Yet by 1944, almost 40 per cent of the population was listening every week. Its scriptwriter, Ted Kavanagh,
calculated that storylines were less important than stock characters – Mrs Mopp: 'Can I do you now, sir', Colonel Chinstrap: 'I
don't mind if I do', and the rest – all orbiting around the series'
star performer, Tommy Handley. Far from tactfully avoiding
the subject of war, *ITMA* made it the backdrop to every scene
before setting out to lampoon all the petty regulations that war
had unleashed: ministry announcements, rationing, restrictions,
careless talk. For its millions of fans, *ITMA* provided a common
reference point and a common vocabulary – a chance to share
punchlines in the street and to revel in the collective joy of prick-
ing pomposity.[31]

If there was one single act of grand policy that contributed
more than anything to the BBC's embrace of popular taste on
the airwaves, it was the decision to launch a full-scale listening
alternative to the Home Service. The BBC had mooted the idea
the moment that war was declared, but it was the pressing need
to entertain bored British troops stationed in France during the
winter months that wore down initial resistance to the idea
in government and military circles. There were wireless sets
aplenty in the soldiers' billets and camp canteens, but reports had

A 1944 episode of *It's That Man Again* – or *ITMA*. Two of its
regular characters, 'Mrs Mopp' (Dorothy Summers) and 'Lady
Poppy-poo-pah' (Jean Capra), are pictured alongside Tommy
Handley. The Variety department, which had spent much of
the war in North Wales, had by now returned to London.

suggested it was the commercial station at Fécamp that was 'listened to morning, noon and night'. In December 1939 the BBC
held urgent discussions with senior officers to design a service for
the army that might also cater for the general listener at home.
Test transmissions began on Sunday 7 January 1940, and a programme 'For the Forces' began properly just over a month later.
Early feedback from troops on the ground revealed an appetite
for news at breakfast and lunchtime, very little enthusiasm for
religion, and requests for a lot more variety and music. If this
important audience was to keep tuning in, the BBC concluded,
the new schedule needed to be light and lively and designed to
work even if it was on in the background. What made the arrival

of the Forces Programme such a momentous event on the home front was that after months of frustration, it gave the British people a choice on the airwaves again. With its generous provision of music, the Forces Programme also offered what Mass Observation called 'a sort of tap listening, available all day as a mental background and relief'. Grace Wyndham Goldie saw it as nothing less than a broadcasting 'revolution'. 'For the first time,' she wrote in the *Listener*, 'the quality of the programmes is being decided from below rather than from above; for the first time the box office, so to speak, is dominant.[32]

*

The BBC's achievements in the early part of the war can be exaggerated, its failures too easily overlooked. Wartime Britain was not always a nation at ease with itself, though it would sometimes have been hard to know it from listening to the wireless. There was scant discussion of shortages in supplies, the break-up of families, public anger over billeting, or, despite the best efforts of *Music While You Work*, the continued low morale and absenteeism on many production lines. Yet if the overall aim of the BBC's programming was to paint a convincing enough picture of a nation pulling together in order to avoid public morale as a whole sinking dangerously low, then it was largely successful. Its emphasis on consensus rather than division meant papering over some very real cracks in the fabric of society, but the BBC's response was never straightforwardly authoritarian or deliberately evasive or monolithic in tone: it could not afford to be. Its programme makers had to accept the mosaic of tastes and moods within the country, and then somehow reflect these back to the audience in ways that suggested the war effort was driven by a sense of common purpose.

To think of this as merely the cynical enactment of policy handed down from on high would be to neglect a vital dimension of the BBC's wartime story. Geoffrey Bridson saw his wartime work at the BBC as part of a crusade to save the world from itself through the power of broadcasting. In the current fight against Nazism, he was happy to be described as a propagandist – a term 'bracketed' in his own mind 'with the Old Testament prophets and the writers of the canonical gospels'. He believed sincerely 'in all we were fighting for', he explained: 'I had only to write what I felt.'[33] Many others inside the BBC also discovered that their work was driven by an emotional commitment to the war effort as much as by a sense of duty. Or, perhaps more accurately, they now found that duty and feeling were indistinguishable.

If there was a single moment when this bond was forged more intensely than any other, it was the autumn of 1940, when the German air raids which had been expected at the outbreak of war finally arrived. As cities and towns all across the country were attacked almost nightly in the Blitz, those who worked at the BBC ceased to be detached observers of the war. As human beings as well as professionals, they came to share with their fellow citizens all the terror and the disruptions – as well as all the excitements and the camaraderie.

The BBC in the Blitz

On Saturday 7 September, wave after wave of German bombers – at least 250 at a time, escorted by countless more fighter planes – passed over London, dropping a deadly cargo of fire bombs and high explosives. The city's anti-aircraft guns responded with a 'terrific barrage', while RAF fighters swooped around the sky frantically. But the attack was overwhelming. Thousands of homes in Woolwich, Silvertown and Rotherhithe were devastated, and whole streets blistered with craters, shattered glass and broken bodies. Throughout the East End, factories, warehouses and docks were engulfed in flames. 'Everywhere you looked was fire. Across the water, north, south, east and west, everywhere.' By the time the all-clear sounded at 5 a.m. on Sunday, 436 people had been killed and another 1,600 seriously injured. Before September was out, the death toll in London alone would reach 5,730. By the time of the last 'big' raid eight months later, in May 1941, more than 43,500 civilians had been killed nationwide, with a further 71,000 seriously injured. Hundreds of thousands of homes and workplaces had been destroyed or badly damaged, while vital supplies had been disrupted across the country. Millions survived the onslaught – prepared, so it seemed, to 'stick it out'. Yet few were untouched completely.[34]

Hitler's aim was to destroy Britain's key national resources: the infrastructure of dockyards, armaments manufacturing, energy supplies, fuel and food. But the national broadcaster's iconic buildings and transmitters were also high on his list of targets. Those who worked for the BBC were not just caught up in the Blitz; they were under direct attack.

Visibility was now a matter of life and death. Enemy bombers were repeatedly helped to their targets in the docklands by the distinctive horseshoe curve of the Thames, which no blackout could prevent from glistening in the darkness. In Portland Place, the white stone hulk of Broadcasting House also 'gleamed brilliantly', especially on moonlit nights. No one inside could fail to be conscious of its ghastly vulnerability. Every morning, Maurice Gorham would walk to work after a noisy night, 'wondering if it would still be there'. Barely a fortnight of the Blitz had passed before bombs 'knocked hell' out of Oxford Street, Berkeley Square and surrounding areas. A direct hit on 'BH' at some point 'seemed inevitable'.[35]

A few basic measures were already in place in the hope of protecting the building and its occupants. A nightly fire watch involved staff taking turns to keep a lookout from the roof. Others volunteered to work with air defence services such as the Observer Corps, which supplied RAF Fighter Command with crucial information about the position of enemy planes. Whenever they came close, a warning bell would send hundreds of their colleagues scurrying to take shelter. The BBC laid on its own armoured bus to get staff home at night, and getting a ride was, for many, 'the only time one really felt safe'. Since the

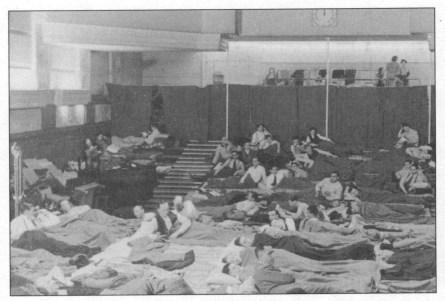

Staff sleeping on mattresses in the concert hall of Broadcasting House in October 1940. The usual seating had been removed and a line of curtains was put up towards the back to create separate zones for men and women.

work of broadcasting was now going on around the clock the BBC also provided emergency sleeping accommodation. The complex task of finding safe space in central London for around 400 men and women every night fell to Stuart Williams. The largest concentration of bedding was in Broadcasting House itself, where seating was removed from the concert hall so it could be pressed into service as a dormitory. Williams hired two experienced box office assistants from a West End theatre to run a nightly booking system. 'Although mattresses had to be removed from certain areas during the day, the House Staff had their plans. They put them down in exactly the same positions the following night, and the individual was given a ticket when he booked his bed, which had on it "Your Bed" and showed the actual location and the actual place where the bed would be.' The delicate issue of cleanliness was less easily solved. At first, anyone staying overnight had to make do with a bare mattress and pillow and just a couple of blankets. Later, sleeping bags were issued that could be laundered weekly. Unfortunately these were often in short supply because local authorities were also busy stockpiling them as shrouds.[36]

One of those who took advantage of the overnight service was Clare Lawson Dick, who worked in the Registry. When her flat in Regent's Park was badly damaged by an incendiary bomb, she joined those taking up semi-permanent residence in what she referred to affectionately as 'our burrows': the Broadcasting House basement. It was a troglodytic experience to which staff adapted remarkably well. Whenever the sirens sounded they would descend into the labyrinth of underground floors where they 'worked and played, ate and drank' –revelling in the exotic encounters the Blitz had suddenly made possible: 'Freedom fighters from France still in their fishermen's blouses in which they had just rowed across the Channel ... secretaries formed into firefighting teams; producers, actors, writers, journalists, war correspondents, and the wonderful members of the BBC's foreign teams who broadcast to Europe and the world' – all trapped together for a few hours by the air raid raging above. When it was time for sleep, Lawson Dick would usually make her way to 'Shelter D', a small brick cellar under the neighbouring Egton House which she shared with Stephen Tallents, now the Controller of the BBC's Overseas Service. Others in possession of one of Williams's tickets would make their way to the numbered mattresses laid out in tiered steps inside the concert hall, where a washing line festooned with blankets divided the men's section at the bottom from the women's at the top. With people coming and going at all hours, there was often little rest to be had and people would start idly wandering the maze of nearby corridors.[37] During one particularly terrifying air raid in which Broadcasting House shook with every explosion, Clare Lawson Dick was with three of her workmates, 'all of us in pyjamas and dressing gowns', when she bumped into the Director-General, Frederick Ogilvie. He immediately offered them the use of his sub-basement redoubt, 'a bare brick room about the size of a bathroom':

We were grateful and lay down on its concrete floor sharing the single cushion between the four of us. Then, through the wall from an adjoining studio we heard the voice of Ed Murrow beginning a broadcast to America with the words, 'This is England's zero hour'. And we felt more wretched than before.[38]

Siege conditions created moments of real intimacy. In one corner could be found the Home news editor, R. T. Clark, living permanently inside Broadcasting House, and, when not asleep in his bunk, smoking and drinking and talking with Murrow until the early hours. In another would be Pat Ryan, lying on his desk or sitting on the floor, as he shared with his team shards of information about the latest turn of events; and in a corridor nearby a stray celebrity, whose studio performance had been interrupted by the latest air raid and who was now looking for a meal or some pleasant company to help pass the time. Through the autumn and winter of 1940 and in the early months of 1941, the BBC's basement retreats possessed what Clare Lawson Dick described as a rich 'communal life': people 'continuously gossiping with one another, eating re-constituted eggs, drinking ersatz coffee, sleeping three hundred at a time, huddled on the floor'. Staff were not entirely cut off from the world outside. At the end of a shift, the newsreader Bruce Belfrage would put on the uniform of a special constable to direct traffic, and Maurice Gorham worked on the streets as an ARP warden. Many of the women in the Duplicating Section travelled in each day from Lambeth and Stepney – two areas of the city that suffered the heaviest bombardment – having spent their nights in the crowded shelters of the London Underground. Dodging the Luftwaffe, travelling past bombed-out houses, making forays into shops to find provisions, doing voluntary shifts alongside other civilians: it was impossible for the BBC's staff not to experience at close quarters the disruption and devastation that now constituted daily life for much of Britain. Yet once inside a BBC building, work offered the kind of intense existence that Clare

Lawson Dick found exhilarating. 'To come in from the blitz ... brought the inner glow of arriving at the place where one was meant to be. Where one joined one's tribe and took part in the rituals we all understood so well.'[39]

★

All sense of routine and relative safety was suddenly shattered in October 1940, when Broadcasting House suffered the direct hit that had long been feared.

The Luftwaffe had been getting closer all the time. St George's Hall next door had been gutted by an incendiary in the final week of September. Soon afterwards, a bomb struck the corner of the Langham Hotel opposite, destroying several rooms reserved for announcers working late shifts. Local residents complained that they were suffering directly as a result of Broadcasting House's 'glaring whiteness' and demanded that it be fully camouflaged. On Tuesday 15 October, the BBC responded by contracting a firm of painters to 'tone down' the building's external surfaces.[40]

The move came too late. That same evening, bombs began to rain down all over London's West End. First, the George, a favourite BBC pub, was hit. Moments later, several bombs landed in Portland Place. It was just after eight o'clock when Olive Shapley got off the tube at Regent's Park station and was walking towards Broadcasting House:

Halfway there the sky suddenly seemed to break overhead and a great noise started up. Bombs screamed and blazing shrapnel danced about in the streets. I realised that this had to be a determined attack on Broadcasting House, but in my panic I continued to try to reach the safety of the building ... Then there was a deafening roar and a cloud of smoke went up, completely enveloping both Broadcasting House and the BBC's nearby Langham building.[41]

A 500 lb bomb had hurtled through a seventh-floor window. Crashing through two more floors, several offices and the BBC's switchboard room, it came to rest in the Music Library on the fifth floor. The whole building shuddered, causing so much damage that no one realised it was a delayed-action bomb that had not yet exploded. As the area was being evacuated, a small group of firefighters and BBC staff tried desperately to drag the bomb towards a window. It was then, at exactly one minute and fifty seconds past nine, that it went off.[42]

Bruce Belfrage was in a basement studio, having just started reading the main evening news. In sitting rooms across the country, listeners heard a faint background rumble as Belfrage paused for a split second to blow the plaster and soot off the script in front of him before carrying on with the rest of the bulletin. Although he was later congratulated for his sangfroid, he actually spent the next few minutes experiencing a severe attack of claustrophobia, not knowing 'whether it was still possible to get out into the street'. Mary Lewis was also in the building, having just left the Duplicating Section to bed down for the night. 'The place seemed to rock a bit and a lot of dust came down, but nothing much happened in the Concert Hall. Then we realised people were trapped in the studio on the third floor and throughout that night you could hear drills trying to get them out … it was pretty unpleasant: nobody quite knew how many people were involved.' By the following morning, the picture was clearer. Most of those trapped on the third floor had been staff using Studio 3A as a 'secure' area. In all, six people – three men and three women – had been killed and twenty-three hurt; another man died of his injuries two days later. Though the core structure of Broadcasting House had survived, the place was a mess and studios on three floors had been put out of action for at least a year.[43]

A few weeks later the BBC suffered a second blow. Just after 10 p.m. on Sunday 8 December 1940, a large landmine floated down on its parachute into Portland Place and became entangled with a lamp post before exploding. The blast killed a

Members of the BBC's house staff help sift through the remains
of the Music Library, which, along with several studios, had been
badly damaged by the bomb which struck Broadcasting House on
the night of 15 October 1940. Seven people died in the attack.

policeman, tore through windows and offices in all directions,
and ruptured a maze of water mains and sewage pipes. An off-
duty recording engineer standing just yards away was thrown
to the ground, from where he watched in horror as chunks
of recently repaired masonry started to fall from Broadcasting House. Gripping the kerb as successive blast waves and a

whirlwind of shrapnel flew into him, he felt as if he were in 'a scene from Dante's Inferno', with flames everywhere and 'a few dark huddled bodies nearby'. Inside the building, electrical fires were breaking out, and water cascading down stairways into studios and control rooms. Staff responsible for programmes already on-air carried on for another hour or so before being ordered out. As people streamed through the exits and dodged the shrapnel, the BBC's contingency plans swung into action. Alec Sutherland, from the Recorded Programmes department, hurriedly gathered up 'about a ton' of discs on which the next day's programmes had just been compiled and flagged down the BBC armoured car, which took him to Maida Vale. Here, the BBC had converted an old skating rink into an emergency back-up facility. 'I figured that I could commandeer a studio and put out the recordings.' In the end 'only one bulletin was missed and that was in Danish'. Early the next day, he made duplicates of every programme yet to be broadcast and sent them by taxi to Wood Norton: the prospect of them being lost forever in another attack was too horrific to contemplate.[44]

A flurry of activity followed in the weeks ahead. A 10,000-ton steel-reinforced concrete 'stronghold', with walls and ceilings some eight feet thick, was hastily constructed at the back of Broadcasting House, to provide a back-up switchboard and four bomb-proof emergency studios. Meanwhile, the slow drift of staff from the regional outposts back to central London, which had been underway since the spring, went into reverse.[45]

For now, the staff of the European language services were packed off to Maida Vale. Few were happy with the arrangement, not least because the building had an enormous glass roof that left its new inhabitants feeling 'like cattle in a market which might at any moment become a slaughterhouse'. Their worst fears were realised the following spring, when a high explosive bomb struck the building, killing one member of the German Service and injuring several others. Bombs also damaged a large part of Bedford College and landed next to the old Peter Robinson department store at 200 Oxford Street – both of which

were now occupied by the BBC. As if to emphasis the continuing danger, a heavy raid on the night of Wednesday 16 April
1941 came horribly close to Broadcasting House again, this time
destroying the best part of a neighbouring street.[46]

By this stage, secret planning for the wholesale departure
of the BBC from its main premises had begun. It had always
been envisaged that, if London should become uninhabitable,
Wood Norton would become the Corporation's main wartime
headquarters. But it wasn't only London that was prey to
German bombing raids. Several BBC transmitters were badly
damaged or destroyed, including one that had been erected in
the grounds of a biscuit factory in Birmingham: on the night
of Tuesday 19 November 1940, three staff on duty there were
killed. On Friday 21 February 1941, the BBC's Swansea studios
burnt down. Manchester, where Val Gielgud had been eager to
relocate his drama team, continued to suffer regular bombard-
ments and blackout conditions 'worse even than in London'.
It was, however, the BBC's Bristol redoubt that bore the brunt
of disruption. After one particularly nasty attack in March 1941,
members of the Music department were swiftly relocated to
Bedford to join Religious Broadcasting, while Variety staff were
divided between a small outpost in Weston-super-Mare and
a larger group who travelled, along with seventeen dogs and
a parrot, up to Bangor in North Wales. It was here that they
remained until the end of the war, producing hit shows such as
ITMA and *Happidrome* from various seaside venues on the North
Wales coast. Those left behind in Bristol were given access to
one of the most bizarre refuges of the whole war: the Clifton
Rocks funicular railway, where seven studios were built in tiers
up its steep surface, each one half-buried and equipped with its
own emergency power supply and food store.[47]

Throughout the tail end of 1940 and most of the following
year, staff everywhere were either pulling down the hatches or
on the move. Billeting officers were having to find accommodation at short notice. Church halls, theatres and country houses
were being kitted out at breakneck speed. By the close of 1941,

the Corporation's 10,000 employees had been broken up into as many as 250 different 'establishments' scattered widely across the country.[48]

In the midst of all this, it was often hard for the legendary 'Blitz spirit' to thrive or for that 'inner glow' that Clare Lawson experienced not to dim a little. Val Gielgud, who had previously enjoyed nothing better than a night at the theatre preceded by a 'capital partridge and a good bottle of claret', filled the pages of his diary with a litany of complaints: not just the constant, disheartening struggle to create decent radio in the face of inadequate studios and frequent interruptions from air raids, but all the inconveniences of daily life, including trains that were dark, unheated and slow, and weather – especially in Manchester – that was beastly. Others were angry at the constant danger they faced from being an enemy target. Reports from Maida Vale, for instance, suggested that staff there were getting 'very bolshie'. But the most common emotional responses echoed those of the civilian population at large: a complex mix of irritation, fear, exhilaration and fortitude. Even Gielgud confessed to 'a certain feeling of stimulation' from being in London during an air raid. Whatever the horrors of the Blitz at its peak, the intense feeling of being under siege had, he thought, produced 'a general gutfulness and an almost "front-line" sense of camaraderie'.[49] Keeping programmes on the air had become a high-wire act, involving hastily arranged contingency plans and working hours lived under extraordinary conditions: taking cover, sleeping rough, being confronted with acute moments of chaos and danger. It had stretched the nerves of the BBC's staff to breaking point. It had also forged bonds of loyalty and friendship as intense as any in the Corporation's history.

Social revolution?

The vast quantities of ordnance dropped on Britain during the Blitz could not blast into oblivion deeply entrenched social divisions. There had been shockingly unequal access to shelter

Audrey Russell interviewing a woman who had just lost her home during a V2 rocket attack in September 1944. Russell valued working for *Radio Newsreel*, but regarded reporting duties covering bombed-out streets or unexploded bombs as 'very unpleasant … I didn't like them at all'.

during the air raids of autumn 1940, with the poorest provision being among the most vulnerable working-class communities. In London's West End, expensive restaurants still managed to have rationed items and many delicacies on the menu, while in the most heavily bombed parts of the East End there were recurring food shortages for aid workers. Iniquities such as these persisted inside the BBC just as they did in the country at large. When the Variety department was exiled from London, one of its star producers, Howard Thomas, talked warmly of the 'comradeship' he and his fellow refugees shared. He also admitted later that he and his fellow producers had 'basked in VIP treatment' in the best billets while their secretaries were herded into hostels. It was an arrangement replicated across the Corporation.[50]

Even so, the notion of a 'People's War' was not entirely mythical. 'Fair shares' and 'equal sacrifice' were the watchwords of civilian life: if anyone tried to pull rank or refused to muck in, their behaviour rarely passed unnoticed – especially since it was ordinary workers who had proved themselves the 'quiet heroes' of the home front. This was as true of life inside the BBC as anywhere else. Clare Lawson Dick remembered vividly being in the basement canteen at Broadcasting House for breakfast one day, when a group of firefighters, 'weary and dirty after fighting fires in the neighbourhood all night' came in and were encouraged by everyone to go to the front of the queue. Everyone that is, except J. B. Priestley, who also happened to be there and who complained to the Director-General, standing nearby, that it was 'disgraceful that people of their importance should be held up'. Ogilvie, 'rightly outraged', replied tartly to Priestley that 'It is by putting over very different views in your *Postscripts* that you have become so much admired by the public'.[51]

The egalitarian society Priestley had mythologised was starting to take fragile root in parts of the BBC. This was the moment when first names started to be used more freely in the newsroom and when Bruce Belfrage refused to put on a coat to meet a cabinet minister because he thought it 'just nonsense in the middle of a total war'. The 'almost perpetual discomfort' of days and nights spent in the cramped and airless Broadcasting House basement, he explained, had produced in him 'a totally unreasoning resentment towards authority'. Stuart Williams turned up to the Control Board every day unshaven and wearing an open-necked shirt, not as an act of rebellion, he said, but because it was hard in extreme conditions 'to pay particular attention to the hour of the day and the seniority of those to whom we were reporting'. The dramatic dispersal of the BBC operation across so many buildings in so many towns and cities had been designed with the hope that London would remain at the apex of a well-planned command-and-control system. But the day-to-day reality was that places like Bristol and Bangor and Wood Norton rapidly developed 'their own little autonomy'. There were edicts and decisions aplenty, but according to Stuart Williams the priority was 'to achieve results very rapidly': 'the old deliberations of major issues, we had no time for.' After all the centralisation of the 1930s, some much-needed room for local initiative was creeping back.[52]

Broadcasters had also put their bodies on the line. It made them not just observers of the war but participants. The impulse to create the image of a People's War, which had begun as a tactical necessity, was emerging from the rubble and the noise as something more human, more organic – more deeply *felt*. When Frank Gillard arrived at Broadcasting House as a newly minted war correspondent in 1941, after several years freelancing for the BBC in Bristol, he discovered an atmosphere transformed from the 'rather detached, slightly cold' environment he had once known. 'I found', he said, 'a great sense of mission and purpose':

> It was a new BBC, and it was a BBC that was, I would say, totally identified with the life of ordinary, everyday people. Every day, twice a day, you had these sessions of *Music While You Work* ... Every day, you had *Workers' Playtime* broadcast from factories ... variety stars entertaining workers and so on. The emphasis was all that way. The BBC was with the people ... And it was quite exhilarating to be in it. Yes, we were working under improvised conditions. We were working with makeshift equipment. We were worn out because we got no sleep at night because of air raids and that sort of thing. But we were doing something that was important for the morale of the country, we were part of the great national war-effort ... The BBC in a couple of years became an absolutely revolutionised institution.[53]

These are striking words, though not untypical. The ethos of collective effort for collective gain was now widely shared, even among staff who usually enjoyed the high life. Through the eight months of the Blitz, Val Gielgud had spent countless nights on Home Guard duty – 'chilly on the roof above Manchester with the autumn fog', sitting with a shotgun in Broadcasting House control room for five hours 'in a draught of refrigerated air' – and dreaming quietly of America. 'What wouldn't I give for one evening in a city with lights', he confided. Yet when the chance eventually came in the form of a lucrative job offer from Hollywood he turned it down in an instant. The movies, he explained, had 'only the remotest connection with the war effort'.[54] Despite all the darkness and the dangers and the discomforts of home – or, more accurately, *because* of them – he knew deep down that the BBC really *was* part of the war effort.

As for that other famous phrase to emerge from the Blitz, that the nation had 'stood alone': it had little basis in reality. The Soviet Union and the United States were not fighting Allies until 1941, but Britain was already dependent on the military, industrial and diplomatic support of the dominions, colonies and dependencies, and the assistance of refugees from occupied Europe. The wartime BBC was a cosmopolitan enterprise, too. One of the reasons Frank Gillard believed it had been transformed after 1939 was through the 'great infusion of new people'. Many of these latest recruits were foreigners. And as the threat of invasion receded and the focus shifted to the liberation of Europe, it was the largely hidden and sometimes totally secret work with which these men and women were engaged that would lay the foundations for the BBC's reputation as an international broadcaster – and contribute materially to the defeat of Nazism.

7

LONDON CALLING

I think we can say without boasting that even in the black days of defeat we managed to convince people that if they wanted the truth they had to listen to London.

Richard Crossman, Political Warfare Executive, 1941

In the summer months leading up to the Blitz, a strange air of paranoia had settled over Britain. The Low Countries and France had fallen, and there were persistent rumours that the country was riddled with treacherous foreigners poised to support an imminent invasion. Several hundred 'enemy aliens' had already been interned or placed under curfew, but there was still talk of the 'enemy in our midst'. People imagined worrying signs wherever they looked: marks left on telegraph poles as a secret code for invading troops; pigeons carrying messages abroad; ice cream sold by Italians that was poisoned. With public anxiety at its height, the cabinet decided that 'Defence Regulation 18B', authorising the internment of suspected traitors, would be applied with renewed vigour.[1]

It was now that the country's spymasters turned their gaze on one of the founding fathers of the BBC. Peter Eckersley had left his post as Chief Engineer back in 1929, dismissed because of a divorce scandal. But he had been keeping up his interest in broadcasting technology. And in the summer of 1939, as Europe was sliding to war, he had been meeting businessmen, raising money, and setting up companies. His ambition: to launch a new commercial radio station somewhere on the coast of northern Holland or Germany, broadcasting to Britain in English.

If Eckersley's ambition had simply been to make himself rich, matters might have rested there. MI5 and Special Branch suspected more sinister motives, however. The previous autumn, officers from New Scotland Yard had interviewed Eckersley's typist. She told them that her boss had posted plans for the radio station to 'an important German official of some sort' in Berlin. The officers had also questioned one of Eckersley's business partners, who told them that Eckersley had been 'continually' travelling to Germany, that he 'was definitely pro-Nazi ... a great admirer of Hitler' and 'violently anti-Semitic'. His wife, Dorothy, had even gone to Germany to attend one of the Nuremburg rallies; she was in Germany now, with her son, working 'hand-in-glove' with the Nazis arranging a number of new radio stations.[2]

More enquiries followed. Special Branch heard that Eckersley was deeply 'mixed up' with Oswald Mosley and various financial backers of the old British Union of Fascists. Mosley, it appeared, had got a concession 'out of Hitler' to create a radio station at the coastal town of Norddeich and had subsequently offered Eckersley £1,500 a year. MI5 now decided that they should interview Eckersley themselves. Unfortunately, by the time they got around to looking for him, he had gone to ground – 'believed to be abroad', though no one knew precisely where.[3]

The evidence against Eckersley remained largely circumstantial. But the investigations against him were a measure of how seriously the threat of radio propaganda emanating from Nazi-occupied Europe was now being taken. William Joyce's broadcasts from Hamburg had already demonstrated that the war on the ground was going to be accompanied by a battle of words across international airwaves. The Nazis had embraced radio as 'the most modern, the strongest and the most revolutionary weapon' in their armoury. Britain could not stand idly by, and although the BBC's official position had been that 'deliberate perversion of the truth' was to be avoided, it could hardly avoid being sucked into the propaganda war.[4] The task of sustaining morale among millions of fellow Europeans in the years between occupation and liberation would demand endless ingenuity and patience from the Corporation. Aside from the inevitable struggle to maintain a degree of editorial independence, it daily faced the awful prospect that broadcasting the wrong words could be a matter of life and death for its clandestine listeners abroad.

'All the tongues of Babel'

Broadcasting to Europe began in the most makeshift of ways. On Tuesday 27 September 1938, the BBC broadcast Neville Chamberlain's famous speech justifying his attempts to secure a deal with Hitler. 'How horrible, fantastic, incredible it is', he told listeners to the National Programme, 'that we should be digging trenches and trying on gas masks here because of a quarrel in a faraway country between people of whom we know nothing.' Only hours earlier, the Foreign Office had contacted the BBC asking it to translate the speech and broadcast it in German, French and Italian. There were French and Italian speakers to hand, but for the German broadcast the BBC had to whisk Robert Lucas, the London correspondent of an Austrian newspaper, to Broadcasting House. As Chamberlain's speech came stuttering through on a telex machine sentence by sentence, a slightly flustered Lucas was asked to translate. Sitting in a studio next door was the illustrator Walter Goetz, who had been plucked out of a cocktail party and asked to read into the microphone Lucas's frantically scribbled translation. It was Goetz's first time on-air, the telex machine kept stopping, and the translations were almost certainly heard by no more than a handful of listeners. But a precedent had been set. Daily broadcasts – just fifteen minutes each in French, German and Italian – continued from the autumn of 1938 onwards. A 'European Service' had been created, *de facto* if not yet *de jure*.[5]

In supporting this new venture, the BBC could draw on nearly six years' experience in broadcasting to other parts of the globe. Its Empire Service, launched back in 1932, had embodied one of John Reith's long-held ambitions: to use broadcasting as a 'consolidatory' influence, not just within Britain but throughout the dominions – Canada, Australia, New Zealand, and South Africa, as part of the white, English-speaking 'British world' – as well as the colonies, in other words, India and Britain's dependent territories in the Caribbean, Africa and the Pacific. By transmitting English-language programmes to these scattered places, the BBC hoped it would help Britons in what it called 'the back of beyond' to stay in touch with their old homeland. It hoped, too, that broadcasting would help the Mother Country 'diffuse its ideas and its culture' more widely. The BBC was soon beaming some fifteen or sixteen hours of programming a day in all directions – not just news, but features, vaudeville, light music, sports commentaries, Big Ben, and the voice of the nightingale.[6]

These first overseas broadcasts made no attempt to provide programmes in local languages. But by the mid-1930s, Italian, American and Russian services for overseas listeners were all expanding – and all increasingly influential. Since 1933, Nazi Germany in particular had been investing heavily in transmitters and sending out programmes with a strong propagandist slant on international affairs. The BBC warned the government that there was a growing need to counteract these foreign stations. Sentimental talk of Empire broadcasting as a means to maintain personal ties to the Mother Country gradually gave way to more muscular talk of the need to 'project' Britain and its democratic traditions.

The Middle East, where Britain assumed a strong strategic interest, became the first flashpoint. The British Foreign Office had become especially alarmed by a radio station at Bari in southern Italy, which had begun spewing out inflammable propaganda in Arabic on behalf of Mussolini's fascists. The government gave the go-ahead for the BBC to begin its own Arabic Service. From Monday 3 January 1938, listeners were provided with just over an hour of broadcasting every evening

– a mixture of music, poetry, talks, drama, all generally high-brow in tone. News bulletins were a key part of the schedule, though the very first one sent shockwaves through Whitehall by reporting the hanging of a Palestinian by order of British military authorities. Rex Leeper, the head of the Foreign Office's news department, was appalled. The BBC, he argued, needed to accept the regular 'selection and omission' of certain items. The BBC's Empire Service news editor replied bluntly that the 'suppression of truth runs counter to the Corporation's policy'. And there the matter rested: an unspoken stalemate, without any formal agreement being inscribed in a sacred text, and with issues of principle shunted aside.[7]

It was an awkward foretaste of the close but fretful relationship between the BBC and the government when it came to international broadcasting in wartime. On one side, ministers and civil servants had accepted that any attempt at spreading official propaganda would most likely succeed if done through a trusted source such as the BBC. This meant the state accepting some loss of control over the process. On the other, the BBC had maintained that its credibility depended on audiences continuing to believe in its complete editorial independence. Given its status as a national broadcaster, however, it also recognised a need to be informed by government policy and thinking. The two parties were now committed, whether they liked it or not, to close and continuous collaboration.

★

From 1939 onwards, the foreign-language services that had slipped quietly into existence in 1938 took on a more confident life and identity of their own. By May 1944, the BBC would be broadcasting in forty-six different languages, its output hours would have trebled, its staff numbers quadrupled, its transmitter-power grown fivefold. The Corporation's burgeoning international activity was by then large enough to be split into two fairly autonomous branches. The old Empire Service had evolved into a new and expanded 'Overseas Service', which was now broadcasting separately to Latin America, North America and the West Indies, the Pacific, Africa, the Near East, and India. Meanwhile, the separately organised 'European Service' was providing regular programmes not just in German, French and Italian, but in Polish, Czech, Slovak, Romanian, Hungarian, Serbo-Croatian, Greek, Dutch, Danish, Flemish, Swedish, Spanish and Portuguese – in fact, in just about every major language spoken on the Continent.[8]

Servicing output on this scale represented an enormous challenge. It was hard enough to get people with the right language skills. But once recruited, their status inside the Corporation was still far from straightforward. The European Service, for instance, ended up being organised around a 'Central Desk' where news was scripted by British-born staff; these stories were then distributed to the different language sections to be translated and assembled into bespoke bulletins by small teams of native language speakers, mostly refugees now exiled in Britain. Each of these teams, in turn, would remain under the watchful eye of a 'supervisor', who had to be British-born but also reasonably fluent in the language concerned. According to the historian Alan Bullock, then a young duty editor on the Central Desk, the supervisor was there just in case any of the foreign staff 'suddenly started to say "Hurrah for Hitler"'. This complex arrangement meant that for each and every language service, the BBC needed to recruit – and get security clearance for – a sizeable pool of writers, translators, supervisors and announcers.[9]

Office space and studio facilities could barely keep pace with demand. Some Overseas staff had been posted to Wood Norton or nearby Abbey Manor from the beginning of the war. After June 1941, many moved back to London, where they made a decent if rather makeshift home for themselves at 200 Oxford Street. Later still, they relocated to one or other of the four hulking blocks of Bush House near the Strand. The European Service, meanwhile, had begun modestly in a small corner of Broadcasting House, though bomb damage forced its relocation to Bedford College and the 'squalid and dangerous' studios at Maida Vale.[10] From January 1941, and much to their relief, its staff were offered the lower ground floor and basement of Bush House. Within three years they had taken over several of the upper floors and were nearly a thousand strong.

'Bush' therefore became very much the beating heart of the BBC's international broadcasting operation, its canteen almost certainly the most culturally diverse meeting place in London. European émigrés were particularly important: they knew intimately the mindsets of listeners back home on the Continent. They were, however, far from being a unified group. Indeed, one Bush House inhabitant described its narrow corridors as the site of what sometimes looked like 'civil war on a cosmopolitan scale'.[11] The different language sections had their own character, defined in part by the people who led them and the people they employed. And although the European Service would constantly try to assert a collective sense of identity, it was at the level of these smaller teams that grand strategy had to be translated into the nuts and bolts of actual programmes.

Giants of Bush House: the German and French Services

The two most powerful language sections at Bush House were the German and the French. What they had in common was their size and a proud spirit of independence. Yet they each had very distinct challenges. One broadcast directly to Britain's enemies; the other to allies living under occupation. The two services were also strikingly different in their working cultures – each one shaped profoundly by the individual personalities who made its programmes.

The German section had always drawn on a group of highly talented refugees, many of them Jewish. They included, among others, the prominent lawyer, Carl Brinitzer; the film actor and director Walter Rilla; the theatre director, Julius Gellner; and, fresh from his experience fighting in the Spanish Civil War, the expressionist writer Karl Otten. One of the youngest recruits was Martin Esslin, born in Budapest but educated in Vienna, and fluent in five languages. Officially, the job of all these native German speakers was to act as translators or occasional script-writers: they were not supposed to speak on-air themselves lest the Nazis accused the BBC of being a mouthpiece for disgruntled exiles. The microphone was therefore reserved in the first instance for people such as the Professor of Political Economy at Aberdeen, Lindley Fraser, or the two young Oxford academics, Richard Crossman and Patrick Gordon Walker. The *Sonderberichte* – special reports that regularly set out British views on international affairs – were the responsibility of another Briton, Leonard Miall, who described his job as 'to get well-known English people to write two scripts per night' and arrange for them to be translated as speedily as possible. Given this formal division of labour along national lines, Alan Bullock's blunt assessment was that the foreign refugees, though distinguished in their own fields, 'regarded themselves as helots, and, on the whole, we regarded them as that, too'.[12]

This was not how the native German speakers saw things. Martin Esslin reckoned they were only cast in the role of 'anonymous handmaidens' because in wartime Britain 'it was obviously "not cricket" to *say* that the German people, or Austrians in my case, contributed something to the actual creative thinking'. But it was actually Esslin, seen as 'the bottle-washer' of the team on account of his extreme youth, who was the true author of 'literally hundreds' of the talks delivered on air by announcers such as Lindley Fraser. In his view, Fraser and the rest 'were merely lending their British voices to *our* commentaries'. Esslin's other contribution to the wartime German Service was his inventive manipulation of Hitler's speeches. He discovered that the library in Broadcasting House possessed recordings of almost every public performance by Hitler since 1933, and he spent his spare time listening to them and making detailed notes so that he 'knew every Hitler speech by heart'. He then turned this deep knowledge into hundreds of pieces of powerful radio propaganda by selecting clips of Hitler's own

A team from the German Service answers questions sent in
by listeners, 1943. The man in shirtsleeves is Hugh Carleton
Greene. Sitting opposite him is one of the Service's most regular
presenters, Lindley Fraser, and on the other side of the glass
is Hans Buxbaum, a native German-speaking producer.

voice and juxtaposing them with snippets of more recent news
in order to demonstrate with stunning clarity quite how many
of the Fuhrer's promises had been broken.[13]

Other programmes were less durable. Originally, most
transmissions to Europe tried to imitate the Home Service by
encompassing lots of different genres, all pulled together into a
richly mixed schedule. But this made it hard to achieve a consistent tone or create a focused message. Senior figures inside the
BBC and government were seriously worried that the German
Service's programmes, many of which reflected the deeply cul-
tured, progressive values of their makers – 'what Goethe had
said about humanism and so on', in Esslin's rather dismissive
judgement – were simply too rarefied for winning the rough-
and-tumble propaganda war.[14]

The appointment in October 1940 of a decisive and powerful

new head unleashed a whirlwind of change. Hugh Carleton Greene had been the *Daily Telegraph*'s star foreign correspondent before the war, reporting from Berlin and Warsaw. More recently, he had worked for military intelligence, where his job had been to interrogate captured Luftwaffe pilots. Those who met him described him as 'courteously quiet' but also 'ruthless', capable of fixing someone with whom he disagreed with a 'sort of basilisk's stare'. Greene arrived 'bursting out of an air force uniform' and armed to the teeth with strong opinions about the need for change. He heartily disliked many of the talks and features for their 'wishy-washy liberal sentimental nonsense about liberty and so on'. 'We want facts, you see', he told his staff. What followed was a general toughening-up of content. Rilla and Otten were sidelined and the British actor Marius Goring, then a sergeant in the Intelligence Corps, was brought in to overhaul features. There was also a determined effort to reach the 'ordinary' German listener in language that was simple and accessible. The schedule now included regular appearances by *Kurt und Willi*, two characters whose dialogue was written in the Berlin dialect, and *Aus der Freien Welt*, which included the hot jazz and swing records that were forbidden in Germany. There was an early-morning 'Workers Programme' along with series targeted at German sea crews and air-force personnel. These listed the names of dead or captured fighters – information that proved a highly effective incentive for concerned relatives to keep tuning in. Above all, Greene ensured that bulletins and talks were up to date. The keenly felt sense of competition with Goebbels' propaganda machine meant that, as Bullock put it, 'everything was to be sacrificed to getting news as promptly as possible … whatever else there was would always be subsidiary'. It had to be accurate, too. Greene knew there was a great deal of 'cross-listening' throughout Europe: people were eavesdropping on all sorts of programmes, including the Home Service in Britain. To protect its reputation for truth, every BBC outlet needed to carry the same basic account of events. It also meant admitting to military defeats as well as victories – something that involved plenty of arguments with the armed services at home but built up trust among audiences abroad.[15]

Over time, the German Service's sober, confident tone created a lasting 'fund of credibility' with listeners in Germany who might otherwise have remained highly sceptical of accounts coming from the enemy. The penalties imposed for any citizen caught listening to foreign radio were ferocious. Yet anecdotal evidence suggested that the numbers tuned to London were growing, and that German audiences were comparing the BBC's matter-of-fact approach more and more favourably with the 'hectic shouting and neurotic heroism' of their own broadcasters. Hitler's military defeats in Russia and North Africa in 1942 helped turn a corner – for the BBC as much as for the Allies. The Nazi's hold over domestic audiences had depended hugely on their success in military attacks. With that disappearing fast, listeners were drifting away. The radio, they had once been taught to believe, was an 'oracle holding the secrets of the future'. And the secrets had migrated to London.[16]

*

By the time Hugh Carleton Greene had finished overhauling his German team, they occupied the whole of one side of Bush House's fourth floor. Arranged on the opposite side was that other teeming giant of the BBC's wartime overseas operations, the French Service. Here, there was the same organisational structure: native language speakers coexisting with a select group of British-born staff in supervisory roles. Yet a very different atmosphere prevailed. While the German Service was, in Alan Bullock's words, 'deadpan and underplayed', the French was 'romantic and *con brio*'. Bullock reckoned that this reflected the contrasting personalities of the two departmental heads. Greene's opposite number was the former *Guardian* correspondent, Darsie Gillie, a man described by colleagues as someone of 'enormous character and personality ... exciting intellectual achievement and radiance'. His impressive height and his habit of gesticulating wildly earned him the affectionate epithet of 'the semaphore'. He was also recognised as having a 'stubborn character and a volcanic temperament'. His most important feature from the BBC's point of view was that he had 'a great feeling for France'.[17]

Gillie's dynamic style set the tone. Yet what truly liberated the creativity of the French Service was its ability to deploy native language speakers before the microphone. Most adopted pseudonyms, though their radio personae usually reflected something of their real selves. Pierre Maillaud, a radical from the Midi, who had been the deputy director of a large press agency in London, broadcast under the *nom de guerre* of 'Pierre Bourdan'; Yves Morvan, a conservative Catholic from Brittany, appeared as 'Jean Marin'; and Michel Saint-Denis, a well-known theatre director who had been attached to the British Expeditionary Force prior to its evacuation from Dunkirk, adopted the name of 'Jacques Duchesne'. Among those who stuck resolutely to their real names was Jean Oberlé, a successful painter and part-time journalist who had suffered from polio in the 1920s and now used a walking stick to navigate the BBC's corridors.[18]

Among these exiles, Duchesne was the senior figure. He would take to the microphone 'as if it was an old friend' and chew over recent events with Bourdan and Oberlé in *Les Trois Amis*, a weekly current affairs series. *Les Trois Amis* was later absorbed into *Les Français parlent aux Français*, broadcast from 9.30 p.m. till 10 p.m. twice weekly from Friday 6 September 1940. This second programme became the dazzling centrepiece of the BBC's output. Tangye Lean, one of the key British members of staff, believed Duchesne's previous experience in the theatre was the crucial ingredient. 'Half an hour's propaganda became more exciting in his hands than any other radio programme I had heard … themes were attacked from all angles, originally, wittily, musically, in dialogue… There was something essentially gay and confident about it.'[19]

One problem that arose from the start was what to do with

A news bulletin being prepared by the French Service at Bush House in March 1944. The Service's head, the volcanic Darsie Gillie, was frequently embroiled in rows with the Free French, who broadcast their own separate programmes on BBC frequencies.

General de Gaulle and his 'Free French'. De Gaulle had arrived in London on the afternoon of Monday 17 June 1940, bringing with him two suitcases, a small stock of francs, and limitless reserves of self-belief. Rejecting the legitimacy of Marshall Pétain's collaborationist Vichy regime, he regarded himself as the head of a French government in exile. And now that his political base was in Britain, he saw the BBC as his best chance of reaching compatriots. Indeed, he recorded in his diary that on meeting Churchill that first afternoon in London, the prime minister had 'put the BBC at my disposal'.[20]

At about 8 p.m. the next day, Tuesday 18 June 1940, the BBC received a message from the Ministry of Information that a French general would arrive at Broadcasting House shortly to broadcast a brief speech during the French Service's 10 p.m. news – his script having been pre-approved by the War Cabinet itself. Soon after, the General strode in with his entourage to deliver a rousing declaration that 'the struggle should go on'. 'The flame of French resistance', he announced, 'must not be extinguished.' Few would have heard his passionate, four-minute-long oration, and fewer still would have been in any position to respond. But in the next few weeks, many came to hear *of* it. De Gaulle was clearly thrilled with his own performance. 'As the irrevocable words flew out upon their way', he recalled, 'I felt within myself a life coming to an end.' He would speak from the BBC studios on several more occasions over the next four years. Indeed, he ended his first speech that Tuesday with a promise to listeners that they would be hearing from him again the very next day – something that took the BBC by surprise, since nothing had yet been cleared with the censors. After a flurry of consultations behind the scenes he was given the microphone once more the following Saturday, and again two days later.[21]

Those handling de Gaulle were less than impressed. Elisabeth Barker, a talks producer in the European Service, had been asked to conduct him to the studio for his broadcast. 'He was immensely tall and I was very much struck with his boots', she recalled, but he came across like 'a dinosaur ... physically as well as perhaps politically'. As for his voice, it was impressively deep, though delivered in an animated style more suited to 'a Racine tragedy', rising and falling seemingly at random. Her most striking memory, however, was the General's extraordinary behaviour when he next visited. After he had finished in the studio, Barker was asked to escort him to the Director-General, who wanted to offer a drink and shake his hand. As they sipped their sherries together, de Gaulle enquired casually as to whether his debut performance on Tuesday had been recorded for posterity. Leonard Miall, who was also in the room, had to tell the General that, alas, no: Churchill had been making his famous 'finest hour' speech that day, and this had tied up the

BBC's extremely limited supply of recording equipment. What Miall called 'quite a scene' then followed: 'I became the first British recipient of the famous de Gaulle temper.'[22]

The BBC's real difficulty with de Gaulle, however, was establishing where his passionate appeals would fit into the overall output. In most of its broadcasts the French Service aimed at combating the worst of Vichy propaganda rather than directly expressing support for one individual, and whatever the private feelings of its staff it felt duty-bound to recognise the strength of Pétainism. Indeed, the BBC's official line was made crystal clear in a directive to staff dated 17 July 1940: broadcasters 'may be derisive about the men of Vichy', it said, but 'we should continue to be polite to Pétain personally'.[23] De Gaulle might believe that the BBC's facilities had been put at his disposal by Churchill, but it was clearly vital for the Corporation to establish that they had never been the prime minister's to give away in the first place.

The solution to all this – and it was a pattern repeated across many of the other language services – was for the BBC to give exiled governments such as de Gaulle's their own ring-fenced corner of the schedule. The 'Free French' would therefore come dashing from their Carlton Gardens headquarters every night to claim their five minutes of 'free time'. At 9.25 p.m., just after the end of the news, a BBC announcer would utter the words, '*Honneur et Patrie – voici La France Libre*'. At this signal, the voice most regularly heard would not be de Gaulle's – he would speak only on major occasions – but that of Maurice Schumann, the General's spokesman. Schumann was an amiable presence, though BBC regulars winced at his declamatory, parade-ground technique. 'His one idea was to seize the microphone and to shout into it at the top of this very high-pitched voice.' *Honneur et Patrie* was viewed by regular French Service staff as 'rather like a party-political broadcast'. Not only did they doubt its claim to speak impartially; they recoiled at its somewhat 'megalomaniac flavour'. Even its inspirational calls for popular resistance gave them headaches: they knew from intelligence briefings in

London that conditions in France would not be ripe for decisive action for some time, and that lives would be put in real danger if anything happened before the Allies were ready. After the first year of operations, the priority for the BBC was no longer merely the raising of morale. In the words of Tangye Lean, 'patience had to be instilled' among French listeners deeply frustrated at British military inaction.[24]

Managing all this required 'great subtlety', and it fell to Darsie Gillie to try his best to rein in the high drama of *Honneur et Patrie*. The strain often showed. Staff would watch Gillie walk up and down the corridors, muttering and kicking and banging the wall as he went, trying to decide whether to 'confront Carlton Gardens' or let things go. There was one guiding principle that Gillie held to, however. It was that neither the French Service nor the Free French owed unquestioning allegiance to the British government. When the South African prime minister Jan Smuts spoke disparagingly about the French war effort, Gillie allowed both Schumann, on behalf of the Free French, and Duchesne on behalf of the BBC's team, to 'go into action, verbally' against the ageing statesman, despite the fact that Smuts was a firm ally of Britain and that doing so on a BBC wavelength was tantamount to putting 'two fingers up'.[25]

It was this self-evident determination to speak to the people of France with genuine passion that encouraged growing numbers to tune into 'Radio Londres'. Reports reached Britain that in Paris 'a veritable pandemonium' of British broadcasts could be heard 'pouring news through balconies, windows and patios', and that many of the slogans from *Les Français parlent aux Français* were being sung 'from the Pas-de-Calais to the Pyrenees'. A letter smuggled to the BBC from Paris in September had proved heart-rending and inspiring in equal measure: 'If only you could see us listening to your broadcasts,' it read, 'we only live for that.' Another letter described how 'At 8.15 the whole family falls silent and drinks in the voice of the English radio, of our Free French ... An invisible thread ties us to you.' At the beginning of 1941, Vichy radio officials estimated the BBC's daily audience in its jurisdiction to be about 300,000; by the end of 1942 the figure had apparently grown tenfold. For many French men and women, the very act of listening was an act of resistance. André Philip, the socialist politician who had worked actively to oppose the Pétain regime, claimed later that 'The underground resistance movement was built up by the BBC' – indeed, that for him and his comrades, the BBC was 'everything'. In 1944, when the time really was right for organised resistance on a massive scale – when *La France Libre* was poised to become *La France Combattante* – the BBC in London was ready to play a full and valuable 'operational' role.[26]

Eavesdroppers

The BBC's acute understanding of what was happening to listeners in occupied Europe was often gleaned from letters smuggled out across the Spanish or Swiss borders. But when it came to events unfolding in real time, or finding out about the latest messages hurled into the ether by Nazi propagandists, the most effective source of intelligence was the BBC's own Monitoring Service – a large and vitally important cog in the Corporation's wartime machinery.

Monitoring's origins were remarkably humble. In the summer of 1939, when Wood Norton was being prepared as a country hideout, a paltry £810 had been spent on kitting out a small cottage in the grounds – 'Mrs Smith's House' – and erecting nearby a wooden hut equipped with six wireless receivers and a set of aerials. Here, away from all the electrical interference in the main house, a small team of men and women were employed to sit, headphones on, eavesdropping on the faint and distant transmissions of foreign broadcasters. Within a couple of years, broadcasts in thirty-two languages were being monitored; signals were being tracked not just from Europe, but from as far away as South Africa and Japan; and Lord Haw-Haw's nightly transmissions were being recorded verbatim. A more sensitive listening station was established higher up on nearby Tunnel

Hill, more huts were built, and dozens – and then hundreds – more Monitors were recruited. Before long a vast system was in place to process all the intelligence gathered. Foreign radio bulletins would be recorded on to wax cylinders that were then carried down the hill in baskets, ready to be played back and analysed by the 'M' unit staff, who were working in the huts in eight-hour shifts to ensure a twenty-four-hours-a-day, seven-days-a-week service. Others were employed in a more secretive 'Y' unit, which tapped private radio channels and broke into communications between German pilots flying over British skies. Until the Blitz forced them out, there was also a team of Monitors based in Broadcasting House dedicated to writing up reports: they were among those killed while working in Studio 3A on the night of 15 October 1940.[27]

Each day, a battery of women typing 'like machine guns' would churn out hundreds of pages of transcripts. By 3 a.m. or 4 a.m. verbatim accounts of countless broadcasts had been stapled into hundreds of quarto-sized booklets – a detailed *Daily Digest* of up to 150,000 words, a more concise three-or-four-page *Daily Monitoring Report*, special 'intake reports', working papers, a *Weekly Analysis* – all in multiple copies ready to be loaded on to cars or trains for their journey to London. Material identified as particularly important was sent over the Wood Norton teleprinters, or taken by military despatch riders to the cabinet, the Foreign Office, the Ministry of Information, the Service Ministries, and various secret intelligence units. Everything, of course, was also circulated throughout the BBC's news teams – and was viewed especially keenly by those making programmes for Europe.[28]

The entire operation, though largely overseen by British-born staff, depended, once again, on a teeming community of highly skilled immigrants. Martin Esslin had begun his career at Monitoring before moving to the German Service in London. At Evesham, he would catch the bus to work every morning in the stimulating company of his colleague Anatole Goldberg, who had been born in St Petersburg, grown up in Berlin,

Inside a Monitoring Service 'Listening Room' at Wood Norton,
1941. Any big speeches from Hitler or Goering broadcast
on German radio would require a special effort at the hut,
with extra Monitors drafted in to work in relays.

and had learned Chinese, Japanese and Spanish before fleeing
to Britain. Inside his hut, Esslin would find himself working
alongside the art historian Ernst Gombrich, who specialised
in monitoring German broadcasts, and the future publisher
George Weidenfeld, who, being the same tender age as Esslin
himself – just twenty-two in 1940 – rapidly became his closest
friend. Sometimes Esslin would be on the rota with the Span-
ish-language team. There his supervisor was the formidable
Ilsa Barea-Kulcsar, who had been involved in a range of radical
left-wing movements in her native Austria before she joined the
Republican forces during the Spanish Civil War.[29]

Most of these immigrants had experienced the rise of fascism
for themselves. And in the judgement of one British member
of staff at Wood Norton, they constituted 'perhaps the most
amazing collection of individuals as well as nationalities ever

gathered together in so small a space' – a rival to the cultural melting pot of Bush House. With the lashed-up buildings, ad hoc aerials, cables, mess and mud, the whole place might have looked 'rather like an army camp' instead of a country estate. But socially it was more like a university: a reservoir of knowledge, a market-place of ideas. It certainly provided ample evidence that, when it came to human capital, fascism's loss was Britain's gain. And for now, it was very much the BBC's gain, too, for the Monitors were far more than just efficient transcribers: they turned listening into a highly developed skill, involving not just linguistic ability but stamina and imagination. Goldberg described how it was only by listening to the same station for months on end – by developing a notion of what 'normal' output sounded like – that it was pos-sible to make sense of subtle changes in enemy thinking. In 1945 it was Ernst Gombrich who guessed that Hitler was dead before it had been announced, simply because he had heard German radio playing a Bruckner symphony and happened to know – had *always* known – that this particular piece had been written for the death of Wagner. In 1940, when lots of unknown radio stations of dubious origin were springing up across Europe, Esslin was recruited into Wood Norton's 'Special Listening Section' and charged with patrolling the far reaches of the dial. It was while tuned into a particularly obscure wavelength that he first heard German press releases being sent over the air to frontline offic-ers. It later emerged that this was the wavelength the Germans used for distributing scrambled messages via their so-called Hell-schreiber machine, one of which was subsequently acquired on the Lisbon black market and brought to Wood Norton. It meant that BBC Monitoring – and, through BBC Monitoring, various government agencies – had vital early access to items of news such as Hitler's speeches or Goebbels' latest propaganda direc-tives, and could then produce their own propaganda responses so quickly that the German high command was convinced they had a spy in their midst. To Esslin's immense satisfaction, 'they never thought that they were broadcasting this entire material themselves to us through the Hellschreibers'.[30]

By the end of the war, the BBC was monitoring something like 1.25 million words a day. Nearly a thousand people were employed, 650 of them directly engaged in eavesdropping, the rest in editorial or clerical roles. The only major disruption to this work was in 1943, when hurried plans for the full-scale evacuation of London required Wood Norton to be cleared out in case it had to become the BBC's emergency headquarters and Monitoring was forced to relocate permanently to Caversham Park near Reading. Throughout this time, there could be no public recognition of the hard work being done behind closed doors. But for many European refugees, the chance to apply their skills to the Allied cause in this way brought immense personal satisfaction. Ernst Gombrich admitted years later that it was impossible to know if the work he and his hundreds of colleagues did as Monitors actually shortened the war in any tangible way. 'We only know that we could not have sustained the effort if we had not hoped to contribute to Hitler's ultimate downfall.'[31]

'Pull and push': the Political Warfare Executive and the BBC

Despite the gargantuan flow of valuable information pouring in from Monitoring, there was always the feeling in government circles that the BBC's broadcasts to Europe needed much tighter control from above if they were to be truly effective as propaganda

Transmissions to neutral countries and to France were supposed to be directed by the Ministry of Information; those to Germany by a more mysterious branch of the Foreign Office based in Electra House and known as 'Department EH'; the Ministry of Economic Warfare, which aimed to disrupt the German war machine, also had a vested interest in the BBC's output, as did the Foreign Office's Political Intelligence Department, and even the Secret Intelligence Service's sabotage branch, 'D' Section. They all recognised that the BBC was by far and away the most effective means of reaching people in occupied Europe – and tried, for that reason, to co-ordinate the content of broadcasts. Representatives of the BBC would travel almost daily to Woburn Abbey, the 'country' headquarters of several government propaganda organisations, to attend meetings with officials and agree a series of 'directives', setting out priorities or suggesting the names of speakers to be invited to the microphone. But in the plethora of competing departments, there was plenty of room for contradictory advice or simple misunderstanding to creep into the system, and officials grumbled loudly at what they saw as the BBC's willingness to ignore guidance.[32]

The first step towards creating a more tightly co-ordinated effort came in February 1941, when the BBC was obliged to accept the appointment of Ivone Kirkpatrick as 'Foreign Advisor' to oversee its transmissions. Kirkpatrick was a highly experienced diplomat who had been serving as director of the Ministry of Information's Foreign Division since April 1940. Although his new post gave him no formal executive power over BBC staff or programmes, the idea was that he should become the sole channel of official information and guidance on overseas news – and that, for its part, the Corporation should pay due 'regard' to his advice. Barely had Kirkpatrick got his feet under the desk, however, when a new set of arrangements emerged. Various intelligence departments charged with sabotaging the enemy had already been merged by Churchill into a new Special Operations Executive – the 'SOE'. Now, in the summer of 1941, a similar reshuffle took place among departments concerned with covert propaganda. This led to the creation of the Political Warfare Executive – or 'PWE'. Neither the SOE nor the PWE replaced entirely all the other Whitehall units, and both operated under the cover name of established entities, such as Electra House or the Political Intelligence Department. But in principle, at least, their creation – and the arrival of the PWE in particular – established the conditions for a more coherent propaganda strategy for foreign broadcasting. As for Kirkpatrick, his personal role changed, but remained no less crucial. He became overall Controller of the BBC's European Service with an office in Bush House, and responsible to the BBC in all administrative matters, though answerable to the PWE for political guidance concerning occupied Europe and answerable to the Ministry of Information in relation to neutral countries. He would attend the PWE's daily committee meetings at its London base in Mayfair. The fact that Kirkpatrick was himself a member of the PWE as well as being a senior BBC official was a clear indication of the extraordinarily intimate relationship being forged between the two organisations. So too was PWE's relocation in February 1942 to the top three floors of Bush House.[33]

On the surface at least, everything was set fair for close co-operation between government and broadcasters. Kirkpatrick was only one floor away from Bruce Lockhart, the PWE's Director-General, and General Dallas Brooks, its military leader. He was, in other words, in the best possible position to be briefed at any time of day or night on all the latest strategic thinking at the heart of the government's intelligence community. When it came to dealing with his BBC colleagues in the rest of the building, Kirkpatrick proceeded on the basis that he was working with 'very high-grade staff' who could be trusted with the day-to-day handling of affairs. 'My aim', he explained, 'was to get policy agreed and then to leave them to execute it without the distraction of outside pressure.' The European Services staff themselves were rather more wary. Alan Bullock thought Kirkpatrick 'wonderfully urbane' but also 'the Government man'. Harman Grisewood, drafted in as Kirkpatrick's assistant, offered a more nuanced assessment, seeing in his new boss a willingness to 'fight the Foreign Office for the independence of the BBC'. Grisewood also thought Kirkpatrick's diplomatic history played well. 'He had served in Berlin, he knew these people, Goering and so on, he had accompanied Chamberlain to those meetings with Hitler, he knew all this at first hand ... That gave him a good deal of prestige over these rather cocky Hugh Greenes and Darsie Gillies and so on, who, if he hadn't had this experience, might not have deferred to his judgement: he could say, "Oh yes, I know exactly what to do, Goering said to me the following things ..."[34]

Kirkpatrick was not the only channel of communication between the BBC and the PWE. The mutual entanglements, though invisible to outsiders, were extensive. Elisabeth Barker, for instance, passed Kirkpatrick in the opposite direction, having been seconded from the BBC's European Service to the Executive's Balkan section. From Woburn Abbey, she supplied former colleagues at Bush House with what she called 'broad guidelines' for propaganda to Yugoslavia. The German Service, meanwhile, was being steered by the forceful presence of Richard Crossman, who had been working at 'SO1', the successor organisation to Department EH, since 1940. Crossman had already appeared on the BBC airwaves, and the script of his July 1941 *War Commentary* offered vital clues to his views on radio propaganda. It was not supposed to be a duel or 'private war' between the BBC in London and Goebbels' ministry in Berlin, he had told listeners. The trick was to speak to 'Herman Muller, dock-worker, of Hamburg, Jean Dumont, baker, of Lille, and Karl Petersen, Norwegian peasant'. Even then, he added, you have to have 'facts on your side'. In 1940 the facts had all been on Germany's side; ever since the Battle of Britain and 'the refusal of Londoners to be beaten by the Blitz', the reverse was true. And, given that people in occupied Europe had spent 'the black days of defeat' learning that 'if they wanted the truth they had to listen to London', there was now a real chance for British propaganda to 'reassert itself'. Listeners should never be given false hope, though: they will be reluctant to fight for ideals, he warned, 'unless the chances of winning are fairly good'. It was precisely this analysis that lay behind Crossman's constant efforts to ensure that German broadcasts emanating from London were ruthlessly aligned with the government's immediate war aims at all times.[35]

The PWE's influence did not go unchallenged. Objections were raised that it was diminishing the broadcasters' 'primary function', which was to give Continental audiences 'pure news'.

'The best Political Warfare', one BBC memo argued, 'is that waged with the weapons of responsible journalism, not that carried out with the instruments of the clever advertiser.' 'News values', another stated, 'are assessed by a professional estimate of what people are interested in and not by propaganda needs.' But what really prevented the PWE from exercising full control over the BBC's European Service was not so much an argument over principles as a series of more practical considerations. Problems often arose, for instance, simply because the decision-making processes of the Executive failed to keep up with the brisk tempo of live broadcasting. From his position as a sub on the Central News Desk, Alan Bullock observed how all the 'crucial questions' of what to report and how to report seemed to arise in the middle of the night 'when everybody had gone home, or the directive wasn't due to be formulated until Thursday afternoon'. The result was that 'you were constantly making snap decisions'. Any post-mortems were usually ineffective: 'they would shake their heads over the sins we had committed the week before, but everybody had forgotten about them by then. They always forgot about them if the news was good. If the news was bad then of course you were in for trouble.'[36]

The Central News Desk in Bush House, where Bullock worked, turned out in fact to be the most bruising battleground in the PWE's ongoing effort to control the European Service. A key part of the Executive's strategy was to introduce into the system its own army of 'Regional Directors'. The job of each Director was to supervise the work of a corresponding language service inside the BBC, ensuring, in the words of their formal brief, that output 'conforms with policy and is adapted to the needs of the Region'. Richard Crossman was the Regional Director for Germany, Ralph Murray directed the Balkan Service, a Colonel Sutton would deal with the French Service, and so on. Guidelines would be established at weekly meetings between these Regional Directors and their BBC counterparts.[37] As a means of ensuring that British propaganda was tailor-made the process made sense, even though staff at Bush House were often far too independent in spirit to follow completely a line laid down by people who were essentially outsiders. The problem was that it was bitterly opposed by two of the most important figures at the BBC. Kirkpatrick himself objected to the PWE's Regional Directors on the grounds that all communication should really pass through his office: he was, after all, the overall Controller of the European Service and saw his role very much as *the* PWE manager inside Bush House. Even stronger objections erupted from one of Kirkpatrick's most senior lieutenants, Noel Newsome, the BBC's own Director of European Broadcasts and, effectively, the Central Desk's Editor-in-Chief.

Newsome was determined to spread his own version of anti-Nazi propaganda, rather than slavishly disseminate formulations handed down by the PWE. He had a profound aversion, in particular, to Crossman's presence: he could see the man's intellectual brilliance, but regarded him as unprincipled – in fact, 'an entirely malevolent influence'. Crossman seemed to embody what he saw as the PWE's profoundly limited purposes: the short-term aim of winning the war. Newsome was more interested in the kind of world that would emerge from victory. He wanted propaganda that argued for democracy, that attempted to *teach* the enemy the virtue of ancient rights, good governance, progress. And he believed that the projection of what he thought of as British values had a special role to play. The rallying cry of liberty, he wrote, was one 'which we are most competent to get across because *we* understand it'.[38]

It was this that drove him to challenge the autonomy of the various language sections in Bush House and try to build some form of common editorial 'voice' that could extend across the entire European Service and reflect its British origin. He would hold two daily conferences with all the various language section editors in attendance, and issue his own daily directive every morning – telling the BBC's own regional editors that 'it was a waste of time' to refer his instructions to the PWE's people, while turning what he called a 'Nelsonian blind eye' to any directive he judged 'reactionary'. He also started popping up regularly on the airwaves as 'The Man in the Street', a series of five-minute commentaries that presented a distinctly progressive image of Britain. Newsome hoped it would help allay the suspicions of the more radical resistance movements on the Continent, who were always being told by Nazi propaganda that Britain was a stronghold of feudalism. Brendan Bracken at the Ministry of Information hated the series, believing it to be nothing but 'red propaganda'. By the early months of 1942, the PWE was so incensed by what they saw as Newsome's attempt to 'sabotage' their strategy that they tried to get him removed from Bush House altogether.[39]

Kirkpatrick was less dogmatic about this struggle between regionalism and centralisation. But like Newsome he became more and more convinced of the need to limit government interference. His loyal assistant, Harman Grisewood, later described the extraordinary flavour of some of the meetings Kirkpatrick chaired. The Foreign Office would have been 'trying to egg us on, either to suppress or invent'. Kirkpatrick would then ask the PWE people to hand over their written directives, 'and he would go through them and biff out what he thought was impossible or undesirable'.

> He would say 'we are not having that, and we are not having this, nor that … Argue as much as you like, but I am not having that here in the BBC. We would lose credibility if we did. Credibility is our weapon: we have got to be believed. We are not going to tell these untruths.'[40]

Naturally, the PWE was aghast to find that their own man was now apparently 'more BBC than the BBC'. And in the end, the PWE had to concede that the 'precise position' of its authority over the BBC was 'never satisfactorily determined'.[41] The relationship between these two proud and powerful organisations was probably summed up most accurately by Alan Bullock, who cast his trained historian's eyes over everything going on around him. There was, he concluded, 'a constant pull and push'. Newsome and Kirkpatrick 'never stopped' fighting their corner, and the individual language services did 'what they could get away with'. The European Service was obliged to conform overall with government policy. Indeed, since its own staff believed in the common cause of defeating Nazism, it did so willingly. But neither the working culture of Bush House nor the commitment of its inhabitants to reporting accurately were compromised beyond repair. Most importantly of all, listeners on the Continent continued to trust what they heard. In its broadcasts, Bullock concluded, 'nobody was making specious promises, nobody was telling lies … we got it right'. 'It's very surprising when I think of all the rows and arguments and so on – in the end, they all died away by comparison with the fact that London had gone on broadcasting and that this was something that people wanted to hear.'[42]

Fate knocking at the door: the V for Victory campaign

The simple fact that people in occupied Europe were listening to the BBC in their millions was precisely what made broadcasting so useful when it came not just to sustaining morale, or winning over hearts and minds, but to making covert attempts to disrupt the enemy and organise outright resistance. By stirring the occupied peoples to acts of sabotage, this 'operational' work was seen as vital in preparing the ground for D-Day, whenever it might come. A remarkable example of the technique had been deployed relatively early in the war – and it was one for which the BBC itself was largely responsible. It provided a striking precedent: an example of what might be achieved – and a warning of what could go wrong if coordination was lacking.

The 'V' campaign had its origins in a broadcast on the Belgian Service on Tuesday 14 January 1941. The BBC's commentator, Victor de Laveleye, had been reading letters smuggled back to London from his homeland, and had noticed references to the initials 'RAF' being chalked up on walls. He had also spotted obscure references in several Continental newspapers to 'Vive de Gaulle' appearing across Paris, Queen Wilhelmina's initial 'W' in the Netherlands, and King Haakon's 'H' in Norway. He thought of the risks for those involved and wondered if something simpler might be safer. That evening, de Laveleye went before the microphone with a proposal for his listeners. He pointed out that there was something that stood for 'victory' in French and for 'vryheid' – freedom – in Flemish. It was something that worked in English, too. And it represented his own name. It was, perhaps, the perfect symbol of Anglo-Belgian understanding. 'I suggest that you should use the letter "V" as a rallying sign.'[43]

Within days, 'V's were being chalked up in Normandy. When they heard of this, Noel Newsome and his deputy, Douglas Ritchie, wondered if de Laveleye's idea might be expanded. Ritchie, especially, was excited by the potential of a simple act of resistance to create a vast 'underground army' among the people of occupied Europe. There were already overt signs of resistance, and Ritchie believed a campaign around the 'V' symbol might bring greater coordination to otherwise isolated rebellions. He thought it would boost the morale of those trapped under Nazi rule by making them feel part of a wider struggle. It could break the resolve of enemy soldiers. And when the time was right, it might even provoke a wave of mass sabotage capable of striking a deadly blow at the entire German war machine.[44]

In May Ritchie set out his vision in a memo, 'Broadcasting as a New Weapon of War'. This was no longer about just graffiti; it was about all sorts of minor acts of resistance. 'The Germans are short of oil: at a word from London sugar can be slipped into petrol tanks all over Europe ... The Germans are short of rubber: at a word from London, motor tyres can be slashed all over the continent ... railway lines all over Europe can be rendered temporarily unsafe by means of rocks and logs.' 'When the British Government gives the word,' he suggested, 'the BBC will cause riots and destruction in every city in Europe.'[45]

Two weeks later, an unofficial 'V Committee' gathered for

the first time to enlist the key language sections based at Bush House. A special edition of *Les Français parlent aux Français* told French listeners all about the V-sign and what it might unleash. The Dutch followed with a similar programme of their own. And before long, the European Service had turned de Laveleye's modest concept into a full-blown campaign. To keep up the momentum, the English-language service adopted the device of a regular presenter, given the moniker of 'Colonel Britton'. The mysterious Colonel was in fact Douglas Ritchie himself. His first talk to Europe went out as part of a regular news bulletin on Friday 6 June 1941. He used the four minutes allotted him to describe pavements and walls across Europe being covered with the letter 'V', and to suggest that factory workers under occupation might 'slow up a bit'. Over the following months, countless ways of disrupting industrial productivity became the bread-and-butter theme of the Colonel's pronouncements: 'The slower you work, the quicker you'll win ... Blunt the tools and instruments, leave a screw loose here, a file there ... see that the food which you have to give the Germans is the worst you have and that it's badly cooked in the dirtiest dishes.'[46]

It was at one of the V Committee's regular meetings in June that it was realised the campaign might be based not just on visual symbols but on sound. John Rayner, from the Ministry of Economic Warfare, had started beating his hands on the table – three soft strikes followed by a louder one: dot, dot, dot, DASH – the letter 'V' in Morse code. The sound recalled the opening bars of Beethoven's Fifth Symphony, with its distinctive rhythm evoking the idea of fate knocking at the door. The confluence of symbolism was delicious, and Ritchie remembers leaving the meeting 'walking on air'. Colonel Britton took to the microphone once more. 'If you or your friends are in a café and a German comes in,' he instructed, 'tap out the V-sign altogether the sign of resistance to tyranny, the sign and rhythm of a great European army.' Within a month, the dot, dot, dot, DASH was being drummed out round the clock as the BBC's new 'interval signal', filling the gaps between each programme on its

European Service. The campaign was rapidly becoming something of a sensation. Churchill himself started to appear with his
hand raised and fingers arranged into the V-sign; the identity of
Colonel Britton – the 'Scarlet Pimpernel of the Radio' – became
a topic of conversation in the gossip columns of the press and
around Britain's dinner tables; in Manhattan, the 'V for Victory
Foxtrot' made its debut on the dance floor – featuring, somewhat inevitably, three short steps followed by a longer one.[47]

Towards the end of 1941, there were signs that the campaign
was having an effect where it mattered most: on the ground in
Europe. Reports came back from Paris to Marseilles that V-signs
were covering walls, pavements, doors, even telegraph posts.
Letters smuggled out of the Netherlands and Belgium claimed
that the Vs 'were everywhere'. A special day of 'mobilisation'
had apparently prompted rioting in Yugoslavia and Czechoslovakia. And output in Škoda's munition factory was said to be
falling. How much of the activity in and around Prague was
due to the broadcasts from London and how much due to the
support for resistance movements coming from Moscow was
unclear. But the Nazis were cornered into claiming that 'The
letter V denotes Germany victory'. This counter-attack went
some way to neutralising the effect of Ritchie's work, but it was
all rather unconvincing and only made it harder for police to
arrest anyone caught tapping out the code.[48]

Ritchie believed that his dream of a pan-European resistance was on the verge of becoming a reality. Yet behind the
scenes there was a gathering sense of unease, both inside the
BBC and out. Some of the exiled national governments in
London felt that no one apart from them had the right to order
their citizens about. Some of the BBC's language sections saw
in the campaign another instance of Newsome's centralising
tendencies. Reprisals were a genuine worry. Ritchie himself
had warned of the danger back in May: 'We must not ask our
friends to do things which are dangerous for them', he told the
V Committee. He soon learned that the death sentence was
being imposed in Norway following acts of sabotage apparently

V signs in a shop window in occupied Prague, 1941. By
now, the Nazis had co-opted the V sign as a symbol of
German victory, undermining its effectiveness for London's
original campaign of support for resistance groups.

inspired by London, and that in France fifty people had been
summarily executed by the Nazis in reprisal for the killing of a
single German officer. In the face of such repression, militant
talk from the safety of a Bush House studio seemed distinctly
irresponsible.[49]

In strategic terms, the bigger objection was that the timing
was all wrong. No matter how often Colonel Britton asked listeners to 'be patient', his stirring pronouncements could not
but help raise expectations that a full-frontal Allied intervention
was imminent, although everyone in British government and
military circles knew that the opening of a Second Front was
at least a year or two away. Something needed to be done to
prevent resistance movements in occupied Europe being stirred
to action too quickly and inadvertently setting back their own
cause. When the Political Warfare Executive took formal charge
of the BBC's European broadcasts in September 1941, official

backing for the V campaign started to evaporate. For the next six months, Ritchie detected a lack of enthusiasm, a watering-down of his ideas. And then, on Friday 8 May 1942, came a personal message from the PWE's director-general, Bruce Lockhart, thanking him for his 'remarkable' work, but explaining that it was necessary to cease the Colonel Britton talks. 'The V campaign must either advance or retreat', Lockhart told him. 'An advance in the desired direction is not yet possible, and I think you will agree that it is better to stop than to go back.'[50]

The war of codes

Though the V campaign was halted in its tracks, it had encouraged the PWE to explore how other kinds of 'operational propaganda' might take advantage of the BBC's transmissions to Europe.[51] There was one approach in particular that had already been tried, and which would end up being deployed extensively in the closing stages of the conflict. It became one of the most vital bits of war work conducted by the BBC – though it was done so covertly that only a handful of BBC staff ever knew of its existence.

Back in December 1940 – in the midst of the Blitz – a Dutch army officer had turned up at the European Service's temporary accommodation in Maida Vale. He explained how he had just escaped from Rotterdam by plane, and needed desperately to get a message to one of his comrades back home that very evening. All that was needed was for the BBC to mention in its 10.45 p.m. news bulletin the name of a mountain in Romania: his friend would be listening and he would then know that a plane was on its way to bring him to safety. Douglas Ritchie was the editor on duty that night. 'I sat down behind my desk in an agony of indecision. Our policy was to broadcast the truth, not descend into lying.' Yet here was someone requesting that the BBC do something that felt neither truthful nor deceitful. Ritchie took the plunge. 'I made up a short news item, including the name of the mountain in Romania and, calling the English news editor, I told him to insert this news item near the end and to tell the announcer to cough twice before and after.'[52]

An extraordinary precedent had been set. A year later, with the PWE laying down policy for the BBC's European broadcasts, the smuggling of coded messages into regular programmes became standard practice. By the end of August 1941, coded messages to British agents or resistance fighters had been transmitted in French, Serbo-Croat, Dutch, Czech, Norwegian and Greek. The purpose of these messages was set out in an internal BBC document. They were, it said, usually for 'confirming that an operation is taking place, or of retarding or cancelling an operation'; they might 'acknowledge the safe arrival of persons or documents'; they might even warn operatives that they 'are in danger and should take the necessary steps to protect themselves'. Usually a line or two was enough. At 6.15 p.m. on 7 September 1942, for example, the French Service announcer included the phrase 'Albertine et Victor pensent a leur Cousin Jackie'; two hours later there was another message – 'Bonjour aux amis de Dominique'. On the French Service alone, there would be roughly fifty such messages over the course of a typical week. Across the European Service as a whole, August 1942 saw 371 coded messages broadcast; just over a year later, the monthly figure had risen to 1,287.[53]

The words themselves arrived at Bush House from a range of sources. The Ministry of Information, the War Office, Department EH, the PWE, the SOE, exiled national governments such as the Free French or the Polish, and military intelligence were all involved. It was by no means easy for those on duty at the BBC on any given day to be sure that every message reaching their desk was legitimate. The risk that fifth columnists would try to sneak false information on to the airwaves was thought to be genuine. There was no guarantee, either, that exiled governments would always send messages that accorded with official British strategy. There was, for instance, some anxiety that the Polish government in exile would use their access to the airwaves to attack Britain's new ally, the Soviet Union; broadcasts to

Yugoslavia also needed to be closely monitored, given the division in London – and even within the BBC – between supporters of the nationalist General Mihailović and the Communist partisans of General Tito. To minimise confusion, security was gradually streamlined, with the SOE and the Secret Intelligence Service, MI6, usually taking responsibility for checking messages before passing them on. As an extra layer of security, the bona fides of everyone phoning Bush House with information was established through agreed code names: 'Napoleon Bonaparte' for messages to Belgium, 'Jack Masters' for Denmark, 'Bing Crosby' for the Netherlands. Last-minute messages would often be hand delivered – usually by trusted BBC secretaries seconded to one or another of the government departments concerned.[54]

Not every coded message was sent out in verbal form. From the end of 1941, bulletins to Poland would sometimes include a minute or two of music instead of a final news item. The arrangements in this case were elaborate – though, alas, not foolproof. Fifteen minutes before each bulletin was due, a Polish officer would arrive at Bush House giving the name 'Peter Peterkin' and deliver the gramophone record to be played on air. For over a year, the scheme ran without a hitch. Then on 13 January 1943 a new member of staff happened to be on duty – someone 'not quite familiar with the routine' or its importance. The record was entirely forgotten. Two months later, another BBC staff member – equally ignorant of the arrangement – decided to tell the Polish officer who brought him the disc that it was 'frivolous' to broadcast music when there was so much serious news to report. Then in June a typographical error in the running order meant that the wrong side of the disc was played. Soon, studio staff were playing different records entirely, prompting Alec Sutherland, an experienced BBC hand, to be brought to the studio to supervise all future broadcasts. 'What was happening', he explained, 'was that the Recorded Programme Assistants would look at this disc ... hold it up to the light and see if it looked kind of scratchy, and they would see a band of equivalent width that they thought would make

a better broadcast. And so they would play the other band ...
and the wrong bridge would get blown up in Poland.' The SOE,
stung by these failures, impressed on the BBC the importance
of getting things right: the scheme, it explained, had 'been of
very great value' to the Polish government and its agents on the
ground.[55]

*

It was hard for BBC people not to be irritated by messages
being forced into their lovingly crafted programmes, especially
when they were never privy to the underlying purpose. Professional instinct kicked in, telling them that the inclusion of
bizarre phrases, clunking slogans or inappropriate music was
horribly distracting for listeners. Even Noel Newsome, though
in the know himself, felt that several news bulletins had been
'completely ruined' by an 'undue flood of messages' and, in
one awkward instance, the requirement to play amid all the
sombre reports from battlefields a recording of 'Pistol Packing
Momma'. There was room for compromise. In January 1943, for
instance, the SOE acceded to a request from the BBC's Norwegian editor that messages be restricted as far as possible to subtle
changes in a broadcast's opening or closing announcements.
The usual phrase, 'Here is London, the news tonight', could, he
had suggested, be changed when required to 'Here is London
with the latest news'.[56] It was the kind of deal that embodied the
same 'pull-and-push' that Alan Bullock had observed between
Newsome, Kirkpatrick and the PWE. The intimacy between
the BBC and the government's intelligence agencies had been
forged by necessity. But the high stakes involved usually pushed
both parties towards a workable relationship.

In any case, by the early summer of 1944 the time for argument was over. Planning for the Second Front invasion was
reaching a critical stage: the flow of 'operational' messages to
resistance groups on the Continent was more important than
ever. It was now impossible for the BBC to refuse any reasonable

request. By May 1944, the Italian Service was transmitting as many as twenty lines of messages in a single bulletin; the French Service was pumping out three times as many.[57]

The climax of the BBC's three-and-a-half-year mission to send vital information covertly to underground Europe came at 9.15 p.m. on the night of Monday 5 June 1944. It was then that the BBC started transmitting an unusually long list of messages across the English Channel. Within twenty-four hours, 1,050 acts of railway sabotage had been initiated via the BBC, 950 of which were successful. By the time a message from de Gaulle had been broadcast the following afternoon, something approaching a national uprising was underway in France. Nestled in among all the strange phrases that had been transmitted from London the previous night, there was one that mattered more than any of the others – a short phrase adapted slightly from a line in the French poet Paul Verlaine's famous 'Song of Autumn': 'Bercent mon coeur d'une langueur monotone'.* It was ninth in a list of twenty-four. And it was the official signal to the French Resistance that D-Day was about to begin.[58]

---

* There is some confusion about the actual words used. '*Blessent* mon coeur d'une langueur monotone' is the line in Verlaine's original poem. This is therefore the version that has been used in many accounts of D-Day ever since. It is also the one that many listeners heard – or, more precisely, *thought* they heard – through the hiss and crackle of their radio sets that night. But in 1939 the popular French singer Charles Trenet had released a version that replaced 'Blessent' (rock) with 'Bercent' (wound). This happens to be the version that appears on the actual script for 5 June 1944 held at the BBC's written archives. It – and not the Verlaine version – is also the one recorded in a French archive of Special Operations Executive messages received that night by the Resistance network 'Ventriloquist'. So, despite the legend, the message that was actually broadcast on the evening of 5 June 1944 was almost certainly '*Bercent* mon coeur d'une langueur monotone': Trenet's lines, not Verlaine's.

8

TURNING THE TIDE

The great history of the world is unfolding before us.
Eyewitness report over Normandy, BBC News, 6 June 1944

Nineteen months earlier, on Saturday 4 November 1942, the BBC had asked listeners on the Home Service and Forces Programme to stand by for what it promised would be the best news in years. At 11 p.m. the announcer took to the microphone. 'This is London, this is Bruce Belfrage speaking', he began. 'Rommel is in full retreat.'[1] It was news that had raised the long-suppressed hope of millions that the worst of the war might just be over, the tide beginning to turn. There were still bombing raids by the Germans, though these were now fairly erratic. The Soviets were holding on in Stalingrad. And in North Africa the battle of El Alamein had represented a decisive and long-awaited victory after months of setbacks for Allied troops.

Over the next eighteen months all the talk was about when and where and how a 'Second Front' would be opened and the German occupation of Western Europe rolled back. When D-Day finally came in June 1944 it represented not just an extraordinary military moment – the biggest seaborne invasion in history – but, for the British people at large, a release from years of siege and stasis. It carried with it the profound hopes and anxieties of a whole nation.

For the national broadcaster it was clearly necessary to match the greatness of the occasion. And not just for a home front audience hungry for news. The BBC's coverage would serve as a vital source of information for the invading Allied troops and for millions of clandestine listeners across occupied Europe eager to know if liberation was at hand. To fulfil its role in June 1944, and to give listeners the most accurate and timely accounts from the battlefield, the BBC would have to develop new technology, new chains of communication, new programmes, new practices – all against a tight deadline, and, given the obvious need to keep D-Day plans from the enemy, all in conditions of utmost secrecy.

The Second Front

The most striking innovation had come as early as July 1940 with the launch of *Radio Newsreel*, one of the classic news programmes of the war. It was broadcast on the Overseas Service in four daily editions, six days a week, each one destined for a different part of the world, and, rather than simply recounting the news of the day, it consciously evoked the magazine style of the cinema newsreel, offering listeners a slick mix of despatches, commentary, interviews and recorded actuality. Among its reporters was Audrey Russell, who described the constant striving to be up to date. 'We'd have a half-hour programme ready to go on the air, and suddenly the whole thing had to be scrapped because of the mercy of events – a completely new script, new inserts, new *everything* had to be put together in as little as an hour and a half.'[2]

Radio Newsreel provided a model for news coverage that was urgent and involving. But the biggest prize had always been eyewitness accounts from the frontline. There had been several useful experiments. Throughout 1942 several reporters had been in North Africa supplying regular updates on the desert battles between Rommel's armoured divisions and British forces under the command of generals Alexander and Montgomery. And in September 1943 Wynford Vaughan-Thomas had flown over Berlin in the back of a Lancaster bomber. The BBC engineer next to him captured his shaking voice as he described the German searchlights and streams of flak being trained on his aircraft while its bombs exploded in flashes on the ground below – 'like watching somebody throwing jewellery on black velvet', he told listeners, 'winking rubies, sparkling diamonds, all coming up at you'.[3]

Remarkable as these dispatches were, they were not yet routine. They were also subject to considerable delay by government officials, which made it hard to imagine how a vast and fast-moving military campaign of the kind now being planned could ever be covered effectively. The sheer range of difficulties to be overcome had been revealed starkly in the coverage of North Africa. Early in the desert campaign, the BBC's correspondent, Richard Dimbleby, had to be recalled after giving rather over-optimistic reports on air, much to the annoyance of soldiers in the battlefield and War Office staff in London, who had listened in to everything he said and were fully aware of its failure to match reality on the ground. The problem had arisen because he had been working mostly from the BBC's Cairo office rather than the actual field of combat, leaving him dangerously reliant on misleading briefings from senior figures in Middle East Command, and only able to offer listeners the most broad-brush of descriptions. When Frank Gillard and Godfrey Talbot were sent out to replace him, they decided it would be better to report only what they had seen with their own eyes. Being out in the desert, however, made it harder to get reports back to London in a timely fashion. To record anything, they had to use disc-machines mounted on cumbersome trucks that needed the assistance of engineers. Many recordings were ruined by sand getting into the mechanism; the needle would also get stuck whenever nearby guns went off. When a disc was eventually cut, it would need to be carried by dispatch rider all the way to Cairo, where it would have to go through as many as four separate censorship offices before catching one of the scheduled transmission 'beams' to London. Even then, it might not survive all the static it picked up on its long journey through the ether, and could end up having to be 're-voiced' by another reporter back in London. The whole process was woefully under-resourced compared with US facilities, and there was real anxiety in London that if this were to be repeated for the Second Front, the British military effort would be completely overshadowed by accounts of American success.[4]

The BBC realised that some sort of fully co-ordinated, properly equipped 'Radio Commando Unit' was needed. The broad principles were set out in December 1942: the Corporation, an internal report stated, should recruit a 'corps of radio war correspondents strong enough in numbers and quality to aim at covering all major battles on land and sea ... air operations, the general picture from GHQ, and interesting activities at bases and behind the lines'. There also needed to be established 'a system of communications between the theatres of operations and the broadcasting centre in London designed to get all material back by the speediest method'.[5]

In March 1943, a huge mock-military exercise, 'Operation Spartan', was held along the river Thames so that the army could practice fighting a major offensive battle. From the BBC's point of view, it was the perfect opportunity to convince senior officers that it could be involved 'without being a nuisance'. Groups of reporters, engineers and feature writers were thrown together into two units that were then attached to 'opposing' armies. Their dispatches were flashed to Broadcasting House, where they were censored and 'broadcast' on dummy bulletins and newsreels. Richard Dimbleby was among those who took part. He was critical of several aspects of the BBC's efforts, including the way in which one young recording engineer 'wore his field cap at a rakish angle' throughout the day. But in general, he concluded, 'the idea of a team in the field has been found workable'. More importantly, government officials and military commanders were sufficiently impressed to agree that the BBC should henceforth be given as much co-operation as possible. Two months later, the 'War Reporting Unit' was established. Seymour de Lotbiniere, the BBC's Director of Empire Programmes, who had years of experience running outside broadcasts, was initially responsible. He immediately picked the well-known commentator Howard Marshall as the new unit's director, and Malcolm Frost, who had set up the Monitoring Service and worked for MI5, as its deputy. Frost in turn recruited some twenty or so correspondents, including, among others, Richard Dimbleby, Frank Gillard, the Canadian Stanley Maxted, and the war-hardened Australian, Chester Wilmot.[6]

The next challenge was to provide each correspondent with decent recording equipment. As the North African campaign showed, 'mobile' recording generally meant a disc-cutting machine mounted on a large lorry. Engineers had also managed, with effort, to squeeze turntables into a couple of Wolseley saloon cars. But creating something small and light enough to be used by a correspondent working alone – and creating it in sufficient numbers for the new War Reporting Unit to do its work – was trickier. By the end of 1943, the BBC's workhorse was still the 'Type C', which weighed a good 450 lb. As the antic-ipated date of Operation Overlord got nearer, engineers set out to install twenty-four of these in a fleet of old Humber mili-tary ambulances, putting yet more of them on board ships and aircraft, so that correspondents would at least have access to a facility of some kind. At the same time, they worked round the clock to develop and build a completely new device, the 'midget' disc recorder. Wrapped in a wooden case, it included batteries, a clip microphone, and twelve double-sided ten-inch discs, each of which gave just under three minutes' recording time per side. The whole thing weighed no more than 40 lb in total: a huge advance. By the end of May 1944, eleven had been assembled; another thirty-seven would be ready within four months. The BBC's newly recruited correspondents were promptly whisked up to Wood Norton for a weekend to be trained in how to use them.[7]

The BBC's D-Day planning now entered its final stages. In March 1944, members of the War Reporting Unit were given 'commando' style training in reconnaissance tech-niques, weapons, signals, map reading, and aeroplane and tank

Frank Gillard, a member of the BBC's War Reporting Unit,
trying out one of the BBC's new – and lighter – portable
recorders. The picture appears to have been taken in
March 1944, during training for Operation Overlord.

recognition; they learned how to live rough and cook in the field; they were even issued with army uniforms. It was hoped that all this would not just make them self-sufficient; it would also win them the respect of the troops with whom they would be embedded. Meanwhile, the BBC's engineers worked on creating a chain of dedicated phone lines and transmitters capable of getting the correspondents' reports from the Front, wherever it might be, all the way back to central London as quickly as possible. This involved setting up 'feed-in' points at various coastal ports from Great Yarmouth to Plymouth, placing microphones and disc-machines in some of the BBC's transmitter stations scattered across southern England, and adding extra lines to Broadcasting House. Finally, several mobile transmitters suitable for use at the Front were loaded on to trucks and moved into the marshalling areas ready for embarkation.

At this point, the BBC could only proceed in close step

with the military. For the most part, this was easy enough to manage. Operation Spartan had been instrumental in smoothing relations with Britain's own top brass. But the BBC's mission also included a vital role in the broader Allied military effort, which for the purposes of Operation Overlord was now led by Supreme Headquarters Allied Expeditionary Force – or 'SHAEF' – and under the ultimate control of the American commander, General Eisenhower. His vision for SHAEF included creating a bespoke radio service for the vast numbers of troops who would soon be fighting on the Continent. The British already had the General Forces Programme, the Americans their Armed Forces Network. But Eisenhower believed passionately that a shared experience would help integrate the British, Canadian and American forces under his command. He wanted output to reflect the rough ratio of military effort on the ground: programmes would be 50 per cent American, 35 per cent British, 15 per cent Canadian. It was, however, the BBC that had the studios, transmitters and personnel in all the right places. So it was the BBC that would, in effect, be running the show. Maurice Gorham was therefore appointed the new Allied Expeditionary Force's Programme Director, while several other senior BBC figures were pulled into its orbit, including Francis McLean, the engineer who was co-ordinating a lot of the technical support for D-Day; Leonard Miall, who was seconded to SHAEF's newly created 'Psychological Warfare' division; and Cecil Madden, the great impresario of the BBC's television service and, more recently, the Empire Variety Unit, where many of the entertainment programmes the new service would require were already being made.

Everyone involved came with the right qualifications. Gorham, for instance, had been helping to run the BBC's North American Service for the past three years, working closely with a team of mostly Canadian broadcasters on loan to the Corporation. In the days before Pearl Harbor, the North American Service had existed largely to challenge isolationism and anti-British feeling in the United States by evoking sympathy for the struggle against Nazism; once the US had entered the war, the aim was to 'maintain friendship and understanding between allies'. Each evening, seven hours or so of programmes were beamed across the Atlantic, including a special North American edition of *Radio Newsreel*, live link-up shows such as *Transatlantic Call* and *Atlantic Spotlight*, and a drama serial, *Front Line Family*, the BBC's first-ever full-blown, regular soap opera, featuring the Robinson family's struggle to endure bombing and blackout. In Gorham's view, *Front Line Family* had communicated the realities of the war in Europe better than any other news report or talk from the BBC. From his base at the underground Criterion Theatre in Piccadilly Circus, Cecil Madden's Empire Variety Unit turned out a stream of live talent shows and musicals. One of his longest-running series, *American Eagle Club*, was rebroadcast in the US on the Mutual Network and featured a mix of messages from GIs stationed in Britain to relatives back home alongside musical sequences from big names such as the Glenn Miller Band. Behind the scenes, the BBC had already set up an American Liaison Unit to provide facilities for broadcasters such as Ed Murrow from CBS and Fred Bate from NBC. In 1942 Leonard Miall had been pulled out of Bush House and despatched to the US as part of a Political Warfare Executive mission to help co-ordinate the sharing of intelligence with the American's own propaganda ministry, the Office of War Information, or 'OWI'.[8]

There were, then, all sorts of well-oiled links between the British and their American counterparts. Unfortunately, before Eisenhower's new service was even launched, co-operation had soured at the highest levels. The difficulties began in 1943 when William Paley, the head of the CBS network, blew into London to take overall charge of the OWI's operations in Europe. Within months he was demanding that the BBC's European Service relinquish large amounts of airtime so that the Americans could use its transmitters. Paley argued that America's own secret operatives in Europe were 'much more important' than what he called the 'little allies who had been making a very small contribution'. The BBC disagreed. It accorded just as much status to the various national resistance movements with which it had been in touch over the years, not to mention the SOE's own agents. When Ivone Kirkpatrick refused to make swingeing cuts in the Bush House broadcasts, Paley complained to the Ministry of Information. The BBC still refused to hand over more than a few extra hours a day. In Kirkpatrick's mind, allowing the Americans even this much access to the enormous audiences built up by the European Service amounted to 'one of the most valuable items of Reverse Lend-Lease' in the entire war. In Paley's mind, the BBC's decision to stand with its 'little' European allies revealed just how 'lousy' the new trans-Atlantic relationship might turn out to be.[9]

The Paley crisis betrayed a deeper issue. Bluntly put, the BBC was wary of fully merging its propaganda effort with the Americans because it regarded its own work as vastly more advanced. When Leonard Miall was in New York for the PWE and monitoring *Voice of America*, he was aghast at what he had heard: 'They were getting facts wrong, they were getting the mood of things wrong, they were so remote from the war that they used to say "good evening" when it was morning in Europe.' In London, Kirkpatrick offered a forthright analysis of the BBC's position: 'we had been longer at the game than they, we had been able to build up a British and foreign staff which had been thoroughly run in ... and our geographical and political proximity to Europe enabled us to understand the mentality and requirements of our listeners.' Given all this, the BBC was at pains to insist in 1944 that its 'orders' would come from PWE, not from SHAEF: it would merely 'give consideration' to its pronouncements.[10]

With a shaky truce in place over propaganda policy, the remaining challenge in the immediate run-up to D-Day itself was keeping all the broadcasting arrangements secret. Correspondents and equipment had to be deployed in such a way that every aspect and phase of the D-Day landings could be covered. Yet a sudden concentration of staff in one place – whether that was Portsmouth or Harwich or Dover – risked giving everything away to the enemy. This meant that a few – though *only* a few – people at the top of the BBC now had to be trusted with the invasion plans themselves. Malcolm Frost at the War Reporting Unit was among this select group. 'Whoever sat in my chair *had* to know', Frost explained. Working for MI5, and having good relations with Eisenhower, was crucial. 'I was the right chap in the right hole … they trusted me.' Meanwhile, the idea of letting something slip on air, even accidentally, was simply too appalling to contemplate: when the TUC leader Walter Citrine attempted to refer in a programme to work going on along the south coast, he had to be swiftly silenced. [11]

Even so, towards the end of May more and more of the BBC's own staff sensed that *something* was up. At *Radio Newsreel*, Audrey Russell was starting to put the pieces together. 'We began to know that it was imminent because the correspondents you knew, your old friends, were disappearing all the time.' The whole of the south of England was becoming one sprawling military camp, and the BBC's reporters were being transported to the units in which they would be embedded. One collecting point was the village of Pangbourne. Susan Ritchie, a clerk for the Monitoring Service at nearby Caversham, was billeted in a scruffy hostel there. 'Several days before D-Day it was obvious what was happening', she recalled. 'About a dozen BBC correspondents arrived' and spent 'a flirtatious few days', as she put it, 'tensed up, ready to go'. As they lazed around the swimming pool, the new arrivals became increasingly impatient. One was soon so bored that he decided to test his kit by jumping 'fully dressed into the pool to see if he would sink' – which, apparently, he did. In fact, the correspondents did not have to wait long. As May ended, Ritchie noticed countless planes flying low overhead and 'truck after truck after truck full of American servicemen' grinding past. Everyone, it seemed, was on the move. Those, like Ritchie, who witnessed it first-hand knew the long-awaited opening of the Second Front was only a matter of days, perhaps even hours away. As for the rest of the country, it was 'expectant, almost hushed'. 'Every time we turn on the radio we expect to hear that the great invasion of Europe has begun.'[12]

'This is the day and this is the hour': D-Day

Behind the scenes at the BBC, highly secret plans for an official announcement were now falling into place, the interlocking machinery of a vast news-gathering operation snapping into gear.

On Thursday 1 June, rotas were amended to make sure that a senior engineer was on duty around the clock, until 'such time as forthcoming events materialise'. Two days later, on the Saturday, a senior news editor at Bush House surreptitiously prepared recordings of special announcements: messages from the prime ministers of Belgium and the Netherlands and the King of Norway, as well as one from Eisenhower himself. De Gaulle was brought back to London from Algiers the same day, though such was the strictness of security arrangements that he was not told of the invasion plan until Sunday – one day before the planned launch date of Monday 5 June. The General was so insulted by this that he declined to record a message until the morning of D-Day itself – and, even then, strode into the studio 'seething with anger'. On Sunday afternoon, the BBC's announcer John Snagge was also confined to Broadcasting House and was instructed by the Director-General, William Haley, to produce, without consulting anyone, a short document detailing how exactly the different programme services of the BBC would all be switched through to the same studio at a moment's notice. 'It was so top secret', Snagge recalled, that he was not even allowed to dictate his plan to a secretary. Instead, the BBC's Controller of Programmes, Benjie Nicolls, came into the room where he was working and asked him to describe his scheme while he wrote it all down.[13]

Everything was now almost ready, but bad weather the following morning pushed D-Day back twenty-four hours: another frustrating wait. Then, as dusk fell on the Monday, over at Bush

House the BBC's French Service started broadcasting its long list of coded messages to listeners across the Channel. Three miles to the north, in Primrose Hill, Minnie Baker was tucked up in bed, though wakeful. In her diary the next day, she noted having had an 'almost sleepless night, owing to planes going over without a break'. Down on the Sussex coast, Muriel Greenway could just about make out in the darkness a sky 'full of planes'. 'I feel very restless and can settle to nothing.'[14]

Inside the BBC, people were also awake and on the move. Benjie Nicolls summoned Mary Lewis from the Duplicating Section to his office. She was on fire-watching duty, passing the time stapling scripts together and chatting with her fellow volunteers, when the phone rang:

> I thought well this is odd, but as it might be to do with the fire-watch I'd better answer it. And it happened to be Mr Nicolls ... When I got there, I was asked if there was anybody who could do any work. I said well in fact we'd closed – it was then about 10 o'clock at night – but that if it was urgent I could probably type it and run it off for them myself. I was then shown this document, and these were the actual instructions for D-Day ... It was quite obvious that it was highly confidential. I ... had to go down and roll it off. I had the greatest difficulty in getting rid of the rest of the fire party who I didn't want to see what I was doing. I took it back and was rewarded with two eggs by Mr Nicolls, who said it was very good of me to do the extra work.[15]

At 3 a.m. John Snagge was summoned, along with Pat Ryan and Ed Murrow, to the London offices of SHAEF, where he was required to sit in a small locked room guarded by military police.

> A piece of paper was then plonked in front of me on which was written 'Top Flight 0732 GMT'. That was all. And I looked at this and I thought now what the hell does this

mean. Obviously, it was the moment of release. And 0732 GMT meant 0932 Double British Summer Time. So that was when the announcement was going to be made.[16]

Snagge immediately rang everyone on standby at Broadcasting House and Bush House – a signal for them to open a safe in which copies of his instructions had been stored. The so-called 'alerting period' began, with transmitters around the country being switched, and announcers interrupting the Home, Overseas and European Services at 9.30 a.m. exactly, so that two minutes later John Snagge himself could read into his microphone the few lines typed on a pink card placed before him:

Supreme Headquarters, Allied Expeditionary Force, have just issued Communique Number One ... Under the command of General Eisenhower, Allied naval forces, supported by strong air forces, began landing Allied armies this morning on the northern coast of France.

He read slowly, before repeating the Communique. The messages from various heads of state that had been recorded three days previously were then brought into a studio and placed carefully on a turntable. Among them were some words from Eisenhower himself, now speaking directly to the 'people of western Europe' and asking resistance fighters to start following the instructions they had recently received. A small huddle of engineers and producers hovered over the discs as they turned, willing the needle not to get stuck as the portentous words they contained were finally released into the ether from 'every transmitter that was not occupied by the Germans'.[17]

There was only one hitch.

Having seen Snagge's plans the previous evening, Mary Lewis had decided to rise at 6 a.m. and leave her bed in the basement concert hall in plenty of time to hear the momentous announcement being made – 'much to the fury of my neighbours on adjoining mattresses, who said why was I getting up

The BBC announcer John Snagge. His reading out of 'Communique Number One' just after 9.30 am on 6 June 1944 was the official confirmation that D-Day had begun, but the Minister of Information accused the BBC of 'having blown the gaff' after it had relayed German reports of the invasion at 8 am.

so early because there wasn't an alert'. Yet by the time she went to the canteen for breakfast, Lewis was aghast to discover everybody already talking about the invasion over their tea and toast. It turned out that at 7 a.m. Monitors at Caversham had picked up reports of the landings that were being carried on German-controlled radio stations, and when this information was passed on to the BBC newsroom it had been dutifully reported on the 8 a.m. bulletin. Among the millions who had tuned in and caught the news was Vere Hodgson, in Holland Park: 'The voice, in suppressed excitement, stated that paratroopers were said to be landing on the Seine estuary, and that German ships were fighting invasion barges in the Channel. Could it really be?' The senior editor on duty at the time had spent the best part of an hour fighting official appeals to stop the news being broadcast, explaining that he would only block it if a formal 'censorship stop' was received – something that never happened. The Minister of Information nevertheless accused the BBC of 'having

blown the gaff'. The BBC responded by saying it had not actually said the landings *were* taking place, only that a radio station
claimed they were. Strictly speaking, this was perfectly true,
though not exactly in the spirit of what had been planned so
carefully for so long.[18]

In any event, after Snagge's official announcement at
9.32 a.m., the BBC had several agonising hours to wait before it
could tell listeners anything more about what was actually happening over on the French coast.

Most members of the War Reporting Unit had already
arrived in the combat zone: several, including Richard Dimbleby, had flown over the channel in bombers or fighter aircraft;
seven were aboard various ships and landing craft; another three
– including the head of the War Reporting Unit, Howard Marshall – were embedded with assault divisions now fighting on
the beaches; Chester Wilmot had arrived by glider; and Guy
Byam had parachuted into Normandy. Robin Duff, who was
originally supposed to parachute in too, had ended up accompanying an American troopship across the Channel. As soon
as he reached dry land, he realised that the portable recorder
he had been carrying so diligently did not like getting wet. 'It
just wouldn't work at all … I recorded everything on the beach,
and then played it back, and of course there wasn't a sound on
it!'[19] Fortunately, William Helmore, an Air Commodore aboard
a Mitchell bomber, had more success with his equipment, and
the description he had been able to record as he flew over the
Normandy coast at 'H-Hour' provided listeners with their first
eyewitness account when it was eventually broadcast just after
the one o'clock lunchtime news:

> We're just going in to drop our bombs; it's a very tense
> moment – just the dawn of the moment when our troops
> are going in on the French beaches; I've seen them with
> my own eyes, practically in the act of touching down on
> the beaches. I feel it a great privilege to be here … we're
> just getting ready to go in and bomb … My God, there's

some bloody nasty flak round this place – very nasty flak, blast it! ... Now I can see the invasion craft out on the sea, like a great armada attacking France. This is history; it's a thing I can't be eloquent about in an aeroplane, because I've got engine-noises in my ears. But this really is a great moment for us, and to feel that I sit here with this weird means of telling you about what I'm seeing gives me a feeling of witnessing a strange pageant – something unreal. I feel detached, and that awful feeling that the great history of the world is unfolding before us at this very moment.[20]

A few hours later, the first eyewitness report from the ground was broadcast. It came from Howard Marshall, whose dogged struggle to get his despatch on air showed the logistical difficulties the BBC news operation faced until it had transmitters of its own in Normandy. He had been in a landing barge during the first assault, from where he witnessed the opening gun battles and the alarming sight of boats all around him sinking as they hit German mines. Having waded ashore, he had had only a few moments on land before hitching a boat ride all the way back across the Channel so that he could reach one of the BBC's transmission points on the south coast. By 7.15 p.m. he was on a hillside near Fareham, where his vivid impressions could be sent on to Broadcasting House in London. 'I'm sitting in my soaked-through clothes with no notes at all', he began. 'All my notes are sodden – they're at the bottom of the sea, so as it's only a matter of minutes since I stepped off a craft, I'm just going to try to tell you very briefly the story of what our boys had to do on the beaches today.' He went on to describe 'the very lowering and difficult morning' the troops had experienced trying to get a foothold in the sand. But he was able to end on an upbeat – and, as it later transpired, rather over-optimistic – note, painting a word picture of Allied forces moving up from the beaches and into the hills. 'We were beating the weather ... we had our troops and our tanks ashore, and ... the Germans weren't really putting up a great deal of resistance.'[21]

By mid-evening, Home Service listeners had heard messages from de Gaulle and the King, as well as a sermon from the Archbishop of Canterbury. There were still only a few accounts from the frontline, though dispatches were starting to arrive thick and fast behind the scenes. Discs recorded in the field by correspondents were being carried back to London by RAF or navy couriers. More often, the reporters' voices – some recorded, others live – were travelling 'up the line' from Fareham, or being sent via the army's own mobile transmitters in the field of combat, and ending up in one of the 'recording channels' at Broadcasting House, where they were immediately cut on to new discs. If anything needed to be removed for security reasons, then fresh copies would be made with the offending passages skipped over. While this was going on, a 'telediphone' converted all the reporters' verbal dispatches into typewritten scripts that could be checked easily by the censors. Once passed, these scripts could then be circulated to a range of news departments and programme teams.[22]

The flow of information was barely enough to meet a by now insatiable public appetite for the very latest news. In west London, Vere Hodgson had been glued to her wireless ever since hearing those first reports at 8 a.m. 'At 1 o'clock I was amazed to hear correspondents' reports, and even the sound of gliders. Someone spoke from a bomber over the French coast with the boys landing below.' In Primrose Hill, Minnie Baker, who had been kept awake the previous night, was rather gloomier. Her own wireless had fused as soon as she turned it on at breakfast time, and she had had to wait until three o'clock in the afternoon before a friendly neighbour brought round a spare set. By then she had retired for the rest of the day to recover and listen. 'I was thankful. I didn't mind having to stay in bed all day, but was so wretched not knowing what was happening.' Those who had been out at work all day had their first chance to catch up when the six o'clock news was broadcast, and now listened attentively: 'the first and last time that there was complete silence' according to one account from a normally bustling

Land Army hostel. Before the day was out, the BBC had also supplied material to an estimated 725 American radio stations. In occupied Europe, millions of French and Belgian and Dutch people were tuning in, too, seeking guidance on what to do or any information about German reprisals.[23]

In Broadcasting House, the strain of meeting the demand was already beginning to tell. Mary Lewis had been printing scripts non-stop in the Duplicating Section for over eighteen hours when she went to the basement canteen for a well-deserved break. But she had barely arrived before one of the few correspondents left in the building, Robert Reid, sauntered up and asked if she would come quickly to the first-floor office where he had set up a dedicated duplicating machine for the War Reporting Unit. 'We really are in the most awful mess upstairs,' he told her, 'the machine is flooding ink everywhere, the secretaries are having hysterics.' Lewis decided that the simplest thing was to take charge for the rest of the night and accept from Reid the promise of 'a good strong drink of Scotch' in return:

> I said, 'Where do you get a drink of Scotch from at 2 o'clock in the morning?' He said, 'If you come with me I will find one for you.' The second wave of correspondents were asleep, waiting to be flown over the following day, and they were sleeping in full kit and they had all been issued with a bottle of Scotch to take with them. And Bob and I went in among these sleeping correspondents and rifled their hip flasks from their pockets, brought them back to the Duplicating Section. And I proceeded to drink Scotch out of a cracked canteen cup and get through an enormous quantity of work.[24]

From the Front

The bottleneck in the BBC's duplicating service earlier that evening had been precipitated by the launch of a new Home Service programme specifically designed to take full advantage of the dispatches flooding in from the Continent. *War Report*, broadcast immediately after the nine o'clock news, promised listeners that 'night-by-night' it would bring 'news of the war from correspondents and fighting men ... live broadcasts and recordings made in the field, special broadcasts from forward areas, and dispatches and expert comment'. It was edited on alternate shifts by Laurence Gilliam from Features and Donald Boyd from News, and if Gilliam's watchword was intimacy, Boyd's was immediacy. Gilliam wanted to immerse listeners in the visceral, rough-and-tumble world of the frontline through using as much 'actuality' sound as possible – enemy planes flying overhead, bombs dropping, shooting, shouting – as well as the intimate stories of those who had been doing the fighting on the ground. Boyd, meanwhile, brought a deep concern for accuracy and an obsession with using the most up-to-date accounts. In their hands, each edition was pulled together in the basement of Broadcasting House at an alarming – indeed, exhausting – tempo: every dispatch arriving on disc would be listened to and edited, every script would need reading and subbing and submitting to the censor – and every censored script would then almost always need replacing by a newer script – or by a newer recording – which in turn needed to be cut and subbed and censored. And when each day's edition was finally on air – with no time for the usual rehearsal – all the recorded 'inserts' would be rushed into the studio and placed quickly on one or another of six turntables, ready to be played out according to a running order that was liable to change yet again while the programme was in full flow. 'My job', Snagge recalled, 'was to sit at a table with the script which was bunged in front of me and frequently taken away from under my nose just before I started and another was substituted and bunged in front of me.' The whole process was so stressful that within two months Snagge was asking to be withdrawn from his duties, complaining that last-minute scripts meant he was making too many mistakes on air.[25]

The series lived up to its bold promise to give listeners 'the latest and fullest picture' of the war. Except for a short rest

Howard Marshall in 1944, using one of the War Reporting Unit's recording trucks to file a despatch. Listeners complained that the BBC's bulletins were sometimes too gruesome but coverage in series such as *War Report* and *Combat Diary* provided an emotional link between battlefront and fireside.

period in the early spring of 1945, it was on the Home Service every night until hostilities in Europe had ceased: a total of 235 editions that traced in kaleidoscopic fashion the Allies' complicated – and sometimes messy – struggle to loosen Germany's military grip. Throughout, the efficient deployment of people and facilities out in the field was key to the programme's success back home. Within a fortnight of the Normandy landings, the BBC had its own mobile transmitters in place. The first, Mike Charlie Oboe, or 'MCO', had been mounted on a three-ton truck and moved to the south coast before D-Day but only got across the Channel on 17 June, once a gale that had been raging for a whole week had died down enough for its safe passage. Within twenty-four hours of coming ashore, it had been erected in a chateau near the town of Bayeux, and was fully operational.

A few weeks later two more arrived: Mike Charlie Nan (call sign MCN) and Mike Charlie Peter (call sign MCP). All three transmitters dramatically improved the ability of the BBC's correspondents to get their dispatches back to London in a timely fashion, especially once a mobile censorship unit had also been established on the ground. But it was always a struggle to ensure that the hardware kept pace with a constantly changing military front-line. MCO, for instance, supplied a fairly weak signal, and when it took to the road to chase after the armies, it was forced to hug the Channel coast all the way. There was greater flexibility as more territory in northern France and the Low Countries was liberated: BBC engineers would quickly seek out and rehabilitate any radio studios they came across during the advance. By drawing on one or another of these facilities, correspondents were able to supply *War Report*, as well as all the BBC's regular news bulletins, with a running commentary of the highs – and lows – of the long Allied campaign: the breakout from the Normandy beachheads; the trapping of German soldiers in the 'Falaise gap'; the bitter struggle to take bridges and cross the Rhine; and the fall of Berlin. There were regular dispatches, too, from the BBC's reporters in Italy, the Balkans and Burma. On one occasion, Chester Wilmot even sent a dispatch via a secret transmitter fitted in a suitcase and dropped by the RAF for the use of the Belgian resistance. The War Reporting Unit's only female correspondent, Audrey Russell, had been excluded from the first landings in Normandy. But by the end of the year she was near Liège, covering life at an anti-aircraft battery and the experiences of Belgian civilians. She knew full well these 'background stories' were keeping her away from what she called the 'hard news'. But her reports proved just as vivid and informative as the frontline dispatches of her male colleagues.[26]

It was, though, the liberation of Paris in the closing days of August 1944 that excited most attention, thanks to the extraordinary accounts beamed back from BBC correspondents embedded with the French and American troops who had entered the city. Robert Dunnett reported from the Place de la Concorde, where General de Gaulle had just narrowly escaped being shot. Amid a confusion of French voices and occasional gunfire, he described the crowds gathering around him, someone waving the flag of the Red Cross from a balustrade, shots coming from nearby buildings and tanks returning fire with 'a terrific salvo'. The 'peculiar whistling noise', he explained, was the sound of 'bullets going past' as he spoke. His colleague, Robert Reid, meanwhile, was just outside Notre Dame, where thousands of Parisians had assembled to await de Gaulle. Reid's account was, if anything, even more astonishing. Against a backdrop of intermittent machine-gun fire, he described the tanks heading towards him covered with people and the General himself entering the cathedral. Shooting suddenly erupted from 'all over the place' and Reid's microphone cable was disconnected in the rush of people taking shelter. At this point, listeners at home heard a brief break in the recording. When he had plugged the cable back in, Reid went on to describe seeing de Gaulle striding down the central aisle, shoulders flung back, 'in what appeared to me to be a hail of fire from somewhere inside the cathedral'. Reid watched as members of the Resistance came bursting in to try to pick off the German snipers, and people in the congregation crouched behind pillars before getting up again to sing the *Te Deum*. Towards the end, Reid told listeners that the shouting and the cheering they could hear in the background was the sound of four of the snipers being caught and hauled away. 'At the moment,' he explained, 'I'm just squatting cross-legged on the floor by the side of the cathedral making this recording … I didn't want to be too conspicuous.' It was, the *National Review* decided, a 'triumph' of reportage: 'There can never have been anything more dramatic.'[27]

It was not always clear how much gory detail listeners at home would tolerate – or how much bad news they could bear whenever the Allies' military progress faltered. Intelligence reports conducted by the Ministry of Information uncovered signs of at least some public disquiet: dispatches were occasionally thought 'too harrowing or gruesome', especially for the families of those fighting; reporters sometimes sounded too much like excited football commentators; interviews with wounded servicemen were just like the 'less reputable newspapers' in their effect on 'grief-stricken' relatives; and so on. Such reactions would have surprised many of the correspondents involved: they felt they were taking a great deal of care over the words they sent back. Military censorship was one aspect of this. But through experience, Gillard said, the correspondents had all become 'self-censors, recognising forbidden ground in advance and keeping well clear of it'. In any case, he added, 'None of us wanted to utter anything on the air that would put a single fighting man in peril.' Nor did they want to say anything that would upset or irritate them. As Robin Duff pointed out, 'When you know perfectly well that the chaps that you're describing and with whom you're working are going to hear what you've said that night, it's no good over-writing.' Nevertheless, there was an obvious determination among those responsible for *War Report* that it should be the 'faithful recorder' of whatever was happening on the ground. The BBC's visceral accounts of enemy soldiers being cornered in the Falaise Gap in August 1944 – 'a graveyard of German equipment and troops', a scene of 'frightful slaughter', the sounds and sights of gunfire pouring down 'like rain' on the desperate, defeated men fleeing the assault: this was 'not glorifying war', said John Snagge, but 'the opposite: indicating the *horror* of the whole thing'.[28]

And clearly for many listeners it was the vivid, immersive realism that was precisely *War Report*'s appeal. It is certainly what captivated Vere Hodgson, from the D-Day landings onwards: 'Marshall was in one of the barges and you could feel the swing of it ...', she recorded breathlessly in her diary. Month after month, between ten and fifteen million Britons tuned in regularly, exhilarated by the sense of following the microphone to the places where things were happening. And although the story unfolding before their ears was by no means one of continuous and rapid Allied victory, the overall narrative was the one they had longed to hear for two years or more – one of success outweighing failure, a war reaching its endgame. Throughout, *War Report* offered an immediate link between the battlefront and the fireside – one that made places like Caen and Arnhem seem far less remote psychologically than, say, Mons or the Somme had been during the First World War. It claimed to offer 'no special appeal other than the simple, human, honest account of what one man had seen and heard'.[29] But if so, this was a simplicity won through extraordinary – and largely hidden – effort. The coverage of D-Day and its long aftermath made the BBC's war correspondents famous, yet they drew on a vast and often unacknowledged machinery of planning, training, engineering, logistics and administration.

There were also enormous hidden difficulties behind the scenes. Despite the well-executed provision of portable equipment and mobile transmitters, for instance, correspondents still struggled to make recordings in the hostile environment of the battlefield. When the weather turned especially cold, as it did in the winter of 1944–45, the ten-inch discs they carried around with them became too hard and brittle to be cut; even swaddling the discs underneath one's clothing, as Audrey Russell frequently did, would rarely get them warm enough to work.[30]

Worse was what Robin Duff called the 'childish' rivalry between American and British military commanders over the content of some radio broadcasts. There had been no sign of trouble when the new 'Allied Expeditionary Forces Programme' began at dawn on Wednesday 7 June 1944 with a tuneful blast of the nursery rhyme 'Oranges and Lemons', before supplying news bulletins every hour from the BBC's Overseas Service. But it was only a matter of weeks before grumbles started to be heard from the Americans. British variety programmes, though popular among British troops, left the GIs cold. *ITMA*, especially, was anathema. Whenever it came on, they would switch over to German stations playing music instead. They also grumbled that there was just not enough American news or American sports coverage, and worse, that 'the news as a whole was slanted too much towards the British'.[31]

American patriotic sensibility continued to be offended right until the end. But as the armies advanced, and city after city was liberated, the BBC was cheered by the startling evidence coming to light about the impact it had had on those who dared to listen to its broadcasts through the dark years of occupation. A fore-taste had come in the early hours of Monday 5 June 1944 – one day before D-Day itself – when Godfrey Talbot, whose reports on the Italian campaign had been heard across the Continent, arrived in Rome along with his fellow correspondent Wynford Vaughan-Thomas:

> As soon as the BBC insignia on our jeep and recording truck was spotted a great shout went up, and in a matter of seconds we were engulfed ... men and women clambered frenziedly on our truck and car crying 'Allo BBC' and 'Viva Radio Inglese!' I stood on the truck's roof to escape, but was pulled down, my battle-dress torn, and was hugged.[32]

A few weeks later Robin Duff was in Paris. 'It was thrilling beyond belief ... I spoke French, and had arrived with Amer-ican forces: there were not many British, but we were much more popular.' Within minutes everyone was streaming on to the streets and plying him with champagne. In Belgium, Audrey Russell found herself constantly showered with gifts of eggs and other presents from local residents. Five hundred miles to the east, as Soviet troops liberated Czechoslovakia, they found loud-speakers in the streets of Prague and other towns blasting out the news bulletins of the BBC's Czech Service.[33]

When the fighting in Europe had ceased altogether, the French Resistance leader Georges Bidault was able to give the BBC an eloquent account of what broadcasts from London had meant for him and his fellow fighters during four long years:

> In the depths of the sheltering forests, in the undergrowth of the watching moors, in the friendly streets of shadowy towns, a word arrived from across the Channel and spread

Wynford Vaughan-Thomas being mobbed by the residents of Marseilles as he tried to conduct an interview in August 1944. Nearby, Allied forces and fighters from the Free French were in the final stages of liberating the city.

in miraculous fashion; and so a web was woven, invisible to the enemy. Patiently, dangerously, the network spread, closely and firmly knit vast coils which at the appointed time brought about his fall.[34]

On Sunday 22 October 1944, with Paris free, the French Service had broadcast *Les Français parlent aux Français* for the last time. Its place on the schedule was given over to the freshly constituted *Radiodiffusion Française*. In its very first broadcast the presenter paid a moving tribute to the Corporation and its staff. 'The BBC was a torch in the darkness and the embodiment of the promise of liberation', he told his listeners. 'The world was in agony; but the BBC played its life-giving music. The world was submerged in lies; but the BBC proclaimed the truth.'[35]

Victory and defeat

By the spring of 1945, listeners back in Britain had reason to cheer, too. The blackout had ended. The BBC was broadcasting weather reports again. And every evening on the Home Service, *War Report* was bringing news of the dramatic final stages of the conflict in Europe.

In May 1945, Chester Wilmot was at Lüneberg Heath to describe the German army's unconditional surrender. 'Hallo BBC, hallo BBC, this is Chester Wilmot speaking from the Second Army Front in Germany', he began. 'I've just got to the transmitter and so I haven't had time to edit these recordings.' He then proceeded to play the first of the discs he had recorded earlier that day. 'It's ten minutes past six on Friday 4 May,' it began, 'the hour and the day for which British fighting men and women and British peoples throughout the world have been fighting and working and waiting for five years and eight months.' He went on to describe the German generals entering and leaving the tent in which the signing ceremony took place, and listeners heard Montgomery declare there and then that 'All hostilities on land, on sea, or in the air' would cease at 8 a.m. the next day. The following Monday Frank Gillard joined Montgomery for the surrender of the German Supreme Command. The field marshal had summoned Gillard by telephone, 'showing a favour' to him personally but also 'to the BBC'. The whole eleven-month campaign, Montgomery explained, had had a 'Crusading Spirit' about it. 'This Spirit had many and deep sources, and the BBC was one of the means by which this Spirit was fostered.'[36]

Back in London, there was no edition of *War Report* that night. The BBC had decided that its work was done. After its last edition on Saturday, the studio attendant on duty in Broadcasting House wiped the chalk off the blackboard in the basement production office, erasing a rich palimpsest of messages and notes and running orders. He then turned to the announcer, John Snagge, and said quietly 'so: it's all over'.[37]

★

And so it was. Except for one last wartime act that the BBC was required to perform: the broadcasting of the VE day celebrations to an expectant country.

On the morning of Tuesday 8 May, the overarching challenge was to capture the mood of the country when there was no single mood to capture: almost everywhere, joy and relief was mingled with exhaustion and foreboding. All through the East End of London the 'battered little streets' were said to be 'gay with bunting'. But in Leeds, a rather more subdued atmosphere was reported. Everyone was somehow 'lost and off their bearings', a nurse wrote in her diary, 'because all at once their best "toy" had been taken away from them – the war!' Another diarist confessed to similar emotions herself: 'I can't say I'm wildly excited ... just a pleasant feeling of "Well, that's over. What now?"'[38]

Showing remarkable prescience, the BBC's Director-General, William Haley, had already warned staff that the Home Service's programmes for the day 'must seek to balance rejoicing, thanksgiving, tribute and warning.' He also hoped that the BBC would 'rise to greatness' for the occasion. The scale of planning certainly gave every indication that it might. As the sun rose, Broadcasting House could be seen decked in the flags of twenty-two Allied nations and floodlit for the first time since 1937. Inside, its programme makers approached the day as if they were covering another large battle on the Western Front: special transmitters and phone lines were leased, outside broadcast units were set up around the country, seasoned war correspondents were stationed at strategic locations, and, through the afternoon and evening, vast numbers of people were put on standby, ready to be paraded before the microphone to share their stories, not just of the day but of the past six years. The prime minister spoke from Downing Street at 3 p.m., and the King had his slot at 9 p.m. There were the chimes of Big Ben, the playing of the national anthem, talk of the Empire. But the moments of high pomp were easily outweighed by hours of dance music and sing-along variety shows: waltzes were played on the organ of

A battered – and still camouflaged – Broadcasting House in London on VE Day, 8 May 1945. The building was decorated for the occasion with the flags of the twenty-two Allied nations. Inside, staff were busy preparing for a whole day of special broadcasts from across Britain and the rest of Europe.

the Granada, Clapham Junction; the Crookhall Colliery Band performed at Gateshead Town Hall; and Lew Stone and his band were at a Southampton hotel. The ringing of church bells was a running theme, with services relayed from York Minster, what was left of Coventry Cathedral, and a church in the Dorset village of Puddletown. As one listener explained, hearing all these peals from different places 'seemed to give the feeling of the whole land rejoicing in the early summer day'. The schedule tried to weave together the various corners of Britain to create a day-long sound-picture of a nation both diverse and unified. There were broadcasts from the streets of Cardiff, Swansea, Birmingham, Liverpool, Newcastle, Glasgow and Portsmouth. There were messages from miners in South Wales and dock-workers in Belfast. There was community singing from Bangor.

The effort to transcend boundaries of class and region and taste was obvious. So, too, was the BBC's desire to let a little unbridled emotion into the proceedings. Just after midnight, Stewart MacPherson was at London's Piccadilly Circus, providing one of the climactic moments of the day's coverage. As crowds cheered in the background, he described the 'terrific throng' around him. People were shimmying up lamp posts to hang British, Soviet and American flags, others launched fireworks. Australian and Canadian soldiers passed by doing a snake-dance. 'Nobody's going in the direction they want to go, and nobody cares less … It's almost been worth waiting for – five years and eight months.' Across the country, listeners had been keeping their wireless sets turned on for long stretches of the day so they could feel part of the unfolding drama. They kept them on well after dark, too, as the soundtrack to long hours of drinking and dancing. The festivities in one Somerset village hall were no doubt typical. 'The radio's lively programme of music was on and dozens of village children appeared on the scene with fireworks and crackers I have never seen such signs of unrestricted merry-making.'[39]

During his Piccadilly Circus commentary, MacPherson had briefly wondered aloud how many of the people he described had relatives still fighting. It injected a small but necessary note of melancholy into the day's proceedings. Earlier in the evening, listeners had heard the moving comments of a Mrs MacDonald in Glasgow. 'For many a mother in the British Isles,' she told listeners, 'this night must hold sad memories as well as joy.' One of her sons had been killed in Italy; another had lost a leg; two more were in the Far East, still fighting, still in danger. 'I can't forget that the war is only half done.' The most sombre moment of the whole day, though, was a despatch from Wynford Vaughan-Thomas. He was in the main square of Lüneburg, from where he described a single white flag dangling from the Town Hall and crowds of Germans milling around in the afternoon heat, hushed and despondent as they listened to the official announcement of the Nazi surrender and the forthcoming military occupation of their country by the Allied Expeditionary Force and the Soviet Army. The plight of those on the defeated side did not go entirely unnoticed among British audiences. 'It must be terrible in Europe. How on earth can we get everyone fed?'[40]

The mixed emotions of the day were apparent inside Broadcasting House, too. Some listeners thought they could detect the sounds of a cocktail party in the studio during the one o'clock news. In fact, the announcer, Stuart Hibberd, had been at the microphone with all his old medals pinned to his chest. It was these that had been clanking noisily as he read the bulletin with patriotic gusto. Upstairs in the Duplicating Section, meanwhile, Mary Lewis and her team were run off their feet once more dealing with all the extra programmes. Volunteers had been drafted in and promised they could go outside as soon as they had printed their scripts and running orders. 'The girls had all brought in paper hats and streamers and food – everybody had given up one sweet coupon so we could all have some sweets. We were singing at the tops of our voices while the machines were running and there was paper on the floor.' The head of administration chose this very moment to drop by, dressed immaculately and wearing his spats for the occasion. 'I think he was a bit appalled … but he spoke to everybody and thanked them for what they had done.' Others on the BBC payroll found it hard to celebrate, even on this special day. Harman Grisewood was feeling the strain of nearly four years helping to run the BBC's programmes to Europe. 'I was extremely tired and exhausted as most of us were … tired of the sheer war service.'[41]

Only a few weeks before, Grisewood had collapsed in his office and had had to be carried out unconscious. He hoped the Director-General might offer him a short holiday to recuperate. It was not to be. An 'air of packing up in the corridors and offices' had already settled on the premises, and he was about to join the busy merry-go-round of job changes as the BBC rapidly adjusted to a post-war world. Dozens of staff who had spent the last year of the war working at SHAEF were returning. Malcolm

Frost arrived back with instructions from the Director-General William Haley to 'go down and clean up' the Monitoring Service – which, his MI5 training told him, meant a clear-out of perceived security risks. He was also told that Churchill wanted the BBC's overseas broadcasting to be 'cut very heavily'. Many of the foreign staff who had been so vital to the BBC's war work now faced losing their jobs. Some took the chance to return to their native countries, while many of their British colleagues departed for prominent roles outside the BBC. Noel Newsome, who had briefly hoped for a post at Bush House running some kind of pan-European organisation, was standing as a Liberal candidate in the forthcoming general election. Ivone Kirkpatrick had already returned to the Foreign Office, from where he now invited Grisewood to join him 'in the intelligence side' – an offer Grisewood rejected in favour of staying with the Corporation. Inevitably, the German Service experienced something of a mass exodus, with many of its members heading to Germany to help rebuild its shattered broadcasting system. Dick Crossman, who had worked for the Political Warfare Executive was now a candidate for the Labour Party in the forthcoming general election. He invited Martin Esslin for lunch to try to persuade him to join too. Esslin politely explained that he was not actually a socialist and that he was staying at Bush House. There, he would become one of the great survivors in a stripped-down European Service, though the path ahead was going to be bumpy. Despite his extraordinary wartime record of countering Nazi propaganda, it was several years before he was given the security clearance required for promotion: he had to stand idly by while others, including the talks producer Guy Burgess, were vetted successfully ahead of him. The security services, Esslin realised, were still 'dazzled by the English gentleman and suspicious of the foreigner, when it should have been the other way around'.[42]

*

In the summer of 1945, the tectonic plates of the wider world seemed to be shifting at breakneck speed. Less than a fortnight after VE day, Mass Observation received a rather despairing diary entry from one of its contributors in London: 'Already the reaction is setting in … Britain and the US seem to be at loggerheads with the USSR … There seems to be nothing but strife and confusion ahead when we should be seeing the bright skies of peace.' Amid the first intimations of increased paranoia about the threat of international communism, Noel Newsome's dream of a united Europe with Britain at its heart was fading fast. Instead, it was ties across the Atlantic that were strengthening. Under Malcolm Frost's guidance, the Monitoring Service quickly forged what he called 'an arrangement' with the CIA – a sharing of costs and of information. The BBC's focus in its eavesdropping activities moved decisively eastwards.[43]

On the home front, the political climate was being dramatically reshaped, too. In July's election, the first for ten years, Britain's voters finally got their chance to punish the Tories for having dragged their feet over social reform. As one Huddersfield woman remarked of Churchill when he visited the town, '*he* hasn't had to queue for potatoes'.[44] The outgoing prime minister had been tired and erratic on the campaign trail. And after Labour's landslide victory with a manifesto promising to 'Face the Future', there was to be a new and all-encompassing emphasis on reconstruction.

The need for bold measures was obvious to anyone who looked around. The country, like the BBC, had won the war. But both were bruised and battered by their efforts. Back in September 1939, John Daligan, the young lift attendant at Broadcasting House, had left the BBC's headquarters to join up and fight. When he arrived back, six months after VE day, 'it was a bit of a shock to see how badly it had been knocked about'.[45] Broadcasting House was no longer its original gleaming white: it was muddy grey and pitted with bomb damage. Nor was there a guaranteed job. In his absence, a wave of fresh arrivals had already settled in to their new careers at the Corporation. It had grown exponentially – from 4,889 employees in September 1939 to 11,479 now. Its range of activities had multiplied: new language services, more entertainment programmes, countless more bulletins to broadcast. There were new voices and person-alities at the microphone and new techniques on the airwaves. Over the past six years the BBC had learned to give a popular, homely touch to much of its output, and in doing so, helped to burnish the powerful, morale-boosting ideal of the 'People's War'. It had established an intimate if chequered working rela-tionship with Whitehall and the murky world of the intelligence services, while at the same time building from scratch a reputa-tion on the international stage for emphasising the truth. It was now a little more open to the world. And, by and large, decent broadcasting principles had triumphed.

Yet all this had been achieved in the extraordinary circum-stances of total war. How much would suddenly disappear, and how much survive, was hard to predict. But it seemed unlikely there could simply be a return to the status quo ante. Like the rest of the country, the Corporation was having to recover, reorientate, rebuild. Broadcasting, the Director-General told his staff, had just proved its power to wage war. For six years it had been used 'as well, as efficiently, and as vigorously as each one of us knew how'. 'Tomorrow', he warned, 'we must turn that same energy to the problems of peace.'[46]

III

CONSENSUS AND CONFLICT

9

A BOMB ABOUT TO BURST

Mass without mind has always come a cropper.
George Barnes, Director of Television, BBC, 1956

At three o'clock on Friday 7 June 1946, a simple, touching chore-ography unfolded in flickering black and white beneath the grey north London sky.

A gleaming Austin roared up to the entrance of Alexandra Palace and out on to the tarmac stepped an immaculately dressed Jasmine Bligh, the BBC's star television announcer from the pre-war days. Smiling warmly into a camera, and clutching in her hands a sheaf of typewritten notes, she began. 'Good afternoon everybody. How are you? Do you remember me?' Some perfunctory speeches from various dignitaries followed, before Bligh introduced Margot Fonteyn dancing, a variety 'party', a George Bernard Shaw play, and the same Mickey Mouse cartoon film that had been running when Alexandra Palace was last on-air. Later that evening there was music from Geraldo and his orchestra and Kenneth More starring in *The Silence of the Sea*, a tense drama about the French Resistance.[1]

The following day was the main event: the Victory Parade. Hundreds of thousands assembled in the drizzle to watch an enormous column of troops, military bands and armoured vehicles snake through London's streets. There were fly-pasts, fireworks, a flotilla along the Thames. The BBC's two outside broadcasting units were at the Mall, Freddie Grisewood and Richard Dimbleby at the microphone. Later in the evening,

Franklin Engelmann was mingling with the crowds, interviewing members of the public live on camera.[2]

Behind the scenes at Alexandra Palace, everyone breathed a sigh of relief. Six years and nine months after its dramatic closedown in September 1939, television was back.

The BBC had dragged the infant medium into life with the shadow of war hanging over everything. Programmes were listed in the *Radio Times* cheek by jowl with adverts showing a country hoping for a better future yet caught in the grinding reality of the present. The Ministry of Food promised increased tea and milk rations, and suggested that packed lunches might avoid wasting 'precious holiday hours in queues'. Its advert even included an enticing sandwich recipe: 'Choose 1-day old bread, and cut fairly thin.' 'A brighter future for the housewife' was being predicted by the British Gas Council, with talk of kitchens fully equipped with cooker, water-heater and refrigerator, though only, of course, when factories had made the 'switch-over to peace'. The Stillmore baking company listed a cornucopia of flours and custards. 'Very soon now you'll get your desserts', they boasted, though adding in the small print that not all their products were available 'at present'.[3] Readers could be left in no doubt that this was to be an age of austerity. Bomb-ravaged towns and cities, currency crises, manufacturing for export rather than the home market, an absence of goods in the high street, expensive loan repayments to the US, the costly maintenance of Britain's Great Power status: one thing after another would diminish the incoming Labour government's room for generosity.

For the best part of the next decade, there would also be severe restrictions on the BBC's own freedom to plan ahead. While wartime censorship powers had lapsed, penny-pinching Treasury oversight of capital expenditure remained. As for its television service, it was still very much the frail child of the BBC family. The opening broadcast of 1946 would be watched by no more than 15,000 people in London and the Home Counties – fewer than the number tuning in for the inglorious shutdown back in September 1939. By now many of the pre-war TV sets in circulation had broken down or been wheeled quietly into storage. As the succession of sounds and images beamed out from Alexandra Palace that June weekend went flying out into the London sky, millions of homes had the wireless on instead – listening to the afternoon's racing from Epsom and the old wartime comedy, *Merry-Go-Round*.[4]

Opening the box

All the same, the sheer speed with which everything had been pulled together in time for the Victory Parade was remarkable.

The BBC's efforts had been led by Maurice Gorham, who had arrived at Alexandra Palace on a foggy Friday in November 1945 to find television's old home looking 'more tumbledown than ever'. The place had been abandoned so suddenly in September 1939 that it was like the *Mary Celeste*: 'offices left all standing with half-finished letters on the table and forsaken cups of tea.' Large parts of the building had been scuffed and scarred by use as a camp for refugees and a holding base for troops. In the two first-floor studios just about every capacitor and resistor and inch of cabling needed replacing. Outside Broadcast vans had been stripped of their machinery. Rats were everywhere.[5]

Waking the old television service from its deep sleep was going to be a gargantuan task. Fortunately, Gorham could draw on the support of a highly experienced group which included Cecil Madden, the great impresario of pre-war entertainment, George More O'Ferrall, who would look after drama, Mary Adams, would take charge of talks, and Philip Dorté and Peter Bax, who would be responsible for outside broadcasts and design. Once the armed services had freed the rest of the BBC's staff from their wartime duties, they too came rushing to Ally Pally, 'mad keen' to return. The real key to progress, though, was a decision taken back in 1945: that instead of waiting for the introduction of new higher-definition technology the BBC would stick to the tried-and-tested, if rather dated, 405-line system that it had been using in 1939. It meant that Alexandra Palace could make good use of the hardware to hand. It also meant that for years ahead, programmes would have to be pulled together not just amid a chaos of dust and decay but with equipment held together on a wing and a prayer.[6]

Obsolescence was only one of several challenges to be navigated. Less than a week after television's triumphant relaunch, word arrived that major sporting venues, commercial theatres and film companies were all refusing to co-operate. The opposition of West End theatres to live relays felt depressingly familiar. But the cinema industry's alarm at television wanting to broadcast the occasional feature film was a new challenge – as were the anxieties of sports promoters, who were scared that major events such as the Derby were going to be beamed by the BBC on to large cinema screens throughout the country. Gorham knew that the payment of generous fees was the best way to buy them off. But his hands were tied by tight control of the purse strings. The end result was hugely frustrating for a BBC trying to create an attractive broadcasting schedule. For every theatre production allowed, five were refused. Tennis from Wimbledon could be shown, but not league football; by 1949 viewers could see *The Birth of a Nation* but not the latest Stewart Granger film. For a while the BBC's sports output was reduced to showing tug of war, table tennis and amateur football.[7]

Television clearly had the potential to do so much more. Coverage of the 1948 London Olympics provided a showcase for what might be done. Two mobile units were used – one at Wembley Stadium, the other at the poolside – each deploying three cameras. Producers were stationed nearby, watching banks of monitoring screens so they could co-ordinate commentary from a dozen different contributors. By the end of the competition, the BBC had provided seventy hours of live programming from the Games, with critics praising the mix of long shots and close-ups and the 'velvety' quality of the images at home. Rights-holders of all kinds recognised that the publicity

value of good-quality television coverage outweighed any financial hit at the turnstile and gradually relented.[8]

Austerity was harder to negotiate away. 'National reconstruction' meant a large slice of Britain's industrial production
being devoted to export, rather than the home market, and a
relentless drive to reduce unnecessary personal consumption.
This also meant tighter rationing of many essential goods such
as meat, butter, potatoes and petrol, as well as restrictions on
foreign travel. Television, like everything else, would have to
submit to a rigorous system of resource allocation. Indeed, as
the BBC's Director-General William Haley acknowledged, any
expansion would be 'controlled absolutely by the Government'.
It would be a while before enough affordable TV sets would
reach British shops and transform viewing from a middle-class
luxury to a mass past-time. It would be a while, too, before the
studios of Alexandra Palace could be kitted out with all the new
equipment that was so desperately needed by the programme
makers themselves.[9]

The greatest damage inflicted by austerity was on the
Corporation's efforts to extend television coverage beyond
London. Even the impressively lofty Alexandra Palace transmitter was incapable of hurling a television signal much beyond
the Chilterns or the North Downs. Most of England and all of
Scotland, Wales and Northern Ireland remained beyond reach.
Yet the government-appointed Plowden Committee, which
considered all requests for capital expenditure, had ruled that
the BBC could build no more than one new transmitter a year.
Haley himself was remarkably sanguine. 'The country was in a
frightful state', he admitted: 'it had to get its industry going on
a peacetime basis; it had to build houses and other things.' The
ruling was nevertheless deeply frustrating for staff at Alexandra Palace, who craved the vast nationwide audiences already
enjoyed by their colleagues in radio.[10]

Television's marginal status did at least offer a creative breathing space. There were still only two cramped studios, offices and
workshops lacked daylight and ventilation, and drama rehearsals

had to be cobbled together in draughty church halls scattered across north London. But the war had demonstrated how much could be achieved through a collective, bloody-minded determination to make do. Lively leadership was crucial, too. Maurice Gorham, an Irishman with socialist leanings who had 'an encyclopaedic knowledge about America and all things American', was always willing to fight ferociously on behalf of television with the BBC's top tier. His successor, Norman Collins, was cut from very different cloth. Harman Grisewood thought him 'cocky'. He was certainly unafraid to hide his thrusting ambition: Gorham described him as looking 'exactly like an advertisement of a young businessman who uses all the right products and is bound to become head of the firm'. Yet for all his faults, Collins oozed an enthusiasm that was infectious.[11]

Necessity was once again the mother of invention. The commercial ban on using certain variety artists encouraged producers to cross the English Channel and bring French jugglers, clowns, mime artists and singers over to London. One result of this initiative was that on Saturday 17 May 1947 television viewers were treated to the 'gala opening' of a new cabaret series, *Café Continental*, which attempted to conjure the atmosphere of 'Gay Paree'. Cameras revealed customers done up in evening dress sitting at tables, while waiters scurried to and fro carrying trays, barmen served exotic-looking drinks, and a compere introduced viewers to each guest performer. It was all an elaborate studio sham. Waiting staff were played by actors, the customers by members of the public; Parisian background noises were supplied by a gramophone sound-effects disc; and the champagne buckets were filled with ginger ale. Yet *Café Continental* served its purpose admirably, plugging the gaping hole left by the absence of home-grown stars and providing viewers with a much sought-after 'fantasy of escape'.[12] Meanwhile, Cecil Madden would be traipsing off to the Windmill Theatre in London's Soho, famous for its dance shows and nude tableaux. It was here that he recruited many of the performers for his variety spectaculars at Alexandra Palace, featuring – as

The Austrian equilibrist 'Jolly' balancing on bottles in the Alexandra Palace studio for a 1949 episode of *Café Continental*. The series plugged the gaping holes that existed for programme makers whenever commercial agencies banned home-grown artists from appearing on BBC Television.

he put it – lots of 'plumed girls coming down the staircase in Oo-La-La style'.[13]

At the rather more highbrow end of the operation, drama staff were concerned most with trying to escape the limitations of television's stagey pre-war formats. To start with, everything was studio-bound, everything live. This created a certain frisson for actors. But directors craved the facility to pre-record or cut swiftly between moving cameras, while schedulers dreamed simply of being able to repeat a successful production without the expense and trouble of bringing an entire cast and crew back to the studio. A handful of technical fixes helped. It soon became possible to film directly from a television monitor in order to make a 'telerecording' for later playback. From 1952 'variable'-lens cameras allowed for much faster shifts between

A scene from the 1953 drama serial *The Quatermass Experiment*, a 'thriller in six parts'. 'Will friends and acquaintances please note that I refuse to answer telephone calls during future instalments', the *Observer*'s television critic informed her readers after the opening episode.

long shots, medium shots and close-ups. The purchase of the old Rank film studios at Lime Grove, near London's Shepherd's Bush, also brought the welcome addition of four extra studios and a large scenery bay. The building itself was charmless. Outside, it looked like a furniture store; inside, it was 'dingy, unkempt, hardly suitable for human occupation'. And after it was acquired, there was little money left in the kitty for anything else. But it gave the television service ten years' breathing space before it would need another base.[14]

Aesthetic innovation was at its most visible in the 'horror plays' – crime thrillers, macabre murder mysteries, supernatural stories and science fiction – which proved so popular among viewers. One of the landmark moments in television's post-war evolution was the 1953 production, *The Quatermass Experiment*, about a space rocket veering off course during an experimental flight then crashing back to earth, leaving its surviving crew member mutating into a monstrous creature. The play's author, Nigel Kneale, had been one of the first recruits to a new Script Unit set up in 1951; its producer was Rudolph Cartier, an Austrian émigré who had joined the BBC in 1952 after working in European cinema. Together, they created a thriller that tapped cleverly into post-war anxieties about the Cold War and the atomic bomb. Cartier used short filmed inserts to 'open up' the range of settings, deployed mobile cameras for 'tracking' shots, and accelerated the tempo of cross-fades at key moments to build dramatic tension. The boldest innovation of all, however, was in the overall format. Instead of being presented as a single play adapted from a book or stage production, *The Quatermass Experiment* was a six-part serial written specially for television. It was a strategy that seemed to hook the viewers. 'I have seen nothing so frightening in my life', one told the *News of the World*. 'I won't look in next Saturday unless I have someone with me, but I must know what happens.' It offered the thrilling immediacy of live theatrical performance *and* a foretaste of the medium's more cinematic future.[15]

One of the leading architects of this future also happened to be one of Alexandra Palace's most troubled characters. Cecil McGivern had been responsible for producing some of the BBC's most remarkable wartime radio features, but he had also spent time working at the Rank film company, and from the moment he arrived as Programme Director in 1947, he showed himself to be manically committed to perfecting the art of television. He was held in extraordinarily high esteem: 'one of the most gifted producers ever' … 'a brilliant creative artist' …. 'the most impressive single human being that I had anything to do with in the whole of the Fifties.' But his perfectionism was a double-edged sword. After evening transmissions had finished, he would retreat to his office and remain glued to the screen watching and re-watching programmes or rushes of film through his

Cecil McGivern in 1943, while still working as a radio features producer. When he later arrived at Alexandra Palace as Programme Director, he rapidly gained a formidable reputation as an obsessive cheerleader for the newer medium – and as someone whose drinks cabinet was always open.

thick-lensed glasses. Producers could expect a long late-night phone call or pages of cramped, handwritten notes at the top of their in tray the next morning. These, Norman Collins recalled, were 'always highly intelligent': 'he was acute on costumes, he was acute on lighting, he was acute on every single aspect of acting, he was acute on news value … He was a man very deeply and morally committed to whatever he believed himself to be doing.'[16]

What McGivern believed himself to be doing was this: attempting to ensure that programmes of every genre were technically and artistically the very best they could be, regardless of cost or policy – regardless, too, of how prickly and demanding others would find him. The result was a series of heated run-ins, especially with Alexandra Palace's engineers, who generally preferred safety over experimentation.[17]

Wednesday 14 November 1951 marked one of many occasions when this tension was exposed to horrible effect. It was then that the BBC's unrepentant pre-war avant-gardist, Lance Sieveking, was given charge of a two-and-a-quarter-hour non-stop live production of one of his own plays, *A Tomb with a View*. The storyline, as always with Sieveking, was absurdly elaborate, and the technical demands it made on the night were mind-boggling: 42 separate scenes, ranging from a Monte Carlo casino to an overgrown graveyard, 112 film inserts, 85 still images. After struggling to get the whole thing on-air amid several breakdowns and much confusion, the engineers rose up as one to demand that 'such programmes' were never attempted again. In the furore that ensued, McGivern vigorously defended the much put-upon Sieveking. *A Tomb with a View*, he confessed, had indeed asked too much of television 'given its present state of development'. But the producer's 'attempt to extend, develop and create' had been entirely legitimate. Discovering which bits worked and which did not was only ever achieved, McGivern insisted, by allowing even flawed ideas to go ahead and 'learn through sharp experience'. He begged his engineers to remember that the creative urge of producers was something they would just have to put up with: 'Controlled it tends to die, to get drunk, to cut its throat or to join films.'[18]

November 1951 was to be Sieveking's first and last involvement with the BBC's post-war television service: afterwards, he returned bruised and battered to the familiar comforts of radio. McGivern, on the other hand, 'lived for television'. He probably died for it, too. 'The strain of work was such that he consoled himself a great deal with drinking', Collins recalled. 'It became distressing.' Years later, McGivern would be eased sideways, before finally leaving the BBC after twenty-five turbulent years. By then even his greatest fans thought him a 'broken reed'.[19] He was not the first employee at the BBC to be destroyed by overwork and overdrink; nor would he be the last. But he embodied more starkly than anyone else how the pursuit of quality often left a heavy human toll on those who felt they were directly responsible for making it happen.

Crowning moments

The one area of activity McGivern had rarely worried about during his time at Alexandra Palace, was 'Outside Broadcasts'. As the Victory Parade and the Olympics had shown, they were among the liveliest areas in television during the late 1940s and early 1950s.

The team making them was led by the not inconsiderable figure of Seymour de Lotbiniere. At six-feet-eight-inches tall, Lotbiniere – or 'Lobby' as he was universally known to friends and colleagues – towered above everyone else in the Corporation and had no difficulty exuding an air of no-nonsense authority. He had been running 'OBs' in both radio and television since the 1930s, and was instrumental in facilitating the BBC's reporting of D-Day: the archetypal safe pair of hands.

Like everyone else in the television service, Lotbiniere had had to make do with out-dated facilities – in his case, the two hulking pre-war mobile control vans rusting away on the forecourt. Fortunately, poor resources were compensated for by the quality of his on-air commentators. 'He had lots of rules,' his deputy Peter Dimmock recalled, 'and the best rule of all for a television commentator was "when in doubt say nowt".' Not everyone could make the leap, especially if they had spent their entire career describing everything in loving detail for a radio audience. But Richard Dimbleby's ability to restrict himself to the short if somewhat portentous phrase at just the right moment quickly made him the established star. He learned faster than anyone that for television he had to become what he called 'the *annotator*, the man who puts helpful notes in the margin'.[20]

The coronation of a new queen at Westminster Abbey on Tuesday 2 June 1953 provided the BBC with what one insider called 'the OB of all OBs'. Indeed, such was the military nature of television's behind-the-scenes operation that one reporter even started referring to the event as 'C-Day'. Most time and energy in advance was expended on persuading royal officials that mere subjects had a right to witness the ceremony in the first place. Neither the young Queen nor Prince Philip fancied television being present. And with Churchill now back as prime minister, the cabinet had also been lukewarm. Peter Dimmock later recalled one of the many incidents he had had to endure during months of tortuous negotiations. Lotbiniere, he said

> came back from a very depressing meeting at the Cabinet Office and said, 'Peter, it's no good, Churchill is adamant. We can't go inside Westminster Abbey.' I said, 'Well this is absolute balls Lobby! People aren't going to stand for it'. He said, 'I know but there you are – Churchill's against it and apparently he's got the whole of the Cabinet with him'. So we lobbied and lobbied and lobbied and in the end the Cabinet said, 'Well very well, as long as you only televise on the west side of the choir screen.' Well that was equally ridiculous because the whole ceremony was at the altar.[21]

Dimmock decided to leak this to the press. Right on cue, the papers howled about a pre-war 'caste system' offering a privileged view to the favoured few. Dimmock was delighted. 'It worked! The pressure then was such that they said, well very well we *could* have an experiment.' This, it turned out, meant a trial run before the Duke of Norfolk, the Archbishop of Canterbury, and various royal aides, the consequence of which was the BBC being told firmly that at no stage could there be a television camera nearer than thirty feet from the Queen. Fortunately, Palace officials were clueless as to how television actually worked. When it came to a rehearsal, Dimmock fitted the camera with a two-inch wide-angle lens so that the image on screen appeared respectfully distant. On the day of the Coronation itself, however, he quietly swapped this for a twelve-inch

Richard Dimbleby in his commentary box in Westminster Abbey
during a rehearsal for the coronation of Queen Elizabeth II in June 1953.
Palace and Abbey officials insisted that the BBC's staff and equipment
remained as discreet as possible throughout the live broadcast.

zoom – with the result that everyone watching at home could enjoy 'the most wonderful close-up'.[22]

On the day itself a vast broadcasting machine was in place. Along the route of the procession from Buckingham Palace to Westminster Abbey there were twelve commentary positions and twenty-one cameras. Inside the Abbey were four more discreetly placed cameras, as well as twenty-nine microphones spread around the building to create a complete 'sound picture'. A 'control room' had been set up in the verger's office, and a small box constructed behind the triforium. It was here that Richard Dimbleby sat hunched from 5.30 in the morning till 2.30 in the afternoon describing the scenes below for viewers at home. Not for nothing had he been christened 'Gold microphone-in-waiting'. By the time the most sacred part of the ritual had reached its climax, he was in full panegyric mode. 'The moment of the Queen's crowning is come' he intoned, in what was perhaps the most sonorously biblical turn of phrase in an epic performance. As one astute analysis put it, Dimbleby's utterances were 'so expertly woven in between the Archbishop's words and the blasts of trumpets that it was as though he were conducting the ceremony himself'.[23]

Across Britain, an estimated 20.4 million – more than half the adult population – had gathered around the screen with friends or relatives. As the press pointed out, the day had turned into not just the Queen's Coronation, but television's, too. It had shown what the new medium could do when the full panoply of resources – both technical and human – were thrown at a single task and organised meticulously: the BBC's own performance was widely, and justifiably, lauded.[24]

As it turned out, not every viewer had spent the day in awed and reverential silence. For many, the picture quality had been disappointing. One viewer described it as like witnessing 'a rather bizarre séance'. Others found all the pomp rather comical. 'Look at the Queen', one viewer remarked. 'She's like a plum pudding by now, they've put so many dresses on her.' Others regarded the broadcast as an endurance test and had fallen asleep. By the end of the evening, a majority of those polled said it was news of the conquest of Everest, not the Coronation, that had been the day's most inspiring moment.[25]

As for the legendary effect on sales of TV sets, numbers had been growing steadily for a while: nearly three-quarters of a million in 1951; nearly one-and-a-half million in 1952; just over two million in 1953. King George VI's funeral in February 1952 had been one stimulus. Sport was another – and perhaps, in the long run, a more important one than royal events. If people decided that the summer of 1953 was the right moment to buy or rent a new TV, it was just as likely to have been for the FA Cup Final at Wembley in May, when Stanley Matthews inspired Blackpool to a thrilling last-minute victory over Bolton Wanderers. It was then that people gathered raucously around their sets at home – hugging cushions, hugging each other, cheering loudly in the 'electric' atmosphere of the match's dying minutes.[26]

Growth in television ownership was also boosted by the loosening of economic restrictions in the high street. In 1947 shortages of components had meant that no more than 2,000 sets a month could roll off Britain's production lines, and the sets cost as much as £150 – far more than the average monthly wage. By 1953, they were being turned out much faster and the price had come down to £60. The previous Labour government's commitment to full employment had bequeathed a welcome degree of financial security for many families. And once restrictions on hire purchases were eased in 1954, it was even possible, with a down payment of £6 or less, to get a set with a whopping seventeen-inch screen.[27]

The greatest spur of all to creating a nation of television viewers was the opening of more transmitters, each one bringing the BBC's signal to a completely new regional audience. In 1949, the government had finally allowed the Corporation to decide for itself how to invest its licence-fee income: its response was to build four high-power – and several more low-power – transmitters as quickly as possible. The 750-feet-high Sutton Coldfield transmitter went live just before Christmas that year, allowing programmes to be received for the first time in millions of homes stretching from the Midlands all the way to the southern fringes of Manchester and Liverpool. Within two years, there was another new mast at Holme Moss on the Pennines, serving the North of England. And less than a year after that, most of Scotland was brought into the television fold with the opening of the Kirk O'Shotts transmitter high up on north Lanarkshire's windswept moorlands.[28]

The public clamour not to be 'left out' was complicated by pride in regional identity. In the early 1950s, North and South could still feel a long way apart, culturally as well as physically. When Holme Moss opened in 1951, and the North had its first look at programmes from Alexandra Palace and Lime Grove, the *Manchester Guardian* pointedly suggested that producers in London 'may have to look again at some of their output'. The people of the North, it said, would show 'a considerable distaste for airy-fairy trifles with a disguised educative purpose'. As to broadcasting's great qualities of connection – its ability to 'make the great new Northern audience feel part of the television "family"' – the paper wondered aloud whether there might soon be an 'alarming side' to this miracle. Its metaphorically minded reporter had noticed that around the base of the BBC's soaring new mast were hundreds of sheep grazing 'incuriously'. And it had put 'horrid thoughts' into his mind. His worry? 'What the world's most powerful influence in mass communication could do to human beings.'[29]

Television's 'true purpose'

Television had lost its reputation as the sickly child of broadcasting only to become a lightning rod for a whole new array of cultural anxieties.

As reception spread northwards and westwards across the land, it was especially hard to separate the BBC's goal of ensuring that every home was in reach of a transmitter from the rather more disturbing spectre of cultural sameness or the dulling of viewers' critical faculties. In Wales, rumblings of discontent over the threat to traditions of singing round the hearth provoked the Camarthenshire poet David Henry Culpitt into condemning aerials as 'The Devil's forks'. In Orkney, older residents also warned that a rich local heritage of communal entertainment would be washed away by 'flickering, over-heated vacuities'. Even in parts of the country where television had been around for years, it was hard to dispel the notion that people were becoming somehow addicted. The anthropologist Geoffrey Gorer wrote despairingly of a 'family life, if not wrecked ... at least emptied of nearly all its richness and warmth'. He was fascinated, in particular, by women knitting or doing needlework as they watched TV. 'The more they watch, the more they knit', he noted, overlooking somewhat the fact that for many women who had been told not to 'waste' time, knitting at least felt like *something* productive – the continuation, rather than the neglect, of domestic duties.[30]

For some commentators, television's greatest danger was that it threatened the fabric of community life. The sociologists Michael Young and Peter Willmott compared the sociability of old working-class districts in London like Bethnal Green with the sprawling new estates on its outskirts like Debden – a place of strung-out streets where it seemed the only interaction between neighbours was glancing at each other through net curtains – and wondered if it was television's 'magic screen' in the sitting room that had encouraged residents to retreat into their own private domains. 'The tellie keeps the family together', one Debden resident explained, 'None of us ever have to go out now.' For another middle-aged couple, the purchase of a set had filled a hole in their relationship. 'After you've been married for a long time,' they told researchers, 'you run out of good conversation.'[31]

The Uses of Literacy, Richard Hoggart's ground-breaking work of social observation published in 1957, barely mentioned television – perhaps because Hoggart himself did not yet own a set. But he was confident enough to describe for his readers thousands upon thousands of families around the country engaged in some sort of unholy communion, an 'undiscriminating looking-in' at the same images on their screens. Every night, 'dead from the eyes downwards … The eyes would register but not connect to the nerves, the heart and the brain; they would connect to a sense of shared pleasure, of pleasure in simply sharing the unifying object, not in the object itself.' The result? A kind of mass enervation in the face of easy entertainment and received opinions. Much the same vision of pernicious mediocrity was on offer from J. B. Priestley, who used his column in the *New Statesman* to grumble about people spending their evenings watching 'idiotic parlour games'. A few more years of this, he suggested, and the nation might be 'permanently half-witted'.[32]

For the programme makers of Alexandra Palace and Lime Grove the more pressing problem was that television was apparently being held back by a High Command at Broadcasting House. Norman Collins called the BBC's most seasoned generation of controllers, departmental heads and administrators a 'Brahmin caste'. Its members still held the reins of power and he felt sure they were incapable of shaking off the idea that radio would always remain the central business of the BBC.[33]

Was he right to be concerned? Possibly. In 1948, when one of radio's most promising Talks producers, Grace Wyndham Goldie, had applied for a job in the television service, the response of her senior colleagues in Broadcasting House had been one of disbelief. *'Television?* But television's not of any importance: it's only a flash in the pan' she was told. 'You don't really want, do you, to work with *vision* when you can work with *words*?'[34]

It was attitudes at the very top that mattered most, of course, since Directors-General set the tone. And William Haley appeared to present a major problem. Wyndham Goldie attended many of the infamous getting-to-know-you staff lunches he hosted in Broadcasting House – occasions that usually passed in an awkward, deathly silence. She did her best to get the conversation moving. But the Director-General, she noticed, even 'resented having television talked about'. His decision in 1950 to create the new title of Director – as opposed to merely 'Head' or 'Controller' – of television might have been seen as a sign of progress, were it not for the fact that Haley passed over the obvious candidate, Norman Collins, in favour of George Barnes, who had been occupying the grandly titled post of Director of Spoken Word. Barnes was humane, clever, high-minded, and supremely well-connected in Cambridge-Bloomsbury circles. But he had no television experience whatsoever, and, in the brutal judgement of one insider his influence on its development was 'absolutely nil'. As one wag put it, 'you might as well put Isaiah Berlin in charge of Chipperfield's Circus'.[35]

As for Haley's successor as Director-General, he was another figure hardly likely to disturb the BBC's established hierarchies. Major-General Ian Jacob had originally been recruited in 1946 to run Bush House. His background was resolutely military and political: a field marshal for a father, army training, and time served in the wartime cabinet as Churchill's Assistant Military Secretary. Jacob acknowledged that television would be a crucial part of the BBC's future. He was even prepared to invest a bigger share of resources in it. But as one senior programme maker pointed out, 'By nature, he was a conservative ... he distrusted intellectuals no less than troublemakers'. His style – brisk, serious, stolid – was hardly the spirit of adventure that the denizens of Alexandra Palace and Lime Grove craved.[36]

Yet, away from the spotlight, the BBC's upper ranks *had* actually been grappling with the implications of television's growth. Whatever his personal forebodings, Haley acknowledged that it represented the future; he just wanted it to be 'civilized and adult'. 'I do not believe it is any primary function of the BBC to be popular', he said. 'The BBC's primary function is to be the BBC and all the BBC stands for.' He later recalled being asked by the Governors 'to "make the BBC a bit more matey".' 'And I said "as long as I'm Director General of the BBC, the BBC will not be matey, it is not in the nature of the BBC to be matey" ... We were doing what we thought was right.' Among the things Haley thought was right was that all parts of the Corporation should work to the same set of standards. That meant that the television service needed to be an 'extension' of the work done by radio, rather than something fundamentally separate. He remained convinced for years that it was his appointment of George Barnes that gave television its 'true BBC purpose'.[37]

What, though, *was* television's 'true purpose'?

Back in July 1945, Clement Attlee's dramatic landslide election victory had marked one of the most decisive breaks with wartime: not just a return to one-party government after years of uneasy coalition, but, with Winston Churchill removed from Downing Street, the opportunity, perhaps, to build a more egalitarian country. Attlee had decided that under him the levers of the state would be used to build a 'New Jerusalem' of nationalised industries and universal welfare roughly along the lines set out by William Beveridge back in 1942. Housing was high on the agenda. But for Aneurin Bevan, the minister in charge, ideals of hearth and family and community mattered as much as bricks and mortar. For him, the social and geographical divide that separated homeowners and council tenants was 'wholly evil ... a monstrous infliction upon the essential psychological and biological one-ness of the community'. Other Labour policies – a comprehensive social security scheme, the creation of the National Health Service, even the distribution of food and other household essentials through the mechanism of rationing – were based on similar ideals of *universal* provision, where welfare would be available to everyone regardless of status or income.[38]

Could broadcasting have a role to play in this grand project? Beveridge had included 'Ignorance' – alongside Want, Disease, Squalor and Idleness – as one of the five 'giants' to be slayed. After 1945, culture and learning, in all its forms, became a vital ingredient of the government's mission to improve. 'We should', Herbert Morrison argued, 'set ourselves more than materialistic aims.' Michael Young, who had composed Labour's winning manifesto, would later write of securing general happiness not by 'multiplying people's wants' but by laying the foundations of a satisfying life based on 'the sense of brotherhood'. If there was going to be a New Jerusalem, he suggested, it would be built in galleries and museums and libraries, in grocery stores and schools, and in the privacy of millions of homes, not just in the great industrial planning departments of Whitehall. Women and children would play their part alongside men. And domestic life or personal relationships would matter as much as state control of industry, cradle-to-grave social welfare, and Aneurin Bevan's National Health Service.[39]

This realm – of home and hearth and family, of thought and leisure and taste – had been radio's domain for years. Might it eventually be television's too? Few committed Bevanites stalked the managerial corridors of the BBC. But the spirit of national renewal promised by Labour's landslide victory spoke to a wider mood and had an obvious affinity with the Corporation's own deeply rooted goal of spreading Matthew Arnold's sweetness and light. As Director-General, William Haley was as adamant as any of his predecessors that if all broadcasting produced was a nation of listeners and viewers it would hardly be a 'social asset'. After all, it was never supposed to be an end in itself. The BBC's responsibility was to 'develop true citizenship and the leading of a full life'. If that all sounded a bit high-minded, even pompous, he also spoke of broadcasting as 'a source of companionship, of recreation, of good humour, of escape and of fun'. With Haley, as with Reith, the mix was everything. A 'full life' was a rounded life, a life of virtue *and* pleasure.[40] It followed that only when every component of the BBC's varied output was accessible to every person equally could this full life become a reality. With public service broadcasting, as with politics, universalism was everything.

None of this turned the BBC into a cheerleader for Labour. Harman Grisewood, who would have an important part to play in the post-war BBC, thought Haley's vision, if anything, reflected a Whig tradition of 'benevolence'. Grisewood himself was a committed Conservative. But even he could see that in 1945 a simple return to the attitudes of the 1930s was neither possible nor desirable. 'The mood was one of disenchantment with the past ... we were now in a world where new feelings and new relationships were being born.' Above all, he believed the BBC's role was to do more than simply hold a mirror to the world and reflect faithfully 'what goes on and what motivates the present-day'; the point, as always, was to *change* the world – and to do so by discriminating in favour of what was 'vital'.[41]

Haley himself had taken a look at the BBC's first-ever study of viewing habits. Flicking through page after page of carefully tabulated data, he was as rattled as anyone by evidence of mealtimes and bedtimes changing, domestic chores being abandoned in the evening, a fall in pub drinking, the rise in home drinking. 'I saw more and more that we had a great social force in our hands ... If light entertainment and a little serious stuff could do *this*, what would a full-blooded service do? I felt the time had come when we really must take this thing very seriously indeed.'[42]

His appointment of George Barnes to television's top job was only one manifestation of this thinking. There was to be a broader influx of radio people at Alexandra Palace and Lime Grove to help ensure that staff there adopted what one official called the BBC's 'tradition of leadership in culture, manners and good behaviour'. Wyndham Goldie described the result as 'a certain atmosphere of non-co-operation on both sides'. Yet as Haley no doubt intended, some of the old Broadcasting House culture rubbed off. Wyndham Goldie herself, for instance, claimed that it was her apprenticeship in radio talks programmes which had taught her to believe that 'nothing should be quick at the cost of quality ... you should aim for distinction in every field you touched'. Television 'doesn't just need pictures', she argued. 'If what you get is through a man talking or a woman talking, that's just as good television as if you see seventeen acrobats dancing, and perhaps better.'[43]

In fact, it was the *combination* of talking heads and dancing acrobats that gave the BBC's post-war television service its distinctive character. In his great sociological analysis, Hoggart had assumed that people watching at home were immersed in an 'endless flux of the undistinguished and valueless'. But this was grossly misleading. The nightly television schedule was actually 'arranged in very much the same way as a good hostess might arrange an evening meal': an inviting hors d'oeuvre, then a more substantial main course, and finished off with something a little lighter on the palate.[44]

The menu was certainly far more varied than the *Manchester Guardian* had implied when it published its great jeremiad on the occasion of the Holme Moss transmitter's opening on Friday 12 October 1951. In the afternoon, viewers across England were treated to fairly standard fare: racing from Ascot, followed by stories and archery lessons for children. But the evening was more celebratory, kicking off at 8 p.m. with thirty minutes of *Television Comes to the North*, featuring speeches live from Manchester Town Hall before an audience of 'distinguished Northern personalities' and Richard Dimbleby politely grabbing interviews with some of the two hundred guests. A fifteen-minute edition of *Newsreel* was followed by a documentary profiling the famous detective, Robert Fabian of Scotland Yard. The centrepiece of the evening's entertainment was the hour-long *Hullo Up There!*, an extravagant gala showcasing the talent available at Alexandra Palace and Lime Grove. It included a brief taster of *Café Continental*, jokes from Terry-Thomas, gardening tips from Fred Streeter, and the TV cook Philip Harben making a three-minute omelette. Puppets were also in abundance, with guest appearances from Muffin the Mule, Mr Turnip, Prudence Kitten, and the Little Grey Rabbit. Celebrations continued on Saturday evening, when a highlight of the schedule was an edition of *Music Hall* from the Theatre Royal in Leeds, featuring homegrown talent from the North like Gracie Fields and the Black Dyke Mills Band. The Toppers swirled and tap-danced their way down a specially built staircase, while the as yet unknown singer Frank Abelson – later famous as Frankie Vaughan – belted out a tune called 'Lucky You, Lucky Me', which he had been asked by the BBC to learn specially for the occasion. It was clearly a moment for frivolity rather than seriousness. But the television schedules that same week included several plays, some ballet, a piano recital, and even Somerset Maugham in conversation with the painter Graham Sutherland. In the week ahead there would be the first of a regular variety show from Blackpool, Wilfred Pickles staging a television version of *Have A Go!* from a miners' convalescent home, amateur boxing from the Royal Albert Hall, the first of six Sherlock Holmes stories, a 'documentary fashion programme' about Nottingham's famous lace garments, and a film portrait of the cellist Pablo Casals. It added up to something miles away from the 'dope-dreams' of Priestley's nightmare.[45]

Not every programme could be slotted crudely into well-worn categories. *Animal, Vegetable, Mineral?*, which began in October 1952, had all the hallmarks of a quaintly educative programme of distinctly minority interest, yet became one of the biggest hits of the fifties. Every other Thursday evening, a panel of experts, including eminent archaeologists and museum curators, would be invited to the Lime Grove studios to identify a series of mystery objects. The *Radio Times* told viewers what to expect: 'One of the objects may be the beak of a cuttlefish, another a Tibetan prayer wheel, another a piece of Sèvres porcelain, and so on.' One of those working on the series was a young David Attenborough. He had been tried out briefly as an interviewer, but Mary Adams had decreed that his teeth were 'too big' to be in front of the cameras. His role on *Animal, Vegetable, Mineral?* was to visit various museums and choose the mystery objects: among his favourites was a Japanese moustache lifter. The programme was also lucky in having the eminent archaeologist Mortimer Wheeler, who could be relied upon to play outrageously to the gallery, 'twirling his moustaches, pretending initially to be baffled, then discovering a clue and finally bringing his identification to a triumphant conclusion'. To help things go with a swing, Attenborough would make sure that every panellist was wined and dined generously before each programme. The tantalising possibility of a row breaking out amid the battling of egos only added further to the programme's allure for those at home.[46]

'Afternoon Women's Programmes' earned much less critical attention. But they were even harder to stereotype. Monica Sims, who had also cut her teeth in radio, was a key member of the team. 'Because they went out in the afternoon we had a chance ... to experiment with all sorts of things.' From her attic office in Lime Grove, she would prepare the usual items – 'you know, the women's interests in fashion, beauty, cooking and all those things, family affairs, medicine.' But she also set out to create a schedule 'carefully planned to try and cover different aspects of women's lives'. 'They had the heading in those days of "Mainly for Women", but ... we thought of them as general television programmes.' Sims therefore also turned out short filmed reports on countryside issues as well as drama serials. Meanwhile, yet another old radio hand, Olive Shapley, presented a series called *Leisure and Pleasure*, which reviewed new books, art shows and plays.[47] Doreen Stephens, who ran Afternoon

Children gathered around the television set in 1950 to watch *Andy Pandy*. The puppet had been designed by Freda Lingstrom, the head of Lime Grove's newly-created Children's department. The voice-over was provided by Lingstrom's partner, Maria Bird.

Women's Programmes, defined her measure of success in words that would have shocked a later generation of broadcasting professionals. She aimed, she said, for 'a constantly *diminishing* audience'. She wanted her viewers, 'to be so stimulated to new activities that they had no time to turn on their sets'.[48]

In this respect, children were taken just as seriously as everyone else: they were, after all, citizens *in the making*. When *Andy Pandy* first appeared on British screens in 1950, young viewers found it hard to tell whether this strange puppet, with its floppy hat, its baggy, striped jumpsuit, and its wide-eyed, slightly startled expression, was actually a boy or a girl. The clown-like androgyny was just as much part of its character as the all-too-visible strings that held it upright and gave it its endearingly jerky walk. Every Tuesday afternoon, Andy would play happily with Teddy and Looby Loo until a sing-song voice announced – as it always would – that it was 'Time to go home, time to go home', and Andy would wave goodbye before disappearing obediently into a little straw basket. Mary Adams, who had commissioned the programme, hoped children at home would respond enthusiastically to Andy's invitations to join in 'by clapping, stamping, sitting down, standing up and so forth'. Monica Sims, who would soon be joining the Children's department, thought the key to *Andy Pandy*'s success was that all the movements and songs mirrored very precisely what an average three-year-old could do. Her new boss, and the woman who had designed *Andy Pandy* in the first place, was Freda Lingstrom. Every programme that Lingstrom went on to develop, Sims reckoned, was 'designed very carefully to cover all aspects of a young child's life'. '*Bill and Ben* was a fantasy ... *Rag, Tag and Bobtail* was the sort of beginnings of natural history, *The Woodentops* were really about relationships within a family.' The guiding philosophy had in fact been laid down by the BBC on the eve of *Andy Pandy*'s launch. Television's 'Children's Hour', it said, should always entertain and be liked. But it also needed to satisfy parents and educational professionals that it would foster children's needs, not just their wants.[49] The BBC saw no reason for denying children the same balanced diet of education, information and entertainment it offered the country's grown-ups: they were to get a full service 'in miniature'.

The approach could get a little nannyish. Throughout the early 1950s, and with the vigorous encouragement of the Postmaster-General, the Corporation imposed a so-called 'Toddlers' Truce'. Around six o'clock every weekday evening, television transmissions ceased for a period so that parents across the country could get their youngest children to bed. But even here, although the practice irritated programme makers, it spoke to a consistently held ethos about the benefits of rationing. In 1949, before the 'Truce' had even been formalised, Norman Collins had made his own heartfelt plea to the thousands of Britons who were now starting to buy new sets: 'Please don't let the children view too much. At least send the little beasts to bed when the time comes.' At the BBC, even television's most passionate advocates believed there would always be better – more active, more creative, more socially responsible – things to do than simply sit and watch the screen for hours on end.[50]

Competition

Trepidation over television's dazzling effect was slowly giving way to a calm acceptance of its ordinariness. The medium might occasionally be viewed with suspicion, but it was no longer seen solely as a disruptive intruder. It was friendly, domesticated, *unremarkable*.

Being taken for granted, however, brought with it new dangers.

Well before the middle of the decade, anyone skilled at reading the tea leaves would have detected a small but growing restlessness towards the Corporation's monopoly over British screens. The BBC was also horribly exposed to the vicissitudes of high politics. From the moment that Churchill's Conservative's returned to government in the autumn of 1951, the BBC's monopoly status looked precarious. Within seven months a White Paper would be introduced calling for 'some element of competition'. Two years after that the 1954 Television Act was passed, paving the way for the first regional commercial television companies to be established. And on Thursday 22 September 1955, 'Independent Television' was launched.

ITV began just after seven o'clock in true BBC fashion, with a relay of stirring speeches from assorted dignitaries at London's Guildhall. At eight o'clock a live variety show starred Billy Cotton and his band, familiar to millions from his many radio appearances, as well as turns from Shirley Abicair, the Australian zither player, and Leslie Welch 'The Memory Man'. Later, there was Edith Evans playing Lady Bracknell, boxing from Shoreditch Town Hall, news read by Christopher Chataway, and a gala cabaret with George Formby at the Mayfair Hotel. The real novelty act of the night, however, came at exactly twelve minutes past eight, when viewers were treated to the first-ever ad break on British television. The camera closed in on a block of ice standing in a stream, a tube of toothpaste was thrust into view, and a clipped voice announced 'it's tingling fresh. It's fresh as ice. It's Gibbs SR toothpaste'.[51]

Something approaching full nationwide coverage would only be achieved by commercial television in 1962. For ITV's opening night, just two regional companies were up and running: Associated Rediffusion and ATV. It meant that fewer than 200,000 viewers, mostly in the London area, tuned in.[52] But as more regions followed – Granada, Scottish, Anglia, and the rest – it was clear that the BBC faced an entirely new prospect. For the first time, several million British families could settle down for an evening in front of the box and choose between two rival channels.

How on earth had this momentous challenge to the BBC's dominance come about? Even before its triumphant display during the Coronation, the BBC's television service had earned more admirers than critics. There was no obvious public clamour for a commercial rival. News reaching Britain that several million American viewers of the Coronation Service had had their coverage interrupted by an advert for deodorant and an 'interview' with a chimpanzee called 'J. Fred Muggs' only served to reinforce the notion that vulgarity was an unavoidable feature of the ratings-led approach. So great were the social and cultural changes wrought by this new medium, the *News Chronicle* told its readers, that it was 'all the more imperative' that in Britain it remained under 'wise but firm control'.[53]

The precise nature of this 'control' had already been scrutinised in a government review of the BBC's activities back in 1949. The process itself had turned into something of a farce. The Liberal peer William Beveridge, who chaired the committee of inquiry, had ruffled feathers by focusing almost entirely on radio and wasting time pursuing narrow personal grievances. Right at the start, the BBC's Director-General William Haley had gone to see him, 'a courtesy visit to welcome him and say we would give him all the help we could'. Yet Beveridge had launched into an extraordinary diatribe, telling Haley that he would be investigating thoroughly why he had not been allowed to do more broadcasting over the years. He even demanded to look at the BBC's files – 'I shall find out who blocked me, I shall find out who put the veto on me, I shall find out the censorship'. Later, Beveridge used an entire day's session to complain about not being given a major role in the BBC's Wordsworth Centenary programmes. Harman Grisewood, who was present, judged it to be 'the most prolonged exhibition of pique and vanity which I have ever witnessed'. Haley thought the performance 'disgraceful'. Despite this, the committee's conclusions, published at the beginning of 1951, had been overwhelmingly favourable: Haley's argument, that, as in Gresham's Law, competition would mean 'the good, in the long run, will inescapably be driven out by the bad', had won the day. The BBC was told to devolve more power to Scotland, Wales and Northern Ireland as well as to the English regions; the Governors were also given a little more influence over the Director-General. But radio, overseas broadcasting and television would all remain the monopoly of a single Corporation.[54]

The general election changed everything, however. Churchill himself still loathed the BBC: 'It kept me off the air for 11 years. It is run by reds', he kept insisting. But the real problem lay with the fresh parliamentary intake of October 1951, which included a number of younger Tories who fervently took up the cause of commercial broadcasting. Breaking the BBC's monopoly presented an obvious opportunity. There was now more money in people's pockets – and, in turn, more opportunities for selling consumer goods: an economic environment that, to the Tory vanguard at least, appeared to require a free market in broadcasting in order to be fully exploited. The group was small in size but benefited from the presence of a much larger group of MPs for whom the BBC's monopoly felt like just another example of socialist nationalisation, of 'somebody else knowing best'.[55]

Harman Grisewood could sense a change of weather at Westminster: a 'weariness with the BBC's self-righteousness and arrogance'. The climate in the country was less easy to gauge.

Though opinion polls showed that most people were still reasonably satisfied with the status quo, public patience with the self-restraint demanded by years of austerity – what Churchill portrayed as some sort of nightmare 'Queuetopia' – was clearly a diminishing resource. One influential analysis of the period wrote of 1945's 'New Jerusalem' being eclipsed by a 'New Elizabethan Age', in which the mythical pastoral ideals of 'Deep England' fought back against the impersonal, rational, interfering, bureaucratic 'onslaught' of the improving state. Hughie Green, one of ITV's new on-screen personalities suggested much the same in rather more prosaic language. 'People do not want three hours of fucking *King Lear* in verse when they get out of a ten-hour day in the fucking coal-pits,' he said, 'and fuck anybody who tries to tell them that they do.'[56]

The Director-General, Ian Jacob, set out the BBC's defence in a wide-ranging memo to senior colleagues. The Corporation, he said, had provided 'a service of television which balances the needs of all parts of the country and of all levels of the population'. Rather than targeting the richest areas, the BBC had ensured the medium was universally accessible. As for the range of programmes on offer, Jacobs explained that it had not been 'a question of deciding what is good for the people and denying them much of anything else'; it was 'a question of remaining in a position to withstand pressure from whatever direction it may come and to be able to steer a steady course in fulfilling the aims of the Charter to inform, educate and to entertain'. In other words, the freedom to plan programmes without constantly worrying about ratings was precisely what guaranteed a schedule neither exclusively uplifting, nor exclusively popular, but serendipitous, balanced, varied. As was often the case at the BBC, America stood as the ultimate warning. It was pointed out that on any given night in New York, the four main television channels 'often broadcast different light entertainments … or different thrillers at the same time'. There, competition had brought 'sameness, not variety'.[57]

Such was the view from the dizzy heights of BBC

management. When it came to the factory floor, the accusation levied against the Corporation was that whatever the grand intentions, its programmes would gradually diminish in quality because the people who made them were growing complacent. But at Alexandra Palace or Lime Grove, this accusation would have mystified everyone. David Attenborough saw a television medium continually nudged forward by an eager, collective spirit of enquiry. 'Our discussions over coffee in the canteen were vigorous and never-ending.' 'What, visually, was the best way to change shots …? When could we justifiably use music? Was it dishonest to mix film sequences shot earlier with live action without making it explicit that we were doing so?' Huw Wheldon also remembered a place filled with 'a very special brand of person': 'people who were young and vigorous but who had been in the army, the navy or the air force during the war', people who 'had enough experience of quarrels to be able to quarrel very fruitfully for long periods of time without buggering everything up'. It was the opinion of this 'extraordinary generation of restless and committed people', a group determined to take television by the scruff of its neck and to make their mark, which weighed most heavily with Wheldon: '*they* were my competitors.' It mattered, too, to Wheldon that he and his colleagues were of a generation that had been brought up to regard the BBC itself as 'immensely impressive and civilized': 'we were working for an important organisation … we took it seriously.' As for editorial scrutiny from above, what struck Wheldon most was the degree of creative freedom he felt he enjoyed, even as he climbed the editorial ladder. 'Nobody ever said to me you can't do this … nobody, not ever.' This attitude, Wheldon believed, 'came from deep sources within the Corporation itself'. The BBC was an institution that had been 'brought up over the years to understand something about the nature of freedom and the nature of freedom to make things'. 'They bore it and they backed it from on high', he reckoned, but it 'came from low down'.[58]

Counter-attack

Even someone as touchingly loyal as Huw Wheldon was forced to recognise that the arrival of ITV changed the broader climate within which the BBC operated.

Like it or not, the commercial companies had cooked up some highly attractive schedules. Among their offerings was the police drama *Dragnet* and the comedy series *I Love Lucy*, the first among several hugely popular American imports. There were also well-crafted home-grown series such as *The Adventures of Robin Hood*, game shows laden with generous prizes, such as *Take Your Pick* and *Double Your Money*, and starry family entertainment in the form of *Sunday Night at the Palladium*. Later, umbrella titles such as *Television Playhouse* and *Armchair Theatre* provided weekly slots for the single play – a genre that the BBC had always treated as its own special domain. And as far as the BBC was concerned, the ratings told their own story. In February 1956, barely five months after launch, ITV was pocketing more than 60 per cent of the audience in homes that were able to receive its broadcasts. By this stage, too, opinion polling revealed the humiliating fact that only 16 per cent of viewers thought the BBC better than ITV. With commercial broadcasters already quietly shunting some of their most serious programmes – documentaries, orchestral concerts and discussions – to late-night slots, so that peak viewing hours were reserved for the biggest light entertainment shows, the competitive outlook offered little hope of improvement.[59]

The BBC had shown that it could summon up the killer instinct if it wanted to. It was only moments before ITV took to the air for its opening night back in September 1955 that a small team of relatively unknown producers in radio had created a national sensation by doing away with one of the main characters in their most popular drama serial, *The Archers*. A quarter of the British adult population tuned in to hear Grace Archer, newly married and pregnant, rushing into the stables at the Grey Gables Country Club to save her horse from a raging fire, only to be felled by a crashing beam and end up expiring in the arms of her beloved husband, Phil. The Corporation tried to deny that the death had been a deliberate spoiler. And there was some credibility to the claim. Scriptwriters had been planning to whittle down cast numbers for a while, and the spotlight might have settled on Ysanne Churchman, who played Grace, after she had campaigned for a pay rise. But the truth was that the Controller of the Light Programme, Rooney Pelletier, had said to colleagues back in May that if a violent death was being planned it should be timed 'if possible to diminish interest in the opening of commercial television'.[60]

Since the newspapers did indeed devote rather more coverage to Grace's demise than ITV's birth, the BBC's tactic evidently paid off. But a bigger, longer-term strategy was clearly needed, especially where it mattered most: in sharpening up the output from Alexandra Palace and Lime Grove.

It was now that Broadcasting House finally turned on the money taps. From 1955, an ever-larger share of the BBC's income flowed into television. Light entertainment, which would most often find itself in the frontline of the ratings war, was first to splash out. In 1956, a lucrative contract secured the *Billy Cotton Band Show*, a highly polished television version of the successful radio series. The faces, as well as the voices, of the BBC's own newsreaders, started to appear on screen. There was a new emphasis on timing, and especially on tightening the gaps between programmes, so that instead of resorting to dreary government information films or the familiar sight of the Potter's Wheel interlude, or even just dead air, the BBC could match the 'gloss and pace' of ITV when it came to the rapidly evolving art of 'Presentation'.[61] In the *Radio Times*, television listings were moved to the front, radio's to the back. A flurry of new appointments to senior positions, and the departure of long-serving figures such as George Barnes and Cecil McGivern, reinforced the impression that a different era was beginning. The arrival of commercial opposition was clearly sending shock waves across the Corporation. People in radio were starting to accept, sometimes grudgingly, that in the competition for audiences it was television that occupied the frontline. People in television, meanwhile, were having to think more ruthlessly – about which programmes had the strongest viewer appeal, or where the weakest slots in the schedule lay. Yet the impact of competition was tangled up with all sorts of other changes taking place: the influx of a less deferential generation of programme makers; the increasing influence of news and current affairs; and novel techniques for producing shows.

The bumpy process of adapting to all these powerful forces probably made its presence felt in Children's Television before anywhere else. And it was there, too, that staff showed how, step by step, it might just be possible to compete aggressively while holding on to the Corporation's core values.

Since 1951, thanks to the influence of its head, Freda Lingstrom, the department had been concentrating heavily on programmes for the very youngest. But neither this neglect of older children nor the Toddlers' Truce could survive the arrival of ITV. Within months a new head was appointed. Owen Reed brought with him the experience of a long and exotic career both in and out of the BBC: acting in radio dramas in the 1930s, war reporting in Egypt, undercover operations with the Partisans in Yugoslavia, running the Balkan Section at Bush House. Nothing, however, had quite prepared him for his arrival at Lime Grove and, 'like a man going to the scaffold', being given first sight of the viewing figures. They showed with brutal clarity that older children were deserting the BBC in even larger numbers than their parents. A shell-shocked Reed remembers being offered a 'very stiff gin' by Cecil McGivern. 'I said to him what is my brief from you? He said it's very simple. You have got to recover the lost child audience without sacrifice of standards ... we've got to turn Freda's standards upside down.'[62]

For the next seven years, Reed's message to his colleagues was clear: 'The middle range of children, the eights to twelves, they're active, fidgety, action-demanding, they must have film ... They have got to be out-and-about rushing around, action, horizons, chases ...' He commissioned new adventure stories, such as *The Silver Sword*, and knockabout dramatisations of the long-running *Jennings* and *Billy Bunter* books. He also encouraged studio-based shows to offer their viewers as much 'action' as possible within the limits of their format. *Crackerjack*, which had first appeared only a matter of days before the launch of ITV in 1955, crammed an increasing number of competitive games and comedy acts into each frenetic edition, while the host, Eamonn Andrews, kept everything moving briskly before a lively theatre full of cheering youngsters.[63]

In October 1958, an entirely new series with a more educative tone was launched, offering fifteen minutes of friendly chat about 'Toys, model railways, games, stories, cartoons' every Thursday afternoon. *Blue Peter* was not exactly original. Reed's main source of inspiration was a series which had been broadcast since 1956: *Children's Television Club*, made in North Region's newly acquired Dickenson Road studios in Manchester, a converted Wesleyan chapel from where, once a month, Wilfred Pickles, Mabel Pickles, and the former child actor Judith Chalmers would demonstrate how to throw pottery, ride go-karts, or take turns handling 'Conker' the dog. Something similar had been tried even earlier on a couple of programmes that had been running since 1950: *Whirligig*, described as 'A Children's Variety Magazine' and its sister programme *Telescope*, in which Cliff Michelmore interviewed children in the studio and introduced items ranging from cookery lessons and piano recitals through to how to build a model theatre.[64]

All these series provided a rich seedbed of ideas – and experience – that *Blue Peter* would use to great advantage, though in Owen Reed's mind, what *Blue Peter* offered that was entirely new was taking its young viewers on imaginative and informative journeys *out* of the studio. *Blue Peter* also represented a leap forward behind the scenes, since it was the most thoroughgoing example yet of a production technique that Huw Wheldon had labelled the 'force-of-arms' approach. Instead of a single all-powerful producer, a series would be given their own permanent production team, with specialist skills on standby so that the full panoply of the BBC's resources, ranging from scriptwriting to outside broadcasts and location filming, could be exploited in one fell swoop.

The same method had been tried out for adults in April 1954 when 'a big team with powerful people' was brought together to produce the magazine show *Sportsview*. Soon afterwards, Grace Wyndham Goldie applied it to *Panorama*, transforming a somewhat sleepy discussion programme into a hard-hitting weekly magazine that rapidly built up a reputation as the BBC's foremost investigative current affairs series. Its opening music – a blast of Rachmaninov – established its authoritative tone. So too did Richard Dimbleby's legendary ability to command the studio space as he linked together each of four or five separate filmed reports, 'almost like a sort of fighter pilot, banking first one way and then another'. In February 1957, there was the first edition of *Tonight*, a lively forty-minute daily topical magazine series that helped fill the early-evening gap previously occupied by the Toddler's Truce. In this case, the 'force-of-arms' approach meant the throwing together of reporters, many recruited from the recently collapsed *Picture Post*, and a production team that could only be described as 'young, ambitious and quite brittle'. Cliff Michelmore, who had already proved his mettle at Children's Television, was brought in as the new show's unflappable host. For the opening episode he presided over twelve separate items, including the FA Cup draw, a report on a statue of Aphrodite upsetting the residents of Richmond-upon-Thames, Jonathan Miller poking fun at Charing Cross Road's shops, an interview with Ed Murrow about post-Suez Britain, film of Toscanini's funeral in Italy, and a topical calypso from Cy Grant. 'We assumed', its editor, Donald Baverstock said, 'that the audience were interested in showgirls, important people, elderly philosophers, cranks, lunatics, attractive girls – and why shouldn't we be interested likewise: we put 'em all together'. Within a matter of months this daring mix of news and entertainment – in 1957, it really *was* a daring combination – proved a huge hit with viewers and critics.[65]

In recruiting staff to *Panorama* and *Tonight*, Grace Wyndham Goldie had valued 'toughness' above almost everything else. Her protégés – Grace's 'boys', as they were known – encompassed politics-savvy journalists, bright young graduates, and a bevy of ex- or future MPs. The group, which included, among others, Michael Peacock, Antony Jay, John Freeman, Alasdair Milne and Donald Baverstock, were able, articulate, opinionated, ambitious. Within the run-down but high-thinking ghetto that was Lime Grove they saw themselves – indeed, were seen by those around them – as a kind of Praetorian Guard. 'We used to call them the Baverstockade', one of their colleagues remembered. Someone else observed tartly that they represented 'professionalism with more than a touch of the self-righteous'. In just a few years, many were rapidly ascending the BBC hierarchy, taking command of large swathes of output. Baverstock was among the most confident and fastest rising of all. Colleagues acknowledged his extraordinary intellectual energy. They also found his belief in the absolute rightness of his own judgement rather wearing. He was certainly part of a distinctly macho culture. Despite this – or perhaps because of it – he soon worked his way up to the rank of Assistant Controller, then Controller.[66]

It was therefore now to Baverstock that Owen Reed, as head of Children's Television, found himself having to pitch ideas on a regular basis. Like the other heads of departments summoned to attend one of Baverstock's 'offers' meetings, Reed was struck by a new obsession with ratings. 'The touchstone for everything, for virtue, for success, validity of programme effort – everything' turned on the latest viewing figures. 'No defence on grounds of philosophy or intent was listened to.' Baverstock's own position was clear. 'We must get rid of bad programmes in order to force good ones in.' For Reed, this meant more and more of his own programme ideas being shot down. On one especially painful occasion, Baverstock turned round and told him 'The trouble with you, boyo, is you're so bloody middle class'. 'It was', one shocked witness to the scene remembers, 'the first time I'd heard a Controller go and rubbish one's programme head in front of a junior member of staff'.[67]

Something beyond the clash of personalities was at work here: the indifference of ambitious current affairs staff towards programmes they deemed soft. As Reed saw it, with people like Baverstock in positions of influence inside the Corporation, 'a sort of horror of anything labelled with the name of children swept through the Television Service'. Before long, Reed found his entire team of drama producers dispersed. *The Sunday Serial*, which had previously been in the hands of specialist programme makers, now became the responsibility of an all-purpose Drama department used only to dealing with adults.

The new regime kicked off in January 1962 with a thirteen-part dramatisation of *Oliver Twist*, a story which the Children's Television department had always avoided on the grounds that it was far too macabre for five o'clock on a Sunday afternoon unless handled in 'a very careful way'. Reed could only stand by helplessly as the advice was ignored.

> There was a horrific treatment of the battering out of Nancy's brains and the slow oozing of blood over the edge of the table which produced nightmares and protests and a fearful rumpus the next day. Among the children who were kept awake the following night and woke screaming were the children of the Director-General, who wanted to know what had been going on. There was an inquest, but it made no difference.[68]

For Reed it was a personal tragedy. But he wondered if the affair also marked the end of an era of innocence in British television.

The medium had grown into early adulthood under the aegis of the BBC. And it had done so largely because, for over a decade, programmes had been 'made-in-the-making', as Wheldon put it. An idea would emerge and no one could be sure it worked until it had been broadcast. Afterwards, it would be criticised internally – roughed up, perhaps by Cecil McGivern or Grace Wyndham Goldie over a glass of whisky. The reactions of the public and the newspaper critics would be debated. It might be changed in the light of everything. Then, finally, another edition would be broadcast, beginning the whole process again. In other words, making television, like making radio, had been an evolutionary process in which success was built on a tolerance of failure.

The arrival of commercial competition had not entirely crushed this working culture. Indeed, given the legal requirement placed on ITV to educate and inform its audiences, as well as entertain them, there were plenty of observers who reckoned that the old monopoly was simply evolving into a new, and equally cosy, public service *du*opoly. Even so, market forces were beginning to percolate through the ecosystem. And Richard Hoggart was surely right to warn in 1957 of a future in which their distorting effect could weaken any lingering belief in cultural 'uplift'. There was, he warned, but the shortest of steps between providing what the public wanted and *over*-providing what the public wanted. There would be a struggle, he warned, 'to ignore the myriad voices of the trivial and synthetic sirens'.[69]

In BBC Television itself, a profound generational shift was also well underway: a rush of new people, new ideas, new programmes. But as Owen Reed knew only too well, there were losses, too. One of the Corporation's most experienced figures, Harman Grisewood, referred with sadness to the inexorable rise of 'Good Television', in which 'what was attractive on the screen should have a place there regardless of other considerations'.[70] The leading lights of BBC Television were now brimming with confidence, ruthless in defending their craft, keen not just to take on the commercial opposition but to challenge the BBC's ancient traditions. Television had well and truly ceased to be a cottage industry. Whether its new, tough-minded professionalism would help it adhere to Reithian principles of public service in the turbulent decade to come was far less certain.

10

BUILDING PYRAMIDS

Who's talking about entertainment? I'm talking about the
BBC! The BBC is part of the English heritage. Like suet
pudding and catarrh.

The Glums, Light Programme, 1954

Television may have been the rising star of the fifties, but for
many Britons the spirit of the decade was best distilled in one
unassuming slice of lunchtime radio.

At midday every Sunday in homes up and down the country
the air would start to thicken with the 'aromas of roast lamb
and gravy, and the sounds of new potatoes being scraped and
mint being chopped'. As this domestic ritual unfolded, another
sound, the soothing voice of Jean Metcalfe, would issue from
the speaker in the corner and drift through the gently warming,
steam-filled atmosphere – as if it, too, was an essential ingredient of the feast to come. 'The time in Britain is twelve noon, in
Germany it's one o'clock', the voice would announce. 'But home
and away it's time for *Two-Way Family Favourites.*' For the next
hour and a quarter, tables would be laid and vegetables boiled to
oblivion against an agreeable background of music and warming
messages passing between the men and women of the armed
forces in Germany and their families back home. The familiar
tunes, Metcalfe's honeyed tones, the cheery contributions from
her co-presenters in Cologne: it all blended so deliciously that
for an entire generation it felt as if 'the digestive juices and the
heartfelt emotions of the nation' were flowing as one.[1]

With its link-up across national boundaries, *Two-Way Family Favourites* was a powerful reminder that Britain's relationship with Europe – and the BBC's own international activities – had survived the coming of peace. The fifties, so often characterised as inward-looking, presented new and startling geopolitical challenges for politicians and broadcasters alike. Radio was still the main means of communicating across whole continents and oceans. The depth of experience the BBC had accumulated in wartime guaranteed it a leading role in the national goal of 'projecting Britain'.

It was a powerful reminder, too, that for most Britons at home these were still wireless days par excellence. In 1952, there were still roughly eight times as many radio-only licences as TV licences. For now at least, radio remained *the* universal medium, embracing all sexes, ages, classes and regions. It was the principal source of home entertainment throughout the week – not just on Sunday lunchtimes.[2]

In the minds of many of the programme makers, the older medium remained the BBC's 'senior' service. Radio people retained a profound belief in the seriousness of their craft and an ability to shape the lives of fellow citizens for the better. Indeed, in an era when ideas of family and fireside appeared more potent than ever it seemed only natural that the one service that already reached so many millions of homes and had woven itself so deeply into the very fabric of domestic life, was the one best placed to deliver that old Reithian dream of spreading culture and enlightenment. Family and radio: like twin planets they danced in orbit, locked in each other's gravitational pull.

A glimpse of a far horizon

In November 1951 there was a nationwide competition to find the 'Typical British Family'. Covering the event, the *Brighton Evening Argus* imagined a husband relaxing with his pipe after a day at work, children playing quietly, and the woman of the house contentedly making a lemon meringue pie. In the official and semi-official rhetoric of the post-war years, the moral and social health of the family was closely aligned to the moral and social health of the nation. The Labour government assumed that home was where good nutrition, healthy habits, decent behaviour and a desire for life-long learning might be inculcated. Successive Conservative governments put the stress on motherhood and marriage as the unassailable norm, and the importance of family cohesion in forging a stable society. Across both parties, there was a strong belief that children were the country's future – that whatever happened in school, it was the family home that provided the irreplaceable crucible for their development. The psychoanalyst John Bowlby was quoted widely on the vital impact of 'mother love' on a child's character. 'If she neglects him when he is small', he warned Britain's parents, 'there will be trouble afterwards.'[3]

Children's radio had always assumed a special role in the BBC's own vision of the domestic moral economy. Not only did programmes for the very young provide a break for parents; they helped mould the intellect and imagination of the next generation. With its familiar opening refrain, 'Are you sitting comfortably? Then I'll begin', *Listen with Mother* had been offering radio audiences a fifteen-minute dose of stories and nursery rhymes at 1.45 p.m. every Monday to Friday since 1950. There had also been a *Children's Hour* of one kind or another on the radio ever since 1922. Derek McCulloch, who ruled over these programmes from London for nearly two decades, had believed in instilling his young audience with what he saw as the Christian virtues of Godliness and neighbourliness. The results were not to everyone's taste: *Children's Hour* could be preachy and cloying. But its famous sign-off, 'Goodnight children everywhere', imprinted itself on millions of Britons, and the famous 'Uncle' and 'Aunt' personas adopted by its presenters fostered what one producer called a 'family feeling ... the feeling of a small community to which you as a listener belonged and which was coming on for you, personally, every day.'[4]

When it came to older children, producers had to grapple

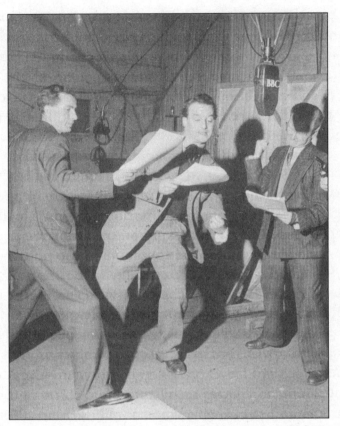

A 1947 episode of the hugely popular adventure series *Dick Barton –
Special Agent*. Noel Johnson, Alex McCrindle and John Mann perform
the roles of Dick Barton, Jock and Snowy for the studio microphone.

with simmering public concern over the potential effects of
broadcasting on volatile young minds. Overheated newspaper
reports of a vast juvenile crime wave created the impression that
civil society – indeed, the nation's moral fibre – was fraying at
the edges, and prompted a row over the hugely popular radio
serial *Dick Barton – Special Agent*. When it had been launched
in 1946 it was not explicitly aimed at a juvenile audience. But
it quickly got one. By 1950, nearly fifteen million were tuning
in five times a week to follow Barton's thrilling exploits as he
battled against a succession of sleazy ne'er-do-wells. In every
struggle our hero remained impeccably upright in manner

and speech. But what might be the effect on listeners of being immersed repeatedly in this sordid world of crime? The BBC felt obliged to seek the opinion of more than seventy child-guidance clinics. Their replies leaned almost two-to-one in favour of the series. The Royal Hospital for Sick Children in Edinburgh even pronounced *Dick Barton* positively beneficial 'for the projection of phantasy'. But there was enough doubt to unsettle the Corporation. 'Nightmares and undue mental tension are produced in some children', one London clinic claimed. 'Many of them look on Barton as a fool who gets away with too much, and miss the moral issues raised.' Broadcasting House, acutely conscious of its responsibilities, decided to act. A new set of rules issued in June 1950 required that every *Dick Barton* now came lumbered with a postscript solemnly explaining the rights and wrongs of the latest episode.[5]

Given the anxiety that many parents harboured over the suitability of programmes for the young, it came as a blessed relief for women at home to have at least some listening all of their own. An investigation by Mass Observation in 1956 had revealed that 'The Housewife's Day' was on average fifteen hours long. In the midst of this non-stop domestic labour, the BBC provided a fixed point when she might, briefly, take a break. When it went on the air for the first time at 2 p.m., Monday 7 October 1946, *Woman's Hour* had been advertised as a programme of 'music, advice, and entertainment for the home' – a blandly generic description that hardly seemed to promise anything radically different from all its predecessors. In the opening week, listeners were offered 'Mother's Midday Meals', 'Your Winter Clothes', 'Children in the Home', and 'Putting your best face forward', a menu of items that prompted the *Daily Mirror* to declare the series 'uninteresting, a waste of time, full of old ideas'. But over coming weeks there were discussions on equal pay and health legislation. In the following year, there were nine separate talks on the currency crisis and a series of reports about women engineers. By 1953, the items on offer in a single edition included a discussion with an academic on the latest scientific research on nutrition, reviews of several plays opening in London's West End, a traveller reflecting on her recent 'Adventures in Africa', and a dramatised profile of the Scottish queen, Mary Stuart.[6]

Woman's Hour had been swiftly recognised in government circles as a valuable channel of communication for reaching women voters. The creation of the NHS, the introduction of a National Insurance Scheme, changes to rationing, new housing schemes: ministers knew each one of these welfare reforms needed to be 'sold' to those who would be impacted most directly. At every turn, a torrent of official information would come pouring out of Whitehall – pamphlets, advertise-ments, travelling exhibitions, films. But it was Aneurin Bevan who consistently made the biggest effort to secure sympathetic coverage from women's radio programmes. Producers, in turn, recognised that 'almost any decision taken in Whitehall' would immediately affect the lives of their listeners. A 'household, a kitchen', one of them told the *Northern Daily Telegraph* in May 1947, was never 'isolated' from questions of public policy.[7]

All this came naturally to those in charge. From 1950, the Talks department, which provided much of *Woman's Hour*'s content and most of its staff, was being led by Mary Somer-ville, a woman William Haley regarded as one of the BBC's most 'remarkable' producers. It was with Somerville's encour-agement that Janet Quigley, who had run the wartime *Woman's Page*, took over as full-time editor, bringing with her nearly two decades of broadcasting experience. There was also Isa Benzie, a contemporary of Quigley's at Oxford who had since run the BBC's Foreign Department: she now specialised in producing many of *Woman's Hour*'s health talks. Together they created what one fresh recruit called a place of 'real blue-stockings'. It was also 'one of the most forward-looking' corners of the entire BBC. Three-quarters of the audience were working-class women, many of whom had been denied a decent formal education. As Quigley told her team in 1952, the programme's mission was to transport such listeners beyond the four walls

Olive Shapley interviewing Eleanor Roosevelt as 'Guest of the Week' for a special Festival of Britain edition of *Woman's Hour* in 1951. Shapley claimed that even in the 1950s the series 'tried to open a window on the world' and was 'at the forefront of changing public perceptions of broadcasting taste'.

of the home and give them 'a glimpse of a far horizon, a new sphere of thought, a strange and unfamiliar subject'.[8]

In a BBC still relatively new to the art of audience research, the *Woman's Hour* team had an unusually strong sense of their listeners' tastes. Soon after the launch of the series they were receiving more than a thousand letters a week. Questions relating to so-called 'marital difficulties' came up regularly, with listeners looking to *Woman's Hour* as a source of reliable advice. In 1952, for instance, four correspondents were invited to the studio to share their views on how to sustain a 'happy marriage':

Guest: I thought our marriage would really go on the rocks, because I'm afraid things were not very satisfactory as regards the intimate side of our married life.
Presenter: Yes. You found sexual relations a little difficult to start with, was that it?
Guest: Yes, it was most unsatisfactory altogether, and in a few weeks I became quite a nervous wreck and very irritable and bad tempered …
Presenter: Yes. And how did you put it right?
Guest: Well, I did seek medical advice, but there was nothing wrong there really … I was just told to go home and have a baby, just like that. So, I said, 'well that's all right. I'd wish you'd show me how to do it.'[9]

The *Daily Mirror* called it 'one of the frankest talks ever broadcast' by the BBC. Discussing it all in such a matter-of-fact manner allowed the *Woman's Hour* team to build a reputation for pushing boundaries. As with television, benign neglect of daytime output by senior management gave *Woman's Hour* the chance, as one producer put it, to 'experiment with all sorts of things that we probably wouldn't have been allowed to do' otherwise. The daytime slot mattered to listeners, too. At 2 p.m., one of them explained, 'all the family are either at school or work, so therefore we can enjoy the talks on current affairs and other talks … I learn things I should be too shy to ask anyone I know for fear of being thought ignorant.' 'The absence of the man of the house', said another, was crucial: sensitive subjects could be listened to without embarrassment.[10]

The letters pouring in from around the country also provided vital information on how to address listeners appropriately. The material conditions of working-class life had to be constantly taken into account. The suggestion of a talk on refrigerators, for instance, was rejected on the grounds that 'the very large majority of our audience have no such helpful appliances … and listeners' correspondence shows that they are intensely irritated by such reminders of comfort beyond their reach'. The idea of the series having a summer break was also rejected, on the grounds that few listeners could afford to take 'holidays away from home'.[11]

The trickiest task facing producers was deciding how to cater for the 'double lives' many women were now leading, juggling paid work outside the home with running a household. By the end of the 1940s roughly a quarter of married women were in the workforce, including many who had joined during the war and wanted to continue. Yet there was a palpable desire among many to embrace homemaking. For some, the post-war home was a place for realising long-held dreams of a better life, and the role of housewife was seen not as constricting but empowering.[12] One way of dealing with this range of experience was to launch a Sunday afternoon edition, *Woman's Hour Digest*, which, from 1951, offered those who had been out at work the chance to catch the highlights of the past week. Another strategy was to discuss the issue openly in the form of dramatised dialogues. This rather stilted performance featuring the married couple 'Isabel' and 'John' was typical of the genre:

Isabel: Sheila rang up today. She wants your advice.
John: Oh! What's wrong this time?
Isabel: She wants to take a job. She saw an advertisement which seemed to be just the sort of thing she would like – and then Peter kicked up a fuss about it. Said he wasn't going to have his wife going out to work.
John: Silly ass!
Isabel: Well, I just told her to go ahead and take it ... It always amazes me that there are still so many of these Victorian men about who just think that a woman's place is at home ...
John: I say the same as you – she ought to be free to take a job if she wants to. Goodness knows industry needs all the women it can get ...[13]

Several months later, it was the homemakers' turn to be

venerated. 'A lot of people seem to think that a domesticated woman is rather a dull and mousy person', a guest explained. 'I think it's the career woman who's much more likely to become stereotyped and develop a one-track mind.'[14]

Woman's Hour's desire to be fair-minded on matters of controversy was palpable. But when Olive Shapley, now one of its regular presenters, claimed that the programme's goal was to be 'balanced, just as life should be ideally', she alluded to something broader: a refusal to see domestic topics and public affairs as mutually exclusive.[15] The production team always claimed that even dedicated homemakers wanted to be stimulated and challenged. By the end of the 1950s the size and loyalty of the audience suggested that their instincts had been right.

Indeed, *Woman's Hour* was soon a flag-bearer for wider change at the BBC. The sprawling Talks department had always enjoyed a reputation for its rigour and serious-mindedness. It was the kind of place where the Master of Balliol College, Oxford, the distinguished philosopher, Sandie Lindsay, could be told by a producer that his script was 'feeble beyond measure' – full of clichés without 'saying anything of significance'. The concern for quality was admirable, but it was starting to create an enervating effect. Anyone who dared suggest giving the microphone to a journalist rather than yet another university don was treated as if they had suggested handing over the airwaves to a pornographer.[16]

Woman's Hour offered a fresh approach. Instead of observing an inviolable rule that all talks should be precisely fifteen minutes long, it commissioned items lasting no more than six minutes. Rehearsals were kept to a minimum so that some sense of spontaneity survived. Each edition aimed to pack into the running order a variety of formats – not just interviews or talks, but live discussions, book reviews, a daily serial. Behind the scenes, meetings were conducted in what staff described as a democratic fashion: producers 'chipped in'. Nor were listeners excluded from these deliberations. Deploying the kind of language rarely heard elsewhere in Talks, Janet Quigley described

Woman's Hour as 'a kind of club'. 'Far from being confined to passive listening,' she said, 'membership of this club takes an active form: listeners write about the programme and about themselves, they criticise, encourage, suggest and occasionally broadcast. This co-operation in building the programme insures that it is really their own.' Norman Collins described the series 'as one of the most important instruments the BBC had'. It 'bore no resemblance to the dignified nature of what the BBC had been doing in the past', he said – and was all the better for it. In 1957 two of its producers, Isa Benzie and Janet Quigley, would be instrumental in the launch of a 'morning miscellany' for the Home Service, conceived in the same spirit. Their new programme went under the catchy title *Today*.[17]

Rebuilding the world

If the BBC saw its primary social role as creating the conditions for British citizens to live a 'full life', it was also acutely conscious of how the war had left it entangled with a range of international obligations. By the time the Allied victory had been declared, some twenty million adult listeners were thought to be tuning into the broadcasts of the different European language services from Bush House. Millions more in North America, Latin America and the Caribbean, Africa, the Middle East, the Far East, and around the Pacific, were listening regularly to one of Bush's many indigenous language programmes or to the English-language programme of its Overseas Service. The BBC, in other words, entered the post-war era as a fully fledged global institution: tuned into the world, broadcasting back to it, acutely conscious of the power of radio to shape international opinion. Plenty of countries also looked to the BBC as *the* model for public service.

Labour's 1946 White Paper on broadcasting expressed the state's position clearly. In the battle for hearts and minds, it argued, 'we cannot afford to let the British viewpoint go by default'. It was a position that ensured government financial support for the BBC's overseas operations – and , equally, the oversight that came with it. One of the characteristic features of the post-war period was therefore the BBC's need to accommodate the strategic concerns of successive governments. Yet the BBC's desire to seed the world with its particular values and standards remained a powerful, deep-rooted force of its own.[18]

In 1945, it had been in Europe where the need for missionary intervention was most keenly felt. Following the declaration of peace, Geoffrey Bridson had travelled through the shattered towns and cities of Germany. 'The utter devastation left by the bombing', he wrote, 'was a sight I am unlikely to forget.' In Hamburg, Maurice Gorham found that street after street had been shelled to oblivion in the final stages of the Allied assault. 'The rubble seemed to have been bulldozed off the roads and pavements and heaped up inside the ruins.' It was here, too, that the only fully functioning radio station could be found in what was now the British zone of occupation. Since Britain was responsible not just for feeding millions of Germans before they died of starvation, but for the rebuilding and de-Nazification of a once vigorous broadcasting system, it was Hamburg that now became the centre of a busy operation in which the BBC played the leading role.[19]

The person appointed overall controller of broadcasting within the British zone was the head of the German Service, Hugh Carleton Greene. When he arrived, Greene saw his mission as ensuring that Nordwestdeutscher Rundfunk, or NWDR, the regional broadcasting organisation that had been established from the ruins of Radio Hamburg, would become 'independent of state and party political influences'. In the longer term, that included being independent of the occupying power. Gathering the station's rather dazed German staff into the station's concert hall for the very first time, Greene's message was simple and striking: 'I am here to make myself superfluous.'[20]

It had already been agreed in London that NWDR should speak with a local voice. This meant recruiting any German who was willing to let differences of opinion reach the airwaves.

On a day-to-day basis, the vital job of winnowing out available talent fell to the twenty-four-year-old Walter Eberstadt, who had served as a psychological warfare officer in the British Army. Eberstadt would screen applicants through a series of one-to-one interviews. 'I'd give them a meal, whisky, cigarettes or pipe tobacco and have them talk, talk, talk. If I concluded they were fundamentally decent, I was not put off by some affiliation with the old system.' Once confirmed in place, production staff would be required to attend a training school organised by Greene and offering a special emphasis on teaching recruits their responsibilities as broadcasters in a democratic society. The vast majority of instructors were German journalists, but the ethos they encouraged would have been familiar to anyone back in Broadcasting House: trainees referred to the instilling of a 'British spirit'.[21]

Grumbles from Hamburg's local politicians, outraged at being denied a direct hand in the operation, were brushed aside, and by the end of 1947 NWDR's public service status was formalised. It reflected what Greene called 'the constitution' of the BBC but with 'sensible modifications'. An Administrative Board was constituted very much along the lines of the BBC's own Board of Governors. This Board in turn appointed a Director-General, Adolf Grimme, a culture minister in one of the regional governments. On Monday 15 November 1948, Grimme took up his post. Four days later Greene left, happy that with his help NWDR had become the first German broadcasting organisation after the defeat of the Nazis to acquire legal status.[22]

*

On his return to London, Greene took charge of the BBC's broadcasts to Eastern Europe and the Soviet Union. As a result of the Communist coup in Czechoslovakia, the Berlin Blockade, the Marshall Plan and other steps being taken to create a new Western alliance, the Cold War was reaching an especially belligerent phase. Given the stalemate in the political and military

arena, the strategy for both sides was fast becoming 'the continuous pursuit of victory by other means' – broadcasting, of
course, included.[23]

Back in 1945, the government had been poised to scale back
Bush House's transmissions to Europe before the chill in Britain's relationship with its former Soviet ally, and the descent
of an Iron Curtain separating East from West, forced a hasty
modification of its plans. There was also a shift in focus. The
BBC's Director-General William Haley acknowledged that once
the Nazi occupation of vast swathes of the Continent had been
rolled back and local broadcasting organisations re-established,
there would 'not be the same overwhelming need for the clerk
and peasant in Europe to listen to the BBC'. In future, the Corporation would use its various language services to reach a
smaller though more influential audience: the decision-makers
and opinion-formers.[24]

Regular broadcasts in Russian began on Sunday 24 March
1946. At first, the flavour was noticeably apolitical, with discussion of world affairs restricted to an urbane weekly talk by Anatol
Goldberg. It was reckoned inside Bush House that Russian listeners would have been 'so oversupplied with Soviet political
propaganda' that they would only be enticed to the BBC with
'a good deal of culture and entertainment'. Greene thought it
foolish in any case to believe 'it should be any part of our objec-
tive to contribute to the overthrow of the Soviet regime or to
"liberate" the Soviet people, who had probably no desire to be
liberated anyway, at least from outside'. A more realistic aim, he
reckoned, was to help nudge Soviet public opinion into being
'not unfriendly to the West'.[25]

This softly-softly approach grated with a Foreign Office
that wanted more overt criticism of communism. When the
Soviets began systematic jamming of transmissions in April
1949, Greene agreed that the time for caution was probably over.
Henceforth, the aim of programmes in Russian would be to
'expose both the expansionist purpose of the foreign policy of
the USSR and also the ruthless and despotic nature of the Soviet

regime itself'. Goldberg's weekly talks became sharper in tone. A weekly Slavonic Orthodox Church service was introduced. And as with other services to the Eastern bloc, there was to be a greater emphasis placed on hard-hitting news, so that, as the BBC itself put it, less time was 'wasted' on air with 'descriptions of camping in Cornwall or recordings of noises at a wildfowl exhibition'.[26]

It was always hard to be sure exactly what impact these broadcasts had. American sources indicated that in the aftermath of the 1948 coup in Czechoslovakia, between a half and three-quarters of radio sets in the country were tuned to the BBC. For nearly three decades after 1949, tens of thousands of personal testimonies were sent to the long-running series, *Letters without Signature*, which the BBC broadcast to listeners in the 'German East Zone'. The individual comments they contained – 'We place our hopes in you', 'I trust you', 'I like your programme very much, because it shows the views of citizens who are not represented in our press' – were certainly encouraging. Information from the USSR proved harder to obtain: Bush House often had to rely on attacks in the Soviet press, or a spike in jamming activity, to assess whether its transmissions had hit a nerve.[27]

What was less in doubt was that the BBC's broadcasts across the Iron Curtain had exposed a subtle but important divide between government and Corporation in how to respond to the Cold War's ideological battle. While he was running the European Service at Bush House, Ian Jacob made clear that he wanted programmes to stress the merits of Western civilisation and British liberal democracy rather than constantly launching attacks on the Soviet system: the idea of a 'voice of NATO' type service was completely out of the question. So too was blindly following a United States that favoured an aggressive 'crusade for freedom'. Jacob saw the BBC's role as being a sort of national weathervane. 'By bringing a great variety of people to the microphone,' he wrote, 'the BBC tries to show to its listeners the different currents of thought, the full and democratic

Nina Rekstin and Tony Cash demonstrate the Bossa Nova for radio
listeners in the Soviet Union. It was the last in a series of introductions
to 'western' dances broadcast on the BBC's Russian Service in 1964.

flow of ideas, and the diverse opinions, that go to make up the
voice of the British people.'[28]

Naturally, the Foreign Office worried that the BBC 'pulled
punches and obscured viewpoints'. So long as its overseas operations were funded by a direct grant-in-aid from the Treasury, the
BBC could hardly ignore these criticisms. Yet the constitutional
understanding reached in 1947 was that while the Foreign Office
could determine the overall nature and scope of the BBC's
broadcasts – which languages were included and how much
money and airtime they were each allocated – the BBC would
have editorial control over actual content.[29]

Potential rows were often defused through personal relationships. On the BBC side, Jacob's career in the War Cabinet
meant he was comfortable moving in military, diplomatic and

intelligence circles; on the Foreign Office side, relations were managed by Ivone Kirkpatrick, whose wartime role at Bush House meant he understood the importance of convincing listeners abroad that the BBC remained independent of party or state. When the relationship worked smoothly, tangible proof of the extraordinary level of trust came in the form of what Martin Esslin called 'the greatest of all secrets': the Foreign Office's willingness to share routinely with senior editors at Bush House highly classified communications from its embassies abroad. There were other times when staff found themselves going head-to-head with what were described as 'ill-conceived and positively dangerous' proposals from more junior Whitehall officials. The BBC's broadcasts across the Iron Curtain were therefore the outcome of what one leading historian of Cold War diplomacy has categorised as 'continuous, complex and often difficult negotiations'. In everything, fudge and compromise were as important as public service ideals.[30]

*

The Cold War acted as a uniquely powerful theme around which the BBC's operations were shaped in the post-war era. But it was not the only international development bearing down on its activities. In May 1947, three months before the independence and partition of India, government ministers announced that the word 'British Commonwealth' was to be used instead of 'Empire'. Before the fifties were out, Burma, Ceylon, Sudan, the Gold Coast and Malaya would also achieve self-government. Many – though not all – of these countries would retain a link with the old imperial centre on renegotiated terms.[31]

Did this notion of a looser, voluntary association represent a genuinely new relationship or merely some new and subtle form of colonialism? When it came to broadcasting, it appeared to be a mixture of both. The BBC's External Services – the new catch-all name for the hitherto separate European and Overseas services – often acted the beneficent missionary when it came to setting up new indigenous broadcasting organisations. It also still envisaged London as the hub of a Britannic world held together by radio.

The BBC had emerged from the war with its reputation in 'Commonwealth' countries such as Australia, New Zealand and Canada at something of a high water mark. George Ivan Smith, who had joined the Australian Broadcasting Corporation back in 1936, was among those who had been seconded to London during the war to boost Britain's ability to speak in friendly terms with its fighting allies. Back home, the library of the ABC had been filled with books about the Corporation, and its announcers had copied the old Savoy Hill custom of wearing a black tie to read the news. Reith himself had been viewed as 'a demi-God'. In short, the BBC's influence in Australia had always been 'absolutely enormous'. For Smith, however, it was the war itself, and his daily experience of running the Pacific Service from the cultural melting pots of 200 Oxford Street and Bush House, which had 'sealed the bond'. 'I'd never been out of New South Wales, let alone Australia ... I knew nothing about Africa until I met Africans at the BBC. I knew nothing about the Caribbean until I met people at the BBC ... all the way down the line there was this admixture of cultural interests and political interests.' Smith described this daily experience as giving him an 'awareness of what the Empire meant in terms of people' – an experience echoed by other colleagues from Australia, as well as a large group of Canadians, all of whom forged 'an extraordinarily strong link' between London and their home countries. An institution that had perhaps once seemed forbidding had also been revealed as more human. 'They always protected their own standards', Smith said, but 'they were open ... they brought in people who could help them to understand'.[32]

While many Commonwealth broadcasters stayed after the war, forging a long career with the BBC, some on the Corporation's own payroll travelled in the opposite direction. Stuart Williams, who had managed sleeping arrangements during the Blitz, spent much of 1947 and 1948 travelling to Egypt, Singapore,

India and what was then Ceylon, to negotiate BBC access to local transmitters – a vital activity if the Corporation's output was to be heard properly throughout the Far East. In 1950, Hugh Carleton Greene followed up his two years running the BBC's Eastern European Services with a spell in Malaya, where he brought his experience of psychological warfare to bear on the crushing of a Communist uprising. That same year, Ian Jacob concluded months of international discussions by being elected the first president of a brand-new entity, the European Broadcasting Union. Throughout the first decade of the post-war period, there was also a steady flow of BBC engineers to the West Indies, Burma and tropical Africa, to undertake surveys, establish studios, and set up transmission facilities.[33]

Whitehall, and indeed many senior figures at the BBC, still regarded broadcasting as a tool of colonial policy, reflecting the view from London that across the former Empire self-government was something only to be achieved after several more years of British tutelage. But in Africa, especially, BBC visitors found themselves increasingly torn between the Corporation's old imperial instincts and their duty as programme makers to report the truth as they found it – a truth that recognised the debilitating effects of colonial rule and the popular clamour for independence. When Martin Esslin visited East and Central Africa in 1950 to make 'endless features on agricultural policy in the Sudan and Uganda', he had no doubt as to the trip's official purpose. 'It was projection of Britain and it was justifying our presence there'. Three years later on a visit to South Africa, he felt morally compelled to reveal to listeners back home a rather more challenging story. As well as interviewing Nelson Mandela and Walter Sisulu from the African National Congress, Esslin met several supporters of apartheid, including members of the South African government whose attitudes appalled him. When he returned to London with hours of recordings packed into his suitcase he found making anything resembling a 'balanced' feature almost impossible. South Africa, though nominally independent, was still a member of the Commonwealth. He knew, therefore that he 'couldn't be too rude'. He settled, instead, for weaving into the script subtle hints about 'how terrible they were'.[34]

Such caution was justified, given what Geoffrey Bridson had gone through when he was a guest of the South African Broadcasting Corporation. Back in 1947, while covering the latest royal tour, he also compiled an account of the country's racial policies for the BBC series *Focus*. 'I stated the relevant facts as I had been quietly collecting them during my stay', he explained. Unfortunately, on the very day on which his documentary, *The Colour Question*, was due to be broadcast, the South African Embassy despatched a delegation to Broadcasting House demanding that the programme be pulled. The BBC refused, saying it was 'a matter of public interest'. The Embassy responded by asking the British government to take the entire BBC off the air 'in the interests of Commonwealth solidarity'. The Director-General, William Haley, still refusing to intervene, instead sent a personal message of support to Bridson while he was putting the finishing touches to the programme in the studio. The programme went ahead. Months of heated exchanges between the South African government and 10 Downing Street ensued, during which it looked at one point as if a £80 million gold loan to Britain would be rescinded. Despite all this, Bridson recorded that he was never reprimanded himself for 'having stirred up such an unholy ruckus'.[35]

A slightly easier ride was had by Tom Chalmers when he went to Nigeria in 1951 to organise its national radio network, declaring himself keen 'to enter very fully' into local life. He knew he needed to forge a decent working relationship with the country's colonial administrators, since they were the ones with access to the resources he needed. Differences started to emerge, however. When it came to making programmes, Chalmers wanted to recruit as many local people as possible. 'If you're going to broadcast at all in a country like Nigeria you *must* have Nigerians, mostly, to do it', he reasoned. Indeed, as far as Chalmers was concerned, it was 'coming from the BBC and not being died-in-the-wool colonial civil servants' that had the biggest bearing on the work his team did: 'we had none of the inhibitions about Africans and Africanisation ... that the civil servants had.' Among those subsequently hired was Fela Sowande – a talented and classically trained composer, jazz pianist, bandleader and choirmaster – who was appointed the Director of Music. A vacancy as Talks producer was filled by Chinua Achebe, who was about to write his first novel, *Things Fall Apart*. Chalmers could see that Achebe 'didn't require much training' – though he was despatched to London nonetheless: even Chalmers still assumed that the BBC's own training school represented the international gold standard.[36]

It was the precise constitutional status of the new Nigerian Broadcasting Service that provoked the trickiest debates with colonial officials in Lagos. They assumed it ought to be under their own centralised control. From Chalmers' perspective, what was required was a regionalised system 'capable of being formed into a national service exactly like the BBC'. He also believed that it needed to be a public corporation rather than government-run, so that it was insulated from direct political interference. As for the schedules, they should be planned, as Chalmers put it, in 'very Reithian' terms: 'the usual mix of education and information and entertainment.' Since all the energy and initiative lay with Chalmers and his staff, rather than the colonial government, what finally emerged by the end of 1956 – a fully fledged Nigerian Broadcasting Corporation – was indeed largely crafted in the BBC's own image. Once this had been achieved, Chalmers' British team packed their bags and returned home: it would have been all too easy, he concluded, 'to get involved far too deeply in a country and a society which was not theirs'.[37]

*

The BBC was at its most imperious in the unshakeable assumption that its own programmes were superior to those made

almost anywhere else in the world. The global trade in programmes still flowed overwhelmingly in an outward direction
from London. A threatened flood of US radio exports never
materialised, largely because the leading American networks
were too busy trying to establish a stranglehold over their
domestic television market. This gave the BBC a vital breathing
space. Radio stations across Australia, New Zealand, Canada,
Southern Africa and the West Indies continued to rebroadcast
hundreds of hours of BBC output every week. Live coverage
of cricket Test matches and rugby tours in particular aroused
a passionate and devoted following, conjuring up the image of
an international community forged through friendly rivalry. For
the 1953 Coronation the BBC masterminded an hour-long programme called *Commonwealth Greetings*, which, according to one
rather over-excited producer, aimed to show 'a multi-coloured,
multi-racial British Commonwealth, with strength and wisdom,
looking towards a bright future'. The BBC's efforts were clearly
tilted towards emphasising the most benign aspects of this imagined community. When its Christmas Day programmes were
rebroadcast later that year, it was telling that while they referred
to insurgencies in Kenya and Malaya, it was the violence of the
rebels rather than the vicious repression of the colonial state
that was highlighted.[38]

Whatever the merits of individual programmes, the extent
of the BBC's success in exporting a marketable vision of Britain
was hard to deny. By 1950 it was getting four times more airtime
on the Canadian CBC than in 1947 – even overtaking the number
of hours devoted to American shows. In Australia, nearly half
of the ABC's variety output came from London, including old
warhorses such as *Take it from Here*, *Variety Bandbox*, and *Much
Binding in the March*. By 1953, the BBC's Transcription Service,
responsible for shipping recordings abroad, was distributing
658 different radio shows on tens of thousands of discs. It was
sometimes hard for Commonwealth broadcasters to conceal
their frustration at this avalanche of material. In September
1952, the head of the CBC's London office wrote despairingly

to his managers back home. 'It is a form of imperialism. They unconsciously feel that they have the best broadcasting system in the world, staffed by the best possible people, producing the best possible programmes in the best possible way.' The awkward truth was that, consciously or unconsciously, many other broadcasters around the world seemed to agree with the BBC's glowing self-assessment. There was a constant stream of fact-finding visits to the Corporation's studios – delegations not just from the dominions and colonies, but from the United States, the Soviet Union, Japan – all eager to learn more about its techniques, its policies, its guiding philosophy. Overseas broadcasting organisations also kept inviting BBC people to come and work with them. Only a matter of months after his contentious trip to South Africa, Geoffrey Bridson was in Australia, helping the ABC establish a feature-making unit.[39]

Above all, there was the as yet unmatched scale and reach of the BBC's own international transmissions. Growth was by no means inevitable: politicians had a tendency to assume that broadcasting could be turned on and off like a tap if and when resources dictated. Between 1951 and 1953, successive cuts were imposed on the General Overseas Service, the European Service, as well as the Portuguese, Spanish and Latin American services, and broadcasts to North America – all while the US and Soviet Union were rapidly expanding their own transmissions. A particularly vicious round of cuts in 1952 prompted Ian Jacobs to write to the Conservative government in desperation. 'It seems to me that at a time when we are doing our utmost to strengthen the Western world in order to prevent war we should be expanding the activities of the BBC's Services rather than … paring them down.' Even the *Daily Mail* understood the ramifications of Whitehall parsimony. 'The Voice of America booms, the Voice of Stalin roars', it warned, yet 'the Voice of Britain must whisper'. It was nothing short of miraculous, therefore, that by mid-decade, the overall number of language services broadcast around the world from Bush House was up from a post-war low of just nineteen to more than forty. Their combined broadcasting time – 552 hours a week – was more than that of all the BBC's domestic radio and television services combined. As for the General Overseas Service in English, it was now on air for twenty-one hours every day. George Ivan Smith summarised the BBC's international achievement neatly: the Corporation had been 'leaving its calling card out all over the world', and as yet no other broadcasting system had the same 'universal spread'. Someone even bothered to calculate the total money involved. It turned out to be roughly one-third of one per cent of the British defence budget.[40]

The envy of the world

International entanglements were never entirely separate from the rest of the BBC's business. They sometimes exerted a subtle but important influence back home. A desire in the corridors of Broadcasting House to see post-war Britain reconnect once more with the best of world culture was one of the motivations behind a brand-new and highly ambitious radio service launched with great fanfare on Sunday 29 September 1946: the Third Programme.

Aside from a forty-five-minute harpsichord recital of Bach's 'Goldberg Variations', some madrigals by Monteverdi, and a speech by the South African prime minister, Jan Smuts, the opening night itself had a distinctly British flavour: a recording of Max Beerbohm talking about the London of 1935, a live concert from Maida Vale featuring Handel, Purcell and Vaughan Williams, and a specially commissioned Festival Overture from Benjamin Britten. Over the following days, however, a proudly internationalist tone seeped through. Listeners were treated to contemporary poetry in French, the Hungarian composer Zoltán Kodály conducting a concert of his own music, and an unabridged production by the twenty-one-year-old Peter Brook of Jean-Paul Sartre's *Huis Clos*. In subsequent weeks there would be Racine's *Phèdre*, several new productions of ancient Greek classics such as Aeschylus's *Agamemnon*, and a flurry of programmes with a German theme to mark the bicentenary of Goethe's birth, including a talk from Thomas Mann and a six-part dramatisation of *Faust*, translated by one of the BBC's young star writer-producers, the poet Louis MacNeice. Speech programmes – plays, features, readings and straight talks – occupied a full two-thirds of airtime. In the opening month alone, there was E. H. Carr on international relations, the Spanish pacifist Salvador de Madariaga on 'The Crisis of Liberalism', and the first episodes of new series on European cinema, sculpture, architecture, poetry, archaeology and science.[41]

When the Third was launched, it was hoped that there would be at least three or four programmes every week that demonstrated a commitment to culture of the highest international standards. In November 1946, the attention of critics was caught by *In Parenthesis*, an ambitious adaptation of David Jones's epic poem, hailed by T. S. Eliot as a work of genius. Its producer, Douglas Cleverdon, set out to honour the shape-shifting style of the original. Jones's story had been inspired by what he had seen and heard and imagined on the Western Front during the First World War, but its modernist refusal to contain itself to a single time or place was nimbly captured through Cleverdon's cutting back and forth between different eras and his artful mixing up of the earthy language of the trenches with the mythic language of the Bible and the ancient Welsh bards. The *Listener*'s critic found *In Parenthesis* a trifle too complex; others declared it brilliant and unforgettable; most agreed that it advertised powerfully the Third's willingness to showcase innovative writers.[42]

If there was one programme above all others destined to go down in history as a creative pinnacle of British radio it was the extraordinary ninety-minute-long broadcast on the Third on the evening of Monday 25 January 1954: Dylan Thomas's drama, *Under Milk Wood*. It offered listeners an affectionate and bawdy journey through the night-time dreams and wakeful days of Organ Morgan, Polly Garter, Captain Cat and a teeming multitude of other characters in the fictional village of Llareggub.

The Welsh poet Dylan Thomas in November 1948. Thomas
had acted in the 1946 Third Programme of *In Parenthesis*;
legend has it that he recited his lines with a cigarette
dangling from his mouth. Until his sudden death in 1954 he
was also due to be the narrator for *Under Milk Wood*.

Both the all-Welsh cast revelling in the poetic rhythm and
texture of their lines, and the imagery evoked by a rich tapestry of sound effects, were vital ingredients in the programme's
success. But the well-publicised story of its tempestuous
creation also contributed to its legendary status. The thirty-
nine-year-old Thomas was supposed to have been the narrator,
but died before what he called his 'wretched script' was ready.
That *Under Milk Wood* ended up as his best-known work therefore owed a great deal to the infinite patience of his producer,
the same Douglas Cleverdon who had worked on *In Parenthesis*
eight years before. Cleverdon spent five years of his life cajoling
a script out of Thomas. The poet's first concept had been for
something called 'The Village That Was Mad', a place where, as
Cleverdon put it, 'everybody behaved in Dylan's usual way of

drinking and making love and talking and having a good time generally'. Cleverdon decided that Thomas was wearing himself to a shred with an over-elaborate storyline, and told him to start afresh. It was Cleverdon who was forced on several occasions to visit pubs and train stations to track down the script after Thomas, the worse for drink, had accidentally mislaid it. And it was Cleverdon who recast the play after Thomas's untimely death so that Richard Burton could step into the role as narrator. It was therefore Burton's rich voice that was woven into the very fabric of the piece right from its opening lines:

> To begin at the beginning: it is spring, moonless night in the small town, starless and bible-black, the cobblestreets silent and the hunched, courters'-and-rabbits' wood limping invisible down to the sloeblack, slow, black, crow-black, fishingboat-bobbing sea.

Kingsley Amis thought Thomas's work 'sentimentalising, ignorant horsepiss'. The *Listener*'s critic was far more enthusiastic. The programme had had him 'spellbound from start to finish'. Thomas's skill, he wrote, was to 'land us in a world more vivid and alive than the physical world we know'. *Under Milk Wood* had 'explored every key, from Rabelaisian humour to profound pathos' and shown a 'dazzling command of language'.[43]

The scheduling of the Third was largely in the hands of Etienne Amyot, a trained concert pianist. As the Third's chief 'planner', it was Amyot who had to ensure that attention-grabbing speech programmes like *Under Milk Wood* were balanced by an equally inviting menu of classical music. On the eve of the 1946 launch, he had promised that 'special regard will be given to those works which, either because of their length or their physical difficulty, are rarely heard'. 'Most of us know a fugue of Bach,' Amyot suggested, 'few are familiar with the entire forty-eight.' What really set the music schedule apart, though, was the heady infusion of Continental influences that the Third brought to the domestic scene. In May 1947 it sent the music critic William Glock on a fact-finding trip across Europe, and he was able to return with a bulging contact book and news of orchestral life flowering in Vienna, Prague, Munich and Berlin. His subsequent series, *Music in Post-War Europe*, was a signal that one section of the national airwaves, at least, would resist all pressure to adopt a parochial outlook. Amyot's own background was a mixture of French, Danish and Dutch; he, too, had excellent contacts in Europe. And it was because of this that he secured for the Third what he regarded as the finest thing it ever broadcast. The Director-General, William Haley, had been chatting to him about Diaghilev and the Ballets Russes, about composers such Mussorgsky and Glazunov and Stravinsky, and about how nobody had really heard of Russian music before it was brought to Paris in the years just before the First World War. Might something similar now be done in London, Haley asked – 'something which will have as lasting an influence..?' Amyot's response was to arrange for the entire Vienna State Opera Company to visit Britain in the autumn of 1947 and perform a series of broadcast concerts. The result, Amyot believed, was to 'set music in London aflame'. 'It was fabulous, a standard of performance people hadn't heard here for years … it had very wide repercussions, not only in music but also in design, costumes, the *mise en scène* – the whole thing.' 'That the British could produce a cultural programme of *such* quality', Haley observed, 'did more for the prestige of Britain among people who really cared about the arts and sciences than anything else that certainly the BBC did and possibly anything else that was done by broadcasting.'[44]

The Director-General could be allowed his moment of triumph. The timing of the Third's launch had been propitious. For a generation of naturally curious, state-educated, working-class or lower-middle-class Britons like Richard Hoggart, the Third seemed to embody the most generous of gifts that a hungry autodidact might wish for at a time of material austerity: cultural enrichment in the form of a free supply of the 'best in every department of human knowledge, endeavour and achievement', something that flew in the face of a traditional British prejudice 'against people being too clever, too literate'. Among the literary establishment, of course, its reputation was already unassailable. The Third, wrote the novelist and music critic Edward Sackville-West with undisguised hyperbole, was becoming 'the greatest educative and civilising force England has known since the secularisation of the theatre in the sixteenth century'.[45]

The radio pyramid

Could such boundless optimism last? The outward signs were promising. Behind the scenes it was a different story.

For a start, the Third Programme had been built on some shaky foundations. It was the fruit of years of argument inside the BBC – and, in the end, the determined advocacy of one man in particular: William Haley himself. It had been conceived in outline as early as the summer of 1944, when the Director-General was already starting to think about the shape of peacetime broadcasting. Literary book sales were on the rise; more people were tuning in to serious drama; the broadcast just seven months after VE day of Louis MacNeice's epic feature, *The Dark Tower*, complete with incidental music from Benjamin Britten, showed not just a public appetite for meaty listening but that the craft of making sophisticated radio was coming of age. It was easy to conclude that culture might form a significant component of post-war broadcasting; indeed, that by embracing it confidently, the BBC could enhance its role as a 'civilizing influence'.[46]

It was also felt widely in the management corridors of Broadcasting House that, whatever their merits, the two existing services – Home and Forces – did not quite add up to giving listeners the full range of programmes they deserved. The Home might continue to be what Haley called 'the main vehicle of the Corporation ... for everything in the Charter – education, entertainment and information'. As for the Forces, he felt 'there ought to be after the ardours of the war ... a lighter programme' in much the same spirit. But the permanent addition of a 'lighter' service, though welcome, threatened to unbalance the BBC's overall mix unless there was a matching commitment to providing listeners with more demanding stuff elsewhere on the airwaves – some sort of 'Programme C'.[47]

Benjie Nicolls proposed a service devoted to the arts called 'the Minerva Programme'. Haley loathed the idea, suspecting it would end up 'just a high falutin' cultural programme'. He wanted something bigger and bolder: 'a free-wheeling programme which was going to have anything on God's Earth in it.' Over cups of tea, Etienne Amyot listened to his Director-General open up. 'He'd say how in the war the BBC had got this immense prestige all over the world for telling the truth ... And the thing that preoccupied Haley's mind almost more than anything else at the time – this was towards the end of the war, the last month – was how this prestige could be sustained.'[48]

Amyot's advice had been to avoid the word 'culture' at all costs. It was 'a word I hate', he explained. 'I like "choosy" ... it's much better. Or "selective".' For Haley, however, the solution was to upend all accepted notions of good broadcasting and simply abolish the idea of fixed points in the schedule. That meant, for instance, that news bulletins were out: schedulers were to enjoy 'a completely blank open space of up to five hours every night, night after night'. Individual items – whether they were plays or concerts or anything else – would get whatever time they deserved. None of this was aimed at listeners of any particular class, Haley stressed. Rather, the network was for an audience he called 'perceptive and intelligent'. The Third's first head, George Barnes, talked in similar terms of it being for 'the listener who is willing to make an effort': there would, he warned, be few props. If all this meant small audiences so be it. The new service could be what Geoffrey Bridson called a 'pace-maker and trend-setter'. Harman Grisewood agreed. If culture was like 'cheese', he said, the Third was the 'activating process'.[49]

What seemed to make all this remotely feasible was that the

Third was designed as just one part of a much bigger architectural concept. In planning the BBC's post-war reorganisation of radio, Haley thought of himself as building a 'pyramid'. At the base was the Forces Programme's natural successor – what, from Sunday 29 July 1945, became the 'Light Programme'. The name spoke for itself. It would offer plenty of music of the popular kind, as well as lots of comedy shows. Though it would neither aspire to the slickness of American radio nor seek to become the radio equivalent of the *Daily Mirror*, the overall style would be crisp and friendly – ideal, in fact, for background listening. As for the audience, it was thought it might attract roughly half the adult population. Occupying the pyramid's broad middle layer would be the Home Service, defined in planning documents as

> carefully balanced, appealing to all classes, paying attention to culture at a level at which the ordinary listener can appreciate it; giving talks that will inform the whole democracy rather than an already informed section; and generally so designed that it will steadily but imperceptibly raise the standard of taste, entertainment, outlook and citizenship.[50]

The Home, in other words, would be the quintessentially 'mixed' Reithian service, by and large continuing both its wartime incarnation and the legacy of the pre-war National and Regional Programmes. It was assumed that roughly forty per cent of the audience would tune in. The Third, naturally enough, occupied the pyramid's glittering summit, where it was hoped that with a fair tailwind the remaining ten per cent of the adult population could be tempted to listen regularly.

When the scheme was complete, the former Director-General John Reith described it as thoroughly 'objectionable' precisely because the Third appeared to ring-fence culture for a tiny minority – a betrayal of that ancient mission to spread it as widely as possible. This mistook Haley's intentions. Although the pyramid appeared to reinforce rather than challenge old cultural hierarchies, it was never supposed to be a static arrangement. Each of the three radio services were designed to overlap in terms of programme content. All three, for instance, would have at least *some* music and *some* drama and *some* talks. Several programmes on the Home would be repeated on the Light – and vice versa. Such items would create bridges and 'crossing points' rather than rigidly policed borders, so that the Light, the Home and the Third would merge into one another. The example Haley chose to illustrate how this might work was Richard Strauss's comic opera *Der Rosenkavalier*. 'I would want the Light Programme to play the waltzes ... Then about a week or ten days later I would hope the Home Service would play one act, the most tuneful act of the opera, and within the month the Third Programme would do the whole work from beginning to end, dialogue and all.'[51]

The three services, in other words, were part of a single co-ordinated whole. This made it possible for listeners to switch freely between the different layers as their curiosity was piqued or their moods fluctuated or the amount of concentration they could devote to the radio set changed over the course of a week or a month. Or, indeed, as their personal tastes evolved over the course of a lifetime. Because ultimately Haley's hope was this: that the British people *as a whole* would gradually move up through the pyramid to the point where, after many decades, the entire structure would be turned upside down – the majority coming to like 'the best' rather than 'the worst'. His grand architectural scheme was therefore intended not as a break with the BBC's past but a repackaging of its original responsibility 'both to satisfy and to lead': 'to satisfy current demand and to lead in raising standards of appreciation so that what is demanded is progressively better.' The difference this time was that instead of suddenly plunging the listener from popular to unpopular material, from highbrow to lowbrow and vice versa, in what Haley called a 'hot and cold process' – one which contributed, he felt, to the BBC's reputation for being 'didactic, arbitrary and something of a governess' – the listener would move on to higher ground of his or her 'own volition'.[52]

The scheme depended on a fair bit of behind-the-scenes coordination that was not always forthcoming. But 'bridges' and 'crossing points' were certainly there if listeners wanted to find them. When Norman Collins took over the Light, he confessed that the very name irritated him. 'It seemed to me to give a frivolous connotation.' From now on, he explained, there would be less music, more talk. The launch of *Woman's Hour* in 1946 had been an early statement of intent – as was finding space on the schedule for one of the heavy hitters of the wartime Overseas Service, *Radio Newsreel*. Collins proceeded on the assumption that most people were interested in almost anything, as long as it was presented in 'palatable form'. Soon, there were new series on science, books, drama, poetry, politics. One of his proudest possessions was *Music in Miniature*, which broadcast fifteen minutes of chamber music every week without ever actually naming any of the pieces played or, indeed, mentioning the dread words 'chamber music' at all.[53]

There were other series that felt as if they might work equally well on *any* of the networks. Two comedies in particular pulled off the unusual feat of breaking down barriers of class and taste. *Take It From Here*, first broadcast on the Light in March 1948, drew on the proven acting talent of three variety stars from the old wartime show *Navy Mixture*: 'Professor' Jimmy Edwards, and the Australian comedians Joy Nichols and Dick Bentley. But it was its duo of writers, Frank Muir and Denis Norden, who were crucial to its success. The two men represented a break with the tradition of what Muir called 'concert-party, end-of-the-pier stand-up, funny men – Ted Ray, Arthur Askey, and so on'. It was strongly working-class in appeal, heavily reliant on catchphrases, mildly subversive on the surface, and fundamentally conservative at heart. Muir and Norden saw themselves as 'younger people, without Music Hall experience or Concert Party experience at all ... we were very literary orientated, we liked pastiche parodies of types of films ... books.' Their invention of 'The Glums' offered listeners a fresh set of cult characters, including Pa Glum, an archetypal male chauvinist, his slow-witted son, Ron, and Ron's fiancée – played by a new cast member, June Whitfield. 'Radio was full of decent families at the time … it was all very cosy and we thought we'd have a nasty family.' Even this bold stroke might not have been enough were it not for the fact that each edition of *Take It From Here* was recorded before a live audience on Sundays. 'It was an organic growth week-by-week and on Monday, willy-nilly, you were influenced by how the show went the previous day: so it was the audience which told us in which direction to move.' When it came to the Glums, Muir and Norden quickly sensed that humorous situations worked better than endless gags. 'We lost the jokes and made it much more little stories.' The result was that much sought-after quality in BBC light entertainment, a combination of 'sophistication and corn'.[54]

The Goon Show echoed this success. They arrived via the Home Service's Monday evening comedy show, *Crazy People*. The *Radio Times* explained that the series was 'based upon a crazy type of fun evolved by four of our younger laughter makers': Spike Milligan, who wrote most of the material, Harry Secombe, Peter Sellers, and Michael Bentine. One of the BBC's own eccentrics, Dennis Main Wilson, who had worked with Hugh Carleton Greene at Nordwestdeutscher Rundfunk and was known for always talking in 'semi-comprehensible' digressions, was given the role of producer. 'Now', the *Radio Times* added, 'it remains to be seen what will happen when their differing brands of comedy are fused.' What actually happened was the melting together of an anarchic, modern idiom with a twisted nostalgia for a Victorian past – 'as though', suggested the *Observer*, 'Britannia were having not a nightmare but a sort of comic dream … as though Dali, Kipling and Dickens had co-operated.' For thirty minutes every week listeners were plunged into a manic swirl of surreal sound effects, absurd plots, and characters with funny names and funny voices – Secombe's 'Neddie Seagoon', Milligan's 'Eccles', and Sellers' 'Bluebottle' among them. The historian and dedicated Goons fan, Peter Hennessy, summed up their work as 'a kind of decade-long "other

ranks" revenge on the Empire and its officer class'. For Frank
Muir the Goons offered something even more fundamental. In
an era when everything seemed so regimented and socially fet-
tered, they provided an unstuffy blast of a world which 'had no
logic at all'.[55]

The success of *Take it From Here* and *The Goon Show* is a
reminder that even in the 1950s – even in the era of what Norman
Collins rather caustically labelled 'steam radio' – the BBC was
far from being stuck in the role of po-faced, hectoring 'Auntie' to
the nation. But any talk of a 'golden age' concealed the widening cracks in Haley's pyramid – cracks that were highly visible
to those working inside, even if not yet to the general public.

The Home, for instance, was supposed to offer 'a catholic programme designed to nourish the whole man': back in
January 1947, it had broadcast twice as much 'variety' as 'talks
or discussion', and some forty per cent of its output consisted of
music, more than half of which was 'light' or 'dance'. Yet, over
the years, more and more of its most entertaining programmes
were being hived off to the Light and more and more of its most
challenging programmes to the Third. The result was that it
became a steadily narrower, more middlebrow service – out-
flanked by popularity on one side, prestige on the other.[56]

This was a failure of leadership. Collins's fizzing energy at
the Light Programme had earned him the moniker of 'Haley's
Comet'. The same could never have been said of Lindsay Wellington, a man described by Geoffrey Bridson as walking rather
than running the Home Service. Wellington had been in the Corporation since 1924, and, in Bridson's view, only ever favoured
ideas that were 'politically and in every other way innocuous'.
Even the Director-General was unimpressed. 'Mr Wellington',
Haley said, 'is not a man who can't see the wood for the trees;
he's a man who can't see the trees for the leaves.'[57] Wellington's
successor was equally lacking in the spirit of invention. Andrew
Stewart, who took over in 1952, was a sober and principled Scot
for whom, as Bridson put it, 'the scrip of Sir John Reith was still
the only legal tender':

When I once suggested changing the name and image of the Home Service, he gazed at me in astonishment as though I had suggested changing the shape of the British Isles. Home, I pointed out, was what all the bright boys and girls were eager to get away from: the label was middle-aged and losing us a generation of up-and-coming listeners. And was it really necessary to deaden every programme gap with the dulcet pealing of Bow Bells? His Grace the Archbishop of Canterbury, he solemnly assured me, would be deeply disturbed if we didn't![58]

The Home was reliable, informative, reasonably varied. It was also a little *stolid*. If its public reputation was sustained through the 1950s, it was largely through having become part of the deeply felt wartime experience of the British people: stolid, it seemed, was what a sizeable minority of the listener-ship wanted.

The Third Programme, of course, was *the* place to take risks. But there the problem was a losing battle to retain even the modest share of the audience its architects had been hoping for. By an unlucky coincidence, its opening months had been hampered by interference from a radio station in Soviet Latvia that had started broadcasting on the same wavelength. The only solution – for the BBC's Droitwich transmitter to reduce its own power – meant that tuning in was like listening to 'someone distantly thrashing a birdcage'. The startling discovery a year later that fewer than one in a hundred Britons were bothering to listen at all suggested a much deeper problem: that the Third's schedule was filled with too much stuff the public regarded as 'difficult'. The *Daily Mirror* cheekily referred to it as 'Third symphony for orchestra and two listeners'. The BBC's own Governors asked why there could not be more Beethoven and Haydn 'instead of music which nobody else ever played'. Meanwhile, the Third's most prominent champions formed a powerful – and very public – counterweight against any attempt to make programmes more accessible. In September 1951, E. M.

Forster launched a subtle attack on the Third's new series of 'light orchestral concerts'. The line-up included the Royal Philharmonic playing Bizet and Fauré and the Vienna Philharmonic performing Strauss and Schubert and Mozart. This struck most observers as perfectly respectable. For Forster the very idea of 'light music' on the Third was a 'discrediting' signal that audience ratings were starting to influence programme planning: the Third's true role was to chase quality, not quantity, he insisted.[59]

What Forster failed to recognise was that Haley's grand vision – indeed, the BBC's whole ethos – depended on combining quality *and* quantity, or at least finding a workable compromise between the two. According to Harman Grisewood, when it came to the Third, the Director-General 'wanted to be sure that the programme was not going to be filled either with Viennese operetta or with expositions of logical positivism'. Haley himself pointed to a more fundamental principle: 'The job of the BBC is to lead, but no leader will have any following if he gets out of sight.'[60]

Finding out how far exactly a programme could go without getting 'out of sight' was the most enduring challenge in everything the BBC did. One thing was certain: no simple solution could be imposed from the top. 'I felt very strongly that the Director-General shouldn't do it', Haley explained. He might 'lay down the principles … set a general feeling'. But 'he cannot step in and control any programme'. 'We diffused this responsibility through eight hundred producers … We will make mistakes but that is the price of freedom.'[61]

Haley's restraint was admirable, yet it meant that the flaws in his radio pyramid went largely untreated. Throughout the decade, the audience for the Third fell consistently. Worse, thanks to the steady rise in television viewing the total number of people available to listen to radio of *any* description in the evenings was declining rapidly: in the battle for ratings, those running the Light, the Home and the Third were competing with each other over a steadily diminishing resource. By the end of the decade, Geoffrey Bridson concluded, radio was most assuredly 'in the doldrums'.[62]

As a producer, what Bridson himself really craved was a Home Service ambitious enough to feature the work he already did for the Third. 'The very verb "to broadcast" means to disseminate widely', he pointed out. 'To confine the best in radio to one exclusive wavelength could only result in disseminating it most narrowly ... I did not want to preach exclusively to the converted.' From Harman Grisewood's perspective, the problem was that thanks to the timidity of the Home Service under its post-war heads, John Reith's warning about the Third Programme ring-fencing culture had alas come true – and meant the betrayal of the BBC's larger sense of purpose. 'There was no point, I felt, at all in artistic sensitivities and intellectual daring, however brilliant, if these attainments floated like duckweed on the dark stagnant water below.'[63]

The British people themselves had not wholly abandoned their devotion to radio. They were listening less, watching TV more. Yet in millions of homes, radio continued, without fanfare, to seep deeply into people's consciousness. 'Our home was full of music', a young Cilla Black remembered of growing up in Liverpool at the time. Peter Hennessy recalled Saturday afternoons as a child in the Cotswolds – 'inseparable in my memory from the Central Band of the Royal Air Force playing-in Eamon Andrews and *Sports Report* on the Light Programme to the sound of "Out Of The Blue".' Whether it was the football results, the 'warm Hampshire burr' of John Arlott's cricket commentaries, or any number of comedy shows, he said, listeners like him somehow developed 'a private relationship' with the invisible men and women behind the microphone.[64]

This heart-warming bond between audience and broadcaster helped radio survive. But the BBC had once had grander ambitions for the medium. And William Haley's judgement of his own achievements, made years later, ends on a dispiriting note. He had been the chief architect not just of the Third Programme but of the whole extraordinary pyramid of which it formed the glorious summit. Yet 'the people', he admitted somewhat forlornly, just 'did not start moving through the pyramid upwards to any great extent'. Most had made up their minds about what they liked best and had left their dial stuck on the same wavelength ever since. Taste remained stubbornly fixed by class. The BBC's own audience research showed that while 65 per cent of those with incomes below £350 a year liked music hall programmes, only 25 per cent of those with incomes above £1,000 felt the same. The BBC had also discovered that while nearly a quarter of those defined as upper middle class might tune into the Third in the evening, only 3 per cent of those defined as working class would do so. People were no different when engaged in other pursuits. In cinemas across the country, the working class were in the stalls, the middle class in the pricier balcony seats. But for the BBC, a 'universal' service with the potential, as Reith once put it, to transcend 'Fortune's twin-keys: Leisure and Money', such findings came as a blow.[65]

Back in 1945 it had not been entirely naïve to believe and hope for something better. Behind the dreariness of austerity there had been 'a bubbling if not a piping prospect ... about future possibilities in a settled but far from static society'. But it was in the fifties that the novelist Nancy Mitford wrote of the distinction between 'U' and 'Non-U' – a supposedly unbridgeable linguistic rift between the upper class and everybody else that may have begun with satirical intent but rapidly became a national obsession. The divisions created by the eleven-plus were particularly pernicious – splitting families as well as whole communities. Whether a child ended up being one of the 25 per cent selected for a grammar school place was determined just as much by where he or she lived as by performance in the exam, but for the large majority who failed the crude process of selection, life trajectories became stubbornly fixed. The secondary moderns these children attended never came near to achieving the parity of esteem with grammars that had been promised, leaving millions underqualified for anything other than a working life of manual jobs. Meanwhile, at the beginning and end of every school day, thousands of buses trundling along the streets of Britain betrayed a striking form of spatial apartheid: back seats for the secondary modern girls, middle seats for secondary modern boys, front seats for the conspicuous minority of grammar school pupils.[66]

Perhaps it had always been unrealistic of Haley, like Reith before him, to imagine that broadcasting could ever tackle the deep class divisions that still scarred Britain. Yet the radio pyramid, so hierarchical in outward form, had embraced a notion of 'uplift' that was too deeply ingrained in BBC thinking to be abandoned now. Evidently, new approaches were needed. Haley's model had relied too much on structures and top-down planning, when making programmes that widened horizons was really achieved through countless everyday decisions taken by those working in the Corporation's production offices, newsrooms and studios. The attitudes and instincts of these men and women – above all their ability to understand and reflect lives that might be very different from their own – were also crucial to the BBC's collective ability to ensure, as its motto promised, that 'Nation shall speak peace unto Nation'. The post-war years would therefore test, as much as anything else, the BBC's grasp, in practical terms, of what defined this 'Nation'. It was nothing if it was not about the millions of people who lived within its boundaries. But in a Britain that was slowly becoming more racially diverse, and where class identities were slowly starting to weaken, did the BBC know yet who these people really were? Even now, could it learn how to speak to and represent *everyone*?

11

STRANGERS

… you stay in the world you belong to and you don't
know anything about what happening in the other ones.

The Lonely Londoners, Sam Selvon, 1956

On the evening of Monday 14 October 1946, in the darkness of
Swansea's windswept harbourside, a BBC producer was bundled
against her will on to a ship bound for the other side of the
Atlantic.

The journey from London had been delayed by her repeated
attempts to sabotage the car in which she was travelling, and it
was only with 'firm handling' that she was forced up a rope ladder
on to the deck of the SS *Tetela* in time. Nearly a month later the
ship would arrive at its final destination: Kingston, Jamaica. The
BBC had covered the £40 cost of passage and continued to pay
her a salary until the end of the year. But a groundbreaking and
all too brief broadcasting career was at an end.

The woman at the heart of this tragic drama was Una
Marson. The 'leaving note' written by her employer on her last
day at Bush House stated bluntly that although she had always
been 'an excellent producer' she would never be re-engaged. Ten
years later, Marson would write to one of her old bosses, Laurence Gilliam. 'My years at the BBC', she told him, 'now seem
like a dream – an exciting dream which ended in a nightmare.'[1]

It had all started so promisingly. Una Marson left Jamaica
in the summer of 1932, just twenty-seven years old and with a
remarkable CV. She had already published two collections of her

own poetry and set up a monthly literary magazine, *The Cosmo-politan*. Once in Britain, she had found work with the League of Coloured Peoples and the League of Nations. Over the next few years, Marson built a growing reputation as a prolific speech-maker, organiser of cultural events, freelance journalist and magazine editor. Within four years of her arrival she was being acknowledged as 'the leading black feminist activist in London'.[2]

Marson had shown no hint of any interest in working at the BBC. But then, right out of the blue, an opening pre-sented itself. She was visiting the 1939 Radiolympia exhibition in the company of Winnie Casserley, the latest in a long line of white-skinned, blue-eyed and blonde-haired 'Miss Jamaica' com-petition winners, when the two women were asked to give an interview for the BBC's television cameras. Cecil Madden was sufficiently impressed to invite Marson to Alexandra Palace. In the few weeks left before September's close-down, she found herself working with him on *Picture Page*: tracking down guests, drafting interview scripts, arranging rehearsals. Once war was declared, the Overseas Service gave her a full-time job produc-ing and presenting *Calling the West Indies*, a series that featured heart-warming messages to families back home from the thou-sands of men and women who had left the Caribbean to come and work for the Allied cause – as pilots, navigators, wireless operators, gunners, ground staff, nurses, mechanics, caterers – or to join the assembly lines of Britain's factories. Marson also appeared on *Voice*, a series produced by George Orwell for the BBC's Indian Section featuring a mix of established and less well known poets. The experience of sharing the microphone with, among others, Mulk Raj Anand, William Empsom and T. S. Eliot inspired her to devise her own version two years later. The series she started, *Caribbean Voices*, would continue almost unin-terrupted until 1958, establishing itself as an influential home for literature from the region and a vital source of patronage for writers like Andrew Salkey, Sam Selvon, George Lamming, V. S. Naipaul and Derek Walcott.[3]

Working for the Corporation had rarely been straightforward.

Una Marson checking a script by Learie Constantine before his talk for the wartime Overseas Service programme *Calling the West Indies*. Before being forced to leave the BBC, she also started *Caribbean Voices*, an influential slot for many leading poets from the region until it ceased running in 1958.

In the 1940s, the fact that a Black Jamaican woman had been recruited at all was remarkable. Indeed, the BBC had 'thought it well to check with the Colonial Office that there would be no objection on their part to our appointment of a coloured British subject'. Staff files record that she was soon deemed 'extremely intelligent, loyal and lively' and, crucially, 'a more experienced broadcaster than most of her colleagues'. They also noted that 'as the only "coloured" producer in the BBC' she faced 'prejudices which undoubtedly exist among some of the staff, with whom she has to work'. This was certainly borne out by the behaviour of Joan Gilbert, who had worked on *Picture Page* and ran many wartime entertainment programmes for Cecil Madden. In May 1941, she complained that Marson had 'got an exaggerated idea of her own position and her own authority'. 'Quite frankly,' she added, 'I wouldn't let anybody speak to me in the way Una does, and certainly not a coloured woman.' At Bush House, Marson did at least have the sympathetic protection both of her immediate manager, the Director of the African Service, John Grenfell Williams, and the wartime Controller of the Overseas Service, J. B. Clark. Both leapt to her defence when the West India Committee, a London-based lobby group representing plantation and white-owned business interests, grumbled about her broadcasts.[4]

The constant hum of prejudice was almost certainly a factor in Marson having some sort of nervous breakdown towards the end of 1945. Within months she was being treated for what doctors called 'delusions' of persecution; by May 1946, she had been certified as suffering from schizophrenia and detained in hospital. The BBC granted her an exceptional period of sick leave and sought regular progress reports from doctors. But some time in the early autumn the decision was taken that Marson should be assisted back to Jamaica to benefit from what one manager called 'her home environment'. Soon after, arrangements were made to drive her to Swansea to catch the SS *Tetela*. The Jamaican poet J. E. Clare McFarlane accompanied her on the journey across the Atlantic. When John Grenfell Williams wrote to thank him for his assistance, he said that it was 'a matter of very great regret' to the BBC that her seven years of service had ended in such sad and turbulent circumstances.[5]

'For Heaven's sake shut up'

In the two decades after the war, Britain – and, in particular, London – proved to be 'both magnet and nightmare' for the country's new colonial citizens.[6] So too, it seemed, did the BBC.

The arrival of the HMT *Empire Windrush* at Tilbury Docks on 22 June 1948, bringing with it nearly 500 West Indians looking for work, was a symbolic moment, though only part of a centuries-long story of British ethnic diversity. And despite the government's desperate calls for more recruits to Britain's factories and its infant National Health Service, immigration remained a slow trickle at first. Between 1948 and 1952, just a few thousand West Indian immigrants turned up. Larger numbers started arriving after 1952: by the early 1960s some 300,000 men, women, and children had made their way to Britain. All these new arrivals were legally – and, more than that, *felt* themselves to be – British citizens. An Act of 1948 had declared them British subjects entitled to a British passport. They had also been told since childhood that Britain was their 'mother country', the centre of *their* empire.[7]

The host country betrayed a striking degree of ignorance about these new arrivals. The description of Britons as 'absent-minded imperialists' felt stunningly appropriate. For many, the Empire had only made its presence felt with any intensity at moments of spectacle such as royal jubilees or coronations. Otherwise, the dominant feeling was merely one of 'detached and tepid pride in its existence'. As for domestic attitudes towards the West Indies, decades of colonial propaganda had conditioned many Britons, if they thought about it at all, to 'view men and women of African descent as lesser peoples who had been defeated and subdued by British power'. Richard Hoggart barely touched on the issue of immigration in his book *The Uses of Literacy*. Yet he revealed a strong pressure among long-established communities to conform, an assumption that most neighbours were 'your sort'. Implicit in almost everything he described was that in many British towns 'outsiders' were viewed warily. It took only a matter of days for the twelve-year-old Mike Phillips, who had arrived with his parents from British Guyana on a cold January day in 1956, to experience the painful absence of hospitality. At school, he and the other 'foreign' boys sat apart in a corner of the classroom; walking home every afternoon, he was met with the 'inevitable' question: 'Why don't you go back where you came from?'[8]

The BBC ought to have had a clear role in introducing Britain's newest citizens to their hosts. Reith had always said that broadcasting's purpose was to build 'a more intelligent and enlightened electorate'. Tolerance of difference was vital to achieving this. The Corporation's programme makers acknowledged that they were creating role models and reinforcing certain standards; many, indeed, enthusiastically embraced the opportunity to intervene and instruct in social affairs. The immigrants of the Windrush era were by no means the first immigrants to arrive in Britain. But they were the first to arrive in a radio-listening, television-watching nation. This should have made their experiences, their histories, the legacies of Empire that brought them across the Atlantic, a legitimate focus of attention from the national broadcaster.

Yet the BBC's track record was uneven and contradictory. As Una Marson's own career illustrated, sincere attempts to avoid offence or address injustices coexisted with what one former employee – himself a child of immigrants – described as 'a back-catalogue of wrongs – major and minor'.[9]

There was a history the BBC could point to of featuring non-white performers on air. In the 1930s, the Guyanese bandleader Rudolph Dunbar, for instance, had made numerous radio appearances along with 'his Coloured Orchestra'. In 1934, the singer Elisabeth Welch even had her own radio series, *Soft Lights and Sweet Music*. And the list of African American artists performing at Alexandra Palace before the war was highly distinguished, including, among others, Paul Robeson, Nina Mae McKinney, Josephine Baker and Adelaide Hall.

There was also evidence that programme makers had become increasingly aware of the risk of causing racial offence. In the later stages of the war, when as many as 130,000 African American GIs were stationed in Britain, producers were reminded that there was 'particularly good reason to be careful not to say anything which might be interpreted as showing colour prejudice'. Such advice suggested a healthy degree of sensitivity at the top. It also suggested that transgressions were common on the ground. In this instance, guidance was issued after the actor Mabel Constanduros had told a group of children during a live show that 'the black man will get you if you don't look out'. Managers explained that such language 'tends to bring up some white children to be afraid of, and therefore hostile to, coloured people'. Editorial intervention could cut both ways, of course. In 1950, the Controller of Television, Norman Collins, bowed to viewers' complaints about a variety show called *Black Magic* in which a Black performer sang a love song to a white woman. Collins did not wish to ban this sort of thing outright, he explained, but he ruled that henceforth 'love songs between white and coloured artists must be very scrupulously considered'.[10]

The most striking aspect of appearances by Black artists on the BBC during this early period was that they were restricted almost exclusively to the role of performers in light entertainment. Whether or not this was due to deeply held racial stereotypes about Black musicality and physicality, the ultimate effect was that the BBC presented them to the public largely as 'exotic' attractions. This would be demonstrated in the most perverse way when it came to the BBC's seemingly unshakeable commitment to *The Black and White Minstrel Show*, which was to survive on British television screens for two decades after its launch in 1958. Mike Phillips remembers being teased at school whenever it was shown. 'I thought, don't they think we have *any* feelings? Doesn't it occur to them that there is *a whole history* behind this caricature!?' The uncomfortable truth was that 'they' – the BBC's senior management – did indeed feel there was a whole history behind the show, but only a positive one. The practice of white performers blacking up for a song-and-dance routine, they suggested, drew on a decades-old American style and a 'perfectly honourable theatrical tradition of the British music hall'. It was offensive only to 'killjoys'. The show's high ratings, they suggested, simply confirmed that the BBC had a popular and well-crafted hit on its hands.[11]

It would not be until 1967 that the voices of protest against *The Black and White Minstrel Show* started to break through. In May that year, the Campaign Against Racial Discrimination submitted a petition calling for it to be axed. The minutes of a

BBC Board of Management meeting record the Corporation's head of publicity turning to the letters page of the *Daily Mail* to gauge what he called the 'general view' of the public. Having adopted this shaky methodology, he concluded that 'the programme was not racially offensive' and decreed that 'no further action was necessary'. There *was* at least one determined voice of opposition within the BBC's ranks. The Corporation's Chief Accountant, Barrie Thorne, had done time in the BBC's New York office and seen something of the civil rights movement. Five years *before* the Campaign Against Racial Discrimination's public attack, he had written privately to the BBC's Director of Television arguing that 'The "Uncle Tom" attitude of the show' was 'a disgrace and an insult to coloured people everywhere'. By 1967, he was writing to the Director-General's Chief Assistant, Oliver Whitley. 'No matter what the outward gloss and size of the audience', Thorne complained, the show was 'underlyingly offensive', and the BBC needed to take more account of 'the continued fight against segregation going on in the United States, here, and elsewhere in the world'. Whatever the 'rights and wrongs' of the matter, Whitley replied, protesting was counterproductive. 'Coloured people', he advised, should 'for Heaven's sake shut up'. Only in 1978 did someone in a position of authority – in this case, the Controller of BBC1, Bill Cotton – grasp what had been obvious to campaigners for some time. 'It's all very well people who are not black saying "I didn't think about it that way"' Cotton told the show's fans, but 'it's the people who are black' whose views surely needed to be taken into account. The decision to cancel had come shockingly late.[12]

On the rare occasions when Black people *did* actually feature on the BBC outside the realm of popular entertainment, it was almost always as part of a journalistic enquiry into the perceived social impacts of immigration on the host community. One BBC radio producer, demonstrating an unusually acute understanding of the role of structural inequality in creating racism, suggested to colleagues that the working-class Briton 'owes his colour feeling to his own position ... which makes him want to boss somebody elsewhere'. What interested her most, though, was the danger of prejudice serving 'a political end'. Can 'revulsion' at those who appeared different be 'overcome', she asked her fellow producers, and if so, 'how?'[13]

It was an important question, and did not go entirely unanswered. In 1952, a whole season, spread between the Light, Home and Third, addressed the issue of race relations. Episodes came with titles such as *The Conflict of Culture: Racial Misunderstanding and Prejudice*, and *Race and Recognition: Growing Colour Problem in Britain*. Three years later, BBC Television screened *Special Enquiry: Has Britain a Colour Bar?*, in which the former war correspondent Robert Reid put to viewers this overarching question concerning West Indian immigrants: 'How do they fit in to our ways and standards of life, coming, as they do, from places where customs, standards of life, are much different, and, very often, lower than our own?' For the programme, René Cutforth was despatched to Birmingham, a city where immigrants from both the Caribbean and the Indian sub-continent had often found work in heavy industry. Cutforth wandered around the factories and the pubs, unearthing appalling examples of racism among employers, landlords and union officials. 'The full acceptance of these strangers', he warned, 'may take time.' The volume of anti-immigration feeling in Britain was clearly rising, fuelled in the latter half of the decade by unhelpful rhetoric from a number of right-wing politicians. In the space of just four weeks in the late summer of 1958, there were no fewer than thirty-two separate reports on BBC Television about attacks on Black people's homes, and about white lynch mobs tooled up 'with iron bars, butcher's knives and weighted leather belts' roaming the streets of Nottingham and London's Notting Hill. By this point, even the somewhat slow-moving Home Service was devoting large slices of airtime to analysing the increasingly violent turn of events.[14]

This kind of coverage was a mixed blessing. The repeated focus on outbursts of prejudice, the highlighting of violence, even the very titles of the programmes – it all reduced the rich tapestry of Black British lives to little more than a 'problem'. But

René Cutforth's journey to Birmingham did at least suggest that programme makers were interested in finding solutions. And by the early 1960s, the solution that came most readily to mind – the one that appeared so obviously 'colour-blind' to the BBC's broadcasters, as well as being in the old 'unifying' traditions of Reith – was the cause of ever-closer *integration*.

The crucial moment came in 1964. After witnessing the incendiary use of racist language by a Conservative parliamentary candidate in Smethwick during the election campaign, Labour's Postmaster-General, Tony Benn, wrote to the BBC's Director-General, Hugh Carleton Greene, suggesting that the BBC might consider a regular programme specially for immigrants 'telling them how to adapt to life in Britain'. In July 1965, the BBC hosted two conferences: one for representatives of the Indian and Pakistani communities in Britain, the other for representatives of the West Indian community. A crucial difference of opinion emerged. While Indian and Pakistani representatives were keen for the BBC to introduce programmes made especially for them, the West Indian representatives thought special programming would only heighten a sense of separation from Britain at large. This meant that when the Corporation's newly constituted 'Immigrants' Programme Unit' was established in Birmingham that year, the first fruit of its efforts was aimed exclusively at Indians and Pakistanis: the Sunday morning series *In Logon Se Miliye*, launched in October 1965 and renamed the following year as *Apna Hi Ghar Samajhiye*.[15]

The English translation of *Apna Hi Ghar Samajhiye* was *Make Yourself at Home*. There was a radio version, broadcast on the Home Service at the unsociable hour of 8.10 a.m. before what the BBC called 'normal' programming began, and a television edition, broadcast at the slightly more civilised hour of 9 a.m. Since it was keen to reach both Indian and Pakistani communities the BBC was involved in a delicate balancing act. The two key members of the programme team were Mahendra Kaul, who had a background in Indian broadcasting, and Saleem Shahed, who had been involved in Pakistani broadcasting; the very first

Mahendra Kaul, one of the key members of the team behind
Apna Hi Ghar Samajhiye, the series 'for Indian and Pakistani
immigrants'. By 1974, when this picture was taken, Kaul was
producing several other programmes made in Birmingham,
including the long-running TV series *Nai Zindagi Naya Jeevan*.

presenter, Aley Hasan, was an Indian Muslim. The language
adopted for the series was Hindustani, described by the BBC as
a 'mixture of simple Hindi and simple Urdu'. Underpinning everything, however, was the programme's obvious purpose: not so
much to provide a link with the audience's former homeland but
to assist with their integration here in Britain. This meant lots
of basic advice on finding jobs, filling in forms, or dealing with
the authorities over housing, education and health. A large slice
of the radio edition was taken up with English language lessons.
And to leaven the mix a little, there were celebrity interviews, live
dramas and Bollywood soundtracks. Despite its rough-and-ready
aesthetic, the programme slowly gained a small but dedicated
audience. The BBC could satisfy itself that it had, as one internal
document put it, 'contributed in a worthwhile measure to the
dismantling of the party wall between "Us" and "Them"'.[16]

By the early 1970s, some influential figures in Broadcasting House were suggesting privately that *Apna Hi Ghar Samajhiye* and its various successors and spin-offs, though part of a worthy public service commitment, irritated 'regular' listeners. As a result, the programme was quietly shunted to an even earlier slot, setting in motion a steady decline in ratings. It would be left to a new generation of local radio stations to put Asian programming on a firmer footing. The absence of any programmes for people from the Caribbean remained a running sore. Colin Grant, a child of Jamaican immigrants, recalled growing up in suburban Britain and feeling 'as if West Indians and their children had been abandoned or, at best, overlooked by the mainstream, as if we were the graft that didn't "take"'. But even those programmes for Britain's Asian communities that had been made always had a strong flavour not of integration but of assimilation. Broadcasters assumed that incomers needed to learn the 'set of rules' by which they would be expected to live. Even the Corporation's more progressive programme makers still saw their role as educating immigrants, not being educated by them.[17]

'An attitude of mind'

Why was it that the one part of the BBC's workforce that we might expect to be most curious about the immigrant experience – its journalists – seemed to be so resolutely *incurious* for so much of this period? There was no simple answer to this question. But both personal and political factors were at play.

In 1946 the BBC had committed itself to providing news that demonstrated 'the most rigid and absolute avoidance of expression of editorial opinion'. The object of bulletins, it said, was 'to state the news of the day accurately, fairly, soberly and impersonally'.[18] It was a dignified position. And the BBC believed that by sticking to such principles its global reputation for veracity would be protected in the years to come. But there was a thin line between rigid sobriety and a stifling of enterprise.

Presiding over the Home News Division, and therefore responsible for setting the overall tone and content, was the domineering and ultra-conservative New Zealander, Tahu Hole. He had been appointed to the job in May 1948 by William Haley, who valued what he saw as the man's 'tremendous streak of independence'. 'I was absolutely certain that whether he did right or wrong, he would not give way to anybody inside or outside the Corporation.' It was an assessment that turned out to be all too accurate. Among Hole's most infamous decrees was the requirement that at least two reliable outside sources were required to verify the accuracy of every news story. Hole illustrated this by describing what would happen if a BBC correspondent called in with 'a news story which said that, let us say, the Wailing Wall in Jerusalem had been damaged by whatever – a bomb or an earthquake'. 'If we got that from our own correspondent we wouldn't use it,' he said bluntly, 'because unless our correspondent had been right next to the Wall when it was damaged he would have got it from someone else and he might conceivably have been the victim of a hoax ... We would have to wait until we had satisfied ourselves from attributable sources that it was so.' For Hole, the over-arching principle was simple: 'Accuracy at all costs.' Leonard Miall, who was now the BBC's Washington correspondent, saw things rather more negatively. 'Tahu Hole's concern was that the News should never make a mistake: it didn't matter how slow it was, how dull it was, as long as it didn't make a mistake.' He remembered how in 1950 he had been among a tiny handful of reporters who had been given advance information from White House sources that there was to be a military response to North Korea's invasion of the South, yet was prevented by Hole from breaking the story. 'I just simply lost my temper, and I said "Well, it's no good trying to expect Correspondents to have any initiative if this is what you do ...".'[19]

Hole believed equally strongly that consistency was as important as accuracy, and that news could not be told properly through pictures. The ensuing conflict between his News

Division and the television department at Alexandra Palace was described by one insider as 'like a battle between a school of whales and a herd of elephants ... two powerful forces locked against each other'. One source of friction was *Television News-reel*, which Alexandra Palace had launched back in 1948 – a short, lively magazine that pulled together brief filmed reports on sporting events, ship launches, disasters, sundry royal visits and the like. Its great strength lay in its camerawork and editing – unsurprisingly, since it was made by television's own film unit. Its ability to deal with the very latest news of the day was less striking, and this provided the excuse for Hole to make a territorial grab, insisting that News Division take charge. When the Hole-approved format, under the title of *News and Newsreel*, was first broadcast in 1954 the *Daily Mail* called it 'a mixture of the dull, trivial and ineffectual'.[20]

Tahu Hole's tenure at the BBC did eventually come to an end – though a rather ignoble one. In 1958, the Director-General Ian Jacob shunted him sideways, putting him in overall charge of the BBC's administration and making room for Hugh Carleton Greene, who would become head of an enlarged 'News and Current Affairs' directorate. Two years later, Greene took over the top job from Jacob. 'I realised when I became Director-General that I must do something':

> Tahu Hole had an appallingly corrupting effect on the characters of otherwise good people. People used to bring him in their little bouquets of flowers from their gardens to present to him as if he was some sort of heathen idol. To speak quite frankly, I have had to do with the Nazi leaders in Germany and I have never had such a sense of evil from any of them as I had from Tahu Hole.[21]

It was a devastating assessment. And it was with the full backing of the Governors that Greene – 'like a snake striking' as one of his colleagues put it – insisted on Hole's immediate resignation.[22]

By the spring of 1960, he was gone for good. But he had not been the only block to progress. There was a wider problem with the BBC's ability to report on social affairs. In television, just as much as in radio, close ties with Whitehall and Westminster meant not just a narrowly conceived view of what constituted an issue worthy of coverage; they ensured that a tone of deference infused almost every interview. The relationship was punctuated by tussles for supremacy, but otherwise involved a great deal of mutual indulgence.

At the most senior level, for instance, government and Opposition made a great deal of fuss about the prospect of television usurping the Palace of Westminster as *the* place where Britain's political differences were aired before the public. Churchill, perennially convinced that the BBC was a hotbed of communists, inevitably complained the loudest. In the dying days of the wartime coalition, the Director-General had been required to sit and listen as Churchill told him that 'the BBC must do no political broadcasting of any kind whatsoever'. Churchill, of course, was quite capable of contradicting himself. After his defeat in the 1945 election, he would frequently ring Haley at home on a Saturday morning to harangue the Director-General down the line. 'If you think you are going to keep me off the air now that I am not Prime Minister as you did in the 1930s, you're not going to be able to do it.' The problem was not radio but television. 'I've spent fifty years on my feet having to watch the effect of what I was saying as I was saying it', he told Haley. 'If I'd also had to worry about how I was looking, politics would have become intolerable.' His Labour counterpart, Clement Attlee concurred. 'And that', Haley reckoned, 'was the end of political broadcasting in television during my time as Director-General.'[23]

Churchill's bluster was really a form of misdirection. MPs of all persuasions knew that politics had to be covered on Britain's airwaves somehow. The crucial issue was *who* controlled it. Politicians believed it should be the party machines; the Director-General believed editorial responsibility lay with the BBC. Haley also harboured a deeper worry: that the more interested the BBC became with politics, the more politicians would take an interest in the BBC. Nor was he alone in thinking this. In 1951, the retired Controller of News, John Coatman, warned his former colleagues that if politicians ever succeeded in asserting a right to scrutinise the BBC's political coverage their oversight would be 'continuous and jealous'. The understandable desire at the top of the BBC to avoid provoking unnecessary conflict was largely responsible for the Corporation inflicting on itself one of the most absurd restrictions on its ability to report the full range of contemporary affairs: the so-called 'fourteen-day rule', which prevented discussion on radio or television of any issue likely to arise in either of the Houses of Parliament in the coming fortnight. The BBC had first operated this self-denying ordinance in wartime, when it deemed it dangerous for the national broadcaster to draw attention to political division. But the same principle was restated in peacetime, and what had started as a convention had calcified into law.[24]

It was the 1956 Suez crisis that finally pushed the BBC into asserting more confidently the right to decide for itself what could and could not be reported. The prime minister Anthony Eden's secret plan, hatched in collusion with France and Israel, to provoke a military attack on Egypt and occupy its Canal Zone, would end in Britain's very public diplomatic humiliation and the resignation of Eden himself. Less obvious to the British people at the time was the angry row rumbling away behind the scenes between the government and the national broadcaster.

On Saturday 3 November, when the first airstrikes on Egypt had already taken place but British paratroopers had not yet landed, Eden went on the BBC to make a televised Prime Ministerial Broadcast. David Attenborough was part of the BBC production team that usually tended to him. He remembers arriving at 10 Downing Street and being taken to one side by Eden's press officer, who told him 'the old man's gone mad, I don't know what to do, he won't see me'. Attenborough dashed upstairs to find the prime minister in bed 'looking dreadful, in his pyjamas', a line of pill bottles extending the full width of a

The Prime Minister Anthony Eden at the BBC's Lime Grove studios,
preparing to speak to the nation about the Suez Crisis in 1956.

shelf above the headboard, his wife frantically dabbing mascara
on to his moustache. Attenborough was asked for his own
detailed opinion about what the prime minister should say:

> He had this speech on a series of jumbo typewriter cards
> and he was reading through it ... "And so my friends" ...
> "do you think 'my friends' is right, David ... is it perhaps
> a bit over the top?" I was appalled ... what was perfectly
> clear was that here was a very, very sick man, and to me as a
> young television producer it seemed dreadful that the fate
> of the world should be in the hands of a very sick man.[25]

Despite everything, Eden managed to get across his key
message: military action in Egypt was justified. By now, though,

public opinion was bitterly divided. In Bush House, the Controller of the Overseas Service sensed the domestic policy implications. 'We had all got used to the fact that there wasn't a great deal of difference in foreign policy between the two main political parties, and here suddenly the nation was split right down the middle ... the BBC felt it its duty to reflect accurately – as accurately as it could – the situation.' Crucially, the Labour Party was also opposed to Eden's adventure. The Leader of the Opposition, Hugh Gaitskell, therefore felt entitled to a televised broadcast of his own. It was a reasonable request. But Eden was insisting that full wartime conditions now applied – conditions that obliged the BBC to support the government of the day in exactly the same way as it had done between 1939 and 1945. The Director-General, Ian Jacob, happened to be in Australia, so the urgent task of sorting out this horrible impasse fell to his political fixer, Harman Grisewood, together with the BBC's Director of Administration, Norman Bottomley. The two men were summoned hastily to a 'War Room' in Whitehall, where, Grisewood recalled, they were promptly given a dressing-down by 'a lot of soldiers and some Air Force people'. 'They reminded us that under the rules of World War Two, we subjected ourselves – the BBC – to the Government of the day and to what was called the "War Effort" ... And we were asked to do the same.' Grisewood and Bottomley refused to comply, a decision that prompted a message from 10 Downing Street that a legal instrument would henceforth be drawn up for taking over the BBC. In effect, Eden was repeating the threat that had been made against the Corporation by Churchill thirty years earlier during the 1926 General Strike. Unlike Reith, however, Grisewood stood firm: 'The country *was* divided and our job, our principles, made us give a voice – a very full one – to those who opposed this venture altogether.' If this was not done, he made clear, he – and many others – would resign. On Sunday 4 November Gaitskell duly appeared on television, launching a blistering attack on the 'criminal folly' of invading Egypt and calling on the prime minister to resign.[26]

The BBC had shown, albeit belatedly, a willingness to assert editorial independence – and, specifically, its programme makers' right to decide not just *what* counted as a legitimate topic of debate but also *who* exactly could be invited on air to speak about it. Yet dramatic fallings-out like this between the Corporation and the government were the exceptions rather than the rule. During this entire period, it is the enduring intimacy between broadcasters and politicians that proved more influential in shaping the BBC's news coverage day-in, day-out. As Director-General, William Haley had been unusual in wanting to keep a distance from politicians; Ian Jacob, with cabinet experience behind him, was far more at ease in the corridors of power, seeing congeniality rather than confrontation as the key to managing relations with Westminster and Whitehall. His right-hand man in this enterprise, Harman Grisewood, would spend the long evening hours in the House of Commons on Jacob's behalf making friends with the party whips, getting to know MPs more personally. Lower down the BBC hierarchy, there was also a natural affinity between individual BBC producers and those who controlled the levers of the state – a shared belief in applying rational top-down solutions to the problems of society. Grace Wyndham Goldie, who as BBC Television's Head of Talks and, later, the head of the whole TV 'Current Affairs Group', was in many ways the perfect embodiment of this outlook. During the war, she had worked at the Board of Trade, organising the distribution of food to bombed-out towns and cities:

> This altered my whole attitude throughout my BBC life to the responsibilities of government and the instruments of government like the Civil Service ... And all the burdens and strains and other things we've been talking about, which have to be undergone by BBC producers, are a fraction of what they are for members of the Government ... So I've always been careful ... that an adequate appreciation is given in any comment or presentation of political subjects to the severe responsibilities which they carry.[27]

Editorial consistency at the BBC was established by cultivating a corporate *sensibility*, so that programme makers instinctively knew what was 'right' without having to be constantly monitored. As Wyndham Goldie explained, it was all 'an attitude of mind' – one 'communicated to you through discussion of programmes with your elders and betters'. Her own overriding ethos, with which all her producers were daily inculcated, was 'balance'. The notion was hardly new: back in the 1920s, Hilda Matheson had promulgated exactly the same editorial principle, what she described as a commitment to 'express all the most important currents of thought on both sides, preserving a carefully balanced diversity'. But by the 1950s, when MPs of all parties were paying closer attention to the workings of the BBC, it seemed more important than ever that the principle was observed, and, even more importantly, was *seen* to be observed. What current affairs did, Wyndham Goldie said, 'sank the BBC ... by dint of falling beneath standards, or it could help the BBC by its carefully controlled yet original and balanced attitude to the problems of the day'. It was, she claimed, 'an amorphous sort of approach which was only worked out in detail ad hoc'. But the BBC's journalists invariably assumed that it was the range of opinions expressed in Parliament that defined the outer limits of reasoned debate on any major issue.[28]

This heavy focus on Westminster had profound consequences. A television series such as *In the News*, which promised viewers 'unrehearsed discussion on topics of the week', relied on regulars such as the Tory MP Bob Boothby, Labour's Michael Foot, the former Independent MP and right-winger, William Brown, and the Oxford historian A. J. P. Taylor. To Wyndham Goldie's way of thinking, they earned their place in the studio because they offered 'a remarkable effervescence of wit, common sense, intellectual honesty and political passion'. But even when *In the News* was at its most sparklingly disputatious, it was still very much a programme that viewed topical events from the rarefied summits of Westminster or the Senior Common Room.[29]

The first spring shoots of a more liberated approach to news coverage would eventually burst through – in television rather more visibly than in radio. Once Tahu Hole had gone, a separate newsroom was set up in a corner of the old Alexandra Palace building. There, Hugh Carleton Greene wasted little time planting a fresh team of senior editors, plucked mostly from the fertile soil of Bush House. Among the most dynamic of the new arrivals was Stuart Hood, who had both a distinguished war record – fighting in Italy, working on Enigma, supporting the Italian partisans – and years of experience helping to run the BBC's German and Southern Europe sections. He came to his new posting in 1959 feeling confident that 'one could try things out and do things'. He was particularly keen to learn from ITN's success. He also wanted to be 'as good as the *Daily Mirror* ... cover the news in an interesting but also serious way'. Stiltedness and the 'impersonality of normal report writing' were to be abandoned.[30]

Yet even Hood's proposed reforms amounted to an overhaul of style rather than substance. There was little sign, even now, of a radical expansion in actual subject matter. Back in 1953, audience research had revealed that viewers of *In the News* wanted something 'besides political items'. Six years later, an internal BBC report was still noting the emphasis its own news programmes placed 'on the arrival and departure of Cabinet Ministers' or 'quotations from nondescript officials and semi-official figures'. Six years on again, a BBC enquiry into the 'Public Mood' concluded that people were tired of hearing about Parliament and politicians and their 'party games'. Journalists, managers were told, needed to turn their spotlight away from 'purely political argumentation' and devote more time and resources to exploring the underlying trends in industrial relations, technology and society.[31]

The sheer repetitiveness of these warnings raised the question of whether practices and organisational structures in the BBC's various news and current affairs departments had simply become too calcified to respond. It had been nearly fifteen years since John Coatman had presented his critique of the relationship between the BBC and the political establishment. Coatman's gloomy prognosis back then, that old habits of 'subordination' would linger, even if 'below the level of consciousness', had proved remarkably prescient. Hood stood firm in his belief that a national broadcaster such as the BBC would always be concerned more than anything with the activities of what he called 'the central powers' of the state: it was, he said, 'in the nature of the beast'. One of his successors would later claim, too, that it was entirely natural that the BBC news operation had economic editors, diplomatic editors, royal correspondents, and a fleet of staff covering Parliament, but that something like a 'community relations correspondent' was an anomaly. Whoever occupied such a post, he suggested, would be open to the charge 'that he is on the side of the racial minorities'.[32]

The long-term cost of this way of thinking would become horribly clear in April 1975. It was then that a young journalist was despatched from Bush House to visit Manchester and report on the Caribbean community living there. The reporter in question was the very same Mike Phillips who had arrived from British Guyana back in 1956: he was now on the BBC's own payroll.

What Phillips found when he arrived in Manchester was 'an entire community which was neither impressed nor interested by the fact the BBC was doing a programme about them'. 'The degree of sympathy with which the programme was to be conducted', he noticed, was 'utterly irrelevant ... the media had failed accurately to reflect the lives, problems and aspirations of immigrant minorities, they felt that they owed us ... nothing.' It was an unequivocal rejection, though Phillips was notably less surprised by it than his BBC colleagues. He had worked in the BBC's Manchester newsroom several years before and found the experience 'really unpleasant'. 'I kept bringing stories, most of them about police harassment', he recalled. He also remembered vividly what his news editor said to him on each occasion: 'Oh, um, I'll deal with that, just leave it alone.'[33]

A social eye

In the 1950s, as in the 1930s, it was often the documentary makers and, even more, the dramatists, who took up the challenge of probing the most neglected corners of British society.

One of the most original productions was broadcast by North Region in October 1953. *The Drifting Sort* featured a variety of homeless people – or what the *Radio Times* characterised as the 'hobo and the busker, criminal and dreamer, the young man with a grievance and the old man without hope' – all talking 'about themselves'. Its producer, Denis Mitchell, was a hugely talented South African documentary maker who had been enticed to the BBC by Geoffrey Bridson. It was while he was based in Manchester that Mitchell developed the series *People Talking*, which provided a regular showcase of his trademark style: allowing those on the margins of society to have their say. For each project he would set out alone, often walking the streets at night, finding people by chance, and then recording their words. Back in the 1930s, when Shapley had left the studio to capture people in their natural habitats, she had needed an enormous recording truck and the assistance of an engineer. But in 1952 the first batch of EMI 'Midget' tape recorders had arrived at the BBC. It meant that Mitchell had equipment small enough and light enough to sling over his shoulder. He could be less obtrusive. his subjects more spontaneous.[34]

It was harder to pull this off in the technically more cumbersome medium of television. But even here, portable equipment was starting to make a difference. When Mitchell left radio in 1955 to work in Lime Grove's small documentary unit, he came across a new generation of lightweight 16 mm film cameras. After returning to Manchester, he used them in a newly established BBC Northern Film Unit to make the documentary that established his international reputation. *Morning in the Streets*, broadcast in 1959, and co-directed by Roy Harris, was Mitchell's 'impression of life and opinion in the back streets of a Northern City' as it came to life at the start of a working day. It was shot in Liverpool, Stockport, Salford and Manchester, and in the opening sequence, viewers saw a montage of striking images – snapshots of dilapidated street corners and rain-soaked rooftops emerging from a gloomy, all-enveloping fog. Later, streets liven up, breakfasts are eaten, glasses of stout are downed in pubs, elderly women do their laundry, children flood into school and out again – all to an accompaniment of local voices commenting on themselves, their families, their memories, the local gossip, the state of the world as they saw it.[35]

There was a whole heap of artifice involved in a documentary like this. Indeed, some of Mitchell's colleagues were seriously alarmed when they discovered more about his methods. 'We loved him dearly', one of them explained. But much of what he produced 'was in strict terms a cheat'. In an earlier programme called *Night in the City*, for instance, Mitchell had opened with a shot of a night watchman, back to camera, sitting over a charcoal burner with his hands outstretched, as a deep male voice discoursed wisely, quoting a long line of philosophers from Plato onwards. 'It emerged later on that the chap who had said this about Plato was a totally different figure', and someone who had since died. 'Mitchell had judged his words to be so poetic that he had overlaid them on the night watchman, a man who was from somewhere else.[36]

One reason Mitchell got away with his sleight of hand was that this 'think-tape' technique, as he called it, was so integral to his style. It involved a fusion of radio and television methods in which taped interviews were edited down to create well-chosen sound bites and then positioned strategically over silently filmed sequences that had been shot separately. The overall effect was always highly impressionistic, though Mitchell no doubt believed it was an approach that revealed its own truths – deeper ones, perhaps, than could ever be revealed by the more conventionally factual approach of current affairs. Mitchell later confessed that he had simply 'fallen in love with the human voice'. He believed that working-class people, especially, had 'a natural poetry' to their voices that demanded to be heard. What captivated him, he said, 'wasn't what they said so much as how they said it'. It was a revealing comment. Like his near contemporary, Charles Parker, who, from his base in Birmingham, was busy producing a much-celebrated series of 'radio ballads' elegantly woven from hours and hours of conversation – with fishermen, boxers, travellers, labourers – Mitchell sometimes seemed to be reducing his interviewees to the function of sound effects, rather than people whose actual opinions were to be taken seriously. It was as if they were walk-on parts – unnamed, uncredited – in projects that were still largely shaped by – *belonged* to – the producer in the edit room.[37]

Fictional portraits of working-class life free of sentimentality or caricature were not entirely absent. But they were unusual. This was a problem that went beyond broadcasting, of course. Shelagh Delaney said that it was seeing too many theatre productions where 'working class people simply appear as imbeciles' that drove her in 1958 to write *A Taste of Honey*, the tale of a teenage girl who leaves her Salford home, has a brief affair with a sailor, and finds herself pregnant. The BBC seemed largely content to stick with older, cosier concerns in its own drama productions. Between 1954 and 1957, it treated its viewers every Friday evening to *The Grove Family*, a serial that followed the joys and tribulations of Mrs Grove, her husband Jack, a self-employed builder, and their Hendon household. The opening episode of what was in effect British television's first soap opera, 'A House of Your Own', very much set the tone, with Jack in celebratory mood, having paid off his mortgage, and his wife planning to buy new curtains. *Punch*'s critic described it as a sensible, efficiently produced 'twenty-minute parade of the accepted suburban lower middle-class virtues, chores, domestic economics and humour'.[38]

By the time *The Grove Family* reached the television screen, two other serials, *Mrs Dale's Diary* and *The Archers*, were already household fixtures for millions of radio listeners – and showed no signs of running out of steam, despite the permanently disgruntled opposition of the head of Radio Drama, Val Gielgud, who dismissed them both as wretched, standardised production-line fare, 'lower than beasts that perish'. Neither was centred on working-class life. *The Archers*, for instance, billed itself as 'the daily events in the life of a farming family'. But the family concerned was part of the rural squirearchy. As for Mrs Dale, she was a well-off doctor's wife with a daily help and a gardener, living somewhere in London's outer suburbs. The nearest the BBC came to a soap opera dedicated to working-class characters and settings was when the writer Tony Warren approached two of its producers, Olive Shapley and Barney Colehan, bearing the outline of a new television serial he wanted to create called *Florizel Street*, and which he thought would 'do very well' on the BBC. 'I can see a little back street in Salford', Warren told Shapley while sharing a train carriage one night, 'a pub at one end and a shop at the other, and all the lives of the people there, just ordinary things …' 'It sounds *so* boring', Shapley replied. When Colehan read Warren's written proposal, he hated the title. It sounded, he said, 'like some disinfectant'. He also told Warren the BBC was just 'not into this kind of programme'. Faced with a singular lack of enthusiasm, Warren's only option was to take his idea to the commercial television company, Granada, where it received a warmer welcome and would be launched in 1960 under a hastily revised title, *Coronation Street*.[39]

Yet the BBC's own serials had an appeal that crossed social boundaries among listeners. At its peak, *Mrs Dale's Dairy* was attracting more than half of the available working-class radio audience. One devotee, the wife of a Carlisle factory worker, told BBC researchers that she loved following *Mrs Dale* 'because it was the life she felt she should have had'. As for *The Archers*, it had built up an equally mixed following of nearly ten million listeners in little more than two years.[40] This was partly because the serial had shown itself to be far more dramatic than anticipated. It had been conceived back in 1948 as a means of infiltrating rural communities with important government advice on sound agricultural practice. But as 'a farming Dick Barton', the emphasis was also very much on entertainment. The actor Norman Painting, for instance, saw his own character, Phil Archer, less as a plodding young farmer and more the 'patron saint of testosterone':

> The very first scene I did was after a New Year's Eve party sitting in the back of a car with Grace, who was the boss's daughter ... and it's quite clear that at the very least he'd got his hand down her blouse and the chances are he was busily undoing her bra... Because it was radio those that didn't want to think such things didn't – it was just 'an affectionate scene'. But it was unmistakable, and we had some very intimate love scenes ... I was sent contraceptives through the post, you know.[41]

For most listeners, the enduring appeal of *The Archers* was not just that very little of *that* sort of thing happened: it was that very little of *anything* happened. Two years into its existence and after interviewing several hundred fans, the BBC's audience researchers concluded that if its popularity lay anywhere it was with 'the appeal of "real" people and ordinary, homely credible incidents'. Similar testimony was offered from listeners to *Mrs Dale's Diary*: 'They are my friends', 'I feel as if the family were relations of mine or very close neighbours', 'I find myself thinking about them all the time'. There was only one conclusion the BBC could come to: what most of the audience wanted most of the time was 'Everyday events, rather than sensational stories'. Within these limits, a serial like *Mrs Dale's Diary* was still quietly capable of handling many of the issues that millions of women were grappling with throughout the 1950s: the pressure to be homemakers, the trials of motherhood, unhappy marriages, sons being called up for National Service. Its main characters might have been steeped in conservative values – 'solid, respectable, unimaginative, dull', as Harold Nicolson put it when he tuned in for the one and only time. But in Mrs Dale's young daughter 'Gwen' listeners found someone not just irked by the restrictions of family life but willing to question whether she wanted a life of domesticity or the chance to get a job outside.

They could hear Gwen's grandmother being wonderfully supportive: 'She can go on with her career after she's married, can't she?... Don't keep harping on marriage, Mary – let the child concentrate on her career.'[42]

The millions of women who followed *Mrs Dale*, so avidly that they were sneeringly referred to in the press as 'addicts', certainly refused to treat the storylines as either totally alien or boringly mundane. Neither did they regard their own role as one of passive acceptance. 'Hear them every day, I *must*', one listener confessed – before telling researchers that she also often found the episodes 'infuriating ... even maddening'. Though the lives portrayed in *Mrs Dale's Diary*, like those in *The Archers* and *The Grove Family*, were not exactly the same as those of most working-class listeners and viewers, they were recognisable enough to touch a chord. And they proved that 'ordinary' lives and 'ordinary' events were of intrinsic interest – that it was possible for the BBC to treat the normal as noteworthy.[43]

Atlantic crossings

As yet, remarkably little of this new-found attentiveness to ordinary lives and ordinary events was being deployed by television or radio when it came to Britain's immigrant communities. George Lamming's 1954 novel, *The Emigrants* and Sam Selvon's 1956 novel, *The Lonely Londoners* both showed what might be achieved on the page. Selvon's novel, in particular, with its cast of utterly believable characters centred on the homesick Moses Aloetta, gave a widely read collective voice to the immigrant experience in London during its first foggy, smog-filled post-war decade. In a BBC with few ethnic minority staff of its own, the possibilities for bringing this thriving literary tradition to the nation's airwaves were too easily overlooked. It was only in 1969, thirteen long years after it had been published, that Selvon would be invited to create radio plays based on characters from the novel.

Again, the BBC had not been entirely inactive. Selvon had first featured on the BBC in June 1947, when John Figueroa read out his poem 'Lucky Lucre' on *Caribbean Voices*. Five years later, he was introduced to British listeners when he read his own short story, 'The Village Washerwoman' on the Light Programme, and, later the same month, when he gave a talk on the *Tea-Time Talk* programme on the Home Service about the village in Trinidad where he grew up.[44]

But in the year in which *The Lonely Londoners* came out, the BBC's most high-profile portrayal of the immigrant experience came not from the obviously talented Selvon but from a white British writer, John Elliott, whose one-hour television play, *A Man from the Sun*, was screened at the peak time of 9 p.m. on Thursday 8 November 1956.

The play was described in the *Radio Times* as 'A Story of West Indians in London'. Its central character was Cleve Lawrence, a skilled carpenter who had arrived in Britain hoping for work but who is gradually forced to accept the realities of his new existence: being treated as a foreigner, being judged by the colour of his skin. 'There is no colour bar in the law, but in people's hearts', 'Daddy' Zacharius, a father figure in the local Black community, tells a disheartened Cleve. The lead role was taken by Errol John, and it was said that the large cast read 'like a directory of African and Caribbean actors' then working in Britain. One, Pauline Henriques, described working with a script unlike anything else 'written about black people for television'. Elliot had been determined to achieve a new level of realism with *A Man from the Sun*. He had spent the summer months in London nosing around Brixton, 'sinking into the background, talking and listening to people, going to parties, to church, to work, and generally being a fly-on-the-wall'. Not everyone showed the same commitment to authenticity. One of the other cast members, Nadia Cattouse, remembers a props woman coming on to the studio set to dress the room her character was supposed to be living in. 'I watched as she messed up the bed clothes, and made the room look as sleazy as possible. This was how she thought people from the Caribbean lived!'[45]

A Man from the Sun highlighted how an even vaguely authentic

A scene from *A Man from the Sun*, broadcast on BBC Television
in November 1956. Around 40 per cent of all adult viewers
watched. From left to right: Sonny McKenzie ('Johnny Todman'),
Gloria Simpson ('Ethlyn'), Earl Cameron ('Joseph Brent'),
Andre Dakar ('Daddy Zacharius'), and Errol John ('Cleve').

portrayal of immigrant life for British audiences still depended
on the active support of a small handful of sympathetic white
producers. Nadia Cattouse reckoned that aside from John Elliott
in television, the key individuals throughout the 1950s and early
1960s were a trio of radio people: Geoffrey Bridson, John Gibson
and Betty Davies. 'If it wasn't for people like them', she said, 'we
wouldn't have worked. They helped make things happen.'[46]

It was the best-known figure in this trio, Geoffrey Bridson,
who was behind one of the most extraordinary radio series
of the whole post-war era: *The Negro in America*, a season of
nineteen programmes broadcast on the Third Programme
between September and December 1964. What made the series

The American poet Langston Hughes at his Harlem home, 1962. Hughes' collaborations with the BBC began in 1944, when Geoffrey Bridson produced his play, *The Man Who Went to War*. It starred an all African American cast depicting a family living through the London Blitz.

so significant was not just the breadth of vision that Bridson brought to the series, it was also that his co-editor throughout the twelve long months that went into making it was the famous African American poet Langston Hughes. Hughes's involvement represented a considerable publicity coup for the Corporation. More importantly, it was Hughes himself who ensured that the BBC gained access to a range of sounds and voices – from the civil rights struggle, from jazz music and from African American literature – which had rarely been heard in Britain.

The series grew out of a professional relationship that stretched right back to the war, when Bridson had been in New York making programmes for the BBC's North America Service and the two men had discovered just how much they had in common: a shared joy in poetry, a love of jazz, a commitment to progressive politics. They had both thought deeply about how mass communication might be used in the service of the underdog rather than the establishment. The purpose of art, Hughes once said, was 'communication, the wider the better'. 'About an idea', he added, 'one must be practical.'[47]

Two decades on, Bridson was finding himself increasingly drawn to what he called 'the Integration Struggle' in America and 'its obvious relevance to the growing influx of immigrants in Britain'. In 1961, he returned to New York, recording two long interviews with Hughes for the Third, in which the writer ranged over his evolution as a poet, the history of Harlem, contemporary politics and literature, and the future of race relations. Then, in 1963, the germ of the idea for *The Negro in America* started to grow from a series of discussions between Bridson, Laurence Gilliam and the Controller of the Third, Howard Newby. The plan was for an ambitious package of plays, documentaries, jazz programmes, gospel shows, poetry recitals and discussion programmes to coincide with the 1964 US presidential election campaign, during which the racial injustices faced by African Americans was expected to loom large. 'At last … an opportunity to rally sympathy to their cause', Bridson wrote. Bridson spent the spring and summer months of 1964 in New York, gathering raw material. After visiting the off-Broadway theatres of Greenwich Village and the jazz clubs and record stores of Harlem, meeting leading members of the civil rights movement in the city, and, most importantly, spending long hours at Hughes's home on East 127th Street, discussing ideas over glasses of whisky, he returned to London to whittle down the hours and hours of tape in his luggage.[48]

Among the programmes that emerged when the series was finally launched in September were several plays that would have been entirely unfamiliar to British audiences, including a special recording of Langston Hughes's latest 'documentary musical' then being staged in Greenwich Village, *Jerico-Jim Crow*. There were also poetry selections introduced by Hughes, showcases of the contemporary African American jazz scene, compilations of what were described as 'Negro folk-songs', and a round-table discussion that included Cannonball Adderley, Quincy Jones, Dizzie Gillespie and Cecil Taylor, among others, talking about jazz. In the opening week of December, listeners heard Bridson in a *Conversation with Langston Hughes*, in which the poet ranged widely over the contemporary American scene.[49]

Many of these episodes had, at best, a distinctly lukewarm reception from critics and listeners. Bridson's interview with Hughes, especially, was regarded as altogether too relaxed and chummy. Where, asked the *Listener,* was the stimulating clash of opinion? It sounded as if Bridson and Hughes were travelling through the United States 'sitting in deep chairs in an observation car, drawing at long cigars and sipping highballs'.[50]

Conversation with Langston Hughes had indeed been a record of two old friends enjoying each other's company. The friendly tone was utterly deliberate on Bridson's part. He had always believed that the best way to ensure listeners were exposed to the hard truths about racial injustice was by retaining the warmth – what he called the 'gurgling laugh' – in Hughes's natural speaking voice. 'We cannot see your beatific smile on radio', Bridson had told the poet, so 'we should very much like to hear it.' As for Hughes, he too had spent his entire career grappling with what he called 'the old problem … how to get everything to suit everybody'. The only solution he had found, he once explained to a close friend, was 'lulling with one hand, while lopping with the other'.[51] Whether it was a production such as *Jerico-Jim Crow* or a round-table debate about jazz, the aim, as both men saw it, was never the avoidance of serious politics; it was for the politics to be introduced with a light touch.

Unfortunately, the racial situation in America had been deteriorating dramatically while the series was being put together. The increasingly heated atmosphere clearly had to be acknowledged more prominently if the remaining programmes were to retain any credibility.

It was, in the end, three very different programmes that really allowed *The Negro in America* to convey to listeners the full, shocking reality of the African American's fight for racial justice. The civil rights struggle had already been reported widely on radio and television in the United States; much less of it had been heard or seen in Britain. Bridson's response was to trawl through hundreds of hours of American news reports to create two startling documentaries of his own featuring a montage of speeches, protest songs, and running commentaries from reporters. The third documentary, and the one that caused the biggest stir, was *Freedom Now*, imported from Pacifica Radio in California. It replayed the explosive events in Birmingham, Alabama in 1963, when civil rights campaigners had fought running battles with the almost entirely white local police, and broadcast almost unedited the visceral account of one radio reporter who happened to be in the thick of it all with his tape recorder running when white racists launched their vicious bombing campaign. All three programmes prompted immediate and widespread praise. 'Superb' and 'horrifying' were typical responses. It was all 'utterly unsentimental, but extremely moving' one listener said. *Freedom Now*, in particular, was 'very gripping', 'stark and moving', 'deeply inspiring'. 'It let us, as it were, be present', explained one member of the audience. And in a comment that must have thrilled Bridson and Hughes to the core, a former missionary wrote that 'There was vigour, compassion and the ring of truth' in everything he had heard. 'It made you feel "surely these people must be free".'[52]

For Bridson it was responses such as this that mattered the most. His documentaries had shown very clearly the direction BBC's programme makers needed to take in the future – moving away from polished scripts, embracing instead a raw and spontaneous approach. But to Bridson, questions of style were always inseparable from broadcasting's moral purpose. The *Guardian*'s complaint, that *The Negro in America* had failed to deliver enough dispassionate analysis, would have struck him as entirely missing the point. The *Listener* demonstrated a firmer grasp of his intentions when it argued that seeing things solely from the African American perspective for a change was precisely what created *real* understanding. *The Glasgow Herald* understood too that the power of the series lay in its rich mix of approaches – something that only a large, wide-ranging and multifaceted broadcasting operation such as the BBC could deliver. A news-and-current-affairs approach would never have worked on its own, it suggested. It was the *combination* of 'plays, poetry, music, and documentaries' that had created 'one composite feature'. The result was 'Not only the best series of the year, but possibly the best of all time'. By this stage, Hughes himself, by no means a fan of Britain or its institutions, had sent Bridson a personal note with a surprising but heart-warming message scribbled on it: 'The BBC is the most – I love it!'[53]

Perhaps the greatest achievement of the series was that while attempting, no matter how imperfectly, to portray an aspect of contemporary life, it had also found space to imagine a different – better – world. As such, it embodied the oldest Reithian instincts of the BBC while being draped in distinctly modern clothing. Harman Grisewood had once suggested that what he called 'the "mirror" theory' was never going to be enough to justify the Corporation's existence. The job of public service broadcasting, he said, was not merely to reflect faithfully – to report – what goes on in the present day. It was to 'discriminate in favour of what is vital'. E. M. Forster put the same point rather differently in one of his broadcasts for the Third, when he described the BBC as an organisation that always needed to have one face turned to the past and the other to the future. 'One of them reflects, the other explores', he said. The point was not so much to describe the present, but to enrich it – through 'the backward look at achievements, the forward look of possibilities: the double vision of Janus'.[54]

*

In December 1964, as *The Negro in America* was coming to its end, the BBC – like the country at large – was certainly poised awkwardly between past and future when it came to the subject of race and British identity.

At peak time on Saturday evening viewers could still lap up *The Black and White Minstrel Show* on television. And as the election result in Smethwick had shown, plenty of people could still feel comfortable electing to Parliament a candidate who deployed hideously racist language. Yet now, when Una Marson herself arrived back in London for the first time since she had been bundled on to the *SS Tetela*, she was delighted to see so many familiar faces from 'back home'. She wandered around Brixton market, looking at the salt fish, buying some hard-dough bread, listening to the calypso drifting out of the record shops. Later, she lunched with Andrew Salkey and spent a 'glorious day of witty, amusing conversation' with George Lamming. In Birmingham, a new Centre for Contemporary Cultural Studies was just being opened at the university, dedicated to the study of popular music, newspapers, advertising – what was coming to be called 'mass culture'. Fittingly, its director was Richard Hoggart, and neither he nor his new research centre would ever be short of things to discuss. Though his 1957 book had only reflected briefly on the place of broadcasting, he had long since become a regular – if discriminating – member of the BBC's audience. Watch enough television, he wrote, 'and you almost feel the cakes of custom being cracked open'. It was now that he started wondered if broadcasting might do more than 'offer a funny and slightly subversive angle on our lives': might it also, he asked, help create a *common* culture, in which the lives of people who did not go to the theatre or to university would, by stealth and serendipity, become as rich and fulfilled as those who had always had their share?[55]

As it happened, the sixties would neither deliver Hoggart's dream of a 'common culture' nor allow the BBC to act freely with stealth and serendipity. The new decade was a blur of sensations and excitements, a time when it seemed that things really *were* going to be different, but also a time when those opposed to change took a stand. And if a 'strange, stirring mixture of possibility and peril' therefore hung over everything – if young were going to be set against old, progressives set against conservatives – it was going to be in broadcasting itself that the battle over the future of British society would have to be played out and fought over with unexpected ferocity.[56]

12

THE SHOCK OF THE NEW

Mucky jokes. Obscenity – it's all the go nowadays.
That Was The Week That Was, BBC TV, 27 April 1963

The last weekend of November 1962, autumn all but a memory. The 'Big Freeze', which would see Britain covered in icy fog and deep drifts of snow had yet to arrive. But the weather was on the turn. The Meteorological Office warned of cold showers from the North and frost in sheltered places.

In London's Television Centre, an audience was assembling in Studio 2, soaking up the heat from overhead lighting, while trolley-loads of warming mulled claret were pushed around by women dressed in black fishnet stockings. As the temperature rose, the cameras rolled into position. At 10.50 p.m., after what was described as 'a wonderful piss-up', the programme they had come to watch took to the air for the very first time. Its strange, somewhat convoluted title was announced in the opening theme tune, performed live in the studio by Millicent Martin. 'That Was The Week That Was', she sang. 'It's over, let it go.'[1]

The *Radio Times* had promised 'An entertainment for late on Saturday night'. The billing, cool as the weather, drastically undersold the programme's red-hot novelty. *That Was The Week That Was* offered a blend of entertainment and current affairs that was not just topical but blisteringly anti-authoritarian. Politics and television were parodied by Roy Kinnear in squaddie's battledress, playing a soldier standing for election. Willie Rushton and Kenneth Cope acted out a skit about the Bomb.

That Was The Week That Was gets ready to go live from Television
Centre in 1962. Millicent Martin is rehearsing her opening song,
while three of her fellow presenters – Willie Rushton, Roy
Kinnear and Lance Percival – watch from behind their desk.

There was a sketch about pre-marital sex, another poking fun at
product placement on commercial television. The acerbic columnist Bernard Levin interviewed a group of public relations
managers, giving them a verbal mauling. Making his television debut as the show's host was the twenty-three-year-old
David Frost, sporting a 'sloppy charcoal suit and overambitious
haircut'. The style was loose, edgy, a little chaotic. Viewers at
home could see cameras trundling around, floor staff lurking
in the wings. The cast fluffed lines and looked into the wrong
cameras. Somehow, none of it mattered. Artifice was exactly
what the show seemed to be thumbing its nose at.[2]

Once the first show was over, the programme team piled
into taxis for a celebratory meal of beef and mango stew on the
King's Road. What, they wondered, would the newspaper critics
and public make of it all?

The following morning's *Sunday Telegraph* provided the

answer. *That Was The Week That Was*, it said, was 'Without reservations ... brilliant'. It had chewed over the week's events
'with intelligence and dislike'. Those PR men interviewed by
Levin 'may have thought they had come to a party but they
ended up at a massacre'. For the first time, it concluded, television had proved itself 'as lethal as a gun'. David Frost, George
Melly wrote in the *Observer*, was the first television compere
who 'instead of helping to keep the children from becoming
over-excited, seemed determined to make them behave even
worse'. As for the public, an audience of one million had been
expected: three and a half times that number had watched. A
phenomenon had been born. And given that its full title was
something of a mouthful, the BBC's bawling infant had already
earned an affectionate alias: *TW3*.[3]

The influence of 'the satire boom' was obvious. Just two
years earlier, the stage revue *Beyond the Fringe* and its four young
performers – Peter Cook, Dudley Moore, Jonathan Miller and
Alan Bennett – had been described in the *Daily Express* as 'brilliant, adult, hard-boiled, accurate, merciless, witty, unexpected,
alive, exhilarating, cleansing, right, true and good'. In sketch
after sketch, the show had poked fun at everything sacred in
British life. Cook's mocking impersonation of the ageing prime
minister, Harold Macmillan – portrayed as a bemused figure
only half-aware of his own country's diminishing status in the
world – had become something of a cause célèbre. 'We hadn't
seen prime ministers actually lampooned, by name', one utterly
enthralled member of the audience recalled, 'it was a shock, a
slap in the face'. The show's success had allowed Peter Cook to
launch 'The Establishment', advertising itself as London's 'First
Satirical Nightclub'. Twenty days later, the first issue of *Private
Eye* hit the newsstands. By the middle of 1962, Britain's leading
young satirists were performing nightly across the capital.
All that remained to be conquered was Broadway, which had
a satire boom of its own, and the BBC, which – rather more
promisingly – did not.[4]

Hugh Carleton Greene, now two years into his term as

Director-General, had already been putting it about that the time was ripe to revive the cabaret spirit of 1930s Berlin. It would, he suggested, 'be healthy for the general standard of public affairs' if pomposity were to be pricked. A recent attempt by Light Entertainment to build a show around the American satirist Mort Sahl had been a failure, largely because it had been a traditional variety show, with a succession of guests and mid-dle-of-the-road musical interludes. The baton had subsequently been passed to Lime Grove and the team behind *Tonight*. Once planning was in the hands of their own producer, the thirty-one-year-old Ned Sherrin, it was inevitable that *TW3* would embrace liveness and topicality. Viewers were promised 'the most irrever-ent hour of the week'.[5]

When he had first seen Sherrin's plans back in February, Donald Baverstock, now the Assistant Controller of Television, was delighted. He hated the humbug of politicians, and their treatment by broadcasters 'as if they were all of one breed, when I knew there were personal ambitions and personal animosi-ties between them'. He also saw *TW3* as offering refreshment to an audience that, thanks to the BBC's unrelenting seriousness, had been over-burdened through the week with a 'philosophy of concern, goodwill and public spiritedness'. 'Late on Satur-day night people are more aware of being persons and less of being citizens', he explained. 'There should be room in this programme for prejudice, for cynicism, for Juvenal's "sacred indignation".' Sherrin put it rather more bluntly. What *TW3* offered, he said, was 'adult chat … the kind of thing one says to one's friends at a time like eleven o'clock on a Saturday night. It has some shock effect simply because it has never been said on television before.'[6]

Despite BBC nervousness around the very word 'satire', *TW3* was clearly designed to capture the mood of the moment. Sherrin felt that his old programme, *Tonight*, had been 'on the side of the audience'. But, like Frost, he wanted *TW3* to take the relationship a step further – 'from a conversation into a conspir-acy'. 'We were looking for a "them" and "us" relationship. "Us" constituted the programme makers ... and the sympathetic part of the audience. "Them" were the public figures or establishment forces whom we investigated, challenged, mocked or pilloried, and those viewers who tut-tutted in shock.'[7]

Grace Wyndham Goldie was nominally in charge, and distinctly nervous. She had dismissed one of *TW3*'s pilot shows as 'politically both tendentious and dangerous'. Unsurprisingly, she opted to stay at arm's length throughout the first series, leaving her colleague Alasdair Milne in day-to-day control. At the very top of the BBC, the Board of Governors was onside, though soon unsettled by accusations of blasphemy. Church leaders had objected, in particular, to a sketch that featured a 'Consumer's Guide to Religions', in which, after poking fun at Catholicism, Judaism, Protestantism, Islam and Buddhism, Frost recommended the Church of England as the 'best buy'. It prompted one Anglican preacher to call on Christians everywhere to 'storm the BBC'. Senior politicians generally had more sense than to react quite so volubly. Harold Wilson, the newly elected Labour leader, pronounced *TW3* 'vastly entertaining'. Harold Macmillan, who had to put up with being regularly impersonated by Willie Rushton, decided that being laughed at was better than being ignored, and instructed his Postmaster-General that he was 'not, repeat not' to take action against the programme.[8]

Like *Beyond the Fringe*, *TW3* fell into the category of what the *Observer*'s critic Kenneth Tynan called 'anti-reactionary without being progressive'. Even so, being anti-reactionary usually meant being anti-government. And for now that meant being anti-Conservative. The consequences were predictable. Conveying the increasingly restless mood among MPs and party officials, the *Sunday Telegraph* suggested that an 'anti-Establishment establishment' was on the march. By the time it came to a second series in the autumn of 1963, Greene was ready to see the show's wings clipped a little. Wyndham Goldie was asked to keep a closer watch, and more and more scripts were referred to the Director-General for his adjudication. Sherrin felt that the result was a more 'stilted and self-conscious' run. Dennis Potter, who happened to be both a contributing writer for the series and a paid television reviewer, talked of 'the shock' of 1962 having all but vanished. Perhaps, he wondered, 'A bomb explodes only once'.[9]

The ending, when it came, was swift. A bout of flu in November gave Greene the opportunity to reach a decision. When he returned from leave he told the Board that he intended to take the programme off air at the end of the year. The line sold to the press was that early termination was for one reason only: 1964 would be a general election year, making the programme's political content 'difficult to maintain'. This was less than honest. The reality was that Greene knew that the deputy Chairman of the Governors James Duff was threatening to resign if *TW3* was allowed to continue, and that as Director-General he, too, might then have to follow. Greene had also simply had enough: enough of Wyndham Goldie calling him every Saturday morning to burden him with her latest anxieties; enough of the Governors getting at him. Above all, Greene had come to the conclusion that *TW3* was 'diverting attention from the real achievements of the BBC'. No single programme was more important than this wider mission – and no single programme was worth sacrificing the cohesion between Governors and Director-General upon which the pursuit of this mission depended.[10]

The final episode was transmitted on Saturday 28 December 1963 – a mere thirteen months and thirty-seven episodes after the series had begun. The programme closed with Willie Rushton swapping his usual Macmillan impression for the role of a BBC commissionaire turning off the studio lights. As he wandered around, one last, suitably irreverent song crossed his lips:

That Was The Week That Was
It's over, let it go ...
The DG is a fleabag,
He couldn't run a bus.[11]

The 'DG', of course, knew *exactly* what he was doing.

When he took over as Director-General in 1960, Greene had said that he wanted to 'open the windows and dissipate the ivory-tower stuffiness' that he thought still clung to parts of the BBC. But as the BBC's windows were flung open, a whirlwind of social change swept in. Much of this was welcomed, even embraced; some was treated with suspicion; and a great deal would provoke agonised debate and fallings-out. Greene might claim that after *TW3* 'Nothing could ever be the same again'. But the BBC always had to operate within the limits set by government and by public opinion. And as programme makers and senior managers alike were to discover, it was often difficult to know how an institution so infused with traditional notions of dignity should respond in practical terms to new ideas, new tastes, new attitudes.[12]

The young ones

It was often the young who most vigorously challenged middle-class values – the very things that viewers and listeners of a certain age still believed would be guarded in perpetuity by a national institution such as the BBC. David Nobbs, who was part of Ned Sherrin's stable of young writers for *TW3*, said that for him the show's greatest appeal had always been that it was 'of my generation and it spoke for my generation'. This was a generation that also showed a new assertiveness in social relations. For a BBC that aimed to provide programmes for people of all classes and all ages – a BBC that was clearly most at ease in a world of consensus – the task of accommodating rapidly diverging tastes on the limited number of channels it controlled was to prove tortuous. But it was already hard to avoid the impression that broadcasting was not just reflecting these trends: it was also starting to amplify them.

In a speech in November 1961, Macmillan referred to the 'hot, pitiless, probing eye' of television. It was in current affairs, in particular, that he felt 'clashes of personality combined with aggressive interviewing' were being engineered for the sake of entertainment. One presenter had established a special reputation for putting the thumbscrews on: Robin Day. Whenever he presented *Panorama* or election night programmes, he would bring to the screen an unusually forensic, indeed abrasive, approach. He always claimed that a set-piece interview 'wasn't an ordeal or anything of the kind'. And, indeed, even Harold Wilson, destined to become, as Day put it, increasingly 'pathological' about the BBC, said he would relish such encounters. 'The harder they were, the better I liked them', Wilson claimed. Yet for all those not yet battle-hardened by Westminster life – a category that included quite a few television critics as well as many members of the public – it sometimes seemed as if the BBC as a whole, and television in particular, was starting to behave, well, *impertinently*.[13]

What further underscored the BBC's symbolic role in the coming decade was broadcasting's new-found enthusiasm for youthfulness in its own ranks. If there was one phrase that popped up more than any other in accounts of the period, it was 'Young Turks'. Everywhere one turned, they were on the rise. In television, men such as Donald Baverstock, Michael Peacock and Stuart Hood were promoted to powerful roles as Controllers or Assistant Controllers while still in their early thirties. In Radio, talent-spotters with hastily drawn-up contracts in their back pockets were despatched to select universities to hunt down the most promising students who were performing in fringe shows. A single reconnaissance trip to Cambridge in 1963 netted for the BBC John Cleese, Bill Oddie, Tim Brooke-Taylor and Graeme Garden. In the following year, another Footlights recruit, David Hatch, began a thirty-year broadcasting career that would eventually take him close to the top of the Corporation and, along the way, enable him to reshape radio comedy for a new generation of listeners.[14]

With the sudden influx of these bright young things, the old-timers increasingly felt like dead wood. When David Hatch arrived at the BBC, he thought it 'thrilling ... full of talented people', but also 'very elderly'. Most staff were in their fifties – a cohort Hatch and others would stereotype, only half-jokingly, as 'chaps with cravats': men such as Charles Maxwell and Con Mahoney, with wartime or national service behind them and the tastes and experiences of their era. They had, Hatch said, 'ruled the roost in the '50s'. But 'life had moved on ... these producers were sitting in a lovely building called Aeolian Hall in Bond Street, opposite Sotheby's, waiting for the artists to come in and say, "We'd like to do a show with you," and of course they weren't coming anymore – they were going up to the Television Service'.[15]

It was in television that the employment of younger talent was most obvious – and most obviously geared towards helping the BBC appeal to a younger audience. The needs of these viewers were reasonably well-understood in outline. Theirs was a generation enjoying unprecedented spending power, attending university in greater numbers, more questioning of the conventions of society, more willing to demonstrate when roused to anger. Defining how this translated into good broad-casting was the challenge, especially when it came to teenagers. A government report in 1960 had suggested that 'shopping, fashion, lounging in coffee bars and jiving the night away' were the 'cultural activities' that offered many young people an outlet for their creativity. But it was music that now seemed to define almost everything else – the clothes to wear, how to talk, the ways to walk.[16]

The BBC's first attempts to capture even the merest hint of this cultural ferment were a little ungainly. For one brief run between 1957 and 1958, television's prime Saturday tea-time slot had been given to *Six-Five Special*. The show was produced by two Oxford graduates still in their twenties: Josephine Douglas and Jack Good. If rock 'n' roll meant anything, Good said, it had to be about 'energy, excitement, novelty and rebellion. Being against toffee-nosed, conventional, culturally dead society. "Kick you in the face, you Tory buggers" stuff.' In this spirit *Six-Five Special* attempted to showcase what sections of the press referred to as the 'hooligan music' of the day, with up-and-coming performers such as Tommy Steele introduced by 'Jo' Douglas and her co-host, the hip young Radio Luxembourg disc jockey, Pete Murray. The fact that Murray's opening remarks to camera – 'Welcome aboard the *Six-Five Special*, we've got almost a hundred cats jumping here, some real cool characters to give us the gas' – were completely scripted rather ruined the spontaneous vibe that Good had been hoping for. But at least viewers could see a studio of gyrating young couples. *Juke Box Jury*, which occupied the same slot in the schedule for most of the following decade, represented something of a backwards step. Its simple formula – a silky and avuncular David Jacobs helping celebrity guests to judge the hit potential of the week's record releases – would attract upwards of twelve million viewers. The BBC delighted in learning that those watching at home ranged in age from four to ninety-four. But something so unthreatening to an older generation was precisely what made teenagers less than enthusiastic.[17]

Although neither programme had been rebellious in anything other than the most superficial way, the response among some of the Corporation's older hands ranged all the way from mild bewilderment to outright alarm. Both the BBC's Controller of Television, Kenneth Adam, and his head of Light Entertainment, Ronnie Waldman remained convinced that jazz, not pop, was the coming thing. Waldman's successor, Eric Maschwitz, who had done so much in the 1930s to keep radio in touch with the sounds of the era, dismissed *Six-Five Special* as cluttering up the screen with 'juvenile delinquents'. Even the usually restrained John Snagge was aghast at the BBC giving airtime to The Beatles. 'They are just noises,' he complained , 'a sort of primitive noise which is made by, I don't know, black countries.'[18]

By the end of 1963, it was obvious that pop really was going to be more than a passing fad. Though London and Liverpool were getting all the publicity, it was in Manchester that the BBC made its next – and boldest – attempt to ride the wave. There, the producer Barney Colehan had been spending the summer trying to devise a show to take on ITV's very successful *Ready Steady Go*. The search for an ideal frontman had brought him to the Mecca ballroom in Leeds, where the manager, a young man called Jimmy Savile, had asked to be auditioned. Savile had already done stints on Tyne Tees Television, as well as appearing on Radio Luxembourg and running his own local show, the 'Teen and Twenty Club'. Colehan recalled finding Savile, his hair died in a tartan pattern, playing records while 'all these girls were jiving around to the music'. He was intrigued enough to invite him, along with 'two or three coachloads' of teenagers, to come to the BBC's Dickenson Road studios for a pilot. Colehan then invited Eric Maschwitz, and his deputy, Tom Sloan, up from Shepherd's Bush to watch:

> They said to me, 'This is absolutely fantastic. We've never seen anything like this, how these kids can enjoy themselves and you get this music in at the same time. They're all dancing around and doing things. Very, very good indeed, but where on earth did you get this idiot? Where did you get the man with the funny hair?' I said, 'That's Jimmy Savile. He's a Mecca manager.' 'Crikey, we can never use him. It's just nonsense. It's just too way out, is that. You've got some good ideas, but how on earth you could have him I don't know.' They said, 'Right, we'll take it. We'll have a look, we'll think about this.' They took the tape away, and six months later they reproduced the 'Teen and Twenty Club' and called it *Top of the Pops*.[19]

Britain's newest music show reached British television screens on New Year's Day 1964, with a line-up that included the Beatles singing 'I Want to Hold Your Hand' and The Rolling Stones' rendition of 'I Wanna Be Your Man'.[20] As for the presenter on that first episode, it turned out after all to be the man from the Mecca ballroom, Jimmy Savile himself. Any qualms about his suitability had apparently been shelved in the rush to secure what appeared to be the embodiment of that mystifying thing, youthful cool.

*

It is hard to imagine John Reith watching the launch of *Top of the Pops*. But the retired Director-General could already see the way things were going under Hugh Carleton Greene. And he was now growling from the sidelines. 'I lead, *he* follows the crowd in all the disgusting manifestations of the age', he wrote in his diary.[21]

The comment was deeply unfair. Greene wanted to lead just as much as Reith: he just wanted to take audiences on a more adventurous journey. He believed fervently that the odd 'shock' might do some good. Stuart Hood recalled his boss hammering this home in meeting after meeting. 'I remember him saying, "if you don't upset part of your audience most of the time, you're not doing your job properly".'[22]

This signal from the top was important. But there were other reasons why staff now felt able to spread their creative wings. During the past half-decade, a steady growth in the number of television viewers had led to a near trebling of licence-fee income. The long-awaited opening of Television Centre in 1960 also provided the Corporation with what was claimed to be the largest and most advanced facility of its kind in the world. Bill Cotton, who was then rising quickly up the ranks in Light Entertainment, described the effect of working in the new doughnut-shaped building that was spread across some twelve acres of west London. It was almost alchemical, he said, 'You just walked that little bit taller'.[23]

More important still was the decision of the government-appointed Pilkington Committee to award a third television channel to the BBC rather than ITV. In 1962, the Committee's members had needed little persuasion to come down in the Corporation's favour. Britain's commercial broadcasters, they felt, were screening a few too many American crime series – and

making just a little bit too much money. The fact that the BBC
also happened to be overtaking ITV in the ratings for the first
time since 1955 only seemed to confirm its continued status as
the national broadcaster. Even so, Greene had used every last
drop of his psychological warfare training to influence the Committee – manoeuvring, lobbying, unveiling evidence of bad
behaviour among commercial operators. There were also some
artfully arranged performances of the BBC at work during the
Committee's 'getting-to-know-you' visits. When it descended
on Lime Grove, a formidable array of experienced programme
makers – Grace Wyndham Goldie, Leonard Miall, Alasdair
Milne and Huw Wheldon among them – had been gathered
up. They proceeded, a little more flamboyantly than usual,
to argue with each other at great length 'about something or
other'. As the meeting came to an end, one of the Committee
members, Richard Hoggart, took Wheldon to one side and said
how impressed they were by the freedom of expression the programme makers evidently enjoyed.[24]

In 1964, the new channel, BBC2, took to the airwaves. What
followed over the next few years was the creation of a channel
very much in the image of David Attenborough, the man who
was eventually appointed Controller. 'We would take programmes from every category one could think of, and find new
approaches and neglected subjects', Attenborough explained.
Archaeology appeared in the form of *Chronicle*, which took
a distinctly global and contemporary approach to the subject
and even commissioned new excavations of its own. *Life* was
launched, featuring the zoologist Desmond Morris reporting on nature and conservation, while a sister programme,
Horizon, covered science more broadly. Classical music was
given prominence through a stream of live concerts, including an 'electrifying' 1965 broadcast of the eighty-three-year-old
Igor Stravinsky conducting his own *Firebird* at London's Festival
Hall. On the drama front, there were adaptations of classics by
George Eliot, Henry James, Sartre, Tolstoy and Dostoyevsky
– along with a lengthy serialisation of *The Forsyte Saga*. Given

that BBC1 already covered lots of the big matches in football, rugby and cricket, BBC2 opted for inventing events of its own. In 1965 there was floodlit rugby league, and, four years later, the novel idea of televising snooker. The balance between modernity and tradition was striking. On Saturday 22 February 1969, viewers could enjoy the latest episode of *Colour Me Pop*, featuring the Glaswegian band, The Marmalade, who had just topped the chart with their song 'Ob-La-Di, Ob-La-Da'. The following evening viewers were offered the opening episode of *Civilisation*, an unashamedly patrician thirteen-part history of art presented by Kenneth Clark. The first episode, 'The Skin of Our Teeth', began with the camera in Paris and Clark turning round to glance admiringly at Notre Dame. 'What is civilisation?', he wonders. 'I can't define it in abstract terms *yet*. But I think I can recognise it when I see it. And I'm looking at it now.' With Clark, there would be no Africa or Asia or Islam, nor any female artists: his themes were the story of how civilisation – as 'we', the West, know it – had been endangered by war, barbarism and decay, and how it needed defending still.[25]

The mere fact that the Corporation now had two television channels instead of one was liberating. It meant that not every programme needed to have the broadest appeal. Just as the Third Programme had carved out a space for providing challenging radio for a discerning minority, BBC2 could act as a channel for trying out new ideas without undermining the frontline ratings war that BBC1 had to wage with ITV. If some viewers were still offended by what they saw on the screen, this, too, was entirely consistent with good Reithian principles. Reading the former Director-General's memoirs for the first time during his 1965 Christmas break, Attenborough's eyes had fallen on one magisterial sentence in particular: 'It is royal to do right and receive abuse.' 'It consoled me then', Attenborough recalled, 'and was to do so frequently in the next few years.'[26]

'Disbelief, doubt and dirt'

For new recruits to the BBC who arrived with high hopes of
bringing radical change, the 1960s were to prove frustrating and
rewarding in equal measure. Young, politically progressive men
and women could see an organisation eager to benefit from
their energy and creativity, and, perhaps in return, a chance for
them to nudge the BBC into closer alignment with the spirit of
the age – *their* age. But those who harboured truly revolutionary ambitions were unlikely to thrive. Alfred Bradley, who had
joined the Leeds studios as a young drama producer in 1959,
warned younger colleagues that life at the BBC always neces-
sitated daily accommodations. It had been the veteran features
producer Jack Dillon who had first explained to him the nature
of the job:

> He told me a story about a young producer who turned
> up ... and for the first few months, he said 'Oh, that's
> beneath my dignity, I couldn't do that.' And then the next
> few months he said, 'Oh that's too difficult, I can't do that',
> and it went on for a long time with him not doing anything.
> Jack Dillon was heard to say, 'Look lad, you've accepted the
> thirty pieces of silver; for God's sake, betray somebody.'
> You've got to work, you are paid ... it's a good organisation
> to work for most of the time.

Dillon's boss, Laurence Gilliam, had provided Bradley with
even blunter advice. 'Regard the BBC as a hermaphrodite', he
said to him. 'Suck its tits but kick it in the balls.'[27]

If there was one place where this happened more than anywhere else it was in the BBC's drama output. Bradley's own
response to Gilliam's advice was to tap into the 'great upsurge
of new writing' that he could see all around him in Leeds. In
1964, he teamed up with a struggling young writer, Alan Plater,
and launched an anthology radio series called *The Northern
Drift*. Scripts from what Bradley called 'the established people'
were out. Instead, short stories and sketches were accepted

from unknown young writers scattered across the BBC's North Region, from Carla Lane in Liverpool to Trevor Griffiths in Manchester and Barry Hines in Barnsley.[28]

Bradley's recruits belonged to a much broader cohort of politically engaged writers who were also finding doors opening for them at Television Centre in London. There the recently appointed Head of Drama, Sydney Newman, had been explicitly instructed by Greene to secure for the BBC all the new talent that he could find – and to bring back to the BBC all those writers first discovered by radio in the late 1950s who had since drifted away.

Newman was more interested in the kitchen sink than in 'tea and crumpets', and he knew how to embrace the latest styles. His previous role running drama at the commercial television company ABC had been only the latest stage of a rich career stretching back to the war. Before coming to Britain, he had worked in his native Canada under the pioneering documentary film-maker John Grierson, and directed outside broadcasts. By the time he started commissioning plays for the BBC in 1963, he was, as he put it, 'very much instilled' with the traditions of documentary reality. For him, entertainment was not the same as escaping reality; it was 'the entertainment of new concepts, new ideas'.[29]

Just months before arriving at the BBC, Newman had sat down one Tuesday evening and watched the first episode of a brand-new BBC1 drama series, *Z Cars*. It thrilled him as much as seeing Osborne's *Look Back in Anger* had done back in 1956. Based on extensive documentary research by its two scriptwriters, Troy Kennedy Martin and John McGrath, the series dramatised the everyday rough and tumble in which ordinary policemen and women were immersed. 'The cops were incidental', McGrath admitted. They were 'the means of finding out about people's lives'. As for the lively camerawork, always following the action, it seemed light years ahead of the static shots and stagey studio settings Newman associated with traditional BBC drama. It represented everything he wanted to see, not just in serials such as

Z Cars but in the revered genre of single plays, a strand of output he regarded as having fallen 'absolutely asleep'.[30]

It was Jimmy MacTaggart's arrival in the department in 1964 that 'brought the magic' Newman was after. MacTaggart proceeded to gather around him a loose nucleus of progressive directors, story editors, writers and producers, including Tony Garnett, Ken Loach, Roger Smith, Ken Trodd, Dennis Potter and Irene Shubik. 'We were in our late-twenties, cheeky, full of brass neck', Loach remembers. The impact of their collective presence was felt first and foremost through *The Wednesday Play*, which began in October 1964 and ran for six extraordinarily successful years before the shift to a Thursday-night slot required it to change its name to *Play for Today*. In the years to come, nearly ten million viewers would switch on every week and, in doing so, witness some of the most iconic television moments of the 1960s and 1970s.[31]

Among *The Wednesday Play*'s seminal early productions were *Up the Junction*, broadcast in November 1965, and *Cathy Come Home*, broadcast a year later. *Up the Junction* was based on a novel – in this case, Nell Dunn's impressionistic portrait of the lives of young, mostly working-class women in south London. But the play's director, Ken Loach, offered television viewers something more cinematic than literary – a kaleidoscope of fragmented images and mis-matched voice-overs. It was also 'funny, and racy, and raucous and full of music'. Most striking of all, Loach took the camera on to the streets, using hand-held equipment and lower-grade film stock in order to achieve the same look of grainy 'immediacy' found in news footage. *Cathy Come Home*, written by Nell Dunn's husband, Jeremy Sandford, and directed again by Loach, also involved a mix of studio and location filming, though on this occasion with the intention of creating something more like a fly-on-the-wall documentary. What the two plays had in common was that both attempted to intervene robustly on highly charged social issues. *Cathy Come Home* drew attention to the appalling housing crisis, and its broadcast offered a huge boost to the newly established charity Shelter and

The 1966 *Wednesday Play, Cathy Come Home*, directed by Ken Loach. It told
the story of Cathy Ward (played by Carol White), a young woman faced
with homelessness and her children being taken away by social services.
A voiceover provided distressing facts about Britain's housing crisis.

led directly to the setting up of a second homelessness charity,
Crisis. *Up the Junction* featured a harrowing scene of a backstreet
abortion: that a Bill to legalise the procedure was being debated
in Parliament at the same time was far from coincidental. The
brief, Loach said, had always been 'to do contemporary drama
that rattled the cages of the Establishment'. 'We thought we
were part of the public discourse.'[32]

During the two series' combined twenty-year run, viewers
were treated to thrillers, comedies, science fiction, farces, even
the occasional 'well-made play' or classic literary adaptation
from copper-bottomed writers such as Evelyn Waugh and John
Mortimer. As one of the series' producers explained, viewers
kept coming back week after week 'not knowing what they were
going to get – and that was part of the point'.[33] Nevertheless,

along with plays by Dennis Potter, David Mercer and others, it was *Up the Junction* and *Cathy Come Home* that stood out as emblematic of the new wave. Their striking visual style was a key factor in the impact the BBC's drama slot had on critics, viewers, and policy-makers. It gave its storylines a veracity that appeared to turn drama into news.

For some, this was also the biggest problem with *The Wednesday Play* and *Play for Today*. And, to the BBC's great discomfort, some of their fiercest critics turned private distaste into a moral crusade. The biggest and most articulate cheerleader of this group was an art teacher from the Midlands: Mary Whitehouse. She had been provoked in the first instance by some throwaway jokes about marriage in a mildly satirical comedy show, *Between the Lines*, though it had not taken long for *The Wednesday Play* to catch her attention. By May 1964, she had gathered 2,000 people in Birmingham Town Hall, many of them churchgoing women like herself, to denounce the series. 'We are told that the dramatists are portraying real life,' she told her audience, 'but why concentrate on the kitchen sink when there are so many pleasant sitting rooms?' Her meeting marked the launch of a much wider 'Clean Up TV' campaign, which accused broadcasters in general of neglecting the morally upright lives of the 'silent majority' and the BBC in particular of using television to project into millions of homes 'the propaganda of disbelief, doubt and dirt'. Whitehouse would soon become the biggest thorn in the BBC's side, rallying an impressive number of like-minded individuals and pressure groups to the cause for the rest of the decade. Greene raised the stakes by steadfastly refusing to meet her, in the belief that she never represented more than a tiny minority. In return, Whitehouse supplied an uncompromising verdict on the Director-General: 'If you were to ask me who, above all, was responsible for the moral collapse which characterised the sixties and seventies, I would unhesitatingly name Sir Hugh Carleton Greene.'[34]

Greene was certainly guilty of underestimating the breadth and determination of the forces arranged against him. For besides Whitehouse's Clean Up TV campaign, there was a dizzying coalition laying siege to the Corporation throughout his term of office. By the end of 1964, *Z Cars* had, for instance, provoked a grand total of nineteen chief constables around the country to join forces with 'Clean Up TV'. A year later, the BBC's hugely popular new comedy series, *Till Death Us Do Part*, which brought to full Rabelaisian life the working-class character of Alf Garnett and his extended East End family, was provoking telegrams to the prime minister and headlines in the Sunday tabloids about 'The TV Show that Shocks the Nation'. In the early 1970s, Whitehouse herself was busy as ever, throwing her weight behind the Christian 'Festival of Light', which held a rally in Trafalgar Square and whose leaders warned the BBC that it should not be 'the place for any and every social experiment'.[35]

Staff at the coalface could try with all their might to explain that series such as *TW3*, or *Play for Today* or *Till Death Us Do Part* were merely honouring the words of Shakespeare's Hamlet – to 'hold as 'twere the mirror up to nature'. But phone calls to the BBC following the broadcast of *Up the Junction* had been roughly twenty to one against the play.[36] Permissiveness was becoming a new preoccupation in a culture war where questions of sex, taste and morality were all connected, all politicised, all polarised. Whether or not standards really were deteriorating mattered less to programme makers at the BBC than the simple fact that listeners and viewers were clearly becoming more sensitive. Staff arrived each morning knowing that every creative decision they took risked a public outcry.

Radio was caught up in this struggle just as much as television. The only difference was that in the older medium arguments revolved around one theme above all others: 'bad' language.[37] Radio had been woven into the very fabric of listeners' lives: anything unusual always came as a much greater shock. For programme makers, the 'rules' as they had existed at the start of the decade were largely unbending. 'The word "damn" was frequently deleted from Home Service and Light

Programme plays' one young radio drama producer recalled. 'The word "bloody" had to be "referred" and the word "bugger" (and worse) was totally proscribed.' Sometimes, the list went even further. A so-called 'Green Book', drawn up back in 1948, supplied the BBC's Variety department with a comically specific list of forbidden subjects. It included a ban on jokes about lavatories or 'effeminacy in men' as well as any 'suggestive references' to subjects such as 'Honeymoon Couples, Chambermaids, Fig leaves, Prostitution, Ladies' underwear, e.g. winter draws on, Animal habits, e.g. rabbits, Lodgers, Commercial travellers'. Staff still referred to it as 'the Bible'. Yet there was room for theological interpretation. At the fastidious end of the spectrum was Charles Maxwell, who 'disliked smut' and 'was like a brick wall'. At the other end, where the department's younger members congregated, there was David Hatch, who preferred to discover the limits of good taste by constantly testing them. Harder to place were Barry Took and Marty Feldman, the co-writers of *Round the Horne*. They opted to create two comic characters – Julian and Sandy – who spoke largely in the gay patois of Polari, thus ensuring that those 'most likely to be outraged would not understand a word of the show's coded filth and innuendo'. After all, nothing in the Green Book explicitly prevented the pair from naming their fictional legal firm 'Bona Law'.[38]

Boundaries were trickier to navigate when it came to drama, largely because playwrights often set out deliberately to unsettle. Nor could producers be expected to work in complete isolation from standards set elsewhere. The failure in 1960 to prosecute *Lady Chatterley's Lover* for obscenity had established very publicly the principle of 'artistic merit' for novels. In cinema, too, censors were adopting a much more tolerant attitude towards nudity and violence. Only stage plays remained subject to the scrutiny of the Lord Chamberlain. But in 1968 even his powers were abolished, ushering in a new age of theatrical opportunities. Inside Broadcasting House, the arrival in 1963 of Martin Esslin as the head of Radio Drama had been a key turning point. Esslin was determined to offer patronage to 'difficult' plays, a category that, inevitably, included plays using language in deliberately challenging ways.[39]

The Third Programme, with its small but dedicated audience, provided the obvious place for a broadcast of Pinter's *Landscape* soon after the play had been denied a stage production in 1968. The dialogue included a few carefully placed expletives, ranging from the occasional 'shit' to a single 'fuck' in the final scene. It was these 'indecencies' that had sent the Lord Chamberlain over the edge. But Esslin knew his Pinter inside out. He argued that since the drama lay 'entirely in the language' the play should be performed uncut or not at all – and that BBC Radio should do it if the British stage could not . The Controller of the Third, Howard Newby, confessed to a strong personal distaste for four-letter words, especially if their use was 'in any way gratuitous'. But after consulting the Director-General he duly consented.[40]

A bigger problem was created by the 'bloodies' and 'damns' of ordinary speech, which often slipped under the radar whenever writers and producers strove for authenticity. In 1970, the BBC's Birmingham studios offered listeners an unusually rambunctious portrait of British teenage life. *Filthy Fryer and the Woman of Mature Years*, written by Andrew Davies, was entirely free of four-letter expletives, which was why it was not referred to London prior to broadcast. But in attempting to paint an accurate portrait of a schoolboy obsessed with sex, it had chalked up seven 'bloodies', four 'Gods', three 'sods', three 'Christs', and two 'arses' – not to mention plenty of lustful talk about 'milk white thighs' and masturbation – all in the space of one hour of afternoon radio. It had also mentioned Hamlet, Sartre, Camus and Marcuse. Managers in Broadcasting House therefore felt duty-bound to take it seriously. In an extended post-mortem held in the Council Chamber, Martin Esslin defended *Filthy Fryer* as 'a very funny play and a completely harmless one'. Its conclusions, he said, 'were highly moral and it contained nothing to which anyone accustomed to television could take exception'. Others wondered if a little judicious editing might have helped avoid the 'gross and unnecessary offence' which some listeners had evidently taken, but even they agreed that the play deserved to be transmitted. The meeting concluded by suggesting that there was no need for producers to 'retreat from recent advances in frankness', though the whole affair had highlighted 'the dangers broadcasting ran in dealing with what to many people were still delicate subjects'.[41]

Determining public taste from the third floor of Broadcasting House often felt like trying to draw a line in the mist, for as one member of Radio's Light Entertainment department declared in frustration, 'it had now become much more difficult to decide what was generally acceptable'. It was obvious that letters or phone calls of complaint could not be ignored entirely: they provided at least *some* measure of offence, especially as it was felt in Britain's suburban heartlands. That was why they were summarised regularly and circulated among senior programme makers. But incoming correspondence represented a small, self-selecting group rather than 'the public' at large: as one senior manager suggested, it would be wrong to ignore such views, and equally wrong to broadcast *only* the kind of programmes of which such listeners approved. Some in the audience evidently regarded naturalistic ways of talking, or merely the appearance before the microphone of a regional accent or a non-RP voice, as an index of moral decline. According to one internal analysis, this offended minority appeared to think that if only the Corporation reverted to some kind of pre-war gold standard in ways of speaking on air 'then society would be different, that is, better'.[42] But the Reithian ethos had always been about using broadcasting to dispel misunderstanding and ignorance. And it was precisely this founding ethos that was elegantly rearticulated by one senior BBC figure in October 1974 in a carefully worded memo distributed to producers:

> We should not allow ourselves to be put in the position of having to demonstrate that broadcasting a certain programme does no damage of any kind ... *Not* broadcasting certain types of programme is also damaging and the good

that we do by airing certain subjects in a responsible way, though it may well be immeasurable, must be set in the balance against any incidental harm ... A broadcasting service which avoids difficult subjects because they create difficult questions of public relations or because they can be shown to have damaging effects in some ways, may be shirking its public responsibilities. Certain questions need to be aired and discussed in a responsible society if that society is to grow in a healthy way.[43]

This was a defence that cut to the heart of the BBC's sense of moral duty. It showed not only that Reithianism had survived into the 1970s but was also a reminder that, even now, if the will was there, it could still be put to vaguely progressive purposes.

'Auntie's first freak out'

The author of that striking memo had other reasons for speaking out so passionately about the treatment of sensitive topics. For in 1974, he was still coping with the tumultuous fallout of a decade of radical reorganisation across the whole of BBC Radio.

His name was Tony Whitby, and the post he held was still relatively new and unfamiliar in the BBC's lexicon: Controller of 'Radio 4'. The new network had been born in the early hours of Saturday 30 September 1967. It was the direct descendant of the Home Service, and shared its birthday with another new network, 'Radio 3', which had inherited the Third Programme's mantle. These apparently simple changes in nomenclature had real and far-reaching implications.

The idea of tinkering with Haley's pyramid of Light, Home and Third had emerged as a response to the alarming bleeding away of radio's audience to the rival attractions of television. Permanent relegation to the status of a background medium seemed likely, a future in which radio sets, sent packing from living rooms, would only be listened to inattentively in the kitchen or bedroom or car. Given that all the plays, documentaries, symphonies, sketch shows and the like that the BBC had always excelled in making relied on listeners concentrating, the question was whether Britain should follow America's lead and focus instead on the kind of stuff that could be listened to casually and in short bursts – some non-stop music here, a steady flow of news there – while also ensuring that each radio service was a bit more consistent in character. At the very least, the solution appeared to be a shift away from a series of 'rich mix' radio channels to something more 'generic', where listeners could predict fairly easily what they would hear whenever they turned on their favourite station.

The first steps had been taken back in August 1964, when the daytime hours on the Third were stripped of various speech programmes and devoted instead to a flow of classical music. The new 'Music Programme', a kind of network-within-a-network, contained nothing so esoteric as to frighten the 'general listener' away – what the BBC's Controller of Music, William Glock characterised as 'an unobtrusive accompaniment of Bach and Mozart and Schubert'. As for the speech programmes that had been displaced, they were rehoused on the Home Service, which sent *Record Review* and *Music in Our Time* in the other direction. The net result was that the Third could promise listeners more uninterrupted music, the Home more talk. 'Talk', of course, included all those tricky plays that the Third had previously accommodated. It was precisely for this reason that Tony Whitby, as Controller of Radio 4, had found himself grappling more and more with the problem of 'difficult' language. It was not just that the scripts were becoming more challenging; it was that they were now being exposed to what Whitby called a 'fairly conservative audience' for whom 'unorthodox ideas tended to produce an unfavourable reaction'.[44]

A renegotiated relationship between the Home and the Third reflected just one half of the BBC's 'generic' radio revolution. Alongside the launch of Radios 3 and 4, there had also been a reckoning for the Light Programme. Here, too, a gradual process of streamlining had been taking place since 1964.

Long-serving series such as *Radio Newsreel* and *The Archers* had been moved across to the Home, and several old favourites, such as *Have a Go*, killed off. By 1967, even these attempts to refashion the Light Programme into a music-only station had failed miserably to keep pace with a 'pop' scene that had exploded into life. For a broadcaster committed to serving every part of the national audience, the implications were horrendous: an entire generation of listeners giving up all hope that the Corporation would offer anything worth tuning in for. It was for this reason that September 1967 marked an even more dramatic rupture in the BBC's existing structures than the end of the Home and the Third: the demise of the Light Programme and its replacement by, not one, but *two* stations – Radio 1 and Radio 2.

The concept of a new service devoted to pop was not entirely anathema to the BBC. But the Corporation faced a huge challenge in offering *any* kind of music more space on the schedules. Copyright laws obliged it to pay a hefty fee to record companies, music publishers, composers and performers. These powerful outside groups also fixed the total number of records it could play. The BBC had made repeated requests for an increase in this so-called 'needle time'; its requests had been consistently rejected. By 1967, the Light, Home and Third were still restricted to barely more than thirty hours a week between them. Even if it had wanted to the BBC was simply unable to offer listeners much more than *Saturday Club* and the Sunday afternoon chart show, *Pick of the Pops*: a pretty meagre ration. Annie Nightingale, then in her early twenties and setting out in her career as a music journalist in Brighton, spoke for many of her generation when she said that as far as the Light Programme was concerned, 'the pop music was utterly atrocious'. 'You had "Twenty Tiny Fingers, Twenty Tiny Toes", you had "Tulips From Amsterdam" … we couldn't understand why it was *so* appalling.' Every Sunday evening she would re-tune her bedside transistor radio to 208 metres medium wave and catch the chart countdown on Radio Luxembourg. The signal was erratic and maddeningly difficult to locate. But it was through listening devotedly through 300 miles' worth of static that Nightingale had first discovered a new and secret teenage culture, 'American pop stars, rhythm and blues – Chuck Berry, Howlin' Wolf'. From Easter 1964, she found an even more appealing alternative. It was on Sunday 29 March that the 'pirate' station Radio Caroline started broadcasting from a ship moored a few miles off the coast near Felixstowe. Flying a Panamanian flag of convenience, and situated just outside the United Kingdom's territorial waters, the station was safely beyond the reach of any law concerning wavelengths or royalty payments. Which meant that it was free to play as many records as it wanted while raking in up to £180 for every advertising spot. The station, like all the other pirates that suddenly burst on to the scene in the mid-1960s, was a hard-headed business operation. But the buccaneering image, burnished by endless tales in the tabloid press of disc jockeys bravely battling the North Sea swell as their battered ships weighed anchor and circumnavigated the British Isles, had an obvious appeal. It was, Nightingale explained, 'the first time we'd heard pop records and commercials played continuously, it was also the first time we'd heard brash young voices between the records ... They didn't talk down to us like some poncey BBC bloke; they were our mates.'[45]

If only because of its obligation to international treaties about wavelengths, the government felt it had to act. The awkwardly named Marine Etc Broadcasting (Offences) Act passed in July 1967 made it illegal to supply the pirate ships and paved the way for the BBC to provide a replacement service paid for out of the licence fee. By the middle of August, and with the assistance of several tons of well-placed dynamite, the assorted disused minesweepers and floating light-ships of the pirate fleet had been sunk and detailed preparations were underway inside Broadcasting House for what was provisionally labelled the 'Popular Music Programme'.

The man responsible for this behind-the-scenes operation was Robin Scott, the recently appointed Controller of the Light Programme. Scott had worked for the Corporation almost continuously since joining the French Service at Bush House in 1942. Colleagues called him 'the White Tornado' on account of his distinctive flock of white hair and the fact that he was always rushing around. He certainly had the appropriate blend of hard-won experience and youthful energy. Once he and his boss, Frank Gillard, had settled on 'Radio 1' as the name of the new service – Scott had originally wanted something like 'Radio 247', but recognised the tidiness of a numerical system – detailed schedules were drawn up.[46]

Inspired by the pirate stations, Scott opted for a pattern of 'sequence' programmes broadcast at the same time every day, each one usually lasting an hour or more and presented by a 'personality' disc jockey. To cover the combined needs of Radio 1 and Radio 2, some thirty disc jockeys were hired. Roughly half were transferred from other parts of the BBC, among them Alan Freeman, Pete Murray and Jimmy Young. Terry Wogan was offered a slot on *Late Night Extra* after Scott heard his audition tape. 'I said yes I'd like him ... he's got to get rid of a bit of the Irishness and then he will be very good indeed.' As for the rest of the team, Scott decided to recruit directly from the pirates. Throughout the summer months, he would go home at the end of every working day and sit in the attic listening to tape recordings of each show. Radio Caroline, he thought 'very much second rate' by this stage: it was Radio London, modelled on the New York Top Forty station WABC, which he admired most. It was therefore to Radio London's ship, the *Galaxy*, that the young BBC producer Johnny Beerling was despatched on a covert mission to make contact with its star presenters.[47]

The first to jump ship and land with both feet in Portland Place was the twenty-five-year-old Tony Blackburn. His new career kicked off in August with a trial shift presenting the Light Programme's *Midday Spin*. The experience proved disorientating. 'The people were very nice ... very gentlemanly', Blackburn remembered. He even put on a suit for the occasion 'to try and fit in', while some of his new colleagues returned the compliment by 'wearing flowery shirts and trying to be cool'. But the BBC's way of doing things came as a shock:

> My producer, Peter Jones – I'd never met a producer before, because out on the pirate ships we didn't have things like that – Peter Jones said to me, 'Could I have your script?' And I said, 'Well, I haven't got a script.' And he said, 'Well, how do you know what you're going to say?' and I said, 'Well, I don't, I ad-lib.' And he said, 'Ooh, not used to that.' And he showed me an Alan Freeman script that said, 'And right now, pop pickers, ah...' And it had the word 'ah' *written in*! And I said, 'Well, I can't do that, I'm sorry' ... Because, you know, I didn't know what I was going to say until I said it.[48]

Henceforth, standard BBC practice of scripting in advance was dispensed with. Rehearsals were still insisted upon. But 'nobody', Blackburn explained, 'ever put pressure on me to write a script ... They just wanted me to do what I'd been doing'. The change of tack also required the BBC to kit out its studios with new 'self-op' equipment, so that the DJs could 'drive' everything for themselves, timing the ebb and flow of their own patter so that they would 'ride' the music instinctively. This only left the issue of jingles, which were a vital ingredient in recreating something of the pirates' punchy upbeat sound. Once more, Scott opted for the line of least resistance. He simply asked the Dallas-based company that had made the jingles for Radio London to come up with an almost identical series for Radio 1. 'In fact', Johnny Beerling later explained, 'some of them *were* the Radio London ones – we just changed the words.'[49]

Radio 1 took to the air at 7 a.m., Saturday 30 September. Tony Blackburn opened his microphone, said 'And good morning everyone – welcome to the exciting new sound of Radio 1', then played the single 'Flowers in the Rain' by The Move. Welcome, George Melly pronounced cheekily in the next day's *Observer*, to 'Auntie's first freak out'.[50]

There had actually been remarkably little freaking out behind

Tony Blackburn rehearses for the opening of Radio 1 in September
1967, watched over by Robin Scott, the new station's Controller. Despite
having worked for pirate radio Blackburn recalls turning up for his first
shifts at the BBC wearing jackets and ties so that he could 'fit in'.

the scenes. It was 'very relaxed', Blackburn recalled. 'I just wrote
out the words that I'd say ... I really wanted to get that right,
because I thought if I mess *that* up I'm going to have to live
with that for the rest of my life.' As for the choice of opening
track, 'It wasn't one of my favourite records ... But it was a nice
record and reflected that era.' Throughout the morning, he was
watched over by his producer, Johnny Beerling, whom Scott saw
as a useful 'shepherd and guide'. But after a week Beerling said,
'look Tony, this is nonsense, me getting up in the middle of Kent
at four o'clock in the morning and driving up to sit there and
produce you. You've worked in pirate radio, you know how to
do it. I will listen at home and then I'll come in, then we'll have
the post-mortem afterwards.'[51]

George Melly suggested that Radio 1 had been 'almost Ger-
manic in its thoroughness' when it came to plagiarising the
pirate sound, yet ended up 'lifeless'. But the arrival of Radio 1

offered a breeziness that had been sorely lacking on the BBC. Only now, Robin Scott felt, was the Corporation talking to its younger listeners in 'the language of the mid-6os'. As Controller, he had been left to run his own ship. 'The high admirals didn't send any signals', he explained, 'There wasn't a committee which would decide how these things were to be done.' A service from the BBC could never offer quite the same romantic appeal as the pirates: the need to avoid unnecessary controversy was ever present. But Radio 1 was at least free of any commercial control from the music industry – free, too, to build its audience gradually rather than competing relentlessly in a ratings war. Soon, all the signs were pointing in the right direction. Listening figures were solid. There was lots of exciting new pop music around, and the station's impact on the music industry itself was demonstrably positive: within eighteen months, record sales had jumped by nearly 10 per cent.[52]

What made this all the more remarkable were the difficulties that Scott and his team grappled with out of public sight. The Controller was running two services – Radio 1 and Radio 2 – in place of the single Light Programme. For this, his extra needle time was a measly two hours a week. The whole point of the new station had been to play hit records. But while the pirates might have been free to put the Beatles' 'A Hard Day's Night' on its studio turntables whenever it wanted, Radio 1 often had to resort to a royalty-free version performed by the BBC's house orchestra at Maida Vale. As Johnny Beerling pointed out, this 'didn't quite hack it as far as the audience was concerned'. Across the schedule, chat had to fill almost as many hours as music. In his own late-morning slot, Jimmy Young resorted to phone-ins and recipes. His show was also one of many throughout the week that had to be shared by Radio 1 and Radio 2 to save money. This made it even harder for the new station to establish a distinct identity. 'It was', Beerling explained, 'like fighting with both hands behind your back.'[53]

Miraculously, Radio 1 still found space in its schedule for some distinctly esoteric sounds – and a strikingly different style

John Peel in the Radio 1 studios, 1969. The Controller, Robin
Scott had been a fan of Peel's old Radio London pirate show,
The Perfumed Garden, which he described as 'a kind of mixture
of music and modern philosophy, a bit of a hotch potch'.

of presenting. It was at two o'clock on the station's second
afternoon of broadcasting, sandwiched between Michael Aspel
presenting *Family Favourites* and Alan Freeman's *Pick of the Pops*,
that John Peel made his debut on *Top Gear*, and first set out
his stall: introducing listeners to music they had little chance
of hearing *anywhere* else on British radio. It was Peel, too, who
would now amuse the critics with a stream of languid, slightly
hippyish commentaries. His description in 1969 of Pink Floyd's
latest LP sounding like 'the cries of dying galaxies lost in sheer
corridors of time and space' was entirely in character.[54]

Peel arrived at Radio 1 having already secured cult status.
His background was solidly middle class and public school,
but he had spent much of his young adult life drifting through
dead-end jobs in Texas, Oklahoma and California. It was while
he was in America that he had found himself listening to the

eclectic music of late-night radio shows and spending his days perusing record stores. His rapidly acquired musical knowledge – and his successful attempts to pass himself off as a Scouser – allowed him to work his way into presenting his own radio shows. By the time he left California to join Radio London in 1967 the confidence he had in his own musical judgement had grown considerably. His show, *The Perfumed Garden*, featured whatever records excited him on the day: The Grateful Dead, Country Joe and the Fish, Jimi Hendrix, Pink Floyd were only among the better known; numerous other bands he championed would disappear without trace, though not before he had discharged what he saw as his civic duty by exposing them to a broader public. The result, according to one description, was that in the few summer months before Radio London was shut down *The Perfumed Garden* became 'a sacred corner of hippydom magically unsullied by commercial forces'. The fact that he was accompanied by the smell of incense wherever he went and frequently dressed in a kaftan or velvet pantaloons only added to his 'Summer of Love' appeal.[55]

For his new role at the BBC Peel was paired with the producer Bernie Andrews – the beginning of a short but joyously collaborative partnership. For the next two years, Andrews would meet Peel ahead of every show to engage in friendly combat over the choice of tracks. 'He'd have a pile of records he'd want in, and I'd have a pile of records that I wanted in: we used to go through them and say, OK, your turn ... I had to be fairly careful, otherwise he would have made a whole programme of two hours of Ultimate Spinach or Quicksilver Messenger.'[56]

Peel did not remain an isolated figure for long. In January 1970, Annie Nightingale was given her own show – the first woman at Radio 1 in a permanent and high-profile disc-jockey role. When she had first contacted Radio 1, Nightingale had been told bluntly that DJs had to be 'husband substitutes' for lonely young housewives: the doors were therefore 'locked, bolted, barred'. Even now, she suspected she had been allowed through the BBC's sacred portals as a token gesture. But she was

After the announcement that she is joining Radio 1, Annie Nightingale is surrounded by press photographers. As the station's first full-time female disc jockey, she wondered if her appointment in 1970 had been designed to deflect rumbling accusations in the media over BBC sexism.

there, at least. And like Peel she extracted from her bosses the right to have a say in the choice of records. Indeed, this struck Nightingale as the single most important aspect of her new job. The producer, Teddy Warrick had offered her this advice: 'You will get the requests you deserve, depending on what you play.' Nightingale understood immediately what he meant: 'If I played an endless stream of crap music people would ask for more of the same, but if I played quality music the audience would reciprocate by writing in with suggestions … for more quality music.' She had to go with her instincts: 'The whole point of it was to be passionate – "I've heard this tune, I want to play it to you, what do you think?"'[57]

The ethos was that supply *could* shape demand: that in opening listeners' ears to unfamiliar music public taste might be widened, enriched, *improved*. In its way, it was old-style BBC paternalism. But Radio 1's most adventurous presenters never sounded as if they were dispensing guidance from on high: they sounded as if they were sharing a tip with friends, siblings, lovers. 'The programmes with which I'm involved', Peel explained in 1972, 'are aimed at turning y'all onto some musicks that you might not otherwise investigate.'[58] Reith might not have used the same words exactly; he would surely have recognised the sentiment.

As for the sharp contrast between what Peel and Nightingale were offering listeners in the evenings and weekends, and the breezy top-twenty patter supplied by presenters like Tony Blackburn in the peak-time hours, this, too, had a kind of Reithian logic. 'Ratings by day, reputation by night', Radio 1's senior executives would proclaim. The personality disc jockeys of the daytime would set out to be 'the housewives' favourite' and ensure that tens of millions tuned in; their night-time colleagues would be the explorers and pioneers, hoping to make the strange familiar. Whether their very different audiences would ever mingle or merge was another matter – one that would only be addressed properly in the 1990s. For now, it worked. The men and women behind Radio 1 had discovered what their BBC ancestors had learned many times before: that in public service broadcasting the only answer to the question of whether to lead public taste or follow it, was that it always had to be both.

Backlash

In December 1968, the artist Yoko Ono and her partner John Lennon turned up as guests on Radio 1's *Night Ride* to discuss the release of their latest album, *Two Virgins*. In the course of their amiable chat with John Peel, Yoko Ono read out a poem on air about her recent miscarriage. Peel knew about it in advance, since Lennon had asked him a month earlier if he might donate some of his blood to help her. To him, talking about it in front of listeners seemed only natural.

Unfortunately, Charles Hill, the former wartime 'Radio Doctor', former Tory Postmaster-General and former head of the Independent Television Authority, had recently been installed as Chairman of the BBC's Governors. And he wanted to make his presence felt. The day after Peel's programme, he called up Robin Scott, to tell him that something 'appalling' had been said on air. Scott duly listened to a recording and went to see Hill. The Chairman was upset not just by the 'physiological' detail in Yoko Ono's interview but by the fact it had been an unmarried mother talking about it. It was, he suggested, 'another example' of the BBC being 'led down the wrong alleys'. 'Your Mr Peel', Hill told Scott, 'ought to be watched a bit.' 'It was my first encounter with a Governor', Scott recalled, 'and it was a bit of a shock, the realisation that there was another power in the BBC and perhaps a new style.'[59]

Scott's instincts were right. Hill's arrival as Chairman marked something of a full stop to the whole Greene era – and with it, the fizzing sense of adventure the Director-General had brought to the BBC. Harold Wilson would later claim that he had only parachuted in the former Chairman of ITA because he wanted to see a 'cross-fertilisation' of ideas between the BBC and the commercial sector. 'There was nothing more to it than that.' But it was a mischievous choice. Martin Esslin spoke for many among the BBC's programme makers when he described Hill as 'the lowbrow philistine incarnate'. With his Rolls-Royce parked outside, his demand for an office suite of his own, and his permanent air of bruising impatience, he was certainly not in the classic mould of the Corporation Man. It was, David Attenborough said, 'as if Rommel had taken over the Eighth Army'. When the new Chairman took the unprecedented decision to hire his own secretary, it was clear that, outsider or not, he intended to be 'Mr BBC'. The woman duly appointed claimed that her boss 'got on well with the staff, once they'd accepted the fact that he intended to run the show'. But very few could accept it was *ever* a Chairman's job to 'run the show'. This was precisely why Greene thought of resigning when he first heard of Hill's appointment. Attenborough contemplated it too, though, like Greene and many others, he held on for a bit, mainly because 'the general feeling was that all good men rallied to the cause'.[60]

When Greene finally decided he had had enough, his replacement, Charles Curran, was dismissed by many as a 'cipher' for Hill. By now, a strange, jittery atmosphere was taking hold in the organisation. Curran's reputation for being dogmatic and short-tempered was one cause of concern. The BBC's standing with politicians, which seemed to be going from bad to worse, was another. The broadcast in June 1971 of a documentary showing how Harold Wilson and his cabinet colleagues were adapting to life after the Conservative's election victory, was merely the first in a series of flashpoints. In this instance, not only did the programme's title, *Yesterday's Men*, appear needlessly spiteful; its jaunty, satirical style and its focus on the trappings of high office such as ministerial cars, seemed to trivialise what public service was all about. Wilson, for one, thought it 'disgraceful'. The following year, Conservatives were working themselves up over *A Question of Ulster*. The programme had been planned as a studio discussion scrupulously balanced between Protestant and Catholic, loyalist and republican, left and right. But backroom manoeuvring by the Stormont government and scare-mongering by the *Daily Telegraph* had ensured that when the programme was transmitted, during a period of intense street fighting in Northern Ireland, it was in a climate in which the expression of radically opposed views, no matter how calmly expressed, was regarded as the height of irresponsibility. By now, there was unease inside the BBC too. Stuart Hood wondered if the robust confidence that BBC journalists showed in their own judgement was turning into 'institutional arrogance'. Ian Trethowan, who had worked on many of television's biggest political programmes, referred rather more succinctly to 'those shits at Lime Grove'.[61]

Trethowan was a close friend of the prime minister, Edward Heath. He knew there was mounting pressure from influential right-wingers for broadcasting to be more closely supervised. He was also the coming man at the BBC – first, as Managing

Director of Radio, then, from 1977, as Curran's successor in the top job. His views on a whole range of BBC policies therefore mattered a great deal. And they often amounted to this: the avoidance of any controversy he deemed 'unnecessary'. In the mind of a political journalist like him, this often meant sacrificing the advances made in drama or entertainment in order to protect news and current affairs – or, as Trethowan put it, fighting only on 'ground worth fighting for'. When vetoing the use of a four-letter word in a radio play in 1972, his reasoning was that broadcasting the word was 'simply not worth the inevitable row'. The 'outstanding argument', he told staff privately, was 'one of political expediency'.[62]

The mood of retrenchment was unmistakeable. But retrenchment from *what*, exactly? The progressive spirit of the sixties had percolated through large parts of the BBC machine, bringing with it a younger generation of broadcasters and notable changes in subject matter, tone and style. But while there had been a new and healthy degree of tolerance for diversity and dissent, permissiveness had never run rampant. There continued to be plenty of what Huw Wheldon called the 'safe stuff' in the schedules. There continued to be powerful figures who argued in favour of tradition. Editorial processes tended to block dramatic change in either direction. One of the greatest BBC institutions was the weekly 'Programme Review Board'. In these Wednesday morning gatherings, senior staff would discuss various programmes the BBC had just broadcast, and attempt to reach a position on any issues of principle they raised. They were living proof of Reith's claim that what the BBC did was a result not of 'what one individual thinks' but something 'coming from a consensus of opinion and experience'. This tribal wisdom, or 'collective consciousness' as Martin Esslin called it, was more than a product of professional instinct: it ceaselessly blended the broadcasters' own gut feelings with the views of listeners and viewers, while giving a nod to institutional precedent and keeping an eye on the prevailing political atmosphere. The BBC, Huw Wheldon explained, was a complex and sometimes contradictory beast: 'a very civilized outfit, a very political outfit, a very Machiavellian outfit *and* an outfit in which principle is involved'.[63]

While striking innovations such as *TW3*, *The Wednesday Play* or Radio 1 provided rejuvenating jolts to the system, the BBC was really a self-sustaining machine which ensured that most television and radio, most of the time, evolved in unremarkable fashion. It continued, as always, to mix the popular with the esoteric, the highbrow with the lowbrow, the entertaining with the informative, the mischievous with the respectable.

This was, of course, the most delicate of mechanisms, always vulnerable to being knocked off course by the shock of external events. At the start of the 1970s, with the election of a government bent on fighting key industrial workers, spiralling violence in Northern Ireland, OPEC's dramatic oil price rises, economic stagflation and power cuts, there would be talk of the country facing what Christopher Booker called a 'weary, increasingly conservative, increasingly apprehensive disenchantment'.[64] By 1979, disenchantment would curdle into outright confrontation. With the election of Margaret Thatcher as prime minister, that much-repeated piece of broadcasting wisdom, that 'The nation divided always has the BBC on the rack', would prove more apposite than ever.

IV

ATTACK AND DEFENCE

13

TRADE AND TREACHERY

The Home Secretary and I think it is time the BBC put its
own house in order.

Margaret Thatcher, 1979

It was on Friday 2 April 1982 that the British public first learned
that the Falkland Islands, 8,000 miles away in the South Atlantic,
had been invaded. Somewhere in the Islands' capital, Stanley, a
lone telephone operator had managed to call HMS *Endurance* and
warn that Argentine soldiers had scrambled ashore to reclaim the
'Islas Malvinas' for their country. The BBC's Latin American correspondent, Harold Briley, heard the message, dialled up London
and went on-air to announce the news. The BBC had been on a
low-level war footing since January, when its Monitoring department had noticed the US-backed Argentine dictator General
Galtieri making louder noises than usual about the Malvinas. In
response, a small television crew had been deployed to Buenos
Aires, another sent to the southern tip of Chile, and a relay post
established by John Simpson in the Uruguayan capital, Montevi-
deo. Now, as the prime minister, Margaret Thatcher, convened
an emergency cabinet, ministers and civil servants kept themselves abreast of the latest information by setting up in their
outer office a radio tuned to the World Service.[1]

Over the next few months, the BBC broadcast sometimes
remarkable coverage of the scrappy, tightly fought war to re-
establish British control over the islands. Journalists accompanied
British forces on their long journey south to provide eyewitness

accounts for listeners and viewers back home. Radio 4 altered its schedule hundreds of times to accommodate extended bulletins. The World Service trebled transmissions to the South Atlantic, providing an information lifeline for the islanders and British ground troops. And in the words of the normally sceptical *Daily Mail*, the television evening news provided viewers with 'a shared national experience'.[2]

Reporting arrangements proved tortuous. The Ministry of Defence allocated no space at all for journalists on the Task Force heading south, and only gave way after pressure from Downing Street's chief press officer, Bernard Ingham. Even then, there seemed a distinct lack of goodwill. Room could be found for the *Wolverhampton Express and Star*, but not for World Service correspondents. Brian Hanrahan managed to scramble aboard HMS *Hermes* for television; Robert Fox followed later on the SS *Canberra* for radio. But the dispatches they sent home were censored twice over, first by Ministry of Defence officials accompanying the Task Force and then by colleagues back in Whitehall. The navy held back any information it feared might be heard by the Argentines, with the result that journalists were banned from mentioning anything to do with the sky, the sea, the keep-fit exercises on board, even the food the troops ate. This air of paranoia lightened a little once the Falklands had been reached and hand-to-hand fighting began. But as British troops moved across the hilly, windswept terrain, engaging in sharp, bloody combat with the enemy, British television cameras were never allowed to show any actual battlefield images – a rule that was easy enough to enforce because of the sheer difficulty in getting *any* footage back to Britain. Recordings had to be taken by boat to Ascension Island before being transmitted north. It meant that three weeks elapsed before viewers in Britain could see even a still picture of the capture of South Georgia – one day longer than it had taken the *Times* to provide a graphic account of the Charge of the Light Brigade in 1854. Lessons learned painfully during the Second World War – be first with news, take reporters into your confidence – had been forgotten. Viewers back

Brian Hanrahan on board HMS *Hermes*, part of the 1982 Falkland Islands
Task Force. Also pictured: sound recordist John Jockel and cameraman
Bernard Hesketh. A prohibition against quantifying British losses inspired
Hanrahan to include one of the war's most memorable lines in his report.

home often had to be content with the thin gruel of brief and
rather solemn appearances by the Ministry's lugubrious spokesman, Ian McDonald.[3]

It was an information vacuum that the BBC's own reporters
attempted to fill with considerable ingenuity. One of the most
memorable lines of the whole conflict was uttered by Brian
Hanrahan while reporting on a successful sortie of Harrier
jets from HMS *Hermes*: 'I counted them all out,' he said, 'and
I counted them all back.' Without having to wait for pictures,
radio often responded faster. The older medium came back into
its own, in the workplace as well as in the home. 'Someone has
brought a radio in and news bulletins are listened to eagerly', a
listener's diary noted at the end of April. 'Tea break discussions
are devoted exclusively to the crisis with opinions on whether
we ought to use force becoming divided.'[4]

'There are traitors in our midst'[4]

Opinions were indeed 'divided'. And this created enormous difficulties for the BBC when dealing with the political atmosphere back home. For while the Corporation had provided audiences across the world with some exemplary reportage from the frontline, some of its domestic coverage was provoking wild accusations of treasonable behaviour from senior Conservative politicians and an increasingly strident tabloid press.

'The problem', as the outgoing Director-General Ian Trethowan put it at the time, was 'how to define the national interest'. The BBC had to balance the public's right to know with the military's need to win. It also had a duty to represent British opinion as fully as possible. And while opinion polls made clear that a large majority of voters were in favour of Thatcher's military response, there was a significant minority – 30 per cent, perhaps – who were opposed. When Mass Observation asked diarists to record their feelings in April and May, many of the responses came back infused with ambivalence. 'We do seem to be using a sledgehammer to crack a nut', one woman wrote. She backed the Task Force but wanted more time for 'talking and cooling down'. When the Argentine cruiser the *General Belgrano* was torpedoed and sunk by a British submarine on Sunday 2 May, leading to the loss of over 300 lives, she felt 'like crying, thinking of those young Argentine men'. 'I have listened to and watched hundreds of news bulletins, discussion programmes and documentaries … and heard many shades of opinion from colleagues, friends, acquaintances and relations', another diarist explained. 'I now find myself firmly on the fence.'[5]

These different shades of opinion had to be chewed over on programmes such as *Panorama* or *Newsnight*. And, predictably, both programmes were under attack as a result.

Newsnight was the first to face scrutiny. A special edition in the aftermath of the Belgrano sinking had opened with the presenter, Peter Snow, speaking to camera. 'There is a stage in the coverage of any conflict where you begin to discern the level of accuracy of the claims and counter-claims on either side', he began. 'Well, tonight ... it must be said that we cannot demon-strate that the British have lied to us so far, but the Argentines clearly HAVE.' It was a script designed to emphasise Argen-tinian rather than British failures. But it was possible to infer an implied moral equivalence between the two regimes. And Snow's detached description of troops as 'British' rather than 'ours' struck a false note with anyone who already suspected that the BBC was not 'on our side'. Strictly speaking, the BBC was never supposed to be on the side of *any* particular gov-ernment, and it was usually assumed that the British national interest was served best by ensuring that the Corporation's rep-utation for impartiality remained intact – a line agreed with the cabinet during the Second World War and reinforced repeatedly since. Now, the policy was underlined again in a memo circu-lated to all newsroom staff. 'We should try to avoid using "our" when we mean "British", it said. 'We are not Britain, we are the BBC; so "our" should be reserved for "our correspondent" and "our reporter" ... we are talking about a BBC correspond-ent, not a British official.' The Ministry of Defence's spokesman, Ian McDonald also referred nightly to 'British forces', but this did not inhibit the *Sun* newspaper from branding the BBC as 'traitors in our midst'. Its own choice of headline when report-ing the death of hundreds of Argentine conscripts aboard the *General Belgrano* would never be mistaken for showing doubt. It simply said 'Gotcha!'[6]

Before the dust had settled from the *Belgrano* incident, a British ship was struck by an Exocet missile and a Harrier shot down over Goose Green. In perhaps the most tense week of the war, hostility to the BBC from the press and from MPs esca-lated to lynching level. This was the moment that *Panorama* now chose to explore the views of those who had strong reservations about Britain's military action. As with *Newsnight*, the opening remarks of *Panorama*'s presenter, Robert Kee, were scripted with delicacy. 'It was Argentina who unquestionably put herself in the wrong by acting unilaterally to settle this long-running diplomatic dispute', he stated, before adding: 'Opinion at home

The Prime Minister Margaret Thatcher, 10 Downing Street,
being interviewed by Richard Lindley and Robert Kee for a
special Falklands War edition of *Panorama* in April 1982.

is now undoubtedly behind Mrs Thatcher if war seems necessary. But there are still reservations ... What weight do such
voices carry, now that we may be poised for an invasion?' There
followed an interview with the Argentinian representative in
New York, and a report by Michael Cockerell which suggested
that among those who had doubts about the campaign were
senior military figures. The programme also included five short
quotations from the prime minister, contributions from other
Conservative MPs, and a live interview with one of Thatcher's
loyal lieutenants, Cecil Parkinson. These editorial attempts at
balance were not enough to stop all hell breaking loose. The
prime minister happened to catch the episode and was apparently
'seething'. That evening, the BBC's Political Editor, John Cole,
found himself surrounded in the Palace of Westminster lobby
by Conservative MPs barracking him about the programme.
Three days later, the BBC's Chairman, George Howard, and its

Director-General designate, Alasdair Milne, were summoned to appear before the Conservative's backbench Media Committee. More than one hundred MPs crammed themselves into the sweltering heat of Committee Room 10 to harangue their guests. Milne was shouted at to 'stand up' whenever he spoke, as though he were in the dock of a criminal court. As they got up to leave, a young MP approached Howard, jabbed a finger at him and said, 'You, sir, are a traitor'. 'Stuff you!' the Chairman snapped back.[7]

The atmosphere of distrust rumbled on until well after the final surrender of Argentine forces in June. Throughout, Britain's tabloid papers – and in particular, the *Sun*, which had chosen to 'back Maggie' unequivocally – took every opportunity to stir things up. It laid bare one of the great battle lines of British public life in the years to come: a concerted attempt by elements of the press to weaken the BBC's position in the media landscape.

The Falklands War also marked a troubling watershed at the highest level of politics. Thatcher had entered the crisis as a deeply unpopular prime minister. Her own future had therefore been tied closely to success in the South Atlantic. The BBC, she believed, 'had a responsibility to stand up for our Task Force, our boys, for our people'. Its consistent failure to do so, as she saw it, was why 'something sulphurous' entered the relationship between Corporation and government. When Alasdair Milne looked back on this period years later, he acknowledged that it was the ten fraught weeks of the war that had sowed the 'seeds of enmity'. Military victory in June 1982 swept Thatcher to a second and much more impressive election victory the following year. This gave her both the confidence and the political capital to pursue her domestic policies more aggressively. 'Economics are the method', she had said back in 1981; but 'the object is to change the heart and soul'. It was an agenda that would have in its sights the radical overhaul of broadcasting itself. For the rest of the decade, the climate within which the BBC operated became a potent brew of political, commercial and personal hostility.[8]

Trench warfare

The case for drastic reform of the BBC was not immediately obvious, either to broadcasters or the public. There were still twenty-five million Britons watching television every night: in programming terms, this was something of a golden age. During the June general election, the BBC schedule had featured, among other morsels: *Dynasty*, *Top of the Pops*, *Tomorrow's World*, *Panorama*, *Question Time* with Robin Day, and *Breakfast Time* with Frank Bough and Selina Scott. An old favourite, *Nationwide*, was about to end, but a new comedy series, *Blackadder*, was just beginning. There was still *Play School* and John Craven's *Newsround*; and *Blue Peter* had Simon Groom seven miles up, flying in a high-performance jet. *Grandstand* featured the Cricket World Cup and Wimbledon. Later in the year there would be *Dad's Army*, *The Generation Game*, *'Allo 'Allo!*, *Only Fools and Horses* and *The Young Ones*. One of the BBC's most popular dramas the previous year had been Alan Bleasdale's *Boys from the Blackstuff* – a mordantly witty take on the humiliations wrought by mass unemployment. Over the next three years other highlights would include the doom-laden nuclear conspiracy thriller *Edge of Darkness*, and Dennis Potter's semi-autobiographical masterpiece, *The Singing Detective*. One of the BBC's very biggest television shows, *That's Life*, was still offering a clever combination of jokey items about strange-shaped vegetables and campaigning consumer journalism. And of course, there was the BBC's family of radio services, quietly pulling in millions of fiercely loyal listeners every day for programmes ranging from large-scale orchestral concerts on Radio 3 to Simon Bates's daily tearjerker, 'Our Tune', on Radio 1, via the pleasing middle ground of *The Archers*, *Desert Island Discs* and *Woman's Hour* on Radio 4.[9]

The prime minister herself was a fan of the BBC2 series *Yes, Minister*, which was unsurprising given that its running theme was how elected politicians were constantly being frustrated by wily Whitehall mandarins. She was also eager to appear on *Jim'll Fix It*, where she hoped to face the softest of questioning from one of her most ardent political supporters, Jimmy

Savile. Otherwise she rarely watched or listened. It was her press secretary, Bernard Ingham, who would summarise for her the day's news stories, and her husband, Denis, who would bring to the Downing Street dinner table regular updates on the latest atrocities committed by what he called the 'British Bastard Corporation'.[10]

As a politician, Thatcher always needed enemies, and in her own mind the BBC fitted the role perfectly. Like the church, the universities, the civil service, and the NHS, it was not just a symbol of the corporate state, or of inefficiency and restrictive practices: it was one of the ideological heartlands of consensus, riddled with attitudes that were at best woolly, and at worst socialist. It was structurally – perhaps pathologically – unable to embrace the era of privatisation, free markets and consumer sovereignty. Indeed, having grown fat on the licence fee – which amounted, she felt, to a kind of compulsory levy or state handout – it was emblematic of the bloated, inefficient, complacent public-sector strongholds that claimed to act for some strange sort of 'common good' purely in the hope of protecting themselves from the correcting force of competition. Worse, it was influential. And worst of all – because perhaps this single irritating fact left the most painful shard of cognitive dissonance in the Thatcher mindset – it was popular.[11]

The prime minister was by no means alone in her thinking. Her minister Norman Tebbit summed up the visceral loathing felt by many a Tory backbencher when he memorably described the BBC as that 'insufferable, smug, sanctimonious, naïve, guilt-ridden, wet, pink orthodoxy of that sunset home of third-rate minds of that third-rate decade, the Sixties'. Yet it was Thatcher who remained the conviction politician par excellence, the animating force. The BBC's political editor, John Cole, who interviewed her on many occasions during her time in office, remembers how she would always grab hold of every encounter and 'impose her will on it'. 'She had a kind of enamelled self-confidence', he said, 'that didn't allow for the kind of dialogue one might have had.' On her occasional visits to Broadcasting

House or Television Centre, she would lay into everyone she met for their alleged left-wing views, bustling through studios 'like the proverbial dose of salts, exuding hostility and insulting everyone regardless of their rank or status'. Bernard Ingham was supposed to provide a buffer on such occasions, but as one of the BBC's Governors observed, he was 'even ruder than she was'. These whirlwind visits were, of course, just one part of a broader, more sustained campaign. As a senior news editor put it, 'the BBC was being beaten up, pushed and shoved and pummelled for a very long time, relentlessly, week after week, month after month'. This went well beyond normal party political axe-grinding, he decided: it showed that the BBC 'in its very nature was anathema'.[12]

When it came to finding ways to pounce on the BBC, one plank of the government's approach was to weaken its competitive position in the broadcasting marketplace. Spending power was the critical factor. In the Corporation's case, this was still determined almost entirely by its income from the licence fee. Since this was something paid directly by members of the public, it was supposed to guarantee independence from commercial and political pressures. Yet it was governments that were responsible for periodically setting its level. And few politicians could resist the opportunity this provided to circumscribe the BBC's freedom of action in ways that suited their own priorities. It was, for instance, a determination to tackle inflation that had prompted Jim Callaghan's Labour government to impose licence-fee settlements that were punitively low, and which meant that the Corporation entered the Thatcher era already making drastic internal economies. It was hugely embarrassing that commercial television produced two of the most lavish and well-received series of the early 1980s, *Brideshead Revisited* and *The Jewel in the Crown*, while the BBC broadcast a sub-par American import, *The Thorn Birds*. But as the Controller of BBC1 explained, 'The fact is we couldn't have afforded to make *Brideshead* or *Jewel in the Crown* ... those budgets were absolutely astronomical.' None of this cut any ice with a political regime convinced that there was more fat to be cut. And among the prime minister's loyal lieutenants there were now ministers like Nigel Lawson and Nicholas Ridley who were pressing for a Corporation shorn of whole radio networks and television channels. Even those in Thatcher's cabinet who were inclined to be supportive were hinting that the licence fee could no longer 'be regarded as immortal'.[13]

This shift in emphasis was given powerful support by a newspaper industry that had aspirations to get into broadcasting and which recognised that, as things stood, the BBC was their strongest competitor. Rupert Murdoch, and the man he installed as editor of the *Sunday Times*, Andrew Neil, were now in the vanguard of attempts to alter this state of affairs. Neil, an admirer of the American television system, was also deeply fascinated by new technology. He believed that cable and satellite, which had already created a radically expanded range of television channels in the US, presented an opportunity to give British viewers the cornucopia of choice they surely wanted and deserved – and which the bloated, overweening BBC had denied them for so long. It was hardly coincidence, therefore, that as the latest round of licence-fee negotiations between the BBC and the government was reaching its climax in January 1985, the Murdoch-owned *Times* published a series of leading articles that challenged the Corporation's historic status as national broadcaster. 'The BBC', it argued, 'should not survive this Parliament in its present size, in its present form and with its present terms of reference intact.' Was it not the consumer, rather than the producer, who was the best judge of the kind of programmes that should be made? Might it not make sense to break the BBC into a series of franchises that could be bought by commercial companies?[14]

Few ideas as radical as these could be introduced as easily as Murdoch demanded. And when Thatcher's government made its only head-on attempt to kill the licence fee completely, it ended in failure. The Peacock Committee, led by a Scottish economist of unimpeachable free-market credentials, was set up in March 1985 with the specific intention that it would recommend that the BBC switched to advertising. After seeing evidence that this would cause terrible damage to existing advertiser-funded services such as ITV, it baulked at the idea. Its final report, published in July 1986, proved a bitter personal disappointment to Thatcher, but the notion of a smaller, less competitive BBC did at least now have a head of steam behind it. And there were plenty of other mechanisms for bringing this about. The licence fee continued to be pegged to the retail price index or below. At a time of steeply rising production costs this meant wave after wave of real-term cuts. In June 1985, well-developed plans for a glittering new Norman Foster-designed radio centre opposite Broadcasting House had to be cancelled, jobs in television's technical areas – scenery, costumes, make-up – were shed, programme budgets squeezed, and the purchase of new equipment frozen. For years, there was the threat of merger or radical change hanging over radio: a scheme to merge local radio with Radio 2, followed by another for local radio to merge with Radio 4, yet another for Radio 4 to be stripped of all its drama and comedy and features so that it could provide uninterrupted news. Meanwhile, legislation in Parliament deregulated the broadcasting industry and expanded the commercial sector: cable and satellite television was sanctioned, quality thresholds removed, and new commercial licences made available in both radio and television. Behind every measure lurked not just the desire to break open the broadcasting duopoly and boost competition, but a determination to push the notion of 'consumer sovereignty', in which listeners and viewers, not 'producer elites', were assumed to be the best judges of their own interests.[15]

Thatcherism was now entering what has been called its Maoist phase, with government policy working in lockstep with a hostile press trying mercilessly to whip up public feeling against the Corporation. This was not just about its size or its alleged profligacy or its lack of commercial nous. It was also about bias or falling editorial standards. The London *Evening Standard* would go on about the BBC's 'remorseless mediocrity'. the *Spectator* would grumble about it being anti-British. The

Daily Mail kept referring to the Corporation as 'Biased, Bankrupt, Corrupt'. The *Sun* would shamelessly accuse it of being 'boring' one day and 'sleazy' the next.[16]

Above all, there would be complaints that something had gone awry at that powerhouse of current affairs television, Lime Grove. Individual programmes often provided the initial target. An early warning shot, predating even the Falklands War, had come in 1979 when a *Panorama* crew had filmed IRA men in balaclavas appearing at a road block in the village of Carrickmore, near Omagh. The footage was never actually shown, but the press played along with the notion – shared by politicians on both sides in Westminster – that any television report that featured paramilitaries amounted to giving legitimacy to men of violence. The incident suggested that the BBC's systems of editorial control were lax, and when Thatcher read about it she announced that it was 'time the BBC put its own house in order'. BBC insiders were convinced that the outrage was being deliberately stoked up. But they could see what was *really* happening. 'It was the first real indication that the politicians were gunning for the BBC', one senior editor recalled. 'And by God, they gunned for years afterwards.'[17]

Enemies within

The delicate task of handling government attacks had always been a matter for the BBC's most senior figures. As Director-General between 1977 and 1982, Ian Trethowan had been a Tory 'wet' who believed in defusing risky programmes before they got anywhere near to rattling the political class – a category that included the Corporation's own Governors. His successor, Alasdair Milne, was a different proposition. He had joined the BBC in 1954 straight out of Oxford and had risen fast as one of Grace Wyndham Goldie's bevy of bright young men – earning his spurs on *Tonight* and *That Was The Week That Was* before running the BBC in Scotland. Now he was the first programme producer in the top job. He was obviously clever, and those who knew him closely found him warm and decent. Yet he could also come across as impatient. One of Milne's most senior lieutenants, Alan Protheroe, saw his own role as protecting Milne's back – acting as a kind of 'flak-catcher' by taking direct responsibility for editorial standards in programme output. The job, he said, was far from straightforward. Milne had a boredom threshold of 'about 17 seconds', a character trait, Protheroe reckoned, left over from school days. 'People who go to Winchester have bred into them in their time in school that if you are not a Wykehamist then you really are quite fortunate to be allowed to draw breath.' The fact that Milne found himself dealing with a Board of Governors who were increasingly his 'intellectual inferiors' – as Protheroe put it rather indelicately – would be one major cause of friction at the top of the BBC over the next few years.[18]

Milne certainly had every reason to be irritated by the Governors he was landed with. All governments wanted friendly faces on the BBC's Board. But convention dictated that, whichever party was in power, overall membership should reflect a rough-and-ready balance across the political spectrum. After all, one of the Board's key roles was to act as a shock absorber between politicians and programme makers – indeed, this was what was supposed to ensure that the Corporation never became an arm of the state. This compact was torn up by Thatcher, who started stacking the Board with individuals she could regard as 'one of us'. For the BBC, the Governors became the 'enemy within'.

The effect was gradual. George Howard, appointed Chairman in 1980, was a country landowner straight out of central casting: outspoken, party-loving, kaftan-wearing, womanising, a man of gargantuan appetites. He was Tory, though not Thatcherite – which is why a fellow 'wet', the Home Secretary, William Whitelaw, had chosen him in the first place. Milne found him to be 'capable of the utmost rudery to everybody in sight … the Grand Whig landlord bit was very obvious'. During the Falklands War, he had clearly struggled to comprehend the BBC's difficulties. When Protheroe revealed that senior Conservatives had been deceiving him, Howard's reply was 'they wouldn't lie to me – they were at school with me!' The biggest problem Howard posed for the BBC was his extravagant lifestyle: repeated requests to host lavish events at the licence-fee payers' expense at his home, Castle Howard, or for young women to be brought up to his hotel suites while on overseas business. Otherwise, he proved himself a decent enough defender of the BBC.[19]

His successor, appointed in 1983, was much more to Thatcher's tastes. Stuart Young, a City accountant whose brother David was in the cabinet, was part of what Protheroe called the 'New Toryism'. He appreciated the arts, even defended the BBC as an idea, but his overwhelming philosophy was of value for money. From 1983 until 1986, when he died of lung cancer, Young's moments of rapport with Milne became progressively rarer. When it came to choosing his replacement. in turn, Thatcher consulted Rupert Murdoch. She presented him with the name of Marmaduke Hussey, who had led the management side during the bitter industrial dispute at Times Newspapers in 1979. 'He's your man', was Murdoch's enthusiastic reply. It seemed such an obscure choice at the time that the BBC's senior managers had to reach for their dog-eared copy of *Who's Who*. There they discovered that Hussey had fought as a Grenadier Guard in the war, lost a leg, and was married to one of the Queen's ladies-in-waiting. When he was unveiled to the press, Hussey revealed that he knew very little about broadcasting, and absolutely nothing about the BBC: he did not even know where in London it was based. As far as the government was concerned, he sounded perfect.[20]

For those inside Broadcasting House, the new Chairman proved something of a culture shock. He would lumber about, braying loudly at people, slapping his subalterns on the back and attempting to overwhelm people with an image of bumbling charm. Hussey's role models were newspaper proprietors such as Rothermere or Murdoch, so he naturally regarded the BBC as somehow 'his'. It was an approach that did not always work. One of the BBC's longest-serving and most experienced

The Board of Governors in 1982. In the middle, sitting, is the Chairman George Howard, flanked by the outgoing Director-General, Ian Trethowan on his right, and incoming Director-General, Alasdair Milne on his left. William Rees-Mogg is on Trethowan's right. By 1986 it was even harder to dispute the Board's Conservative bias.

secretaries stayed just one month in his office before moving on. 'Absolute chaos ... Papers everywhere ... most things lived on the floor ... I didn't like his patrician manner, I'm afraid.' What mattered most, however, was the line from Conservative Central Office: that Hussey had been appointed to 'get in there and sort it out'. Protheroe, too, assumed the new Chairman's brief was to ensure that 'the financial bottom line really would prevail' and 'to lay to rest this great business that the BBC is entirely populated by concealed Marxists'.[21]

By now, the Tories had been in power long enough to ensure that the Board had accumulated more and more Governors who shared Thatcher's highly sceptical attitude towards the Corporation. Even the Board's most prominent Labour figure, Joel Barnett, came from his party's anti-union, fiscally conservative wing. The most troubling figure of all, however, was Barnett's immediate predecessor as Vice-Chairman, the former editor of the *Times*, William Rees-Mogg. Protheroe thought Rees-Mogg 'the most malevolent man' he had ever met: 'a man who regarded the BBC with contempt ... He disliked the BBC to his marrow, to his very core, to the depths of his soul if he had one'. His method was to 'nit-pick': 'to erode confidence, to erode performances, to criticise unthinkingly ... he really was a malign influence'. Rees-Mogg had persuaded himself that 'the powers of the Board went well beyond advising and warning': it 'had ultimately the executive authority'. It was a mindset that many fellow Governors now shared, and the result was years of bitter wrangling between a Board of Management desperate to protect their independent authority over day-to-day editorial decisions, and a Board of Governors who, as Protheroe put it, seemed to regard everything the BBC's programme makers did as 'wrong, foolish, unnecessary, irrelevant, wasteful'.[22]

One of the biggest and most damaging of these rows between Governors and programme staff erupted in August 1985. Once again, it was over the BBC's coverage of Northern Ireland.

One of BBC Television's most experienced documentary makers, Paul Hamann, had wanted to explore why people on either side in the Troubles were attracted to politicians holding extreme views. The programme he created, *Real Lives: At the Edge of the Union*, probed the issue in highly personal terms by portraying the 'ordinary' lives of two men who happened to be elected representatives of their communities: Martin McGuinness of Sinn Féin, and the hard-line loyalist, Gregory Campbell. McGuinness was already suspected of being the IRA's Chief of Staff; Campbell had openly advocated a shoot-to-kill policy against the republican paramilitaries. Politically, they were polar opposites. Yet both men were young, working-class, teetotal and church-going. They advocated violence while being good 'family' men. They seemed an ideal pairing.

The series editor for *Real Lives*, Edward Mirzoeff, liked the idea from the start: he knew that Hamann was an expert on the Troubles and could be trusted to tread carefully. Both men knew, too, that either the BBC's Northern Ireland Controller,

James Hawthorn, or the Head of Programmes, Cecil Taylor, would have to be consulted for editorial clearance at every step. Hamann remembers phoning the BBC's Belfast offices 'more often than I've ever phoned any Controller in Northern Ireland about any particular programme ... we both knew it was sensitive ...' In fact, since both McGuinness and Campbell appeared fairly regularly on radio and television in Northern Ireland, the BBC's Belfast operation regarded Hamann's documentary as relatively uncontroversial. Hamann himself saw the two politicians in question as 'both fairly appalling people' and hoped his film would demonstrate this. His biggest struggle was getting a decent balance: he had found that McGuinness was 'the more approachable man and more skilled at using the camera'. Even so, the final edit seemed to satisfy everyone who had been consulted that the programme was both fair and revealing. Cecil Taylor's comments to Mirzoeff as he departed for his summer holidays were unequivocal: 'I'm completely happy with it.'[23]

Real Lives: At the Edge of the Union was a remarkable if sometimes dispiriting piece of television. In among shots of rain-soaked, slate-grey skies, McGuinness and Campbell were seen standing in separate graveyards and walking on different stretches of the beach, each accompanied by his own family. At one point a woman's voice is heard saying 'Every time he goes out I am wondering will he get back safe?', and it is hard to be sure to whom she is referring. Elsewhere, McGuinness expresses his belief that 'there are circumstances in which the use of the gun is quite justified and the freedom of Ireland is a just cause'. Campbell counters with perhaps the most chilling line in the whole documentary, that he was unashamed about saying 'Christmas had come early' when two IRA men were shot.[24]

Once the final edits had been made, the programme was scheduled for transmission. It had been put together in the midst of a summer in which newspaper front pages had been dominated by terrorist bombings and hijackings, and when the atmosphere surrounding Northern Ireland, especially at Westminster and among the London-based press, was more febrile than ever. Fleet Street was on the lookout for anything that could be spun as evidence of the BBC's bad faith.

Just days before the documentary was to be broadcast, a reporter from the *Sunday Times* who had got wind of it alerted the Home Secretary, Leon Brittan, and 10 Downing Street. The reporter was subsequently given the opportunity to meet Thatcher, who was in the United States at the time, and put to her a hypothetical question about whether it was right for a 'British television company' to screen an interview with a suspected IRA commander. 'I would condemn it utterly', was her unequivocal answer. Back in London, the Home Secretary then published a letter saying Hamann's programme was too dangerous to broadcast because it would 'materially assist the terrorist cause'. Putting this in writing was a hugely provocative act. All governments had the right to ban the BBC from showing something: it was a 'large, looming' power that had been written into the Charter and the licence. But it was a power that was only supposed to be invoked in conditions of utmost national emergency, such as war. Eden had threatened to do so during the Suez crisis, before being forced to retreat. Now Brittan backed off, too, saying, rather ingenuously, that his letter had merely expressed a 'personal view'. The damage, however, was already done, since the Board of Governors had now been alerted to a programme they had known nothing about. They decided to call an emergency meeting.[25]

The Director-General was on a fishing holiday in Scandinavia. Michael Checkland, who was deputising in his absence, managed to track Milne down by phone and warn him that the Governors were on the warpath and might ask to view the film before it was broadcast. 'You say to them that there's no tradition of this in the BBC', Milne replied. 'They should not do it if they can possibly avoid it, but in the end, of course, if they insist they have that right.' By the time he was back in London it was too late. The Governors had indeed exercised their ultimate right. As they sat and watched the documentary in the Boardroom of Broadcasting House, they had rapidly worked themselves into a froth of indignation. Amid loud tutting, William Rees-Mogg declared the programme 'vile propaganda for the IRA'. None of the Governors sought the advice of the BBC's senior managers in Belfast – experienced figures who could have reassured them that editorial scrutiny had taken place and the letter of the law fully complied with. They simply assumed that there had been a duplicitous attempt to get something past them, and proceeded to issue a formal instruction that the programme should be withdrawn. The Welsh Governor, Alwyn Roberts, was the lone voice of dissent.[26]

Milne, Protheroe, Checkland and other members of the Board of Management had predicted that the Governors would be offended by *At the Edge of the Union*. But they had also expected them to support the principle of it going ahead 'in the interests of public service broadcasting, the nation and public information.' The Governors, however, had failed to separate their professional role from their own personal prejudices. As far as an infuriated Paul Hamann was concerned, they had also shown themselves to be 'naïve and uneducated'.[27]

Their interference sent shockwaves across the BBC. On Wednesday 7 August, the day Hamann's programme was supposed to be broadcast, hundreds of news programmes on radio and television had to be cancelled after the Corporation's journalists, recognising an infringement of the BBC's editorial independence, walked out in protest. 'They were mutinous and furious and angry,' Milne recalled, 'and the Governors couldn't understand.' The documentary team at Kensington House, where Hamann and Mirzoeff were based, were also bewildered – unsure if the BBC's own senior managers were really on their side. 'The great thing about the BBC for many, many years', Mirzoeff claimed, was that programme makers were 'bollocked in private, but in public you were backed ... but it wasn't happening here ... it was totally catastrophic'.[28]

In fact, the Director-General *was* working behind the scenes to get the Governors' ban reversed. Milne shared the view of most of his professional colleagues, that there was 'nothing wrong' with the programme, nor with the programme team's 'meticulous' referrals to the BBC's most senior figures in Belfast. As a way out of the impasse, some minor changes were made. Nothing was deleted, but nineteen seconds of stock footage of a bomb going off in Belfast were inserted. Hamann regarded it as a cliché that he had studiously avoided including in the first place: 'it's something they do on *Panorama*, we don't.' But he was willing to accept it in the spirit of compromise, and it seemed to be enough to reassure the Governors. On Wednesday 16 October, *At the Edge of the Union* was finally broadcast. In the *Guardian* the following morning, Nancy Banks-Smith wrote that the bomb footage had 'spoiled' an otherwise 'lovely, sad, quiet' forty-five minutes. *The Observer*'s critic Russell Davies reckoned that to viewers at home Gregory Campbell 'visibly lost' what he called the BBC's 'minimalist charm contest'. 'Perhaps it was felt by the Establishment objectors that the personal contrast between the two central figures of the film ... panned out the wrong way.'[29]

The Director-General had won a hard-earned victory. But his relationship with the Governors had been left in tatters. Over the following year, rows broke out like wildfire, with the Murdoch press, in Milne's words, ceaselessly 'going for the BBC's jugular'.[30]

One ugly dispute involved an investigative programme about the government concealing the vast sums of public money it had spent on a spy satellite, Zircon – a fracas that ended with the BBC's production offices in Scotland being raided by police. It was, however, an edition of *Panorama* broadcast back in January 1984 that brought matters to a head. The episode in question, *Maggie's Militant Tendency*, had uncovered allegations of racist and anti-Semitic attitudes by members of the Conservative Party with links to the hard right. It was based on a confidential report from within the party itself. *Panorama* had done its own investigations, gathered sworn statements from witnesses, and had checked everything with the BBC's lawyers. When it was transmitted, the programme had provoked fury at Conservative Central Office, as well as headlines of 'Lies, Damn Lies, and

Panorama' from the *Daily Mail*. It had also prompted libel actions from several MPs who had been named on-air.[31]

It was these actions that were finally coming to court in October 1986. Milne, Protheroe, the BBC's lawyers and the production team all still regarded the programme's evidence as 'bomb proof'. When it was first screened, the Chairman, Stuart Young, had also been convinced, reassured by well-placed personal contacts that the programme had got its facts right. But now, three years on, it was not Young but the Vice-Chairman, Joel Barnett, and the incoming Chairman, Marmaduke Hussey, who were in control. Neither man trusted the BBC's journalism or Milne's reassurances that the case could be won. To make matters worse, reports started circulating that some of *Panorama*'s original witnesses were under pressure to withdraw their testimony. Barnett immediately instructed the Corporation's lawyers to settle out of court before they had even presented their case: the BBC had been forced to cave in by its own Governors.

The fatal blow was delivered early the following year. On Thursday 29 January, the Board gathered for one of its regular meetings at Television Centre. With Milne's most loyal supporter, the Welsh Governor Alwyn Roberts, having retired the previous evening, Hussey and Barnett were free to make their move. At lunchtime they ushered Milne into the Chairman's office. 'I am afraid this is going to be a very unpleasant interview', Hussey announced. In fact, there was no interview. Hussey simply said they wanted the Director-General to leave immediately, and that unless he agreed to the fiction that he was resigning for personal reasons, his pension would be at risk. In a state of utter shock, Milne signed a letter and handed it over. Only later that evening when he was back home would he feel the humiliation – 'being discarded by such people without a word of explanation or discussion'.[32]

Hussey had wanted David Dimbleby as Milne's successor. The job went instead to the BBC's most senior financial officer, Michael Checkland. Many of the Corporation's journalists sneered at the news, regarding the appointment as uninspired.

Yet Checkland's ability to describe the BBC as a 'billion pound business' and licence-fee payers as 'shareholders' was the kind of language that removed much of the poison from relations with Downing Street. Moreover, the new Director-General was a loyal Corporation man – still seen as 'unquestionably one of us' by staff. On his rise up the ranks, Checkland had demonstrated a knack for conjuring up badly needed pots of money at short notice from reserves prudently set aside. As Director-General, he quietly tightened the BBC's belt, while showing that good financial management could be a means to an end – 'making programmes happen'.[33]

It was, however, a second appointment made in 1987 that would be of greater long-term significance: the man brought in to take charge of news and current affairs as Checkland's deputy and heir apparent – John Birt.

Birt's background was unusual for a top job at the BBC: Liverpool, Catholic, working class. His meteoric media career had also been forged entirely in the commercial sector, most recently at London Weekend Television, where he had been responsible for the austere current affairs programme *Weekend World* and the rather more populist *Blind Date*. Though professing to have had 'faintly left-wing' ideas in his youth, he was by his own account 'a convert to free-market mechanisms': colleagues described him as a 'punk monetarist'. He certainly had the right image. Corporation lore had it that the traditional BBC man was someone with 'a secret spangled tutu worn under his suit'. Checkland was invariably clad in something sensible from Marks & Spencer. Birt, everyone noticed, was an Armani-and-Gucci-loafers man. His status as an outsider made him, in his own words, as 'welcome as a Protestant made Pope'. But he arrived at Broadcasting House looking very much like a man intending to make his mark.[34]

A mission to explain: John Birt and BBC News

At one of his first editorial meetings, Birt was asked which BBC current affairs programmes he liked. 'To be honest,' he replied, 'there's nothing I like.'[35] No one could doubt that radical change was now on the cards. But what *kind* exactly?

Those with good memories would have recalled Birt's authorship, along with Peter Jay, of a controversial series of articles published in the *Times* in 1975 that launched a very public assault on the values of broadcast news. The 'Birt-Jay thesis', as it came to be known, had claimed that most coverage was guilty of a systematic 'bias against their audience's understanding of the society in which it lives'. 'Devoting two minutes on successive nights to the latest unemployment figures or the state of the stock market, with no time to put the story in context, gives the viewer no sense of how any of these problems relate to each other', they complained. Birt clearly believed that little had changed in the twelve years since those words had been printed. In a series of meetings and directives, he now set out his prescription: more specialist journalism in areas such as economics and home affairs, more analysis, more focus on stories of historical significance, more scripting and planning in advance. The truth of a news story, he told staff, could be arrived at through proper research, not just by the more random tradition of journalists digging around and following their noses. Above all, good journalism at the BBC was best secured through a rigorous system of managerial control – control that would steer the BBC away from the 'J'accuse' style of journalism associated with Lime Grove and that might stop 'mistakes' such as Carrickmore, *Real Lives*, and *Maggie's Militant Tendency* ever happening again. If the structures were there, Birt believed, the programmes would follow. This meant not just new posts and job titles, new working parties, new editorial guidelines – in short, a new way of working – it meant a wholesale reorganisation of departments. The most significant of these was the total merger of News and Current Affairs across both radio and television, creating a new, unified and immensely powerful Directorate.[36]

This did not go down well. The BBC's more seasoned reporters resented the fact that their new overlord had never worked

John Birt in 1975, when he was working for London Weekend Television. He had just published a series of influential articles in *The Times* in which he argued that there was a 'bias against understanding' in broadcast news.

at the 'sharp end' of journalism. They also believed he was libelling the past. How, Charles Wheeler asked, was 'Birtian' analysis any different to what was already provided on *Newsnight*? Could journalism really be 'pre-planned'? Might Birt's apparent obsession with layer upon layer of centralised editorial scrutiny not only kill off any tradition of investigative journalism but undermine the individual character of programmes such as *Panorama* or *The World Tonight*? Stories of despair and minor acts of rebellion soon started to circulate. One much ridiculed example of the new fashion for micro-management was the issuing to every producer and presenter of a lengthy 'pro-forma' on interviewing. It was, Sue MacGregor said, 'a strange guide to send to experienced broadcasters'. Over at *Panorama*, a team busy investigating what looked like irregular financial practices inside the Conservative Party claimed that they were suffering 'referral fatigue' after their script had been subjected to extensive rewriting by committee – rewriting that appeared to turn a decent scoop into a finished programme dismissed by reviewers as timorous.[37]

Birt had his defenders. In his role as Controller of Editorial Policy, John Wilson was in the top tier of those now involved in the 'vetting' of programmes such as *Panorama*. He would sit with colleagues around a table and go through each script line by line. It was, he admitted, a long and difficult process. But it made several programmes 'significantly stronger than they would have been'. In January 1991, the broadcast of a *Panorama* that threatened to expose the secret role of the Department of Trade and Industry in the development of an Iraqi 'supergun' had to be cancelled not once but twice, provoking an outcry in Parliament. This, Wilson explained, was simply because 'it needed more evidence'. The whole idea, he said, was not to make programmes politically safe: rather, 'it was to make them legally sound'.[38] As for Birt's wider impact, there was no doubting the sheer level of investment that was now taking place in news and current affairs. Nor could anyone miss the thrusting sense of expansion. By 1990, new specialist correspondents were in post, each endowed with a team of reporters and researchers; extra overseas offices had been opened, boosting the coverage of foreign affairs; and the sharing of resources between different outlets had been encouraged through new electronic technology and clearer chains of command.

Would the gains from Birtism soon start to outweigh the losses? This was, perhaps, a question that could only be answered when the re-engineered news and current affairs machine was placed under real stress for the first time.

As it happened, the litmus test on this occasion would be Britain's involvement in a Middle Eastern war as part of a US-led coalition. In August 1990, the Iraqi leader Saddam Hussein invaded Kuwait. Five months later, after diplomatic efforts to persuade him to leave voluntarily had faltered, 'Desert Storm' was launched to drive him out by force. At 9.50 p.m., London time, on Wednesday 16 January 1991, US and coalition warships in the Gulf launched a fusillade of cruise missiles, many of them targeted on the Iraqi capital Baghdad. Aerial bombing continued for several more weeks, followed in the early hours of Sunday

24 February by a ground assault that lasted just four days before overwhelming Saddam's forces.

From start to finish, the size and complexity of the military campaign was reflected in the media operation put in place to report it. The BBC's overseas bureaux in the US, the Soviet Union, Israel and Jordan were reinforced with extra staff. Stephen Sackur and Kate Adie were embedded with the British First Armoured Division. Other reporters were on board Royal Navy ships in the Gulf, or billeted at command headquarters in Riyadh and Dhahran. In Baghdad itself, two other BBC correspondents, Bob Simpson and his namesake John, had disobeyed an order to return home and remained hunkered down with a small team in the Al-Rashid Hotel – which, rather alarmingly, happened to be directly above the Iraqi leader's own secret bunker. From there, they tried to make as much use as they could of a satellite phone smuggled in just days before the start of hostilities. After being forced to leave, Jeremy Bowen and Allan Little took their place, accompanied by a cameraman, Rory Peck. Meanwhile, back in London, the nine o'clock news was extended, and Radio 4 was split so that long wave would carry the usual mix of programmes while FM would be free to provide seventeen hours a day of non-stop war coverage. The official title for the service was 'Radio 4 News FM', but the BBC's announcers were the only people ever to use it. Taking inspiration from Iraq's once feared but apparently ineffective missile defence system, newspaper journalists quickly dubbed it 'Scud-FM'. Most of the producers and reporters drafted in to run the service simply referred to it as 'Rolling Bollocks'.[39]

To begin with there was plenty to report. At military headquarters in Saudi Arabia, General Norman Schwarzkopf and Group Captain Niall Irving were on hand to deliver a series of bravura performances from the podium, where they would describe the latest air strikes and, to the delight of television picture editors everywhere, unveil video footage of smart bombs gliding towards their targets. Once the initial onslaught was over, however, these airless news conferences had diminishing appeal. In Baghdad, nightly bombing raids, interference from Iraqi minders, and the inevitable difficulties of moving around a malfunctioning city combined to limit the number of dispatches Jeremy Bowen or Allan Little could offer viewers or listeners back home. Correspondents embedded with British troops had to follow Ministry of Defence rules that required them to submit scripts for 'review' by officers. And with so much of the war being fought in the air, there was often little to report other than a vague atmosphere of expectation. When the land offensive began, the Pentagon even imposed an all-embracing forty-eight-hour news blackout. The inevitable result was that a great deal of airtime had to be filled with what felt like endless studio chatter. Sue MacGregor remembers one presenting shift on Scud-FM when she was given a piece of paper with the names of two experts and a succinct instruction: 'Discussion on water supplies in the Middle East. Keep going for twenty minutes.'[40]

Many of those tuning in at home expressed a growing weariness: 'News did come in', one listener told Mass Observation, 'great waves of it. So much so, that saturation coverage was reached by about 11.30am with me. Endless interviews with "experts" and military men.' The BBC's own audience research department also uncovered signs of unease. '*News*, yes, we want *News*', a listener explained. 'Endless speculation and discussion by journalists and "expert" civilians, no I do *not* want.' 'The number of complaints about excessive coverage is striking', the researchers concluded rather despairingly. '"Armchair generals" and other "pundits"', they pointed out, 'were especially disliked.'[41]

It sometimes felt as if the BBC's news machine had expanded beyond the capacity of real events to feed it. Yet by the end of hostilities the widespread charge that there had been nothing but endless speculation looked harder to sustain. For a start, some extraordinary first-hand reportage had pushed its way on to the airwaves. On 13 February 1991, Allan Little broadcast a grisly account of the carnage at al-Amiriyah, a Baghdad suburb, where coalition planes had incinerated a large civilian shelter. Arriving in the immediate aftermath, he had been able to describe the black smoke billowing out of the rubble, and the chaos as distraught local residents dragged out the charred and mutilated bodies of their relatives and piled them into the back of trucks. Most of the victims would have been women and children, Little explained, 'no one knows how many have been killed'. But he had time to gather evidence from relatives and rescue workers, and offered an estimate: hundreds. It was a figure the British and US authorities tried their best to dispute. Within hours of his report, the BBC was being denounced as 'the Baghdad Broadcasting Corporation'. Agitated by growing scepticism in London and Washington, Little decided to return with his fellow journalist Marie Colvin to the hospital he had visited the day before.

> There were bodies piled on top of each other on every flat surface – dissection tables, slabs, worktops around the walls and of course all over the floor. Marie and I counted 311 and gave up when we came to a vast pile, taller than me, of body parts so fragmented that it made it impossible to count further … We knew hundreds had been killed because we had counted the bodies. The claim was verifiable.

Two weeks later, BBC news carried another equally distressing report, this time from Stephen Sackur, who told of apocalyptic scenes on the Basra road, where a column of Iraqis fleeing Kuwait had been burnt beyond recognition by an onslaught of cluster bombs dropped from above – 'saloon cars, tanks, military vehicles sitting nose-to-tail in a stalled procession' as far as the low grey clouds allowed him to see. The scale of it was staggering. From what Sackur saw, hundreds upon hundreds had perished while apparently in full retreat – an example, perhaps, of the coalition's much-vaunted 'maximum force' being applied out of all proportion to what was required.[42]

Despatches like these were, as John Simpson put it, 'conspicuously more rounded and descriptive than the "Holy Cow!"

offerings of CNN'. For reporters like Allan Little, they were examples of good old-fashioned eye-witnessing that allowed him 'to close down propaganda, to challenge myth-making'. As for those studio discussions that filled the quieter moments of the Gulf War, they sometimes provided the necessary ballast of a bird's-eye view. 'I have never heard an American all-news station which even aims at the depth of background, at the range of reference, which is going out on Radio Four News FM', the *Daily Telegraph*'s critic Gillian Reynolds wrote. Drawing on the BBC's growing ranks of correspondents, its banks of information, its power to attract big-hitting interviewees and experts, it had, she said, created a service that was 'instant, informed, urgent without being hysterical ... describing with sober tact the reality of what is going on'. Despite the grumbles, more than a million were listening regularly. Viewing figures for the nine o'clock news on BBC1 were up by a fifth. And ratings for some of the BBC's international coverage were soaring: in Egypt and the United Arab Emirates around half the adult population had tuned into the Arabic Service during the conflict – a doubling of the previous figure.[43]

The outgoing Director of Television, Paul Fox, was in no doubt: the Gulf War showed that John Birt had bashed the Corporation's news and current affairs into 'exceptionally' good shape.[44]

But this was only partly true when accounting for the success of the coverage. Birt's push for more expert analysis, and his ability to secure decent resources for his Directorate, had certainly given the BBC extra depth and context. But old-style boots-on-the-ground reporting had played its role, too. And in the end, what made the journalism so impressive was the variety of approaches and perspectives it encompassed. *Panorama*, the nine o'clock news, *Today*, *The World Tonight*, even Scud-FM: as yet, none of these programmes sounded or looked quite like the others. Birt had made a concerted drive for stronger managerial control. But the bland uniformity of output this came close to creating had to some extent been held in check by powerful countervailing forces: the impossibility of micro-managing split-second editorial decisions on the ground; the stubborn survival of that gut instinct for a good story; and the deep, almost tribal loyalty staff felt for their own programmes. If the Birtist over-haul of news and current affairs could be judged a success, it was only because – for now at least – it had been only half-fulfilled.

Permanent revolution?

When Birt finally took over from Michael Checkland as Director-General in 1992 he was, however, poised to introduce a second wave of reform even more sweeping than the first. This time, his intention was to align the entire Corporation more closely with the prevailing fashion for market forces.

On his arrival in 1987, Birt had described the BBC as a 'bureaucratic monolith' with no proper budget control, full of staff and facilities that had 'accreted for years, relentlessly expanding without challenge', lacking a 'governing brain' to guide its responses to government, and cut off from the wider, brisker, more entrepreneurial world of 1980s Britain – more civil service, church, or public-school common room than 'Covent Garden or Soho'. It was an assessment that conveniently overlooked the long and very real history of cost-cutting and job losses that the Corporation had gone through ever since the 1960s. But Birt's rhetorical emphasis on this break with the past was entirely intentional, a means of persuading a sceptical government that the BBC really was reforming *itself*. Thatcher might no longer be in charge – the more emollient John Major was now installed in Downing Street – but the ruling Conservative nostrums of choice and value for money still needed to be observed. Just as importantly, they needed to be *seen* to be observed.[45]

The main plank of Birt's latest master plan was the introduction of an 'internal market' under the innocent-sounding title of 'Producer Choice'. It came into effect, appropriately enough, on April Fools' Day 1993.

Put simply, Producer Choice turned the BBC's entire

operation – production departments, research teams, libraries, facilities and so on – into hundreds of separate 'business
units' that were then required to buy or sell to each other everything from programmes and services to studio slots and office
stationery. Each individual programme team or department
would be charged a nominal share of the BBC's overheads, such
as the cost of maintaining studios, catering, administration
or transport. Studio sessions allowed to overrun, unnecessary
trips, more actors than strictly necessary: all this waste would
be squeezed out of the system as programme makers faced
what the Director-General called 'the full blast of market pressure'. The age-old distinction between 'Radio' and 'Television',
which his 'bi-media' News and Current Affairs Directorate had
already started to dismantle, was now far less important than
the distinction between 'purchaser' and 'provider'. The logical
next step was the creation in 1996 of an all-encompassing split:
between 'BBC Broadcast' – the TV channels and radio networks
that commissioned material – and 'BBC Production' – the programme-making departments that offered up their goods for
sale.[46]

This internal market also depended on the growth outside
the BBC of an independent sector of small-scale production
companies and facilities houses. Many of these had sprung up
in response to the launch in 1982 of Channel 4, which acted
as a kind of publisher, transmitting programmes made by a
panoply of 'indies' rather than making its own. Four years later,
the Peacock Report had recommended that the BBC should
source at least a quarter of its television output from this fledgling sector. Birt now embraced the idea wholeheartedly, hoping
that outsiders would gradually inject a new style on air and
encourage a more entrepreneurial culture behind the scenes.
The presence of an independent sector also meant that *in-house*
producers could see if the studios they wanted were available
outside at a better price. The Corporation's own facilities were
not themselves allowed to pitch for custom from the indies:
they could lose business, but never win it. The arrangement

was therefore highly destabilising. Any in-house resource that was no longer in full demand counted as 'excess capacity' to be got rid of. By the end of the decade more than 10,000 employees were either made redundant or had 'transferred out' to the independent sector.[47]

Production staff across the Corporation soon learned that in order to survive they would have to work up proposals that were 'honed more finely than any actual programme', knowing all the time that the vast majority would be rejected and that any that were accepted would be at someone else's expense. Each act of commissioning also generated a mountain of paperwork that seemed out of all proportion to the benefits gained. Economies of scale that the BBC had enjoyed for decades suddenly evaporated. The BBC's vast Gramophone Library housed an unrivalled range of recordings – and an unrivalled depth of knowledge among its staff – all of which was available to anyone in the Corporation. Yet now that it was obliged to make an internal charge of £8 for each separate loan, programme makers calculated that it was slightly cheaper to buy their own copy of a record from a nearby shop. It meant that each business unit 'saved' a notional amount of money. It also meant that with dozens of producers descending on the High Street, the BBC as a whole was spending more. As for the Library, fewer transactions meant having to levy even higher charges – and becoming steadily less cost-effective. Either that, or letting staff go. And to make matters worse, while creative or support staff were disappearing fast, hundreds of administrators and advisers were turning up in their place. The Policy and Planning unit established in 1987 became just one part of a fast-expanding Corporate Centre said to be costing £90 million a year.[48]

The effect on staff morale was predictable: a widespread cynicism, angry and bemused, swept through the Corporation. Apart from understandable unease over job security, it expressed the feeling that an old and valuable BBC was about to be lost forever. It was this lurking sense of betrayal that motivated one of the BBC's most respected voices, its Delhi correspondent

Mark Tully, to speak out very publicly. In the summer of 1993, he told an audience at the Edinburgh Television Festival that a broadcaster that relied so much on individual talent needed to retain 'some flexibility, perhaps even an element of chaos, to allow for experimenters and eccentrics'. Instead there was bureaucracy, even fear, and programme-making being treated as though it were simply 'biscuit making'.[49]

The elegiac mood was captured poignantly in a novel, *The Silent Sentry*, set in Broadcasting House and written by a producer, Chris Paling, who worked there during the 1990s. In the novel, Paling's hero, a BBC lifer, sees himself as part of a dying profession overwhelmed with feelings of worthlessness. 'Real art', he believes, 'has to be allowed to ferment among the inertia of creative inactivity.' 'Change. Revolution. The arrival of the market economy', his doctor explains, 'It's no different, I imagine, from what's happened to those of us in the Health Service ... Like alcohol, food, and, ah, sex, change is good in moderation. One can have too much of it.' Further up the BBC hierarchy, among the lower reaches of senior management, another of Paling's characters, who once upon a time made programmes, leads a life defined by endless hours in 'liaison meetings, strategy meetings, meetings with resources, meetings with editors, meetings with controllers, watching dull people in ill-fitting suits writing dull things on whiteboards, projecting inane statements onto screens ... patronising me with gobbets of American management speak'. He hates it but puts up with it. After all, in the BBC those who complained most vociferously 'were those who loved it the most wholeheartedly'. They did not know how the Corporation worked, but they knew it just did. And they were loyal. Yet ever since the 1980s commercialism and now managerialism had taken hold of the collective consciousness. 'The fabric was crumbling.'[50]

*

In 1993, Margaret Thatcher wrote in her memoirs that after

spending more than a decade in office being irritated by the BBC, she regarded Marmaduke Hussey and John Birt as representing 'an improvement in every respect' on the previous regime.[51] Hussey had rid the BBC of Alasdair Milne and replaced him with an accountant; Birt had roughed up the meddlesome folk at Lime Grove and exposed the Corporation to the energising blast of market forces.

Birt's own view was that he had simply tried to 'get ahead of the game', and that everything achieved since 1987, especially the introduction of Producer Choice, 'made it easier' for the government to back off. 'The radicalism of that, the fact that ten thousand people left the BBC or were made redundant – plainly the BBC was taking efficiency seriously.' His cool engineer's mind, valuing processes and systems, never quite found the language to bring the rest of the BBC with him. And there were clearly plenty who saw the cure as worse than the disease. But for admirers among the media's entrepreneurial class, Birt's 'monomania' was 'the quality needed to reform an organisation that seemed, in the 1980s, unreformable'. Whether or not the BBC was quite as badly in need of reform as this implies was, in the end, a question of political belief rather than hard economics. But the unavoidable reality was that the BBC had faced a sustained period of Conservative rule, and those at the top of the BBC had deemed it necessary for the Corporation's survival to present itself to the government in terms that were broadly acceptable to the prevailing climate.[52]

One of the Corporation's most consistent and incisive academic critics, Tom Mills, sees this as a reminder that the BBC does not stand apart from the world of politics and power: it is *part of it*, with many of its most senior staff, especially in news and current affairs, far too comfortable in the worlds of Westminster and Whitehall. As for Producer Choice, Mills suggests that by instituting a 'business-like ethos', it changed the Corporation's culture, as Birt himself would later claim, 'fundamentally – for ever'.[53]

Yet the rows over the Falklands, over the coverage of

Northern Ireland, over the ways in which the BBC was supposedly out of control – like the rows about the General Strike in
1926 or the alleged sapping of morale during the Second World
War – were evidence that the relationship between the BBC
and the government of the day, though always close, was rarely
frictionless. Thatcher's attempts to bully the BBC had been
relentless; the unwavering support she was offered by a hostile
press a deeply disturbing harbinger of things to come. But
interference from above was often contested by the broadcasters themselves, sometimes fiercely: politicians did not always
get their way. As for Birt's own 'Maoist phase', it had come up
against what the anthropologist Georgina Born described as 'a
powerful and recalcitrant professionalism'. Journalists and programme makers at the BBC had never been simply 'the creatures
of the governors': they had tried to keep quietly doing what they
thought was right – what made for good radio or television. The
fact that Birt never quite managed to take the BBC with him was
less a failure on his part and more a healthy sign that he was in
charge of a complex and not always biddable machine – one that
worked best through an organic, almost alchemical process of
change. As always, it was the programme makers who kept 'the
mother ship of values' in the BBC moving forward.[54]

14

THE EXPANDING LABYRINTH

America has Hollywood and Britain has the BBC.

Bill Cotton, 1993

It was, the BBC's Moscow correspondent Bridget Kendall said, 'one of the most vividly memorable episodes of my life' – a moment when history 'hung in the balance'.[1]

In August 1991, the politics of the global Cold War had reached a fork in the road. After two years of convulsions across Eastern Europe, which had seen Communist regimes fall one after another in countries from Poland to Romania, the prospects for similarly dramatic change in the biggest Communist state of all, the Soviet Union, remained uncertain. Since the late 1980s, its leader Mikhail Gorbachev had promulgated the twin policies of perestroika (restructuring) and glasnost (openness) in order to reinvigorate the stagnating fortunes of the former superpower – and prove, perhaps, that Communism itself had a progressive and dynamic future. Yet the economy was now flat, food shortages rife, nationalist unrest growing in the republics, and the Party was losing its grip. If there were tangible benefits from the years of disruption, they remained invisible to most ordinary citizens: the pace of change needed either to be accelerated or reversed. Gorbachev was in no doubt about the need to keep moving forward. For hardliners in the Party, the Defence Ministry and the KGB, his reforms had already gone too far. Might now be their moment to act?[2]

Mid-August was the time of year when the Soviet capital

was usually at its hottest and sleepiest. Muscovites with dachas would have departed for the countryside, foreign correspondents were abroad on their summer vacations. By chance, Kendall had decided to stay behind, planning to use the quiet season to play a bit more tennis. But then at around six o'clock in the morning of Monday 19 August, she was woken by the phone ringing in her flat: the duty editor in the BBC's Bush House newsroom was on the line. 'Has there been a coup?' 'Not as far as I know,' Kendall replied. She pulled clothes over her pyjamas and rushed down to the BBC office on the seventh floor. Inside, the printers were already churning out reports from the various news agencies, the telex machine chattering away. Information was fragmentary and confusing. There was ominous talk of Gorbachev being taken ill at his dacha in the Crimea and an 'emergency committee' running the country. There was nothing so far to prove that a group of people had actually succeeded in seizing power. She decided to provide London with a carefully worded piece of 'holding copy', saying that it had 'all the hallmarks of a Soviet coup' but going no further.[3]

'Then, in the next hour, things began to happen.'

Kendall turned on the television to find that normal programming had been interrupted. Something unsettled her. When she had been a student at Oxford and Harvard, learning Russian, Kendall had spent a great deal of time in the Soviet Union. That was in the late 1970s and early 1980s, the dying days of the Brezhnev era: she had learned then all about the ways of a Kremlin-controlled media. And she immediately recognised the on-screen announcer who was now before her: the very same granite-faced man who had presented the news for the old regime. 'He'd been retired as inappropriate for the reform years, and he was back reading this stuff in a gloomy voice.' When his announcements were over, the television switched to Swan Lake. 'And I remembered from my earlier years as a student, that when Brezhnev died, and they didn't know what to do as a party to prepare the nation for this traumatic moment … they always switched to Swan Lake.' 'It was Swan Lake that

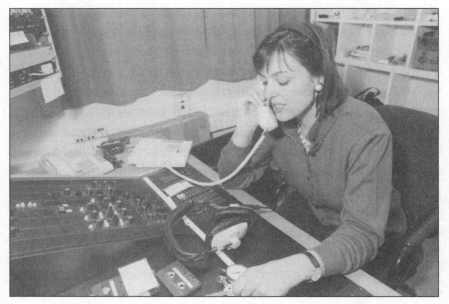

The BBC Moscow correspondent, Bridget Kendall. As the attempted
Soviet coup unfolded in the early hours of 19 August 1991, the situation
on the streets of the capital city was confused, and at first Kendall
had to gather as much extra information as possible by phone.

convinced me: no one would do that unless they were rolling
the clock back.'[4]

Soon, the evidence was piling up, the tone of Kendall's dispatches darkening by the hour. Peter Hitchens, in Moscow for
the *Daily Express*, rang to warn her of a column of tanks trundling
down Kutuzovsky Prospekt towards the city centre. Moments
later her own producer, Ben Rich, called: 'Actually, there's some
tanks outside on the bridge near our office.' It sounded as if
everything Gorbachev had achieved was about to be undone.
But when Kendall ventured outside, she sensed an air of chaos,
even signs of open defiance. She watched as her elderly clean-
ing lady, Masha, still in her apron and headscarf, went up to the
tanks outside the BBC compound and rebuked the soldiers as
they emerged from their turrets. 'You should be ashamed of
yourself! Go home to your mothers!' The man recently elected
to the role of President of the Russian Republic on a reformist

platform, Boris Yeltsin, had evaded arrest and had dashed to the Russian parliament building, the White House. From there he was captured by the world's television cameras standing on a tank, denouncing the emergency committee and calling on the military to ignore its commands. There were rumours that special forces might yet try to storm the parliament building, but crowds of people were also turning up, and barricades were being erected using buses and trams. 'They were building open fires, there were great vats of soup, women with pushchairs, someone had a guitar.' Elsewhere in the city, illegally photocopied flyers were being pasted up on walls. Most important of all, there was still no sign of a concerted military clampdown, and, back at the BBC's office, reports were coming in that the Baltic republics and the mayors of Moscow and St Petersburg were all defying the new emergency committee. By the end of the second day it was, in the words of one American journalist, starting to feel like a coup more out of the Marx Brothers than Dostoevsky.[5]

The situation at Gorbachev's holiday villa by the Black Sea remained a worrying mystery. It was by no means clear at first whether the coup plotters were going to shoot him or try to win him over. On the Wednesday, however, two delegations arrived at the dacha – one representing the emergency committee, another sent by Yeltsin. And it was to Yeltsin's team that the Soviet leader turned. A short while later, the coup leaders were arrested and Gorbachev brought back to Moscow.

In the face of popular opposition and international pressure the hardliners had lost their nerve. In just three days, their plot had collapsed and the Soviet leader restored to his old position. Gorbachev's victory, however, proved hollow. He had been unpopular among Soviet citizens for some time, but in the few days he was held captive political power in the country had shifted – visibly and irreversibly – to Boris Yeltsin. In the course of the next four months, Yeltsin proceeded to dismantle the remaining trappings of Soviet rule, and at the end of the year the red flag was lowered at the Kremlin to make way for the

Russian tricolour. The Soviet Union, once a global power and Communist monolith had, in Bridget Kendall's words, 'quietly dismantled itself and vanished with barely a murmur'.[6]

★

In the immediate aftermath of the failed coup, the Corporation's publicity team back in London seized on one incident that seemed to offer unimpeachable evidence of the BBC's success. On the day after his return to Moscow, Gorbachev had given a news conference and was questioned about how isolated he had been during his captivity. He replied that his son-in-law had managed to rig up a small short-wave radio and aerial. 'So what did you listen to?' one journalist then asked. With the world's television cameras and microphones trained on him, Gorbachev mentioned the BBC. It was, he said, 'the best of all'. The Corporation wasted little time in taking out newspaper adverts that showed Gorbachev at his desk, and the words printed underneath: 'When you need to know what's going on in the world.' Rather embarrassingly, the BBC's own Monitoring Service later explained that he had been referring not to the content of the BBC's broadcasts but simply the quality of reception at his dacha.

Yet, if Gorbachev's initial remark did not really deserve to be enshrined in Corporation mythology, he made several other comments that *were* revealing about the BBC's global reputation. At the same news conference that Thursday, he had asked aloud if any BBC reporters were present. 'I'll take a question from them', he said. Unfortunately, Bridget Kendall had already left. 'Never mind,' Gorbachev said with a smile. 'The BBC knows everything already.' A few days later, when he was leaving the parliament building and waving the press away, Grigory Nekhroshev called out that he was from the BBC Russian Service. The Soviet leader stopped and shook his hand warmly. The BBC, he then explained, had indeed been his main source of information during his confinement. Its reports had been the most reliable and thorough. And it was listening to the BBC that had confirmed in his mind that the coup was doomed to failure.[7]

It was no accident that the BBC's coverage of the events of August 1991 had an impact. Resources – both human and material – had made all the difference. Few foreign correspondents posted to Moscow could speak Russian as fluently as Kendall, or have the same depth of knowledge about Soviet affairs. They found themselves relying on official sources, agency wires or what some friendly translator might relay to them from the papers and television news; Kendall could, as she put it, 'get at the stuff under the surface … make connections with people'. She could also draw on the BBC's vast news-gathering machinery and the reservoir of collective knowledge that came with it. John Birt's recent investments in foreign bureaux had entailed a generous upgrade to the BBC's two Moscow offices. When Kendall had first arrived in July 1989, there was just one direct-dial phone for reporters to use to contact the London newsroom, and recordings had to be flown back to Britain. By 1991, a dedicated phone 'circuit' had been created, allowing material to be filed around the clock. The old telex machine now provided direct access to updates from the BBC's Monitoring Service: it was the Russian-language experts at Caversham who had first alerted the rest of the BBC to the possibility of a coup in the early hours of Monday 19 August. Within days, the BBC's Moscow operation had a small battalion of reporters spread around the city, including Martin Sixsmith for television, Tim Whewell for radio and the World Service, and Grigory Nekhroshev and Masha Slonim for the Russian-language service. Kendall's other radio colleague, Kevin Connolly, had been on holiday, but was whisked back in time to report on the coup's final collapse. Yet more reporters and producers had been flown in from London to supply special reports for just about every outlet, ranging from the *The World Tonight* on Radio 4 to *Newsnight* on BBC2. It was Whewell and Nekhroshev who managed the biggest journalistic coup of the whole crisis by getting to the White House, barricading themselves inside an abandoned office, and broadcasting live as tanks

circled menacingly outside. When their words were rebroadcast from Bush House, they were heard by listeners throughout
Russia.[8]

In the heat of the crisis, formal job demarcations barely mattered. Radio correspondents popped up on television, television
correspondents filed for radio, producers cut tape for whoever
needed it first. As ever when a major crisis was unfolding, the
demands of output editors back home seemed insatiable, the
hours of work intolerable. But on this occasion, the BBC's news
machine had had the capacity to respond: the human capital to
ensure deep knowledge of the local scene, the technical infrastructure to keep open the channels of communication between
London and Moscow, the staff to redeploy at a moment's notice,
the cash to book flights, hire drivers and pay translators. Well-
oiled, and with the benefit of what engineers would call a high
degree of inbuilt 'redundancy', the different components had
clicked into place, creating something bigger and better than
the sum of its parts. The failed Soviet coup of August 1991 was
not just an example of journalistic endeavour: it was an object
lesson in the rewards to be reaped from a Corporation spending
generously.

Forces of nature: Attenborough, the BBC and the natural world

As reporters gathered in Moscow in December 1991 to witness
the death throes of Soviet Communism, a small team of film-
makers were setting out for the world's southernmost region to
capture the dying moments of an Adélie penguin.

The remarkable footage they brought back appeared in
the 1993 television series *Life in the Freezer*. Millions of Britons
watched transfixed as a hungry nine-foot-long leopard seal lay
in ambush, and then, just as a young penguin slipped into the
water for its first-ever swim, pounced with deadly effect. In previous weeks viewers had seen whales and elephant seals feed on
krill, albatrosses and snow petrels nest on icy cliffs, and penguins

of every variety clamber over rocky slopes and march slowly in their huddled thousands across vast, white plains. *Life in the Freezer*'s six-part natural history of Antarctica showed that even in the coldest place on earth, an abundant – if perilous – ecosystem could survive through every season.

The series, though three years in production, had been half a century in gestation. In using film-making techniques that offered images of 'revolutionary' quality, it drew on a tradition of making natural history programmes that the BBC had nurtured carefully since the Second World War. In having David Attenborough as its presenter, *Life in the Freezer* also represented the latest project for an individual who had been at the forefront of wildlife television since the 1950s. The format had been established in 1979 by the epic series *Life on Earth* and its two follow-ups, *The Living Planet* and *The Trials of Life*. But in bringing together once more the unique talents of Attenborough and the BBC's Natural History Unit, *Life in the Freezer* provided a stunning showcase for what might be achieved when broadcasting played the long game.[9]

Attenborough had been introduced to the public in 1954 when BBC Television launched *Zoo Quest*. At the time, the series delighted viewers. Rather like some nineteenth-century animal-capturing expedition, a curator from London Zoo would head off with Attenborough to New Guinea or Madagascar and haul back to the studio a snake or bird or some other creature that they had tracked down in the undergrowth. The short films shot on location allowed viewers to see the animal's natural habitat for themselves, and the studio chat would be informative. Yet it was all a little quaint. And by 1973, when Attenborough had emerged from a decade toiling in the higher reaches of BBC management and was hungry to make programmes again, a more ambitious approach was required. Kenneth Clark's 1969 series *Civilisation* and Jacob Bronowski's follow-up, *Ascent of Man*, had both demonstrated how a series of thirteen weekly episodes could, as Attenborough put it, 'build up into something that *really* told you something'. Thus inspired, he set about outlining a thirteen-part series that would tell the story of Darwinian evolution. He would present it himself, and he would illustrate it using living creatures. 'I wrote it with no consideration of cost or practicability or anything.'[10]

The initial treatment for what became the 1979 series *Life on Earth* has been described as 'revolutionary in its idealism'. The script was driven by the shape of Attenborough's argument. And since his words swooped across continents, so too would the programme's sounds and images: if Attenborough referred to a coelacanth, then a crew would be dispatched to capture it on camera. Given the scale of the task, the production process took years. The BBC's film crews were often in so many places at once that it was impossible for Attenborough to accompany every expedition. But for most of the big set pieces he would be in the thick of the action: riding a donkey in the Grand Canyon, diving among corals off the Great Barrier Reef in a gaudy crimson wetsuit, swishing his way through hot, humid jungles in Central America.[11]

Life on Earth began with single-cell organisms. The first few weeks also featured sea snails and shrimps, millipedes and scorpions, lungfish and newts – as well as that incredibly elusive coelacanth. In fact, the series would be more than halfway through before it served up any giant lizards or big cats. It was an audacious approach. Behind the scenes at the BBC, Attenborough had to face down complaints that 'green slime is not the way to start off a big series'. Yet the gamble paid off, not least because the opening episodes featured images of such startling close-up intimacy that even some of the world's tiniest creatures kept everyone glued to their sets. In the penultimate episode, viewers witnessed the most extraordinary sequence of all. The idea, Attenborough explained, had been for him to be filmed on a Rwandan mountainside explaining the evolution of the opposable thumb while gorillas moved about some distance away. It did not quite work out as planned:

I turned round to talk to the camera to give this

thumb-and-forefinger story when I felt a weight lying by
my feet and I looked down – and there were two baby
gorillas undoing my shoelaces. Well, I couldn't really talk
about the thumb-and-forefinger while that was going on,
so I stopped … and then I felt a tap on my shoulder and I
turned round and there was a huge female gorilla and she
put her hand on me and put her hand on my head and
turned round and looked at my face. And this went on for,
it seemed to me, an age. And it was paradise – it was such
a privileged delight. I couldn't believe it was possible. And
eventually they left, and I crawled back.[12]

It was then Attenborough discovered that, in order to save
the BBC's dwindling film stock, the cameraman, Martin Saun-
ders, had only taken a couple of shots just to 'give the boys
a laugh' back in the cutting room. These out-takes were what
ended up being shown to millions in the finished programme.
Fortunately, Attenborough had also managed to fill those fleet-
ing moments with some inspired ad-libbing. 'There is more
meaning and mutual understanding in exchanging a glance with
a gorilla than any other animal I know', he said quietly to the
camera as the animals caressed him. 'It seems really very unfair',
he went on, 'that man should have chosen the gorilla to sym-
bolise everything that is aggressive and violent, when that is the
one thing that the gorilla is not – and that we are.' As Attenborough lamented years later, 'it could have been a twenty-minute
mind-blowing thing'. Yet the little there was turned out to be
more than enough to turn it into an iconic moment of British
television history.[13]

After just two episodes of the series the *Observer*'s television
critic Clive James declared himself 'slack-jawed with wonder and
respect': 'you practically need a seat-belt, the aesthetic effect is
so stunning.' By the end, he admitted to having been 'distracted
only by envy of my own children, for whom knowledge was
being brought alive in a way that never happened for my generation or indeed for any previous generation in all of history'.[14]

James was among the first, though not the last, to draw attention to the vital role that Attenborough played as presenter. It was in his hands, he wrote, that television had become an 'instrument of revelation'. 'To Attenborough all that lives is beautiful: he possesses, to a high degree, the quality that Einstein called *Einfühlung* – the intellectual love for the objects of experience.' The subject matter in *Life on Earth* was titanic. But its presenter had a gift for 'the simple statement that makes complexity intelligible'.[15]

It was an astute description. But Attenborough's programmes were also the product of team intelligence. And the real powerhouse behind *Life on Earth*, and later series like *Life in the Freezer*, was the Natural History Unit based in Bristol.

The Unit had grown steadily in size and scope since 1945. It was then that the former war correspondent Frank Gillard, who had just taken charge of the BBC's West Region, decided to encourage a local specialism in natural history programmes. He asked Desmond Hawkins, a young amateur bird-watcher, to develop a slew of radio series, including *Birds of Britain*, *Birdsong of the Month*, and *The Naturalist*. At first, Hawkins had no one to support him. But he teamed up with a young studio manager, Tony Soper, and together they started to build an impressive network of contacts among the country's amateur and semi-professional naturalists, sound recordists and photographers. They worked particularly closely with the German refugee Ludwig Koch, as well as the BBC's own Eric Simms – two leading ornithologists with legendary collections of bird recordings. The famously perfectionist Koch would spend months at a time enduring 'horrid conditions' in the Scottish Highlands to capture the courtship notes of the greenshank. Soper would head off to Pembrokeshire and Fair Isle armed with a Bolex – 'the serious amateur's 16mm camera' – to practise filming puffins and fulmars. By the mid-1950s, both Hawkins and Soper were ready to switch from radio to television. They dismissed existing series, the kind presented by Armand and Michaela Denis, as sentimental and dishonest.

It was 'husband-and-wife-venturing-into-the-deepest-darkest-Africa stuff', Soper recalled. 'We wanted to talk about animals as they genuinely are and not as they can be made into by a sort of anthropomorphic treatment.'[16]

The one thing they needed was good quality footage to illustrate their ideas. It was one of their regular collaborators, Peter Scott, the owner of a wildfowl sanctuary in Slimbridge, who provided their breakthrough. In 1954, Scott had come rushing back from Switzerland with news of an extraordinary thirteen-minute film by a German naturalist, Heinz Sielmann, about woodpeckers. The close-ups it featured were stunning: Sielmann had even used infrared technology to film *inside* a tree trunk. His footage was snaffled up by the BBC in Bristol and shown nationwide at peak time on Saturday, 15 January 1955. 'It was a sensation', Hawkins remembers. 'The supervisor of the switchboard in London rang me up and said, "You may like to know that our switchboard was totally jammed for three hours ... We simply couldn't cope".' More importantly from Hawkins' and Soper's point of view, the audience reaction had been noticed by BBC management. 'It was what really made the Natural History Unit possible.' Sielmann himself was given a contract with what now became a fully fledged department. In June 1955, there was the first episode of *Look*, introduced by Peter Scott from 'the BBC's West of England television studio', promising viewers 'a fly's eye' view of insects, toads, squirrels and foxes. In 1959, a seven-part spin-off, *Faraway Look*, showcased footage that Tony Soper and Peter Scott had shot during a three-month trip to the Galápagos Islands.[17]

In the twenty years between this first attempt to tell 'the Darwin story' and the broadcasting of *Life on Earth*, the Natural History Unit had grown exponentially in size, confidence and expertise. It had discovered – and trained up – hundreds of talented film-makers. Some were now employed in Bristol, others were part of a global network of freelancers eager to work with the Unit on whatever its latest project might be: it was already regarded as the world's leading centre for wildlife documentaries, a place teeming with highly skilled and zoologically literate producers. When David Attenborough first drew up his prospectus for a new story of evolution, the Unit was more than prepared. Indeed, two of its leading producers, Chris Parsons and John Sparks, had actually presented their own detailed plans several months *before*: 'a wildlife version of Kenneth Clark's "Civilization"', 'the story of life on this planet' – a blockbuster series, perhaps with Attenborough as presenter.[18]

By the end of the 1970s producers at the Unit exerted a powerful influence on the evolution of television wildlife documentaries at the BBC. Typically, they would consult in the region of 500 scientists for any given series. In making *Life on Earth*, researchers visited 183 different institutions in person. When it came to *The Trials of Life*, a huge database was compiled of suggestions and information from researchers around the world who had come up with arresting stories of individual animal behaviour that could be translated into filmed sequences. 'You might think that a scientist might be reluctant to reveal to a television producer behaviour that he has taken years of sitting in some rain-drenched, insect-ridden jungle to observe and understand,' one member of the Unit explained, 'but once they were convinced that their discoveries would not be distorted but presented as truthfully as we could manage, they welcomed us enthusiastically.'[19]

Time and again, it was this coming together of two precious BBC resources – on the one hand, a reservoir of specialist skills nurtured over decades, on the other a remarkable individual talent for communicating complex ideas to a very large public – which ensured that the BBC's biggest wildlife series ended up as both critical *and* popular successes. In their effort to make visible the previously invisible, the *Life* programmes had stimulated the development of new cameras, new lenses, new ways of lighting a scene. By revealing previously unknown animal behaviour, they occasionally changed scientific consensus. As for their impact on ordinary viewers, Clive James offered his own prediction. 'It was obvious,' he wrote after *Life on Earth*, 'that thousands of new zoologists would all be conceived at

David Attenborough and crew during a break from filming in
the Ecuadorian rainforest for the 1984 series *The Living Planet*.
They wanted to show viewers how a tropical eco-system
could support an immense variety of flora and fauna.

once, like a population bulge.' There were, James thought,
wider lessons to be learned, too – about the BBC's capacity for
making good programmes in general. Its knack for the blockbuster, he claimed, had 'attained the status of collective genius'.
And it had happened, he believed, because of the way things
were organised: the ecology of British television and of the BBC
in particular. 'The programme makers have been brought up
in a tradition of pride in work … the kind of tradition which
radical criticism is least equipped to understand.'[20]

Right on cue, the *Sunday Telegraph*'s own resident critic, A. N. Wilson – trained in the skills of priesthood and medieval literature, though not, it would appear, in media studies – decided that he knew *exactly* how television programmes were made: cynically. In 1990, he accused *The Trials of Life* of faking a sequence in which a bird kicked soil into Attenborough's face – an accusation that ended with a printed apology in his newspaper.

Undaunted, Wilson now accused *Life in the Freezer* of faking its famous footage of that leopard seal attacking a penguin. 'The chances of a cameraman being in the right place at the right time', he wrote, were 'inconceivably remote.' 'One wonders how many live penguins they had to feed to the seal before they got the desired effect.' Given that five cameramen had been working on location for two weeks, and that one of them had gone into the water in a near-suicidal attempt to get close-up footage of a natural event, the series producer Alastair Fothergill felt duty-bound to threaten legal action. It was true that some wildlife sequences *had* to be filmed in studio conditions because it was often impractical to do otherwise. Eggs hatching, insects eating, caterpillars moving: these could only be seen properly with special lighting and magnification. On location, too, a certain amount of setting up was sometimes needed: male and female scorpions had to be surrounded by plastic barriers to stop them escaping before filming had finished. But when it came to a leopard seal killing a penguin or a lion killing a wildebeest it would, Attenborough explained, be 'very difficult to do it in a way which either would be convincing but also which would be tolerable morally – and so you don't.'

The programmes he made were built not just around scientific accuracy: they were built around ethical practices. Since sequences filmed on location were not supposed to be faked, they could only be captured by observing nature's own entirely unpredictable timetables. One of the recurring aspects of life in a Natural History Unit production was therefore long periods spent waiting for something to happen. It was one of the reasons programmes like these were so expensive to make – and why, in the end it was an institution such as the BBC that could make them. 'What organisation is it who's going to say, "We're going to start investing in this and there will be no return at all for three years?"' Attenborough asked. 'No other broadcasting organisation I know.'[21]

As for Wilson's troubling allegation about the broadcaster's filming techniques, it ended with Alastair Fothergill and the BBC winning their case. The out-of-court settlement involved not just a grovelling retraction from the writer but a sizeable sum of money. The BBC gave it to the Falkland Islands Conservation Society's latest penguin appeal.[22]

BBC Online and iPlayer

By the middle of the 1990s, David Attenborough's wildlife series had reached the status of rock-solid global brands, sold in their millions as DVDs and rebroadcast on hundreds of overseas television networks. Their commercial success reflected the BBC's growing activity in the arena of international programme sales – a useful supplement to the licence fee that also burnished its worldwide image as a blue-chip broadcaster.

But for eighty years the BBC's reputation had been built around the twin pillars of radio and television, and the closing years of the twentieth century were to witness a profound challenge to these two traditional media. The technological landscape was changing fast, and although the precise nature of this future was unknowable, the mere possibility that radio and television might one day be eclipsed by new ways of consuming entertainment or accessing information was something that the BBC needed to take seriously. Not everyone in the organisation could see this at the time. But some did, and the Director-General himself, John Birt, was among them. Whatever his mistakes over the management of news or the introduction of Producer Choice, as an ardent technophile he was the right man at the right time when it came to embracing this digital future.

It was in this spirit that in July 1997 Birt took a flight across the Atlantic – a trip that would turn out to be the most important of his entire BBC career.

The Director-General prided himself on being a 'blue skies' thinker. Since joining the BBC, he had spent one week each summer trying to step back from his day-to-day duties and expand his horizons. In 1997, his latest fascination was with the ideas of Nicholas Negroponte, the author of a recent bestselling book, *Being Digital*. The two men first met at the World Economic Forum in Davos and had had several conversations together since. At these meetings, Negroponte had laid out a startling techno-utopian vision of the near future. He believed that 'old' media would become obsolete. In their place the weightless electronic 'bits' of the information superhighway, whizzing around the world at the speed of light, would create entirely virtual newspapers and forms of entertainment – 'new' media that could be personalised by each individual consumer into a portable, digital 'Daily Me'. It was stimulating stuff. 'He made me think and understand what some of the significance of the new technology was likely to be', Birt explained. Now, the Director-General wanted to follow up these conversations with a week-long visit to the American west coast. He knew that his trip would end in Seattle, so he could meet Bill Gates at Microsoft's headquarters. The rest of his itinerary was the responsibility of Jamie Reeve, who had joined Birt's Policy and Planning team two years earlier. Reeve had spent the summer of 1995 in New York, where he had watched as an old friend had put together a database of cinema showtimes that anyone with a dial-up internet connection could access. Reeve thought it 'unbelievably amazing'. Once back in London, he had spent time looking up other interesting websites. By the time he accompanied the Director-General on his trans-Atlantic flight in July 1997, he had lined up visits to the most dynamic-looking internet companies he had come across, including Geocities and Netscape in California. A meeting had also been arranged in Seattle: at Progressive Networks – the forerunner of the audio-streaming company RealNetworks.[23]

Before he had even arrived in Seattle, however, Birt's head was spinning. 'This was a wholly new world ... the power and extent and functionality of the internet came through to me, personally, for the first time.' He had reached a firm conclusion: 'that this was a Very Big Thing that was going to change the world, and that the BBC had to be at the centre of it.' On his flight from San Francisco, Birt pulled out a sheaf of paper from his briefcase and proceeded to sketch out what he thought the BBC needed to do. 'And rather immodestly I waved these bits of paper to Jamie across the plane at the end of the day, saying, "This is the BBC's internet strategy".'[24]

By the autumn, Birt's Policy and Planning unit had been charged with taking the lead. In his new role as the head of Digital Strategy, Reeves worked closely with Ed Richards, the Controller of Corporate Strategy and a future Chief Executive of Ofcom. Richards recalled the air of excitement in their offices. 'Almost every day something new, from somewhere around the world, came to our attention.'[25]

It was then, too, that Birt and his policy-makers noticed for the first time quite how much experimental work had already been going on right under their noses. In what Birt conceded was a BBC that remained, despite his own efforts, 'uncontrollable, slightly anarchic, slightly chaotic', it was perhaps inevitable that people did things slightly covertly. But the whole 'computer revolution' had also been embraced enthusiastically in many programme-making departments. Back in January 1979, BBC2 had broadcast 'Now the Chips Are Down', an edition of *Horizon* highlighting a shortage of 'tech' skills in the British economy. Three years later, the BBC's education department launched a computer literacy project built around a series of programmes, instructional books, and support networks for teachers. A key component of the project was a bespoke personal computer, the 'BBC Micro', designed to be affordable and easy to use for viewers at home. Working with the BBC's in-house Research and Development team, BBC Education had created the brief: a machine allowing people with no previous experience to learn the so-called 'BASIC' computer language. A team of young scientists from Cambridge had come up with the design, and the company they worked for, Acorn, had manufactured it. With its chunky keyboard and orange function keys, the Micro became a distinctive fixture of many British households and classrooms in the 1980s, with thousands of children in particular spending hour after hour creating colourful graphics or playing video games such as *Frogger* and *Pac-Man* while also – it was hoped – learning to programme.[26]

The project provided something of a template for a new television series launched in 1994 with a focus on the internet, called, appropriately enough, *The Net*. The production company making the series, Illuminations, was keen to establish a dialogue with viewers while the programmes were still on air. So it set up bulletin boards, placed an email address in the closing credits, and even made plans for a users' club of some kind. Soon after, BBC Education created its own 'BBC Networking Club' to help viewers get online. By this stage, one of the Corporation's most internet-savvy engineers, Brandon Butterworth, had also built an internal network called 'Reith' that linked desktop computers across different departments, and had secured for his employer a website domain name: 'bbc.co.uk'.[27]

As staff in different corners of the Corporation had begun to explore the internet, they had also started to create web pages. It was all very ad hoc. Alongside a site for the BBC's Hungarian Service, there would be 'Trumptonshire Web', a fan site for the children's television programme. Over at Radio 1, staff were creating 'live chat' facilities. At the recently launched news and sport radio network, Five Live, the '606' phone-in for football fans evolved into what was quite possibly the busiest message board in the entire country. And by May 1997, small groups of BBC journalists at Television Centre and White City were building an 8,000-page site for the general election results. It had not really been 'planned' as such, one of the senior editors there explained, 'it just evolved really quickly on the hoof … you didn't have to consult everybody before you did what you wanted to do ... it felt as if you could do anything, really'.[28]

A great deal of this creative ferment was only uncovered by the Director-General and his team through casual conversations or social networks. But in the wake of Birt's transformative visit to California the clear view from the centre was that an informal economy of local initiatives needed to be pulled together into a grander, more coherent vision. So much of what was happening was 'half-understood', Birt thought, 'it wasn't coalescing, it didn't gleam'. Some £2.6 million was now allocated from existing funds to start weaving together an online service that could encompass far more than just news. This was when, in the words of one policy official, 'there was a bringing together of all the people who had the good ideas, plus a corporate push'. The Chairman, Marmaduke Hussey, remained highly sceptical. According to one source, Hussey regarded the internet as 'bollocks'. This antediluvian attitude, Birt later admitted, was the cause of 'a serious dispute' between the two men at the top. In programme-making departments there were also staff who worried about their own already very tight budgets being cannibalised for something that still felt rather peripheral. But doubters were invited to parties in the Council Chamber of Broadcasting House, where they could chat to some technical whiz kids and order pizza or sushi online. 'This was seen as absolutely amazing', Birt remembers. Enthusiasm 'spread like wildfire'.[29]

It was the News people who now made the running. They were supposed to be launching their own full-scale online service in the autumn. But the sudden death of Princess Diana at the end of August jolted everyone into pre-emptive action. As the dramatic story unfolded, it was quickly realised that the BBC's web pages needed constant updating. Journalists drafted in at short notice started experimenting with embedding little clips of video and audio grabbed from television and radio. A tribute site was assembled, a webcast arranged for the funeral. Only in the second week of September could staff finally draw breath. When the main News online site was formally launched on

Monday 15 December 1997, a hasty investment in extra servers meant that it was able to stream the one, six and nine o'clock television news bulletins: the BBC's first full video-on-demand service. Over the next twenty-four months, the rest of the BBC followed suit. The 'multimedia' character of the internet, and its status as something more than a mere adjunct to television and radio, was starting to be realised.[30]

Creating BBC Online had been neither cheap nor risk-free. The BBC could not launch new services without approval from the government, and for a year or two it had to switch large pots of existing money from one budget to another in the hope that something would emerge and its efforts be rewarded. Fortunately, the licence fee settlement of 2000, the first under the new Labour government of Tony Blair, turned out to be one of the most generous in the BBC's history: set at 1.5 per cent *above* the inflation rate for the next seven years. In return, the BBC would take the lead in building the country's digital infrastructure and encourage digital take-up among the public. John Birt was ecstatic, convinced it was BBC Online itself that had swung the deal. 'We had a vision to take to the Government', he said, and it 'excited them.'[31]

Many of the Corporation's commercial competitors had also dabbled with the internet, but few had yet managed to establish a successful online presence of their own. Their need was for the quick return, their focus on the here and now. But turning what had once been an obscure backroom technology into a service offering millions of users the same editorial and production standards that they were used to in radio and television required patience. And in Britain it was the BBC that had the capacity to find out, bit by bit, what worked and what did not, what navigation should look like, or how multimedia and social media could be integrated into a web page. BBC Online only came to fruition when the different parts of the BBC connected with each other. But it drew on a tradition of curiosity and an institutional willingness to make mistakes. It was, as someone astutely pointed out, 'the product of opportunity, not fear'.[32]

*

The BBC's digital reinvention was not quite over yet. Seven years later, on Christmas Day 2007, the British public had its first taste of the 'iPlayer'. And as with BBC Online, a rather tangled story lay behind its creation.

One crucial moment came during an alcohol-fuelled brain-storm. Tony Ageh had joined the BBC in 2002 after a publishing career spent developing magazines such as *City Limits* and the first digital content at the *Guardian*. In his new role at the Cor-poration he was responsible, among other things, for overseeing the online pages of the two digital television networks, BBC3 and BBC4. When the *Evening Standard* noticed one day that the BBC3 website featured the model Jordan dressed 'inappropri-ately', Ageh was instructed to 'make the problem go away' and then sack the person responsible. Instead, he took Robin Price, the editor in charge of the team that had updated the offending site, to a late bar at Bush House and told him that they were not going to leave until they had come up with an idea 'so good' that the BBC would keep him in post. After many hours drinking and dreaming up some truly terrible ideas, the pair eventually hit on the notion of somehow allowing people to access BBC3's programmes using their personal computers: they could then watch what they liked when they liked. The two men even came up with a name – the '3VO'. It sounded as if this might just do the job; the only problem was that, having had so much to drink, they weren't sure they would remember it the next morning. So in his late night taxi home Ageh called his friend and BBC colleague Bill Thompson – who had worked with him on the *Guardian*'s website – and asked him to write down the idea and then email it back to him. 'The next morning an email arrived from Bill ... I gave the note to Robin, told him simply to remove Bill's name and send it back to me with his own name on it instead.' Overnight, Thompson had embellished the original concept. It was now a document that set out the future iPlayer in embryonic form. 'Too busy to catch every episode of your favourite BBC Three shows?', it began. 'Then use 3VO – BBC Three's streaming video on demand service.'[33]

The iPlayer offered a practical means of delivering what others at the BBC had been grappling with conceptually for years. One of John Birt's key strategists, Jeremy Mayhew, remembers the whole notion of video on demand as being very much 'in the air' in the mid-1990s while BBC Online had been in development. Birt himself described video on demand as his 'obsession', and believed that every other digital innovation under his watch would eventually come together in this final merging of television, radio and the internet. In 1996, Radio 1 had found a way to post on its website recordings of recent broadcasts so that anyone in the world could 'listen again' by clicking on a virtual mixing desk: it was the template for the 'BBC Radio Player', which was unveiled to the public in 2001 and included most of the programmes broadcast by the BBC's national radio networks and local stations. It was cleanly designed, easy to use, and, being funded by the licence fee, entirely free of advertising.[34]

Tony Ageh's challenge in 2002 was to find a way of adapting this kind of work to the medium of television. His first move was to find someone with the ability to build something. This turned out to be Ben Lavender, a young engineer in the BBC's New Media Technology department. Lavender brought not just the skills of a trained computer scientist – inspired, he said, by a childhood playing around with the BBC Micro – but a career working on distributing music and videos over the internet. He already had detailed plans worked up for what he called an 'Internet Personal Video Recorder'. Over the next six months, he would design a new user interface, hire developers, apply for a patent and run pilots. Lavender also had to resolve the issue of performance rights, and had to set out proposals for how taste and decency could be managed on a platform that had no obvious 'watershed'.[35]

By November 2003, Lavender and Ageh were ready to present a working prototype. The 'Executive Committee' of the Director-General, Greg Dyke, only voted to support the project by the narrowest of margins: Lavender got a further slice of development money and the chance to test it out on a sample of 5,000 viewers, but institutional inertia was already setting in. 'TV folks hated it', Ageh remembers. 'So did marketing. And the policy teams initially refused to even discuss it.' Lots of people, it seemed, simply found it difficult to imagine that anyone would *ever* want to watch television on a computer screen. In the end it took two more years and endless staff presentations – Ageh and Lavender stopped counting at eighty-four – before Mark Thompson, Dyke's successor as Director-General, announced that what he called 'MyBBCPlayer' would go ahead. Even then, Thompson warned that everything would be subject to 'approval from our Governors and all necessary consents'.[36]

What this meant in practice was a so-called 'public value test', a consultation process designed to reassure commercial rivals that any new BBC service would avoid damaging their interests. It also meant yet another lengthy delay for iPlayer's creators. Lavender's original hope was that his new platform would include programmes from ITV, Channel 4 and Channel 5 as well as the BBC's own. He and Ageh called it 'competing on content, collaborating on technology'. The advantage of this 'unified' approach, they believed, was that the British public would avoid having to install a different service for each separate television channel. Neither the broadcasting companies concerned, nor the Secretary of State for Culture at the time, Jeremy Hunt, were interested. Then, in November 2006, while Ageh's team were waiting for the last stage of formal approval, Channel 4 poached several of the BBC's developers and launched an online service of its own, 40D. It was immensely frustrating. By July 2007, when there had still been no formal decision from the top of the Corporation, one insider complained that the BBC had 'gone from market leader to market laggard'. The Christmas launch five months later came not a moment too soon.[37]

★

Back in 2003, Greg Dyke had told the team behind the iPlayer's development that they had 'saved the BBC'. Was he right?

The team was certainly responsible for bringing the concept of 'catch-up' television to a wider public. As one newspaper put it, iPlayer had shown the world how 'it should be done ... glossy, navigable and without too much fiddling around'. Before long, a third of the country's entire internet capacity was taken up by people using it. By March 2012, it had been voted the UK's number one brand. With iPlayer and Online combined, the BBC could boast that viewers and listeners need 'never miss a moment' when it came to major sporting, cultural or news events. The BBC's dogged commitment to testing the potential of 'the digital' had paid off, holding out the prospect that even in a future dominated by the internet, new social platforms and 'always on' mobile phones, the Corporation might retain for itself a centre-stage role.[38]

It had been touch-and-go at times. In an organisation more tightly managed and market conscious than ever, looking to the future had sometimes been seen as wasteful effort. This was one reason why John Birt's early enthusiasm for video on demand failed to ensure unqualified support for the iPlayer once he had left. Fortunately, the stories of Online and iPlayer also showed that the BBC still had on its payroll what one insider called 'nippy, smart people working around the edges trying things out – and failing'. Their success – not just for the BBC but in building 'Digital Britain' – also provided an important lesson for policy-makers: the large-scale risks from which commercial companies recoiled could be taken on very effectively by a public institution such as the BBC – so long, of course, as it was allowed the capacity for long-term thinking and as long as failure was tolerated as a vital component of innovation.[39]

Where the BBC *was* vulnerable was in the very moment of its triumph. Once it had done the heavy lifting in testing a product, commercial companies were free to pile in. In 2012, the BBC basked in the warm glow of a successful London Olympics – its coverage more extensive and more highly rated than ever, thanks in large part to the combined effect of Online and iPlayer. But it was in 2012, too, that the US company Netflix arrived in Britain, promising its own well-funded cornucopia of online entertainment. 'The iPlayer really blazed the trail', the company's chief executive admitted – a generous acknowledgement of the debt he owed. His company, though, was in the business of competition, not collaboration. It was also rich, and free from the regulation that prevented the BBC from developing iPlayer to its full potential. For the next seven years, while the BBC was blocked from including 'box sets' of its most popular series, Netflix grew steadily in popularity – and the Corporation's share of the UK audience for on-demand video declined from 40 to 15 per cent. By 2019, the BBC warned that it had lost its chance to catch up. In the very market it had created, its future looked like one of managed decline.[40]

'Low art with guts'

BBC Online and the iPlayer had been seen as investments for a future arriving at breakneck speed. But one of the great surprises of the 'new' media age was just how popular the 'old' media remained. We showed a powerful attachment to watching and listening to the same programmes as our families, friends and neighbours. We still seemed to be fond of the shared experience, the 'water-cooler' moment. And it was still network television and radio that supplied these in abundance.

With radio, a programme's place in the schedule was so deeply enmeshed with the rituals and rhythms of domestic life that the BBC messed around with it at its peril. In 1990, when Radio 4 first announced it was going to shift *Woman's Hour* from its age-old afternoon slot to mid-morning, questions were raised in Parliament and a newspaper called for a mass burning of the *Radio Times*. Two years later, when plans were unveiled for Radio 4 to hand over its long-wave frequency to a rolling news service, listeners marched on Broadcasting House and tore up their licences. 'Radio isn't like TV or newspapers, which burst in on us from the world outside,' Jenny Diski wrote, 'it's more like running water or electricity, just there, part of everyday life, always has been, unthinkable that it shouldn't be.' Radio offered a tidal flow of the reassuring and the familiar, with the occasional undercurrent of the esoteric and the surprising.[41]

For television, the key to survival was novelty. It is what made it 'a widescreen view of subtle and incremental social shifts … a palimpsest of the national mood'. John Howard Davies, who had been the BBC's entertainment impresario in the late 1970s and early 1980s, once said that the producer's job was simply to feel 'vibrations in the air'. But for a broadcaster required to balance ratings with reputation, this was never straightforward. Staff had to come up with programmes that were 'classy but not prissy, fun but not brash, red-blooded but not loutish'. The BBC also had to relate to viewers in *all* of their moods. Huw Wheldon's old formula, about making the good popular and the popular good, still felt like a useful rule of thumb. It avoided the BBC being tied to making 'quality' programmes in the narrowest sense, and meant that popular programmes could be defended as part of the Corporation's remit. 'After all,' Clive James had pointed out, 'triviality is one of the things that free people like to consume.' He thought the golden rule for programme makers was this: 'anaemic high art is less worth having than low art with guts.'[42]

The first big television hit of the new millennium, Channel 4's *Big Brother*, came too late to get a mention in James's *Observer* column, but it probably fitted his favoured category. Over nine weeks, dozens of cameras eavesdropped on a group of young adults confined together in a purpose-built east London 'bungalow'. The raw material, full of petty squabbles and long stretches of banal inactivity, seemed unpromising at first. But viewers' growing obsession with the nightly highlights and the weekly expulsions of household members voted out by the public, offered a vivid demonstration of television's ability to draw an audience slowly but surely into an unfolding drama – even if it was a drama of television's own making.

The two biggest stars of the BBC's 1997 series *Driving School*:
the hapless learner Maureen Rees and her husband Dave. The
series proved to be one of the first examples of a new and
highly popular genre on British screens, 'reality TV'.

Big Brother was a bit brash for the Corporation's tastes. But
its 'reality' format echoed deeper traditions of 'observational'
entertainment found at the BBC. In 1994, for instance, BBC1
had screened *Animal Hospital Week*, which featured Rolf Harris
taking viewers on a nightly tour of an RSPCA hospital in north
London. The story of Floss the Alsatian, who could walk just
a few steps before his back legs collapsed, prompted tears on
camera and a jump in the ratings to 9.5 million. Sick animals
– and the high-stakes drama of their recovery or, in Floss's
case, demise – proved they could be a huge draw. As did stories
showing the human ability to combine heroism and fallibility.
The 1997 series *Driving School*, which set out to follow a group
of learners preparing for their test, made a minor celebrity out
of Maureen Rees, who had to write 'L' and 'R' on her hands and
who, on one memorable occasion, ran over her husband's foot.[43]

A new genre was emerging: documentary reborn as 'a soap opera of the mundane'. In television, a formula as easily repeatable as this tended to spread through the schedules like Japanese knotweed. And it took no time at all for the 'docusoap' format to be so ubiquitous as to attract the attention of the nation's satirists. Radio 4 was first off the mark with its 1995 'mockumentary' series *People Like Us*, featuring Chris Langham as the inept BBC reporter 'Roy Mallard' and his bumbling day-in-the-life portraits of various professions. In 2001 there was BBC2's *The Office*; four years later, BBC4's *The Thick of It*.[44]

Even satires as sharp as these could not erase the docusoap's essential pleasures. With its immersive, fly-on-the-wall style, it had the vaguely educational feel of a traditional piece of investigative reporting. But its narrative power came from classic soap opera ingredients: a 'cast' of characters carefully selected to guarantee a little conflict, a lurking sense of jeopardy, some powerful journeys of redemption. If this was manipulative, it was no more so than any good soap opera, or indeed any conventional drama. It was after watching a man being told that his cat's cancer was inoperable that the writer Peter Conrad declared *Animal Hospital* to be 'as gut-wrenching as King Lear'. When the Australian import, *Neighbours*, was first screened in Britain in 1986, sociologists had discovered that British Asian teenagers were among the most avid followers of suburban Melbourne's sun-soaked 'Ramsay Street'. They gossiped about its characters as a way of commenting indirectly on their own families, and in particular the importance in Punjabi culture of family honour or *izzat*. But schoolchildren of all kinds, students, even the retired also watched *Neighbours* in their millions. It brought together people of very different ages, social classes and ethnic backgrounds. For a while it was 'as near to a communal culture as the nation possessed'.[45]

The most successful soap opera of all had first reached British television screens just a year before: *EastEnders*. It was a serial that would be going strong thirty-five years later – still winning audiences of up to fifteen million viewers, stacking up its tenth BAFTA award, and being described as 'one of the most gripping, skilful and important programmes in British television history'.[46] Its origins, however, had been highly unusual. In contrast to most BBC programmes, *EastEnders* emerged not through the ferment of ideas bubbling up from the production departments, but as a result of hard-headed decisions by senior managers.

Back at the beginning of 1983, the BBC's income had been stagnant, while ITV's was booming. And the commercial channel used its superior bank balance to spend heavily on big, popular programmes for the lucrative mid-evening slots. It was screening more than three times as many game shows as BBC1, twice as many variety shows, more than twice as many situation comedies. The result: in terms of numbers, reach, and loyalty, five of the top six series were ITV's. The BBC might once have responded by scheduling a big-hitting programme just after supper time in the comforting assumption that viewers would then stick with the same channel for an entire evening's viewing. But viewers now had remote controls. They were zapping promiscuously from channel to channel. The BBC always wanted to be in touch with popular taste: its apparent inability to produce anything that embraced ordinary working lives as confidently and consistently as ITV's *Coronation Street* had started to feel like a creative failure that needed correcting urgently.[47]

A new peak-time soap opera of its own was the BBC's highly strategic answer. By the spring of 1983, the new serial had already been commissioned by the Controller of BBC1, Alan Hart; the man in charge of the BBC's resources, Michael Checkland, had ring-fenced a pot of more than £1.6 million pounds; and a dedicated producer and scriptwriter had been recruited – Julia Smith and Tony Holland, two people who had worked together on *Z Cars*. There was an intense debate behind the scenes about where exactly the serial should be set. The Managing Director of Television, Bill Cotton, favoured a northern setting. Both Tony Holland and the head of Television Drama, Jonathan Powell, favoured London. An early suggestion that it

Filming on the set of *EastEnders* in 2000. The dedicated 'Albert Square' set, at the BBC's Elstree Studios, had taken two years to plan and build. The 'Queen Vic' pub, seen here in the background, remains the setting for some of the soap's most dramatic episodes.

should be centred on a caravan park was rejected as 'unbearably dispiriting', leaving the idea of an East End location as front runner. Once the shape and feel of the fictional 'Albert Square' had been fleshed out, work began on constructing a dedicated set at Elstree, where a group of staff from Television Drama were located. Smith brought in hand-picked directors, many of them young and straight from the Royal Court theatre. Holland drew on his own experience of growing up in London's East End, mapping out storylines that self-consciously tackled pressing social issues while also offering viewers a touch of 'the Blitz spirit in a mythic "cockney" world'.[48]

After two packed years of planning and building, researching and writing, casting and rehearsing, the first two episodes were broadcast at 7 p.m. on Tuesday 19 February and Thursday 21 February 1985. More than twelve million people watched as the theme tune played over a swirling aerial shot of London's docklands and, in a suitably dramatic opening scene, three of the leading characters, Den Watts, Arthur Fowler and Ali Osman, were seen breaking down the door to Reg Cox's flat only to find him slumped in a chair on the brink of death. In less than a month more than twenty million people – roughly half the adult population of the entire country – were watching every week, tuning in to see 'born-and-bred' East End characters such as Dot Cotton and Ethel Skinner, the Beales and the Fowlers go about their lives, making friends, gossiping, and sometimes falling out with each other and with newcomers like the Osmans and the Jefferys or with young racist thugs like Nick Cotton. A worrying dip in ratings during the serial's first summer was promptly reversed when the start time was shifted to 7.30 p.m. so that it no longer clashed with ITV's *Emmerdale Farm*. Its sheer popularity would soon be unrivalled. The 1986 Christmas Day edition featured the landlord of the Queen Vic pub, 'Dirty Den', discovering that his wife Angie had lied to him about being terminally ill and serving divorce papers on her in cold-blooded revenge. Thirty million watched – the biggest British television audience of the decade.[49]

EastEnders was an instant marketing dream for the BBC. Viewers and critics have occasionally accused the serial of being overly didactic, its characters too diagrammatic, its plot lines melodramatic. Yet over the years it has managed to embrace the generic essentials of a soap opera – archetypes, cliffhangers, vigorous emotionality – while exploring an extraordinary range of life-changing problems: unemployment, imprisonment, rape, drugs, alcoholism, attempted suicide, murder, homophobia, infidelity, AIDS, abortion, ageing, death. When Arthur Fowler experienced a slowly spiralling nervous breakdown, doctors said that they had never seen the trauma and distress of mental illness so well depicted. It was praised for standing in a literary tradition that stretched back more than a hundred years – to Charles Booth's study of East End poverty, George Sims's *How the Poor Live*, and the novels of Charles Dickens. It was also praised for acknowledging Britain's increasingly complex, multi-ethnic nature. Characters of African Caribbean, Asian and Turkish Cypriot heritage, it was pointed out, were not just transient visitors brought in to embody racial 'problems': they owned the grocery, they ran the café, they were a normal part of Albert Square's communal life. The portrayal of diversity was always a work in progress: there were critics who felt that for much of the 1980s and 1990s, *EastEnders'* Black or Asian or gay characters were still distinctly underdeveloped. But a storyline in 2010 demonstrated just how determinedly the serial's scriptwriters were attempting to make up for lost ground. After careful consultation with several British Muslim and gay rights organisations, the relationship between the characters of Christian Clarke and Syed Masood was allowed to develop in a nuanced and sympathetic way while exploring the tensions between faith and sexual identity. 'There's a danger of being too careful with black and Asian characters', the executive producer explained. 'But it seems to me if we steer away from any controversy, they don't stand a chance of being a great *EastEnders* family – they'll just be in their kitchen unit making curries for years and years and that's not going to be very interesting.'[50]

*

Even in the most formulaic of genres, broadcasters were involved in a task of constant, if sometimes nervous, reinvention. Programmes had to respond to the tiniest shifts in public mood, standards of behaviour, values and tastes, while somehow always remaining true to themselves. Often, this was a matter of pouring new wine into old bottles.

Doctor Who had its own in-built device for achieving this: the periodic regeneration of its main character, and with each regeneration a new group of companions and a subtle shift in tone. Even the show's most popular villains, the Nazi-like Daleks, could be given the occasional refresh. After a quarter of a century of being restricted to trundling around on level ground, a 1988 episode pulled a rabbit out of the proverbial hat

– and ratcheted up the nation's anxiety levels – by showing a Dalek effortlessly levitating up a staircase.

Other series required wholesale re-engineering. When it was first broadcast in 1977, *Top Gear* had been a mild-mannered motoring magazine featuring informative reports about car insurance or Angela Rippon commentating on road conditions as she drove from London to Birmingham. A 2002 revamp brought in a trio of new presenters, led by Jeremy Clarkson, and turned it almost overnight into a blaring carnival of amusing crashes, naughty stunts and male banter. Much to the Corporation's delight, it also turned it into one of Britain's most lucrative programme exports.

The most successful makeover of all came two years later, when BBC1 unveiled its eye-popping reinvention of ballroom dancing for the reality era. There was already a rich tradition to draw on: dance lessons had been a feature of the schedule since television's birth. In 1936, Home Counties viewers could watch the professional pairing of Pat Kilpatrick and Alex Moore dressed to the nines and hoofing their way around numbered squares on the floor of the Alexandra Palace studio. After the war, there was earnest instruction from Victor Silvester's *Television Dancing Club* – tagline: 'evening dress only' – and one of the longest-running television series in the world, *Come Dancing*. The show's first episode came live from London's Lyceum Ballroom for the 1950 final of the British Formation Dancing Trophy. Harry Roy and his band provided the music, Wally Fryer and Violet Barnes demonstrated the New Charleston.[51] *Come Dancing*'s unbending adherence to the rules of ballroom dancing would eventually make it feel dated – especially once Baz Luhrmann's 1992 hit film *Strictly Ballroom* had shown how exuberant the dance steps of the paso doble could be if performers were allowed to cast convention aside.

Given all this, it seemed either a stroke of genius or an act of madness for the BBC to attempt to build a new Saturday night ratings winner out of this raw material. Yet the opening episode of *Strictly Come Dancing* on Saturday 15 May 2004 augured well.

There were tailcoats and sequined dresses and no shortage of traditional Latin and ballroom dance steps. But all the classic ingredients of a twenty-first-century reality TV format were there too: showbiz celebrities, including in this instance the almost inevitable presence of an actor from *EastEnders*; touching journeys of personal growth from participants; audience interaction through phone-in voting; judges ready to perform their allotted pantomime-villain role; and an atmosphere of suspense while everyone waits to learn who will be knocked out. The show's reality-TV wrapping undoubtedly owed a great deal to its original producer, Richard Hopkins, who had been an instrumental figure in launching *Big Brother* before he joined the BBC. But unlike ITV's *X Factor*, *Strictly Come Dancing* took pains to exude a benign and inclusive atmosphere of escapism and nostalgia: no one was going to be intentionally humiliated, no dance would be halted by a crowing klaxon. And having the seventy-six-year-old former *Generation Show* host Bruce Forsyth as Tess Daley's co-presenter ensured that older viewers could enjoy a warm reminder of the family-friendly Saturday night television they had grown up with. Brucie's well-timed double takes to the camera were part of an old-school vaudevillian act stretching back to his days at the Windmill Theatre, but he could also attract an adoring crowd at Glastonbury. After five decades of presenting big entertainment series on both ITV and the BBC he could appeal to viewers as 'surrogate brother, boyfriend, husband, father and ultimately grandad'.[52]

Above all, *Strictly* delivered on that most basic promise of entertainment: sheer escapism. By 2015, more than five million Britons were applying for a ticket to be in the studio during the live broadcast. For the final episode of 2020, more than thirteen million people were watching at home. The dancers were the undoubted stars. But it was also thanks to an army of studio managers, musicians, stagehands, lighting engineers, builders and carpenters creating a series of sets in two minutes flat, and dozens of wardrobe assistants gluing 2,500 sequins on to a single dress by hand, that for ninety minutes every week viewers could immerse themselves in a gaudy, sparkling, austerity-free bubble.[53]

*

Not every new programme ended up a roaring success. So how could broadcasters predict the winners and losers?

The short answer was: they couldn't.

A sun-soaked version of *EastEnders* sounded like a sure-fire hit. Yet *Eldorado*, a prime-time soap set among the British migrant community in Spain and launched with a great deal of razzmatazz in July 1992, proved a disaster. It lasted exactly a year before soaring costs, uneven acting, a shortage of production staff, and ratings lower even than *Panorama*'s, forced scriptwriters to manoeuvre their star characters on to a boat and sail them towards the horizon. Nor was it easy for viewers or seasoned critics to spot the potential of a winning formula. Fewer than 1.5 million watched the first series of *The Office*. After the opening episode of *The Great British Bake Off* in 2010, the *Guardian*'s reviewer declared competitive baking 'a contradiction in terms'. 'Once you've seen one person cream butter and sugar together, haven't you seen them all?'[54]

Market logic was of little help. It asked simply that commissioning editors gave the public more of what past experience showed they wanted. If commercial instincts had been followed to the letter, broadcasters would have ended up endlessly replicating the same old stuff, again and again. In his history of British television, Joe Moran reminds us that when people are sitting in front of their screens they rarely behave like the 'carefully deliberating consumers that focus groups assume them to be'. Anticipating what viewers *really* want is 'a hazardous and unpredictable business', he concluded, precisely because they usually need to see something before making up their minds.[55] The virtue of public service broadcasting was that it could hold fast to the idea that a leap into the dark would make possible more – not fewer – of these unbidden pleasures.

Clive James had warned against theorising about television. It was, he wrote, an 'expanding labyrinth', too large, too varied, too mutable to be characterised easily. One generalisation he did offer, however, was that the BBC kept coming up with more than its share of 'prodigies'. And even if this had been a hazardous and unpredictable process, it had never been *entirely* a matter of chance. James pointed to 'a tradition of pride in work'.[56] But there was more to it than that. What linked news coverage of the Moscow coup with the swirling success of *Strictly*, and everything in between, was the BBC's deep reservoir of capital – human, technical, ethical. Programming decisions – minute by minute or year by year – were based on instincts honed by experience, and then underpinned by a working environment that allowed for experimentation, collaboration, changes of mind.

Big institutions are often portrayed as lumbering beasts, ill-fitted to the modern world. But, in the case of the BBC, it was the enormous range of its operations, its complex layering of traditions – what Charlotte Higgins called its 'noisy jumble of cultures' – which ensured that a remarkable variety of skills and interests and perspectives could be brought to bear on the creative process. There were always a few blockages clogging up the machinery. But when it was well-oiled, ideas flowed – from department to department, from factory-floor to management and back again. The Director-General, Alasdair Milne, had understood this well. Once, when asked by MPs to name those bits of the BBC that were truly 'public service', his reply had been succinct: *all* of it. If British broadcasting was an 'expanding labyrinth', it was thanks to an entire ecology, a whole machine.

15

ON THE RACK

If one thing is certain about the BBC, then it is that crisis
will always be around the corner. Its enemies are on the
hunt, constantly ...

Charlotte Higgins, 2015

In 2020, an observer of the contemporary broadcasting scene
felt compelled to make this unsettling judgement: 'So far', he
wrote, 'the twenty-first century has been desperately difficult
for the BBC. It has fallen out with government. It has got too
close to the government. It has traduced the reputations of the
innocent and given a free pass to the guilty. It has, like many
British institutions, struggled in the face of change; far too
often, it has become the story.'[1]

To which one is tempted to add: was it not ever thus?

Yet the BBC's difficulties really *do* seem to have intensified
in recent years, and perhaps especially since 2010. In the past
decade, attacks against the BBC have become more persistent,
more organised, more vitriolic – and more destructive. The
BBC has often conspired in its own misfortune: its obligation
to be publicly accountable, and the degree of scrutiny it consequently faces, has made it nervy and defensive. But it's had
good reason to be wary. Labour governments have an uneasy
relationship with the BBC – constantly disappointed, especially, with its apparent failure to compensate for the right-wing
partisanship of the British press. Conservative governments
have shown a deeper ideological distrust, sensing something

disturbingly *collectivist* about the BBC's entire demeanour and purpose. Popular feeling has generally remained on the BBC's side. But one of the changes in public life has been the emergence of a media world possessed of a voracious appetite for sharing instant judgement. It has become easier for the BBC's opponents to mobilise and shift attitudes. Slip-ups – large and small – can be seized on and amplified with intent. 'The BBC is a mortal enemy', one of Boris Johnson's future advisers, Dominic Cummings, wrote in 2004. Its 'credibility' needed to be undermined, its public funding closed down, 'its very existence ... the subject of a very intense and well-funded campaign'.[2] In short, the game was now not just to hack away from the top with the usual levers of political control; it was to make *us*, the people, slowly but surely fall out of love with our own broadcaster.

★

The BBC's first major crisis of the new century concerned the invasion of Iraq by British and American forces, and precipitated a bitter falling-out not with the Conservatives but with the Labour government of Tony Blair.

At seven minutes past six on the morning of Thursday 29 May 2003, the *Today* programme's defence correspondent, Andrew Gilligan, a journalist with a reputation for delivering scoops, offered Radio 4 listeners his latest revelation in the long-running saga of Iraq's weapons of mass destruction. The presenter, John Humphrys, provided the cue. 'The government is facing more questions this morning', Humphrys announced. 'This in particular, Andy, is Tony Blair saying, they'd be ready to go within forty-five minutes ...?' 'That's right', Gilligan replied:

> That was the central claim in his dossier which he published in September, the main ... erm ... case if you like against ... erm ... against Iraq and the main statement of the British government's belief of what it thought Iraq was up to and what we've been told by one of the more senior officials in

charge of drawing up that dossier was that ... actually the
government probably ... erm ... knew that that 45-minute
figure was wrong, even before it decided to put it in.

A few seconds later, Gilligan added this:

Downing Street, our source says, ordered a week before
publication, ordered it to be sexed up, to be made more
exciting and ordered more facts to be ... erm ... to be
discovered.[3]

Here was a BBC correspondent alleging, in effect, that to
send troops into battle the prime minister had deliberately
and consciously misled the nation. It was an incendiary claim.
Within thirty minutes Downing Street had phoned *Today* to
state bluntly that the story was '100 per cent untrue'. Under the
direction of Tony Blair's chief press officer, Alastair Campbell,
New Labour had turned instant rebuttal into a fine art. But the
unwavering certainty of this first denial was unusual. And there
was no let-up over the days and weeks that followed. As the rest
of the British media seized on Gilligan's claims, Campbell took
personal charge of the government's counter-attack. 'I find it
incredible', Campbell told the Foreign Affairs Select Committee at Westminster, 'that people can report based on one single
anonymous uncorroborated source ... that the Prime Minister,
the Cabinet, the intelligence agencies, people like myself con-
nived to persuade Parliament to send British forces into action
on a lie.' As the television cameras looked on, he pointed to a
hefty folder he had with him. 'I tell you, until the BBC acknowledge that is a lie, I will keep banging on, that correspondence
file will get thicker and they had better issue an apology pretty
quickly.' The Director-General, Greg Dyke, who had been on
holiday in Ireland when the allegations were first broadcast, now
got involved. Having received assurances about the accuracy of
Gilligan's report, he accused Campbell of 'misrepresenting our
journalism'. 'My view was straightforward', Dyke explained, 'if

the Government was going to try to bully the BBC then I was going to fight back.'[4]

There were signs in July that the row might peter out. But a shocking turn of events brought everything to a new and awful climax. After frenzied speculation in the media, Gilligan's anonymous source was revealed to be David Kelly, a British biological warfare expert who had been in Iraq as a weapons inspector for the United Nations. On Friday 18 July his body was found slumped against a tree near his Oxfordshire home. He had committed suicide. The government immediately announced an inquiry, to be led by the former Lord Chief Justice of Northern Ireland, Brian Hutton. A few days earlier, Dyke had questioned Gilligan in Television Centre, aware of the high stakes involved. 'You'd better be fucking right', the Director-General had told the reporter, before turning to his Director of News, Richard Sambrook, and his deputy, Mark Damazer, who were also present. 'He'd better be fucking right.'[5]

The Hutton Inquiry sat between the beginning of August and the end of September, and published its report four months later on Wednesday 28 January 2004. The press conference was carried live on the World Service. At the end of proceedings, its presenter Robin Lustig summed up decisively: 'Well, that's very good news for the government, and very bad news for the BBC.' Over in Broadcasting House, the Director-General had been skimming frantically through Hutton's text. Before he had even reached the closing paragraphs he flew into the next door room, where Sambrook and Damazer sat waiting. 'Well, boys', he said to them, 'we've been fucked.'[6]

Hutton's devastating conclusion was that Gilligan's central allegations had been entirely 'unfounded'. But he had gone further. 'False accusations of fact impugning the integrity of others, including politicians, should not be made by the media', he stated. The editorial system that had allowed Gilligan to say what he had said was 'defective'. The BBC's management had also been at fault for 'failing to investigate properly the Government's complaints'.[7]

Greg Dyke, who had just resigned as Director-General in the
wake of the Hutton Report, is mobbed by BBC staff outside
Television Centre in Wood Lane, London, January 2004.

The BBC's response was sudden and dramatic. Before the
day was out its Chairman, Gavyn Davies, had resigned – hoping,
perhaps, that his own departure might allow Dyke to stay.
Unfortunately for the Director-General, the BBC's Governors
happened to have one of their regular meetings scheduled that
very same evening. As Dyke later put it, 'they turned inwards,
talked to each other, and panicked'. He, too, was asked to
resign.[8]

The following morning he sat in his office and composed an
'all staff' email. 'I've sadly come to the conclusion that it will be
hard to draw a line under this whole affair while I am still here
… We need closure to protect the future of the BBC, not for you
or me but for the benefit of everyone out there.' As snow began
to fall, Dyke left Broadcasting House and drove to Television
Centre, where he was mobbed by hundreds of cheering staff. At
other BBC premises around the country, staff carrying placards
walked out. But it was too late. Back at Broadcasting House, the

BBC's new acting Chairman, the Tory peer Richard Ryder, with his new acting Director-General Mark Byford standing next to him, had already gone before the cameras to broadcast a grovelling statement to the watching world. 'On behalf of the BBC', Ryder had said, 'I have no hesitation in apologising unreservedly for our errors.'[9]

There now began what became known inside the Corporation as 'The Process', a quasi-judicial internal inquiry into what had really happened behind the scenes. There would also be the 'Neil Report', in which the BBC's former Director of News and Current Affairs, Ron Neil, would unveil new, tighter rules for the Corporation's journalists: better note-taking, greater editorial scrutiny of anonymous testimonies, speedier investigation of government complaints, more rigorous training. Dyke had wanted closure. None was in sight.

'The Process' did at least mean that one key figure Hutton had failed to call as a witness finally had the opportunity to give his side of the story. Kevin Marsh had been just a few months into his job as *Today*'s editor when Gilligan made his fateful broadcast. He did, however, have years of experience working on programmes such as *The World at One*: he knew what he had to do when he first got wind of Gilligan's 'exclusive'. He had checked it 'against what else I knew and what my own, very senior, sources were telling me'. He had recently enjoyed an off-the-record lunch with Richard Dearlove, the head of MI6, and had been told, in typically gnomic Whitehall language, that 'On any Cartesian analysis, Iraq was not the main threat'. Gilligan was relying on a single source, but the source was well-placed, and Marsh decided it rang true. He discussed with his reporter what he was going to say, asked him to write a script, and pointed out that the government would need to be offered a right of reply. As was typical with most big stories on *Today*, it was agreed that Gilligan would also do a so-called 'two-way' at the start of the programme: a live 'conversation' between him and the presenter, John Humphrys, which, though designed to sound fairly spontaneous would, in fact, have been carefully prepared to follow closely the agreed script. Hutton had claimed that the programme's editor had neither seen a script nor 'considered whether it should be approved'. Yet Marsh was adamant: proper editorial processes *had* been in place.[10]

As for the veracity of Gilligan's claim about 'sexed up' intelligence, dismissed by Hutton as 'unfounded', even that started to look steadily more convincing as other accounts emerged. Later in 2004, the Butler review showed that much of the original intelligence suggesting Iraq had weapons of mass destruction had been 'seriously flawed'. In 2016, the Chilcot Inquiry found that judgements about Iraq's capabilities had been presented with a certainty that was unjustified. By this stage many journalists had already come to believe what Marsh and the Director-General had maintained at the time: that Gilligan had been 'overwhelmingly right', and that Alastair Campbell's war of attrition against the BBC during the Kelly affair had been designed simply to shift the news agenda away from scrutinising the government's own role – part of what Kevin Marsh called 'flinging handfuls of grit into the machine'. As far as Dyke could see, his resignation as Director-General had only been necessary because of a craven capitulation by the 'very Establishment figures' placed above him in the Board of Governors. He had, he said, been fired 'by a bunch of the great and good' who 'knew absolutely nothing about the media'.[11]

There remained the nagging issue of Gilligan's own performance on 29 May 2003. The *Today* programme's editor had been in the back of a taxi on the way to work when he heard the infamous 6.07 a.m. two-way. It was, he thought, a 'dog's breakfast ... the story he'd offered, the story he'd intended to broadcast, was very well-founded' but the phrasing had been loose: 'not much of it sounded like the script I'd read before leaving for the office.' In suggesting that the government 'probably knew' that the forty-five-minute claim was wrong when it was put into the dossier, Gilligan had attributed to his source, Dr Kelly, 'inferences that were his own'. In a draft of his annual staff appraisal of Gilligan – a document later made public at the

Hutton Inquiry – Marsh would write about 'good journalism marred by flawed reporting'. What the *Today* editor was equally at pains to stress was that all this was being properly managed: reporters like Gilligan were usually kept on 'the shortest possible leash'.[12] He was therefore intensely irritated when Richard Ryder had issued his unreserved apology in response to Hutton. It was as if the BBC was owning up to serious weakness in its entire journalistic operation.

It was only to be expected that one immediate effect of the whole affair was sinking morale across the Corporation's news teams, as they saw for themselves the brutal consequences of making a mistake. It was, according to Robin Lustig, 'a dismal time to be a BBC journalist'. But what of the longer term? Over the next few years there was no shortage of outside commentators willing to speak of a chilling effect on the national broadcaster. John Kampfner summarised what would become a commonly held view when he wrote in the *New Statesman* of a BBC that was 'broken, beaten and cowed' – 'excessively risk averse … deliberately avoiding giving offence to the government and the establishment'. The man who had weathered the storm as the BBC's Director of News, Richard Sambrook, also admitted that the outer limits to the BBC's autonomy had been laid bare. When covering the failures of politicians, he explained, 'the BBC has to be very, very careful because it is in the end dependent on a political deal to exist'.[13]

Most of the BBC's own journalists took a more sanguine view. Roger Mosey, who was in charge of Television News at the time, described a self-correcting mechanism taking hold: a return to 'the right balance between journalistic enterprise and accuracy'. As for Kevin Marsh, the person who had been more closely involved in the initial reporting than anyone else, he, too, detected very little permanent change as a result of Hutton. 'BBC journalism had always been safer … It had always been more restrained, its standard of proof higher than the press. And so it continued.'[14]

Yet some of the tectonic plates *were* shifting – and with

potentially greater longer-term consequences for the Corporation's internal culture. When Marsh took over at *Today* in
December 2002, he had found, he said, a place that had been
turned 'into something close to an independent republic within
the BBC', a place with an armour-plated self-confidence in its
ability to 'set the agenda'. In 1997, one of its more maverick producers, Rod Liddle, had been put in charge. As Editor, Liddle had
wanted to bring to *Today* some of the thinking from Fleet Street.
And indeed some of the people: it was Liddle who had hired
Gilligan from the *Sunday Telegraph*. It was around this time, too,
that Marsh sensed a new mood at the top of the BBC. John Birt,
a Director-General with 'an unrivalled reputation for risk aversion', was leaving, to be replaced by the 'much less buttoned up'
Greg Dyke. And alongside this change of regime: 'The idea that
we were too cautious. That we didn't break enough stories and
weren't taking on the press as aggressively as we should.'[15]

As he had chatted to his team for the first time, Marsh discovered over-stretched producers, reporters' notes and scripts
going unchecked, correspondents allowed to broadcast from
home, stories presented at the last possible moment. Gilligan
himself also kept one foot in Fleet Street, writing articles for
the *Mail on Sunday* and the *Spectator*. Marsh's mission became
ending what he called 'the "tabloid" *Today* experiment'. And he
clearly believed that by the time the BBC was introducing the
recommendations of its post-Hutton Neil Report in 2004, the
proper balance between 'enterprise and accuracy' had already
been largely restored. But other aspects of the working environment remained unresolved. He left his post in 2006 saying that
he was 'finding the relentless negativity of "devil's advocacy"
interviewing – *Today*'s staple – as pointless as it was damaging to sensible debate and discussion'. This was nothing to do
with the Kelly affair, he claimed, but a wider, deeper problem
– one touched on by the *Financial Times* journalist John Lloyd,
who described it as 'the product of a culture, a mindset and a
practice'. Lloyd called it 'laser journalism': reporting that was
ravenous for conflict, constantly shining 'a bright and relentless

light on one spot in the chaos of detail and riot of opinion that makes up real events', when what was needed was 'journalism-in-the-round'. The cause of this failure? A 'newspaper culture' dedicated to attack – and a BBC that had come to believe that 'this was the way true journalists should behave'.[16]

It was an analysis that overlooked quite how much 'journalism-in-the-round' there still was on the BBC's airwaves, especially in its coverage of foreign affairs: on *The World Tonight*, on *File and Four*, on numerous World Service programmes, on BBC2's *Newsnight*. But it was true that in many of the Corporation's newsrooms the border between Fleet Street and the BBC was now highly porous – more porous, perhaps, than was good for the BBC's wider reputation. In 2004, some 7,000 people worked in BBC journalism. In some areas there was an 11 per cent turnover of staff every year. Many were moving back and forth between the BBC and jobs on newspapers. After leaving *Today*, Rod Liddle went on to write for the *Spectator*, where Andrew Gilligan was also quickly snapped up by its editor, Boris Johnson. Moving in the opposite direction was Andrew Neil, the former *Sunday Times* editor and arch BBC critic, who now hosted a variety of its political programmes.

The BBC had been here before. In the mid-1970s, the editor of the radio newsroom, himself an ex-Fleet Street man, boasted that broadcasters and newspaper reporters were like peas in a pod, sharing the same values and instincts. But the BBC was more than news. It had other traditions, other values, other aims. The Controller of Radio 3 at the time, Stephen Hearst, said that a gulf existed at the heart of the BBC: 'between people reared in a tradition of public service broadcasting and those whose background lay in journalism'. These were not entirely incompatible traditions. But Grace Wyndham Goldie had warned that news and current affairs could always sink the rest of the BBC 'by falling beneath standards'.[17] In the opening years of the twenty-first century, there was little sign that this gulf in values had been healed – or even fully acknowledged. And whenever the next big journalistic misstep came along – something that, on the law of averages, was bound to happen sooner or later – there would be little public interest in distinguishing between 'BBC News' and the BBC as a whole when it came to apportioning blame.

'A tsunami of filth': 'Sachsgate' and Savile

As it turned out, it was not the Corporation's journalists but its celebrity entertainers who inflicted the next lot of wounds.

One problem arose when Jonathan Ross was joined on his Radio 2 show by the comedian Russell Brand. In October 2008, they were scheduled to do a telephone interview with the seventy-eight-year-old actor Andrew Sachs, best known as the man who had played Manuel, the Spanish waiter in *Fawlty Towers*. What Radio 2 listeners ended up hearing was Ross and Brand leaving a series of voice messages on Sachs's answering machine. In one of them, Brand was trying to speak when Ross shouted 'he fucked your granddaughter'. Much giggling ensued.

It was the kind of lapse of judgement that could occasionally happen in a live broadcast. But this had been recorded two days earlier: if anyone at Radio 2 had heard it ahead of transmission they had clearly thought it acceptable. A week later, the *Mail on Sunday* drew attention to what had been going on and the complaints started flooding in. Before long, Ofcom had launched an investigation, both Brand and Radio 2's Controller, Lesley Douglas, had resigned, and Ross – reputed to be the BBC's highest-paid presenter at the time – was suspended without pay. The Corporation eventually issued a very public apology, calling the voicemail messages 'grossly offensive' and a 'serious breach of editorial standards'. It all came a little too late. The former *Daily Telegraph* editor, Charles Moore, was already denouncing it as a 'classic example of the sort of arrogance of power that organisations like the BBC get, where they think they can do what the hell they like'. How, he wondered, 'did a public-service organisation think that its highest-paid person should be a sort of foul-mouthed comedian?' His own response was to refuse to pay the licence fee until both men had left the BBC completely.[18]

Moore had been silly to see the broadcast as the result of a conscious Corporate decision. All the evidence pointed to a temporary lapse of judgement in one tiny corner of the machine. Most BBC Radio staff thought that Brand and Ross's misbehaviour was not a hanging offence. Yet they knew it was serious: Fi Glover described it as 'a whole heap of unpleasantness'; Lorna Clarke, who was working as a producer in the Radio 2 building at the time, was adamant 'it should not have happened'. Both could see that, once again, a relatively isolated incident was bringing the whole BBC into disrepute. Both noticed the effect it had. It was not just that heads rolled. 'The culture of radio changed overnight', Clarke remembers. 'Compliance' arrived with a vengeance: a rigorous process of form-filling designed to flag any programme content that was vaguely risky; checks against ethical and legal benchmarks; and the closer scrutiny of scripts and running orders, with editorial sign-offs required at every stage. 'The whole operation became really big', and staff became 'terrified of making a mistake'. Whether or not this level of anxiety fed into the programmes that listeners heard at home was harder to discern. Fi Glover claimed that as a presenter she still felt free to skate close to the edge: the burden of compliance was being 'picked up by people behind-the-scenes'. Form-filling was a pain, yes, but in the end it was less about timidity than the tighter observance of existing – and perfectly proper – editorial standards.[19]

Even the trauma of 'Sachsgate' did little to prepare the BBC for the firestorm that engulfed it four years later, when the entertainer, charity fundraiser, and former BBC presenter Jimmy Savile died.

His death, in October 2011, prompted a flurry of activity in two very different corners of the BBC. In one, tribute shows were being prepared for the Christmas TV season. In the other, investigative reporters on *Newsnight* were pulling together what promised to be a shocking exposé of the presenter's prolific history of sexually abusing children and teenagers. The following year, as newspapers starting to report the first detailed

allegations against Savile, an ITV documentary broadcast traumatic accounts from some of his victims. Many institutions
were tainted by the evidence – hospitals, children's homes,
charities, other celebrities. But it was the BBC that had built
him into a national figure, and some of the abuse had been
connected with his television and radio career. The unmasking
of Savile as a predatory paedophile was shocking enough for
a country that had trusted him as a benign if slightly eccen-
tric public figure. More shocking still was the revelation that so
many people – including, perhaps, people at the BBC – had had
their suspicions and had done nothing. *Newsnight* could have
aired many of these revelations in 2011. But its report had never
been broadcast: as the world now learned, the investigation had
been shelved – though on whose orders, exactly, remained for
the moment a mystery.

It looked awful, since the BBC appeared to be implicated
twice over: for allowing Savile to abuse people in the first place,
and for what had the whiff of a hasty cover-up when exposure
threatened to ruin its Christmas eulogies. Past and present were
murkily connected. And the question everyone asked was this:
how much had the BBC *really* known about Savile – then *and*
since? The Corporation decided that it had little choice but to
expose itself to another gruesomely public investigation.

It was the recent turn of events that caused trouble first. The
BBC asked the former ITN and Sky journalist, Nick Pollard, to
investigate why the *Newsnight* report had been dropped. While
his inquiries got underway, and staff had their hard drives seized
and emails searched, the rumour mill went into overdrive.
Newspapers busied themselves with lurid speculation about sex
offenders lurking within the BBC. MPs fired off letters full of
new allegations. The Corporation's press officers would find
themselves fielding hostile enquiries from 6.30 a.m. through to
midnight every day. Even *Panorama* got in on the action by investigating what had happened at *Newsnight*. Whether or not this
was intended to lance the boil, it felt as though the BBC was
eating itself alive. It was at this delicate point in proceedings,

on Friday 2 November, that *Newsnight* – in what looked like a belated attempt to demonstrate its own commitment to investigative journalism – broadcast the very serious allegation that a senior Conservative figure had been involved in child abuse. No one was mentioned, but in the era of social media and easy internet searches, it did not take long for people to come up with a name: the former Tory Party treasurer, Alistair McAlpine. A week later, the *Guardian* published a front-page splash showing that *Newsnight's* investigation had been based on a case of mistaken identity: McAlpine was innocent.

The timing was terrible. The BBC's Director-General, George Entwistle, was new – just weeks into the job and having to firefight on every front. He now faced a BBC Trust that was agitating for a decisive intervention. Its Chairman, the Tory Peer Chris Patten, talked ominously about 'a tsunami of filth' engulfing the Corporation. Others on the Trust argued that because News International had closed down the *News of the World* in response to the phone-hacking scandal, the BBC should axe *Newsnight*. Entwistle considered the idea, but thought it would be an extraordinary overreaction. Instead, he wanted the programme to make a full on air apology while another investigation was launched. The following morning, he went on the *Today* programme to explain the measures he was taking. Unfortunately, his interview was a car crash: the Director-General did not appear fully briefed about the latest press revelations; his own grasp of events seemed shaky. Members of the BBC's executive board promptly received an email asking them to be on standby for a conference call later in the evening. In the meantime, Patten spoke to Entwistle privately. After twenty-three years' service at the BBC – rising up the ranks from trainee to editor and finally to Controller – but just fifty-four days in the top job – Entwistle announced his resignation. 'The sadness flooded over me', Roger Mosey recalled. 'George's decency and intelligence were sorely needed by the BBC, and it was the cruellest of outcomes that someone so full of promise for the future should have been destroyed by the evils of the past.'[20]

Six weeks later Nick Pollard published the results of his investigation into *Newsnight*. After examining more than 10,000 documents and interviewing nineteen witnesses, he concluded that the decision back in 2011 to drop the report on Savile 'was flawed and the way it was taken was wrong'. Yet he also believed 'it was done in good faith. It was not done to protect the Savile tribute programmes or for any improper reason.' If there had been a mistake, it was that *Newsnight*'s editor, Peter Rippon, had set his reporters too high a bar of proof by deciding that the testimony of Savile's victims was not in itself sufficient evidence to proceed with the broadcast. There had been a missed opportunity. There had also been a great deal of chaos behind the scenes. But there had been no deliberate cover-up.[21]

As for those historic claims of abuse by Savile, the BBC had appointed the High Court judge Janet Smith to examine what exactly had happened back in the 1960s, 1970s and 1980s. When her report was finally published on 25 February 2016, it made deeply uncomfortable reading. Smith had interviewed over 380 witnesses and had heard seventy-five separate allegations of inappropriate conduct, including serious sexual assaults, associated in some way with Savile's work at the BBC – most while he had been presenting *Top of the Pops* or *Jim'll Fix It*. Relatively few incidents took place at BBC premises: Savile would usually meet his victims during the recording of a show before taking them elsewhere. But if he could 'gratify himself sexually' while on duty he would. It happened at Radio 1's offices in Egton House, at Lime Grove, at Television Centre, at the Shepherd's Bush Theatre, at regional studios in Leeds and Manchester and Glasgow. And there had been warnings that had gone unheeded. Eight separate complaints about Savile's behaviour were made at the time – five of them from the BBC's own staff. The complainants included witness C16, a sixteen-year-old girl who had gone to a recording of *Top of the Pops* with some school friends in September 1969 and was assaulted by Savile while dancing next to him on a podium. After complaining to a member of the studio floor staff, she was told she must have been mistaken: a security guard

Janet Smith presents her Report on the sexual abuse carried out
by the disgraced BBC presenter Jimmy Savile, February 2016.
Her inquiries uncovered a culture of 'reverence' for celebrities
that had allowed him to abuse victims unhindered for years.

was told to escort her off the premises and she was 'left on the
street'. In 1976, witness B8 was also assaulted at *Top of the Pops*.
When she complained to 'a man with earphones' she was told
not to worry; it was just 'Jimmy Savile mucking about'. The man
with earphones neither passed on the complaint to more senior
personnel nor recorded it in any paperwork. 'He saw what Savile
was doing as harmless fun and B8 as a nuisance.' When witness
C51, a junior BBC employee, was sexually assaulted in 1989, her
supervisor said to her 'keep your mouth shut, he is a VIP'.[22]

For Smith, the crucial issue of whether 'the BBC' had any
knowledge of these goings-on had to be judged on strictly legal
grounds. Clearly, several junior staff had been aware of what
Savile was doing. But the BBC as an institution could only be

said to have been involved in a cover-up if senior staff – heads of department or above – had known and done nothing. Awareness of 'mere gossip or rumour', Smith explained, did not count: it had to be awareness of actual misconduct or hearing an admission from Savile himself. The fact that nothing had been passed up the management line meant that there was 'no evidence that the BBC as a corporate body' had known.[23]

In this strictly legalistic sense, the BBC was off the hook. But its failings were obvious. Junior and middle-ranking staff never thought of passing on what they witnessed because 'they personally thought that such conduct was not seriously wrong'. Such attitudes, Smith pointed out, 'were not unknown in British society in the late 1960s and 1970s. It appears that they were not uncommon in the BBC.' The closest anyone in the Corporation ever came to cornering Savile had been in 1973, when rumours reached the ears of Douglas Muggeridge, the Controller of Radios 1 and 2. Muggeridge arranged for his two closest colleagues, Derek Chinnery and Doreen Davies, to ask Savile himself if there was any truth in the rumours. Savile said not, and he was believed. Muggeridge, Smith decided, had been more concerned with 'the risk of damage to the BBC's reputation' than with the welfare of victims. And there were other features of working life at the Corporation that had got in the way of unmasking Savile: a 'silo mentality' that stopped the sharing of intelligence across departments; staff on precarious short-term contracts afraid to say anything in case they were treated as troublemakers; a BBC too willing to overlook bad behaviour for 'fear of losing talent'; and a 'macho culture' with too few women in senior positions.[24]

The Corporation had had nearly four years to steady itself for Janet Smith's findings. It was poised to respond quickly. By the end of 2016, new child protection and whistle-blowing guidelines were in place, compensation had been paid out, internal procedures overhauled, staff-awareness training introduced. But the scars were deep. As with the Hutton Inquiry in 2004 and the furore surrounding Russell Brand and Jonathan Ross in

2008, the BBC's fallibility had been laid bare. It had repeatedly started out by making a sluggish and overly defensive response to complaints, only to swing dramatically to the other extreme of full-scale self-laceration. On each occasion serious mistakes had been made and individuals had paid the price with their careers. On each occasion the BBC had been subject to intense and unrelenting scrutiny, including from newspapers that had always been hostile towards it. Given the BBC's public status and immense influence, this kind of scrutiny was unavoidable. But in the fierce glare of public accountability, seemingly small decisions by not terribly senior people – a single badly worded report, a momentary lapse in taste, a failure to deliver the right message at the right time – had destabilised the entire Corporation.

Culture Wars

Janet Smith's 2016 report had largely been concerned with the past. As she took pains to point out, both the BBC and wider social attitudes had changed in the half-century since Savile's abuses first occurred. But she had also revealed aspects of the Corporation's working culture that were unsettling. The fact that the BBC had already undertaken its own 'Respect at Work Review' showed that the problem was at least being recognised internally. But reviews were one thing, change another. And it soon became clear that one long-term impact of the Savile affair was that staff who had long felt that something might be awry in their own conditions of employment were now emboldened.

The first flashpoint was over pay inequality. In 2017, the BBC was compelled to release details of every employee with a salary over £150,000. The preponderance of men in the published list was hard to miss. The BBC's China Editor, Carrie Gracie, discovered that she was earning considerably less than two of her male counterparts, the Middle East Editor, Jeremy Bowen, and the North American Editor, John Sopel. After a series of fruitless confrontations with managers, she was driven to write an open letter to the *Times* announcing that she was resigning from her post. The BBC's initial response was to wave around a report by external consultants which suggested that there was no systemic gender bias – merely more men than women occupying senior posts and more men with years of experience behind them. But already a staff pressure group called 'BBC Women' was voicing its collective support for Gracie: within a month the BBC had apologised, agreed to parity, and had offered to backdate her pay. It also promised a renewed effort to close the gender pay gap by 2020. The BBC's own Media Editor, Amol Rajan, concluded that the BBC had gone 'much further' than most other institutions both in terms of equal pay and transparency. Yet he also noted a sense of 'accumulated injustice'. 'Such is the strength of feeling', he warned, that the issue could rumble on. Which it did. Two years later, the Corporation found itself on the losing side again after another of its leading presenters, Samira Ahmed, argued successfully in an employment tribunal that while her role on the television series *Newswatch* was virtually identical to Jeremy Vine's on *Points of View*, she had been paid less than a sixth of his fee. By now another ninety claims over unequal pay were in the pipeline. It was, Carrie Gracie suggested, time for the BBC to 'stop digging'.[25]

In July 2019, another internal dispute reached the newspaper front pages after the apparent mishandling of a complaint against the *BBC Breakfast* presenter Naga Munchetty. The US President, Donald Trump, had just attacked four Democratic congresswomen of colour. Three of them had been born in the United States, the fourth had lived there since she was ten, but Trump called for them to 'go back to the totally broken and crime-infested places from which they came'. In covering the story, one of the BBC's two studio presenters, Dan Walker, asked his co-presenter how she felt on hearing Trump's remarks and whether she had experienced anything similar herself. Munchetty replied,

Every time I have been told, as a woman of colour, to go

back to where I came from, that was embedded in racism
… And I imagine a lot of people in this country will be
feeling absolutely furious that a man in that position feels
it's OK to skirt the lines with using language like that …
Anyway, I'm not here to give my opinion.

A single viewer's complaint, accusing both presenters of a
'left-wing and anti-Trump bias' and 'personal commentary on
controversial issues', led to the BBC's Complaints Unit declaring
that Munchetty had breached editorial guidelines: Trump's *comments* had been racist, but she should not have suggested that
Trump *himself* was a racist. Before long, an array of presenters
and commentators came out in public support of Munchetty,
many of them pointing out that it was her colleague – white and
male – who had prompted the discussion, yet it was only Munchetty who was being censured. With accusations now swirling
around that the BBC was failing not just women but staff from
Black or other minority backgrounds, the Director-General,
Tony Hall, was forced to intervene. Munchetty's words, he
announced, had not been 'sufficient to merit' the Complaints
Unit's original response after all.[26]

For the *Guardian*'s media editor, Jim Waterson, the saga
revealed an important generational divide: between older BBC
hands who had a more absolute approach to 'impartiality' and
a younger cohort that saw it as entirely reasonable to draw on
– indeed, refuse to stay silent about – one's own experiences
and opinions. But an even more profound social and political
divide was taking hold in Britain, with troubling implications
for the BBC. No matter how progressive the Corporation was
as an employer – and in terms of equal pay and ethnic diversity, the hard data suggested that it was indeed better than most
of its competitors – it seemed obvious to most employees that
there was still room for improvement. In-house initiatives, such
as the 50:50 Campaign, Creativity Diversity and 2021's 'Diversity
and Inclusion Plan', which focused on bringing the representation of women, disabled people, and Black and minority people,

both on-air and behind the scenes, into closer alignment with the population at large, all seemed rationally defensible and overdue, no more than a recognition of the BBC's historic duty towards serving all sections of the community. To an increasingly vocal body of critics, however, any attempt to fashion a more inclusive BBC represented merely the latest triumph of metropolitan, left-liberal values – attitudes that pulled the Corporation not closer but *further away* from what were said to be 'true' British values. As one horrified opponent complained, the BBC was turning into a place where '"sexism" and "homophobia" are deadly sins', '"Judgemental" attitudes' were no longer allowed, and it was even 'frowned upon to disapprove of unmarried mothers'.[27]

This was hardly an original line of attack. Back in 2007, the *Daily Mail*'s editor Paul Dacre had raged against the BBC for its 'cultural Marxism', a 'closed thought system' that disenfranchised millions of Britons 'who don't subscribe to the BBC's worldview' – an argument rehashed repeatedly in the pages of his own paper. Over the past decade, academic study after academic study has concluded that by most measures the BBC's news output – the area of programming that most people use to judge its political neutrality – has been, if anything, tilted slightly towards the right. A detailed survey of its coverage of immigration and Europe conducted in 2007 and 2012 showed that, under Labour, government voices had slightly more airtime than the Conservatives, while under the Conservatives, government voices dominated by a much wider margin. Another survey from 2017 showed that 70 per cent of the BBC News channel's late-night review of the front pages featured stories published in Conservative-supporting papers. Most striking of all has been the evidence for a shift over time. A Cardiff University study that looked at references in 30,000 BBC news and current affairs programmes concluded that in 2009, when Labour was in power, there had been a broad balance in references to left- and right-leaning think tanks; by 2015, when a Conservative-led coalition was in power, a clear bias was shown towards those on the right.

For critics on the left and centre, this was only to be expected, given what seemed like an unhealthily busy trade in personnel between the upper reaches of the BBC and the Conservative Party, or its allies in big business, not just through appointments to the Board of Governors or its successors, the Trust and the Executive, but among senior journalists and presenters. But it was perhaps the absorption of Fleet Street values that had been detected in the aftermath of the Gilligan affair that had had most effect. The BBC's Economics Editor Robert Peston spoke in 2014 of a culture that had since become 'completely obsessed with the agenda set by newspapers', especially the *Telegraph* and the *Mail*, with the result that it 'quite often veers in what you might call a very pro-establishment, rather right-wing direction'. Claims that the BBC was left-wing were, he said, 'bollocks really'.[28]

None of this could dissuade the organisers of a remarkable piece of reactionary agitprop theatre that was staged the following year. On Friday 20 March 2015, a man wearing a helmet and white jumpsuit clambered out of a 'tank' parked outside Broadcasting House and proceeded to brandish before the cameras a petition bearing almost one million names. He was dressed as 'The Stig', the anonymous racing driver from *Top Gear*, and the subject of his petition was the suspension of the show's main presenter, Jeremy Clarkson. Clarkson's removal from one of the BBC's most lucrative television formats had been prompted by an incident during which he reacted to being denied a steak supper after a day's filming by punching his producer, Oisin Tymon. Given the clear guidelines introduced by the BBC after Savile, suspension seemed entirely in order. But as the *Guardian*'s television writer Phil Harrison pointed out, *Top Gear* was no longer a programme about cars, or even about grown men behaving like adolescents: it was a vehicle for poking fun at joyless, prissy 'political correctness'. By going on the attack, Clarkson's defenders were offering a coded warning to the BBC, and, by extension, 'to all the people who might be characterised as representing the metropolitan liberal consensus – from the nation's emergent radical traditionalists'. The show's disgruntled fans were, 'to coin an as yet undefined phrase, Taking Back Control'.[29]

It was no coincidence that the driver of the tank that had been parked outside Broadcasting House was Harry Cole, one of the men behind the right-wing website Guido Fawkes and soon to be political correspondent for the *Mail*. A latent 'culture war' was being weaponised by an array of right-wing newspapers, websites, and pressure groups, and age-old grumbles about BBC editorial bias were getting tangled up with newer arguments about identity. Throughout 2015 and 2016, as the BBC negotiated with the government over its Charter renewal and the level of the licence fee, the *Mail*, the *Telegraph*, the *Express* and the various Murdoch papers carried out a series of frontal attacks on the BBC, accusing it of being 'grotesquely bloated', 'arrogant', or run by an 'incestuous luvvie clique'. Journalists often drew inspiration from a cluster of organisations – the TaxPayers' Alliance, the Adam Smith Institute, Newswatch – which busied themselves pumping out report after report that purported to show how expensive or biased or unpopular the national broadcaster really was. Amid this endless onslaught, the BBC's Director-General, Tony Hall was even receiving death threats.[30]

It was a fictional television character who perhaps best summed up the Corporation's dilemma. Ian Fletcher was the 'Head of Values' in a new BBC comedy series, *W1A*, which gently satirised working life inside New Broadcasting House. In the opening scene of the first episode, he voiced what sounded like a suppressed bellow of existential confusion. 'You're at the centre of something genuinely important', he intoned. 'And the really exciting thing is to think that part of my job is going to be to establish where that centre is, and exactly what it's in the middle of.' For an organisation founded on the belief that its job was to hold the ring in the middle of a national debate the approaching 'culture war' was clearly going to be disorientating.[31]

What made the BBC's task harder still was what the veteran

political journalist Peter Oborne called 'a moral emergency in British public life'. It was an emergency he traced back across half a decade, and for which he blamed two politicians in particular: Donald Trump and Boris Johnson. Both men, Oborne argued, treated truth as 'a weapon which can be reshaped, cancelled or deployed according to the needs of the moment'. There was now a blatant intention to deceive; common standards of factual accuracy on which 'people of goodwill could agree' were gone; and in the shape of Boris Johnson in particular a senior politician who 'lies and fabricates so regularly, so shamelessly and so systematically' that Oborne had never encountered anyone like him in three decades of reporting. He offered multiple examples from the 2019 general election campaign trail, ranging from Johnson's misleading claim that forty new hospitals would be built to the temporary rebranding of the Conservative Party Twitter account as the neutral-sounding '@factcheckUK' during a televised leaders' debate. The 'lies and distortions', Oborne concluded, were not just common; they were 'cynical, systematic and prepared in advance'. But worse was the collective failure of Britain's newspapers and broadcasters to challenge these deceptions. How could any voter ever make an informed political choice, Oborne asked, when it was hard to know who was telling the truth and who was not?[32]

Since the days of Reith, the BBC had generally assumed good faith on the part of those it interviewed and that impartiality therefore required no more than giving equal treatment and equal airtime to opposing views. If the self-policing code of conduct that the historian Peter Hennessy memorably described as the 'good chap' theory of government really was now breaking down as Oborne suggested then a culture change was surely needed inside the Corporation's news departments. The BBC's former Political Editor and *Today* programme presenter, Nick Robinson, once explained that his role was simply 'to report what those in power were doing and thinking'. But for Oborne, journalism had to be more than explanatory. 'We should not go into our trade to become passive mouthpieces of politicians', he wrote, for 'There is only one good reason to be a journalist: to tell the truth.' Few BBC journalists would disagree in principle that impartiality was more important than balance – that truth did not lie halfway between right and wrong. But calling out falsehoods did not come naturally to a Corporation brought up believing in the virtues of even-handedness and wanting to behave with decorum. It had got itself into difficulties before, when the *Today* programme had given airtime to climate-change deniers such as Nigel Lawson, even though the overwhelming weight of scientific opinion was against him. On that occasion Ofcom had ruled that *Today* should have made Lawson's maverick status much clearer to its listeners. But the issue of 'false balance' kept raising its head again during the drawn-out aftermath of Brexit. One of the most striking instances was in early 2019, when the host of BBC1's *Question Time*, Fiona Bruce, responded to an audience member's claim that Leave had run a 'dirty campaign' by saying that there had been 'questions over both Leave and Remain'. Strictly speaking, she was right. But it was an answer that equated the flawed economic forecasts of the Remain campaign with serious investigations into elements of the Leave campaign by the National Crime Agency. The *Question Time* incident was not exactly proof of bias, Phil Harrison decided, more a case of carelessness or confusion. Covering Brexit, he said, was like trying to balance apples and oranges: reason pitched against emotion. 'How could *any* broadcaster give equal weight to the nebulous, wildly varied, often seemingly irrational multiplicity of views (and motivations) that underpinned the arguments?'[33]

The obvious answer was: with difficulty. Yet in April 2019, when BBC1's *Politics Live* featured a debate between the economics professor Mariana Mazzucato and the controversialist Toby Young, there were worrying signs that even now not enough hard thinking had been applied to the problem. For here was one guest who had written a whole book on macroeconomics having to cross swords with another who confessed that he had only read the press release. As an example of the way in which false

balance and a contempt for expertise militated against construc-
tive, informed discussion of important issues, Harrison thought
it was 'hard to think of a more perfect illustration'.[34]

Distinctiveness

Inconsistency, hesitancy, the occasional but striking editorial
misstep: all these spelled danger to the BBC when the political
weather was choppy. Back in 2008, it had taken only a couple of
weeks after Russell Brand's and Jonathan Ross's prank phone
messages before David Cameron, then the Leader of the Opposition, put pen to paper for the *Sun* to argue about the BBC's
lack of regulation and its 'squeezing and crushing of commercial competition'.[35]

For the Corporation's enemies, it was like digging a mine
during a medieval siege: the edifice of Broadcasting House
would be more swiftly destroyed if one kept undermining its
foundations. Among the bewildering variety of techniques
deployed, the main line of attack, from which many others
flowed, has been that the twenty-first-century BBC is doing too
many things – that its size and range of activities leaves no room
for commercial operators that might otherwise thrive. Why
should the licence fee pay for Radio 1 when there are hundreds
of commercial radio stations pumping out pop music? Why
run a twenty-four-hour television news channel when there is
Sky or CNN? Why bother with *anything* when there is Netflix?
The BBC, so the argument goes, should abandon its efforts to
do everything from football and dance shows to online news
and podcasts, and concentrate on whatever the market fails to
provide – opera, say, or reporting Parliament. It is a persuasive
argument, and all too conveniently confronts the BBC with a
horrible catch-22. The more successfully the BBC competes –
by innovating, or by engaging more listeners and viewers and
online users – the more complaints there are from its competitors about its 'market impact'. Yet if its ratings drop, or it
retreats from whole areas of programming, it is attacked for

being irrelevant or too slothful to respond in a fleet-footed way to changing social trends. In short, it is caught in a pincer movement: punished for growing, punished for shrinking.

The rise of social media and streaming services such as Netflix provides a case study in the danger the BBC faces – though a lesson, too, in how the Corporation's continued agility has been grossly underestimated in recent years.

At first glance, the figures seem daunting. In 2018, Ofcom showed that sixteen- to thirty-four-year-olds, the 'digital natives' who would normally be expected to make up the next generation of dedicated listeners and viewers, were consuming less than half as much BBC output as the national average. Back in 2014 the BBC's own researchers tracked a fourteen-year-old's computer activity from the end of the school day until bedtime. They followed his clicks and scrolls as he checked out Facebook, watched football on YouTube, Skyped friends, and used Wikipedia for his homework. What he did not do at any point was access BBC material. Other evidence has been more encouraging: older teenagers still use the BBC more than younger ones, and although the current generation are spending fewer hours listening to Radio 1 than their parents, the overall numbers tuning in have been rising recently. Even so, the BBC appears to have been shrinking fast in the global online league table. At the turn of the century, it was the same size as Apple; by 2014 Apple was already twenty times bigger. In the same period, Sky grew from being roughly the same size to twice as big. As for Netflix, the number of its users in the UK overtook those for the BBC iPlayer in the summer of 2019. 'Online,' Charlotte Higgins points out, 'our lives, and our routes to BBC material, increasingly pass through the great ecosystems built by American conglomerates.'[36]

The situation, though, is not yet terminal. Take Radio 1. For the past few years it has been hyperactively diversifying, scattering its output as widely as possible rather than keeping it tethered to the old FM dial. In March 2006, it created its own YouTube channel: as of June 2021 it had 7.3 million subscribers, making it 'the most subscribed to Radio station on YouTube'. Here, 'users' – they are no longer 'listeners' in the traditional sense – can watch videos of performances, interviews, curated playlists, and mini-documentaries. The station is reaching out to teenagers in the multimedia environment they already inhabit: in an echo of the Reithian mission to 'inform, educate and entertain', the strategy now is to 'listen, watch, share'. As for iPlayer, the BBC has been busy making it more like Netflix, providing viewers with a much richer back catalogue of old TV series so the public appetite for box-set binge-viewing can be satisfied. The irony is that the BBC could have done this five years *before* Netflix had even been launched if it had been allowed to at the time. Back in 2007, its 'Project Kangaroo', bringing together the BBC, ITV, and Channel 4 in an all-singing, all-dancing UK-based free-at-the-point-of-delivery video on demand service, had been in the advanced stage of development and was only prevented from coming into being when it was blocked by the Competition Commission after intensive lobbying from commercial operators such as Sky and Virgin Media. Then and since, the BBC has proved its ability to be an 'early mover' with new technologies. But successive governments have demanded that *any* new BBC proposal goes through some kind of 'Public Interest Test' to see whether or not there is the slightest risk of it harming the commercial interests of rival companies. Whether a new service from the BBC might be of direct and immediate benefit to the public is deemed to be of secondary importance.[37]

What might happen if, instead of being constrained, the BBC was actually allowed to *expand*? Thanks to series such as *Strictly Come Dancing*, the UK is already the biggest exporter of television formats in the world, and thanks to series such as *Doctor Who*, it is second only to the United States in the international trade in recorded programmes. The BBC itself remains the world's largest news-gathering operation, and BBC Radio the world's largest commissioner of original drama. Yet the hard evidence suggests that far from squeezing rivals out of existence, its large footprint creates a net gain. In 2021 a wide-ranging economic study argued that the BBC should be seen as a catalyst or 'market shaper'. It is, the report suggested, 'by definition a creative institution' with the potential to be an 'investor of first resort'. When new markets emerge, it is often the one organisation able to take on the risks involved, not just by developing new technology but by trying out new writers, performers, formats. It stimulates a 'virtuous circle' from which the whole sector benefits. The impact of all this has even been quantified. In March 2021, economists calculated that every £1 spent in the UK by the BBC generated activity worth £2.63 in the wider economy; every new job at the BBC created another 1.7 outside.[38]

The logical conclusion is that the bigger the scale and reach of the BBC, the better. But the aim of the Corporation's critics remains resolutely to make it smaller – and, they hope, a *lot* smaller. One of their most powerful means of achieving this has been to encourage the idea that the BBC should only broadcast programmes that are 'distinctive'. The term is slippery. But essentially it is a rhetorical rebranding of the old 'market failure' argument: asking the BBC to withdraw gracefully from making popular programmes because the commercial sector will provide. In 2015 the term was embraced enthusiastically by the newly elected Conservative government led by David Cameron. The need for the Corporation to be smaller, narrower and more 'distinctive' was the dominant theme in his government's Green Paper later that year and in a follow-up report in 2016. During the negotiations over Charter renewal which, conveniently, were also taking place at this time, the Culture Secretary John Whittingdale spoke of how 'pointless and wasteful' it was for the BBC to be 'competing with – and potentially crowding out – other providers'. Radio 4 made sense, his thinking went; but the public service argument for making hits like *Strictly Come Dancing* was 'debatable'. 'The one thing in my view the BBC should not be thinking about is ratings', Whittingdale said emphatically.[39]

The implications for the BBC were ominous – and deliberately so. In a scathing attack on 'distinctiveness' as the latest form of 'media bullshit', the comedian David Mitchell suggested that 'these ideas have not been arrived at in order to improve the BBC, but specifically to make it do less well'. The government, he said, 'doesn't advocate highbrow content *despite* the fact that it might not be popular, but *because* of it'. The strategy was clear. 'An overt challenge to the corporation's existence remains politically unfeasible – the public would miss it too much. The first step, then, is to turn it into something that fewer people would miss – and eventually, over time, to make it so distinctive that hardly anyone likes it at all.'[40]

The BBC was alert to this danger. In April 2016, it published its own report, 'A Distinctive BBC'. It pointed out how distinctive Radio 1 and Radio 2 already were compared to other commercial stations. This was not just because they had more news and documentaries: around 90 per cent of the songs on Radios 1 and 2 were also not being played on any other station. A sample of four commercial rivals showed that on average they each played a rather modest total of 1,857 different songs a year: Radio 1 played 13,729; for Radio 2 the figure was 21,329. Back in 1982, the report pointed out, BBC1's peak-time schedule included a lot of expensively acquired US series, like *Starsky & Hutch*, *The Dukes of Hazzard*, *Dallas*, *Kojak* and *The Rockford Files*: in 2016, in contrast to its rivals, there were none. The key message, however, was this: that as well as producing 'some of the very best programmes and services in the world', the BBC's commitment to universality meant 'reaching everyone with good things' – things not just of public value but 'personal value', and things that remained accessible regardless of wealth, age, background or location. In other words, this broader commitment to programme *range* and social *reach* was where the BBC's 'distinctiveness' lay, not in individual programmes.[41]

It was a robust response, entirely consistent with age-old Reithian principles. But there was no guarantee that this more capacious definition of distinctiveness would be adopted by Ofcom when the new Charter gave it responsibility for regulating the BBC in 2017 – the first time in the Corporation's history that it would be regulated by an external body. In fact, Ofcom simply aped the government line in promising 'a particular focus on distinctiveness'. The latest phrase in David Mitchell's lexicon of 'media bullshit' was hard-wired into official policy.[42]

Even now, the gravest threat lay elsewhere. For the most lethal weapon in any government's armoury remained its ability to set the level of the licence fee – and slash the BBC's spending power. In 2010, the newly appointed Conservative Chancellor George Osborne froze it for six years. At the same time, the BBC was asked to take on the cost of the Welsh language TV channel S4C and the World Service, which had previously been funded by the Foreign Office. The 2015 licence-fee settlement was worse. Back in November 1999, the Labour Chancellor Gordon Brown had announced that every household with one or more members aged seventy-five or over, regardless of household size or income, would no longer have to pay for a licence – and since this was a government welfare policy, that the government would cover the resulting shortfall in the BBC's income. In 2015, George Osborne announced that this funding would be phased out and then withdrawn completely by 2020. It left the BBC with a horrible dilemma: either it picked up the entire bill for a welfare benefit initiated by the state – a bill that by 2019 stood at £745 million, roughly a fifth of the BBC's income – or it would have to end the scheme altogether.[43] Having tied its hands, the government left the BBC to face the consequences. It had to choose between upsetting millions of licence-fee payers by taking a scythe to some of their favourite programmes, even whole channels, or upsetting millions of pensioners by removing a benefit to which they had become accustomed.

Either way, a piecemeal and relentless shrinkage in the BBC's range of activities was unavoidable. Between 2010 and 2019, and adjusted for inflation, public funding of its domestic services was cut by a staggering 30 per cent.[44] Unless it acted fast, the already enormous cost of free licences for the over-seventy-fives would also keep rising. In 2019, the BBC opted for compromise: it would

keep covering the cost of free licences for anyone on means-
tested pension credit and have to ask everyone else – the majority
– to start paying again. By this stage, painful economies had been
made on several fronts: shifting BBC3 online, losing *The Great
British Bake Off* to Channel 4 after failing to meet the higher price
its independent production company demanded, cutting staff
and news programmes in Scotland, Wales and Northern Ireland
and across English local radio and regional TV, axing the Victoria
Derbyshire show and the politics programme *This Week*, reducing the amount of drama on Radio 4 and the number of filmed
reports on *Newsnight*, ending original programming on BBC4,
and closing a whole host of languages on the World Service.

Even cuts on this scale were not enough to satisfy the appetite
among those on the political right for a radically smaller BBC. In
2020, the government launched a public consultation on whether
non-payment of the licence fee should remain a criminal offence.
It was a nod and a wink towards anyone contemplating evasion:
'decriminalisation' now became a dog-whistle cause to an army
of social media culture warriors who shared stories of individuals
taken to court and threatened with jail after struggling to pay the
fee and for whom the BBC was just another mainstream media
'fake news' outlet. By June, a Twitter campaign with the hashtag
#DefundTheBBC was up and running, apparently started by an
eighteen-year-old Tory activist who described himself as 'just a
student' but also happened to receive co-ordinated coverage in
the press and tens of thousands of pounds of funding. BBC insiders calculated that if the non-payment plan were to succeed the
Corporation would end up somewhere between £200 million
and £1 billion poorer – 'as close as it gets to oblivion', in the
words of one senior editor. The government's announcement in
January 2021 that, purely for practical reasons, it would not in fact
be pressing ahead with decriminalisation offered little comfort.
The Culture Secretary, Oliver Dowden, stated baldly that it
remained under 'active consideration'. It was a threat that could
be dangled menacingly over the BBC throughout the period it
was negotiating its next funding agreement.[45]

Endgame?

Dowden had taken the opportunity of his 2021 announcement to hint darkly at the prospect of 'alternative schemes'. There was now the real prospect that this would be the last licence-fee settlement the BBC would ever receive.

If it were really to be phased out or abandoned altogether, would it mean the end of the BBC as we know it – a *coup de grâce*, delivered with untimely poor taste just as the Corporation reached its centenary?

Some of the BBC's own supporters have accepted the idea of a switch to, say, a household levy or an earmarked tax – options that would maintain the BBC as a well-resourced, universal service. But for those wanting the BBC to *shrink* in size and influence, a subscription model is more appealing: it means that only those who actively wanted BBC programmes would pay for them. The practical objection is obvious. Whenever lots of people contribute to something everyone gets more for less: in 2021 the licence fee provided the BBC with enough money to run nine national TV channels, fifty-six radio stations, the BBC website, iPlayer, BBC Sounds, the World Service, as well as several orchestras and online services such as Bitesize, News, Sport and Weather – all while costing each individual no more than 43p a day, or considerably less than the price of a pint of beer a week.[46] In a subscription system, the number opting to pay would be lower – perhaps a lot lower. Supporters of the idea might imagine a premium service of high-quality drama, arts programmes or documentaries – something, perhaps, a little bit like BBC4 or Radio 4. But achieving this would require a subscription far in excess of the current licence fee.

The bigger objection to subscription, though, is ethical. And it is rooted in our understanding of the BBC's history. For David Elstein, a long-standing advocate of subscription, the licence fee has always been just a mechanism. It has, he says, 'no moral significance'.[47] Yet Reith saw it as a passport to equality, a means of ensuring that no one would get a better BBC simply because they could afford to pay more. Whatever the precise mechanics of collecting the money, the fact that it was universally paid for and that the services it funded were then universally accessible has been fundamental to the BBC's identity from the beginning. Indeed, to think of payment as a purely personal transaction to access a 'commodity' for oneself is to misunderstand why the BBC exists in the first place. It has always been about more than satisfying individual desires. It has been about contributing to a reservoir of shared knowledge or collective experience – and about securing benefits for society as a whole. It assumes not just that we have personal tastes and opinions, but that we are capable of transcending them. It is, and always has been, about spreading Matthew Arnold's sweetness and light.

In public service broadcasting, it is the word 'public' that matters most. For the BBC, it is not an inert 'mass' or some nameless 'target demographic', but something dynamic. It involves treating viewers and listeners as living beings, in a relationship with each other, capable of growth and development – and it assumes that on the whole this relationship, this growth and development, is a good, even at times a *joyous* thing. The television writer and producer Armando Iannucci has spoken affectionately of what it meant to him when he was growing up in the 1970s and 1980s. He would watch *Monty Python*, a *Horizon* documentary on space flight, *Morecambe and Wise* and Bruce Forsyth's *Generation Game*, without anyone telling him that 'only one type of show was for me and not the other'. It was, he said, a kind of broadcasting that loudly proclaimed 'that everything, the whole world of knowledge and creativity is on offer, is for you, all of you'.[48]

The standard riposte to this heart-warming vision is to say 'that was then, this is now': that in the era of Netflix and YouTube, listeners and viewers are just not finding the BBC useful any more. This vision of a silent majority voting with their feet has been relentlessly promoted by the Corporation's critics. But the refuseniks have been found out. In 2015, a sample of households that claimed the licence fee to be poor value for money agreed to be deprived of *all* BBC services in return for a refund. By the second week of the experiment, two-thirds had changed their minds. They said they had not realised radio and online were covered by the licence fee; the BBC had been a bigger part of their daily routines than they had thought; they had felt detached from national life. And they were not alone. In 2020, it was still the case that in any given week, over 91 per cent of UK households were using one BBC service or another. In the rest of the world, a further 468 million were watching or listening – a steadily rising number.[49]

There are moments, too, when large numbers of us still cleave to the BBC to savour something together: the 2012 London Olympics, a royal wedding, the finale of a hit drama like *Line of Duty*, Saturday nights for *Strictly*. In 2020 it was Covid-19. The pandemic brought not just a running news story about a public health emergency and government incompetence, but the closure of schools, cinemas, pubs and gyms – an entire nation in lockdown at home. In the thirst for information and distraction people logged on to social media and took out subscriptions to Netflix. But they also turned to the national broadcaster. As the first social distancing measures were introduced in the middle of March, the proportion of households using the BBC jumped from 91 to 94 per cent and BBC News Online was accessed eighty-one million times. Over the following months, viewers could see daily press conferences from Downing Street, or, if they wanted to find out what was really happening, watch the BBC's health correspondent Fergus Walsh deliver a series of distressing but sensitively handled daily updates on the crisis inside Britain's hospitals. When the BBC's local radio stations launched a campaign for anyone struggling, over a million called their helpline. When theatres shut their doors, the BBC broadcast stage plays that had faced cancellation. For children at home struggling to keep their schoolwork going, the Corporation provided its largest ever package of educational programmes in the form of Bitesize Daily.[50]

Since it involved barely dressed strangers pressing their bodies together for months on end, the one programme that

The comedian Bill Bailey and his professional dance partner Oti Mabuse, winning the 2020 series of *Strictly Come Dancing*. In 2015, the Conservative Secretary of State for Culture, John Whittingdale, had complained that it was 'pointless and wasteful' for the BBC to be making such programmes.

seemed least likely to survive pandemic conditions was *Strictly Come Dancing*. But a way through was eventually found. With studio audiences banished, social bubbles for performers and crew, and the clever use of virtual set designs, the series began, a little later than usual, in October. The final episode, on Saturday 19 December, started just minutes after Boris Johnson had appeared on TV to announce a forbidding set of last-minute Covid restrictions for the holiday period. In that moment, the show appeared to judge the national mood well. Craig Revel Horwood announced to everyone watching that to compensate for the sudden cancellation of Christmas, he would offer only positive feedback. A spirit of mutual support spread throughout the rest of the show. As Bill Bailey and Oti Mabuse twirled towards victory, the atmosphere was celebratory but touchingly fragile. 'Saturday nights have been a wilderness in 2020, and collective experiences have been almost non-existent', one of the next day's newspaper reviews explained. 'We all desperately needed something to rally around. We needed joy. That's what *Strictly Come Dancing* was designed to give us. And against all odds, thank God, it delivered.'[51]

*

There was much talk in pandemic Britain of the 'Blitz spirit'. It was a strained metaphor, as misleading in 2020 as it was in 1940. But when it comes to the BBC, we *can* still hear the echoes of a twentieth century that shaped – and reshaped – its fundamental character.

In 1922, John Reith, Cecil Lewis, Arthur Burrows and the small group of men and women they gathered around them, had set out to redeem a world still shadowed by the Great War. They had gazed in wonder at the limitless ether and grabbed hold of a communication technology that they realised could be – and therefore *should* be – placed in the service of society. Their extraordinary achievement was to begin a decades-long process of working out how exactly this should be done: who should speak on air, what they should speak about, the image of Britain that was being presented to the world. For an organisation paid for by the public yet lodged right at the centre of the country's political life, there were few easy answers to such questions: the BBC's failures have been just as much a part of its story as its successes. The Corporation has been increasingly circumscribed by a superstructure of guidelines, regulation and political interference. It has faced competition and technological upheaval and a whirlwind of changing tastes. Sometimes, it has forgotten its own heritage and traditions, been too timid, too defensive, too convinced of its own good judgement. Yet the day-to-day work of making programmes has by and large remained in the hands of thoughtful, fallible human beings. If anything guides them in their labours it is not – or at least, not *yet* – some Mosaic law handed down from on high. It is an ethos that lurks deep – sometimes only half-remembered – in their collective psyche: that foundational injunction to bring 'the best of everything into the greatest number of homes'. Ten years after Reith wrote those words, Hilda Matheson insisted that what still distinguished public service broadcasting from other kinds was its determination to nurture our capacity to 'think, feel and understand'. Sixty-five years on, the Deputy Director of BBC Television, David Docherty, put it even more boldly: that, in the end what marked out the BBC was not its elevated national status but that it was 'on the side of the people: *all* the people'.[52]

How can reality possibly match a sentiment as noble as this? Perhaps we just have to be glad that it is still being expressed at all – that, whatever its current failings, the BBC still has a *conscience*, still has *us* in mind. And when its political enemies are circling with such murderous intent, the crucial question we should ask ourselves is surely this: will the people – *all* the people – return the favour and stand on the side of the BBC?

POSTSCRIPT

The Beeb is a great institution, always to be defended
against its enemies, which include itself.

Clive James, television critic and poet

In January 2021, the BBC entered its hundredth year. A moment
of celebration approached, and it would have been tempting to
imagine that the Corporation was entering calmer waters at last.

There *were* encouraging signs. Those huge spending cuts
seemed to be on target. Television, radio and online were still
responding well to the pandemic. A new Director-General was
installed at Broadcasting House, while Boris Johnson's controversial adviser and arch BBC critic, Dominic Cummings, had
left his job. The government seemed to be distracted by bigger
issues – the continuing battle against Covid-19, the fall-out from
Brexit, a crisis in social care, redecorating Downing Street. And
the BBC was stacking up an impressive list of series hotly tipped
for the coming awards season, including *Strictly Come Dancing*,
This Country, *Inside No. 9*, and two of the previous year's standout
dramas, Michaela Coel's *I May Destroy You* and Steve McQueen's
Small Axe. Meanwhile, after a shaky start, the BBC Sounds app
was clocking up well over a billion 'plays', thanks to hit series
such as *Grounded with Louis Theroux* and *That Peter Crouch Podcast*.
The BBC's news website, growing by 43 per cent year-on-year,
was still the biggest English-language online outlet in the world.

Behind the scenes, though, new crises were already brewing.
And they all had an ominously familiar feel about them.

A few weeks before Christmas, the BBC had been cornered into launching another investigation into past misdemeanours. The approaching twenty-fifth anniversary of *Panorama*'s 1995 interview with Diana, Princess of Wales, had prompted renewed questions over how the BBC's reporter, Martin Bashir, had obtained his world-famous scoop. On the night, twenty-three million Britons had watched as Diana spoke candidly on camera about her husband's infidelity – and uttered that memorable line, 'there were three of us in this marriage, so it was a bit crowded'. The interview was a sensation and secured for Bashir a lucrative twenty-year career as a star reporter on ITV and several American television networks.

Now, a quarter of a century on, the *Daily Mail* and Channel 4 were both reporting old and half-forgotten allegations that Bashir had used fake bank statements to win the Spencer family's trust and secure his interview. The bank statements had appeared to show that staff in the Princess's entourage were selling stories. But a graphic designer employed by the BBC at the time had since revealed that they were mock-ups that he had been ordered to make by Bashir. Diana's brother, Charles Spencer, was now on the warpath, demanding a full apology from the BBC for its 'sheer dishonesty'. 'If it were not for me seeing these statements, I would not have introduced Bashir to my sister', he wrote in an open letter to the new Director-General, Tim Davie. A formal apology for the twenty-five-year-old misdemeanour would normally have closed the matter. But there were horrid complications that made this impossible. Though Bashir had left BBC News in 1999, he had been re-employed in 2016 as its religious affairs correspondent, and later promoted to Editor, Religion – a post that, in British establishment terms, has been described as 'just one step down from the Archbishop of Canterbury'. He was, in other words, still very much the BBC's problem. The timing of the latest allegations was especially awkward because Bashir was seriously unwell after contracting Covid-19, and therefore unable to be questioned. Even more embarrassing for the BBC, a handful of people at the Corporation had actually known about the fake bank statements back in 1996: Bashir had even been investigated over them. As a result of those investigations, Matt Wiessler, the graphic designer involved, had been cast adrift by the BBC while Bashir stayed in post. The head of News at the time, Tony Hall, had justified this leniency on the basis of a handwritten note from Diana in which she said that the forged bank statements had played no role in persuading her to do the interview. But there were still questions to answer over why the 1996 investigation had been kept quiet for so long and why, despite that investigation, despite the fake documents, and despite a reputation in the industry for securing other interviews by dubious means, Bashir had still been given a plum job.[1]

With Charles Spencer accusing the BBC of a 'whitewash', the new Director-General appeared to have no option but to commission a fresh and independent inquiry. In November 2020, the former Supreme Court Justice, John Dyson, was appointed. As had happened many times before, a *Panorama* team also swung into action to investigate the Corporation's previous failings. When the Dyson Report was published on Thursday 20 May 2021, the only good news for the BBC was its finding that by 1995 Diana was probably willing and ready to give a television interview to pretty well any respectable reporter, faked bank statements or not. Otherwise, it was grim reading all round. Dyson confirmed that by using false statements to gain Charles Spencer's trust Bashir had indeed been in 'serious breach' of the BBC's guidelines on straight dealing. In giving Bashir the benefit of the doubt, and in not speaking to Spencer, the BBC's 1996 internal inquiry had been 'flawed and woefully ineffective'. The BBC had also been evasive in response to newspaper enquiries at the time, covering up in its press logs 'such facts as it had been able to establish about how Mr Bashir secured the interview'. The BBC accepted the report in full, issued another apology, and handed back every award the original *Panorama* interview had won.[2]

This was not quite the end of the story, however. The Corporation boasted of its high standards of integrity and transparency. The fact that it had been evasive and that Bashir had been re-employed seemed to suggest broader failings in the News department. Within a month of the Dyson Report, another hurried internal inquiry and *Panorama*'s own investigation had uncovered more unpalatable details from 2016. It seemed that Bashir had got the religious affairs correspondent job after dazzling the head of news and current affairs, James Harding, with his knowledge of Pauline doctrine. Remarkably, he had not been asked about the Diana interview or his record at ITV. The innocent explanation was that 'none of those involved in rehiring Bashir had knowledge of the deceitful methods he had used'. But since Bashir's transgressions had first been reported back in 1996 this raised the question of why Tony Hall – who certainly knew about Bashir's past and was Director-General by 2016 – had not warned the panel about it. Strictly speaking, Hall's lack of involvement was admirable proof that there had been no undue interference from above over Bashir's appointment: the decision was taken by BBC News alone. Yet Harding could have approached Hall to discuss the 1996 investigation and had not done so.[3]

By now, even the BBC's most committed supporters were unnerved. One of Bashir's former BBC News colleagues tried his best to lower the temperature by arguing that after the phone-hacking scandal that had engulfed News International, the missing weapons of mass destruction in Iraq, and a tidal wave of fake news, there had been a wider break down in trust, and it was this breakdown that had led to an old story being blown out of all proportion. 'There is also, perhaps, an anti-BBC agenda at play', he suggested.[4] In a very public tirade delivered while he was hosting *Have I Got News for You* the comedian David Mitchell put the blame much closer to home. 'The thing which makes people love the BBC', he had seethed, 'is not the ruddy news':

The news is a boring programme – we all know it. And in their desperate attempts to make the news watchable,

they stoop to tabloid tactics, and that is going to destroy a
Corporation that is loved for the drama and comedy and
documentaries that it has produced for decades. And the
Tories will cheerfully get rid of that, and use this bullshit
as an excuse, and Martin Bashir may have unwittingly been
the executioner of the BBC.[5]

In fact, the affair was already proving a gift to the BBC's
critics. Immediately after the publication of the Dyson Report,
Robin Aitken claimed in the *Spectator* that this was 'the worst
day in the Corporation's 100 years', revealing, as it did, 'a culture
of corporate corruption'. 'Wholesale, radical and urgent reform
of the BBC is now essential if it is to survive', he concluded. 'As
presently constituted the BBC is virtually unaccountable. That
has to change.'[6] It's been said that under Boris Johnson one reads
the *Spectator* today to find out what the Tory government will
be saying tomorrow. So it came as no surprise that less than
twenty-four hours after Aitken's article had been published, the
Secretary of State for Culture, Oliver Dowden, was in the *Times*
calling for 'cultural change' across the BBC. Its leaders were
guilty of 'groupthink', he argued. It needed to provide more
'distinctively British programmes' so that it was in tune with 'all
parts of the nation it serves'. Dowden's call for a more narrow-
minded nationalism on air was a well-worn Conservative trope.
But in the summer of 2021, he had timing on his side, for as the
Home Secretary Priti Patel warned, the BBC happened to be
facing a 'very, very significant moment' in its life.[7]
    It wasn't just that the next licence fee was still under consid-
eration. It was that Dowden had also spent the tail end of 2020
setting up a ten-strong panel 'to help shape the future of public
service broadcasting'. Its hand-picked members, which included
former executives from Facebook, Sky, ITN, British Telecom and
Channel 4 – but no one from the BBC – were asked to advise ministers 'whether public service broadcasting remains relevant'.
Among the other panellists was Robbie Gibb, a former head of
the Corporation's Westminster politics programmes who had

also been Theresa May's director of communications and had worked closely with Andrew Neil on setting up the right-wing television channel GB News. Since April 2021, Gibb had gained even more influence over his old employer after Downing Street appointed him as a non-executive director of the BBC Board. His arrival, so soon after the appointment of the ex-Goldman Sachs banker and Tory donor Richard Sharp as Chairman, and Tim Davie, who had been an active Conservative Party member in the 1990s, as Director-General, gave every impression of solid-ifying a right-of-centre dominance at the top of the Corporation that had not been seen since the 1980s. The usual self-denying ordinance, about leaving one's personal politics 'at the door' when joining the BBC, was still in place. It could also be argued that having senior figures viewed by the government as not being intrinsically hostile could be strategically advantageous for the Corporation. But subtle political interference was always the risk, and in this respect the omens in 2021 were often unprom-ising. In July, when the BBC was in the middle of appointing someone to oversee its news channels, and Jess Brammar, the former deputy editor of *Newsnight* and editor of HuffPost UK, appeared to be the front runner, it was reported that Gibb had texted the BBC's Director of News and Current Affairs, saying that she 'cannot make this appointment'. He apparently added that if Brammar were to be appointed, the government's 'fragile trust in the BBC will be shattered'. The BBC explained valiantly that 'as a general principle, board members are able to discuss issues with other board members or senior executives'. Yet anyone familiar with the role of the Governors in the sacking of Alasdair Milne back in 1987 would have spotted the potential dangers. The following day, the deputy leader of the Labour Party, Angela Rayner, called for Gibb to resign, adding that 'if he won't resign he should be sacked'. Rayner was not alone in noting that one of the duties of non-executive directors on the Corporation's board was supposed to involve 'upholding and protecting the independence of the BBC'.[8]

By midsummer, almost all the usual torments that had been

inflicted on the BBC over recent years appeared to be piling up, one on top of the other – proof, if yet more proof were needed, of Charlotte Higgins's characterisation of the BBC as an institution having 'crisis in its bones'. A self-inflicted row over editorial failures in News, the press baying for blood, a vague atmosphere of political interference, the tantalising opportunities for a viscerally hostile government to overreact: the only threat that seemed to be in temporary abeyance was the pressure from commercial rivals to hack away at the Corporation's range of programme output. But then, on Friday 23 July, the Tokyo Olympics began, and the British television audience was suddenly made aware of what life with a severely diminished BBC looked like. In 2012 and 2016 the BBC had offered dozens of free live streams for the London and Rio Olympics, ensuring that almost every sport and every competition could be watched at the press of a button. This time the International Olympic Committee had sold all the European television rights for Tokyo to the commercial US company Discovery, putting the vast majority of coverage behind a paywall and restricting the Corporation to just two live streams at any one moment. The deal had been struck with little public fanfare back in 2016, but its full implications only became apparent once the Games were underway. Outraged British viewers complained to the BBC in their thousands. But the stark reality was that with a declining share of income from the licence fee, it had been impossible for the Corporation to offer anything like the £920 million fee paid by the Americans. The BBC's chances for future Olympic Games looked no more promising.[9]

*

Might the BBC's hundredth year witness the first stirrings of an organised fightback on behalf of the BBC?

Lost amid the whirlwind of controversy surrounding Bashir was the launch of a pressure group called 'The British Broadcasting Challenge'. On 20 May 2021, the very same day the

Dyson Report was published, it wrote an open letter to Oliver Dowden, signed by 120 public figures, including journalists, actors, writers, musicians, film-makers and academics, calling for 'an open and transparent debate' on the 'severe threat' facing public service broadcasting. Dowden's advisory panel, they pointed out, was meeting in secret with no public record of its agenda, discussions or recommendations – and the government's short-sighted political and financial attacks needed to stop. Britain could count itself lucky in having created a system characterised by public ownership, enlightened funding, and institutional independence. Its core value was that it was 'For Us, By Us, About Us'. And in a post-Brexit, post-Covid world of misinformation and weaponised opinion, it was being diminished when it was needed most. 'It's time to look at what we have and construct a shared vision for making it better.'[10]

One can only hope that the British Broadcasting Challenge succeeds in its campaign. But when even the most supportive newspapers refer to its signatories as 'cultural grandees', it is a reminder that high-level lobbying is only one half of the pincer movement that might now be required. If the BBC really is 'For Us, By Us, About Us', the government's animosity needs to be met, too, by a wider, fiercer show of public outrage. In short, there needs to be an outbreak of people power. As yet, the signs of this happening are few and far between. But *something* is perhaps starting to shift in popular sentiment.[11]

My home town, Lewes, is famous for its November Bonfire celebrations, the largest – and by some accounts the most rumbustious – in Britain. Once a year this respectable English county town becomes a carnival of burning crosses and effigies. In the evening darkness, torchlit processions wind through the narrow streets accompanied by drumbeats and firecrackers exploding while the air thickens with the smell of tar and paraffin. Members of the seven different Bonfire 'societies' wear the striped tops of eighteenth-century Sussex smugglers, or dress as First World War officers, women suffragists, monks, Vikings, Tudor courtesans, colonial officers in their pith helmets, celebrants of the

Mexican Day of the Dead, Native Americans, Zulu warriors. As papier-mâché effigies of Pope Paul V, Guy Fawkes, and assorted contemporary figures of ridicule – Donald Trump, Kim Jong-un, Jacob Rees-Mogg – are trundled over the cobbles on their 'tabs', crowds of locals and visiting tourists packed on to the narrow pavements respond with enthusiastic shouts of 'burn him, burn him!' The writer David Barnes has described Lewes Bonfire as a 'confusing jumble of history and culture'. It celebrates the victories of the Establishment and Empire over the treasonous rebel but 'at the same time it steals the rebels' clothes, takes a large part of its energy from the desire to light the gunpowder fuse, to burn down the house.'[12]

The pandemic has put paid to Bonfire recently. But the last time it was held I made my way to the High Street to watch the spectacle unfold for myself. I had just passed the house where Asa Briggs lived while completing his monumental five-volume history of the BBC when I turned a corner and suddenly glimpsed one of the tabs being wheeled along by 'Borough' Bonfire Society. It was an unexpected sight: instead of the usual politician, an outsized pilot flying a Lancaster Bomber. He was dropping TV sets, like bombs, on to the crumpled bonnet of a licence-detector van below. The idea, one of the effigy's makers later told me, was to declare open opposition to the ending of free TV licences for the over-seventy-fives. 'We had a lot of support and positive feedback from it', he explained.

Later that night the poor old licence-detector van had arrived at its final resting point. There, along with all the other effigies, it was set alight while people gathered round to watch. I'd been brooding darkly all evening as to why the chosen victim had not been George Osborne, the man actually responsible for withdrawing government funding for the over-seventy-fives. But now, thinking about it more, I could sense a strange and promising ambivalence in the whole affair. Yes, the BBC was being blamed for the actions of a politician, which struck me as unfair. Yet the desire to have a TV licence in the first place – and to enjoy all that it offered – was also present, also being *fought for*. After all, why would anyone take to the streets about something if it didn't matter?

As the effigy slowly collapsed into the flames, the vision before us became gradually more and more distorted. Soon, it was hard to tell whether this really was a bomber pilot we were seeing before us or Guy Fawkes himself. David Barnes said Lewes Bonfire was a form of time travel, a portal opening up to 'monsters climbing through the gates of history', a moment when one can feel the rumbles and echoes of the past, 'a judder in the continuum'.[13] As the last remnants of the BBC effigy turned to ash, and the crowds started to head homewards – to warm up, have a drink, perhaps even watch some of their favourite TV – the judder in the continuum I experienced for myself was a memory of what the retired nurse Muriel Greenway wrote in her diary during the opening months of the Second World War. She had turned off her radio in despair at all the 'high-toned' music and sloppy jazz. But when her set was broken for three full weeks, she had declared herself 'lost … as though a friend has gone from the house'. The message she now sent 'climbing through the gates of history' to those of us marking the BBC's centenary is one full of regret over lost opportunities and at the same time a powerful call to arms: a simple reminder that we sometimes never know just how much we need or want something until it is gone.

NOTES

Unless otherwise indicated, all interviews are those from the BBC Oral History Collection, transcripts of which are held at the BBC Written Archives Centre, Caversham (hereafter 'BBC WAC'). They are copyright BBC and are quoted with the permission of the Corporation.

Preface

1   Asa Briggs, *The History of Broadcasting in the United Kingdom, Vol. I: The Birth of Broadcasting 1896–1927* (Oxford: Oxford University Press, 1995): xiii.

2   David Hendy, *Life on Air: A History of Radio 4* (Oxford: Oxford University Press, 2007): 1; Michael Tracey, *The Decline and Fall of Public Service Broadcasting* (Oxford: Oxford University Press, 1998): viii; 'Taste and Standards in BBC Programmes', General Advisory Council (GAC 362), 21 March 1972, BBC WAC.

3   Charlotte Higgins, *This New Noise* (London: Guardian, 2015): 7, 63–4.

4   Ibid: 121–2, 185; Hendy, *Life*: 8.

5   David Attenborough, *Life on Air* (London: BBC, 2003): 14; Higgins, *Noise*: 230; Raphael Samuel, 'The Voice of Britain', in Alison Light (ed.), *Island Stories: Unravelling Britain. Theatres of Memory, Vol. II* (London: Verso, 1998), 188.

6   Clive James, *The Crystal Bucket: Television Criticism from the Observer 1976–79* (London: Picador, 1981): 13–15; Clive James, *Glued to the Box: Television Criticism from the Observer 1979–82* (London: Jonathan Cape, 1983): 19–20.

7   Jean Seaton, 'Writing the History of Broadcasting', in David Cannadine (ed.), *History and the Media* (London: Macmillan, 2004): 152.

1: Making a New World

1   Roy Porter, *London: A Social History* (London: Penguin, 2000): 378–9, 391; Jerry White, *London in the 20th Century* (London: Bodley Head, 2016): 11, 20; *Times*, 19 December 1922: 7, 9, 12; *Times*, 20 December 1922: 8.

2   Brian Hennessey, *Savoy Hill: The Early Years of British Broadcasting* (Romford: Ian Henry Publications, 1996): 4; Charles Stuart (ed.), *The Reith Diaries* (London: Collins, 1975): 128–9; Andrew Boyle, *Only the Wind Will Listen: Reith of the BBC* (London: Hutchinson, 1972): 120–2.

3   J. C. W. Reith, *Broadcast Over Britain* (London: Hodder & Stoughton, 1924): 23.

4   Richard Overy, *The Morbid Age: Britain Between the Wars* (London: Allen Lane, 2009): 9–11.

5   Lancelot Sieveking, *The Cud* (London: Mills & Boon, 1922): 47–8.

6   Cecil Lewis, *Never Look Back* (London: Hutchinson, 1974): 72.

7   Val Gielgud interview; Lewis, *Never*: 54, 90.

8   Lewis, *Never*: 26–7.

9   Cecil Lewis, *Sagittarius Rising* (London: Warner Books, 1993): 59, 198–9.

10 Ibid: 56–7, 66, 158–62; Lewis, *Never*: 35; Cecil Arthur Lewis, 'The Great War Interviews', BBC.

11 Ibid; Lewis, *Sagittarius*: 66–7, 154.

12 Ibid: 57, 93.

13 Nigel Fountain (ed.), *When the Lamps Went Out: From Home Front to Battle Front Reporting the Great War 1914–1918* (London: Guardian Books, 2014): 306–8; Adrian Gregory, *The Last Great War: British Society and the First World War* (Cambridge: Cambridge University Press, 2008): 250–51; Lewis, *Sagittarius*: 255; Lewis, *Never*: 41.

14 Lewis, *Sagittarius*: 134, 266, 271–329; Lewis, *Never*: 45.

15 Lewis, *Sagittarius*: 95, 121–4, 186, 237; Overy, *Morbid*: 2–3; Lewis, *Never*: 23.

16 Ibid: 59–75.

17 Ibid: 60–1.

18 Ibid: 64; Ian McIntyre, *The Expense of Glory: A Life of John Reith* (London: Harper Collins, 1993): 187; Boyle, *Only*: 22, 27.

19 Marista Leishman, *Reith of the BBC: My Father* (Saint Andrew Press, Edinburgh, 2008): xxvi; John Reith interview, T52/84/2.

20 Matthew Arnold, *Culture and Anarchy: An Essay in Political and Social Criticism*, 2nd edn (London: Smith, Elder and Co., 1875).

21 McIntyre, *Expense*: 8; Boyle, *Only*: 40–1.

22 Stuart, *Diaries*: 23; Boyle, *Only*: 40–1.

23 John Reith, *Wearing Spurs* (London: Hutchinson, 1966): 13; Boyle, *Only*: 83; McIntyre, *Expense*: 58.

24 Ibid: 53; Reith interview; Reith, *Spurs*: 33–7.

25 McIntyre, *Expense*: 65–6, 72; Stuart, *Diaries*: 33; Reith interview.

26 Reith interview; Stuart, *Diaries*: 38; John Foster, 'Strike action and working-class politics on Clydeside 1914–1919', *International Review of Social History*, 35 (1990): 33–70: 34, 38–51.

27 McIntyre, *Expense*: 105, 112; Reith interview.

28 Charles Myers, *Shell Shock in France 1914–18* (Cambridge: Cambridge University Press, 1940): 24–5.

29 Major J. C. W. Reith, Royal Engineers: Ministry of Pensions and successors: Selected First World War Pensions Award Files/Officers,

National Archives PIN26/22370; Leishman, *Reith*: 32; McIntyre, *Expense*: 100, 112; Stuart, *Diaries*: 40.

30 Ibid: 79–88; Boyle, *Only*: 110–11; McIntyre, *Expense*: 96; Leishman, *Reith*: 18.

31 Boyle, *Only*: 118–19; McIntyre, *Expense*: 114; Stuart, *Diaries*: 129.

32 Reith, *Wind*: 83.

33 Cecil Lewis interview, R73/519/1.

34 'Arthur Richard Burrows, 1882–1947', S236/21, BBC WAC.

35 Oliver Lodge, *Past Years: An Autobiography* (London: Hodder and Stoughton 1931): 231–2.

36 Marc Raboy, *Marconi: The Man Who Networked the World* (Oxford: Oxford University Press, 2016): 6, 31, 106; Guglielmo Marconi, 'The Progress of Electric Space Telegraphy', (London: Marconi's Wireless Telegraph Company, 1902).

37 David Hendy, 'The Dreadful World of Edwardian Wireless', in Siân Nicholas and Tom O'Malley (eds) *Moral Panics, Social Fears and the Media* (London: Routledge, 2013): 76–89; *Wireless World*, April 1913: 5.

38 *Wireless World*, September 1914: 375–382; Jonathan Reed Winkler, 'Information Warfare in World War I', *The Journal of Military History*, 73/3 (2009): 845–67; Heidi J. S. Evans, '"The Path to Freedom"? Transocean and German Wireless Telegraphy, 1914–1922', *Historical Social Research*, 35/1 (2010), 209–33; *Wireless World*, April 1917: 24–5; *Wireless World*, July 1917: 244–5.

39 Arthur Burrows: unpublished memoir, S236/21, BBC WAC; *Wireless World*, April 1918: 23–4.

40 Gabriele Balbi, 'Wireless's "Critical Flaw": The Marconi Company, Corporation Mentalities, and the Broadcasting Option', *Journalism and Mass Communication Quarterly*, 2017.

41 *Wireless World*, July 1917; 244–5; 'Broadcasting as a Means of Education', undated note, c.1923, S236/3, BBC WAC.

42 *Wireless World*, April 1917: 40; Velimir Khlebnikov, *The King of Time*, trans. Paul Schmidt, edited by Charlotte Douglas (Cambridge, MA and London: Harvard, 1985): 155–59; Secretary-General of the League of Nations to Arthur Burrows, Marconi's Wireless Telegraph Co., Ltd., Marconi House, Strand, London, 12 January 1921 S236/15, BBC WAC; 'Broadcasting as a Means of Education', (n.d), S236/3, BBC WAC.

43 *The Standard*, 28 December 1912, S236/18, BBC WAC.

44 Arthur Burrows, *The Story of Broadcasting* (London: Cassell & Co., 1924): 44–5; Balbi, 'Critical': 8.

45 Hendy, 'Dreadful': 85–6; *Wireless World*, April 1918: 24.

46 Burrows, *Broadcasting*: 46–53; Balbi, 'Critical': 12.

47 Ibid: 9–10, 16–7.

48 Peter Eckersley, *The Power Behind the Microphone* (London: Scientific Book Club, 1942): 41–4; Burrows, *Broadcasting*: 57–9; Briggs, *History I*: 64–6.

49 Ibid: 54–6.

50 *The Broadcaster*, August and September 1922.

51 Oliver Lodge, *My Philosophy: Representing My Views on the Many Functions of the Ether of Space* (London: E. Benn Limited, 1933); David Hendy, 'Oliver Lodge's Ether and the Birth of British Broadcasting', in James Mussell and Graeme Gooday (eds), *A Pioneer of Connection* (Pittsburgh: University of Pittsburgh Press, 2020): 183–97; Lodge, *Past*: 233–4, 333.

52 'Broadcasting as a Means of Education' (n.d.), S236/3, BBC WAC; Speech on Educational Broadcasting (n.d.), S236/4, BBC WAC; *The Broadcaster*, August 1922: 42.

53 Briggs, *History I*: 56–63; Burrows, *Broadcasting*: 56; David Prosser, 'Marconi Proposes: Why it's time to rethink the birth of the BBC', *Media History*, 25/3 (2019): 265–78; James Curran and Jean Seaton, *Power Without Responsibility* (London: Routledge, 1997): 113–15.

54 Briggs, *History I*: 85–130.

55 Ibid: 113.

56 Reith, *Broadcast*: 23–4.

57 Alan Kramer, *Dynamic of Destruction: Culture and Mass Killing in the First World War* (Oxford: 2007): 278; Eric Maschwitz, *No Chip on My Shoulder* (London: Herbert Jenkins, 1957): 49; Medical Report, 12 July 1929, Correspondence (Box 1926–1935), Sieveking Manuscripts, Lilly Library, Indiana University Bloomington (hereafter 'Sieveking MSS, Lilly'); John Snagge interview, R143/116/1.

58 Paul Fussell, *The Great War and Modern Memory* (Oxford: Oxford University Press, 2000 1975): 113, 188; Hilda Matheson, *Broadcasting* (London: Butterworth, 1933): 52.

59 Lionel Fielden, *The Natural Bent* (London: Andre Deutsch, 1960): 42–73, 92–7; Maurice Gorham, *Sound and Fury: Twenty-One Years in the BBC* (London: Percival Marshall, 1948): 16.

60 Lance Sieveking, *The Stuff of Radio* (London: Cassell, 1934): 18; Fielden, *Bent*: 97.

61 Mark Jackson, *The Age of Stress: Science and the Search for Stability* (Oxford: Oxford University Press, 2013); David Hendy, 'The Great War and British Broadcasting: Emotional Life in the Creation of the BBC', *New Formations*, 82 (2014): 82–99; Reith, *Broadcast*: 168–9; Lewis interview.

62 Fielden, *Bent*: 100–3.

63 Ibid: 99–102; Sieveking, *Stuff*: 8, 50.

2: Riding the Tiger

1 'Notes on the First Broadcast by the British Broadcasting Company, 14th November 1922', C19/2, BBC WAC.

2   Maurice Deloraine interview, R143/185/1; *Times*, 14 November, 1922: 7.

3   Burrows, *Broadcasting*: 72; Lewis interview.

4   Ibid; Reith, *Wind*: 87; C .A. Lewis, *Broadcasting from Within* (London: George Newnes, 1924): 27.

5   Richard Lambert, *Ariel and All His Quality* (London: Gollancz, 1940): 45; Gorham, *Sound*: 11; Hennessey, *Savoy*: 13–17; Kate Murphy, *Behind the Wireless: A History of Early Women at the BBC* (Basingstoke: Palgrave, 2016): 44.

6   Gorham, *Sound*: 15; Lambert, *Ariel*: 9.

7   *Radio Times*, 28 September 1923.

8   Lewis, *Broadcasting*: 26; Reith, *Broadcast*: 23; Reith, *Wind*: 88.

9   Lewis interview.

10   Ibid.

11   Reginald Jordan interview; Basil Vernon Harcourt interview; Ian Hartley, *2ZY to NBH: An Informal History of the BBC in Manchester and the North West* (Altrincham: Willow Publishing, 1987): 11–33; Gorham, *Sound*: 12.

12   Deloraine interview.

13   David Pat Walker, *The BBC in Scotland: The First Fifty Years* (Edinburgh: Luath Press, 2011): 27–31; John Davies, *Broadcasting and the BBC in Wales* (University of Wales Press, Cardiff, 1994): 1–18.

14   Burrows, *Broadcasting*: 69.

15   Reith, *Broadcast*: 34; *Vox*, 16 November 1929: 50.

16   Fielden, *Bent*: 110.

17   Ibid: 102; Val Gielgud, *Years of the Locust* (London: Nicholson & Watson, 1947): 69; Letter, 26 September 1930, Sieveking MSS, Lilly.

18   Michael Carney, *Stoker: The Life of Hilda Matheson OBE 1888–1940* (Pencaedu: 1999): 13–19; Gorham, *Sound*: 32; Gielgud, *Locust*: 69. Fielden, *Bent*: 114.

19   Diary, 1926, Sieveking MSS, Lilly; Kate Whitehead, 'Broadcasting Bloomsbury', *The Yearbook of English Studies*, 20 (1990): 121–31; 'History of Education and Talks Organisation' (n.d.), R13/419/1, BBC WAC.

20   *Vox*, 16 November 1929: 46.

21   Fielden, *Bent*: 106; Stuart Hibberd, *This – Is London* (London: Macdonald & Evans, 1950): 27; Briggs, *History I*: 259–60; Whitehead, 'Bloomsbury': 125.

22   Fielden, *Bent*: 103.

23   Whitehead, 'Bloomsbury': 123; Tod Avery, *Radio Modernism: Literature, Ethics, and the BBC, 1922–1938* (London: Routledge, 2016): 52.

24   Letters, 4 October and 21 November 1924, RConti/910, BBC WAC; Briggs, *History I*: 152–7, 244–8.

25   Letter, 29 October 1929, RConti/910, BBC WAC; Lance Sieveking, *The Eye of the Beholder* (London: Hulton Press, 1957): 30–1, 153.

26 Virginia Woolf, 'Middlebrow', in *The Death of the Moth and Other Essays* (London: Hogarth Press, 1942); Reith, *Broadcast*: 217; Carney, *Stoker*: 20.

27 Ibid: 54.

28 D. L. LeMahieu, *A Culture for Democracy: Mass Communication and the Cultivated Mind in Britain Between the Wars* (Oxford: Clarendon Press, 1988): 183; Avery, *Modernism:* passim; Reith, *Broadcast*: 78, 133–4.

29 Burrows, *Broadcasting*: 112; *Listener*, 30 October 1929: 572.

30 Briggs, *History I*: 75.

31 *Radio Times*, 5 October 1923; Lewis, *Broadcasting*: 34–5, 51–2; Burrows, *Broadcasting*: 80.

32 Harold Bishop interview, R143/11/1.

33 Briggs, *History I*: 252; *Radio Times*, 5 October 1923: 39.

34 Burrows, *Broadcasting*: 80–1.

35 Briggs, *History I*: 183; 'Notes on Technique of Playwriting' (n.d.), R19/276, BBC WAC.

36 *Radio Times*, 5 September 1924: 449: Val Gielgud, *British Radio Drama 1922–1956* (London: Harrap & Co., 1957): 19, 24–6; *Vox*, November 1929: 24; Maschwitz, *Chip*: 52–3; Gielgud, *Locust*: 9–29, 68, 70–1.

37 Murphy, *Behind:* 15–46.

38 Interview with Olive Bottle (née May).

39 Hennessey, *Savoy*: 26–9; Gorham, *Sound*: 23–5.

40 Alison Hess, 'From Hidden Technology to Exhibition Showpiece: The Journey of 2LO, the BBC's First Radio Transmitter, 1922–2012', unpublished PhD thesis, Royal Holloway, 2012: 35–49; Maschwitz, *Chip*: 49.

41 Hennessey, *Savoy*: 18–22; Burrows, *Broadcasting*: 100.

42 Hibberd, *London*: 2–3; Burrows, *Broadcasting*: 100.

43 Lewis interview; Lindsay Wellington interview.

44 Lewis interview; Gielgud interview; Fielden, *Bent*: 107.

45 John Snagge interview; Murphy, *Behind*: 126–7.

46 Harold Bishop interview.

47 Gorham, *Sound*: 25; Fielden, *Bent*, 106–7; Gielgud, *Locust*: 72; Sieveking, *Stuff*: 82.

48 *Radio Times*, 11 February 1927: 333; Maschwitz, *Chip*: 54.

49 'The Kaleidoscope', Sieveking MSS, Lilly; David Hendy, 'Painting with Sound: The Kaleidoscopic World of Lance Sieveking, a British Radio Modernist', *Twentieth Century British History*, 24/2: 169–200; Paul Sieveking (ed.), *Airborne: Scenes from the Life of Lance Sieveking, Pilot, Writer and Broadcasting Pioneer* (London: Strange Attractor Press, 2013) 194–201; 'Autobiographical Sketches of Lance Sieveking', S61, BBC WAC.

50 Sieveking, *Stuff*: 15; P. Sieveking, *Airborne*: 201.

51 Maschwitz, *Chip*: 54; Gielgud, *Drama*: 29.

3: Professionals

1   Sieveking, *Stuff*: 83; Gorham, *Sound*: 25; *Radio Times*, 14 February 1930: 373; Owen Reed interview, R143/106/1.
2   Lewis, *Broadcasting*: 36–7.
3   *Vox*, 9 November 1929: 2–3; Gielgud, *Locust*: 75.
4   Asa Briggs, *The History of Broadcasting in the United Kingdom, Vol. II: The Golden Age of Wireless 1927–1939* (Oxford: Oxford University Press, 1995): 417.
5   'Napoleon of the BBC', Scrapbook: News Cuttings, 1926–1930, Sieveking MSS, Lilly.
6   Fielden, *Bent*: 100; Gorham, *Sound*: 19; Harman Grisewood interview; Maschwitz, *Chip*: 49–50; Gielgud interview; Lambert, *Ariel*: 9–13.
7   Ibid: 26–7; Boyle, *Wind*: 147; Maschwitz, *Chips*: 46–7; Wellington interview; McIntyre, *Expense*: 117.
8   Boyle, *Wind*: 148; Grisewood interview; Fielden, *Bent*: 100; Maschwitz, *Chips*: 50.
9   Fielden, *Bent*: 104; Lewis interview; Reed interview.
10 Fielden, *Bent*: 103; Letter, 19 December 1926, Correspondence, Sieveking MSS, Lilly; Lewis interview.
11 Burrows, *Story*: 94; Lewis interview.
12 Ibid.
13 *Vox*, 9 November 1929: 2–3; Gielgud, *Drama*: 26; *Saturday Review*, 30 November 1929.
14 Lewis, *Broadcasting*: 48; Maschwitz, *Chip*: 49; Reith, *Broadcast*: 119; Hennessey, *Savoy*: 30.
15 Martin Dibbs, *Radio Fun and the BBC Variety Department, 1922–67* (London: Palgrave, 2019): 15; Bishop interview; Burrows, *Story*: 42–3; Briggs, *History I*: 211; Paddy Scannell and David Cardiff, *A Social History of British Broadcasting, Vol. 1 1922–1939* (Oxford: Blackwell, 1991): 361; Eckersley, *Power*: 73–4; Davies, *Wales*: 13–14; Reed interview.
16 Eckersley, *Power*: 63, 68; Davies, *Wales*: 16; Wellington interview.
17 *Radio Times*, 28 September 1923: 12; Reith, *Broadcast*: 78, 123.
18 Ibid: 27; Lewis, *Broadcasting*: 44; Lewis interview.
19 *Listener*, 14 January 1931: 62; Scannell and Cardiff, *Social History*: 370–4.
20 Eckersley, *Power*: 69; Walker, *Scotland*: 30–1.
21 Edward Pawley, *BBC Engineering 1922–1972* (London: BBC, 1972): 34; *Radio Times*, 7 March 1930: 577–9; Briggs, *History II*: 25–9.
22 *Radio Times*, 7 March 1930: 557, 580; Eckersley, *Power*: 126; Scannell and Cardiff, *Social*: 307, 325–7.
23 Walker, *Scotland*: 32; Davies, *Wales*: 28; Memo, 3 March 1924, R13/419/1, BBC WAC.
24 LeMahieu, *Culture*: 143.
25 Reith, *Broadcast*: 161, 219–24; Briggs, *History I*: 221–2; Briggs, *History*

II: 433; Arthur Lloyd James, *The Broadcast Word* (London: Kegan Paul, Trench, Trubner & Company, 1935): 24, 34–5, 41; BBC, *Broadcast English: Recommendations to Announcers Regarding Certain Words of Doubtful Pronunciation, with an Introduction by A. Lloyd James*. 3rd edn (London: BBC, 1935): 10–11.

26 Briggs, *History I*: 266; Ross McKibbin, *Classes and Cultures: England 1918–1951* (Oxford: Oxford University Press, 1998): 460; Scannell and Cardiff, *Social*: 298–9.

27 Tony Crowley, *Proper English? Readings in Language, History and Cultural Identity* (London: Routledge, 1991): 196–218; Barbara Storey, *The Way to Good Speech* (London: Nelson, 1937); Jonathan Rose, *The Intellectual Life of the British Working Classes* (New Haven, CT and London: Yale University Press, 2001): 223–36; Reith, *Broadcast*: 161.

28 Scannell and Cardiff, *Social*: 277–303; Sieveking, *Airborne*: 164–71.

29 Michael Guida, 'Birds, bombs, silence. Listening to nature during wartime and its aftermath in Britain, 1914–1945', unpublished PhD thesis, University of Sussex, 2018.

30 *Radio Times*, 22 December 1933: 894–6, and 23 December 1932: 910; Scannell and Cardiff, *Social*: 280.

31 *Radio Times*, 20 January 1928: 109.

32 Rex Cathcart, *The Most Contrary Region: The BBC in Northern Ireland 1924–1984* (Belfast: The Blackstaff Press, 1984): 60–105.

33 Scannell and Cardiff, *Social*: 310–29; Reith, *Broadcast*: 37, 64.

34 Letter, 9 June 1928, Correspondence, Sieveking MSS, Lilly; Fielden, *Bent*: 110; Lewis interview.

35 Eckersley, *Power*: 58; D. G. Bridson, *Prospero and Ariel – The Rise and Fall of Radio, A Personal Recollection* (London: Victor Gollancz, 1971): 43; Grisewood interview; Charles Siepmann interview, R143/114/1; Frank Gillard interview, R143/50/5.

36 Gorham, *Sound*: 30; Murphy, *Behind*: 28–9.

37 Briggs, *History I*: 205, 215, 301–27.

38 Eckersley, *Power*: 172; Maurice Farquharson interview, R143/42/1; Grisewood interview.

39 Briggs, *History I*: 363–5; Gorham, *Sound*: 26.

40 Ibid: 40; Mark Hines, *The Story of Broadcasting House, Home of the BBC* (London and New York: Merrell, 2008): 24–5, 29.

41 Ibid: 34; John Daligan reminiscence, R143/32/1.

42 Daligan reminiscence; Bishop interview; Snagge interview; Gorham, *Sound*: 42, 44, 54.

43 Gielgud interview; Fielden, *Bent*: 108.

4: Us and Them

1 *Times*, 19 April 1930; *Manchester Guardian*, 19 April 1930.

2   Reith, *Broadcast*: 15–16; Scannell and Cardiff, *Social*: 23–4, 27–8, 32; Briggs, *History II*: 120–1.

3   Selina Todd, *The People: The Rise and Fall of the Working Class 1910–2010* (London: John Murray, 2014): 46–50; Keith Laybourn, *The General Strike: Day by Day* (Stroud: Sutton, 1999): 40–51; *Daily Mail*, 6 May 1926.

4   Details in the section on the General Strike are drawn from a wide range of documents in these BBC WAC files: CO37/General Strike/Staff Arrangements; CO31/1–3/General Strike/News bulletins; CO30/BBCo/General Strike/News Arrangements; CO34/Policy of the Company; CO36/Scripts; CO27/Relations with Labour; Co23/BBCo/General Strike/Archbishop of Canterbury's Message; CO32/2–3/BBCo/General Strike/News bulletins; CO28/BBCo/General Strike/Listeners' Correspondence. Other sources cited are: Reith interview; Laybourn, *Strike*: 58; Todd, *People*: 46–50; Hibberd, *London*: 19–21; Briggs, *History I*: 336–8; Stuart, *Diaries*: 94–139; McIntyre, *Expense*: 141; Tom Mills, *The BBC: Myth of a Public Service* (London: Verso, 2016): 13; Scannell and Cardiff, *Social History*: 23, 39–41; Boyle, *Wind*: 159; P. Sieveking, *Airborne*: 129; Gorham, *Sound*: 13.

5   H. L. Beales and R. S. Lambert (eds), *Memoirs of the Unemployed* (London: Victor Gollancz, 1934): 64–70; *Listener*, 25 April 1934: 700.

6   Lambert, *Ariel*: 21–2; J. B. Priestley, *English Journey* (Great Northern Books: Bradford, 2018): 231, 259–72; Lambert and Beale, *Memoirs*: 8, 49.

7   Reith, *Broadcast*: 16, 153; Todd, *People*: 62; Grisewood interview.

8   Siepmann interview.

9   'Wireless Discussion Groups' (BBC: London, 1931); Siepmann interview; Carney, *Stoker*: 39–41.

10 Todd, *People*: 61–2; Peter Kingsford, *The Hunger Marchers of Britain 1920–1939* (London: Lawrence & Wishart, 1982): 129–65; *Listener*, 24 January 1934: 8–11.

11 Briggs, *History II*: 138–9; Scannell and Cardiff, *Social*: 69–70.

12 Ibid: 71; Siepmann interview.

13 Scannell and Cardiff: 138–40, 339–40; *Radio Times*, 5 June 1931: 581; Godfrey Talbot interview; Bridson, *Prospero*: 28–30.

14 Ibid: 25; Scannell and Cardiff, *Social*: 335–7.

15 Bridson, *Prospero*: 19, 2849–52; Memos, 29 and 30 May 1935, L1/1821/2, BBC WAC.

16 *Radio Times*, 11 November 1938: 8; Scannell and Cardiff, *Social*: 343–4.

17 Olive Shapley interview; Scannell and Cardiff, *Social*: 344; D. G. Bridson, L1/1821/2, BBC WAC; Bridson, *Prospero*: 70.

18 Ibid: 35–6.

19 Oliver Shapley, *Broadcasting A Life* (London: Scarlet Press, 1996): 31–3.

20 Shapley interview; Bridson, *Prospero*: 31; Shapley, *Life*: 36; Scannell and Cardiff, *Social*: 344–5.

21 Ibid: 346.

22 Shapley interview; Scannell and Cardiff, *Social*: 348–9.

23 Shapley interview.

24 Siepmann interview.

25 Ibid; Charles Siepmann, L2/190/2, BBC WAC; John Green interview, R143/198/1; Briggs, *History II*: 144–5.

26 Siepmann interview; Jean Seaton, *Pinkoes and Traitors: The BBC and the Nation 1974–1987* (London: Profile, 2017): 300; John Green interview.

27 Stuart, *Diaries*: 153, 164; David Hendy, 'J. H. Whitley at the BBC 1930–35', in John Hargreaves, Keith Laybourn and Richard Toye (eds), *Liberal Reform and Industrial Relations: J.H. Whitley, Halifax Radical and Speaker of the House of Commons* (London: Routledge, 2017): 143–54.

5: Stardust

1 Dibbs, *Fun*: 22; Briggs, *History II*: 43.

2 Dibbs, *Fun*: 22; Briggs, *History I*: 357; Briggs, *History II*: 34–52.

3 Ibid: 12; Reith, *Broadcast*: 17.

4 Martin Pugh, *We Danced All Night: A Social History of Britain Between the Wars* (London: Vintage, 2009): 216–32; James J. Nott, *Music for the People: Popular Music and Dance in Interwar Britain* (Oxford: Oxford University Press, 2002): 168–83.

5 Scannell and Cardiff, *Social*: 214; Briggs, *History II*: 54.

6 Dibbs, *Fun*: 27–9, 42; Scannell and Cardiff, *Social*: 225–7; Briggs, *History II*: 73–88.

7 Dibbs, *Fun*: 29–30; Matheson, *Broadcasting*: 160.

8 Briggs, *History II*: 24; Dibbs, *Fun*: 24, 91–2.

9 Seán Street, *Crossing the Ether: British Public Service Radio and Commercial Competition 1922–1945* (Eastleigh, John Libbey: 2006): 229–59; Julia Taylor, 'From Sound to Print in Pre-War Britain: the Cultural and Commercial Interdependence between Broadcasters and Broadcasting Magazines in the 1930s', unpublished PhD thesis, Bournemouth University, 2013.

10 Reith, *Broadcast*: 196; *Radio Times*, 17 January 1930: 143–5.

11 Nott, *Music*: 68–79; Dibbs, *Fun*: 82–3; Briggs, *History II*: 52–3.

12 Louis Barfe, *Turned Out Nice Again: The Story of British Light Entertainment* (London: Atlantic Books, 2008): 1–22; *Radio Times*, 11 November 1932: 461; *Radio Times*, 30 December 1932: 1002.

13 Maschwitz, *Chip*: 17–57; *Radio Times*, 1 January 1932: 37.

14 Daligan reminiscence; Maschwitz, *Chip*: 69–71.

15 Dibbs, *Fun*: 49–50; David Porter interview; Dibbs, *Fun*: 57–9.

16 Nott, *Music*: 66, 84–5; Dibbs, *Fun*: 85–9; Maschwitz, *Chip*: 64.

17 Ibid: 71–4; Dibbs, *Fun*: 54–5; Porter interview; *Radio Times*, 20 May 1938: 42.

18 Jennifer J. Purcell, *Mother of the BBC: Mabel Constanduros and the*

Development of Popular Entertainment on the BBC, 1925–1957 (London: Bloomsbury Academic: 2020): 1; Mabel Constanduros, *Shreds and Patches: Autobiographical Memoirs of Mabel Constanduros* (London: Lawson & Dunn, 1946): 5, 39–43.

19 Briggs, *History II*: 101; *Radio Times*, 10 November 1933: *Radio Times* 456; 17 November 1933: 536; Daligan reminiscence; J. C. Cannell, *In Town Tonight: The Story of the Popular BBC Feature Told from Within* (London: George G. Harrap & Co., 1935): 15–17, 84–6.

20 Ibid: 20–23, 45–9.

21 *Radio Times*, 4 May 1934: 406, and 17 December 1937: 53. Scannell and Cardiff, *Social*: 172–5, 269–73; Grace Wyndham Goldie interview, R143/139/4.

22 Dibbs, *Fun*: 55.

23 Ibid: 35–6, 39–40, 77; Gorham, *Sound*: 38; Maschwitz, *Chip*: 59, 68–9; *Radio Times*, 5 February 1932: 298, 7 January 1938: 36, 17 February 1933: 387.

24 Ibid; Scannell and Cardiff, *Social*: 188–9; Dibbs, *Fun*: 73–4; Nott, *Music*: 62.

25 Ibid: 60–1, 173; Scannell and Cardiff, *Social*: 123; Dibbs, *Fun*: 36–7.

26 Ibid: 3; Maschwitz, *Chip*: 79–80.

27 Ibid: 75.

28 Briggs, *History II*: 483–4; Joe Moran, *Armchair Nation: An Intimate History of Britain in front of the TV* (London: Profile, 2013); John Swift, *Adventure in Vision: The First Twenty-Five Years of Television* (London: John Lehmann, 1950): 26–32.

29 Briggs, *History II*: 448.

30 Ibid: 492–3; Bishop interview; Moran, *Armchair*: 16.

31 Ibid: 17–18; Tony Bridgewater interview, R143/170/1.

32 Ibid.

33 'Autobiographical Sketches of Lance Sieveking', S61, BBC WAC; Hendy, 'Painting': 169–200.

34 P. Sieveking, *Airborne*: 226–8, 232; Swift, *Adventure*: 47.

35 P. Sieveking, *Airborne*: 231–2; Moran, *Armchair*: 22; 'The Man with the Flower in His Mouth', R5/07/01, BBC WAC; *Times*, 15 July 1930; *Observer*, 27 July 1930; Letter, 12 July 1930, Correspondence: 1926–35, Sieveking MSS, Lilly.

36 Moran, *Armchair*: 23.

37 Ibid: 24; Swift, *Adventure*: 56–8.

38 Ibid: 55; Moran, *Armchair*: 17; Briggs, *History II*: 507–8, 417; Bridgewater interview; Eckersley, *Power*: 237–9.

39 Briggs, *History II*: 539–47.

40 Moran, *Armchair*: 28–9; Swift, *Adventure*: 72–3; Jennifer Lewis (ed.), *Starlight Days: The Memoirs of Cecil Madden* (London: Trevor Square, 2007): 68–70.

41 Eckersley, *Power*: 240; Cecil Madden interview; Briggs, *History II*: 555–8;

Sarah Johnson, *A Memoir of my Mother, Jasmine Bligh, The First Lady of Television* (unpublished MS): 39–44; Swift, *Adventure*: 74; Lewis, *Starlight*: 70.

42   Ibid: 8; Bridgewater interview.

43   Madden interview; Lewis, *Starlight*: 11; Moran, *Armchair*: 32.

44   Lewis, *Starlight*: 17.

45   Wyndham Goldie interview.

46   Moran, *Armchair*: 31–2; Bridgewater interview.

47   Ibid; Madden interview.

48   *Radio Times*, 30 October 1936: 88–9, and 4 December 1936: 82–3; Moran, *Armchair*: 33–4; Madden interview.

49   Ibid; *Radio Times*, 17 February 1939: 16; Stephen Bourne, *Black in the British Frame: The Black Experience in British Film and Television* (London and New York: Continuum, 2001): 61.

50   Lewis, *Starlight*: 71–2, 100–2; Madden interview; 'Viewers and the Television Service', 5 February 1937, R9/09/01, BBC WAC.

51   Bridgewater interview.

52   Briggs, *History Vol. II*: 553; Bishop interview; Lewis, *Stardust*: 74–85.

53   Pawley, *Engineering*: 236.

6: Under Siege

1   Gorham, *Sound*: 87.

2   Pawley, *Engineering*: 219–24; Briggs, *History III*: passim.

3   Stuart, *Diaries*: 113–5; Pawley, *Engineering*: 215–7; Bishop interview; Bridgewater interview.

4   Mary Lewis interview, R143/85/1; Daligan reminiscence.

5   Richard Overy, *The Bombing War: Europe 1939–1945* (London: Penguin, 2014): 25–6; 'Defence', n.d., R42/217/1, BBC WAC.

6   *War Factory: A Report by Mass-Observation* (London: Gollancz, 1943): 96–104; Gielgud, *Mirror*: 96; Mary Lewis interview.

7   Gorham, *Sound*: 90; Gielgud, *Mirror*: 96; Stuart Williams reminiscence, R143/147/1; Bruce Belfrage, *One Man in His Time* (London: Hodder & Stoughton, 1951): 103–4.

8   Briggs, *History III*: 56–8; Pawley, *Engineering*: 217–8; Francis McLean interview, R143/92/1.

9   Diarist 5399, Mass Observation Archive.

10   Dorothy Sheridan (ed.), *Wartime Women: A Mass Observation Anthology 1937–45* (London: Phoenix, 2000): 50–2.

11   Pawley, *Engineering*: 236–8; Godfrey Talbot interview; Shapley, *Broadcasting*: 67.

12   Daligan reminiscence.

13   Document C: Interim notice of Amendment, 31 August 1939, R34/348; Instructions to Announcer, R58/2, BBC WAC.

14 Talbot interview; Daniel Todman, *Britain's War: Into Battle 1937–1941* (London: Penguin, 2017): 195–6; Clare Lawson Dick interview, 'Memories of the 1939–45 War', R143/83/1.

15 'First Report of Defence Sub-Committee', 11 January 1939, R34/266, BBC WAC.

16 Diarist 5399, Mass Observation Archive; Siân Nicholas, *The Echo of War: Home Front Propaganda and the Wartime BBC, 1939–45* (Manchester: Manchester University Press, 1996): 30–1.

17 Briggs, *History III*: 128–45; M. A. Doherty, *Nazi Wireless Propaganda: Lord Haw-Haw and British Public Opinion in the Second World War* (Edinburgh: Edinburgh University Press, 2000): 6, 93–5.

18 Briggs, *History, III*: 29, 78–80; Nicholas, *Echo*: 18.

19 Ibid: 18–19; Briggs, *History, III*: 23, 29, 40–1, 78–9; 'News Department in Wartime', 29 June 1939, R42/217/1, BBC WAC.

20 Gorham, *Sound*: 113.

21 Alec Sutherland interview, R143/123/1.

22 Gorham, *Sound*: 113; Malcolm Frost interview, R143/46/1; Norman Collins interview, R143/28/1; Briggs, *History III*: 14–15, 45, 91.

23 Ibid: 91–3; Dibbs, *Fun*: 112; Nicholas, *Echo*: 74–85; Briggs, *History III*: 504; Charles Hill interview, R73/515/1.

24 Todd, *People*: 122–40.

25 Richard Toye, *The Roar of the Lion: The Untold Story of Churchill's World War II Speeches* (Oxford: OUP, 2015): 51–65; Todd, *People*: 119.

26 Briggs, *History III*: 139, 192–4; Nicholas, *Echo*: 57–60; Ian Whittington, *Writing the Radio War: Literature, Politics and the BBC, 1939–1945* (Edinburgh: Edinburgh University Press, 2018): 30–64.

27 Angus Calder, *The Myth of the Blitz* (London: Pimlico, 1992): 195–203; Whittington, *Writing*: 45–7, 56–7; Briggs, *History III*: 193–5, 293–5; Nicholas, *Echo*: 60–1.

28 Bridson, *Prospero*: 77–79.

29 *Workers Playtime*, BBC Home and Forces Programme, Thursday 29 October 1942; Dibbs, *Fun*: 127–8; George Budden interview; *Radio Times*, 27 September 1940: 27; Various, R27/257/1 and R27/257/2, BBC WAC; Christina L. Baade, *Victory through Harmony: The BBC and Popular Music in World War II* (Oxford: Oxford University Press, 2012): 65–79.

30 Nicholas, *Echo*: 133; Snagge interview.

31 Ibid; Nicholas, *Echo*: 23–4, 130–2.

32 Ibid: 52; Briggs, *History III*: 115–19.

33 Bridson, *Prospero*: 76.

34 Juliet Gardiner, *The Blitz: The British Under Attack* (London: Harper Collins, 2011): 16–17, 23–6, 359.

35 Todman, *War*: 474; Gorham, *Sound*: 94; Gielgud, *Mirror*: 105; Shapley, *Broadcasting*: 74.

36 Alec Sutherland interview; Mary Lewis interview; Clare Lawson Dick, 'Memories'; Comment from Leonard Miall in Elisabeth Barker interview, R143/6/1; S. G. Williams reminiscences, R143/137/1.

37 Lawson Dick, 'Memories' and 'Sir Stephen Tallents: a Portrait', R73/518/1.

38 Lawson Dick, 'Memories'.

39 Snagge interview; Lawson Dick, 'Memories'; Belfrage, *One Man*: 122; Gorham, *Sound*: 92–4, 100; Mary Lewis interview.

40 R42/35/1 and R42/33, BBC WAC.

41 Belfrage, *One Man*: 111; Briggs, *History III*: 268; Shapley, *Broadcasting*: 74–5.

42 Sutherland interview; Snagge interview; Bishop interview; R60/4, BBC WAC.

43 Snagge interview; Belfrage, *One Man*: 112; Mary Lewis interview; S. G. Williams interview; Bishop interview; R49/60, BBC WAC.

44 Sutherland interview; 'The Landmine in Portland place', L. D. Macgregor, R49/321, BBC WAC; Briggs, *History III*: 267–9; Barker interview; Gorham, *Sound*: 95.

45 McLean interview; Pawley, *Engineering*: 233.

46 Briggs, *History III*: 319; Leonard Miall comment in Elisabeth Barker interview; Noel Newsome, *Giant at Bush House: The Autobiography of Noel Newsome* (London: The Real Press, 2019): 277.

47 Pawley, *Engineering*: 230, 244; Gielgud, *Mirror*: 99; Gorham, *Sound*: 99; John Ammonds interview; David Davis interview, R143/142/1; Briggs, *History III*: 517.

48 Ibid: 24–6.

49 Gielgud, *Mirror*: 95–123; Leonard Miall in Elisabeth Barker interview; S. G. Williams interview.

50 Overy, *Bombing*: 144–48, 150; Todd, *People*: 126, 132; Dibbs, *Fun*: 111; Susan Ritchie interview.

51 Overy, *Bombing*: 128; Todd, *People*: 131, 138; Lawson Dick, 'Memories'.

52 Barker interview; Belfrage, *One Man*: 125; Stuart Williams interview; Snagge interview.

53 Frank Gillard interview, R143/50/5.

54 Gielgud, *Mirror*: 104–8, 113, 117–18.

7: London Calling

1 Christopher Andrew, *The Defence of the Realm: The Authorized History of MI5* (London, Penguin: 2010): 221–3.

2 Note, Special Branch, 8 December 1939, HO 45/23741, The National Archives (TNA).

3 Note, 'N.K', 1 November 1939, HO 45/23741, TNA; Notes, Home Office/MI5, 5 July 1940, 1 August 1940, 30 August 1940, 2 February 1941, HO 45/23741, TNA.

4   Briggs, *History II*: 5–7, 39–41; Michael Stenton, *Radio London and Resistance in Occupied Europe* (Oxford, Oxford University Press, 2000): 117.

5   Leonard Miall interview, R73/522/1; Richard Dove, *Journey of No Return: Five German-speaking Literary Exiles in Britain, 1933–1945* (London: Libris, 2000): 196.

6   Briggs, *History II*: 342–7; Simon J. Potter, *Broadcasting Empire: The BBC and the British World, 1922–1970* (Oxford: Oxford University Press, 2012): 7.

7   Briggs, *History II*: 361–75; Peter Partner, *Arab Voices: The BBC Arabic Service 1938–1988* (London: BBC, 1988): 5, 19–21.

8   Briggs, *History III*: 18, 58–60; Andrew Walker, *A Skyful of Freedom: 60 Years of the BBC World Service* (London: Broadside Books, 1992): 60–9; Pawley, *Engineering*: 254–6.

9   Alan Bullock interview, R143/174/1; Leonard Miall interview.

10   Ivone Kirkpatrick, *The Inner Circle* (London: Macmillan, 1959): 157.

11   Alan Bullock interview; Tangye Lean, *Voices in the Darkness: The Story of the European Radio War* (London: Secker and Warburg, 1943): 37.

12   Dove, *Journey*: 196–7; Briggs, *History III*: 164–5; Miall interview; David Garnett, *The Secret History of PWE: The Political Warfare Executive 1939–1945* (London: St Ermin's Press, 2002): 19; Bullock interview.

13   Martin Esslin interview, R143/40/1.

14   Ibid; Briggs, *History III*: 253.

15   Hugh Carleton Greene interview, R143/56/1; Maurice Latey interview, R143/218/1; Donald Edwards interview, R143/39/1; Harman Grisewood interview; Esslin interview; Briggs, *History III*: 388–93, 163–4.

16   Ibid: 390; Latey interview; Lean, *Voices*: 58–60, 63–4.

17   Bullock interview; Latey interview; Robin Scott interview, R143/111/1.

18   Stenton, *Radio London*: 129–30; Briggs, *History III*: 226–7.

19   Lean, *Voices*: 157–63; Barker interview; Briggs, *History III*: 226.

20   Julian Jackson, *A Certain Idea of France: The Life of Charles de Gaulle* (London: Allen Lane, 2018): 128.

21   W. W. Kulski, *De Gaulle and the World: The Foreign Policy of the Fifth French Republic* (Syracuse University Press, 1966): 5; Jackson, *Certain Idea*: 113–28; Barker interview.

22   Ibid.

23   Briggs, *History III*: 231.

24   Barker interview; Stenton, *Radio London*: 138; Lean, *Voices*: 149–50.

25   Bullock interview; Scott interview.

26   Briggs, *History III*: 230–2; Lean, *Voices*: 149, 160–1; Robert Gildea, *Fighters in the Shadow: A New History of the French Resistance* (London, Faber & Faber, 2015): 63; Stenton, *Radio London*: 133.

27   Marjory Todd, *Snakes and Ladders: An Autobiography* (London: Longmans, 1960): 197; Pawley, *Engineering*: 280–2; Briggs, *History III*: 170–1; Olive Renier and Vladimir Rubinstein, *Assigned to Listen: The Evesham Experience*

1939–43 (BBC, 1986): 66; Oliver Whitley interview, R143/135/2; Esslin interview; Miall interview.

28　Susan Ritchie interview; Briggs, *History III*: 172; Williams reminiscence; Laure Marie Johnson, 'Establishing Broadcasting Monitoring as Open Source Intelligence: the BBC Monitoring Service during the Second World War', unpublished PhD thesis, Kings College, London, 2013: 232–3.

29　Williams reminiscence; Esslin interview.

30　Ibid; Todd, *Snakes*: 197; Briggs, *History III*: 171; Ernst Gombrich obituary, *New York Times*, 7 November 2001; Miall interview.

31　Oliver Whitley interview; Johnson, 'Monitoring': 234–7; Renier and Rubinstein, *Assigned*: 7.

32　Garnett, *PWE*: 17–21; 48; 79–81; 124; Kirkpatrick, *Inner Circle*: 156; Newsome, *Giant*: 207.

33　Kirkpatrick, *Inner Circle*: 156–7.

34　Ibid: 166–7; Garnett, *PWE*: 21; Briggs, *History III*: 379–80; Bullock interview; Grisewood interview.

35　Barker interview; 'War Commentary', R. H. S. Crossman, 13–14 July 1941, 154/4/BR/1/143, Crossman archives, Warwick Modern Records Centre; Esslin interview; Garnett, *PWE*: 20, 84, 112–13.

36　Ibid: 91–6; Bullock interview.

37　Garnett, *PWE*: 86.

38　Stenton, *Radio London*: 71, 76, 113.

39　Briggs, *History III*: 381–3; Newsome, *Giant*: 235, 260, 299; Garnett, *PWE*: 96–7.

40　Grisewood interview.

41　Ibid; Briggs, *History III*: 383; Malcolm Frost interview; Garnett, *PWE*: xviii, 76, 90–4; Latey interview; Grisewood interview.

42　Bullock interview.

43　Adam Ritchie (ed.), *V**** for Victory: The 1940 BBC Campaign against the Nazis, by Douglas Ritchie* (unpublished memoir): 24.

44　Ritchie, *V*: 24–5; Newsome, *Giant*: 282; Briggs, *History III*: 334–5.

45　Ritchie, *V*: 29–30; Briggs, *History III*: 337.

46　Ritchie, *V*: 47, 120–7.

47　Ibid: 50–5, 84, 110.

48　Ibid: 75–9; Briggs, *History III*: 335–6; Garnett, *PWE*: 101.

49　Ritchie, *V*: 39, 65, 99, 114.

50　Ibid: 167; Stenton, *London*: 100–101; Garnett, *PWE*: 102–4.

51　Ibid: 104.

52　Ritchie, *V*: 6–7.

53　'Messages in code', 28 August 1941; 'Handling of BBC messages for the fighting French' (n.d.); 'Special messages broadcast in French Service'; 'Code messages dealt with by D. Eur. B.'s office, November 1943' – all E2/90, BBC WAC.

54 Kirkpatrick, *Inner Circle*: 161; Stenton, *Radio London*: 315–84; Elisabeth Barker interview; 'Handling of BBC messages for the fighting French' (n.d.), Memo, 30 April 1942, Instructions to Regional Directors, 15 July 1942 – all E2/90, BBC WAC.

55 'Gramophone Records in Polish Bulletins', 24 December 1941; Senter, 22 January 1943; Newsome, 23 January 1943; Senter, 18 March 1943; Newsome, 18 March 1943; Macdonald, 21 June 1943 – all E2/90, BBC WAC; Sutherland interview.

56 Newsome, 7 March 1944; Senter, 4 January 1943; Winther, 7 January 1943; Newsome, 9 January 1943; Senter, 17 January 1943 – all E2/90, BBC WAC.

57 'Operational messages in the European Service', 3 May 1944, E2/90, BBC WAC.

58 Briggs, *History, III*: 608; Edward Stourton, *Auntie's War: The BBC During the Second World War* (London: Doubleday, 2017): 357; personal communications from Rebecca Scales, Diane de Vignemont, and the Musée de la Résistance de Bondues.

8: Turning the Tide

1   Belfrage, *One Man*: 129; Briggs, *History III*: 544.

2   Audrey Russell interview, R143/526/1; Gorham, *Sound*: 103.

3   Briggs, *History III*: 110.

4   Frank Gillard interview; Talbot interview; Reed interview; Russell interview; Desmond Hawkins (ed.), *War Report: BBC Dispatches from the Front Line, 1944–45* (London, BBC Books, 1994): 19, 27; Briggs, *History III*: 590; Frost interview.

5   Report to Controller (News), 8 December 1942, R28/280/1, BBC WAC.

6   'Broadcasting About the Second Front', 1 March 1943, and 'Report on Spartan Exercise', 15 March 1943, both R28/280/2, BBC WAC; Pawley, *Engineering*: 293; Briggs, *History III*: 591–2; Hawkins, *War*: 24; Malcolm Frost interview.

7   Bishop interview; Pawley, *Engineering*: 270–9; Briggs, *History III*: 594; Hawkins, *War*: 32.

8   Gorham, *Sound*: 107–33; Michele Hilmes, 'Front Line Family: "Women's culture" comes to the BBC', *Media, Culture & Society*, 29/1 (2006): 5–29; Madden interview; Briggs, *History III*: 369–70; Garnett, *PWE*: 271–3.

9   Kirkpatrick, *Circle*: 164–7; William Paley interview; Garnett, *PWE*: 361–3.

10 Miall interview; Kirkpatrick, *Circle*: 164–5; Briggs, *History III*: 580.

11 Frost interview; Collins interview.

12 Russell interview; Susan Ritchie interview; Briggs, *History III*: 596.

13 Briggs, *History III*: 597–607; Scott interview; Snagge interview.

14 Briggs, *History III*: 605; 6 June 1944, diarists 5325 and 5399, Mass Observation Archive.

15 Mary Lewis interview.

16 Snagge interview.

17 Sutherland interview.

18 Mary Lewis interview; *Few Eggs and No Oranges: The Diaries of Vere Hodgson 1940–45* (London: Persephone Books, 1999): 479; Snagge interview; Briggs, *History III*: 597.

19 Hawkins, *War*: 41, 63; Robin Duff interview.

20 Original broadcast, BBC, 6 June 1944.

21 Original broadcast, BBC, 6 June 1944; Hawkins, *War*: 83–5.

22 Ibid: 42–3.

23 *Vere Hodgson*: 479; Diarist 5325, Mass Observation Archive; Briggs, *History III*: 597–8, 614.

24 Mary Lewis interview.

25 Hawkins, *War*: 64; Snagge interview; Snagge memo, 5 August 1944, R28/282, BBC WAC.

26 Hawkins, *War*: 46–7, 64; Pawley, *Engineering*: 297–8; Briggs, *History III*: 601–12; Gillard interview; Russell interview.

27 Hawkins, *War*: 224–30; Briggs, *History III*: 610.

28 Home Intelligence Weekly Report, No. 193, 15 June 1944, MOI Digital, http://www.moidigital.ac.uk; Hawkins, *War*: 19–20, 193–209; Duff interview; Snagge interview.

29 *Vere Hodgson*: 479; Hawkins, *War*: 22–6; Briggs, *History III*: 601–3.

30 Russell interview.

31 Gorham, *Sound*: 145–7; Memorandum, 21 December 1944, R34/185, BBC WAC.

32 Godfrey Talbot, *Ten Seconds From Now: A Broadcaster's Story* (London: The Quality Book Club, 1974): 93.

33 Duff interview; Russell interview; Briggs, *History III*: 618–19.

34 Ibid: 405–6.

35 Ibid: 611.

36 Hawkins, *War*: 15, 479–83; Gillard interview.

37 Snagge interview.

38 Sheridan, *Women*: 232; Juliet Gardiner, *Wartime Britain 1939–1945* (London: Headline, 2004): 566–9.

39 Briggs, *History III*: 630–42; 'Home Service Programme: Tuesday 8.5.1945', BBC WAC; Programmes as Broadcast, HS/1–18 May 1945; *Victory Report*, BBC Home Service, 8 May 1945; Gardiner, *Wartime*: 569; Sheridan, *Women*: 245.

40 *Victory Report*, BBC Home Service, 8 May 1945; Gardiner, *Wartime*: 577.

41 Talbot interview; Mary Lewis interview; Grisewood interview.

42 Briggs, *History III*: 651; Frost interview; Grisewood interview; Esslin interview.

43 Sheridan, *Women*: 236; Frost interview.

44 Sheridan, *Women*: 253.

45 Daligan reminiscence.
46 Briggs, *History III*: 642.

9: A Bomb About to Burst

1   BBC Television, 7 June 1946; *Radio Times*, 31 May 1946: 4; Moran, *Armchair*: 52.
2   David Kynaston, *Austerity Britain, 1945–51* (London: Bloomsbury, 2007): 115–16; *Radio Times*, 31 May 1946: 3–4.
3   *Radio Times*: 6 July 1945: 1, 4; 13 July 1945: 1, 3, 20; 27 July 1945: 2, 8, 17; 3 August 1945: 23.
4   Briggs, *History IV*: 9–10; *Radio Times*, 31 May 1946: 16–17.
5   Gorham, *Sound*: 174–82; Pawley, *Engineering*: 354–5; Peter Dimmock interview, R143/143/1; *Times*, 2 November 1945: 5.
6   Briggs, *History IV*: 161–2, 177–8; *Times*, 2 November 1945: 5; McLean interview.
7   William Haley interview; Gorham, *Sound*: 205, 209; Briggs, *History IV*: 190.
8   Ibid: 248–51.
9   Kynaston, *Austerity*: 103, 133–4, 227–9, 246–80, 301, 461; Haley interview.
10 Ibid.
11 Collins interview; Tom Chalmers interview; Grisewood interview; Gorham, *Sound*: 137.
12 *Radio Times*, 11 May 1947: 32; Gorham, *Sound*: 218; Moran, *Armchair*: 68–9; Lewis, *Starlight*: 261.
13 Ibid: 256.
14 Briggs, *History IV*: 218; Haley interview; Gorham, *Sound*: 215; John Grist, *Grace Wyndham Goldie: First Lady of Television* (Sandy, Beds: Authors Online, 2006): 100.
15 Lez Cooke, *British Television Drama: A History* (London: BFI, 2003): 14–22; David Kynaston, *Family Britain 1951–57* (London: Bloomsbury, 2009): 316.
16 Haley interview; Grisewood interview; Huw Wheldon interview, R73/530/1; Collins interview; Williams interview; Sutherland interview; Briggs, *History IV*: 205–6.
17 Collins interview; Dimmock interview.
18 T5/534/Plays/A Tomb with a View, BBC WAC; Briggs, *History IV*: 257–8.
19 Haley interview; Collins interview; Wheldon interview.
20 Dimmock interview; Gorham, *Sound*: 221; Briggs, *History IV*: 251.
21 Ibid: 422; Wheldon interview; Dimmock interview.
22 Ibid; Moran, *Armchair*: 73.
23 Briggs, *History IV*: 423–8; Snagge interview; Peter Hennessy, *Having It So Good: Britain in the Fifties* (London: Allen Lane, 2006): 244; Moran, *Armchair*: 80, 136.
24 Briggs, *History IV*: 421–35.

25 Moran, *Armchair*: 78–79; Kynaston, *Family*: 300–1.

26 Briggs, *History IV*: 221; Moran, *Armchair*: 75–6.

27 Ibid: 81; Kynaston, *Austerity*: 297–99.

28 Moran, *Armchair*: 59, 63.

29 *Manchester Guardian*, 10 October 1951: 5, and 11 October 1951: 5.

30 Moran, *Armchair*: 111–17, 123–4, 131; Claire Langhamer, *Women's Leisure in England, 1920–1960* (Manchester: Manchester University Press, 2000): 41.

31 Moran, *Armchair*: 115; Kynaston, *Family*: 51–2, 341–42, 671.

32 Ibid: 324–5; Richard Hoggart, *The Uses of Literacy: Aspects of Working-Class Life* (London: Penguin, 2009): 166–73.

33 Collins interview.

34 Wyndham Goldie interview.

35 Ibid; Grisewood interview; Wheldon interview.

36 Harman Grisewood, *One Thing at a Time* (London: Hutchinson, 1968): 183–5; Bridson, *Prospero*: 224–5.

37 Briggs, *History IV*: 409; Haley interview.

38 Kynaston, *Austerity*: 20, 102, 156, 592–7; Todd, *People*: 153–63.

39 Kynaston, *Austerity*: 37, 139, 539–40.

40 Peter Hennessy, *Never Again: Britain 1945–1951* (London: Vintage, 1993): 449; Briggs, *History IV*: 148.

41 Grisewood, *One Thing*: 178, 150–3, 167.

42 Haley interview.

43 Briggs, *History IV*: 216; Wyndham Goldie interview.

44 Hoggart, *Literacy*: 171; Attenborough, *Life*: 19.

45 *Radio Times*, 5 October 1951: 47–51, 12 October 1951: 48–51; Barney Colehan interview; Moran, *Armchair*: 65.

46 *Radio Times*, 17 October 1952: 44; Attenborough, *Life*: 13–22.

47 Monica Sims interview.

48 Shapley, *Broadcasting*: 160 (emphasis added).

49 Kynaston, *Austerity*: 526–7; Sims interview.

50 Ian Jacob interview, R143/73/1; Kynaston, *Austerity*: 587, 357.

51 Kynaston, *Family*: 507–8; Barfe, *Turned*: 88–9; Hennessy, *Having*: 227.

52 Kynaston, *Family*: 508.

53 Briggs, *History IV*: 433, 805–6.

54 Ibid: 265–356; Collins interview; Haley interview; Bridson, *Prospero*: 159–60; Grisewood, *One Thing*: 176; Hennessy, *Never*: 449.

55 Hennessy, *Having*: 230; Haley interview; Briggs, *History IV*: 390–1.

56 Grisewood, *One*: 175; Briggs, *History IV*: 807–14; Kynaston, *Austerity*: 392; Kynaston, *Family*: 33, 44, 375, 506, 538; Robert Hewison, *Culture and Consensus: England, Art and Politics since 1940* (London: Methuen, 1995) 66–7; Moran, *Armchair*: 105.

57 Briggs, *History IV*: 9, 820–1.

58 Attenborough, *Life*: 15–16; Donald Baverstock interview, R143/166/1; Wheldon interview.
59 Barfe, *Turned*: 98; Kynaston, *Family*: 607.
60 Ibid: 506–7; Norman Painting interview; Briggs, *History IV*: 921–3.
61 Barfe, *Turned*: 105–6; Kynaston, *Family*: 505; Joanna Spicer interview, R143/119/1; Rex Moorfoot interview, R143/96/1.
62 Reed interview; Cooke, *Drama*: 30–1.
63 Reed interview; Sims interview.
64 *Radio Times*, 10 October 1958: 18, 17 November 1950: 45, 24 November 1950: 49.
65 *Radio Times*, 2 April 1954: 38; Wheldon interview; Richard Francis interview, R143/54/1; Michael Bunce interview, R143/175/1.
66 Grist, *Grace*: 87, 102, 129, 132, 136–7; Bunce interview.
67 Grahame Miller interview, N41/7/1; Donald Baverstock interview; Reed interview.
68 *Radio Times*, 4 January 1962: 15–17; Reed interview.
69 Hennessy, *Having*: 101.
70 Grisewood, *One*: 189–91.

10: Building Pyramids

1   Kynaston, *Family*: 557; Hennessy, *Having*: 83.
2   Ibid: 107; Kynaston, *Austerity*: 306.
3   Kynaston, *Family*: 46–47, 570.
4   David Davis interview, R143/142/1.
5   Hennessy, *Never*: 445; Kristin Skoog, 'The "Responsible" Woman: the BBC and Women's Radio 1945–1955', unpublished PhD thesis, University of Westminster, 2010: 25–6; Kynaston, *Family*: 105–6; Briggs, *History IV*: 52–3; Kynaston, *Austerity*: 211–12, 364–5, 505.
6   Kynaston, *Family*: 585; Kynaston, *Austerity*: 124; Skoog, '"Responsible" Woman': 131, 157, 164, 172, 182.
7   Ibid: 162.
8   Haley interview; Kate Murphy, 'Relay Women: Isa Benzie, Janet Quigley and the BBC's Foreign Department, 1930–38', *Feminist Media Histories*, 5/3 (2019): 114–39; Monica Sims interview; Skoog, '"Responsible" Woman': 158.
9   Ibid: 131, 171–2; Sims interview.
10 Ibid; *Radio Times*, 4 October 1946: 5; Skoog, '"Responsible" Woman': 134, 179.
11 Ibid: 175.
12 Todd, *People*: 161–2; Kynaston, *Austerity*: 208–9, 416; Claire Langhamer, 'The Meanings of Home in Postwar Britain', *Journal of Contemporary History*, 40/2 (2005): 341–62.

13 *Radio Times*, 27 March 1953: 11; *Woman's Hour*, Light Programme, 4 February 1947.

14 *Woman's Hour*, Light Programme, 6 June 1947.

15 Shapley, *Broadcasting*: 127.

16 Wyndham Goldie interview.

17 Collins interview; Shapley, *Broadcasting*: 125; Skoog, '"Responsible" Woman': 145–6, 184.

18 Alban Webb, *London Calling: Britain, The BBC World Service and the Cold War* (London: Bloomsbury, 2014): 2–4, 53.

19 Bridson, *Prospero*: 127–31; Gorham, *Sound*: 169; Sutherland interview.

20 Hugh Greene, *The Third Floor Front: A View of Broadcasting in the Sixties* (London: Bodley Head, 1969): 42–7.

21 David Welch, 'Political "Re-education" and the Use of Radio in Germany after 1945', *Historical Journal of Film, Radio and Television*, 13/1 (1993): 75–81; Hans-Ulrich Wagner, 'Repatriated Germans and "British Spirit": The Transfer of Public Service Broadcasting to Northern Post-War Germany (1945–1950)', *Media History*, 21/4 (2015): 443–58; Greene, *Third Floor*: 49.

22 Ibid: 50–6.

23 Webb, *London*: 35–6.

24 Ibid: 16.

25 Greene, *Third Floor*: 29; Webb, *London*: 56–8.

26 Ibid: 47, 59–65.

27 Ibid: 64; Will Studdert, 'Letters without Signature', *The BBC and the Cold War*, BBC Online, https://www.bbc.com/historyofthebbc/100-voices/coldwar/letters-without-signatures; *London Calling: Cold War Letters*, BBC Four, 8 November 2019.

28 Webb, *London*: 30, 41–2; Briggs, *History IV*: 467–8.

29 Webb, *London*: 22–5; Briggs, *History IV*: 466–7.

30 Ibid: 469; Webb, *London*: 7, 27–31, 33; Esslin interview.

31 Hennessy, *Never*: 220; Peter Hennessy, *Winds of Change: Britain in the Early Sixties* (London, Allen Lane, 2019): 185–7; Potter, *Empire*: 144–7.

32 George Ivan Smith interview, R143/72/1; Miall interview; Potter, *Empire*: 143.

33 Williams interview; Greene, *Third Floor*: 33–8; Briggs, *History IV*: 443; Potter, *Empire*: 149.

34 Esslin interview.

35 Bridson, *Prospero*: 133–41; Potter, *Empire*: 191.

36 Tom Chalmers interview, R73/505/1.

37 Ibid.

38 Potter, *Empire*: 144, 146–47, 161, 170; Briggs, *History IV*: 143; Hennessy, *Having*: 91, 245.

39 Potter, *Empire*: 154–5, 161–3; *Radio Times*, 20 July 1945: 3; Briggs, *History IV*: 131–6; Gorham, *Sound*: 217–8.

40 Ivan Smith interview; Briggs, *History IV*: 463–83.

41 *Radio Times*, 27 September 1946: 4, 8–24, and 4 November 1946: 35.

42 Etienne Amyot interview, R143/2/1; Douglas Cleverdon interview; *Radio Times*, 15 November 1946: 16.

43 Kynaston, *Family*: 358–9; Cleverdon interview; *Radio Times*, 22 January 1954: 22; *Listener*, 4 February 1954: 236; Hugh Chignell, *British Radio Drama, 1945–63* (London: Bloomsbury, 2019): 49–51.

44 Humphrey Carpenter, *The Envy of the World: Fifty Years of The BBC Third Programme and Radio 3* (London: Weidenfeld and Nicolson: 1996): 57–8; Briggs, *History IV*: 68; Amyot interview; Haley interview.

45 Hennessy, *Having*: 102; Carpenter, *Envy*: xii; Reith, *Broadcast*: 34; Briggs, *History IV*: 66.

46 Kate Whitehead, *The Third Programme: A Literary History* (Oxford: Clarendon Press, 1989): 10.

47 Briggs, *History III*: 647; Haley interview.

48 Ibid; Amyot interview.

49 Ibid; Haley interview; *Radio Times*, 27 September 1946: 1, 5; Bridson, *Prospero*: 182; Reith, *Broadcast*: 64; Kynaston, *Austerity*: 176.

50 Briggs, *History IV*: 58.

51 Carpenter, *Envy*: 110; Haley interview; Briggs, *History IV*: 70.

52 Ibid: 70, 411.

53 Collins interview; Chalmers interview.

54 Frank Muir interview, R143/232/1; Briggs, *History IV*: 498; Kynaston, *Austerity*: 309; Barfe, *Turned*: 45–6.

55 Ibid: 52–3; *Radio Times*, 25 May 1951: 16; Hennessy, *Never*: 448; Muir interview.

56 Collins interview; Briggs, *History IV*: 501, 503; Hendy, *Life*: 27–8.

57 Collins interview; Bridson, *Prospero*: 225; Haley interview.

58 Bridson, *Prospero*: 227.

59 Briggs, *History IV*: 62, 69; Whitehead, *Third Programme*: 18; Kynaston, *Austerity*: 176–7; *Fifth Anniversary of the Third Programme: Some Reflections by E.M. Forster*, 29 September 1951, BBC Third Programme.

60 Grisewood, *One*: 173; Haley interview.

61 Ibid.

62 Hennessy, *Having*: 112; Bridson, *Prospero*: 224.

63 Ibid: 180–1, 228; Grisewood, *One*: 169.

64 Kynaston, *Family*: 166; Hennessy, *Having*: 89, 107, 114.

65 Haley interview; Kynaston, *Family*: 137; Reith, *Broadcast*: 16.

66 Hennessy, *Having*: 5, 75, 99, 106, 131; Kynaston, *Family*: 115–7, 327–8, 412.

11. Strangers

1 Una Marson staff file, L1/290/1–2, BBC WAC.

2   Delia Jarrett-Macauley, *The Life of Una Marson 1905–65* (Manchester: Manchester University Press, 1998: 78.

3   Ibid: 144–7; Clair Wills, *Lovers and Strangers: An Immigrant History of Post-War Britain* (London: Allen Lane, 2017): 141–4; James Procter, 'Una Marson at the BBC', *Small Axe* 48 (2015): 23–4.

4   Note, 28 January 1941, E1/1297, BBC WAC; 'Staff Training School: Special Confidential Report', *c.* June 1941 and Note, 1 May 1941, L1/290/1–2, BBC WAC; Jarrett-Macauley, *Marson*: 151–3; Procter, 'Marson': 13–15.

5   Notes, 3 May and 13 November 1946, L1/290/1–2, BBC WAC.

6   Susheila Nasta, 'Introduction', in Sam Selvon, *The Lonely Londoners* (London: Penguin, 2006): v.

7   David Olusoga, *Black and British: A Forgotten History* (London: Macmillan, 2016): 407–20, 451–91; Colin Grant, *Homecoming: Voices of the Windrush Generation* (London: Jonathan Cape, 2019): 2–3; Hennessy, *Never*: 440.

8   Hennessy, *Having*: 274; Hennessy, *Winds*: 179–80; Olusoga, *Black and British*: 461; Hoggart, *Literacy*: 21–9, 46; Kynaston, *Family*: 242; Mike Phillips, *London Crossings* (London: Continuum, 2001): 10–15; Mike Phillips, interview with author, 30 May 2018.

9   Colin Grant, 'Whose version?', *Tortoise*, 12 August 2020.

10 Note, 1 May 1943, R34/306, BBC WAC; Darrell M. Newton, *Paving the Empire Road: BBC Television and Black Britons* (Manchester: Manchester University Press, 2011): 27.

11 Olusoga, *Black and British*: 422–3; Mike Phillips, interview with author; *Time Shift: Black and White Minstrels Revisited*, BBC Four, 8 August 2005; Note, 11 September 1962, T16/175/2, BBC WAC.

12 Board of Management minutes, 22 May 1967, R78/1921/1; Thorne, 10 September 1962, T16/175/2; Thorne, 19 May 1967 and Whitley, 30 May 1967, R78/1921/1, all BBC WAC; *Time Shift*, BBC Four, 8 August 2005.

13 Newton, *Empire* 39.

14 Ibid: 41, 84–7; *Special Enquiry: Has Britain a Colour Bar?* BBC Television, Monday 31 January 1955; Grant, *Homecoming*: 132.

15 'Broadcasts to Immigrant Groups', January 1965, R78/1816/1; Note by DG, 19 May 1965, R78/1816/1; Note of a meeting held on 6 July 1965, T16/562/1; Note of a meeting held on 13 July 1965, T16/562/1; 'The Launching of the Programmes for Immigrants', October 1965, R34/1303/2 – all BBC WAC; Gavin Schafer, *The Vision of a Nation: Making Multiculturalism on British Television, 1960–1980* (Basingstoke: Palgrave, 2014): 18–66.

16 BBC Radio News, 5 October 1965; 'The Launching of the Programmes for Immigrants', October 1965, R34/1303/2; Report, 1 October 1970, R34/1303/2, BBC WAC; *Archive Hour*, BBC Radio 4, 25 August 2007.

17 'Programmes for Immigrants', 11 May 1972, R34/1303/2; 'Make Yourself

at Home', 13 November 1972, R34/1303/2, BBC WAC; Grant, *Homecoming*: 9; Wills, *Lovers*: 154; Grisewood, *One*: 167; Kynaston, *Family*: 106.

18 Briggs, *History IV*: 522.

19 Haley interview; Tahu Hole interview, R73/516/1; Miall interview.

20 Briggs, *History IV*: 210–11, 528, 543–5; Paul Fox interview, R143/193/1; Gorham, *Sound*: 233.

21 Hugh Carleton Greene interview.

22 Stuart Hood interview, R143/69/1.

23 Haley interview.

24 Ibid; John Coatman, 'The BBC. Government and Politics', *The Public Opinion Quarterly*, 15/2 (1951): 287–98; Briggs, *History IV*: 554–60; Jacob interview.

25 David Attenborough interview, Part 1, R143/4/2.

26 Whitley interview; Grisewood interview; Grisewood, *One*: 196.

27 Wyndham Goldie interview, 1977.

28 Ibid; Carney, *Stoker*: 75.

29 Briggs, *History IV*: 549–64; Barfe, *Turned*: 82; Kynaston, *Austerity*: 525.

30 Hood interview; Briggs, *History V*: 152–3.

31 Briggs *History IV*: 552; Briggs, *History V*: 153; 'A Shift in the Wind', 12 August 1965, R51/1078/1, BBC WAC.

32 Coatman, 'BBC': 293; Hood interview; Richard Francis interview, R143/45/2.

33 'Antipathy', 15 April 1975, R78/1816/1, BBC WAC; Mike Phillips, interview with author.

34 *Radio Times*, 16 October 1953: 36, and 21 May 1954: 37; Pawley, *Engineering*: 390.

35 *Morning in the Streets*, BBC Television, 25 March 1959; *Radio Times*, 20 March 1959: 9.

36 Stephen Hearst interview, R143/263/1.

37 Joe Moran, 'Vox Populi?: The Recorded Voice and Twentieth-Century British History', *Twentieth Century British History*, 25/3 (2014): 461–83; Briggs, *History V*: 349; Paul Long, 'British Radio and the Politics of Culture in Post-war Britain: the Work of Charles Parker', *The Radio Journal*, 2/3 (2004): 131–52.

38 Todd, *People*: 237–41; *Radio Times*, 2 April 1954: 15, 44; Kynaston, *Family*: 375–6; Cooke, *Drama*: 18.

39 Gielgud interview; *Radio Times*, 26 May 1950: 18; Todd, *People*: 237; Barney Colehan interview; Olive Shapley interview; Shapley, *Broadcasting*: 161.

40 Kynaston, *Family*: 158; Briggs, *History IV*: 99.

41 Norman Painting interview.

42 Skoog, '"Responsible" Woman': 203–4, 210–15; Todd, *People*: 237.

43 Ibid: 237; Skoog, '"Responsible" Woman': 203.

44 *Caribbean Voices*, No. 130, June 1947; *Radio Times*, 6 June 1952: 13, and 13 June 1952: 24.

45 *Radio Times*, 2 November 1956: 38; Bourne, *Frame*: 112–16.

46 Bourne, *Frame*: 117; Newton, *Empire*: 79.

47 'A Writer's Responsibility', October 1965, Folder 12256, Series XIII, Box 484, and 'My Collaborator: Kurt Weill', 27 October 1955, Folder 5203, Box 318, Langston Hughes Papers, James Weldon Johnson Collection in the Yale Collection of American Literature, Beinecke Rare Book and Manuscript Library, Yale University (hereafter 'Langston Hughes Papers, Beinecke').

48 Bridson, *Prospero*: 231, 297–310; *Conversations with Langston Hughes*, BBC Third Programme, 28 April and 5 May 1962; Notes, 2 July and 4 November 1963, R19/2211/3, BBC WAC.

49 *Langston Hughes at the Third*, BBC Radio 3, 4 December 2016.

50 *Listener*, 10 December 1964.

51 Bridson, 22 February 1962, Folder 474, Langston Hughes Papers, Beinecke; Evelyn Louise Crawford and Marylouise Patterson (eds), *Letters from Langston: from the Harlem Renaissance to the Red Scare and Beyond* (University of California Press, 2016): 313.

52 BBC Audience Research Report, 14 December 1964.

53 *Glasgow Herald*, 2 January 1965; Letter, 16 December 1964, Box 1: Correspondence, Writings, Miscellaneous, Folder 1963–64, Bridson Manuscripts, Lilly Library, Indiana University Bloomington (hereafter 'Bridson MSS, Lilly').

54 Grisewood, *One*: 167; *Fifth Anniversary of the Third*, BBC Third Programme, 28 May 1951.

55 Jarrett-Macauley, *Marson*: 218–19; Moran, *Armchair*: 155.

56 Hennessy, *Winds*: 317–20.

12. The Shock of the New

1 Humphrey Carpenter, *That Was Satire That Was: The Satire Boom of the 1960s* (London: Phoenix, 2002): 217–18.

2 *Radio Times*, 24 November 1962: 8–9; Ned Sherrin, *The Autobiography* (London: Little, Brown, 2005): 112–14.

3 Carpenter, *Satire*: 215, 220–7; Hennessy, *Winds*: 370.

4 Carpenter, *Satire*: 103–8, 116–22; Barfe, *Turned*: 162; Briggs, *History V*: 353–4.

5 Carpenter, *Satire*: 227–31; Sherrin, *Autobiography*: 116; Briggs, *History V*: 356.

6 Baverstock interview; Carpenter, *Satire*: 214–31.

7 Sherrin, *Autobiography*: 99.

8 Ibid: 131; Carpenter, *Satire*: 245; Grace Wyndham Goldie, *Facing the Nation: Television and Politics 1936–76* (London: The Bodley Head, 1977): 222; Harold Wilson interview, R143/148/1; Briggs, *History V*: 359–60, 365.

9   Carpenter, *Satire*: 123, 238–73; Briggs, *History V*: 253, 366–7; Greene interview.

10   Grisewood interview; Hood interview; Briggs, *History V*: 372; Greene interview.

11   Carpenter, *Satire*: 282.

12   Greene, *Third Floor*: 13–14, 74–94, 134–5.

13   Robin Day interview, R143/33/1; Wilson interview.

14   Stephen Bonarjee interview, R73/503/1; Hendy, *Life*: 31–3; David Hatch interview, R143/63/1.

15   Ibid; Hendy, *Life*: 76.

16   Todd, *People*: 241; Ray Gosling, *Personal Copy: A Memoir of the Sixties* (London: Faber & Faber, 1980): 25–93.

17   Barfe, *Turned*: 106–8; Briggs, *History V*: 200–7; Hennessy, *Winds*: 457–9.

18   Briggs, *History V*: 200–7; Barfe, *Turned*: 119–20; Snagge interview.

19   Colehan interview.

20   Hennessy, *Winds*: 457–8.

21   Stuart, *Diaries*: 510.

22   Hood interview.

23   Briggs, *History V*: 289, 387; Bill Cotton interview, R143/181/1.

24   Briggs, *History V*: 259–308, 312–14; Wheldon interview.

25   Rex Moorfoot interview, R143/96/1; Spicer interview; Attenborough, *Life*: 203–17; Paul Betts, *Ruin and Renewal: Civilizing Europe After World War II* (New York: Basic Books, 2020): 383–5.

26   Attenborough, *Life*: 205.

27   Alfred Bradley interview.

28   Ibid.

29   Briggs, *History V*: 395–6; Sydney Newman interview, R143/233/1.

30   Cooke, *Drama*: 56–9; Moran, *Armchair*: 159; Briggs, *History Vol. V*: 309; Newman interview.

31   *Drama out of a Crisis: A Celebration of Play for Today*, BBC4, 12 October 2020.

32   Ibid; Cooke, *Drama*: 71–4.

33   *Drama out of a Crisis*, BBC4.

34   Moran, *Armchair*: 158; Briggs, *History V*: 309, 333; Greene interview.

35   Cooke, *Drama*: 56–9; Moran, *Armchair*: 159; Briggs, *History V*: 527–9; General Advisory Council Paper GAC 368, December 1971, BBC WAC.

36   R. Stevenson, *The Oxford English Literary History, Vol. XII: 1960–2000* (Oxford: Oxford University Press, 2004): 301–31.

37   See David Hendy, 'Bad Language and BBC Radio Four in the 1960s and 1970s', *Twentieth Century British History*, 17/1 (2006): 74–102; Hendy, *Life*: 101–17.

38   John Tydeman, 'Bad Language and Radio Drama: A Personal View', in A. M. Hargrave (ed.), *A Matter of Manners? The Limits of Broadcast*

Language (London: Broadcasting Standards Council, 1991): 65–9; Barfe, *Turned*: 51–2, 128; Muir interview; Hatch interview.

39 Esslin interview; John Tydeman interview, R143/129/1; Programme Review Board, 22 September 1971, BBC.

40 Tydeman interview; Howard Newby interview.

41 Hendy, *Life*: 107.

42 Programme Review Board, 14 October 1970 and 26 May 1971, BBC; Hendy, 'Bad Language': 92–3; Notes, 24 June and 15 September 1971, R101/315/1.

43 Whitby, 22 October 1974, R51/1147/1.

44 William Glock, BBC Third Programme, 30 August 1964; Programme Review Board, 28 January 1970, 14 October 1970, 27 September 1972, BBC.

45 Briggs, *History V*: 509–11; Annie Nightingale, interview with author, 9 February 2018; Annie Nightingale, *Wicked Speed* (London: Pan Books, 2000): 16–17, 69.

46 Scott interview.

47 Scott interview; Johnny Beerling, interview with Alban Webb, 18 September 2017, Connected Histories of the BBC, University of Sussex.

48 Tony Blackburn, interview with author, 16 September 2017.

49 Ibid; Terry Wogan interview; Scott interview; Beerling interview, Connected Histories of the BBC.

50 Briggs, *History V*: 575.

51 Blackburn interview; Scott interview; Beerling interview, Connected Histories of the BBC.

52 Briggs, *History V*: 575–6; Scott interview; Blackburn interview.

53 Briggs, *History V*: 572; Scott interview; Beerling interview, Connected Histories of the BBC.

54 John Peel and Sheila Ravenscroft, *Margrave of the Marshes* (London: Bantam Press, 2005): 170.

55 Ibid: 170, 233–4; Scott interview.

56 Bernie Andrews interview, British Entertainment History Project.

57 Blackburn interview; Nightingale interview; Nightingale, *Wicked Speed*: 97.

58 Peel and Ravenscroft, *Margrave*: 185.

59 Scott interview; Peel and Ravenscroft, *Margrave*: 215.

60 Interviews: Stuart Hood; Frank Gillard; Harold Wilson; Hugh Greene; David Attenborough; Hazel Fenton; Hugh Wheldon; Stephen Bonarjee.

61 Wheldon interview; Wilson interview; Briggs, *History IV*: 551, 892–915; Tom Burns, *The BBC: Public Institution and Private World* (London, 1977): 123; Bunce interview.

62 Hendy, 'Bad Language': 96–102.

63 Burns, *BBC*: xiii; Wheldon interview; Esslin interview.

64 Hendy, 'Bad Language': 95.

13. Trade and Treachery

1   Alasdair Milne, *DG: The Memoirs of a British Broadcaster* (London: Hodder & Stoughton, 1988): 85–95; Seaton, *Pinkoes*: 167–8; John Simpson, *Strange Places, Questionable People* (London: Macmillan, 1998): 260–1.

2   Milne, *DG*: 85–95; Seaton, *Pinkoes*: 167.

3   Ibid: 173–6; Milne, *DG*: 86–7; Robert Harris, *Gotcha! The Media, the Government, and the Falklands Crisis* (London: Faber & Faber, 1983): 87; Walker, *Skyful*: 146.

4   Milne, *DG*: 87, 94; Seaton, *Pinkoes*: 178; *Times*, 24 May 1982; Hendy, *Life*: 263.

5   Seaton, *Pinkoes*: 170; Directive 5, The Falkland Islands Crisis 1982: Men A–Z, Mass Observation.

6   Seaton, *Pinkoes*: 178–81; Milne, *DG*: 88–9.

7   Ibid: 90–2; John Cole interview, R143/260/1.

8   Seaton, *Pinkoes*: 7–8, 182; Milne, *DG*: 96; Peter Clarke, *Hope and Glory: Britain 1900–1990* (London: Penguin, 1996): 379.

9   Moran, *Armchair*: 248, 254; Seaton, *Pinkoes*: 256–74.

10 Seaton, *Pinkoes*: 24, 242; Chris Horrie and Steve Clarke, *Fuzzy Monsters: Fear and Loathing at the BBC* (London: Heinemann, 1994): 9.

11 Steven Barnett and Andrew Curry, *The Battle for the BBC: A British Broadcasting Conspiracy* (London: Aurum Press, 1994); Peter Goodwin, *Television under the Tories: Broadcasting Policy 1979–1997* (London: BFI, 1998); Tom O'Malley, *Closedown: The BBC and Government Broadcasting Policy 1979–92* (London: Pluto Press, 1994).

12 John Birt, *The Harder Path* (London: Time Warner, 2002): 339; John Cole interview; Seaton, *Pinkoes*: 190; Horrie and Clarke, *Fuzzy*: 13–14; William Rees-Mogg interview, R143/107/1; John Wilson interview, R143/138/1.

13 Horrie and Clarke, *Fuzzy*: 21; Seaton, *Pinkoes*: 27–49; Alan Hart interview, R143/62/1; Birt, *Harder*: 333–7; Barnett and Currie, *Battle*: 56–72.

14 Horrie and Clarke, *Fuzzy*: 19–37.

15 Richard Francis interview, R143/45/2, Part 3; Hendy, *Life*: 247–77, 293–7.

16 Ibid: 282.

17 Alan Protheroe interview, R143/104/1.

18 Ibid; Seaton, *Pinkoes*: 313.

19 Ibid: 316; Alasdair Milne interview, R143/95/1, Part 2; Protheroe interview.

20 Ibid; Seaton, *Pinkoes*: 316–28; Horrie and Clarke, *Fuzzy*: 42–53.

21 Rosemary Haynes interview, R143/65/1; Protheroe interview.

22 Ibid; Haynes interview; William Rees-Mogg interview; Seaton, *Pinkoes*: 316; Horrie and Clarke, *Fuzzy*: 60–1.

23 Edward Mirzoeff interview; Paul Hamann interview.

24 *Radio Times*, 16 October 1985: 54–7; *Observer*, 20 October 1985: 26; *Guardian*, 17 October 1985: 10.

25 Hamann interview; Mirzoeff interview; Milne interview; Seaton, *Pinkoes*: 321–2; Horrie and Clarke, *Fuzzy*: 47.

26 Milne, *DG*: 141; Seaton, *Pinkoes*: 323.

27 Ibid: 323; Hamann interview.

28 Milne interview; Mirzoeff interview.

29 Milne interview; Hamann interview; *Observer*, 20 October 1985: 26; *Guardian*, 17 October 1985: 10.

30 Milne interview.

31 Protheroe interview.

32 Milne, *DG*: 202.

33 Horrie and Clarke, *Fuzzy*: 80; Seaton, *Pinkoes*: 336; Fox interview; Barnett and Currie, *Battle*: 98–9, 155.

34 Mills, *Myth*: 154; Horrie and Clarke, *Fuzzy*: 88; Libby Purves, *Radio: A True Love Story* (London: Hodder & Stoughton, 2002): 35; Birt, *Harder*: passim.

35 Horrie and Clarke, *Fuzzy*: 97.

36 *Times*, 28 and 30 September 1975; Birt, *Harder*: 248–9, 256–60; Hendy, *Life*: 160, 285.

37 Horrie and Clarke, *Fuzzy*: 103, 116, 124, 166–9; Sue MacGregor, *Woman of Today: An Autobiography* (London: Headline, 2002): 253.

38 John Wilson interview.

39 John Simpson, *From the House of War: John Simpson in the Gulf* (London: Arrow Books, 1991): 281–7; Simpson, *Strange*: 367–415; Susan L. Carruthers, *The Media at War: Communication and Conflict in the Twentieth Century* (Basingstoke: Palgrave, 2000): 133–5.

40 MacGregor, *Woman*: 274.

41 Hendy, *Life*: 346–7.

42 BBC Radio News, 13 February 1991; Allan Little, personal communication, 26 April 2021; Stephen Sackur, *On the Basra Road* (London: London Review of Books, 1991): 20–6.

43 Simpson, *House*: 298; Allan Little, personal communication, 26 April 2021; Allan Little, 'In Defence of the Non-embed', in Richard Keeble and John Mair (eds), *Afghanistan, War and the Media: Deadlines and Frontlines* (Bury St Edmunds: Arima, 2010): 6–12.

44 Fox interview.

45 Birt, *Harder*: 248–60; Horrie and Clarke, *Fuzzy*: 96–121.

46 Birt, *Harder*: 323–7; Barnett and Currie, *Battle*: 180–7; 'New BBC Production Structure', BBC News Release, 6 November 1996; Jenny Abramsky, 'Bi-Media: A Strategy for Radio?', lecture, 6 February 2002, Green College, Oxford; Hendy, *Life*: 288–93.

47 Ibid: 289; Georgina Born, *Uncertain Vision: Birt, Dyke, and the Reinvention of the BBC* (London: Vintage, 2005): 44–52.

48 Hendy, *Life*: 290–1; Born, *Vision*: 77, 287.

49 Ibid: 109; Hendy, *Life*: 292–3; Mark Tully interview with Alban Webb, 31 May 2018, Connected Histories of the BBC, University of Sussex.

50 MacGregor, *Woman*: 255; Purves, *Radio*: 258; Chris Paling, *The Silent Sentry* (London: Vintage, 2000).

51 Horrie and Clarke, *Fuzzy*: 288.

52 Charlotte Higgins, *This New Noise* (London: Guardian, 2015): 104, 107; *Observer*, 27 October 2002; Born, *Vision*: 64.

53 Mills, *Myth*: 139, 165–6.

54 Born, *Vision*: 31, 77; Seaton, *Pinkoes*: 336–7.

14: The Expanding Labyrinth

1   Bridget Kendall, *The Cold War: A New Oral History* (London: Penguin, 2017): xi.

2   Odd Arne Westad, *The Cold War: A World History* (London: Penguin, 2018): 541–612.

3   Bridget Kendall, interview with author, 12 June 2019; Elisabeth Robson Elliot, interview with Alban Webb, 28 May 2019, Connected Histories of the BBC, University of Sussex.

4   Kendall interview.

5   Elliot interview; Kendall, *Cold*: xi, 590–3.

6   Ibid: 583; Kendall interview.

7   Ibid; Walker, *Skyful*: 138–9.

8   Ibid: 92, 138–9; Kendall interview.

9   *Radio Times*, 18 November 1993: 87–8.

10 Attenborough interview.

11 Seaton, *Pinkoes*: 113.

12 Attenborough interview.

13 Ibid; *Life on Earth*, BBC2, Tuesday 3 April 1979.

14 Clive James, *The Crystal Bucket: Television Criticism from the Observer 1976–79* (London: Picador, 1981): 15, 163–4.

15 Ibid: 164–5.

16 Desmond Hawkins interview, R143/262/1; Higgins, *Noise*: 50–1; Tony Soper interview, R143/117/1.

17 Ibid; Hawkins interview; *Radio Times*, 10 June 1955: 21, and 11 September 1959: 21.

18 Jean-Baptiste Gouyon, *BBC Wildlife Documentaries in the Age of Attenborough* (London: Palgrave Macmillan, 2019): 206–8.

19 Ibid: 218–38; Seaton, *Pinkoes*: 131–40.

20 James, *Crystal*: 15.

21 Attenborough interview.

22 Attenborough, *Life*: 342–3.

23 John Birt interview, R143/323/1; Jamie Reeve, 'Witness Seminar', R143/343/1.

24 John Birt, 'Witness Seminar'; Birt interview.

25 Ed Richards, 'Witness Seminar'.

26 Birt interview; Yvonne Rogers et al., 'From the BBC Micro to micro:bit and beyond: a British Innovation', *Interactions*, 24/2 (2017): https://dl.acm.org/doi/10.1145/3029601; Chris Garcia, 'The BBC Micro', *Computer History Museum Blog*, August 2012: https://computerhistory.org/blog/the-bbc-micro/

27 John Wyver, personal communication, 13 April 2021; 'Dreams, data and downloads', https://www.bbc.com/historyofthebbc/research/dreams-data-downloads; Brandon Butterworth, 'Witness Seminar'; Brandon Butterworth, 'Brandon's History of BBC Online', https://www.bbc.co.uk/blogs/bbcinternet/2007/12/brandons_history_of_bbc_on_the_2.html

28 Birt interview; Butterworth, 'Brandon's History'.

29 John Birt, 'Witness Seminar'; Robin Foster, 'Witness Seminar'; Birt interview.

30 Foster, 'Witness Seminar'; Bella Hurrell, 'Dreams, data and downloads'; Butterworth, 'Brandon's History'.

31 John Birt, 'Witness Seminar'.

32 Jemima Kiss, 'Dreams, data and downloads'; Richards, 'Witness Seminar'.

33 Tony Ageh, personal communications, 7–10 May 2021; personal communication from Robin Price, 15 August 2021.

34 Jeremy Mayhew, Simon Walker, John Birt: 'Witness Seminar'; Chris Kimber and Simon Nelson: 'Dreams, data and downloads'.

35 Ben Lavender, *Extrology*: https://www.extrology.com/podcast/creating-the-uks-largest-online-streaming-service-with-chief-product-officer-at-dazn-ben-lavender ; Ian Hunter, 'iPlayer Day: The blue-eyed boy', *BBC Internet Blog*, 12 December 2008: https://www.bbc.co.uk/blogs/bbcinternet/2008/12/iplayer_day_the_blueeyed_boy.html

36 Ageh, personal communication, 7 May 2021; Mark Thompson, Edinburgh International Television Festival, 27 August 2005: http://www.bbc.co.uk/pressoffice/speeches/stories/thompson_edinburgh05.shtml

37 Ageh, personal communication, 7 May 2021; Hunter, 'iPlayer Day'.

38 *Independent*, 30 November 2016; Lavender, *Extrology*; Paul Grainge and Catherine Johnson, 'From catch-up TV to online TV: digital broadcasting and the case of BBC iPlayer', *Screen*, 59/1 (2018): 30.

39 Sophie Walpole, 'Dreams, data and downloads'.

40 Daniel Wilson, 'Distribution policy consultation', https://www.bbc.co.uk/blogs/aboutthebbc/entries/c01f95f4-c4f4–446b-94bb-362995863f84 ; *Guardian*, 25 April 2019; 'BBC iPlayer Public Interest Test', April 2019, BBC, http://downloads.bbc.co.uk/aboutthebbc/reports/consultation/iplayerpit/pit-submission.pdf

41 Hendy, *Life*: 288, 349–62.

42 Phil Harrison, *The Age of Static: How TV Explains Modern Britain* (London:

Melville House): 7–8; Seaton, *Pinkoes*: 239–41; James, *Glued*: 17, 28–9; James, *Crystal*: 60.

43 Moran, *Armchair*: 309–10.

44 Ibid: 310.

45 Ibid: 280–1.

46 Andy Medhurst, *Observer*, 5 February 1995: 75.

47 Anthony McNicholas, 'Wrenching the machine around: EastEnders, the BBC and institutional change', *Media, Culture & Society*, 26/4 (2004): 491–512; Seaton, *Pinkoes*: 285.

48 Ibid: 286; McNicholas, 'Wrenching': 506–9.

49 Ibid: 509; Moran, *Armchair*: 253, 280.

50 Kathryn Dodd and Philip Dodd, 'From the East End to EastEnders: Representations of the working class, 1890–1990', in Dominic Strinati and Stephen Wagg (eds), *Come on Down? Popular Media and Culture in Post-war Britain* (London: Routledge, 1992): 116–32; Peri Bradley, 'Romancing the Soap: Representations of Gay Love and Relationships in EastEnders', in Pamela Demory and Christopher Pullen (eds), *Queer Love in Film and Television: Critical Essays* (Basingstoke: Macmillan, 2013): 33–45.

51 *Radio Times*, 6 November 1936: 91 and 22 September 1950: 43.

52 *Guardian*, 18 August 2017 and 30 June 2013.

53 *Guardian*, 18 December 2015 and 20 December 2020.

54 Horrie and Clarke, *Fuzzy*: 253–8; Moran, *Armchair*: 341; *Guardian*, 18 August 2010.

55 Moran, *Armchair*: 309.

56 James, *Crystal*: 13–17.

15: On the Rack

1   Harrison, *Static*: 126.

2   *Guardian*, 21 January 2020.

3   Kevin Marsh, *Stumbling Over Truth: The Inside Story of the 'Sexed Up' Dossier, Hutton and the BBC* (London: Biteback, 2012): 319–20.

4   Ibid: 127, 168–9; Greg Dyke, *Inside Story* (London: Harper Perennial, 2005): 255.

5   Marsh, *Stumbling*: 172.

6   Robin Lustig, *Is Anything Happening? My Life as a Newsman* (London: Biteback, 2017): 330; Dyke, *Inside*: 2.

7   *Report of the Inquiry into the Circumstances Surrounding the Death of Dr David Kelly C.M.G. by Lord Hutton*, HC247 (London: The Stationery Office, 28 January 2004): 319–23.

8   Dyke, *Inside*: 13.

9   Ibid: 7–8, 20–2; Marsh, *Stumbling*: 16.

10 Ibid: 9–17, 115–17.

11 Roger Mosey, *Getting Out Alive: News, Sport & Politics at the BBC* (London:

Biteback, 2015): 254; Higgins, *Noise*: 150–1; Marsh, *Stumbling*: 128; Dyke, *Inside*: 13–15, 28–29, 253.

12 Marsh, *Stumbling*: 6, 86, 125–7, 156.

13 Mosey, *Getting*: 257; Lustig, *Anything*: 330; Marsh, *Stumbling*: 308; Higgins, *Noise*: 151; Mills, *Myth*: 95–103.

14 Higgins, *Noise*: 153; Mosey, *Getting*: 257; Marsh, *Stumbling*: 310.

15 Ibid: 78–87.

16 Ibid: 102–5, 307–11; John Lloyd, 'Media power', *Index on Censorship: Law on Trial*, 32/4 (2003): 84–92; John Lloyd, *What the Media Are Doing to Our Politics* (London: Constable, 2004): 2–24, 187–95.

17 Hendy, *Life*: 157; Wyndham Goldie interview.

18 Lustig, *Anything*: 330; Higgins, *Noise*: 168.

19 Fi Glover interview with Margaretta Jolly, 16 January 2020, Connected Histories of the BBC, University of Sussex; Lorna Clarke interview with author, 14 November 2018.

20 Mosey, *Getting*: 11, 20–2.

21 *The Pollard Review Report*, 18 December 2012, BBC Trust; 'Newsnight and Jimmy Savile', *The Editors*, BBC News Online, Tuesday 2 October 2012.

22 *The Dame Janet Smith Review Report*, BBC Trust, 25 February 2016: 2–5, 46–68.

23 Ibid: 7–9, 14.

24 Ibid: 15–23.

25 Patrick Barwise and Peter York, *The War Against the BBC* (London, Penguin Books: 2020): 222–223; *Observer*, 2 September 2019; *Guardian*, Friday 10 January 2020.

26 Barwise and York, *War*: 223–7.

27 Ibid: 227; Robin Aitken, *Can We Trust the BBC?* (London, Continuum, 2007): 60–1.

28 Higgins, *Noise*: 164; Harrison, *Static*: 163; Barwise and York, *War*: 138–41; Mills, *Myth*: 31, 106.

29 Harrison, *Static*: 89–98.

30 Ibid: 97; Barwise and York, *War*: 39–51.

31 Harrison, *Static*: 156.

32 Peter Oborne, *The Assault on Truth: Boris Johnson, Donald Trump and the Emergence of a New Moral Barbarism* (London: Simon & Schuster, 2021): 6–9, 16–18, 34–7, 94, 113, 162–3.

33 Mills, *Myth*: 135–6; Oborne, *Assault*: 7; Higgins, *Noise*: 145–6; Barwise and York, *War*: 153–4; Harrison, *Static*: 138–9.

34 Ibid: 152–3.

35 Higgins, *Noise*: 133.

36 Harrison, *Static*: 211; *Times*, 3 August 2019; Higgins, *Noise*: 220–3.

37 Ibid: 222; Barwise and York, *War*: 23–5.

38 Ibid: 14–15; Mariana Mazzucato et al., 'Creating and measuring dynamic public value at the BBC', UCL and BBC, December 2020; KPMG, 'An

assessment of the economic impact of the BBC', March 2021; Higgins, *Noise*: 198.

39 Barwise and York, *War*: 61–2; *Guardian*, 14 July 2015; *Guardian*, 7 October 2015.
40 *Observer*, 6 March 2016.
41 'A Distinctive BBC', BBC, April 2016.
42 'BBC distinctiveness report', OFCOM, 17 July 2017.
43 Barwise and York, *War*: xv–xvi; *Guardian*, 20 October 2010.
44 Barwise and York, *War*: xv.
45 Ibid: 274; Harrison, *Static*: 231–2; 'Government publishes response to decriminalising TV licence evasion', https://www.gov.uk/government/news/government-publishes-response-to-decriminalising-tv-licence-evasion; *Guardian*, 21 January 2021.
46 Barwise and York, *War*: 29.
47 Higgins, *Noise*: 173.
48 Barwise and York, *War*: xii.
49 Ibid: 32–3; BBC Group Annual Report and Accounts 2019/20: 3.
50 Ibid: 5.
51 *Guardian*, 19 December 2020.
52 Higgins, *Noise*: 99, 210; Matheson, *Broadcasting*: 17; James Butler, 'The BBC on the Rack', *London Review of Books*, 19 March 2020; Born, *Uncertain*: 79.

Postscript

1   *Guardian*, 21 October 2020, 3 November 2020, 4 November 2020, 9 November 2020, 13 November 2020, 16 June 2021.
2   *Guardian*, 3 November 2020; *Report of The Dyson Investigation*, 14 May 2021, BBC http://downloads.bbc.co.uk/aboutthebbc/reports/reports/dyson-report-20-may-21.pdf; 'BBC publishes Lord Dyson's Report': press release, 20 May 2021, https://www.bbc.co.uk/mediacentre/2021/dyson-report
3   *Guardian*, 29 May 2021, 14 June 2021; *Observer*, 30 May 2021.
4   *Observer*, 25 April 2021.
5   *Have I Got News For You*, BBC1, 28 May 2021.
6   *Spectator*, 23 May 2021.
7   *Guardian*, 24 May 2021.
8   'Public Service Broadcasting Advisory Panel', https://www.gov.uk/government/collections/public-service-broadcasting-advisory-panel; *Guardian*, 10 July 2021; *Observer*, 11 July 2021.
9   Higgins, *Noise*: 122; *Guardian*, 25 July 2021.
10 'Open Letter', https://britishbroadcastingchallenge.com/open-letter/
11 *Financial Times*, 20 May 2021.
12 David Barnes, *Weird England: Bonfire*, BBC Radio 3, 19 December 2018.
13 Ibid.

ACKNOWLEDGEMENTS

It takes a village, they say. And, truly, I'm in awe of just how many people there are to thank for helping to get *The BBC: A People's History* into the world.

First, and foremost, I owe this book's very existence to my agent Caroline Dawnay and her team at United Agents, as well as to Clive Priddle, Michelle Welsh-Horst and their colleagues at PublicAffairs. I should also thank all the right people at my UK publisher, Profile Books: Andrew Franklin, Penny Daniel, Cecily Gayford and Susanne Hillen. Thanks are due, too, to Charles Drazin, who offered timely assistance in reducing what was once a much larger book to its present size. They've all been a model of professionalism, support and endless patience.

This is an 'authorised' history of the BBC, and I should explain briefly what that means. One thing it *doesn't* mean is any right of editorial control by the Corporation. At no point have I been told what to say or what not to say: I've had a totally free hand, and, for good or bad, this is *my* version of the BBC story, not an officially approved one. What being 'authorised' *has* meant is simply this: several years of invaluable help from the BBC accessing and navigating my way through its archival treasures – including not just its written documents and programme recordings, but also, in my case, getting unrivalled access to the Corporation's Oral History Collection. I therefore have to thank, above all, Robert Seatter and John Escolme in the Secretary's office, who made this access possible and who offered help on a continuous basis, often at short notice and often at unearthly hours. I also want to offer profuse thanks to: James Codd, Louise North, Matthew Chipping and Jeff Walden at the Written Archives Centre; Luke O'Shea, Tadege Bay and James Edwards, who spared no effort in tracking down and preparing images from the Corporation's vast picture library; and the staff of Radio 3 who supplied archive recordings for various programmes I made for them between 2014 and 2016.

Research in the early stages of this book was assisted by the award in 2008–09 of a Visiting Fellowship at the Centre for Research in the Arts, Social Sciences and Humanities (CRASSH) at the University of Cambridge; the Marjorie G. Wynne Fellowship in British Literature at the Beinecke Rare Book and Manuscript Library, Yale University; and an Everett Helm Visiting Fellowship at the Lilly Library, Indiana University, Bloomington. I also benefited from invitations to present findings at Macquarie University in Sydney; the National University of Ireland in Galway; the Charles III University of Madrid; the universities of Bamberg, Bergen, Bonn, Siena, Lund, Aarhus, Copenhagen, Westminster, St Andrews, and Aberystwyth; and at Roma Tre and RAI in Rome; the Prix Italia in Turin; the Australian Media Traditions Conference in Canberra; Wolfson College in Cambridge; the Beinecke Rare Book and Manuscript Library at Yale; the Royal College of Music in London; the European Communication Research and Education Association; the 20s–30s Group; the Cambridge Centenary Authors Seminar; the Transnational Radio Encounters group in Berlin; and the Keep in Brighton. Speculative early versions of several chapters have appeared in other forms – in the *Cambridge Literary Review* and in a number of BBC Radio 3 programmes, namely *The Essay*, the *Sunday Feature: Langston Hughes at the Third*, and *Power of Three*.

From 2016, the task of gathering together many of the personal recollections referred to in this book was boosted by the award, first of a University of Sussex Research Development Fund, and then of a substantial grant from the Arts and Humanities Research Council to support what became the 'Connected Histories of the BBC' project. The core 'Connected Histories' team who worked with me for the past five years – Alban Webb, Margaretta Jolly, Tim Hitchcock, Ben Jackson, Anna-Maria Sichani and Denice Penrose – were instrumental in making accessible the BBC's oral history recordings, creating new interview recordings, and identifying a multitude of associated archival documents. They've shared with me all the pains and all the joys of running a big research project, and have been a vital part of this whole process. The project pulled into its orbit a long list of other contributors and helpers, who also deserve thanks: John Hughes, Mathilde Davidson, Catalina Balan, Louisa Streeting, Josh Harris, Naresh Bedi, Jeannine Baker, Kate Murphy, Jamie Medhurst, Lucy Robinson, Helen Wood, Jilly Boyce Kay, James Procter, Aasiya Lodhi, Emma Sandon, Kate Terkanian, Sejal Sutaria, David Butler, Will Studdert, Hans-Ulrich Wagner, Samira Ahmed, Martha Kearney, Jenni Murray, Lyse Doucet, Nicholas Witchell, and Sue Inglish. 'Connected Histories of the BBC' worked with several key partners: Mass Observation, for which thanks are due to Fiona Courage at the University of Sussex Library Special Collections; the Science Museum Group, for which thanks are due to Tim Boon as well as Elinor Groom at the National Science and Media Museum in Bradford; and the British Entertainment History Project, for which thanks are due to Mike Dick and Sue Malden. Our key partner was the BBC, for which thanks are due not just to Robert Seatter and John Escolme, but also Bill Thompson, Rob Cooper and their team at BBC Research and Development.

The 'Connected Histories of the BBC' project allowed me, and others on the core team, to interview several people who have played an important role in recent broadcasting history, and whose accounts have informed this book: Tony Blackburn, Annie Nightingale, Johnny Beerling, Mike Phillips, Mark Tully,

Satish Jacob, Elisabeth Robson Elliot, Peter Udell, Eugeniusz Smolar, Bridget Kendall, Lorna Clarke, Fi Glover, Joan Bakewell and Esther Rantzen. I'm also grateful for communications and advice from Tony Ageh, Allan Little, Samira Ahmed and Robin Price.

Several formal acknowledgements are also due. BBC images, extracts from the BBC's Written Archives Centre, and quotations from the BBC's oral history collection are all BBC copyright and are reproduced with permission of the BBC. Extracts from Mass Observation are reproduced with permission of Curtis Brown Group Ltd, London on behalf of The Trustees of the Mass Observation Archive © The Trustees of the Mass Observation Archive. Passages by Langston Hughes from the Langston Hughes Papers in the James Weldon Johnson Collection of the Yale Collection of American Literature, Beinecke Rare Book and Manuscript Library, and from the Bridson Manuscripts collection, Lilly Library, Indiana University, Bloomington, are reproduced with the permission of David Higham Associates Limited, London. Extracts from the Sieveking Manuscripts are published courtesy Lilly Library, Indiana University, Bloomington, Indiana, and, along with Lance Sieveking's other writings at the BBC Written Archives Centre, are reproduced with the kind permission of his son, Paul Sieveking. Extracts from Douglas Ritchie's unpublished memoir, *V**** for Victory: The 1940 BBC Campaign against the Nazis*, are reproduced with the kind permission of his son, Adam Ritchie. Extracts from my interview with Annie Nightingale CBE, D.Litt. are reproduced with the permission of the Curtis Brown Group Ltd, London on behalf of Annie Nightingale. Official records related to John Reith and Peter Eckersley held at The National Archives are Crown Copyright, and contain public sector information licensed under the Open Government Licence v3.0.

More personal thanks are due to several friends, colleagues or fellow authors, who were kind enough to read early drafts of the book and provide incredibly valuable feedback. They include: Robert Gildea, Matt Houlbrook, Dan Todman, Alban Webb, John Wyver, Jamie Medhurst, Anthony McNicholas, Robin Price, Tony Ageh and Allan Little. They've all saved me from error: any mistakes that remain are now mine alone.

The second half of this book was written during a global pandemic, and for much of the past eighteen months friends and colleagues have responded heroically to my own 'Long Covid' by lifting from my shoulders some of my normal university duties and offering far more moral and practical support than I've been entitled to expect. I owe special thanks to Alban Webb, Kate O'Riordan, Pollyanna Ruiz, Dolores Tierney, Ben Highmore, Michael Bull, Kate Lacey, Lesley Model, Hope Wolf and Rachel O'Connell. Really, I also owe it to everyone in the School of Media, Arts and Humanities at the University of Sussex: individually, and collectively, they've made my academic home not just intellectually vibrant, but – perhaps more importantly – the kindest and friendliest of places to work. Given the malign political and financial climate within which British universities have been operating for the past decade, that is no mean achievement.

My biggest debt, by far, is to my immediate family – Henrietta, Eloise and Morgan – and to my parents, Jim and Gaynor Hendy. They've all had to put up with more than five years of me being unavailable, distracted, messy, moody, anxious. But it is Henrietta who deserves the greatest thanks of all. She's borne a far larger share of domestic labour than she has any right to expect – and for far too long. She's picked me up and calmed me down too many times to count. She's stood alongside me and kept me company. In short, she's the one who kept me going. It's no exaggeration to say that without her none of the rest would have been possible. And so it is to her that I dedicate this book with all my love and gratitude.

INDEX